How do you Spell Häagen-Dazs®?

How do you Spell Häagen-Dazs?®

The How to Say It® Spelling Dictionary of Brands, Companies, Places and Products

**CARL HAUSMAN, PH.D., and
SHERRY HAUSMAN, M.P.H.**

A Stonesong Press Book

Prentice Hall Press

PRODUCED BY THE STONESONG PRESS
President: Paul Fargis
Vice President, Editorial: Ellen Scordato
Vice President, Development: Alison Fargis
Design Production: Judy Pray

ISBN 0-7352-0302-4

 Paramus, NJ 07652

http://www.phpress.com

To Mark and Carl III

Acknowledgments

Our thanks to the many people, far too numerous to list by name, who patiently answered our questions. We were helped enormously by all those folks who sweat the details.

Carl and Sherry Hausman

Introduction

As Mark Twain once noted, the difference between the right word and the almost-right word is the difference between lightning and the lightning-bug. While we're relatively sure he wasn't addressing the precise problem this book is designed to meet, his epigram holds true for writers and editors grappling with trade names, company names, acronyms and all the other arcane and mysterious words that don't show up in a standard dictionary.

How Do You Spell Häagen-Dazs®? is a collection of abbreviations, terms, acronyms, company and product names, place names, sports-team names, titles and call letters of news and media organizations and colleges and university names.

We have selected material for the book that we believe will be of maximum use to editors, writers, reporters, attorneys, public relations and advertising practitioners and anyone involved in business, institutional or scientific and technical writing. Part of the selection criteria was drawn from the editors' experience: Carl has worked as an editor and reporter in print, broadcast and online venues, and is currently the chair of the journalism department at Rowan University in Glassboro, New Jersey. Sherry has worked as a medical editor, a United Nations program adviser and a data analyst.

In sum, we both came to realize how time-consuming it is to hunt down spellings in various almanacs or on the web. As part of the research for this book, we tracked what kinds of material we frequently searched for when editing copy. We also analyzed several months' of news and media coverage and recorded the frequently used names, words and abbreviations not found in a standard dictionary. Finally, we consulted with others in the word business, particularly newspaper copy editors, to learn which words they frequently had to track down.

The result is a collection of about 25,000 entries. Most of the organization is self-explanatory, but there are a few points worth noting.

Chapter 1, Abbreviations and Acronyms, includes hard-to-find entries such as government agency abbreviations, state-name abbreviations, military acronyms and rank abbreviations, acronyms used by associations and businesses, computer lingo, Internet shorthand, WWW domain-name country codes, airport abbreviations and something we believe business writers will find extremely useful: major stock-exchange abbreviations for companies and selected funds. We generally give the full company name. You will, however, encounter some abbreviations in the names of funds because the abbreviations are part of the official fund name.

Throughout the book we have kept definition to a minimum, because spelling is the prime focus of the work and the user, but in Chapter 1, we do consistently provide the definition following an abbreviation or acronym. This is done to provide context and to distinguish among multiple meanings and usages.

A word about form for acronyms and abbreviations: the stylebook you follow will in many cases determine capitalization and use of periods. In this book, we follow AP style, which is recognized as the most widely used style in media and journalism and is summarized in *The Associated Press Stylebook* and *Briefing on Media Law*. Book editors often opt for the University of Chicago Press style, from *The Chicago Manual of Style*, while others may use *The New York Times Manual of Style and Usage*. You or your organization may use differing or supplementary style guides. In any event, there is more similarity than difference in stylebooks. For example, both the AP and the *Chicago Manual of Style* specify the use of acronyms in the manner presented in this book: all capitals, with certain exceptions as noted in the listings. (For example, "Nasdaq" is written with one capital and the rest of the word lowercase. Nasdaq itself, interestingly, spells it both ways.) *The New York Times* uses uppercase for the first letter and lowercase for the remaining letters of all acronyms if the word is used as a proper noun and exceeds four letters.

Style guides generally opt for sparing use of periods in abbreviations except as noted in the chapter. As a general rule, U.S., U.N., academic degrees and state abbreviations in print style (as opposed to Post Office abbreviations) use periods between the letters (B.A.) after the letters (Ltd.) or in some cases between groups of letters (Ph.D.).

Chapter 2 lists colleges and universities alphabetically.

Chapter 3 lists companies and products, including pharmaceutical names. We have also included many nonprofit organizations, including foundations, in this chapter. Again, we have kept definition to a minimum, but we do define a word when there are two or more listings with a similiar spelling. For example, after "Eagle" you will find both "[snacks]" and "[tires]." Throughout this chapter, the listings are defined in brackets as company, product or nonprofit.

We provide you with full company names as well as other derivations of the names used informally (such as "Kodak" for "Eastman Kodak Co."). Most publishing style guides specify the use of the abbreviation "Co." for "company," and we typically use it. Either way, as long as it consistently conforms to your style, is acceptable.

In written material you will typically omit the comma before the abbreviation "Inc." (for example, "Smith Books Inc.," not "Smith Books, Inc."); AP and NYT specify that form, while Chicago does not specifically address comma usage in its entries on company names. We follow the AP and NYT style in our listings. Consult your style guide for its policy on using abbreviations such as "Co." and "Ltd." on first reference of a company name.

Chapter 4, National Places of Interest, includes place names typically not found in most references, such as military bases, hospitals, monuments, stadiums, airports and embassies. We have also included the official names of about one hundred United States ships because they so often figure in news coverage.

Chapter 5, News and Media, includes names of newspapers, magazines, news services, and call letters for television stations. We omitted radio stations because TV is mentioned in news coverage more often than radio. The listings will give you the call letters and the city and state to which the station is licensed. The newspaper listings contain the locality and state where the paper is published, but if the city name is part of the title (*Fresno Bee*) only the state name will be listed in brackets.

Use of the word "the" in the title of newspapers is tricky. Some styles, such as the stylebook of *The New York Times*, recommend capitalization of "The" for every newspaper title. Others recommend using "The" only when the paper uses it as part of its official title. The problem is that newspapers themselves are inconsistent in the use of "The" in their titles or in listings the papers report to the major media directories. We have included the word "The" in newspaper titles when the publication is listed that way in a major directory. The periodicals listed should appear in italic type in most print and online publications. They appear here in roman type for readability.

Chapter 6, Political, Governmental and International Associations and Institutions, lists organizations in the U.S. but includes some international organizations that operate in the U.S. or are likely to be mentioned in domestic media coverage. Occasionally, we will define where the organization resides "[Department of Commerce, U.S.]" when there is a possibility of confusion with a similar or identical name in another governmental entity.

The book concludes with a listing of sports-team names in Chapter 7.

We believe that you will find this book useful, whether you are writing editorial copy or articles, drafting legal documents or sending out solicitations. Moreover, we hope the book will assume a well-thumbed place on your bookshelf among the dictionary, thesaurus and style manual.

Carl Hausman
Sherry Hausman

Abbreviations and Acronyms

1st Lt. – first lieutenant
1st Sgt. – first sergeant
2nd Lt. – second lieutenant
4DDA – four-dimensional data assimilation
4GL – Fourth-generation language
510(k) – medical device premarket notification
6G4 – Wynkoop Airport
A&D – Admission and Disposition
A&P – Analysis and Prediction
A&P – Great Atlantic & Pacific Tea Co. Inc.
A&SM – appointing and scheduling module
A.A. – associate of arts degree
A.D. – anno Domini, in the year of the Lord
a.m. – midnight to noon
A/L – approach and landing
A/OGCM – coupled atmosphere/ocean GCM
A/QA – professional affairs/quality assurance
A.S. – associate of science
A – Agilent Technologies Inc. [stock listing]
AA – Alcoa Inc. [stock listing]
AA – analysis of alternatives
AA – Armed Forces Americas
AA – assistant administrator
AAA – American Automobile Association
AAAS – American Association for the Advancement of Science
AABB – American Association of Blood Banks

AABW – Antarctic bottom water [also known as ABW]
AAC – Ableauctions.com Inc. [stock listing]
AAC – acquisition advice code
AAC – Arcadia Financial Ltd. [stock listing]
AAFES – Army Air Force Exchange Service
AAG – Association of American Geographers
AAI – AirTran Holdings Inc. [stock listing]
AAIW – Antarctic intermediate water
AAM – atmospheric angular momentum
AANA – American Association of Nurse Anesthetists
AAP – Affirmative Action Plan
AAPC – Accounting and Auditing Policy Committee
AAPOR – American Association for Public Opinion Research
AARI – Arctic and Antarctic Research Institute
AARP – American Association of Retired Persons
AAS – advanced automation system
AAS – American Astronautical Society
AAS – American Astronomical Society
AAS – American Astrophysical Society
AAS – Amerisource Health Corp. [stock listing]
AASHTO – American Association of State Highway and Transportation Officials

AAT – All-American Term Trust Inc. [stock listing]

AAW – aeromedical airlift wing

AB – air base

AB – asymmetric balance

AB – Cannon Express Inc. [stock listing]

ABB – ABB Ltd. [stock listing]

ABC – American Broadcasting Companies

ABC – accounting, billing, and collecting

ABEDA – Arab Bank for Economic Development in Africa

ABF – Airborne Inc. [stock listing]

ABG – Groupe AB S.A. [stock listing]

ABI – Applera Corp. [stock listing]

ABJ – Alabama Power Co. [stock listing]

ABK – Ambac Financial Group Inc. [stock listing]

ABL – American Biltrite Inc. [stock listing]

ABL – atmospheric boundary layer

ABM – ABM Industries Inc. [stock listing]

ABM – antiballistic missile

ABMC – American Battle Monuments Commission

ABN – ABN AMRO Holding N.V. [stock listing]

ABP – American Business Products Inc. [stock listing]

ABQ – Albuquerque International Sunport

ABR – Atlantic Premium Brands Ltd. [stock listing]

ABS – Albertsons Inc. [stock listing]

ABT – Abbott Laboratories [stock listing]

ABX – Barrick Gold Corp. [stock listing]

ABY – Abitibi-Consolidated Inc. [stock listing]

AC – Alliance Capital Management L.P. [stock listing]

ACA – Alabama Power Co. [stock listing]

ACA – American Cartographic Association

ACBUD – assistant comptroller for budget

ACC – Administrative Committee on Coordination

ACC – advanced computer communications

ACC – Air Combat Command

ACC – Alaska coastal current

ACC – Arab Cooperation Council

ACCAD – Advisory Committee on Climate Applications and Data

ACCP – Atlantic Climate Change Program

ACCS – Army Command and Control Computer System

ACCT – Agence de Cooperation Culturelle et Technique

ACDA – Arms Control and Disarmament Agency

ACDA – United States Arms Control and Disarmament Agency

ACE – ACE Ltd. [stock listing]

ACES – Annual Capital Expenditures Survey

ACF – active contract file

ACF – address control file

ACF – Administration for Children and Families

ACF – Americredit Corp. [stock listing]

ACFIN – assistant comptroller for finance

ACG – ACM Government Income Fund Inc. [stock listing]

ACG – Advanced Computing Group

ACH – Army community hospital

ACHP – Advisory Council on Historic Preservation

ACI – Arch Coal Inc. [stock listing]

ACIC – Aeronautical Charting and Information Center

ACIR – Advisory Council on Intergovernmental Relations

ACK – Armstrong Holdings Inc. [stock listing]

ACLU – American Civil Liberties Union

ACM – assistant chief of mission

ACMA – American Coin Merchandising Inc. [stock listing]

ACME – Advisory Committee on the Marine Environment

ACMP – Advisory Committee on Marine Pollution

ACMRR – Advisory Committee of Experts on Marine Resources Research

ACO – Amcol International Corp. [stock listing]

ACO – Association of Commissioned Officers

ACOH – Advisory Committee for Operational Hydrology

ACOMR – Advisory Committee on Oceanic Meteorological Research

ACOPS – Advisory Committee on Protection of the Sea

ACOS – American College of Surgeons

ACP Group – African, Caribbean and Pacific Group of States

ACP – American Real Estate Partners L.P. [stock listing]

ACP – application certification process

ACR – advance census report

ACR – American College of Radiology

ACR – American Retirement Corp. [stock listing]

ACS – Affiliated Computer Services Inc. [stock listing]

ACS – automated control system

ACSM – American Congress on Surveying and Mapping

ACT – Allegiant Bancorp Inc. [stock listing]

ACTUR – Automated Central Tumor Registry

ACU – Acme United Corp. [stock listing]

ACUS – Administrative Conference of the United States

ACV – Alberto Culver Co. [stock listing]

ACX – Arguss Communications Inc. [stock listing]

ACY – AeroCentury Corp. [stock listing]

ACYF – Administration for Children, Youth and Families

AD – Advo Inc. [stock listing]

AD – Andorra

ADA – Americans with Disabilities Act of 1990

ADANS – airlift deployment analysis system

ADAPSO – Association of Data Processing Service Organizations

ADAS – airborne data acquisition system

ADB – Apple desktop bus

ADB – Asian Development Bank

ADC – Agree Realty Corp. [stock listing]

ADC – assistant division chief

ADCP – acoustic Doppler current profiler

ADD – Administration on Developmental Disabilities

ADEOS – advanced Earth observing satellite

ADF – ACM Managed Dollar Income Fund Inc. [stock listing]

ADF – African Development Foundation, The

ADF – Astrophysics Data Facility

ADI – Analog Devices Inc. [stock listing]

Adm. – admiral

ADM – Archer Daniels Midland Co. [stock listing]

A-DMIS – Army defense medical information system

ADN – advanced digital network

ADO – Adecco S.A. [stock listing]

ADO – Army Digitization Office

ADP – automated data processing

ADP – Automatic Data Processing Inc. [stock listing]

ADPCM – adaptive pulse-coded modulation

ADPL – average daily patient workload

ADR – adverse drug reaction

ADR – alternative dispute resolution

ADR – Andrews Municipal Airport

ADS – Addison Airport

ADS – alternative delivery system

ADSL – asymmetric digital subscriber line

ADT – admission, disposition and transfer

ADV – Advest Group Inc. [stock listing]

ADX – Adams Express Co. [stock listing]

AE – Adams Resources & Energy Inc. [stock listing]

AE – United Arab Emirates

AEA – American Economic Association

AEC – Associated Estates Realty Corp. [stock listing]

AEC – Atomic Energy Commission

AECC – Aeromedical Evacuation Control Center

AECGIS – automated electrocardiogram interpretive system

AED – Banco de A. Edwards [stock listing]

AEE – Ameren Corp. [stock listing]

AEE – application execution environment

AEG – AEGON N.V. [stock listing]

AEHA – Army Environmental Hygiene Agency

AEIDC – Arctic Environmental Information and Data Center

AELT – Aeromedical Evacuation Liaison Team

AEM – Agnico-Eagle Mines Ltd. [stock listing]

AEN – AMC Entertainment Inc. [stock listing]

AEP – affirmative employment plan

AEP – American Electric Power Co. Inc. [stock listing]

AER – Aegis Realty Inc. [stock listing]

AERC – Association of Ecosystem Research Centers

AEROCE – Atmosphere/Ocean Chemistry Experiment

AES – aeromedical evacuation squadron

AES – AES Corp., The [stock listing]

AES – Application Environment Specification

AET – Aetna Inc. [stock listing]

AEWC – Alaska Eskimo Whaling System

AF – Afghanistan

AF – Argentina Fund Inc., The [stock listing]

AFA – Air Force Academy

AFAIK – as far as I know

AFAUI – as far as I understand it

AFB – air force base

AFC – Allmerica Financial Corp. [stock listing]

AFC – automatic frequency control

AFCAC – Air Force computing acquisition contract

AFDB – African Development Bank

AFDC – Aid to Families with Dependent Children

AFDO – Association of Food and Drug Officials

AFEA – abbreviated functional economic analysis

AFEAS – Alternative Fluorocarbons Environmental Acceptability Study

AFESD – Arab Fund for Economic and Social Development

AFF – Morgan Stanley Dean Witter Africa Investment Fund Inc. [stock listing]

AFFAC – Air Force Finance and Accounting Center

AFFIRM – Association for Federal Information Resource Managers

AFG – American Financial Group Inc. [stock listing]

AFGWC – Air Force Global Weather Center [USA]

AFIP – Armed Forces Institute of Pathology

AFIS – American Forces Information Service

AFL – AFLAC Inc. [stock listing]

AFLC – Air Force Logistics Command

AFMLL – Air Force Medical Logistics Letter

AFMLO – Air Force Medical Logistics Office

AFMSA – Air Force Medical Support Agency

AFNET – Air Force Network

AFOMS – Air Force Office of Medical Support

AFOS – Automation of Field Operations and Services

AFOSH – Air Force Occupational Safety, Fire Prevention and Health

AFP – United Capital Corp. [stock listing]

AFRC – Air Force Reserve Command

AFRL – Air Force Research Laboratory

AFROTC – Air Force Reserve Officer Training Corps

AFRTS – Armed Forces Radio and Television Service

AFS – American Fisheries School

AFS – Associates First Capital Corp. [stock listing]

AFSC – Air Force Systems Command

AFSC – Alaska Fisheries Science Center

AFSC – Armed Forces Staff College

AFSCME – American Federation of State, County and Municipal Employees

AFSCN – Air Force Satellite Control Network

AFSOC – Air Force Special Operations Command

AFSPC – Air Force Space Command

AFT – American Federation of Teachers

AFT – automated file transfer

AFTRA – American Federation of Television and Radio Artists

AFVP – Aviation Forecast Verification Program

AG – Agco Corp. [stock listing]

AG – Antigua and Barbuda

AGARD – Advisory Group for Aerospace Research and Development

AGASP – Arctic Gas and Aerosol Sampling Program

AGC – American General Corp. [stock listing]

AGD – Applied Graphics Technologies Inc. [stock listing]

AGE – Edwards AG Inc. [stock listing]

AGGG – Advisory Group on Greenhouse Gases

AGH – Atlantis Plastics Inc. [stock listing]

AGI – ALPINE Group Inc. [stock listing]

AGI – American Geological Institute

AGL – Angelica Corp. [stock listing]

AGM – Federal Agric Mtg Corp. [stock listing]

AGN – Allergan Inc. [stock listing]

AGR.A – Agere Systems Inc. [stock listing]

AGR – Agricultural Section (USDA/FAS)

AGS – Saga Systems Inc. [stock listing]

AGT – AIMGlobal Technologies Co. Inc. [stock listing]

AGU – Agrium Inc. [stock listing]

AGU – American Geophysical Union

AGUPR – Agrium Inc. [stock listing]

AGV – automatic guided vehicles

AGX – Agribrands International Inc. [stock listing]

AGY – Argosy Gaming Co. [stock listing]

AH – Armor Holdings Inc. [stock listing]

AH – Army hospital

AHA ID NO – American Hospital Association identification number

AHA – American Hospital Association

AHB – Amerus Group Co. [stock listing]

AHB – Amerus Life Holdings Inc. [stock listing]

AHC – Amerada Hess Corp. [stock listing]

AHCFMS – Army Health Care Financial Management System

AHCPR – Agency for Health Care Policy and Research

AHE – American Health Properties Inc. [stock listing]

AHG – Apria Healthcare Group Inc. [stock listing]

AHI – Allied Holdings Inc. [stock listing]

AHO – Ahold [stock listing]

AHP – American Home Products Corp. [stock listing]

AHPCRC – Army High Performance Computing Research Center

AHR – Anthracite Capital Inc. [stock listing]

AHRQ – Agency for Healthcare Research and Quality

AI – Anguilla

AI – artificial intelligence

AI – ATSI Communications Inc. [stock listing]

AIA – American Insured Mortgage Investors [stock listing]

AIAA – American Institute of Aeronautics and Astronautics

AIANA – American Indian and Alaska Native Areas

AIB – Allied Irish Banks P.L.C. [stock listing]

AICS – automated inventory control system

AID – Agency for International Development

AIDE – automated inventory distribution and exchange

AIDS – acquired immune deficiency syndrome; acquired immunodeficiency syndrome

AIEA – American Indian, Eskimo and Aleut

AIF – Acceptance Insurance Cos. [stock listing]

AIG – American International Group Inc. [stock listing]

AIH – Ablest Inc. [stock listing]

AII – American Insured Mortgage Series 85 [stock listing]

AIJ – American Insured Mortgage Series 86 [stock listing]

AIK – American Insured Mortgage Series 88 [stock listing]

AIM – Aerosonic Corp. [stock listing]

AIMS – Administrative Information and Management System

AIN – Albany International Corp./DE [stock listing]

AIP – American Israeli Paper Mills Ltd. [stock listing]

AIR – AAR Corp. [stock listing]

AIR – American Indian Reservation

AIS – administrative information system

AIS – automated information system

AIT – Applied Industrial Technologies Inc. [stock listing]

AIT – Asian Institute of Technology

AIUI – as I understand it

AIV – Apartment Investment & Management Co. [stock listing]

AIZ – Amcast Industrial Corp. [stock listing]

AJA – Appalachian Power Co. [stock listing]

AJG – Arthur J. Gallagher & Co. [stock listing]

AJX – Standard Automotive Corp. [stock listing]

AK – Ackerley Group Inc. [stock listing]

AK – Alaska

aka – also known as

AKB – Ambac Financial Group Inc. [stock listing]

AKC – Access Pharmaceuticals Inc. [stock listing]

AKK – Armstrong World Inds Inc. [stock listing]

AKOA – Embotelladora Andina [stock listing]

AKOB – Embotelladora Andina S.A. [stock listing]

AKR – Acadia Realty Trust [stock listing]

AKS – Ak Steel Holding Corp. [stock listing]

AL – Alabama

AL – Albania

AL – Alcan Inc. [stock listing]

AL – Arab League

Ala. – Alabama [standard newspaper abbreviation]

ALA – Alcatel [stock listing]

ALACE – Autonomous Lagrangian Circulation Explorer

ALB – Albany County Airport

ALB – Albemarle Corp. [stock listing]

ALC – Alltrista Corp. [stock listing]

ALC – assembler language code

ALCT – address list compilation test

ALE – Allete [stock listing]

ALF – Assisted Living Concepts Inc. [stock listing]

ALG – Alamo Group Inc. [stock listing]

ALGOL – algorithmic language

ALI – Alterra Healthcare Corp. [stock listing]

ALK – Alaska Air Group Inc. [stock listing]

ALL – Allstate Corp. [stock listing]

ALM – Allmerica Securities Trust [stock listing]

ALN – Allen Telecommunication Inc. [stock listing]

ALO – Al Pharma Inc. [stock listing]

ALOS – average length of stay

ALR – Allied Research Corp. [stock listing]

ALS – Alstom [stock listing]

alt – alternative [Internet domain]

ALT – Alteon Inc. [stock listing]

ALT – alternate

ALU – Allou Health & Beauty Care Inc. [stock listing]

ALV – Autoliv Inc. [stock listing]

ALX – Alexanders Inc. [stock listing]

AM – American Greetings Corp. [stock listing]

AM – amplitude modulated radio

AM – Armenia

AMA – American Management Association

AMA – American Marketing Association

AMA – American Medical Association

AMB – AMB Property Corp. [stock listing]

Amb. – ambassador

AMBPRA – AMB Property Corp. [stock listing]

AMC – American Mortgage Acceptance Co. [stock listing]

AMC – Army medical center

AMD – Advanced Micro Devices Inc. [stock listing]

AMDF – Army master data file

AMDL – Air Force Master Data List

AME – Ametek Inc. [stock listing]

Amex – American Stock Exchange

AMF – ACM Managed Income Fund Inc. [stock listing]

AMF – Arab Monetary Fund

AMG – Affiliated Managers Group [stock listing]

AMI – ALARIS Medical Inc. [stock listing]

AMIP – Atmospheric Model Intercomparison Project

AMK – American Technical Ceramics Corp. [stock listing]

AML – AMLI Residential Properties Trust [stock listing]

AMM – Advantage Marketing Systems Inc. [stock listing]

AMN – Ameron Internation Corp. [stock listing]

AMO – Alliance All-Market Advantage Fund Inc. [stock listing]

AMOS – Automated Meteorological Observing System

AMR – AMR Corp. [stock listing]

AMS – American Meteorological Society

AMS – American Shared Hospital Services [stock listing]

AMSCO – Army management structure code

AMSP – Asbestos Medical Surveillance Program

AMSU – advanced microwave sounding unit

AMT – American Tower Corp. [stock listing]

Amtrak – American Travel by Track [National Railroad Passenger Corp.]

AMU – ACM Municipal Securities Income Fund Inc. [stock listing]

AMV – AmeriVest Properties Inc. [stock listing]

AMVETS – American Veterans of World War II, Korea and Vietnam

AMW – Amwest Insurance Group Inc. [stock listing]

AMZ – American Medical Security Group Inc. [stock listing]

AN – Netherlands Antilles

AN – Autonation Inc. [stock listing]

ANA – Acadiana Bancshares Inc. [stock listing]

ANA – Administration for Native Americans

ANBPRA – Abbey National P.L.C. [stock listing]

AND – Andrea Electronics Corp. [stock listing]

ANDA – abbreviated new drug application

ANE – Alliance Bancorp of New England Inc. [stock listing]

ANF – Abercrombie & Fitch [stock listing]

ANG – Air National Guard

ANGB – Air National Guard base

ANH – Anworth Asset Mortgage Corp. [stock listing]

ANK – Atlantic Tele-Network Inc. [stock listing]

ANL – American Land Lease Inc. [stock listing]

ANN – Anntaylor Stores Corp. [stock listing]

ANOVA – analysis of variance

ANS – Airnet Sys Inc. [stock listing]

ANSI – American National Standards Institute

ANWR – Arctic National Wildlife Refuge

ANX – Antex Biologics Inc. [stock listing]

ANZ – Australia and New Zealand Banking Group Ltd. [stock listing]

ANZUS – Australia-New Zealand-United States Security Treaty

AO – Angola

AOAC – Association of Official Analytical Chemists

AOC – aircraft operations center

AOC – AON Corp. [stock listing]

AOF – ACM Government Opportunity Fund Inc. [stock listing]

AOG – Alberta Energy Co. Ltd. [stock listing]

AOIPS – Atmospheric and Oceanographic Information Processing System

AOL – AOL Time Warner Inc. [stock listing]

AOML – Atlantic Oceanographic and Meteorological Laboratory

AOO – American Oceanic Organization

AOPRA – Amerco [stock listing]

AOR – area of responsibility

AOR – Aurora Foods Inc. [stock listing]

AOS – Smith AO Corp. [stock listing]

AOSB – Arctic Ocean Science Board

AOT – Apogent Technologies Inc. [stock listing]

AP – AMPCO Pittsburgh Corp. [stock listing]

AP – applications processor

AP – Armed Forces Pacific

AP – Associated Press

APA – Apache Corp. [stock listing]

APB – Asia Pacific Fund Inc. [stock listing]

APC – account processing code

APC – Anadarko Petroleum Corp. [stock listing]

APD – Air Products and Chemicals Inc. [stock listing]

APDU – Association of Public Data Users

APEC – Asia-Pacific Economic Cooperation

APES – Automated Patient Evacuation System

APF – Morgan Stanley Dean Witter Asia-Pacific Fund Inc. [stock listing]

APF – Naples Municipal Airport

APH – Amphenol Corp. [stock listing]

APHIS – Animal and Plant Health Inspection Service

API – Advanced Photonix Inc. [stock listing]

API – Application Programming Interface

API – Asian and Pacific Islander

APL – Applied Physics Laboratory

APL – Atlas Pipeline Partners L.P. [stock listing]

APMIS – Administrative and Publications Management Information System

APMIS – automated project management system

APN – Alpena County Regional Airport

APO – American Community Properties Trust [stock listing]

APO – Army post office

APO – Properties Trust [stock listing]

APOC – advance post office check

APPN – advanced peer-to-peer networking

APR – agency procurement request

APR – American Precission Industries Inc. [stock listing]

APS – alternate payload specialist

APS – automated procurement system

APS – CollegeLink.com Inc. [stock listing]

APSD – Administrative and Publications Services Division

APT – Alpha Pro Technology Ltd. [stock listing]

APU – Amerigas Partners L.P. [stock listing]

APU – auxiliary power unit

APW – APW Ltd. [stock listing]

APX – Apex Municipal Fund Inc. [stock listing]

AQ – Antarctica

AQA – AquaCell Technologies Inc. [stock listing]

AR – acceptance report

AR – Argentina

AR – Arkansas

AR – Army Reserve

ARA – Aracruz Celulose [stock listing]

Arabsat – Arab Satellite Communications Organization

ARADS – Army Recruiting and Accession Data System

ARB – Arbitron Inc. [stock listing]

ARC – American Red Cross

ARC – Appalachian Regional Commission

ARC – Atlantic Richfield Co. [stock listing]

ARE – Alexandria Real Estate Equities Inc. [stock listing]

AREP – Atmospheric Research and Environment Program

AREPRA – Alexandria Real Estate Equities Inc. [stock listing]

ARG – Airgas On-line [stock listing]

ARH – Asia Pacific Resources International Holding Ltd. [stock listing]

ARI – acute respiratory infections

ARI – Arden Realty Inc. [stock listing]

ARIS – Administrative Records Information System

Ariz. – Arizona [standard newspaper abbreviation]

ARJ – Arch Chemical Inc. [stock listing]

Ark. – Arkansas [standard newspaper abbreviation]

ARK – Senior High Income Portfolio Inc. [stock listing]

ARL – Air Resources Laboratory [ERL]

ARL – American Realty Investors Inc. [stock listing]

ARL – Army Research Laboratory

ARM – ArvinMeritor Inc. [stock listing]

ARMC – Army regional medical center

ARNG – Army National Guard

ARO – Army Research Office

ARPA – Advanced Research Project Agency

ARS – Agricultural Research Service

ARTCC – Air Route Traffic Control Center

ARTS – accounts receivable tracking system

ARTS – annual retail trade survey

ARV – Arvin Industries Inc. [stock listing]

ARW – Arrow Electronics Inc. [stock listing]

AS – American Samoa

AS – Armoc Inc. [stock listing]

ASA – American Statistical Association

ASA – Asa Ltd. [stock listing]

ASAP – as soon as possible

ASAR – advanced synthetic aperture radar

ASB – Salomon Smith Barney Holdings Inc. [stock listing]

ASBP – Armed Services Blood Program

ASC – Accredited Standards Committee

ASC – administrative support center

ASCE – American Society of Civil Engineers

ASCII – American Standard Code for Information Interchange

ASD – account subset definition

ASD – American Standard Co. Inc. [stock listing]

ASDAR – aircraft-to-satellite data relay system

AsDB – Asian Development Bank

ASDM – automated source data maintenance

ASDS – Accunet Spectrum of Digital Services

ASE – airborne support equipment

ASE – American Science and Engineering Inc. [stock listing]

ASE – Aspen-Pitkin County Airport/Sardy Field

ASEAN – Association of Southeast Asian Nations

ASF – Administaff Inc. [stock listing]

ASG – Liberty All-Star Growth Fund Inc. [stock listing]

ASGPI – Association of Sea Grant Program Institutes

ASH – Ashland Inc. [stock listing]

ASI – American Safety Insurance Group Ltd. [stock listing]

ASIC – application-specific integrated circuit

ASIMS – Army Standard Information Management System

ASL – Ashanti Goldfields Co. Ltd. [stock listing]

ASL – atmospheric surface layer

ASM – appointing and scheduling module

ASN – allotment serial number

ASN – Archstone Communities Trust [stock listing]

ASO – Amsouth BanCorporation [stock listing]

ASO – aviation supply office

ASOS – automated seismological observation system

ASP – American Strategic Income Portfolio Inc. [stock listing]

ASPCA – American Society for the Prevention of Cruelty to Animals

ASPEI – Association of South-Pacific Environmental Institutions

ASPR – Armco Inc. [stock listing]

ASPRS – American Society for Photogrammetry and Remote Sensing

ASR – Grupo Aeroportuario Del Surest S.A. de C.V. [stock listing]

ASRS – automatic storage and retrieval system

ASSET – automated software support entry tracking

ASTC – Association of Science and Technology Centers

ASTM – American Society for Testing and Materials

ASV – Ag Svcs Amer Inc. [stock listing]

ASX – Advanced Semiconductor Engineering Inc. [stock listing]

ASXPR – Advanced Semiconductor Engineering Inc. [stock listing]

ASY – Elecsys Corp. [stock listing]

ASYNC – an IBM protocol

async – asynchronous

ASYNC – asynchronous communication

AT&T – American Telephone and Telegraph

AT – advanced technology

AT – ALLTEL Shareholder Services [stock listing]

AT – Austria

ATA – actual time of arrival

ATA – American Tunaboat Association

ATC – air traffic control

ATD – actual time of departure

ATF – Alcohol, Tobacco and Firearms [Treasury Dept. Bureau]

ATF – Equity Income Fund, First Exchange Series [stock listing]

ATG – AGL Resources [stock listing]

ATI – Allegheny Technologies Inc. [stock listing]

ATJ – AT Plastics Inc. [stock listing]

ATK – Alliant Techsystems Inc. [stock listing]

ATL – Atalanta Sosnoff Capital Corporate Delaware [stock listing]

ATM – asynchronous transfer mode

ATM – automated teller machine

ATMS – advanced traffic management system

ATO – Atmos Energy Corp. [stock listing]

ATOC – Acoustic Thermography of Ocean Climate

ATOC – Air Terminal Operations Center

ATP – Argo Bancorp Inc. [stock listing]

ATPR – Alltel Corp. [stock listing]

ATR – Aptargroup Inc. [stock listing]

ATS – annual trade survey

ATS – application technology satellite [NASA]

ATS – APT Satellite Hldgs Ltd. [stock listing]

ATU – Actuant Corp. [stock listing]

ATW – Atwood Oceanics Inc. [stock listing]

ATX – Cross (A.T.) Co. [stock listing]

AU – Anglogold Ltd. [stock listing]

AU – Australia

AUV – autonomous underwater vehicle

AV – audiovisual

AV – Avaya Inc. [stock listing]

AVA – Avista Corp. [stock listing]

AVB – Avalonbay Communities Inc. [stock listing]

AVC – Audio Visual Services Corp. [stock listing]

AVD – American Vanguard Corp. [stock listing]

AVE – Aventis S.A. [stock listing]

AVEPR – Aventis [stock listing]

AVI – Avis Group Holdings [stock listing]

AVIRIS – airborne visible and infrared imaging spectrometer

AVL – Aviall Inc. [stock listing]

AVM – Advanced Magnetics Inc. [stock listing]

AVN – AVANIR Pharmaceuticals [stock listing]

AVP – Avocet Capital Management L.P. [stock listing]

AVR – Avitar Inc. [stock listing]

AVS – application visualization system

AVS – Aviation Sales Co. [stock listing]

AVT – Avnet Inc. [stock listing]

AVX – Avx Corp. [stock listing]

AVY – Avery Dennison Corp. [stock listing]

AVZ – AMVESCAP P.L.C. [stock listing]

AW – Allied Waste Industries Inc. [stock listing]

AW – Aruba

AWA – America West Holding Corp. [stock listing]

AWAWS – America West Airlines Inc. [stock listing]

AWB – air waybill

AWC – Asia Pacific Wire & Cable [stock listing]

AWE – AT&T Corp. [stock listing]

AWG – Alliance World Dollar Government Fund [stock listing]

AWIS – Army WWMCCS Information System

AWK – American Water Works Co. [stock listing]

AWOL – Absent without official leave

AWP – Average wholesale price

AWR – American States Water Co. [stock listing]

AWX – Avalon Holdings Corp. [stock listing]

AXA – Axa Uap [stock listing]

AXBT – airborne expendable bathythermograph

AXC – Ampex Corp. [stock listing]

AXCP – airborne expendable current profiler

AXE – Anixter Intl Inc. [stock listing]

AXF – AXA Financial Inc. [stock listing]

AXL – American Axle & Manufacturing Holdings Inc. [stock listing]

AXM – Apex Mortgage Capital Inc. [stock listing]

AXO – AXS-One Inc. [stock listing]

AXP – American Express Co. [stock listing]

AXR – AMREP Corp. [stock listing]

AXS – Altus Municipal Airport

AXT – American Municipal Term Trust Inc. [stock listing]

AXV – Neil Armstrong Airport

AYE – Allengheny Energy Inc. [stock listing]

AZ – Allianz A.G. [stock listing]

AZ – Arizona

AZ – Azerbaijan

AZA – ALZA Corp. [stock listing]

AZC – Azco Mining Inc. [stock listing]

AZD – Arizona Pub Svc Co. [stock listing]

AZL – Arizona Land Income Corp. [stock listing]

AZN – AstraZeneca Group P.L.C. [stock listing]

AZO – Autozone Inc. [stock listing]

AZR – Aztar Corp. [stock listing]

AZX – Azurix Corp. [stock listing]

AZZ – Azz Inc. [stock listing]

B.A. – bachelor of arts

B.C. – before Christ

B.S. – bachelor of science

B – Barnes Group Inc. [stock listing]

b – bit

BA – Bosnia-Herzegovina

BA – Boeing Corp. [stock listing]

BAB – British Airways P.L.C. [stock listing]

BAC – Bank of America Corp. [stock listing]

BAC – Budget Advisory Committee

BAD – Banque Africaine de Developpement

BAFO – best and final offer

BAL – Balanced Care Corp. [stock listing]

BAO – Boulder Atmospheric Observatory

BAP – Credicorp Ltd. [stock listing]

BAS – Bass P.L.C. [stock listing]

BASIC – Beginner's All-Purpose Symbolic Instruction Code

BAT – Blackrock Advantage Term Trust Inc., The [stock listing]

BAU – BACOU USA Inc. [stock listing]

BAX – Baxter International Inc. [stock listing]

BB – Barbados
BB – BBVA Banco BHIF [stock listing]
BBA – Bombay Co. Inc. [stock listing]
BBC – Bergen Brunswig Corp. [stock listing]
BBDP – Block Boundary Definition Project
BBH – Merrill Lynch Biotech HOLDRS [stock listing]
BBI – Blockbuster Inc. [stock listing]
BBR – Butler Manufacturing Inc. [stock listing]
BBS – bulletin board software
BBSP – Block Boundary Suggestion Project
BBT – BB&T Corp. [stock listing]
BBVPRA – Bbva Preferred Capital Ltd. [stock listing]
BBX – Bankatlantic [stock listing]
BBXRT – Broad Band X-ray
BBY – Best Buy Co. [stock listing]
BC – Brunswick Corp. [stock listing]
BCAO – Branch Cultural Affairs Officer (USIS)
BCC – blind carbon copy
BCC – Boise Cascade Corp. [stock listing]
BCD – binary coded decimal
BCE – BCE Inc. [stock listing]
BCF – Burlington Coat Factory Warehousse [stock listing]
BCM – Canadian Imperial Bank of Commerce [stock listing]
BCP – Balchem Corp. [stock listing]
BCR – Bard Cr Inc. [stock listing]
BCS – Barclays P.L.C. [stock listing]
BCT – BlackRock Broad Investment Grade 2009 Term Trust Inc., The [stock listing]
BCU – Borden Chemicals and Plastics L.P. [stock listing]
BCV – Bancroft Convertible Fund Inc. [stock listing]
BD – Bangladesh
BD – Budget Group Inc. [stock listing]
BDE – Brigade
BDE – Brilliant Digital Entertainment Inc. [stock listing]
BDG – Bandag Inc. [stock listing]

BDJ – Morgan Stanley Dean Witter & Co. [stock listing]
BDK – Black and Decker Corp. [stock listing]
BDL – Flanigan's Enterprises Inc. [stock listing]
BDM – Merrill Lynch & Co. Inc. [stock listing]
BDN – Brandywine Realty Trust [stock listing]
BDR – Blonder Tongue Laboratories Inc. [stock listing]
BDX – Becton Dickinson & Co. [stock listing]
BDY – Bindley Western Industries Inc. [stock listing]
BE – Belgium
BEA – Bureau of Economic Analysis
BEC – Beckman Coulter Inc. [stock listing]
BED – Bedford Property Investors Inc. [stock listing]
BEI – Boardwalk Equities Inc. [stock listing]
BEL – Bell Atlantic Corp. [stock listing]
BEM – Bergstrom Capital Corp. [stock listing]
BEMEX – Bering Sea Experiment
BEN – Franklin Resources Inc. [stock listing]
BEP – Bureau of Engraving and Printing
BERT – bit-error-rate test
BET – Bethlehem Corp. [stock listing]
BEV – Beverly Enterprises Inc. [stock listing]
BEZ – Baldor Electric Co. [stock listing]
BF – BASF A.G. [stock listing]
BF – Burkina Faso
BFA – Brown Forman Corp. [stock listing]
BFC – Blackrock California Insured Municipal 2008 Term Trust Inc., The [stock listing]
BFD – BostonFed Bancorp Inc. [stock listing]
BFN – Bloemfontein J.B.M. Hertzog [South Africa]
BFO – Best Foods [stock listing]
BFS – Saul Centers Inc. [stock listing]
BFT – Bally Total Fitness Holding Corp. [stock listing]
BG – Bulgaria
BGC – General Cable Corp. [stock listing]
BGG – Briggs & Stratton Corp. [stock listing]

BGO – Bema Gold Corp. [stock listing]

BGP – Borders Group Inc. [stock listing]

BGR – Bangor Hydro Electric Co. [stock listing]

BGS – British Geological Survey

BGS – Morgan Stanley Dean Witter [stock listing]

BGT – Blackrock Strategic Term Trust Inc., The [stock listing]

BGY – British Energy P.L.C. [stock listing]

BH – Bahrain

BHB – Bar Harbor Bankshares Inc. [stock listing]

BHC – BHC Communications Inc. [stock listing]

BHE – Benchmark Electronics Inc. [stock listing]

BHH – Merrill Lynch B2B Internet HOLDRS [stock listing]

BHI – Baker Hughes Inc. [stock listing]

BHL – Berkshire Hills Bancorp Inc. [stock listing]

BHM – Merrill Lynch & Co. Inc. [stock listing]

BHO – B+H Ocean Carriers Ltd. [stock listing]

BHP – Broken Hill Proprietary Ltd. [stock listing]

BHW – Bell & Howell Co. [stock listing]

BHY – Blackrock High Yield Trust, The [stock listing]

BI – Bell Industries Inc. [stock listing]

BI – Burundi

BIA – Bureau of Indian Affairs

BIAC – Business and Industry Advisory Committee

BIB – Board for International Broadcasting

BIC – Business Information Center

BID – Sothebys Holdings Inc. [stock listing]

BIDC – business and industry data center

BIGCAT – block-level intercensal geographic changes and transactions

BIO/A – Bio-Rad Laboratories Inc. [stock listing]

BIOS – Basic Input Output System

BIR – Birmingham Steel Corp. [stock listing]

BIS – Bank for International Settlements

BIS – Barrister Global Services Network Inc. [stock listing]

BISYNC – Binary Synchronous Communication

BIT – binary digit

BIW – Birmingham Utilities Inc. [stock listing]

BJ – Benin

BJ – BJ's Wholesale Club Inc. [stock listing]

BJA – Bureau of Justice Assistance

BJS – BJ Services Co. [stock listing]

BJS – Bureau of Justice Statistics

BK – Bank of New York Co. [stock listing]

BKC – American Bank of Connecticut [stock listing]

BKE – Buckle Inc., The [stock listing]

BKF – BKF Capital Group Inc. [stock listing]

BKH – Black Hills Corp. [stock listing]

BKI – Buckeye Technologies Inc. [stock listing]

BKN – Blackrock Investment Quality Municipal Trust, The [stock listing]

BKP – Bank United Corp. [stock listing]

BKR – Baker (Michael) Corp. [stock listing]

BKS – Barnes & Noble Inc. [stock listing]

BKT – Blackrock Income Trust Inc., The [stock listing]

BL – Blair Corp. [stock listing]

BLC – A.H. Belo Corp. [stock listing]

BLD – Baldwin Technology Co. Inc. [stock listing]

BLIPS – Benthic Layer Interactive Profiling System

BLK – Blackrock Inc. [stock listing]

BLL – Ball Corp. [stock listing]

BLM – Blimpie International Inc. [stock listing]

BLM – Bureau of Land Management

BLN – Blackrock New York Insured Municipal 2008 Term Trust Inc., The [stock listing]

BLS – Bell South Corp. [stock listing]

BLS – Bureau of Labor Statistics

BLT – Blount International Inc. [stock listing]

BLU – Blue Chip Value Fund Inc. [stock listing]

BLX – Banco Latinoamericano de Exportaciones S.A. [stock listing]

BM – Bermuda

BMA – Bromma Airport-Stockholm

BMC – BMC Software [stock listing]

BMDO – Ballistic Missile Defense Organization

BMET – Biomedical Equipment Technician

BMG – Battle Mountain Gold Co. [stock listing]

BMI – Badger Meter Inc. [stock listing]

BMIS – budget management information system

BMM – BMC Industries Inc. [stock listing]

BMN – Blackrock Municipal Target Term Trust Inc., The [stock listing]

BMO – Bank of Montreal [stock listing]

BMOMIS – Ballistic Missile Office Management Information System

BMS – Belz Richard [stock listing]

BMT – Blackrock Insured Municipal Term Trust, The [stock listing]

BMY – Bristol Myers Squibb Co. [stock listing]

BN – Brunei Darussalam

BN – Banta Corp. [stock listing]

BN – battalion

BNA – brand name authorization

BNA – Bureau of National Affairs

BNA – Nashville International Airport

BNA – Blackrock North American Government Income Trust, The [stock listing]

BND – Boundless Corp. [stock listing]

BNE – Bowne & Co. Inc. [stock listing]

BNG – Benetton Group S.P.A. [stock listing]

BNI – Burlington Northern Santa Fe Corp. [stock listing]

BNK – CNB Bancshares Inc. [stock listing]

BNL – Bunzl P.L.C. [stock listing]

BNN – Brascan Corp. [stock listing]

BNO – Benton Oil & Gas Co. [stock listing]

BNP – BNP Residential Properties Inc. [stock listing]

BNS – BNS Co. [stock listing]

BNT – Bentley Pharmaceuticals Inc. [stock listing]

BNX – Merrill Lynch & Co. Inc. [stock listing]

BO – Bolivia

BO – Branch Office

BOA – Bush Boake Allen Inc. [stock listing]

BOAD – Banque Ouest-Africaine de Developpement

BOB/EUR – Board of Broadcasting/European Office

BOB – Merrill Lynch & Co. Inc. [stock listing]

BOC – Bureau of the Census

BOG – Belco Oil & Gas Corp. [stock listing]

BOH – Pacific Century Financial Corp. [stock listing]

BOI – Boise Air Terminal Gowen Field

BOL – Bausch & Lomb Inc. [stock listing]

BOM – bill of materials

BOO – Collegiate Pacific Inc. [stock listing]

BOP – Federal Bureau of Prisons

BOQ – bachelor officer's quarters

BOR – Bureau of Reclamation

BOS – Boston Celtics L.P. [stock listing]

BOW – Bowater Inc. [stock listing]

BOX – Boc Group P.L.C. [stock listing]

BOY – Boykin Lodging Co. [stock listing]

BP – BP Amoco P.L.C. [stock listing]

BPAO – Branch Public Affairs Officer

BPC – Banco Comercial Portugues S.A. [stock listing]

BPD – Budget Planning Document

BPD – Bureau of the Public Debt

BPL – Buckeye Partners L.P. [stock listing]

BPO – Brookfield Pptys Corp. [stock listing]

BPP – Burnham Pacific Properties Inc. [stock listing]

bps – bits per second

BPS – Blackrock Pennsylvania Strategic Municipal Trust, The [stock listing]

BPT – BP Prudhoe Bay Royalty Trust [stock listing]

BQT – Blackrock Investment Quality Term Trust Inc., The [stock listing]

BR – Brazil

BR – Burlington Resources Inc. [stock listing]

BRAC – Base Realignment and Closure

BRB – be right back

BRB – Benefits Review Board

BRB – Brunswick Bancorp [stock listing]

BRC – Brady Corp. [stock listing]

BRE – BRE Properties Inc. [stock listing]

BRF – Blackrock Florida Insured Municipal 2008 Term Trust, The [stock listing]

BRG – Bg P.L.C. [stock listing]

BRHC – Companhia Cerve Jaria Brahma [stock listing]

Brig. Gen. – brigadier general

BRKA – Berkshire Hathaway Inc. [stock listing]

BRKB – Berkshire Hathaway Inc. [stock listing]

BRL – Barr Laboratories Inc. [stock listing]

BRM – Blackrock Insured Municipal 2008 Term Trust Inc., The [stock listing]

BRN – Barnwell Industries Inc. [stock listing]

BRO – Brown & Brown Insurance [stock listing]

BRP – Brasil Telecom Participacoes [stock listing]

BRP – business recovery plan

BRR – Barrett Resources Corp. [stock listing]

BRS – Banco Rio de la Plata S.A. [stock listing]

BRT – BRT Realty Trust [stock listing]

BRW – Broadwing Inc. [stock listing]

BRX – Morgan Stanley Dean Witter & Co. [stock listing]

BRY – Berry Petroleum Co. [stock listing]

BS – Bahamas

BS – Bethlehem Steel Corp. [stock listing]

BSB – Banco Santander-Chile [stock listing]

BSC – Bears Stearns & Co. Inc. [stock listing]

BSC – business service centers

BSF – Bureau of Commercial Fisheries

BSH – Bush Industries Inc. [stock listing]

BSI – Blue Square-Israel Ltd. [stock listing]

BSL – Basel Basel/Mulhouse EuroAirport

BSP – American Strategic Income Portfolio Inc.-II [stock listing]

BSPR – Bethlehem Steel Corp. [stock listing]

BST – British Steel P.L.C. [stock listing]

BSX – Boston Scientific Corp.

BSY – British Sky Broadcasting Grp. [stock listing]

BT – Bhutan

BTAPRA – Totta & Acores Financing Ltd. [stock listing]

BTC – Booktech.com Inc. [stock listing]

BTF – Boulder Total Return Fund Inc. [stock listing]

BTH – Blyth Industries Inc. [stock listing]

BTI – British American Tobacco Industries P.L.C. [stock listing]

BTJ – Bolt Technology Corp. [stock listing]

BTM – Blackrock 2001 Term Trust Inc., The [stock listing]

BTN – Ballantyne Omaha Inc. [stock listing]

BTO – John Hancock Bank and Thrift Opportunity Fund [stock listing]

BTS – Bureau of Transportation Statistics

BTT – Blackrock Target Term Trust Inc., The [stock listing]

BTU – British thermal unit

BTW – by the way

BTX – BioTime Inc. [stock listing]

BTY – British Telecommunications P.L.C. [stock listing]

BTZ – Berlitz International Inc. [stock listing]

BUCEN – Bureau of the Census

BUD – Anheuser Busch Cos. Inc. [stock listing]

BUR – Burbank-Glendale-Pasadena Airport

BUR – Burlington Industries Inc. [stock listing]

BV – Bouvet Island

BVA – Bionova Holding Corp. [stock listing]

BVA – Board of Veterans Appeals

BVB – Bridge View Bancorp [stock listing]

BVC – Bay View Capital Corp. [stock listing]

BVF – Biovail Corp. [stock listing]

BW – Botswana

BW – Brush Wellman Inc. [stock listing]

BWA – Borgwagner Inc. [stock listing]

BWC – Belden Inc. [stock listing]

BWE – BancWest Corp. [stock listing]

BWG – Bouygues Offshore [stock listing]

BWI – Baltimore/Washington International Airport

BWL/A – Bowl America Inc. [stock listing]

BWP – Banco Wiese Surameris [stock listing]

BWS – Brown Shoe Company Inc. [stock listing]

BWYWS – Broadway Stores Inc. [stock listing]

BXA – Bureau of Export Administration

BXG – Bluegreen Corp. [stock listing]

BXL – Bexil Corp. [stock listing]

BXM – Biomatrix Inc. [stock listing]

BXP – Boston Properties Inc. [stock listing]

BXS – BancorpSouth Inc. [stock listing]

BXT – American Municipal Term Trust Inc.-II [stock listing]

BY – Belarus

BY – Bway Corp. [stock listing]

BYD – Boyd Gaming Corp. [stock listing]

BYH – Beijing Yanhua Petrochemical [stock listing]

BYL – Baylake Capital Trust I [stock listing]

BYS – Bay State Bancorp [stock listing]

BYX – Bayou Steel Corp. [stock listing]

BZ – Bairnco Corp. [stock listing]

BZ – Belize

BZF – Brazil Fund Inc., The [stock listing]

BZH – Beazer Homes USA Inc. [stock listing]

BZL – Brazilian Equity Fund Inc., The [stock listing]

c.o.d. – cash on delivery, or collect on delivery

C.P. – Caixa Postal

C/SA – client/sever architecture

C – Citigroup Inc. [stock listing]

C – commonwealth

C – computer programming language

C – consulate

C2 – a designated level of trust for unclassified automated systems

C2 – command and control

C2PO – Census 2000 Publicity Office

CA – California

CA – Canada

CA – Computer Associates International Inc. [stock listing]

CA – Consular Agency/Agent

CAA – Capital Alliance Income Trust Ltd. [stock listing]

CAA – Civil Aviation Administration

CAAP – Consolidated Accommodations Acquisition Program

CAAS – Contract Advisory and Assistance Services

CAC – Camden National Corp. [stock listing]

CAC – Census Advisory Committee

CACC – computer-assisted clerical coding

CACGP – Committee on Atmospheric Chemistry and Global Pollution

CACM – Central American Common Market

CAD – computer-aided design

CAD-CAM – computer-assisted design/computer-assisted manufacturing

CADD – computer-aided design & drafting

CAE – Cascade Corp. [stock listing]

CAE – Columbia Metropolitan Airport

CAE – computer-aided engineering

CAEU – Council of Arab Economic Unity

CAFM – computer-aided facilities management

CAG – ConAgra Foods Inc. [stock listing]

CAH – Cardinal Healthy Inc. [stock listing]

CAI – computer-assisted interviewing

CAI – computer-assisted instruction

CAIS – college applicant information system

CAJ – Canon Inc. [stock listing]

CAL – Continental Airlines Inc. [stock listing]

CALA – Continental Airlines Inc. [stock listing]

Calif. – California [standard newspaper abbreviation]

CALS – computer-aided acquisition and logistic support

CAM – computer-aided manufacturing

CAM – Cooper Cameron Corp. [stock listing]

CAMEO – computer-aided management of emergency operations

CAMIS – computer-assisted medical interactive video systems

CAN – American National Can Group Inc. [stock listing]

CAN – Center for Naval Analysis

CANDA – computer-assisted new drug application

CAO – CSK Auto Corp. [stock listing]

CAO – cultural affairs officer

CAP – College of American Pathologists

CAP – Computer/Electronic Accommodations Program Office

CAP – Creative Computer Applications Inc. [stock listing]

CAPCOM – capsule communicator

Capt. – captain

CAR – Carter Wallace Inc. [stock listing]

CAR – commerce acquisition regulations

CARB – California Air Resources Board

CARE – Cooperative for American Relief Everywhere

CARP – Cluster Analysis and Regression Program

CAS – Castle (A.M.) & Co. [stock listing]

CASE – computer-aided software engineering

CASE – computer-aided system engineering

CAST – China Association for Science and Technology

CAT – Caterpillar Inc. [stock listing]

CAT – control and analysis tool

CAU – Canyon Resources Corp. [stock listing]

CAV – Cavalier Homes Inc. [stock listing]

CB – Chubb Corp. [stock listing]

CB – citizens band [radio]

CBA – Brilliance China Automotive Holdings Ltd. [stock listing]

CBA – cost benefit analysis

CBC – Centura Banks Inc. [stock listing]

CBD – Commerce Business Daily

CBE – Cooper Inds Inc. [stock listing]

CBF – Chase Cap V [stock listing]

CBF – Chesapeake Bay Foundation, The

CBG – CB Richard Ellis Services Inc. [stock listing]

CBH – Commerce Bancorp Inc. [stock listing]

CBHPRT – Comed Financing [stock listing]

CBI – Chicago Bridge & Iron Co. [stock listing]

CBI – computer-based instruction

CBJ – Cambior Inc. [stock listing]

CBL – Cbl & Associates Properties Inc. [stock listing]

CBL – convective boundary layer

CBM – Cambex Corp. [stock listing]

CBN – Cornerstone Bancorp Inc. [stock listing]

CBO – Congressional Budget Office

CBOS – Chesapeake Bay Observing System

CBR – CIBER Inc. [stock listing]

CBS – Columbia Broadcasting System

CBSS – Council of the Baltic Sea States

CBT – Cabot Corps. [stock listing]

CBT – computer-based training

CBU – Community Bank Systems Inc. [stock listing]

CBWRA – Census Bureau Welfare and Recreation Association

CBZ – Cobalt Corp. [stock listing]

CC – carbon copy

CC – Circuit City Stores Inc. [stock listing]

CC – Cocos Islands (also Keeling Islands)

CCA – Colonial California Insured Municipal Fund [stock listing]

CCAFS – Cape Canaveral Air Force Station

CCC – Calgon Carbon Corp. [stock listing]

CCC – Commodity Credit Corp.

CCC – Customs Cooperation Council

CCE – Coca-Cola Enterprises Inc. [stock listing]

CCF – Chase Corp. [stock listing]

CCF – collection control file

CCH – Campbell Resources Inc. [stock listing]

CCI – Census of Construction Industries

CCI – Crown Castle International Corp. [stock listing]

CCIS – command and control information system

CCJ – Comeco Corp. [stock listing]

CCK – Crown Cork & Seal Co Inc. [stock listing]

CCL – Carnival Corp. [stock listing]

CCl – Commission for Climatology

CCM – corporate cost management

CCMPR – Carlton Communications P.L.C. [stock listing]

CCN – Chris Craft Industries Inc. [stock listing]

CCR – Commission on Civil Rights

CCR – Countrywide Credit Industries Inc. [stock listing]

CCS – collection control system

CCS – Lehman ABS Corp. [stock listing]

CCSR – Center for Climate System Research

CCSS – Coordinated-Care Support System

CCT – Lehman ABS Corp. [stock listing]

CCTV – closed-circuit televison

CCU – Clear Channel Communications Inc. [stock listing]

CCWCP – Coordinating Committee for the World Climate Program

CCZ – Comcast Corp. [stock listing]

CD – certificate of deposit

CD – civil defense

CD – commerce department

CD – compact disc

CDA – Cordiant Communications Group [stock listing]

CDB – Caribbean Development Bank

CDBG – Community Development Block Grants

CDC – Centers for Disease Control and Prevention

CDCC – Caribbean Development and Cooperation Committee

CDCP – Centers for Disease Control and Prevention

CDD – central data dictionary

CDD – Cordant Technologies Inc. [stock listing]

CD-E – CD-erasable

CDE – Coeur D Alene Mines Corp. [stock listing]

CDER – Center for Drug Evaluation and Research

CDF – common data format

CDG – Paris Charles de Gaulle Airport

CDI – CDI Corp. [stock listing]

CDL/A – Citadel Holding Corp. [stock listing]

CDL/B – Citadel Holding Corp. [stock listing]

CDMA – Code Division Multiple Access

CDMS – Command and Data Management Systems Officer

CDN – Cadence Design Systems Inc. [stock listing]

CDO – Comdisco Inc. [stock listing]

CDP – census designated place

CDPD – cellular digital packet data

CDPRG – Cendant Corp. [stock listing]

Cdr. – commander

CD-R – compact disc-recordable

CD-ROM – compact disc-read-only memory

CD-RW – compact-disc-rewritable

CDS – Credit Store Inc., The [stock listing]

CDT – Cable Design Technologies Corp. [stock listing]

CDTR – common data transfer record

CDV – Consolidated Delivery & Logistics Inc. [stock listing]

CDX – Catellus Development Corp. [stock listing]

CE – civil engineer

CEA – China Eastern Airlines Corp. Ltd. [stock listing]

CEA – Council of Economic Advisors

CECON – chief economist

CED – Canadian Natural Resources Ltd. [stock listing]

CEE – Central European Equity Fund Inc., The [stock listing]

CEES – Committee on Earth and Environmental Sciences

CEF – Central Fund of Canada Ltd. [stock listing]

CEG – Constellation Energy Group Inc. [stock listing]

CE-HEO – chief executive-highest elected official

CEI – Central European Initiative

CEI – Crescent Real Estate Equities Co. [stock listing]

CEIP – CHCS Engineering Improvement Program

CEIS – corporate executive information system

CEL – Nuevo Group [stock listing]

CELADE – Centro Latinoamericano de Demografia

CEM – Chemfirst Inc. [stock listing]

CEN – Ceridian Corp. [stock listing]

CEN – Comite Europeen de Normalization

CENDATA – census electronic data dissemination

CENR – Committee on Environment and Natural Resources

CEO – chief executive officer

CEO – CNOOC [stock listing]

CEO – cultural exchange officer

CEOS – Committee on Earth Observation Satellites

CEPS – Center for Earth and Planetary Studies

CEQ – Council on Environmental Quality

CERCLA – Comprehensive Environmental Response, Compensation and Liability Act

CES – consumer expenditures survey

CEST – Central European standard time

CET – Central Securities Corp. [stock listing]

CEV – Eaton Vance California Municipal Income Trust [stock listing]

cf. – confer

CF – Central African Republic

CF – Charter One Financial Inc. [stock listing]

CFB – Commercial Federal Corp. [stock listing]

CFC – chlorofluorocarbon

CFD – call for discussion

CFD – Conseco Strategic Income Fund [stock listing]

CFE – contractor-furnished equipment

CFE – Lehman ABS Corp. [stock listing]

CFES – continuous flow electrophoresis system

CFI – Culp Inc. [stock listing]

CFIB – Corporate Functional Information Board

CFK – CE Franklin Ltd. [stock listing]

CFO – chief financial officer

CFPPRC – California Federal Bank [stock listing]

CFR – Code of Federal Regulations

CFR – Code of the Federal Register

CFR – Cullen/Frost Bankers Inc. [stock listing]

CFS – COMFORCE Corp. [stock listing]

cfs – cubic feet per second

CFSAN – Center for Food Safety and Applied Nutrition

CFX – CCA Colonial Insured Municipal Fund [stock listing]

CG SEC – Consul General's Secretary

CG – Columbia Energy Group [stock listing]

CG – Congo

CG – consul general, consulate general

CGA – color graphics adapter

CGC – Cascade Natural Gas Corp. [stock listing]

CGCP – Climate and Global Change Program

CGE – Centris Group Inc. [stock listing]

CGI – common gateway interface

CGI – Commerce Group Inc. [stock listing]

CGK – Lehman ABS Corp. [stock listing]

CGL/A – Cagle's Inc. [stock listing]

CGM – Congoleum Corp. [stock listing]

CGMW – Commission for the Geological Map of the World

CGN – Cognitronics Corp. [stock listing]
CGO – Atlas Air Worldwide [stock listing]
CGP – Coastal Corp. [stock listing]
CGR – Cooker Restaurant Corp. [stock listing]
CGS – College Park Airport
CGS – Committee on Geological Sciences
CGX – Consoilidated Graphics Inc. [stock listing]
CGX – Merrill C. Meigs Airport
CGZ – Cotelligent Inc. [stock listing]
CH – Switzerland
CH – Chile Fund Inc., The [stock listing]
CHA – Champion International Corp. [stock listing]
CHB – Champion Enterprises Inc. [stock listing]
CHC – Charter Municipal Mortgage Acceptance Co. [stock listing]
CHCM – Comprehensive Health Care Management
CHD – Church & Dwight Co. Inc. [stock listing]
CHE – CHEMED CORP. [stock listing]
CHG – Central Hudson Gas & Electric Corp. [stock listing]
CHG – chargé d'Affaires
CHH – Choice Hotels International Inc. [stock listing]
CHID – combined health information database
CHK – Chesapeake Energy Corp. [stock listing]
CHL – China Mobile [stock listing]
CHN – China Fund Inc., The [stock listing]
CHO – Charlottsville-Albemarle Airport
CHP – C&D Technologies Inc. [stock listing]
CHR – Gener S.A. [stock listing]
CHS – Chico's FAS Inc. [stock listing]
CHS – Comprehensive Health Services
CHT – Chart House Enterprises Inc. [stock listing]
CHU – China Unicom Ltd. [stock listing]
CHV – Chevron Corp. [stock listing]
CHX – Pilgrims Pride Corp. [stock listing]

CHY – Chyron Corp. [stock listing]
CHZ – Chittenden Corp. [stock listing]
CI – Cigna Corp. [stock listing]
CI – configuration item
CI – Ivory Coast
CIA – Central Intelligence Agency
CIA – Citizens Inc. [stock listing]
CIAD – Climate Impact Assessment Division
CIB – BanColombia S.A. [stock listing]
CICS – customer information control system
CID – Chieftain International Inc. [stock listing]
CID – U.S. Army Criminal Investigation Command
CIDA – Canadian International Development Agency
CIE – communications interface equipment
CIF – Colonial Intermediate High Income Fund [stock listing]
CIF – cost, insurance and freight
CIFAR – Cooperative Institute for Arctic Research
CIK – Credit Suisse Asset Management Income Fund Inc. [stock listing]
CIM – CIM High Yield Securities [stock listing]
CIM – Center for Information Management
CIM – CIM High Yield Securities [stock listing]
CIM – computer-integrated manufacturing
CIMAS – Cooperative Institute for Marine and Atmospheric Studies
CIMS – chemical ionization mass spectrometer
CIMS – corporate information management system
CIN – Cinergy Corp. [stock listing]
CINC – commander-in-chief
CINCAFSOUTH – Commander-in-Chief Allied Forces Southern Europe
CINCEUR – Commander-in-Chief U.S. European Command
CINCLANTFLT – Commander-in-Chief U.S. Atlantic Fleet

CINCUSAFE – Commander-in-Chief U.S. Air Forces Europe

CINCUSAREUR – Commander-in-Chief U.S. Army Europe

CINPRA – Cincinnati Gas & Elec Co. [stock listing]

CIO – chief information officer

CIO – Computerized Thermal Imaging Inc. [stock listing]

CIS – Commonwealth of Independent States

CIT – CIT Group Inc. [stock listing]

CITES – Convention on International Trade in Endangered Species of Wild Fauna and Flora

CIV – Conectiv Inc. [stock listing]

CIX – CompX International Inc. [stock listing]

CIZ – Citizens Holding Co. [stock listing]

CJA – Columbus Southern Power Co. [stock listing]

CJR – Corus Entertainment Inc. [stock listing]

CK – Cook Islands

CK – Crompton Corp. [stock listing]

CKC – Collins & Aikman Corp. [stock listing]

CKE – Carmike Cinemas Inc. [stock listing]

CKH – Seacor Smit Inc. [stock listing]

CKP – Checkpoint Systems Inc. [stock listing]

CKR – CKE Restaurants Inc. [stock listing]

CL – Chile

CL – Colgate Palmolive Co. [stock listing]

CLB – Core Laboratories [stock listing]

CLC – Clarcor Inc. [stock listing]

CLE – Claires Stores Inc. [stock listing]

CLF – Cleveland Cliffs Inc. [stock listing]

CLI – Mack Cali Realty Corp. [stock listing]

CLJ – Crestline Capital Corp. [stock listing]

CLL – Celltech Group P.L.C. [stock listing]

CLM – Clemente Strategic Value Fund Inc. [stock listing]

CLN – Celsion Corp. [stock listing]

CLNP – connnectionless network protocol

CLO – customer liason office

CLP – Colonial Properties Trust [stock listing]

CLQ – Cold Metal Products Inc. [stock listing]

CLR – Clarion Commercial Holdings Inc. [stock listing]

CLS – Celestica Inc. [stock listing]

CLT – Cominco Ltd. [stock listing]

CLU – Canada Life Financial Corp. [stock listing]

CLX – Clorox Corp. [stock listing]

CM – Cameroon

CM – chief of mission

CM – Coles Myer Ltd. [stock listing]

CM – configuration management

CMA – Comerica Inc. [stock listing]

CMC – Commercial Metals Co. [stock listing]

CMDF – catalog master data file

Cmdr. – commander

CME – Core Materials Corp. [stock listing]

CMEA – Council for Mutual Economic Assistance

CMG – Commission on Marine Geology

CMH – Clayton Homes Inc. [stock listing]

CMH – Cleveland Hopkins International Airport

CMHS – Center for Mental Health Services

CMI – Caribbean Meteorological Institute

CMI – case mix index

CMI – CMI Corp. [stock listing]

CMIP – common management information protocol

CMM – Criimi MAE Inc. [stock listing]

CMMI – Census of Manufacturers and Mineral Industries

CMO – Capstead Mortgage Corp. [stock listing]

CMO – civil military operations

CMOC – Civil Military Operations Center

CMS – CMS Energy Corp. [stock listing]

CMS – configuration management system

CMSA – consolidated metropolitan statistical area

CMU – Colonial Municipal Income Trust [stock listing]

CMV – Chase Capital [stock listing]

CMX – Caremark Rx Inc. [stock listing]

CN – Calton Inc. [stock listing]
CN – China
CNA – CNA Financial Corp. [stock listing]
CNB – Colonial Bancgroup Inc. [stock listing]
CNC – Conseco Inc. [stock listing]
CNE – CareerEngine Network Inc. [stock listing]
CNE – certified netware engineer
CNF – CNF Transportation Inc. [stock listing]
CNH – CNH Global N.V. [stock listing]
CNI – Canadian National Railroad [stock listing]
CNJ – Cole National Corp. [stock listing]
CNL – Cleco Corp. [stock listing]
CNM – Colonial New York Insured Municipal Fund [stock listing]
CNMI – Commonwealth of the Northern Mariana Islands
CNN – Cable News Network
CNN – Cna Income Shares Inc. [stock listing]
CNO – chief of naval operations
CNO – Cornerstone Propane Partnership L.P. [stock listing]
CNPP – Center for Nutrition Policy and Promotion
CNS – Consolidated Stores Corp. [stock listing]
CNSTAT – Committee on National Statistics
CNT – Centerpoint Properties Trust [stock listing]
CNTPRA – Centerpoint Properties Trust [stock listing]
CNU – Continucare Corp. [stock listing]
CNV – CVF Corp. [stock listing]
CNX – Consol Energy Inc. [stock listing]
CNY – Carver Bancorp Inc. [stock listing]
CO – Colombia
CO – Colorado
CO – Corrpro Cos. Inc. [stock listing]
COA – Coachmen Industries Inc. [stock listing]
COB – Columbia Laboratories Inc. [stock listing]
COB – coordination of benefits

COBFR – COB (coordination of benefits) field representative
COBOL – Common Business Oriented Language
COCA – Conoco Inc. [stock listing]
COCC – Center for Ocean Climate Chemistry [IOS, Canada]
COCOM – Coordinating Committee on Export Controls
COD – Chiles Offshore Inc. [stock listing]
COE – Cone Mills Corp. [stock listing]
COEs – centers of excellence
COF – Capital One Finanical Corp. [stock listing]
COFI – Committee on Fisheries
COG – Cabot Oil & Gas Corp. [stock listing]
COH – Coach Inc. [stock listing]
COHPRMCL – Commonwealth General L.L.C. [stock listing]
Col. – colonel
COL – Council on Ocean Law
Colo. – Colorado [standard newspaper abbreviation]
COM – command [file name extension]
com – commercial [Internet domain]
Comecon – Council for Mutual Economic Assistance (CEMA)
Command Sgt. Maj. – command sergeant major
COMSEC – communications security
Conn. – Connecticut [standard newspaper abbreviation]
Conrail – Consolidated Rail Corp.
CONUS – continental United States
COO – Cooper Cos. Inc., The [stock listing]
COPAFS – Council of Professional Associations on Federal Statistics
COPS-91 – Cooperative Oklahoma Profiler Studies-1991
COSPAR – Committee on Space Research
COSSC – Compton Observatory Science Support Center, The

COSTED – Committee on Science and Technology in Developing Countries

COTS – commercial off-the-shelf

couns – counselor

COV – Covanta Energy Corp. [stock listing]

COX – Cox Communication Inc. [stock listing]

COY – Corporate High Yield Fund Inc. [stock listing]

CP – Canadian Pacific Ltd. [stock listing]

CP – census of population

CP – command post

CP – control processor

CPB – Campbell Soup Corp. [stock listing]

CPC – Central Parking Corp. [stock listing]

CPCI – computer program configuration item

CPD – central processing and distribution

CPE – Callon Petroleum Co. [stock listing]

CPE – customer-provided equipment

CPFF – cost plus fixed fee

CPG – Chelsea Property Group Inc. [stock listing]

CPH – Capital Pacific Holdings Inc. [stock listing]

CPH – census of population and housing

CPH – Copenhagen Airport

CPI – Capital Properties Inc. [stock listing]

CPI – characters per inch

CPI – consumer price index

CPJ – Chateau Communities Inc. [stock listing]

CPK – Chesapeake Utilities Corp. [stock listing]

Cpl. – corporal

CPM – Control Program for Microcomputers

CPM – cost per thousand

CPM – critical path method

CPN – Calpin Corp. [stock listing]

CPO – Corn Products International Inc. [stock listing]

CPP – Cornerstone Properties Inc. [stock listing]

CPQ – Compaq Computer Corp. [stock listing]

CPS – characters per second

CPS – Choicepoint Inc. [stock listing]

CPSC – Consumer Product Safety Commission

CPSR – contractor purchasing system review

CPT – Camden Properties Trust [stock listing]

CPU – central processing unit

CPU – CompUSA Inc. [stock listing]

CPUC – California Public Utility Commission

CPV – Correctional Properties Trust [stock listing]

CPY – CPI Corp. [stock listing]

CQB – Chiquita Brands International Inc. [stock listing]

CR – Costa Rica

CR – Crane Co. [stock listing]

CRA – Applera Corp. [stock listing]

CRB – Carbon Energy Corp. [stock listing]

CRC – Chromcraft Revington Inc. [stock listing]

CRDA – Crawford & Co. [stock listing]

CRE – CarrAmerica Realty Corp. [stock listing]

CRF – Cornerstone Strategic Return [stock listing]

CRG – Craig Corp. [stock listing]

CRG – Craig Municipal Airport

CRIM – Council on Regulatory and Information Management

CRK – Comstock Resources Inc. [stock listing]

CRN – Cornell Cos. Inc. [stock listing]

CRO – Crown Pac Partners L.P. [stock listing]

CRP – Corpus Christi International Airport

CRR – CARBO Ceramics Inc. [stock listing]

CRS – Carpenter Technology Corp. [stock listing]

CRS – Catholic Relief Services

CRS – Congressional Research Service

CRT – carrier route

CRT – cathode-ray tube

CRT – Cross Timbers Royalty Trust [stock listing]

CRV – Coast Distribution System Inc., The [stock listing]

CRW – Crown Crafts Inc. [stock listing]
CRY – CryoLife Inc. [stock listing]
CS – Cabletron Systems Inc. [stock listing]
CS – customer support
CS – Czechoslovakia
CSA – Careside Inc. [stock listing]
CSB – Ciba Specialty Chemicals Holding Inc. [stock listing]
CSC – Computer Sciences Corp. [stock listing]
CSC – computer software configuration item
CSCE – Conference on Security and Cooperation in Europe
CSE – Case Corp. [stock listing]
CSE – certified systems engineer
CSG – Cadbury Schweppes P.L.C. [stock listing]
CSI – Chase Industries Inc. [stock listing]
CSI – consumer safety inspector
CSJ – Columbus Southern Power Co. [stock listing]
CSK – Chesapeake Corp. [stock listing]
CSL – Carlisle Cos. Inc. [stock listing]
CSM – Merrill Lynch & Co. Inc. [stock listing]
CSO – consumer safety officer
CSP – American Strategic Income Portfolio Inc.-III [stock listing]
CSR – customer service representative
CSREES – Cooperative State Research, Education and Extension Service
CSRS – Civil Service Retirement System
CSS – CSS Industries Inc. [stock listing]
CST – central standard time
CST – Toulouse Space Center
CSTD – Center for Science and Technology for Development
CSU – Capital Senior Living Corp. [stock listing]
CSV – Carriage Services Inc. [stock listing]
CSW – Combat Support Wing
CSX – CSX Corp. [stock listing]
CT – Capital Trust Inc. [stock listing]
CT – Connecticut
CTA – Center Trust Inc. [stock listing]

CTB – Cooper Tire & Rubber Co. [stock listing]
CTC – Compania de Telecomunicaciones de Chile S.A. [stock listing]
CTD – cartridge tape drive
CTE – Cardiotech International Inc. [stock listing]
CTF – combined task force
CTF – CVS Automatic Common Exhange Security [stock listing]
CTI – Chart Industries Inc. [stock listing]
CTL – Century Telephone Enterprises Inc. [stock listing]
CTO – Consolidated-Tomoka Land Co. [stock listing]
CTOS – convergent technologies operating system
CTP – Central Maine Power Co. [stock listing]
CTR – Cabot Industries Trust [stock listing]
CTS – CTS Corp. [stock listing]
CTT – Competitive Technologies Inc. [stock listing]
CTU – Chad Therapeutics Inc. [stock listing]
CTV – Commscope Inc. [stock listing]
CTX – Centex Corp. [stock listing]
CTY – Community Banks Inc. [stock listing]
CU – Cuba
CUAP – College and University Affiliations Program
CUB – Cubic Corp. [stock listing]
CUM – Cummins Inc. [stock listing]
CUO – Continental Materials Corp. [stock listing]
CUR – Current Income Shares Inc. [stock listing]
CUS – Customs Service
CUZ – Cousins Properties Inc. [stock listing]
CV – Cape Verde
CV – Central Vermont Public Service Corp. [stock listing]
CV – coefficient of variation
CV – Curriculum Vitae
CVB – CVB Financial Corp. [stock listing]

CVC – Cablevision System Corp. [stock listing]

CVD – Covance Inc. [stock listing]

CVF – Castle Convertible Fund Inc. [stock listing]

CVG – Convergys Corp. [stock listing]

CVI – Cv REIT Inc. [stock listing]

CVM – Cel-Sci Corp. [stock listing]

CVR – Chicago Rivet & Machine Co. [stock listing]

CVRD – Companhia Vale Rio do Doce [stock listing]

CVS – CVS Corp. [stock listing]

CVT – TCW Convertible Securities Fund Inc. [stock listing]

CVU – CPI Aerostructures Inc. [stock listing]

CW – Curtiss Wright Corp. [stock listing]

CWEPRK – Commonwealth Edison Co. [stock listing]

CWF – Chartwell Dividend and Income Fund Inc. [stock listing]

CWG – Canwest Global Communications Corp. [stock listing]

CWN – Crown American Realty Trust [stock listing]

CWP – Cable & Wireless P.L.C. [stock listing]

CWS – Church World Service

CWT – California Water Services Group [stock listing]

CX – Cemex Inc. [stock listing]

CX – Christmas Island

CXB – Salomon Inc. [stock listing]

CXE – Colonial High Income Municipal Trust [stock listing]

CXH – Colonial Investment Grade Municipal Trust [stock listing]

CXI – Commodore Applied Technologies Inc. [stock listing]

CXM – CoBiz Inc. [stock listing]

CXP – Centex Construction Products Inc. [stock listing]

CXR – Cox Radio Inc. [stock listing]

CXT – American Municipal Term Trust Inc. II [stock listing]

CXW – Corrections Corp. of America [stock listing]

CXY – Cheniere Energy Inc. [stock listing]

CY – calendar year

CY – contract year

CY – Cypress Semiconductor Corp. [stock listing]

CY – Cyprus

CYB – Cybex International Inc. [stock listing]

CYD – China Yuchai Intl Ltd. [stock listing]

CYE – Corp. High Yield Fund III Inc. [stock listing]

CYH – Community Health Systems Inc. [stock listing]

CYL – Community Capital Corp. [stock listing]

CYN – City National Corp. [stock listing]

CYT – Cytec Industries Inc. [stock listing]

CZ – Celanese A.G. [stock listing]

CZ – Czech Republic

CZCS – coastal zone color scanner

CZN – Citizens Utilities Co. [stock listing]

D&F – determination and finding

D.B. – bachelor of divinity

D.C. – District of Columbia [standard newspaper abbreviation]

D.D. – doctor of divinity

D.D.S. – doctor of dental surgery

D.Litt (D.LITT) – doctor of letters

D.O. – doctor of osteopathy

D.V.M. – doctor of veterinary medicine

D – Dominion Resources Inc. [stock listing]

DA – data administration

DA – Department of the Army

DA – Groupe Danone [stock listing]

DAB – Dave & Busters Inc. [stock listing]

DAB – Defense Acquisition Board

DAJ – Daimler Benz A.G. [stock listing]

DAL – Dallas Love Field

DAL – Delta Air Lines Inc. [stock listing]

DALIS – Disaster Assistance Logistics Information System

DAO – Defense Agency Operations

DAO – Office of the Defense Attache

DAP – Discount Auto Parts Inc. [stock listing]

DAPA – distribution and pricing agreement

DAR – Darling International Inc. [stock listing]

DARPA – Defense Advanced Research Projects Agency

DART – Disaster Assistance Response Team

DASA – Defense Atomic Support Agency

DASD(HMS) – Deputy Assistant Secretary of Defense for Health

DASD(HSO) – Deputy Assistant Secretary of Defense (Health Services)

DASD – deputy assistant secretary of defense

DASD – direct access storage device

DAT – digital audiotape

DAY – Dayton Mining Corp. [stock listing]

DBA – database administrator

DBA – doing business as

DBAd – database administrator

DBCP – Data Buoy Cooperation Council

DBD – Diebold Inc. [stock listing]

DBG – Dyerburg Corp. [stock listing]

DBL – Bradley International Airport

DBMS – database management system

DBT – Dbt Online Inc. [stock listing]

DC – direct current

DC – District of Columbia

DCA – Defense Communications Agency

DCA – DQE Capital Corp. [stock listing]

DCA – Washington National Airport

DCAA – Defense Contract Audit Agency

DCASR – Defense Contract Administrative Services Region

DCF – data capture file

DCH – DCH Technology Inc. [stock listing]

DCI – Donaldson Co. Inc. [stock listing]

DCM – deputy chief of mission

DCM – Dreyfus California Municipal Income Inc. [stock listing]

DCN – Dana Corp. [stock listing]

DCN – Defense Logistics Agency Corporate Network

DCO – Ducommun Inc. [stock listing]

DCP – Dominion Resources Inc. [stock listing]

DCRI – Diversified Corporate Resources Inc. [stock listing]

DCRT – Division of Computer Research and Technology

DCS – Doncasters P.L.C. [stock listing]

DCU – Dryclean USA Inc. [stock listing]

DCX – DaimlerChrysler A.G. [stock listing]

DD – Dupont EI Nemours & Co. [stock listing]

DDC – Detroit Diesel Corp. [stock listing]

DDD – Chequemate International Inc. [stock listing]

DD-EFT – direct deposit–electronic funds transfer

DDF – Delaware Group Dividend & Income Fund Inc. [stock listing]

DDI – director, defense information

DDN – Dynamex Inc. [stock listing]

DDR – Developers Diversified Realty Corp. [stock listing]

DDS – Dillards Inc. [stock listing]

DE – Deere & Co. [stock listing]

DE – Delaware

DE – Germany

DEA – Drug Enforcement Administration

DEA – Drug Enforcement Agency

DEC – Decatur Airport

DECCO – Defense Commercial Communications Office

DED – data element dictionary

DEERS – Defense Enrollment Eligibility Reporting System

DEG – Delhaize Group [stock listing]

Del. – Delaware [standard newspaper abbreviation]

DEL – Deltic Timber Corp. [stock listing]

DEO – Diageo P.L.C. [stock listing]

DER – De Rigo S.P.A. [stock listing]

DES – data encryption standard

DES – Desc Sa De Cv [stock listing]

DES – Division of Earth Sciences

DES – Division of Environmental Sciences

DESA – Department of Economic and Social Affairs

DESC – Defense Energy Support Center

DEW line – distant early warning line

DEX – Dexter corp. [stock listing]

DF – Dean Foods Co. [stock listing]

DFAS – Defense Finance and Accounting Service

DFC – Delta Financial Corp. [stock listing]

DFG – Delphi Financial Group Inc. [stock listing]

DFS – Department 56 Inc. [stock listing]

DFT – Downey Financial Corp. [stock listing]

DFW – Dallas/Fort Worth International Airport

DG – Dollar General Corp. [stock listing]

DGF – Delaware Group Global Dividend and Income Fund Inc. [stock listing]

DGS – Dollar Gen Strypes Tr [stock listing]

DGT – streetTRACKS Dow Jones Global Titans Index Fund [stock listing]

DGX – Quest Diagnostics Inc. [stock listing]

DHA – Duck Head Apparel Co. Inc. [stock listing]

DHA – United Nations Department of Humanitarian Affairs

DHC – Danielson Holding Corp. [stock listing]

DHCP – decentralized hospital computer program

DHF – Dreyfus High Yield Strategies Fund [stock listing]

DHHS – Department of Health and Human Services

DHI – Horton DR Inc. [stock listing]

DHR – Danaher Corp. [stock listing]

DHY – DLJ High Yield Bond Fund [stock listing]

DIA – Defense Intelligence Agency

DIA – Diamonds Trust Series I [stock listing]

DIG – digital image generation

DIG – Disney Walt Co. Walt Disney Internet Group [stock listing]

DII – Decorator Industries Inc. [stock listing]

DIMM – dual in-line memory module

DIN – Consorcio G Grupo Dina [stock listing]

DIS – Walt Disney Co., The [stock listing]

DISA – Defense Information Systems Agency

DIT – AMCON Distributing Co. [stock listing]

DIV – John Hancock Patriot Select Dividend Trust [stock listing]

DJ – Djibouti; Jibuti

DJ – Dow Jones & Co. Inc. [stock listing]

DJM – Merrill Lynch & Co. Inc. [stock listing]

DJT – Trump Hotels & Casino Resorts Inc. [stock listing]

DK – Denmark

DK – Donna Karan International Inc. [stock listing]

DKE – Duke Energy Corp. [stock listing]

DL – Dial Corp. [stock listing]

DLA – Defense Logistics Agency

DLA – Delta Apparel Inc. [stock listing]

DLI – Del Laboratories Inc. [stock listing]

DLJ – Donaldson Lufkin & Jenrett New [stock listing]

DLK – Semotus Solutions Inc. [stock listing]

DLL – dynamic link library

DLM – Del Monte Foods Co. [stock listing]

DLP – Delta and Pine Land Co. [stock listing]

DLSA – Defense Legal Services Agency

DLSC – Defense Logistics Services Center

DLW – Delta Woodside Industries Inc. [stock listing]

DLX – Deluxe Corp. [stock listing]

DM – Dominica

DMA – Defense Mapping Agency

DMA – direct memory access

DMC – Dairy Mart Convenience Stores Inc. [stock listing]

DMC – data management coordinator

DME – Dime Bancorp Inc. [stock listing]

DMF – Dreyfus Municipal Income Inc. [stock listing]

DMH – Ducati Motor Holding S.P.A. [stock listing]

DMI – DepoMed Inc. [stock listing]

DMM/A – Dia Met Minerals Ltd. [stock listing]

DMMSP – Defense Medical Material Strategic Plan

DMN – Dimon Inc. [stock listing]

DMP – data management plan

DMP – disk-storage management program

DMS – dimethylsulfide

DNA – deoxyribonucleic acid

DNA – digital network architecture

DNA – Genentech Inc. [stock listing]

DNB – Dun & Bradstreet Corp. Del [stock listing]

DNFSB – Defense Nuclear Facilities Safety Board

DNM – Dreyfus New York Municipal Income Inc. [stock listing]

DNP – Duff & Phelps Utilities Income Inc. [stock listing]

DNR – Denbury Resources Inc. [stock listing]

DNR – Department of Natural Resources

DNS – domain name server; domain name service

DNS – domain name system

DNY – Donnelley RR & Sons Co. [stock listing]

DO – delivery order

DO – Diamond Offshore Drilling Inc. [stock listing]

DO – Dominican Republic

DOA – dead on arrival

DOA – Department of Agriculture

DOALOS – Division for Ocean Affairs and the Law of the Sea

DOB – date of birth

DOC – Department of Commerce

DOC – Medical Advisory Systems Inc. [stock listing]

DOD – Department of Defense

DODD – Department of Defense Directive

DOE – Department of Energy

DOEd – Department of Education

DOI – Department of the Interior

DOJ – Department of Justice

DOL – Department of Labor

DOL – Dole Food Co. Inc. [stock listing]

DOM – Dominion Resources Black Warrior Trust [stock listing]

DOMSAT – domestic satellite

DON – Donnelly Corp. [stock listing]

DOR – Endorex Corp. [stock listing]

DOS – Department of State

DOS – disk operating system

DOT – Department of Transportation

DOTREX – Deep Ocean Tracer Experiment

DOV – Dover Corp. [stock listing]

DOW – Dow Chemical Co. [stock listing]

DOX – Amdocs Ltd. [stock listing]

DP – data processing

DP – Diagnostic Products Corp. [stock listing]

DPA – Delegation of Procurement Authority

DPC – Domestic Policy Council

DPH – Delphi Automotive Systems Corp.[stock listing]

DPI – dots per inch

DPL – DPL Inc. [stock listing]

DPM – deputy program manager

DPRB – Defense Planning and Resources Board

DPS – data processing system

DPW – Department of Public Works

DPW – Digital Power Corp. [stock listing]

DQE – DQE Inc. [stock listing]

DRAM – dynamic random access memory

DRC – Dain Rauscher Corp. [stock listing]

DRD – Duane Reade Inc. [stock listing]

DRE – Duke Realty Investments Inc. [stock listing]

DRF – Dan River Inc. [stock listing]

DRG – Diagnosis-Related Group

DRH – Driver-Harris Co. [stock listing]

DRI – Darden Restaurants Inc. [stock listing]

DRI – Dynamic Resources Inc.

DRM – diagnosis-related management

DRMS – Defense Reutilization and Marketing Service

DRO – Durango-La Plata County Airport

DRQ – Dril-Quip Inc. [stock listing]

DRS – DRS Technologies Inc. [stock listing]

DS – Dallas Semiconductor Corp. [stock listing]

DSD – Dayton Superior Corp. [stock listing]

DSI – Dreyfus Strategic Governments Income Inc. [stock listing]

DSL – deep scattering layer

DSL – digital subscriber line

DSL – Downey Financial Corp. [stock listing]

DSM – Dreyfus Strategic Municipal Bond Fund Inc. [stock listing]

DSN – defense switched network

DSP – digital signal processor

DSP – DSP Communications Inc. [stock listing]

DSS – decision support system

DSS – Quantum Corp. [stock listing]

DSW – Southwestern Bell Telephone Co. [stock listing]

DT – Deutsche Telekom A.G. [stock listing]

DTA – Detroit Edison [stock listing]

DTC – Domtar Inc. [stock listing]

DTE – DTE Energy Co. [stock listing]

DTF – Duff & Phelps Utilities Tax-Free Income Inc. [stock listing]

DTG – Dollar Thrifty Automotive Group Inc. [stock listing]

DTH – Detroit Edison Co. [stock listing]

DTL – Dal Tile International Inc. [stock listing]

DTN – Defense Telecommunications Network

DTP – desktop publishing

DTP – diphtheria, tetanus, pertussis

DTW – Detroit Metropolitan Wayne County Airport

DUC – Duff & Phelps Utility & Corporate Bond Trust [stock listing]

DUK – Duke Energy Corp. [stock listing]

DUR – Durban Louis Botha [South Africa]

DV – Devry Inc. [stock listing]

DVA – Davita Inc. [stock listing]

DVD – digital versatile disc

DVD – Dover Downs Entertainment Inc. [stock listing]

DVI – DVI Inc. [stock listing]

DVN – Devon Energy Corp. [stock listing]

DVX – Denver International Airport

DW – Drew Industries Inc. [stock listing]

DWL – DeWolfe Cos. Inc., The [stock listing]

DWRS – dental workload reporting system

DWT – deadweight

DWT – deadweight ton

DXR – Daxor Corp. [stock listing]

DXT – Diversified Corporate Resources Inc. [stock listing]

DXT – Dixon Ticonderoga Co. [stock listing]

DY – Dycom Industries Inc. [stock listing]

DYN – Dynegy Inc. [stock listing]

DYX – DiaSys Corp. [stock listing]

DZ – Algeria

DZA – Delhaize America Inc. [stock listing]

E – Eni S.P.A. [stock listing]

EAC – Encore Acquisition Corp. [stock listing]

EAFB – Edwards Air Force Base

EAG – Eagle Wireless International Inc. [stock listing]

EAP – employee assistance program

EAPC – Euro-Atlantic Partnership Council

EAR – Export Administration Regulations

EAR – HEARx Ltd. [stock listing]

EAS – Energy East Corp. [stock listing]

EAT – Binker International Inc. [stock listing]

EBB – Kampala Entebbe Airport

EBCDIC – extended binary coded decimal interchange code

EBF – Ennis Business Forms Inc. [stock listing]

E-BPR – enhanced bottom pressure recorder

EBRD – European Bank for Reconstruction and Development

EBS – Eagle Bancshares Inc. [stock listing]

EBS – emergency broadcast system

EBT – extended benchmark test

EBTA – Enterbank Holdings Inc. [stock listing]

EC – Ecuador

EC – electronic commerce

EC – Engelhard Corp. [stock listing]

EC – European Community

ECA – Economic Commission for Africa [United Nations]

ECA – Encal Energy Ltd. [stock listing]

ECAB – Employees' Compensation Appeals Board

ECC – ECC Intl Cp [stock listing]

ECDIS – electronic chart display information system

ECE – Economic Commission for Europe [United Nations]

ECF – Ellsworth Convertible Growth and Income Fund Inc. [stock listing]

ECHO – European Community Humanitarian Office

ECL – Ecolab Inc. [stock listing]

ECLAC – Economic Commission for Latin America and the Caribbean

ECO – Echo Bay Mines Ltd. [stock listing]

ECO – Economic Cooperation Organization

ECOSOC – Economic and Social Council

ECS – European Coal and Steel Community

ECT – Lauder Estée Automatic Com E [stock listing]

ED – Consolidated Edison Inc. [stock listing]

EDA – Economic Development Administration

EDE – Empire District Electric Co. [stock listing]

EDF – Emerging Markets Income Fund II Inc. [stock listing]

EDG – EpicEdge Inc. [stock listing]

EDGAR – electronic data gathering, analysis and retrieval

EDI – Edinburgh, Scotland Airport

EDI – electronic data interchange

EDIS – electronic data imaging system

EDL – Consolidated Edison Inc. [stock listing]

EDO – Edo Corp. [stock listing]

EDO – export development officer

EDP – Electricidade de Portugal [stock listing]

EDP – electronic data processing

EDS – Electronic Data Sys Corp. [stock listing]

EDT – eastern daylight time

EDT – e-dentist.com Inc. [stock listing]

EE – El Paso Electric Co. [stock listing]

EE – Estonia

EEC – Environmental Elements Corp. [stock listing]

EEC – European Economic Community

EEE – Canadian 88 Energy Corp. [stock listing]

EEI – Ecology and Environment Inc. [stock listing]

EEM – Merrill Lynch & Co. Inc. [stock listing]

EEO – equal employment opportunity

EEOC – Equal Employment Opportunity Commission

EEPROM – electronically erasable programmable read-only memory

EEX – EEX Corp. [stock listing]

EF – Europe Fund Inc. [stock listing]

EFC – EFC Bancorp Inc. [stock listing]

EFM – Merrill Lynch & Co. Inc. [stock listing]

EFS – Enhance Financial Services Group Inc. [stock listing]

EFTA – European Free Trade Association

EFU – Eastern Enterprises [stock listing]

EFX – Equifax Inc. [stock listing]

EG – Egypt

EGA – enhanced graphics adapter

EGE – Eagle County Regional Airport

EGI – encoder/grouper interface

EGN – Energen Corp. [stock listing]

EGP – Eastgroup Properties Inc. [stock listing]

EGR – Earthgrains Co. [stock listing]

EGS – European Geophysical Society

EGSWG – European Geophysical Society Working Group on Tsunami

EGT – estimated ground time

EGX – Endorex Corp. [stock listing]

EGX – Engex Inc. [stock listing]

EH – Western Sahara

EHIS – Environmental Health Information Service

EI – Ecology and Environment Inc. [stock listing]

EI – employer identification

EI – Energynorth Inc. [stock listing]

EI – entry interface

EIA – Electronic Industries Association

EIA – Energy Information Administration

EIA – environmental impact assessment

EIB – European Investment Bank

EIJ – Salomon Smith Barney Holdings Inc. [stock listing]

EIL – Electrochemical Industries Ltd. [stock listing]

EIM – electronic image management

EIN – Eindhoven Airport

EIN – employer identification number

EIR – Eircom P.L.C. [stock listing]

EIS – EIS Fund [stock listing]

EIS – environmental impact statement

EIS – Environmental Information Services

EIS – executive information system

EIX – Edison International [stock listing]

EK – Eastman Kodak Co. [stock listing]

EKC – Ek Chor China Motorcycle Co. [stock listing]

EKH – Merrill Lynch Europe 2001 HOLDRS [stock listing]

EKT – Grupo Elektra S.A. de C.V. [stock listing]

EL – Estée Lauder Cos. Inc. [stock listing]

EL – Genesis Energy L.P. [stock listing]

ELC – Electric City Corp. [stock listing]

ELE – Endesa S.A. [stock listing]

ELG – executive-level group

ELI – Elite Pharmaceuticals Inc. [stock listing]

ELK – Elcor Corp. [stock listing]

ELN – Elan Corp. P.L.C. [stock listing]

ELP – Companhia Paranaense de Energia-COPEL [stock listing]

ELT – Elscint Ltd. [stock listing]

ELY – Callaway Golf Co. [stock listing]

EMA – eMagin Corp. [stock listing]

email – electronic mail

e-mail – electronic mail

EMAP – Environmental Monitoring and Assessment Program

EMD – Emerging Markets Income Fund Inc. [stock listing]

EME – Emcor Group Inc. [stock listing]

EMF – Templeton Emerging Markets Fund Inc. [stock listing]

EMI – Eaton Vance Michigan Municipal Income Trust [stock listing]

EMI – electromagnetic interference

EMIS – employee management information system

EML – Eastern Co., The [stock listing]

EML – environmental measurement laboratory

EMN – Eastman Chemical Co. [stock listing]

EMR – Emerson Electric Co. [stock listing]

EMS – C-MAC Industries Inc. [stock listing]

EMS – Emergency Medical Service(s)

EMT – El Monte Airport

EMU – European Monetary Union

ENC – Eisenhower National Clearinghouse

ENC – Enesco Group Inc. [stock listing]

ENDEX – environmental index

ENE – Enron Corp. [stock listing]

ENI – Enersis S.A. [stock listing]

ENL – Elsevier N.V. [stock listing]

ENMOC – El Niño Monitoring Center

ENN – Equity Inns Inc. [stock listing]

ENO – Enodis P.L.C. [stock listing]

ENP – Entreport Corp. [stock listing]

ENP – Kinder Morgan Energy Partners L.P. [stock listing]

ENR – Energizer Holdings Inc. [stock listing]

ENS – European Network for Science

ENSPRF – Enserch Corp. [stock listing]

ENT – Equant N.V. [stock listing]

ENUM – enumerator

ENV – CET Environmental Services Inc. [stock listing]

ENZ – Enzo Biochem Inc. [stock listing]

EO – executive order

EOB – executive office building

EOB – explanation of benefits

EOC – Endesa Chile [stock listing]

EOG – EOG Resources Inc. [stock listing]

EOM – Earth Observation Missions

EON – E.On Ag [stock listing]

EOP – Equity Office Properties Trust [stock listing]

EOR – element of resource

EOSAT – Earth Observation Satellite Co.

EOSDIS – Earth Observing System Data and Information System

EOT – Eott Energy Partners L.P. [stock listing]

EOUSA – Executive Office for United States Attorneys

EOWS – Executive Office of Weed and Seed

EPA – Environmental Protection Agency

EPC – Economic Policy Council

EPC – Epcos Ag [stock listing]

EPCD – Economic Planning and Coordination Division

EPD – Enterprises Products Partners L.P. [stock listing]

EPG – El Paso Corp. [stock listing]

EPGPR – El Paso Tennessee Pipeline Co. [stock listing]

EPI – Consolidated Edison Co. of New York Inc. [stock listing]

EPL – Energy Partners Ltd. [stock listing]

EPOC – Eastern Pacific Oceanic Conference

EPOCS – Equatorial Pacific Ocean Climate Studies

EPORTS – enhanced ports

EPOS – earthquake phenomena observation system

EPR – east Pacific rise

EPR – Entertainment Properties Trust [stock listing]

EPRI – Electric Power Research Institute

EPS – equipment planning system

EQJ – Salomon Smith Barney Holdings Inc. [stock listing]

EQR – Equity Residential Properties Trust [stock listing]

EQS – Equus II Inc. [stock listing]

EQT – Equitable Resources Inc. [stock listing]

EQUALANT – Equatorial Atlantic Survey

EQY – Equity One Inc. [stock listing]

ER – emergency room

ER – entity relationship

ER – error resolution

ERA – earned run average

ERA – Equal Rights Amendment

ERD – entity relationship diagram

ERDA – Energy Research and Development Administration

EREC – Enlisted Records and Evaluation Center

ERF – Enerplus Resources Fund [stock listing]

ERFEN – Regional Study of the El Niño Phenomenon

ERI – Economics Research Inc.

ERIC – Educational Resources Information Center

ERICA – Experiment on Rapidly Intensifying Cyclones over the Atlantic

ERIM – Environmental Research Institute of Michigan

ERJ – Embraer-Empresa Brasileira de Aeronautica [stock listing]

ERL – environmental research laboratories

EROD – Education Resources Organizations Directory

EROS – Earth Resources Observing Satellite

ERS – Economic Research Service

ERS – Empire Resources Inc. [stock listing]

ERT – emergency response team

ERTS – Earth Resources Technology Satellite

ES – executive secretariat

ES – expert system

ES – Spain

ESA – Economics and Statistics Administration

ESA – Employment Standards Administration

ESA – Endangered Species Act

ESA – Enterprise System Architecture

ESA – European Satellite Agency

ESA – European Space Agency

ESA – Extended Stay America Inc. [stock listing]

ESAC – enhance system access control

ESC – Emeritus Corp. [stock listing]

ESC – executive steering council

ESCAP – Economic and Social Commission for Asia and the Pacific

ESCWA – Economic and Social Commission for Western Asia

ESDI – enhanced small-device interface

ESDIM – Earth System Data and Information Management

ESE – Esco Techologies Inc. [stock listing]

ESF – Espirito Santo Finl Grp S.A. [stock listing]

ESF – European Science Foundation, The

ESH – Earl Scheib Inc. [stock listing]

ESI – ITT Educational Services Inc. [stock listing]

ESL – Esterline Technologies Corp. [stock listing]

ESM – Merrill Lynch & Co. Inc. [stock listing]

ESO – European Support Office

ESOC – European Space Operations Center

ESP – Espey Mfg. & Electronics Corp. [stock listing]

ESR – Encompass Services Corp. [stock listing]

ESRIN – European Space Research Institute

ESS – Essen Airport

ESS – Essex Property Trust Inc. [stock listing]

EST – eastern standard time

ESTEC – European Space Research and Technology Center

ESV – Ensco International Inc. [stock listing]

ESX – Essex Bancorp Inc. [stock listing]

ESY – Merrill Lynch & Co. Inc. [stock listing]

ET – E*TRADE Group Inc. [stock listing]

ET – Ethiopia

ETA – Employment and Training Administration

ETA – Entrade Inc. [stock listing]

ETA – estimated time of arrival

etc. – et cetera (and so on) [Latin]

ETC – Environmental Tectonics Corp. [stock listing]

ETD – estimated time of departure

ETE – estimated time en route

ETF – Emerging Markets Telecommunications Fund Inc., The [stock listing]

ETH – Ethan Allen Interiors Inc. [stock listing]

ETI – Environmental Technologies Industries

ETL – Environmental Technology Laboratory

ETM – Entercom Communications Corp. [stock listing]

ETN – Eaton Corp. [stock listing]

ETP – Eastern Tropical Pacific

ETP – Enterprise Oil P.L.C. [stock listing]

ETP – exception to policy

ETR – Entergy Corp. [stock listing]

ETS – encounter tracking system

ETS – enhancement tracking system

ETT – Elder Trust [stock listing]

ETV – E4L Inc. [stock listing]

ETW – E'town Corp. [stock listing]

ETZ/A – ETZ Lavuad Ltd. [stock listing]

EU – European Union

EUA – Eastern Utilities Associates [stock listing]

EUC – equatorial undercurrent

EUCOM – European Command

EUM – Merrill Lynch & Co. Inc. [stock listing]

EUMETSAT – European Organization for the Exploitation of Meteorological Satellites

EUN/WS – Merrill Lynch & Co. Inc. [stock listing]

EUO – Eurotech Ltd. [stock listing]

EURATOM – European Atomic Energy Community

EUROSTAT – Statistical Office of the European Community

EUTELSAT – European Telecommunications Satellite Organization

EUV – extreme ultraviolet

EV – Eaton Vance Corp. [stock listing]

EVA – extravehicular activity

EVAC – evacuation

EVC – Entravision Communication Corp. [stock listing]

EVF – Eaton Vance Senior Income Trust [stock listing]

EVG – Evergreen Resources Inc. [stock listing]

EVJ – Eaton Vance New Jersey Municipal Income Trust [stock listing]

EVN – Eaton Vance Municipal Income Trust [stock listing]

EVO – Eaton Vance Ohio Municipal Income Trust [stock listing]

EVP – Eaton Vance Pennsylvania Municipal Income Trust [stock listing]

EVV – Environmental Elements Corp. [stock listing]

EVV – Environmental Safeguards Inc. [stock listing]

EVY – Eaton Vance New York Municipal Income Trust [stock listing]

EW – Edwards Lifesciences Corp [stock listing]

EWA – iShares MSCI-Australia [stock listing]

EWB – Blanch E.W. Holdings Inc. [stock listing]

EWC – iShares MSCI-Canada [stock listing]

EWD – iShares MSCI-Sweden [stock listing]

EWF – European Warrant Fund Inc., The [stock listing]

EWG – iShares MSCI–Germany [stock listing]

EWH – iShares MSCI-Hong Kong [stock listing]

EWI – iShares MSCI-Italy [stock listing]

EWJ – iShares MSCI-Japan [stock listing]

EWK – iShares MSCI-Belgium [stock listing]

EWL – iShares MSCI–Switzerland [stock listing]

EWM – iShares MSCI-Malaysia [stock listing]

EWN – iShares MSCI - Netherlands [stock listing]

EWO – iShares MSCI - Austria [stock listing]

EWOS – European Workshop on Open Systems

EWP – iShares MSCI-Spain [stock listing]

EWQ – iShares MSCI-France [stock listing]

EWR – engineering work request

EWR – Newark International Airport

EWS – iShares MSCI-Singapore [stock listing]

EWT – iShares MSCI-Taiwan [stock listing]

EWU – iShares MSCI-United Kingdom [stock listing]

EWW – iShares MSCI–Mexico [stock listing]

EWY – iShares MSCI-South Korea [stock listing]

EWZ – iShares MSCI-Brazil [stock listing]

EX – Excide Corp. [stock listing]

EXC – Exelon Corp. [stock listing]

EXEA – Extendicare Inc. [stock listing]

EX-IM – export-import

Ex-Im – Export-Import Bank of the United States

EXM – Excel Maritime Carriers Ltd. [stock listing]

Exosat – European Space Agency's X-ray Observatory

expat – expatriate

EXT – Exeter

EXX/A – EXX Inc. [stock listing]

EY – Ethyl Corp. [stock listing]

EYE – VISH Inc. [stock listing]

EZM/A – E-Z-EM Inc. [stock listing]

EZR – Easyriders Inc. [stock listing]

EZU – iShares MSCI-EMU Index Fund (European Monetary Union) [stock listing]

f.o.b. – free on board

F/C – flight controller

F/CIM – Functional/Corporate Information Management

F – Ford Motor Co. [stock listing]

FA – Fairchild Corp. [stock listing]

FAA – Federal Aviation Administration

FAA – Foreign Assistance Act of 1961

FAB – Firstfed America Bancorp Inc. [stock listing]

FACA – Federal Advisory Committee Act

FACT – film and automated camera technology

FACTS – facilities complaint tracking system

FACTS – Florida Atlantic Coast Transport Study

FAF – First American Corp., The [stock listing]

FAH – First American Health Concepts Inc. [stock listing]

FAJ – Frontier Adjusters of America Inc. [stock listing]

FAMOUS – French-American Mid-Ocean Undersea Study

Fannie Mae – Federal National Mortgage Association

FAO – Food and Agriculture Organization

FAPM – Functional Activity Program Manager

FAPS – field automated payroll system

FAQ – frequently asked questions

FAR – Federal Acquisition Regulation

FARB – Federal Assistance Review Board

Farmer Mac – Federal Agricultural Mortgage Corp.

FARS – financial accounting and reporting system

FAS – Foreign Agricultural Service

FAS – Foreign Agricultural Service

FASAB – Federal Accounting Standards Advisory Board

FASINEX – Frontal Air-Sea Interaction Experiment

FASS – financial analysis support system

FAT – Fresno Air Terminal Georgetown Airport

FATE – Fisheries and the Environment

FATT – Free Trade Area of the Americas

FAWG – Flight Assignment Working Group

FAX – Aberdeen Asia-Pacific Income Fund Inc. [stock listing]

fax – facsimile

FB – FBR Asset Investment Corp. [stock listing]

FBA – First Banks America Inc. [stock listing]

FBF – FleetBoston Financial Corp. [stock listing]

FBI – Credit Suisse Asset Management Strategic Global Income Fund Inc. [stock listing]

FBI – Federal Bureau of Investigation

FBIS – Foreign Broadcast Information Service

FBK – First City Bank [stock listing]

FBN – Furniture Brands Intl Inc. [stock listing]

FBP – First BanCorp [stock listing]

FBR – Friedman Billings Ramsey [stock listing]

FBSC – Fixed Base Crew Stations

FC – Franklin Covey Co. [stock listing]

FCA – Farm Credit Administration

FCB – Falmouth Bancorp Inc. [stock listing]

FCC – Federal Communications Commission

FCC – Flight Clinical Coordinator

FCCSET – Federal Coordinating Council for Science, Engineering and Technology

FCEA – Forest City Enterprises Inc. [stock listing]

FCF – First Commonwealth Financial Corp. [stock listing]

FCG – federal coordinator for geology

FCG – functional coordinating group

FCH – FelCor Lodging Trust [stock listing]

FCM – feature change map

FCM – Franklin Telecommunications Corp. [stock listing]

FCMAREP – Federal Coordinator for Marine Environmental Prediction

FCMSSR – Federal Coordinator for Meteorological Services and Supporting Research

FCN – FTI Consulting Inc. [stock listing]

FCO – First Commonwealth Fund Inc. [stock listing]

FCOMP – Federal Coordinator for Ocean Mapping and Prediction

FCP – Falcon Products Inc. [stock listing]

FCPWG – Federal Credit Policy Working Group

FCS – Fairchild Semiconductor Corp. [stock listing]

FCST – Federal Council for Science and Technology

FCT – Flight Crew Trainer

FCTS – Flight Crew-Trainer Simulator

FCX – Freeport Momoran Copper & Gold Inc. [stock listing]

FCY – Furon Co. [stock listing]

FCZ – Fishery Conservation Zone

FD – facility division

FD – Federated Department Stores Inc. [stock listing]

FD – flight director

FD – functional description

FDA – Food and Drug Administration

FDAd – functional date administrator

FDC – First Data Corp. [stock listing]

FDC – food, drug & cosmetic

FDDI – fiber-distributed data interchange or interface

FDIC – Federal Deposit Insurance Corp.

FDO – Family Dollars Stores Inc. [stock listing]

FDO – flight dynamics officer

FDP – Fresh Del Monte Produce Inc. [stock listing]

FDS – Factset Research Systems Inc. [stock listing]

FDWSC – Federated Department Stores Inc. [stock listing]

FDX – FDX Corp. [stock listing]

FDY – Atichison Casting Corp. [stock listing]

FE – FirstEnergy Corp. [stock listing]

FEA – Federal Energy Administration

FEA – functional economic analysis

FEARS – field employees automated retirement system

FEB – Federal Executive Board

FEC – Federal Election Commission

FECA – Federal Employees' Compensation Act

FED – Firstfed Financial Corp. [stock listing]

FEDIX – Federal Information Exchange Inc.

FEDLINK – Federal Library and Information Network

FEDRIP – Federal Research in Progress Database

FEDSIM – Federal Systems Integration and Management Center

FEDSTRIP – Federal Standard Requisitioning and Issuing Procedures

FEF – FORTUNE e-50 Index Tracking Stock [stock listing]

FEFU – failed edit follow-up

FEG – Fletcher Challenge Energy Division [stock listing]

FEI – Federal Executive Institute

FEI – Frequency Electronics Inc. [stock listing]

FEMA – Federal Emergency Management Agency

FEP – Franklin Electronic Publishers Inc. [stock listing]

FEP – front-end processor

FERC – Federal Energy Regulatory Commission

Fermilab – Fermi National Accelerator Laboratory

FERS – Federal Employees Retirement System

FETC – Federal Energy Technology Center

FEV – Eaton Vance Florida Municipal Income Trust [stock listing]

FEWS – Famine Early Warning System Project

FF – First Financial Fund Inc.

FFA – Franchise Finance Corp. of America [stock listing]

FFB – Federal Financing Bank

FFD – Fairfield Communities Inc. [stock listing]

FFF – FORTUNE 500 Index Tracking Stock [stock listing]

FFG – FBL Financial Group Inc. [stock listing]

FFH – Farm Family Holding Inc. [stock listing]

FFMC – Federal Financial Managers Council

FFP – FFP Partners L.P. [stock listing]

FFS – Fletcher Challenge Ltd. [stock listing]

FFZ – Falcon Field Airport

FG – thick fog

FGDC – Federal Geographic Data Committee

FGI – Friede Goldman International Inc. [stock listing]

FGP – Ferrellgas Partners L.P. [stock listing]

FHA – Federal Housing Administration

FHC – Foundation Health Corp.

FHFB – Federal Housing Finance Board

FHS – Foundation Health System Inc. [stock listing]

FHWA – Federal Highway Administration

FHWAR – Fishing, Hunting, Wildlife and Associated Recreation

FI – fiscal intermediary

FI – Finland

FIA – Federal Insurance Administration

FIA – Fiat S.P.A. [stock listing]

FIAMS – Flinders Institute for Atmospheric and Marine Sciences

FIC/JSC – Finance Committee/Joint Support Committee

FIC – Fair Isaac & Co. Inc. [stock listing]

FIC – Federal Information Center

FICCDC – Federal Interagency Coordinating Committee on Digital Cartography

FID – Fidelity BancShares (N.C.) Inc. [stock listing]

FIDES – Forecaster's Intelligent Discussion Experiment System

FIDI – Fishery Information, Data and Statistics Service

FIF – Financial Federal Corp. [stock listing]

FIFO – first in, first out

FIG – fishing industry grants

FII – Federated Investors Inc. [stock listing]

FIM – functional integration manager

FIMA – financial management system

FIMIS – Fishery Management Information System

FINCEN – Financial Crimes Enforcement Network

FIO – Florida Institute of Oceanography

FIP – Federal Information Processing

FIPS-PUB – Federal Information Processing Standards Publication

FIPS – Federal Information Processing Standards

FIRE – First ISCCP Regional Experiment

FIRMR – Federal Information Resources Management Regulation

FISC – Federal Integrated Systems Corp.

FIT – FAB Industries Inc. [stock listing]

FITS – Flexible Interchange Transport System, The

FIX – Comfort Systems USA Inc. [stock listing]

FIZ – National Beverage Corp. [stock listing]

FJ – Fiji

FJ – Fort James Corp. [stock listing]

FJA – Fedders Corp. [stock listing]

FJC – Fedders Corp. [stock listing]

FJC – Federal Judicial Center

FK – Falkland Islands

FKL – Franklin Capital Corp. [stock listing]

FKNMS – Florida Keys National Marine Sanctuary

FL – Florida

Fla. – Florida [standard newspaper abbreviation]

FLA – Florida East Coast Industries Inc. [stock listing]

FLB – Fletcher Building Ltd. [stock listing]

FLC – Federal Laboratory Consortium

FLD – Full Line Distributors Inc. [stock listing]

FLE – Fleetwood Enterprises Inc. [stock listing]

FLETC – Federal Law Enforcement Training Center

FLH – Fila Holdings S.P.A. [stock listing]

FLIS – Federal Logistics Information System

FLM – Fleming Cos. Inc. [stock listing]
FLMSO – Fleet Material Support Office
FLO – Flowers Industries Inc. [stock listing]
FLR – Fluor Corp. [stock listing]
FLRA – Federal Labor Relations Authority
FLS – Flowserve Corp. [stock listing]
FLSA – Federal Labor Standards Act
FLTWS – Fleet Financial Group Inc. [stock listing]
FLY – Airlease Ltd. [stock listing]
FM&P – Force Management and Personnel
FM – Federated States Of Micronesia
FM – frequency modulation [radio]
FM – Micronesia
FMBPR – Allfirst Financial Inc. [stock listing]
FMC – Federal Maritime Commission
FMC – Financial Management Center
FMC – FMC Corp. [stock listing]
FMCS – Federal Mediation and Conciliation Service
FMCSA – Federal Motor Carrier Safety Administration
FMFIA – Federal Managers Financial Integrity Act
FMI – Franklin Multi-Income Trust [stock listing]
FMIS – financial management information system
FMIS – forms management information system
FMK – Fibermark Inc. [stock listing]
FML – Merrill Lynch & Co. Inc. [stock listing]
FMLA – Family and Medical Leave Act
FMM – FFP Marketing Co. Inc. [stock listing]
FMN – F&M National Corp. [stock listing]
FMO – Federal-Mogul Corp. [stock listing]
FMO – Flatland Meteorological Observatory
FMP – Fisheries Management Plan
FMS – Financial Management Service
FMS – Fresenius Medical Care [stock listing]
FMSHRC – Federal Mine Safety and Health Review Commission
FMT – Fremont General Corp. [stock listing]

FNC – First National Corp. of Orangeburg SC [stock listing]
FND – LCM Internet Growth [stock listing]
FNF – Fidelity National Financial Inc. [stock listing]
FNG – Front Range Capital Trust I [stock listing]
FNL – Fansteel Inc. [stock listing]
FNM – Fannie Mae [stock listing]
FNMA – Federal National Mortgage Association
FNMPRH – Fannie Mae [stock listing]
FNOC – Fleet Numerical Oceanography Center
FNS – Food and Nutrition Service
FNT – Frontline Communications Corp. [stock listing]
FNV – Finova Group Inc. [stock listing]
FNVPRA – Finova Finance Trust [stock listing]
FO – Faeroe (Faroe) Islands
FO – Fortune Brands Inc. [stock listing]
FOA – Field Operating Agency
FOB – Boyd Collection Ltd. [stock listing]
FOCI – Fisheries-Oceanography Coordinated Investigations [NOAA]
FOCUS – Fisheries Oceanography Cooperative Users System
FOD – Flight Operations Directorate
FODAG – Food and Agriculture Organizations
FOE – Ferro Corp. [stock listing]
FOE – Flight Operations Engineer
FOI – freedom of information
FOIA – Freedom of Information Act
FOIRL – fiber-optic inter-repeater link
FOMC – Federal Open Market Committee
FON – Sprint Corp. [stock listing]
FOPG – Flight Operations Planning Group
FOPRA – Fortune Brands Inc. [stock listing]
FOR – Fortis Securities Inc. [stock listing]
FORTRAN – Formula Translation/Translator [computer language]
FORTRAN – formula translator

FOSE – Federal Office System Expo

FOSO – flight operations scheduling officer

FOUO – for official use only

FOX – Fox Entertainment Group Inc. [stock listing]

FPC – Florida Progress Corp. [stock listing]

FPDS – Federal Procurement Data System

FPF – First Philippine Fund Inc., The [stock listing]

FPGA – field programmable gate array

FPI – fixed-price incentive

FPI – functional process improvement

FPL – FPL Group Inc. [stock listing]

FPM – Federal Personnel Manual

FPMR – Federal Procurement Management Regulations

FPO – fleet post office

FPRB – Ford Motor Co. [stock listing]

FPU – floating point unit

FPU – Florida Public Utilities Co. [stock listing]

FQR – Formal Qualification Review

FR – Federal Register

FR – field representative

FR – First Industries Realty Trust Inc. [stock listing]

FR – France

FRA – Federal Railroad Administration

FRA – Frankfurt Rhein-Main Airport

FRB – Federal Reserve Board

FRC – Federal Records Center

FRC – First Republic Bank [stock listing]

FRC – flight control room

FRCS – forward reaction control system

FRD – Friedman Industries Inc. [stock listing]

FRE – Freddie Mac [stock listing]

FRF – France Growth Fund Inc., The [stock listing]

FRG – Federal Republic of Germany

FRG – Furr's Restaurant Group Inc. [stock listing]

FRK – Florida Rock Industries Inc. [stock listing]

FRMAC – Federal Radiological Management Assessment Center

FRN – Friendly Ice Cream Corp. [stock listing]

FRR – flight readiness review

FRS – Federal Reserve System

FRS – Federal Relay Service

FRS – Frisch's Restaurants Inc. [stock listing]

FRT – Federal Realty Investment Trust [stock listing]

FRTIB – Federal Retirement Thrift Investment Board

FRW – First Washington Realty Trust Inc. [stock listing]

FRX – Forest Labs Inc. [stock listing]

FS – Forest Service

FS – Four Seasons Hotels Inc. [stock listing]

FSA – Farm Service Agency

FSA – Financial Security Assurance Holdings Ltd. [stock listing]

FSC – federal supply code

FSC – functional steering committee

FSCPE – Federal-State Cooperative Program for Population Estimates

FSCPP – Federal-State Cooperative Program for Population Projections

FSD – feasibility study document

FSD – Financial Services Division

FSD – Finl Sec Assurn Hldgs Ltd. [stock listing]

FSE – flight-simulation engineer

FSH – Fisher Scientific International Inc. [stock listing]

FSIS – Food Safety and Inspection Service

FSL – Forecast Systems Laboratory

FSM – Federated States of Micronesia

FSM – Foodarama Supermarkets Inc. [stock listing]

FSR – field service representative

FSR – Firstar Corp. [stock listing]

FSS – Federal Signal Corp. [stock listing]

FSS – federal supply schedule

FSS – federal supply service

FSS – fixed service structure

FSSP – forward-scattering spectrometer probe
FST – Forest Oil Corp. [stock listing]
FT – Franklin Universal Trust [stock listing]
FTA – Federal Transit Administration
FTAM – file transfer, access and management
FTC – Federal Trade Commission
FTD – Federal Test Demonstration
FTD – Foreign Trade Division
FTD – Fort Dearborn Income Securities Inc. [stock listing]
FTE – France Telecom [stock listing]
FTE – full-time equivalent [employee]
FTG – Farmstead Telephone Group Inc. [stock listing]
FTI – Financial Technology Inc.
FTIR – Fourier transform infrared radiometer
FTN – First Tenn Natl Corp. [stock listing]
FTO – Frontier Oil Corp. [stock listing]
FTP – file transfer protocol
FTR – Frontier Insurance Group Inc. [stock listing]
FTS – Federal Technology Service
FTS – Federal Telecommunications System
FTS – Footstar Inc. [stock listing]
FTSR – Foreign Trade Statistical Regulation
FTU – First Union Corp. [stock listing]
FTW – Ft. Worth Meacham International Airport
FUN – Cedar Fair L.P. [stock listing]
Fund – Colonial California Insured Municipal [stock listing]
FUR – First Union Real Estate Equity & Mortgage Investment [stock listing]
FV – firm verification
FVB – First Virginia Banks Inc. [stock listing]
FVH – Fahnestock Viner Holdings Inc. [stock listing]
FVOG – Fishing Vessel Obligation Guarantee
FWC – Fosterwheeler Corp. [stock listing]
FWG – Federal Home Loan Mortgage Corp. [stock listing]
FWIW – for what it's worth
FWJ – Public Steers Trust [stock listing]

FWPCA – Federal Water Pollution Control Act
FWS – Fish and Wildlife Service
FWTA – Firstier Bancorp Inc. [stock listing]
FWV – First West Virginia Bancorp Inc. [stock listing]
FX – France
FXM – fiber-optics expansion module
FXN – Sprint Corp. [stock listing]
FY – fiscal year
FYI – for your information
FYROM – Former Yugoslav Republic of Macedonia
FYSB – Family and Youth Services Bureau
FZ – Franc Zone
FZ – freezing
G&A – general and administrative
G – general audiences [MPAA rating]
G – Gillette Co., The [stock listing]
G-2 – Group of 2
G-3 – Group of 3
G-5 – Group of 5
G-6 – Group of 6
G-7 – Group of 7
G-8 – Group of 8
G-9 – Group of 9
G-10 – Group of 10
G-11 – Group of 11
G-15 – Group of 15
G-19 – Group of 19
G-24 – Group of 24
G-30 – Group of 30
G-33 – Group of 33
G-77 – Group of 77
Ga. – Georgia [standard newspaper abbreviation]
GA – Gabon
GA – General Assembly
GA – Georgia
GAAP – generally accepted accounting principles
GAB – Gabelli Equity Trust Inc., The [stock listing]
GAC – global area coverage
GAF – GA Financial Inc. [stock listing]

GAGE – Global Atmospheric Gases Experiment

GAI – Global Tech Appliances Inc. [stock listing]

GAIM – global analysis, interpretation and modeling

GAM – General American Investors Co. Inc. [stock listing]

GAME – GEWEX Asian Monsoon Experiment

GAN – Garan Inc. [stock listing]

GAO – General Accounting Office

GAP – Great Atlantic & Pacific Tea Co. Inc. [stock listing]

GARM – Geographic Areas Reference Manual

GARP – Global Atmospheric Research Program

GAS – Nicor Inc. [stock listing]

GASP – general and annual survey processing

GAT – government acceptance test

GATES – government automated time entry system

GATT – General Agreement on Tariffs and Trade

GAW – global atmospheric watch

GB – Great Britain

GB – gigabyte

GB – Wilson Greatbatch Technologies Inc. [stock listing]

GBC – GBI Capital Management Corp. [stock listing]

GBE – Grubb & Ellis Co. [stock listing]

GBF – geographic base file

GBH – GB Holdings Inc. [stock listing]

GBI – BioLabs Inc. [stock listing]

GBL – Gabelli Asset Mgmt Inc. [stock listing]

GBL – government bill of lading

GBP – Gables Residential Trust [stock listing]

GBR – Greenbriar Corp. [stock listing]

GBT – Global Light Telecommunications Inc. [stock listing]

GBX – Greenbrier Cos. Inc. [stock listing]

GC/MS – gas chromatography/mass spectrometry

GC – gas chromatograph

GC – ground control

GCC – global climatic change

GCC – Gulf Cooperation Council

GCDIS – Global Change Data and Information System

GCFI – Gulf and Caribbean Fisheries Institute

GCG – General Chemical Group Inc. [stock listing]

GCH – Greater China Fund Inc., The [stock listing]

GCI – Gannett Co. Inc. [stock listing]

GCJ – Johannesburg Grand Central Airport

GCM – Greenwich Street California Municipal Fund Inc. [stock listing]

GCMD – Global Change Master Directory

GCO – Genesco Inc. [stock listing]

GCOS – global climate observing system

GCPS – global climate perspectives system

GCR – Gaylord Container Corp. [stock listing]

GCRP – Global Change Research Plan/Program

GCS – Gray Communications Systems Inc. [stock listing]

GCTE – Global Change and Terrestrial Ecosystems

GCTM – Global Chemical Transport Model

GCV – Gabelli Convertible Securities Fund Inc., The [stock listing]

GCW – Gerber Childrenswear Inc. [stock listing]

GCX – GC Cos. Inc. [stock listing]

GD&R – grinning, ducking and running

GD – Applied Graphics Technologies Inc. [stock listing]

GD – General Dynamics Corp. [stock listing]

GD – Grenada

GDC – General Datacomm Industries Inc. [stock listing]

GDF – Global Partners Income Fund Inc. [stock listing]

GDI – Gardner Denver Inc. [stock listing]

GDO – guidance officer

GDP – Goodrich Petroleum Corp. [stock listing]

GDP – gross domestic product

GDPS – global data-processing system

GDR – geophysical data record

GDS – general data systems

GDT – Guidant Corp. [stock listing]

GDW – Golden West Financial Corp. [stock listing]

GDX – general data expansion

GE – General Electric Co. [stock listing]

GE – Republic of Georgia

GEB – Genetronics Biomedical Ltd. [stock listing]

GEBA – Global Energy Balance Archive

GEC – global environmental change

GEEP – Group of Experts on Effects of Pollutants

GEF – Global Environmental Facility

GEG – Spokane International Airport

GEL – Genesis Energy L.P. [stock listing]

GEM – Gulf Ecosystem Monitoring

GEM – Pepsi-Gemex SA De CV [stock listing]

GEMPC – government's estimate of most probable cost

GEMS – Global Environment Monitoring System

Gen. – General

GEN – GenRad Inc. [stock listing]

GEO-CAT – Geographic-Catalog of Political and Statistical Areas

GEODAS – geophysical data system

GEOSAT – geodetic satellite

GER – Germany Fund Inc., The [stock listing]

GES – Guess Inc. Et Al [stock listing]

GESAMP – Joint Group of Experts on the Scientific Aspects of Marine Environmental Protection

GET – Gaylord Entertainment Co. [stock listing]

GEWEX – Global Energy and Water Cycle Experiment

GF – French Guiana

GF – New Germany Fund Inc., The [stock listing]

GFD – Guilford Mls Inc. [stock listing]

GFDL – Geophysical Fluid Dynamics Laboratory

GFE – government-furnished equipment

GFF – Griffon Corp. [stock listing]

GFP – government-furnished property

GFPTS – government-furnished property tracking system

GFR – Great American Financial Resources Inc. [stock listing]

GFX – Cadapult Graphic Systems Inc. [stock listing]

GG – Goldcorp Inc. [stock listing]

GGB – Gerdau [stock listing]

GGC – Georgia Gulf Corporated [stock listing]

GGG – Graco Inc. [stock listing]

GGP – General Growth Properties Inc. [stock listing]

GGT – Gabelli Global Multimedia Trust Inc., The [stock listing]

GGY – Comp Generale Geophysique [stock listing]

GH – Ghana

GHCN – Global Historical Climate Network

GHG – greenhouse gas

GHI – Global High Income Dollar Fund Inc. [stock listing]

GHM – Graham Corp. [stock listing]

GHS – Invesco Global Health Sciences Fund [stock listing]

GI – Giant Industries Inc. [stock listing]

GI – Gibraltar

GIAT – Government Installation Acceptance Test

GIB – Groupe Cgi Inc. [stock listing]

GID – Grupo Indl Durango Sa De CV [stock listing]

GIF – general image format

GIF – Global Income Fund Inc. [stock listing]

GIF – graphics interchange format

GIFA – Governing International Fisheries Agreement

GIG – GTR Group Inc. [stock listing]

GIGO – garbage in, garbage out

GIL – Gildan Activewear Inc. [stock listing]

GILS – Government Information Locator Service

GIM – Templeton Global Income Fund, Inc. [stock listing]

GIN – Greenland, Iceland, Norway

Ginnie Mae – Government National Mortgage Association

GIPME – Global Investigation of Pollution in the Marine Environment

GIPSA – Grain Inspection, Packers and Stockyards Administration

GIQD – inquiry database

GIS – General Mills Inc. [stock listing]

GIS – geographic information system

GISS – Goddard Institute for Space Studies

GITS – Government Information Technology Services

GIX – Global Industries Technologies Inc. [stock listing]

GIX – Government Information Xchange

GK – Gentek Inc. [stock listing]

GL – Great Lakes REIT [stock listing]

GL – Greenland

GLA – Glasgow, Scotland Abbotsichn Airport

GLAMIS – Grants and Loans Accounting and Management Information System

GLAS – Goddard Laboratory of Atmospheric Sciences

GLB – Glenborough Realty Trust Inc. [stock listing]

GLC – Galileo International Inc. [stock listing]

GLCFS – Great Lakes Coastal Forecasting System

GLE – Gleason Corp. [stock listing]

GLE – Global Election Systems Inc. [stock listing]

GLERL – Great Lakes Environmental Research Laboratory

GLFC – Great Lakes Fisheries Commission

GLFS – Great Lakes Forecasting System

GLG – Glamis Gold Ltd. [stock listing]

GLH – Gallaher Group P.L.C. [stock listing]

GLIN – Great Lakes Information Network

GLIS – Geographic and Land Information Society

GLK – Great Lakes Chemical Corp. [stock listing]

GLL – Laidlaw Global Corp. [stock listing]

GLM – Global Marine Inc. [stock listing]

GLP – good laboratory practice

GLPRA – Great Lakes REIT Inc. [stock listing]

GLR – G&L Realty Corp. [stock listing]

GLS – ground launch sequencer

GLT – P.H. Glatfelter Co. [stock listing]

GLW – Corning Inc. [stock listing]

GM – computer graphics metafiles

GM – Gambia

GM – General Motors Corp. [stock listing]

GMA – General Motors Acceptance Corp. [stock listing]

GMAF – general merchandise, apparel and furniture

GMDSS – Global Maritime Distress and Safety System

GMH – General Motors Corp. [stock listing]

GMIS – Grants Management Information System

GMK – Gruma [stock listing]

GMM – Merrill Lynch & Co. Inc. [stock listing]

GMP – good manufacturing practice

GMP – Green Mountain Power Corp. [stock listing]

GMS – Geostationary Meteorological Satellite

GMT – Gatx Corp. [stock listing]

GMT – generic mapping tools

GMT – Greenwich mean time

GMTPR – Gatx Corp. [stock listing]

GN – ground network

GN – Guinea

GNA – Gainsco Inc. [stock listing]

GNC – guidance, navigation & control systems engineer

GNI – Great Northern Iron Ore Properties [stock listing]

GNIB – generic network interface board

GNIS – geographic names information system

GNL – Galey & Lord Inc. [stock listing]

GNMA – Government National Mortgage Association

GNMP – government network management profile

GNP – gross national product

GNT – GenStar Therapeutics Corp. [stock listing]

GNY – Granby-Grand County Airport

GO – guest observer

GO3OS – Global Ozone Observing System (GOOS)

GOA – Gulf of Alaska

GOATS – government outpatient automated tracking system

GODAE – Global Ocean Data Assimilation Experiment

GOES – geostationary operational environmental satellite

GOIN – Global Observation Information Network

GOP – Grand Old Party

GOS – Global Observing System

GOSIP – government open system interconnection profile

GOT – Gottschalks Inc. [stock listing]

GOTS – government off-the-shelf

GOU – Gulf Canada Resources Ltd. [stock listing]

GOV – Gouverneur Bancorp Inc. [stock listing]

GOWON – Gulf Offshore Weather Observing Network

GP – Georgia Pacific Corp. [stock listing]

GP – government property

GP – Guadeloupe

GPB – Georgia Power Co. [stock listing]

GPC – general purpose computer

GPC – Genuine Parts Co. [stock listing]

GPC – graphical performance characterization

GPCC – Global Precipitation Climatology Center

GPCP – Global Precipitation Climatology Project

GPD – Georgia Power Co. [stock listing]

GPF – Georgia Power Co. [stock listing]

GPI – Group 1 Automotive Inc. [stock listing]

GPIAT – Government Preinstallation Acceptance Test

GPK – Graphics Packaging Corp. [stock listing]

GPM – Getty Pete Marketing Inc. [stock listing]

GPMC – Global Patient Movement Center

GPN – Global Payments Inc. [stock listing]

GPO – Government Printing Office

GPRA – Government Performance and Results Act

GPS – GAP Inc. [stock listing]

GPS – Global Positioning System

GPT – Greenpoint Financial Corp. [stock listing]

GPU – GPU Inc. [stock listing]

GPW – Georgia Pacific Corp. [stock listing]

GPX – GP Strategies Corp. [stock listing]

GQ – Equatorial Guinea

GQ – group quarters

GR – BF Goodrich Co. [stock listing]

GR – Greece

GRA – WR Grace & Co. [stock listing]

GRAS – generally recognized as safe

GRASP – Generic Retrieve/Archive Services Protocol

GRASS – geographic resource analysis support system

GRB – Gerber Scientific Inc. [stock listing]

GRC – Gorman-Rupp Co., The [stock listing]

GREAT – Gorda Ridge Eruption Assessment Team

GRH – Grc International Inc. [stock listing]

GRI – Gristede's Foods Inc. [stock listing]

GRIB – gridded binary

GRID – Global Resource Information Database

GRIN – Geographic Reference Identification Number

GRL – Gulf Indonesia Resources Ltd. [stock listing]

GRM – Geographic Reference Manual

GRM – Geophysical Research Mission

GRO – Mississippi Chemical Corp. [stock listing]

GRP – Grant Prideco Inc. [stock listing]

GRQ – Groningen Eelde Airport

GRR – Asia Tigers Fund Inc., The [stock listing]

GRT – Glimcher Realty Trust [stock listing]

GRT – gross register ton

GS – Goldman Sachs Group Inc. [stock listing]

GS – Gulf Shelf

GSA – General Services Administration

GSA – Geological Society of America

GSA – GS Financial Products U.S. L.P. [stock listing]

GSAT – Global Satellite Data Acquisition Team

GSB – Golden State Bancorp Inc. [stock listing]

GSD – Government Systems Division

GSE – ground support equipment

GSE – Gundle Slt Environmental [stock listing]

GSF – ACM Government Securities Funds Inc. [stock listing]

GSFC – Goddard Space Flight Center

GSG – government systems group

GSH – Guangshen Railway Ltd. [stock listing]

GSK – GlaxoSmithKline P.L.C. [stock listing]

GSS – Chieftain International Inc. [stock listing]

GSS – geographic support system

GSY – Guest Supply Inc. [stock listing]

GT – Goodyear Tire & Rubber Co. [stock listing]

GT – Guatemala

GTA – Golf Trust of America Inc. [stock listing]

GTBOS – glad to be of service

GTE – GTE Corp. [stock listing]

GTK – Gtech Holdings Corp. [stock listing]

GTN – Global Technovations Inc. [stock listing]

GTN – Global Trends Network

GTOS – global terrestrial observing system

GTR – Golden Triangle Regional Airport

GTR – government transportation request

GTR – Grupo Tribasa S.A. [stock listing]

GTS – global telecommunication system

GTS – Global Telesystems Group Inc. [stock listing]

GTUB – geographic tabulation unit base

GTW – Gateway Inc. [stock listing]

GTY – Getty Realty Corp. [stock listing]

GTZ – German Technical Assistance Agency

GU – Guam

GUC – Gucci Group N.V. [stock listing]

GUC – Gunnison County Airport

GUI – graphical user interface

GUS – Geographic Update System

GUT – Gabelli Utility Trust, The [stock listing]

GV – Goldfield Corp., The [stock listing]

GVA – Granite Constr Inc. [stock listing]

GVG – Global Vacation Group Inc. [stock listing]

GVP – GSE Systems Inc. [stock listing]

GVT – Morgan Stanley Dean Witter [stock listing]

GW – Grey Wolf Inc. [stock listing]

GW – Guinea-Bissau

GWE – Global Weather Experiment

GWFPAS – general workforce performance appraisal system

GWI – Greenhouse Warming Index

GWL – Great-West Life Assurance Co.,The [stock listing]

GWM – Merrill Lynch & Co. Inc. [stock listing]

GWO – Genesis Worldwide Inc. [stock listing]

GWP – global warming potential

GWP – gross world product

GWPAS – general work force performance appraisal system

GWS – Glenwood Springs Municipal Airport

GWW – Grainger WW Inc. [stock listing]

GX – Global Crossing Ltd. [stock listing]

GXY – Galaxy Nutritional Foods Inc. [stock listing]

GY – Gencorp Inc. [stock listing]

GY – Guiana

GYM – Sport Supply Group Inc. [stock listing]

Gy. Sgt. – Gunnery Sergeant

H – Harcourt General Inc. [stock listing]

HA/OA – Health Affairs/Office Automation

HA – Hawaiian Airlines Inc. [stock listing]

HA – health affairs

HAB – HIV/AIDS Bureau

HACCP – hazard analysis critical control point

HAE – Haemonetics Corp. [stock listing]

HAF/EC – Hallmark Financial Services Inc. [stock listing]

HAI – Hampton Industries Inc. [stock listing]

HAL – Halliburton Co. [stock listing]

HAMS – hospital aseptic management system

HAN – Hanson P.L.C. [stock listing]

HAR – Harman International Ind. Inc. [stock listing]

HARM – hazardous atmospheric release model

HAS – Hasbro Inc. [stock listing]

HAST – Humanitarian Assistance Survey Team

HAT – Hatteras Income Securities Inc. [stock listing]

HAZ – Hayes Lemmerz International Inc. [stock listing]

HAZMAT – Hazardous Materials Response and Assessment Division

HB&P – health budget and programs

HB – Hillenbrand Industries Inc. [stock listing]

HBA – health-benefits adviser

HBc – hepatitis B core antigen

HBC – HSBC Holding P.L.C. [stock listing]

HBI – HomeBase Inc. [stock listing]

HBP – Huttig Building Products Inc. [stock listing]

HBs AG – hepatitis B surface antigen

HC – Hanover Compressor Co. [stock listing]

HCA – HCA-The Healthcare Co. [stock listing]

HCA – head of contracting activity

HCA – Hospital Corp. of America

HCB – H&CB [stock listing]

HCBP – hexachlorobiphenyl

HCC – HCC Insurance Holdings Inc. [stock listing]

HCFA – Health Care Financing Administration

HCFC – hydrochlorofluorocarbon

HCHB – Herbert C. Hoover Building

HCIS – Health Care Institutional Services

HCM – Hanover Capital Mortgage Holdings Inc. [stock listing]

HCM – hardware configuration model

HCN – Health Care REIT Inc. [stock listing]

HCO – Head of Contracting Office

HCO – Huntco Inc. [stock listing]

HCP – Health Care Property Investors Inc. [stock listing]

HCP – health care provider

HCPR – health care provider record

HCR – Manor Care Inc. [stock listing]

HCSCIA – Health Care Studies and Clinical Investigation Activity

HCSPO – Health Care Systems Program Office

HCSR – health care service record

HCSSA – health care systems support activity

HCT – Hector Communications Corp. [stock listing]

HD – Home Depot Inc. [stock listing]

HDC – Hadco Corp. [stock listing]

HDD – Quantum Corp. [stock listing]

HDF – hierarchical data format

HDGECP – Human Dimensions of Global Environmental Change Program

HDI – Harley-Davidson Inc. [stock listing]

HDL – Handleman Co. [stock listing]

HDLC – high-level data link control

HDN – Yampa Valley Airport

HDR – HPSC Inc. [stock listing]

HDS – hospital discharge survey

HDTV – high-definition television

HE – Hawaiian Electric Industries Inc. [stock listing]

HE – human engineering

HEA – Headway Corporate Resources Inc. [stock listing]

HEAO 1 – High Energy Astronomy Observatory 1

HEASARC – High Energy Astrophysics Science Archive Research Center

HEB – Hemispherx BioPharma Inc. [stock listing]

HEC – Harken Energy Corp. [stock listing]

HED – Head N.V. [stock listing]

HEDF – hundred-percent edited detail file

HEI – HEICO Corp. [stock listing]

HEO – highest elected official

HET – Harrahs Entertainment Inc. [stock listing]

HEW – Health, Education and Welfare

HF – high frequency [radio]

HF – Heller Financial Inc. [stock listing]

HFC – hydrofluorocarbon

HFD – Homefed Corp. [stock listing]

HFO – Health Facilities Office

HFPA – Health Facilities Planning Agency

HFT – Heartland Financial USA Inc. [stock listing]

HGA – Heritage U.S. Government Income Fund [stock listing]

HGR – Hanger Orthopedic Groups Inc. [stock listing]

HGT – Hugoton Royalty Trust [stock listing]

HH – Hooper Holmes Inc. [stock listing]

HHED – hand-held entry device

HHH – Merrill Lynch Internet HOLDRS [stock listing]

HHS – Department of Health and Human Services

HHS – Harte Hanks Inc. [stock listing]

HHT – hand-held terminal

HI – Hawaii

HI – Household International Inc. [stock listing]

HIB – Hibernia Corp. [stock listing]

HIBCC – Health Industry Business Communications Council

HIC – Healthcare Industry Council

HIC – Highlands Insurances Group Inc. [stock listing]

HIDA – Health Industry Distributors Association

HIF – Salomon Brothers High Income Fund Inc. [stock listing]

HIG – Hartford Financial Services Group Inc. [stock listing]

HIG – Hawaii Institute of Geophysics

HII – Healthcare Integrated Services Inc. [stock listing]

HIISC – Healthcare Information Integration Support Committee

HIL – Dot Hill Systems Corp. [stock listing]

HIN – health industry number

HIO – High Income Opportunity Fund Inc. [stock listing]

HIPO – hierarchy input process output

HIPRF – Household International Inc. [stock listing]

HIR – Diversified Corporate Resources Inc. [stock listing]

HIRIS – high-resolution imaging spectrometer

HIRS – Health Information Resources Service

HIRS – high-resolution infrared sounder

HIS – Cigna High Income Shares [stock listing]

HIS – health interview survey

HIS – high-resolution interferometer spectrometer

HIS – Home Security International Inc. [stock listing]

HIS – hospital information system

HIS – Indian Health Service

HIT – Hitachi Ltd. [stock listing]

HIV – human immunodeficiency virus

HIW – Highwoods Properties Inc. [stock listing]

HIWPRD – Highwoods Properties Inc. [stock listing]

HIX – Salomon Brothers High Income Fund II Inc. [stock listing]

HK – Hong Kong

HKF – Hancock Fabrics Inc. [stock listing]

HKG – Hong Kong Kai-Tak International Airport

HL – Hecla Mining Co. [stock listing]

HLD – Harold's Stores Inc. [stock listing]

HLI – Hartford Life Inc. [stock listing]

HLMS – high-latitude monitoring station

HLR – Hollinger International Inc. [stock listing]

HLT – Hilton Hotels Corp. [stock listing]

HM – Heard and McDonald Islands

HM – Homestake Mining Co. [stock listing]

HMA – Health Management Associates Inc. [stock listing]

HMC – Honda Motors Inc. [stock listing]

HMD – HLM Design Inc. [stock listing]

HMDA – Home Mortgage Disclosure Act

HME – Home Properties of New York Inc. [stock listing]

HMF – Hastings Manufacturing Co. [stock listing]

HMF – Hypergolic Maintenance Facility

HMG – HMG/Courtland Properties Inc. [stock listing]

HMIS – hazardous material information system

HMIS – health manpower information system

HMK – HALO Industries Inc. [stock listing]

HMMFC – House Merchant Marine and Fisheries Committee

HMMWV – highly mobile multipurpose wheeled vehicle

HMN – Horace Mann Educators Corp. [stock listing]

HMO – health maintenance organization

HMP – Horizon Medical Products Inc. [stock listing]

HMS – health management system

HMS – Host Marriott Services Corp. [stock listing]

HMSC – Hatfield Marine Science Center

HMT – Host Marriott Corp. [stock listing]

HMX – Hartmarx Corp. [stock listing]

HMY – Heilig Meyers Co. [stock listing]

HN – Honduras

HNI – Hon Industries Inc. [stock listing]

HNL – Honolulu International Airport

HNP – Huaneng Power International Inc. [stock listing]

HN-SN – house number-street name

HNT – Health Net Inc. [stock listing]

HNV – Hanover Direct Inc. [stock listing]

HNZ – Heinz HJ Co. [stock listing]

HOB – House Office Building

HOC – Holly Corp. [stock listing]

HOC – hydrophobic organic compound

HOLDRS – holding company depository receipt

HOMES – housing operations management system

HON – Honeywell International Inc. [stock listing]

HOO – Glacier Water Services Inc. [stock listing]

HOSS – housing sales survey

HOT – Starwood Hotel & Resorts Worldwide Inc. [stock listing]

HOV – Hovnanian Enterprises Inc. [stock listing]

HP – Helmerich & Payne Inc. [stock listing]

HP – Hewlett-Packard

HPC – Hercules Inc. [stock listing]

HPCC – high-performance computing and communications

HPCCIT – high-performance computing and communications program and information technology

HPD – hourly precipitation data

HPG – Heritage Propone Partners L.P. [stock listing]

HPLC – high-performance liquid chromatography

HPM – health program management

HPN – Westchester County Airport

HPP – Healthcare Integrated Services Inc. [stock listing]

HPP – Healthy Planet Products Inc. [stock listing]

HPPF – horizontal payloads processing facility

HPRA – Harcourt Gen Inc. [stock listing]

HPS – human performance services

HPSP – health-professional scholarship program

HPT – Hospitality Properties Trust [stock listing]

HQ – Hambrecht & Quist Group [stock listing]

HQ – headquarters

HQAF – Headquarters, Air Force

HQAFOMS – Headquarters, Air Force Office of Medical Systems

HQDA – Headquarters, Department of the Army

HQH – H&Q Healthcare Investors [stock listing]

HQL – H&Q Life Sciences Investors [stock listing]

HQMAC/SG – Headquarters, Military Airlift Command/Surgeon General

HR – Croatia

HR – Healthcare Realty Trust Inc. [stock listing]

HRA – Humanitarian and Refugee Affairs Office

HRB – H&R Block Inc. [stock listing]

HRC – HealthSouth Corp. [stock listing]

HRD – Human Resources Division

HRD – Hurricane Research Division

HRH – Hilb, Rogal & Hamilton Co. [stock listing]

HRI – high-resolution imager

HRIR – high-resolution infrared radiometer

HRL – Hormel Foods Corp. [stock listing]

HRP – HRPT Properties Trust [stock listing]

HRPRA – Healthcare Rlty Tr [stock listing]

HRPT – high-resolution picture transmission

HRS – Harris Corp. [stock listing]

HRS – high-resolution spectrometer

HRSA – Health Resources and Services Administration

HRT – Arrhythmia Research Technology Inc. [stock listing]

HRTWN – Hawaii Regional Tsunami Warning Network

HRY – Hallwood Realty Partners L.P. [stock listing]

HRZ – Hertz Corp., The [stock listing]

HSB – HSB Group Inc. [stock listing]

HSC – Harsco Corp. [stock listing]

HSC – Health Services Command

HSCT – high-speed civil transport

HSD – Homestead Village Inc. [stock listing]

HSE – HS Resources Inc. [stock listing]

HSF – Health Services Financing

HSI – Home Security International Inc. [stock listing]

HSM – Hussmann International Inc. [stock listing]

HSP – Hispanic Broadcasting Corp. [stock listing]

HSPMO – Health Systems Procurement Management Office

HSPO – Health Systems Program Office

HSR – Hi-Shear Technology Corp. [stock listing]

HSRP – High Speed Research Program

HST – Hubble Space Telescope

HSY – Hershey Foods Corp. [stock listing]

HT – Haiti

HT – Hersha Hospitality Trust [stock listing]

HTB – Hyperion 2002 Term Trust Inc. [stock listing]

HTC – Hungarian Telephone & Cable Corp. [stock listing]

HTI – Heartland Technology Inc. [stock listing]

HTL – Heartland Partners L.P. [stock listing]

HTML – hypertext markup language

HTN – Houghton Mifflin Co. [stock listing]

HTO – Hyperion 2005 Investment Grade Opportunity Term Trust Inc. [stock listing]

HTR – Hyperion Total Return Fund Inc., The [stock listing]

HTTP – hypertext transfer protocol

HTV – Hearst Argyle Television Inc. [stock listing]

HU – housing unit

HU – Hudson United Bancorp [stock listing]

HU – Hungary

HUBA – Hubbell Inc. [stock listing]

HUBB – Hubbell Inc. [stock listing]

HUD – Department of Housing and Urban Development

HUF – Huffy Corp. [stock listing]

HUG – High Energy Astrophysics Science Archive Research Center User's Group

HUG – Hughes Supply Inc. [stock listing]

HUM – Humana Inc. [stock listing]

HUN – Hunt Corp. [stock listing]

HURL – Hawaii Underwater Research Laboratory

HVAC – heating, ventilation & air-conditioning

HVC – hepatitis virus C

HVS – housing vacancy survey

HVT – Haverty Furniture Cos. Inc. [stock listing]

HWC – Hurricane Warning Center

HWD – Hollywood Casino Corp. [stock listing]

HWG – Hallwood Group Inc. [stock listing]

HWK – Hawk Corp. [stock listing]

HWL – Howell Corp. [stock listing]

HWM – Howmet International Inc. [stock listing]

HWO – Hurricane Warning Office

HWP – Hewlett Packard Co. [stock listing]

HWS – Hotelworks.com Inc. [stock listing]

HWY – Huntway Refining Co. [stock listing]

HX – Halifax Corp. [stock listing]

HXL – Hexcel Corp. [stock listing]

HXT – Reliant Energy Inc. [stock listing]

HYB – New America High Income Fund Inc., The [stock listing]

HYC – Hypercom Corp. [stock listing]

HYF – Managed High Yield Plus Fund Inc. [stock listing]

HYI – High Yield Income Fund Inc., The [stock listing]

HYP – High Yield Plus Fund Inc., The [stock listing]

HZO – Marinemax Inc. [stock listing]

HZP – Horizon Pharmacies Inc. [stock listing]

I&I – integration and implementation

I&S – interchangeability and substitutability

i.e. – id est (that is) [Latin]

I/O – input/output

IA – Iowa

IABO – International Association of Biological Oceanography

IAD – Washington Dulles International Airport

IADB – Inter-American Development Bank

IADO – Instituto Argentino de Oceanografía

IADRWG – Interagency Alternative Dispute Resolution Working Group

IAEGC – Inter-Agency Electronic Grants Committee

IAF – Aberdeen Australia Equity Fund Inc. [stock listing]

IAF – Inter-American Foundation, The

IAGA – International Association of Geomagnetism and Aeronomy

IAGLR – International Association for Great Lakes Research

IAH – Merrill Lynch Internet Architecture HOLDRS [stock listing]

IAHS – International Association of Hydrological Sciences

IAI – Inter-American Institute for Global Change Research

IAL – International Aluminum Corp. [stock listing]

IAOS – International Association for Official Statistics

IAPG – Interagency Arctic Policy Group

IAPSO – International Association for the Physical Sciences of the Ocean

IARC – International Arctic Research Center

IAS – IASIS Healthcare Corp. [stock listing]

IASC – International Association for Statistical Computing

IASI – Inter-American Statistical Institute

IASS – International Association of Survey Statisticians

IAU – International Astronomical Union

IAVCEI – International Association of Volcanology and Chemistry of the Earth's Interior

IBA – Industrias Bachoco S.A. de C [stock listing]

IBB – International Broadcasting Bureau

IBB – iShares Nasdaq Biotechnology Index Fund [stock listing]

IBC – Interstate Bakeries Corp. [stock listing]

IBCWP – International Bathymetric Chart of the Western Pacific

IBEC – International Bank for Economic Cooperation

IBEW – International Association of Electrical Workers

IBF – iSshares Nasdaq Biotechnol [stock listing]

IBI – Intimate Brands Inc. [stock listing]

IBK – Independent Bankshares Inc. [stock listing]

IBM – International Business Machines Corp.

IBM – International Business Machines Corp. [stock listing]

IBN – ICICI Bank Ltd. [stock listing]

IBP – IBP Inc. [stock listing]

IBP – International Biological Program

IBRD – International Bank for Reconstruction and Development [United Nations]

IBRD – International Bank for Reconstruction and Development [World Bank]

IBSFC – International Baltic Sea Fishery Commission

IBX – Ralston Purina Co. [stock listing]

IC – ICICI Ltd. [stock listing]

IC – integrated circuit

ICA – Empresas Ica Soc Contrladora [stock listing]

ICA – independent cost analysis

ICA – International Cartographic Association

ICA – International Communications Association

ICAO – International Civil Aviation Organization

ICAS – Interdepartmental Committee for Atmospheric Sciences

ICB – information collection budget

ICB – Morgan Stanley Dean Witter [stock listing]

ICBM – intercontinental ballistic missile

ICC – Integration Control Committee

ICC – International Chamber of Commerce

ICC – Interstate Commerce Commission

ICD – International Classification of Diseases

ICD-9-CM – International Classification of Diseases-9th Revision-Clinical

ICEM – Intergovernmental Committee for European Migration

ICF – iShares Cohen & Steers Realty Majors Index Fund [stock listing]

ICF – Kaiser Engineers [stock listing]

ICFTU – International Confederation of Free Trade Unions

ICG – International Coordination Group

ICH – Instituto Cubano de Higrafía

ICH – Investors Capital Holdings Ltd. [stock listing]

ICI – Imperial Chem Inds P.L.C. [stock listing]

ICJ – International Court of Justice

ICLEI – International Council for Local Environmental Initiatives

ICM – Intergovernmental Committee for Migration

ICMP – internet control message protocol

ICMS – Interdepartmental Committee for Meteorological Services

ICMSE – Interagency Committee on Marine Science and Engineering

ICN – ICN Pharmaceuticals Inc. [stock listing]

ICN – internal control number

ICNAF – International Convention of the Northwest Atlantic Fisheries

ICO – Inacom Corp. [stock listing]

ICP – inventory control point

ICR – internal control review

ICRC – International Committee of the Red Cross

ICRM – International Red Cross and Red Crescent Movement

ICRSDT – International Committee on Remote Sensing and Data Transmission

ICS – Morgan Stanley Dean Witter [stock listing]

ICSPRO – Intersecretariat Committee on Scientific Programs Relating to Oceanography

ICSU – International Council for Science

ICTP – International Center for Theoretical Physics

ICWG – International Coordination Working Group

ICWWP – Interagency Committee for the World Weather Program

ICY – Packaged Ice Inc. [stock listing]

ID – Idaho

ID – identification

ID – Indonesia

IDA – Idacorp Inc. [stock listing]

IDA – Institute for Defense Analyses

IDA – Integrated Disbursing and Accounting

IDA – International Development Association

IDB – Inter-American Development Bank

IDB – Islamic Development Bank

IDC – independent duty corpsman

IDC – insulation displacement contact

IDE – integrated drive electronics

IDEF – integrated computer-aided manufacturing definition

IDF – intermediate distribution frame

IDG – Industrial Distribution Group Inc. [stock listing]

IDH – IPI Inc. [stock listing]

IDIDAS – interactive digital image display and analysis system

IDIQ – indefinite delivery, indefinite quantity

IDK – I don't know

IDL – interactive data language

IDMS – integrated database management system

IDN – Intelli-Check Inc. [stock listing]

IDN – International Directory Network

IDNX – Integrated Digital Network Exchange

IDR – Intrawest Corp. [stock listing]

IDS – Industrial Data Systems Corp. [stock listing]

IDT – IDT Corp. [stock listing]

IDTC – indefinite delivery type contract

IDU – iShares Dow Jones U.S. Utilities Sector Index Fund [stock listing]

IDX – Identix Inc. [stock listing]

IE – information engineering

IE – Ireland

IEA – International Energy Agency

IEC – Pec Isreal Economic Corp. [stock listing]

IEE – Intergrated Electrical Services Inc. [stock listing]

IEEE – Institute of Electrical & Electronics Engineers

IEI – Indiana Energy Inc. [stock listing]

IEM – Merrill Lynch & Co Inc. [stock listing]

IESR – input error summary report

IETF – internet engineering task force

IEU – IES Utilities Inc. [stock listing]

IEV – iShares S&P Europe 350 [stock listing]

IEX – Idex Corp. [stock listing]

IF – Indonesia Fund Inc., The [stock listing]

IFAD – International Fund for Agricultural Development

IFB – invitation for bid

IFC – International Finance Corp.

IFCTU – International Federation of Christian Trade Unions

IFD – interface functional description

IFF – International Flavors & Fragrances Inc. [stock listing]

IFIAS – International Federation of Institutes for Advanced Study

IFICS – integrated financial control system

IFN – India Fund Inc. [stock listing]

IFRC – International Federation of Red Cross and Red Crescent Societies

IFRCS – International Federation of Red Cross and Red Crescent Societies

IFS – Insignia Financial Group Inc. [stock listing]

IFS – International Foundation for Science

IFX – Infineon Technologies A.G. [stock listing]

IG – IGI Inc. [stock listing]

IG – inertial guidance

IGAD – Inter-Governmental Authority on Development

IGADD – Inter-Governmental Authority on Drought and Development

IGC – International Geological Congress

IGC – Interstate General Co. L.P. [stock listing]

IGCE – independent government cost estimate

IGES – initial graphic exchange specification

IGF – India Growth Fund Inc., The [stock listing]

IGL – IMC Global Inc. [stock listing]

IGM – interplanetary global model

IGM – iShares Goldman Sachs Technology Index Fund [stock listing]

IGOSS – industry government open system specification

IGR – Integra Inc. [stock listing]

IGT – International Game Technology [stock listing]

IGU – International Geographical Union

IH – I.C.H. Corp. [stock listing]

IHI – Information Holdings Inc. [stock listing]

IHM – Merrill Lynch & Co. Inc. [stock listing]

IHP – Ihop Corp. [stock listing]

IHS – Integrated Health Services Inc. [stock listing]

IHT – InnSuites Hospitality Trust [stock listing]

II – InterSystems Inc. [stock listing]

IIASA – International Institute for Applied Systems Analysis

IIB – International Investment Bank

IIC – Morgan Stanley Dean Witter [stock listing]

IIF – Morgan Stanley Dean Witter India Investment Fund Inc. [stock listing]

IIH – Merrill Lynch Internet Infrastructure HOLDRS [stock listing]

III – Insteel Industries Inc. [stock listing]

IIM – Morgan Stanley Dean Witter [stock listing]

IIR – Iri International Corp. [stock listing]

IIS – Cigna Investment Securities Inc. [stock listing]

IIT – Indonesian Satellite Corp. [stock listing]

IITA – information infrastructure technology applications

IITF – Information Infrastructure Task Force

IJC – International Joint Commission

IJH – iShares S&P MidCap 400 Index Fund [stock listing]

IJJ – iShares S&P MidCap 400/BARRA Value [stock listing]

IJK – iShares S&P MidCap 400/BARRA Growth [stock listing]

IJR – iShares S&P SmallCap 600 Index Fund [stock listing]

IJS – iShares Small Cap 600/BARRA Value Index Fund [stock listing]

IJT – iShares Small Cap 600/BARRA Growth Index Fund [stock listing]

IJX – Equidyne Corp. [stock listing]

IKC – iShares S&P TSE 60 Index Fund [stock listing]

IKN – Ikon Office Solution Inc. [stock listing]

IKTA – Intrust Capital Trust [stock listing]

IL – Illinois

IL – Israel

ILA – Aquila Inc. [stock listing]

ILAB – Bureau of International Labor Affairs

ILC – International Law Commission

ILI – Interlott Technologies Inc. [stock listing]

Ill. – Illinois [standard newspaper abbreviation]

ILM – New Hanover International Airport

ILO – International Labor Organization

ILS – Instrument Landing System

ILX – ILX Resorts Inc. [stock listing]

IM – information management

IM – immunoassay

IM – information management

IM – Ingram Micro Inc. [stock listing]

IMA – Inverness Medical Technology Inc. [stock listing]

IMB – Morgan Stanley Dean Witter [stock listing]

IMC – International Multifoods Corp. [stock listing]

IMC – International Medical Corps, The

IMG – Intermagnetics General Corp. [stock listing]

IMGG – Institute of Marine Geology and Geophysics

IMH – Impac Mortgage Holdings Inc. [stock listing]

IMHO – in my humble opinion

IMI – San Paolo-Imi S.P.A. [stock listing]

IMJ – Indiana Michigan Power Co. [stock listing]

IML – Merrill Lynch & Co. Inc. [stock listing]

IMLS – Institute of Museum and Library Science

IMM – Immokalee Airport

IMN – Imation Corp. [stock listing]

IMO – Imperial Oil Ltd. [stock listing]

IMO – in my opinion

IMO – International Maritime Organization

IMP – Imperial Bancorp [stock listing]

IMR – Imco Recycling Inc. [stock listing]

IMS – information management system

IMS – Institute of Museum Services

IMS – Morgan Stanley Dean Witter [stock listing]

IMSL – International Mathematics and Statistics Library

IMT – information management team

IMT – Morgan Stanley Dean Witter [stock listing]

IMU – inertial measurement unit

IMX – Implant Sciences Corp. [stock listing]

IMY – Grupo Imsa S.A. [stock listing]

IN – India

IN – Indiana

IN – Infonet Services Corp. [stock listing]

Ind. – Indiana [standard newspaper abbreviation]

IND – American Industrial Properties REIT [stock listing]

IND – investigational new drug

INEEL – Idaho National Engineering and Environmental Laboratory

INF – Infinity Broadcasting Corp. [stock listing]

INF – intermediate range nuclear forces

ING – Inactive National Guard

ING – ING Groep [stock listing]

INM – integrated network management

INMARSAT – International Maritime Satellite Organization

INS – Immigration and Naturalization Service

INS – Intelligent Systems Corp. [stock listing]

INSCOM – U.S. Army Intelligence and Security Command

INSRP – Interagency Nuclear Safety Review Panel

INT – World Fuel Services Corp. [stock listing]

INTERPOL – International Criminal Police Organization

INV – American Residential Investment Trust Inc. [stock listing]

INZ – Ina S.P.A.-Istituto Nazionale Delle Assicurazioni [stock listing]

IO – British Indian Ocean Territory

IO – information officer

IO – input output

IO – Input Output Inc. [stock listing]

IO – international organization

IOC – initial operating capability

IOC – Intergovernmental Oceanographic Commission

IOC – International Olympic Committee

IOF – Income Opportunities Fund 1999 Inc. [stock listing]

IOG – Innogy Holdings P.L.C. [stock listing]

IOM – International Organization for Migration

IOM – Iomega Corp. [stock listing]

IOM – Isle of Man Ronaldsway Airport

ION – Ionics Inc. [stock listing]

IOO – S&P Global 100 Exchange-Traded Fund [stock listing]

IOT – Income Opportunity Realty Trust [stock listing]

IOX – Iomed Inc. [stock listing]

IP – implementation procedures

IP – information processing

IP – International Paper Co. [stock listing]

IP – Internet protocol

IPA – Intergovernmental Personnel Act

IPACS – Information Processing Allocation and Costing System

IPG – Interpublic Group of Cos. Inc. [stock listing]

IPK – Imperial Parking Corp. [stock listing]

IPL – initial program load

IPL – Ipalco Enterprises Inc. [stock listing]

IPO – initial public offering

IPOE – inpatient order entry

IPR – International Power P.L.C. [stock listing]

IPS – information processing system

IPS – Ipsco Inc. [stock listing]

IPT – integrated product team

IPT – iParty Corp. [stock listing]

IPX – Interpool Inc. [stock listing]

IQ – Iraq

IQC – Morgan Stanley Dean Witter [stock listing]

IQTOC – indefinite quantity task order contract

IQW – Quebecor World Inc. [stock listing]

IR – infrared

IR – Ingersoll Rand Co. [stock listing]

IR – Iran

IRC – International Rescue Committee

IRC – Internet relay chat

IRDS – information resource dictionary system

IRE – Ireland Bk [stock listing]

IRF – International Rectifier Corp. [stock listing]

IRI – International Remote Imaging Systems Inc. [stock listing]

IRL – interactive reader language

IRL – Irish Investment Fund Inc., The [stock listing]

IRM – information resource management

IRM – Iron Mountain Inc. [stock listing]

IRMO – Integration and Research Management Office

IRR – individual ready reserve

IRS – Internal Revenue Service

IRS – IRSA Inversiones y Representaciones S.A. [stock listing]

IRT – IRT Property Co. [stock listing]
IS – Iceland
ISA – industry standard architecture
ISA – Santa Isabel S.A. [stock listing]
ISAM – index sequential access method
ISBN – international standard book number
ISD – Information Service Division
ISDN – integrated services digital network
ISH – International Shipholding Corp. [stock listing]
ISI – International Statistical Institute
ISIR – initial system impact report
ISL – First Israel Fund Inc., The [stock listing]
ISM – information systems manager
ISO – International Standards Organization
ISP – integrated support plan
ISP – International Specialty Products Inc. [stock listing]
ISP – Internet service provider
ISSAA – Information Systems Selection and Acquisition Agency
ISSC – International Social Science Council
ISSD – information support services division
IST – Ispat International [stock listing]
ISV – InSite Vision Inc. [stock listing]
IT – Gartner Inc. [stock listing]
IT – Italy
ITA – International Trade Administration
ITA – Italy Fund Inc., The [stock listing]
ITC/EC – Intelligent Controls Inc. [stock listing]
ITC – Information Technology Center
ITC – International Trade Commission
ITC – United States International Trade Commission
ITG – Investment Technology Group Inc. [stock listing]
ITH – Tompkins County Airport
ITMS – Interactive Tsunami Modeling System
ITN – Intertan Inc. [stock listing]
ITP – Intertape Polymer Group [stock listing]
ITPB – Information Technology Policy Board

ITPC – Information Technology Policy Council
ITPRB – Gartner Inc. [stock listing]
ITRMS – information technology resource management system
ITT – International Telephone and Telegraph
ITT – ITT Inds Inc. Ind [stock listing]
ITU – International Telecommunication Union
ITW – Illinois Tool Works Inc. [stock listing]
ITX – IT Group Inc., The [stock listing]
ITY – Imperial Tobacco Group P.L.C. [stock listing]
IUBS – International Union of Biological Sciences
IUCN – International Union for Conservation of Nature and Natural Resources
IUD – intrauterine device
IUSSP – International Union for the Scientific Study of Population
IV&V – independent verification and validation
IV – intravenous
IV – Mark IV Industries Inc. [stock listing]
IVC – Invacare Corp. [stock listing]
IVD – IVAX Diagnostics Inc. [stock listing]
IVE – iShares S&P 500/BARRA Value Index Fund [stock listing]
IVX – IVAX Corp. [stock listing]
IW/WS – ImageWare Systems Inc. [stock listing]
IW – ImageWare Systems Inc. [stock listing]
IWB – iShares Russell 1000 Index Fund [stock listing]
IWC – International Whaling Commission
IWD – iShares Russell 1000 Value Index Fund [stock listing]
IWF – iShares Russell 1000 Growth Index Fund [stock listing]
IWM – iShares Russell 2000 Index Fund [stock listing]
IWN – iShares Russell 2000 Value Index Fund [stock listing]
IWO – iShares Russell 2000 Growth Index Fund [stock listing]

IWV – iShares Russell 3000 Index Fund [stock listing]

IWW – iShares Russell 3000 Value Index Fund [stock listing]

IWZ – iShares Russell 3000 Growth Index Fund [stock listing]

IX – Orix Corp. [stock listing]

IXX – Ivex Packaging Corp. [stock listing]

IYC – iShares Dow Jones U.S. Consumer Cyclical Sector Index Fund [stock listing]

IYD – iShares Dow Jones U.S. Chemicals Index Fund [stock listing]

IYE – iShares Dow Jones U.S. Energy Sector Index Fund [stock listing]

IYF – iShares Dow Jones U.S. Financial Sector Index Fund [stock listing]

IYG – iShares Dow Jones U.S. Financial Services Sector Index Fund [stock listing]

IYH – iShares Dow Jones U.S. Healthcare Sector Index Fund [stock listing]

IYJ – iShares Dow Jones U.S. Industrial Sector Index Fund [stock listing]

IYK – iShares Dow Jones U.S.Consumer Non-Cyclical Sector Index Fund [stock listing]

IYKWIMAITYD – if you know what I mean and I think you do

IYM – iShares Dow Jones U.S. Basic Materials Sector Index Fund [stock listing]

IYR – iShares Dow Jones U.S. Real Estate Index Fund [stock listing]

IYSWIM – if you see what I mean

IYV – iShares Dow Jones U.S. Internet Index Fund [stock listing]

IYW – iShares Dow Jones U.S. Technology Sector Index Fund [stock listing]

IYY – iShares Dow Jones U.S. Total Market Index Fund [stock listing]

IYZ – iShares Dow Jones U.S. Telecommunications Sector Index Fund [stock listing]

J – J Net Enterprises Inc. [stock listing]

JAD – joint application development

JAD/RAD – joint application development/rapid application development

JAG – judge advocate general

JASA – Jo-Ann Stores Inc. [stock listing]

JAX – J. Alexander Corp. [stock listing]

JBL – Jabil Circuit Inc. [stock listing]

JBPO – Joint Blood Program Office

JBX – Jack in the Box Inc. [stock listing]

JC – Craig, Jenny Inc. [stock listing]

JCAHO – Joint Commission on the Accreditation of Healthcare

JCC – Jilin Chem Indl Ltd. [stock listing]

JCI – Johnson Controls Inc. [stock listing]

JCL – job control language

JCP – Penney JC Co. Inc. [stock listing]

JCS – joint chiefs of staff

JDN – JDN Realty Corp. [stock listing]

JEC – Jacobs Engineering Group Inc. [stock listing]

JEDA – Joint Environmental Data Analysis Center

JEF – Jefferies Group Inc. [stock listing]

JEM – Merrill Lynch & Co Inc. [stock listing]

JENEX – Japanese El Niño Experiment

JEQ – Japan Equity Fund Inc., The [stock listing]

JERS-1 – Japan Earth Resources Satellite

JFC – Jardine Fleming China Region Fund Inc. [stock listing]

JFI – Jardine Fleming India Fund Inc. [stock listing]

JFK – John F. Kennedy International Airport

JFMIP – Joint Financial Management Improvement Program

JFSC – Joint Forces Staff College

JFSP – Joint Forecast System Project

JGOFS – Joint Global Ocean Flux Study

JH – John H. Harland Co. [stock listing]

JHF – John Hancock Financial Services [stock listing]

JHI – John Hancock Investors Trust [stock listing]

JHMS – joint healthcare manpower standards

JHS – John Hancock Income Securities Trust [stock listing]

JIA – Jackson International Airport

JII – Johnston Industries Inc. [stock listing]

JIT – just in time

JIT – Pentacon Inc. [stock listing]

JLC – Joint Logistics Center

JLG – JLG Industries Inc. [stock listing]

JLK – JLK Direct Distribution Inc. [stock listing]

JLL – Jones Lang Lasalle Inc. [stock listing]

JLN – Jaclyn Inc. [stock listing]

JM – Jamaica

JM – Johns Manville Corp. [stock listing]

JNC – Nuveen John Co. [stock listing]

JNJ – Johnson & Johnson [stock listing]

JNS – Chic By His Inc. [stock listing]

JNY – Jones Apparel Group Inc. [stock listing]

JO – Jordan

JOB – General Employment Enterprises Inc. [stock listing]

JOE – St Joe Co. [stock listing]

JOF – Japan Otc Equity Fund Inc. [stock listing]

JOL – Joulé Inc. [stock listing]

JOS – Jostens Inc. [stock listing]

JP – Japan

JP – Jefferson Pilot Corp. [stock listing]

JPEG – Joint Photographic Experts Group

JPEWG – joint patient evacuation work group

JPL – Jet Propulsion Laboratory

JPM – J.P. Morgan Chase & Co. [stock listing]

JPR – JP Realty Inc. [stock listing]

JPT – J.P. Morgan Chase Capital IX [stock listing]

JPW – J.P. Morgan Index Funding Co. I [stock listing]

JQH – John Q. Hammons Hotels Inc. [stock listing]

Jr. – junior

JRC – Journal Register Co. [stock listing]

JRL – Cincinnati Gas & Electric Co. [stock listing]

JS – Jefferson Smurfit Group P.L.C. [stock listing]

JSC – Johnson Space Center

JST – Jinpan International Ltd. [stock listing]

JTF – joint task force

JUMPS – Joint Uniform Militay Pay System

JUS/CIV – Department of Justice/Civil Division

JUSMAG – Joint United States Military Advisory Group

JWA – Wiley, John & Sons Inc. [stock listing]

JWC – JW Charles Fncl Svc Inc. [stock listing]

JWL – Whitehall Jewellers Inc. [stock listing]

JWN – Nordstrom Inc. [stock listing]

K – Kellogg Co. [stock listing]

K – kilo

K-12 – kindergarten through high school

KAB – Kaneb Services Inc. [stock listing]

Kan. – Kansas [standard newspaper abbreviation]

KAP – Star Struck Ltd. [stock listing]

KAPL – Knolls Atomic Power Laboratory

KB – kilobyte

KBA – Kleinwort Benson Australian Income Fund Inc. [stock listing]

KBH – KB Home [stock listing]

KBK – KBK Capital Corp. [stock listing]

KBL – Keebler Foods Co. [stock listing]

kbps – kilobytes per second

KCC – Structured Products Corp. [stock listing]

KCI – Kansas City International Airport

KCJ – Structured Products Corp. [stock listing]

KCP – Cole, Kenneth Productions Inc. [stock listing]

KCS – KCS Energy Inc. [stock listing]

KDE – 4 Kids Entertainment Inc. [stock listing]

KDN – Kaydon Corp. [stock listing]

KE – Kenya

KE – Koger Equity Inc. [stock listing]

KEA – Keane Inc. [stock listing]

KEF – Korea Equity Fund Inc. [stock listing]

KEG – Key Energy Services Inc. [stock listing]

KEI – Keithley Instruments Inc. [stock listing]

KEM – Kemet Corp. [stock listing]

KEP – Korea Elec Pwr Co. [stock listing]

KES – Keystone Consolidated Industries Inc. [stock listing]

KEX – Kirby Corp. [stock listing]

KEY – Keycorp [stock listing]

KF – Korea Fund Inc., The [stock listing]

KFI – Krause's Furniture Inc. [stock listing]

KFL – Lifestream Technologies Inc. [stock listing]

KFX – KFX Inc. [stock listing]

KFY – Korn Ferry International [stock listing]

KG – King Pharmaceuticals Inc. [stock listing]

KG – Kyrgyzstan

KGB – Soviet secret police [Komitet Gosudarstvennoi Bezopasnostef]

KGC – Kinross Gold Corp. [stock listing]

KGCPRB – Kinam Gold Inc. [stock listing]

KGL – key geographic location

KGT – Kemper Intermediate Government Trust [stock listing]

KH – Cambodia

KH – Kelvin-Helmholtz

KHI – Kemper High Income Trust [stock listing]

kHz – kilohertz

KI – Kiribati

KIC – Mesa del Rey Airport

KIF – Korean Investment Fund Inc. [stock listing]

KIM – Kimco Realty Corp. [stock listing]

KIN – Kinark Corp. [stock listing]

KIT – Kit Manufacturing Co. [stock listing]

KIX – Kansai International Airport

KLM – KLM Royal Dutch Airlines [stock listing]

KLT – Kansas City Power & Light Co. [stock listing]

KLU – Kaiser Aluminum Corp. [stock listing]

km – kilometer

KM – Kmart Corp. [stock listing]

KMB – Kimberly Clark Corp. [stock listing]

KME – Key3Media Group Inc. [stock listing]

KMG – Kerr Mcgee Corp. [stock listing]

KMI – Kinder Morgan Inc. Kans [stock listing]

KML – Carmel Container Systems Ltd. [stock listing]

KMM – Scudder Multi-Market Income Trust [stock listing]

KMT – Kennametal Inc. [stock listing]

KMX – Circuit City Stores Inc. [stock listing]

KN – Saint Kitts-Nevis

KNK – Kankakee Bancorp Inc. [stock listing]

KNL – Knoll Inc. [stock listing]

KNMI – Royal Netherlands Meteorological Institute

KNP – KN Energy Inc. [stock listing]

KNT – Kent Electronics Corp. [stock listing]

KO – Coca-Cola Co. [stock listing]

KODC – Korea Oceanographic Data Center

KOF – Coca-Cola FEMSA [stock listing]

KOR – Koor Industries [stock listing]

KP – Key Production Co. Inc. [stock listing]

KP – North Korea

KPA – Innkeepers USA Trust [stock listing]

KPC – Kentucky Power Co. [stock listing]

KPG – Group Co. Ltd. [stock listing]

KPG – King Power International Group Co. Ltd. [stock listing]

KPN – KPN [stock listing]

KPP – Kaneb Pipe Line Partners L.P. [stock listing]

KPT – Konover Property Trust Inc. [stock listing]

KR – Kroger Co. [stock listing]

KR – South Korea

KRB – MBNA Corp. [stock listing]

KRC – Kilroy Realty Corp. [stock listing]

KRG – KRUG International Corp. [stock listing]

KRI – Knight Ridder Inc. [stock listing]

KRT – Kramont Realty Trust [stock listing]

KRTPRD – Kramont Realty Trust [stock listing]

KRX – QK Healthcare Inc. [stock listing]

KRY – Crystallex International Corp. [stock listing]

KS – Kansas

KSA – Structured Products Corp. [stock listing]

KSC – Kennedy Space Center

KSE – Keyspan Corp. [stock listing]

KSK – Corts Trust Ford Debs [stock listing]

KSM – Scudder Strategic Municipal Income Trust [stock listing]

KSO – Corts Trust IBM Debs [stock listing]

KSS – Kohls Corp. [stock listing]

KST – Scudder Strategic Income Trust [stock listing]

KSU – Kansas City Southern Industies Inc. [stock listing]

KSUPR – Kansas City Southn Inds Inc. [stock listing]

KT – Katy Inds Inc. [stock listing]

kt – knot [nautical mile per hour]

KTB – Cort Tr Bellsouth Deb [stock listing]

KTC – Korea Telecom [stock listing]

KTE – Structured Products Corp. [stock listing]

KTF – Scudder Municipal Income Trust [stock listing]

KTJ – Structured Production Corp. [stock listing]

KTO – K2 Inc. [stock listing]

KTR – Keystone Property Trust [stock listing]

KTX – Corts for Xerox Capital Trust I [stock listing]

KTZ – Cort Trust for Countrywide Capital [stock listing]

KUB – Kubota Ltd. [stock listing]

KVA – KV Pharmaceutical Co. [stock listing]

kW – kilowatt

KW – Kuwait

KWD – Kellwood Co. [stock listing]

kWh – kilowatt hour

KWK – Quicksilver Resources Inc. [stock listing]

KWP – King World Productions Inc. [stock listing]

KWR – Quaker Chemical Corp. [stock listing]

Ky. – Kentucky [standard newspaper abbreviation]

KY – Cayman Islands

KY – Kentucky

KYF – Kentucky First Bancorp Inc. [stock listing]

KYO – Kyocera Corp. [stock listing]

KYT – Corporate High Yield Fund III Inc. [stock listing]

KZ – Kazakstan

L – Liberty Financial Cos. Inc. [stock listing]

La. – Louisiana [standard newspaper abbreviation]

LA – Laos

LA – Louisiana

LAB – labor officer

LAB – Labranche & Co. Inc. [stock listing]

LAD – Litha Motors Inc. [stock listing]

LAES – Latin American Economic System

LAF – Lafrage Corp. [stock listing]

LAIA – Latin American Integration Association

LAM – Latin America Investment Fund Inc., The [stock listing]

LAN – Lancer Corp. [stock listing]

LAN – local area network

LANDSAT – land satellite

LANL – Los Alamos National Laboratory

LANTCOM – Atlantic Command

LAP – link access procedure

LAQ – Latin America Equity Fund Inc., The [stock listing]

LARMC – Landstuhl Army Regional Medical Center

LAS – League of Arab States

LAS – live-access server

LAS – McCarran International Airport

laser – light amplification by stimulated emission of radiation

LAT – local area transport
LATA – local access and transport area
LB – LaBarge Inc. [stock listing]
LB – Lebanon
LBB – Lubbock International Airport
LBC – Laboratorio Chile S.A. [stock listing]
LBF – Scudder Global High Income Fund Inc. [stock listing]
LBI – Liberte Investors Inc. [stock listing]
LBY – Libbey Inc. [stock listing]
LC – Liberty Corp. [stock listing]
LC – Library of Congress
LC – Saint Lucia
LC50 – lethal concentration in environment resulting in 50 percent mortality
LCD – liquid crystal display
LCD – lowest common denominator
LCG – La Coruna Airport
LCK – Rickenbacker International Airport
LCP – Loews Cineplex Entertainment Corp. [stock listing]
L. Cpl. – Lance Corporal
LD – Louis Dreyfus Natural Gas Corp. [stock listing]
LDC – less developed country
LDF – Latin American Discovery Fund Inc., The [stock listing]
LDG – Longs Drug Stores Corp. [stock listing]
LDGO – Lamont Doherty Geological Observatory
LDL – Lydall Inc. [stock listing]
LDP – London Pac Group Ltd. [stock listing]
LDR – Landauer Inc. [stock listing]
LDY – Londonderry, Northern Ireland, Eglinton Airport
LE – Lands' End Inc. [stock listing]
LE – low energy
LEA – Lear Corp. [stock listing]
LED – light-emitting diode
LEE – Lee Enterprises Inc. [stock listing]
LEG – Leggett & Platt Inc. [stock listing]
LEIFS – Lake Erie Information Forecasting System

LEN – Lennar Corp. [stock listing]
LEO – Dreyfus Strategic Municipals Inc. [stock listing]
LEQ – Lehman Brothers Hldgs Inc. [stock listing]
LEV – Leviathan Gas Pipeline Partners L.P. [stock listing]
LEVP – El Paso Energy Partners L.P. [stock listing]
LFB – Longview Fibre Co. [stock listing]
LFG – Landamerica Financial Group Inc. [stock listing]
LFL – Lan Chile S.A. [stock listing]
LFP – Lifepoint Inc. [stock listing]
LFRA – League of Federal Recreation Associations
LG – Laclede Gas Co. [stock listing]
LGA – La Guardia Airport
LGB – Long Beach Airport Daugherty Field
LGE – LG&E Energy Corp. [stock listing]
LGF – Lions Gate Entertainment Corp. [stock listing]
LGL – Lynch Corp. [stock listing]
LGW – Gatwick Airport
LH – Laboratory Corp. of America Holdings [stock listing]
LHO – Lasalle Hotel Properties [stock listing]
LHP – Lakehead Pipeline Partners [stock listing]
LI – Liechtenstein
LIC – Lynch Interactive Corp. [stock listing]
LIDS – logon-ID system
LII – Lennox International Inc. [stock listing]
LIM – laser interface modules
LIN – line item number
LIN – Linens N Things Inc. [stock listing]
LIS – land information system
LIT – Adams Field Airport
LIT – Litton Industries, Inc. [stock listing]
LITPRB – Litton Inds Inc. [stock listing]
Litt.D. – doctor of letters
LIU – light interface unit
LIZ – Claiborne, Liz Inc. [stock listing]

LJC – Louisville International Airport
LK – Sri Lanka
LKI – Lazare Kaplan International Inc. [stock listing]
LL.D. – doctor of laws
LLB. – bachelor of laws
LLB – Computrac Inc. [stock listing]
LLC – limited liability Co.
LLDC – least developed country
LLL – L3 Communication Holdings Inc. [stock listing]
LLNL – Lawrence Livermore National Laboratory
LLY – Eli Lilly and Co. [stock listing]
LM – Legg Mason Inc. [stock listing]
LMAO – laughing my ass off
LMGA – AT&T Corp. [stock listing]
LMM – Laser Mortgage Management Inc. [stock listing]
LMS – Lamson & Sessions Co. [stock listing]
LMT – Lockheed Martin [stock listing]
LNC – Lincoln National Corp. [stock listing]
LND – Lincoln National Income Fund Inc. [stock listing]
LNN – Lindsay Manufacturing Co. [stock listing]
LNR – Lnr Ppty Corp. [stock listing]
LNS – connectionless network service
LNT – Alliant Energy Corp. [stock listing]
LNV – Lincoln National Convertible Securities Fund Inc. [stock listing]
LNY – Landry's Seafood Restaraunts Inc. [stock listing]
LO – liaison officer
LOC – Library of Congress
LOCIS – Library of Congress Information System
LOD – Lodgian Inc. [stock listing]
LOL – laughing out loud
LOR – Loral Space & Communications Ltd. [stock listing]
LORAN – long-range navigation
LOS – law of the sea

LOS – length of stay
LOS – level of security
LOW – Lowes Cos. Inc. [stock listing]
LOX – liquid oxygen
LPC – Lompoc Airport
LPLPRB – Entergy La Cap I [stock listing]
LPM – lines per minute
LPS – launch processing system
LPX – Louisiana Pacific Corp. [stock listing]
LQ – living quarters
LQU – Quilmes Industrial (Quinsa) [stock listing]
LR – Liberia
LR – Lyanier Worldwide Inc. [stock listing]
LRC – Lewis Research Center
LRT – LL&E Royalty Trust [stock listing]
LRW – Labor Realty Inc. [stock listing]
LRY – Liberty Property Trust [stock listing]
LS – Lesotho
LSA – Launch Services Agreement
LSC – Legal Services Corp.
LSDM – Lagrangian stochastic dispersion model
LSG – large-scale geostrophic
LSI – large-scale integration
LSI – LSI Logic Corp. [stock listing]
LSOPRA – Lasmo P.L.C. [stock listing]
LSR – Laser Technology Inc. [stock listing]
LSS – Lone Star Technologies Inc. [stock listing]
Lt. Cmdr. – lieutenant commander
Lt. Col. – lieutenant colonel
Lt. Gen. – lieutenant general
Lt. j.g. – lieutenant junior grade
Lt. – lieutenant
LT – Lithuania
Ltc. – lieutenant colonel
LTC – LTC Properties Inc. [stock listing]
ltd. – limited
LTD – Limited Inc., The [stock listing]
LTD – live test demonstration
LTG – Catalina Lighting Inc. [stock listing]
LTR – Loews Corp. [stock listing]

LTV – LTV Corp. [stock listing]
LU – logical unit
LU – Lucent Technologies Inc. [stock listing]
LU – Luxembourg
LUB – Luby's Inc. [stock listing]
LUCC – land use cover change
LUK – Leucadia National Corp. [stock listing]
LUV – Southwest Airlines Co. [stock listing]
LUX – Luxembourg Findel Airport
LUX – Luxottica Group [stock listing]
LV – Latvia
LVB – Steinway Musical Instrs Inc. [stock listing]
LVC – Lillian Vernon Corp. [stock listing]
LWR – Lutheran World Relief
LXA – LCA Group Inc. [stock listing]
LXK – Lexmark Intl Inc. [stock listing]
LXP – Lexington Corporate Properties Trust [stock listing]
LXV – Lake County Airport
LY – Libya
LYO – Lyondell Chemical Co. [stock listing]
LZ – Lubrizol Corp. [stock listing]
LZB – La-Z-Boy Inc. [stock listing]
M.A. – master of arts
M.B.A. – master of business administration
M.S. – master of science
m – meter
MA – Massachusetts
MA – master of arts
MA – metropolitan area
MA – Morocco
MAA – Mid-America Apartment Communities Inc. [stock listing]
MAAG – Military Assistance Advisory Group
MAB – Mid-America Bancorp [stock listing]
MAC/SG – military airlift command/surgeon general
MAC – Macerich Co. [stock listing]
MAC – military airlift command
MACOM – major command
MAD – Madeco S.A. [stock listing]
MADD – Mothers Against Drunk Driving

MAF – master address file
MAF – Midland International Airport
MAF – Municipal Advantage Fund Inc. [stock listing]
MAFAC – Marine Fisheries Advisory Committee [NFMS]
MAG – Magnetex Inc. [stock listing]
MAI – Medical Assurance Inc. [stock listing]
Maj. Gen. – major general
Maj. – major
MAJ – Michael Anthony Jewelers Inc. [stock listing]
MAJCOM – major command
MAL – Malan Realty Investors Inc. [stock listing]
MAM – Maxxim Medical Inc. [stock listing]
MAN – Manpower Inc. [stock listing]
MAN – metropolitan area network
MAP – Maine Public Service Co. [stock listing]
MAP – manufacturing automation protocol
MAPI – messaging application programming interface
MAPS – manpower analysis and planning system
MAPS – map-plotting system
MAR – Marriott International Inc. [stock listing]
MARAD – Maritime Administration
MARC – machine-readable cataloging
MARTS – advance monthly retail trade survey
MAS – Masco Corp. [stock listing]
MASF – Mobile Aeromedical Staging Facility
Mass. – Massachusetts [standard newspaper abbreviation]
Master Gunnery Sgt. – master gunnery sergeant
Master Sgt. – master sergeant
MAT – Mattel Inc. [stock listing]
MAU – math acceleration unit
MAV – Mavesa S.A. [stock listing]
MAW – Military Airlift Wing
MAX – Mercury Air Group Inc. [stock listing]

MAY – May Department Stores Co. [stock listing]

MB – Marine Board

Mb – megabit

MB – megabyte

MB – Molecular Biosystems Inc. [stock listing]

MBD – MBIA Inc. [stock listing]

MBDA – Minority Business Development Agency

MBE – MBIA Inc. [stock listing]

MBH – Midwest Banc Holdings Inc. [stock listing]

MBK – Bank of Tokyo Mitsubishi Ltd. [stock listing]

MBO – management by objective

MBP – Mid Penn Bancorp [stock listing]

Mbps – megabits per second

Mbps – megabytes per second

MBT – Mobile Telesystems Inc. [stock listing]

MC – machine code

MC – Maritime Commission

MC – Matsushita Elec Indl Ltd. [stock listing]

MC – Monaco

MCA – Micro Channel Architecture

MCA – MuniYield California Insured Fund II Inc. [stock listing]

MCAS – managed-care analysis system

MCB – MCB Financial Corp. [stock listing]

MCC – Mestek Inc. [stock listing]

MCC – Mission Control Center

MCDN – Marine Corps Data Network

MCF – Contango Oil & Gas Co. [stock listing]

MCH – Millennium Chems Inc. [stock listing]

MCHB – Maternal and Child Health Bureau

MCI – Massmutual Corporate Investors [stock listing]

MCJ – Mcdonalds Corp [stock listing]

MCK – McKesson HBOC Inc. [stock listing]

MCL – Moore Corp. Ltd. [stock listing]

MCM – Controladora Comml Mexicana [stock listing]

MCN – Mcn Energy Group Inc. [stock listing]

MCO – Moodys Corp [stock listing]

MCO – Orlando International Airport

MCP – Managed Care Program

MCP – Military Construction Project

MCR – Mfs Charter Income Trust [stock listing]

MCR – Military Census Report

MCS – Marcus Corp. [stock listing]

MCT – Monsanto Co. [stock listing]

MCX – MC Shipping Inc. [stock listing]

MCY – Mercury General Corp. [stock listing]

Md. – Maryland [standard newspaper abbreviation]

MD – Maryland

MD – mission director

MD – Moldavia

MDA – Media Arts Group Inc. [stock listing]

MDB – Multilateral Development Bank

MDC – M.D.C. Holdings Inc. [stock listing]

MDCS – mobile data collection system

MDD – meteorological data distribution

MDG – Meridian Gold Inc. [stock listing]

MDH – MuniHoldings Michigan Insured Fund II Inc. [stock listing]

MDJ – Merrill Lynch & Co. Inc. [stock listing]

MDM – Medium4.com Inc. [stock listing]

MDP – Meredith Corp. [stock listing]

MDR – Mcdermott International Inc. [stock listing]

MDS – Midas Group Inc. [stock listing]

MDT – Medtronic Inc. [stock listing]

MDT – mountain daylight time

MDU – Mdu Resources Group Inc. [stock listing]

MDW – Chicago Midway Airport

MDY – MidCap SPDR Trust Series I [stock listing]

MDZ – MDS Inc. [stock listing]

ME – Maine

MEA – Mead Corp. [stock listing]

MED – e-Medsoft.com [stock listing]

MEDIX – medical data interchange

MEDSEP – medical support enhancement program

MEE – Massey Energy Co. [stock listing]

MEF – multiprocessor enhancement feature

MEG/A – Media General Inc. [stock listing]

MEH – Midwest Express Holdings Inc. [stock listing]

MEI – Marquette Electronics Inc.

MEL – Mellon Financial Corp. [stock listing]

MEM – Memphis International Airport

MEM – Merrill Lynch & Co. Inc. [stock listing]

MEMO – Medical Equipment Management Office

MEN – Munienhanced Fund Inc. [stock listing]

MEQC – Marine Environmental Quality Committee

MER – Merrill Lynch & Co. Inc. [stock listing]

MERB – Medical Examination Review Board

MESA – model experimental systems analysis

MESL – Marine Environment Studies Laboratory

MET – MetLife Inc. [stock listing]

MET – mission elapsed time

METSAAT – meteorological satellite

MEW – Vasogen Inc. [stock listing]

MF – Malaysia Fund Inc., The [stock listing]

MFA – America First Mortgage Investments Inc. [stock listing]

MFAPM – medical functional activities program manager

MFC – Manulife Financial Corp. [stock listing]

MFGA – Compass Bancshares Inc. [stock listing]

MFI – Microfinancial Inc. [stock listing]

MFL – MuniHoldings Florida Insured Fund Inc. [stock listing]

MFLOPS – millions of floating-point operations per second

MFM – Mfs Municipal Income Trust [stock listing]

MFT – MuniYield Florida Insured Fund Inc. [stock listing]

MFV – MFS Special Value Trust [stock listing]

MFW – M&F Worldwide Corp. [stock listing]

MG – Madagascar

MG – Morgan Group Inc., The [stock listing]

MGAPRB – Magna International Inc. [stock listing]

MGB – Morgan Stanley Dean Witter Global Opportunity Bond Fund Inc. [stock listing]

MGC – Morgan Grenfell Smallcap Fund Inc. [stock listing]

MGF – MFS Government Markets Income Trust [stock listing]

MGG – MGM Grand Inc. [stock listing]

MGI – MGI Properties [stock listing]

MGL – Magellan Health Services Inc. [stock listing]

MGM – Metro-Goldwyn-Mayer Inc. [stock listing]

MGP – Merchants Group Inc. [stock listing]

MGS – Metrogas S.A. [stock listing]

MH – Marshall Islands

MHC – Manufactured Home Communities Inc. [stock listing]

MHCMIS – Military Health Care Management Information System

MHCS – Military Health Care System

MHD – MuniHoldings Fund Inc. [stock listing]

MHE – Massachusetts Health and Education Tax-Exempt Trust [stock listing]

MHF – Municipal High Income Fund Inc. [stock listing]

MHG – Meritage Hospitality Group Inc. [stock listing]

MHI – Morrison Management Specialists Inc. [stock listing]

MHK – Mohawk Industries Inc. [stock listing]

MHN – MuniHoldings New York Insured Fund Inc. [stock listing]

MHO – MI Schottenstein Homes Inc. [stock listing]

MHP – McGraw Hill Inc. [stock listing]

MHPCC – Maui High Performance Computer Center

MHR – Magnum Hunter Resources Inc. [stock listing]

MHT – Manchester Airport

MHU – MIIX Group Inc., The [stock listing]

MHX – Meristar Hospitality Corp. [stock listing]

MHY – Managed High Income Portfolio Inc. [stock listing]

MHz – megahertz

MI – Marshall & Ilsley Corp. [stock listing]

MI – Michigan

MIA – Miami International Airport

MIA – missing in action

MIAS – Marine Information and Advisory Service

MIB – management information base

MIC – MuniYield Califormia Insured Fund Inc. [stock listing]

Mich. – Michigan [standard newspaper abbreviation]

MICS – medical inventory control system

MID – management information department

MIDI – military item disposal instruction

MIDI – musical instrument digital interface

MIF – MuniInsured Fund Inc. [stock listing]

MIG – Meadowbrook Insurance Group Inc. [stock listing]

MII – streetTRACKS Morgan Stanley Internet Index Fund [stock listing]

MIJ – Merrill Lynch & Co. Inc. [stock listing]

MIL – Millipore Corp. [stock listing]

MILCON – military construction

MilDep – military department

MILGP – military group

MilsBills – military standard billing system

MIL-STD – military standard

MIM – Merrill Lynch & Co Inc. [stock listing]

MIME – multipurpose Internet mail extensions

MIN – Mfs Intermediate Income Trust [stock listing]

Minn. – Minnesota [standard newspaper abbreviation]

MINUGUA – United Nations Verification Mission in Guatemala

MINURSO – United Nations Mission for the Referendum in Western Sahara

MIPONUH – United Nations Civilian Police Mission in Haiti

MIPS – millions of instructions per second

MIR – Mirant Corp. [stock listing]

MIS – management information system

MIT – Massachusetts Institute of Technology

MIX – Merrill Lynch & Co. Inc. [stock listing]

MIY – MuniYield Michigan Insured Fund Inc. [stock listing]

MJI – MuniYield New Jersey Insured Fund Inc. [stock listing]

MKG – Mallinckrodt Inc. New [stock listing]

MKH – Merrill Lynch Market 2000+ HOLDRS [stock listing]

MKL – Markel Corp. [stock listing]

MKS – Mikasa Inc. [stock listing]

MKT – Advanced Marketing Services Inc. [stock listing]

ML – Mali

MLF – Merrill Lynch & Co. Inc. [stock listing]

MLFPIP – medical logistics functional process improvement program

MLG – Musicland Stores Corp. [stock listing]

MLH – Merrill Lynch & Co. Inc. [stock listing]

MLH – Mulhouse Basel/Mulhouse EuroAirport

MLI – Mueller Inds Inc. [stock listing]

MLJ – Merrill Lynch & Co. Inc. [stock listing]

MLK – Malta International Airport

MLK – Matlack Systems Inc. [stock listing]

MLM – Martin Marietta Materials Inc. [stock listing]

MLN – Merrill Lynch & Co. Inc. [stock listing]

MLP – Maui Land & Pineapple Co. Inc. [stock listing]

MLR – Miller Industries Inc. [stock listing]

MLS – Mills Corp. [stock listing]

MLSDG – Medical Logistics Strategic Development Group

MLT – Mitel Corp. [stock listing]

MM – Mutual Risk Mangement Ltd. [stock listing]

MM – Myanmar

MMA – MuniMae [stock listing]

MMC – Marsh & Mclennan Cos. Inc. [stock listing]

MMD – Moore Medical Corp. [stock listing]

MME – Mid Atlanta Medical Services Inc. [stock listing]

MMG – Metromedia International Group Inc. [stock listing]

MMH – Meristar Hotels & Resorts Inc. [stock listing]

MMI – man-machine interface

MMI – MMI Products Inc. [stock listing]

MMM – Minnesota Mining & Manufacturing Co. [stock listing]

MMR – Mcmoran Exploration Co. [stock listing]

MMS – Maximus Inc. [stock listing]

MMS – Minerals Management Service

MMT – Mfs Multimarket Income Trust [stock listing]

MMU – Managed Municipals Portfolio Inc. [stock listing]

MMU – memory management unit

MMU – Morristown Municipal Airport

MMV – Eaton Vance Massachusetts Municipal Income Trust [stock listing]

MMX – Maxx Petroleum Ltd. [stock listing]

MN – Minnesota

MN – Mongolia

MNA – Minnesota Municipal Term Trust Inc. [stock listing]

MNC – Monaco Coach Corp. [stock listing]

MND – Mitchell Energy and Development Corp. [stock listing]

MNI – McClatchy Co., The [stock listing]

MNM – Merrill Lynch & Co. Inc. [stock listing]

MNP – Municipal Partners Fund Inc. [stock listing]

MNS – Msc. Software Corp. [stock listing]

MNY – Mony Group Inc. [stock listing]

Mo. – Missouri [standard newspaper abbreviation]

MO – Macau

MO – Missouri

MO – Philip Morris Cos. Inc. [stock listing]

MOA – memorandum of agreement

MOCNESS – multiple opening-closing net environmental sampling system

MODEM – modulator-demodulator

MOE – major organizational entity

MOG/A – Moog Inc. [stock listing]

MOHAVE – measurement of haze and visual effects

MOIL – Marine Operations and Instrumentation Laboratory

MOLIS – minority on-line information service

MOM – modular ocean model

MON – Monsanto Co. [stock listing]

Mont. – Montana [standard newspaper abbreviation]

MONUA – United Nations Observer Mission in Angola

MONUC – United Nations Organization Mission in the Democratic Republic of the Congo

MOR – Morgan Keegan Inc. [stock listing]

MOT – Motorola Inc. [stock listing]

MOU – memorandum of understanding

MP – Northern Mariana Islands

MP3 – Moving Picture Experts Group layer-3 audio

MPA – monthly product announcement

MPA – MuniYield Pennsylvania Fund Inc. [stock listing]

MPC – most probable cost

MPEG – Moving Picture Experts Group

MPF – master personnel file

MPF – Merrill Lynch & Co. Inc. [stock listing]

MPH – Championship Auto Racing Teams Inc. [stock listing]

mph – miles per hour

MPNA – Monongahela Power Co. [stock listing]

MPO – Metropolitan Planning Organization

MPO – Motivepower Industries Inc. [stock listing]

MPP – General Cigar Holdings Inc. [stock listing]

MPR – Met Pro Corp. [stock listing]

MPS – main propulsion system

MPS – Modis Professional Services Inc. [stock listing]

MPV – Massmutual Participation Investors [stock listing]

MPX – Marine Products Corp. [stock listing]

MQ – Martinique

MQY – MuniYield Quality Fund Inc. [stock listing]

MR – Mauritania

MR – Morgan's Foods Inc. [stock listing]

MRA – Medical Resource Administration

MRA – Meritor Automotive Inc. [stock listing]

MRAO – Mullard Radio Astronomy Observatory

MRD – Macdermid Inc. [stock listing]

MRE – meal, ready to eat

MRE – Medco Research Inc. [stock listing]

MRF – American Income Fund Inc. [stock listing]

MRG – Morton's Restaurant Group Inc. [stock listing]

MRI/A – McRae Industries Inc. [stock listing]

MRI – magnetic resonance imaging

MRK – Marco Island Airport

MRK – Merck & Co Inc. [stock listing]

MRL – Marine Drilling Cos. Inc. [stock listing]

MRM – medical readiness model

MRM – Merrimac Industries Inc. [stock listing]

MRO – medical regulating office

MRO – USX Marathon Oil Co. [stock listing]

MRP – manufacturer's recommended price

MRP – Mississippi River Plume

MRR – mail return rate

MRR – medical regulating request

MRR – Mid-Atlantic Realty Trust. [stock listing]

MRRD – Marine Resources Research Division

MRS – Midcoast Energy Resources Inc. [stock listing]

MRX – Medicis Pharmaceutial Corp. [stock listing]

MRY – Memry Corp. [stock listing]

MRY – Monterey Peninsula Airport

MS DOS – Microsoft disk operating system

MS Word – Microsoft Word

MS – Milestone Scientific Inc. [stock listing]

MS – mission specialist

MS – Mississippi

MS – Montserrat

MS – multiple sclerosis

MSA – metropolitan statistical area

MSA – Mine Safety Appliances Co. [stock listing]

MSB – Mesabi Trust [stock listing]

MSBOS – maximum surgical blood order schedule

MSC – Material Sciences Corp. [stock listing]

MSD – Morgan Stanley Dean Witter Emerging Markets Debt Fund Inc. [stock listing]

MSE – Morgan Stanley Finance P.L.C. [stock listing]

MSF – Médecins Sans Frontières [Doctors Without Borders]

MSF – Morgan Stanley Dean Witter Emerging Markets Fund Inc. [stock listing]

MSFC – Marshall Space Flight Center

MSG – monsodium glutamate

MSHA – Mine Safety and Health Administration

MSI – Movie Star Inc. [stock listing]

MSK – Grupo Indl Maseca S A De Cv [stock listing]

MSL – mean sea level

MSL – MidSouth Bancorp [stock listing]

MSM – Micronetics Standard MUMPS (Massachusetts General Hospital Utility Multi-Programming System)

MSM – Msc Industries Direct Co Inc. [stock listing]

MSM-UNIX – Micronetics Standard MUMPS UNIX software

MSN – Emeritus Corp. [stock listing]

MSN – Emerson Radio Corp. [stock listing]

MSO – Martha Stewart Living Omnimedia [stock listing]

MSO – Missoula International Airport

MSP – Minneapolis-St. Paul International Airport

MSP – Morgan Stanley Fin P.L.C. [stock listing]

MSPB – Merit Systems Protection Board

MSRC – Marine Sciences Research Center

MSRP – manufacturer's suggested retail price

MSS – management support system

MSS – Measurement Specialties Inc. [stock listing]

MST – Main Street Bancorp Inc. [stock listing]

MST – mountain standard time

MSV – Manufacturers' Services Ltd. [stock listing]

MSW – Mission West Properties Inc. [stock listing]

MSX – Mascotech Inc. [stock listing]

MSY – Morgan Stanley High Yield Fund Inc., The [stock listing]

MT – Malta

MT – Meditrust Corp. [stock listing]

MT – Montana

MTA – Matav Rt. [stock listing]

MTB – M&T Bank Corp. [stock listing]

MTC – Monsanto Co. [stock listing]

MTD – Mettler Toledo International Inc. [stock listing]

MtDNA – mitochondrial deoxyribonucleic acid

MTF – Mitsubishi Tokyo Financial Group Inc. [stock listing]

MTG – Mgic Invt Corp Wis [stock listing]

MTH – Meritage Corp. [stock listing]

MTIM – medical technical integration manager

MTJ – Montrose Regional Airport

MTK – streetTRACKS Morgan Stanley High Tech 35 Index Fund [stock listing]

MTN – Vail Resorts Inc. [stock listing]

MTP – Montana Power Co. [stock listing]

MTPR – Meditrust [stock listing]

MTR – Mesa Royalty Trust [stock listing]

MTS – Montgomery Street Income Securities Inc. [stock listing]

MTT – Merrill Lynch & Co. Inc. [stock listing]

MTTPRX – Met-ed Capital Trust [stock listing]

MTU – Managed Municipals Portfolio Ii Inc. [stock listing]

MTW – Manitowoc Co. Inc. [stock listing]

MTX – Minerals Technologies Inc. [stock listing]

MTY – Marlton Technologies Inc. [stock listing]

MTZ – Mastech Corp. [stock listing]

MU – Mauritius

MU – Micron Technology Inc. [stock listing]

MUA – Muniassets Fund Inc. [stock listing]

MUC – MuniHoldings California Insured Fund Inc. [stock listing]

MUD – multiple-user dungeon

MUH – MuniHoldings Fund II Inc. [stock listing]

MUI – Metals USA Inc. [stock listing]

MUJ – MuniHoldings New Jersey Insured Fund Inc. [stock listing]

MUMPS – Massachusetts General Hospital Utility Multi-Programming System

MUO – Pioneer Interest Shares [stock listing]

MUR – Murphy Oil Corp. [stock listing]

MUS – Muniholdings Insured Fund Inc. [stock listing]

MUST – Manned Undersea Science and Technology

MV – Maldives

MVC – MVC Draper Fisher Jurvetson Fund I [stock listing]

MVF – MuniVest Fund Inc. [stock listing]

MVK – Maverick Tube Corp. [stock listing]

MVL – Marvel Enterprises Inc. [stock listing]

MVS/XA – multiple virtual storage/extended architecture

MVT – Munivest Fund II Inc. [stock listing]

MW – Malawi

MW – Men's Wearhouse Inc. [stock listing]

MWB – My Web, Inc.com [stock listing]

MWD – Morgan Stanley Dean Witter [stock listing]

MWH – BayCorp Holdings Ltd. [stock listing]

MWL – Mail-Well Hldgs Inc. [stock listing]

MWN – Morgan Stanley Dean Witter [stock listing]

MWP – MarkWest Hydrocarbon Inc. [stock listing]

MWS – microwave spectrometer

MWT – McWhorter Technologies Inc. [stock listing]

MWY – Midway Games Inc. [stock listing]

MX – Metso Corp. [stock listing]

MX – Mexico

MXA – Minnesota Municipal Income Portfolio Inc. [stock listing]

MXB – Marnetics Broadband Technologies Ltd. [stock listing]

MXC – MATEC Corp. [stock listing]

MXE – Mexico Equity And Income Fund Inc., The [stock listing]

MXF – Mexico Fund Inc., The [stock listing]

MXG – Maxim Group Inc. [stock listing]

MXM – MAXXAM Inc. [stock listing]

MXO – Maxtor Corp. [stock listing]

MXR – Medix Resources Inc. [stock listing]

MXT – Metris Cos. Inc. [stock listing]

MY – Malaysia

MYC – MuniYield California Fund Inc. [stock listing]

MYD – MuniYield Fund Inc. [stock listing]

MYF – MuniYield Florida Fund Inc. [stock listing]

MYG – Maytag Corp. [stock listing]

MYI – MuniYield Insured Fund Inc. [stock listing]

MYJ – MuniYield New Jersey Fund Inc. [stock listing]

MYL – Mylan Laboratories Inc. [stock listing]

MYM – MuniYield Michigan Fund Inc. [stock listing]

MYN – MuniYield New York Insured Fund Inc. [stock listing]

MYR – Mayor's Jewelers Inc. [stock listing]

MYS – Masisa S.A. [stock listing]

MZ – Milacron Inc. [stock listing]

MZ – Mozambique

MZA – MuniYield Arizona Fund Inc. [stock listing]

N.B. – nota bene (note well) [Latin]

N.C. – North Carolina [standard newspaper abbreviation]

N.D. – North Dakota [standard newspaper abbreviation]

N.H. – New Hampshire [standard newspaper abbreviation]

N.J. – New Jersey [standard newspaper abbreviation]

N.M. – New Mexico [standard newspaper abbreviation]

N.Y. – New York [standard newspaper abbreviation]

N – Inco Ltd. [stock listing]

NA – NABISCO Hldgs Corp. [stock listing]

NA – Namibia

NA – not applicable; not available

NAACP – National Association for the Advancement of Colored People

NAB – National Alliance of Businessmen

NAB – National Australia Bank Ltd. [stock listing]

NAC – National Association of Counties

NACC – North Atlantic Cooperation Council

NACIC – National Counterintelligence Center

NACOA – National Advisory Committee on Oceans and Atmosphere

NADC – Naval Air Development Center

NADP – National Atmospheric Deposition Program

NAE – National Academy of Engineering

NAFTA – North American Free Trade Agreement

NAG – New Accounts Group

NAHB – National Association of Home Builders

NAHRO – National Association of Housing and Redevelopment Officials

NAIC – National Association of Insurance Carriers

NAICS – North American Industry Classification System

NAL – National Agricultural Library

NAM – National Association of Manufacturers

NAM – nonaligned movement

NAMLS – Navy Automated Medical Logistics System

NAMMIS – Navy Automated Medical Materiel Information System

NAP – National Processing Inc. [stock listing]

NAR – National Association of Realtors

NARA – National Archives and Records Administration

NARC – National Association of Regional Councils

NARFE – National Association of Retired Federal Employees

NAS – Narcotics Affairs Section

NAS – National Academy of Science

NAS – Naval Air Station

NASA – National Aeronautics and Space Administration

NASABF – North America Statistical Areas Boundary File

NASAR – National Association for Search and Rescue

NASBIC – National Association of Small Business Investment Cos.

NASC – North Atlantic Salmon Convention

NASCAR – National Association for Stock Car Auto Racing

NASCO – National Academy of Sciences Committee on Oceanography

NASCOM – NASA Communications Network

NASDAQ – National Association of Securities Dealers Automated Quotations

NASM – National Air and Space Museum

NASS – National Agricultural Statistics Service

NAT – Nordic American Tanker Shipping Ltd. [stock listing]

NAU – National Australia Bank Ltd. [stock listing]

NAV – Navistar Intl Corp. New [stock listing]

NAVAIR – Naval Air Systems Command Headquarters

NAVELEX – Naval Electronic Systems Command Headquarters

NAVEUR – Naval Command Europe

NAVFAC – Naval Facilities Engineering Command Headquarters

NAVHOSP – Naval Hospital

NAVMASSO – Navy Management Systems Support Office

NAVMEDCOMINST – Naval Medical Command Instruction

NAVNET – Naval Network

NAVORD – Naval Ordnance Systems Command Headquarters

NAVSAT – navigational satellite

NAVSHIPS – Naval Ship Systems Command Headquarters

NAWAS – national warning system

NAZ – Nuveen Arizona Premium Income Municipal Fund Inc. [stock listing]

NBAC – National Bioethics Advisory Commission

NBC – National Broadcasting Co.

NBD – NB Cap Corp. [stock listing]

NBG – National Bank of Greece S.A. [stock listing]

NBL – New Brunswick Laboratory

NBL – Noble Affiliates Inc. [stock listing]

NBM – Nations Balanced Target Maturity Fund Inc. [stock listing]

NBN – Northeast Bancorp [stock listing]

NBP – Northern Border Partners L.P. [stock listing]

NBR – Nabors Industries Inc. [stock listing]

NBS – national biological survey

NBS – National Bureau of Standards

NBT – National Bancshares Corp. of Texas [stock listing]

NBX – Jefferson Pilot Corp. [stock listing]

NBY – NBC Capital Corp. [stock listing]

NC – Nacco Industries Inc. [stock listing]

NC – New Caledonia

NC – North Carolina

NC-17 – no one under the age of 17 admitted [MPAA rating]

NCA – National Cemetery Administration

NCA – National Command Authority

NCA – Nuveen California Municipal Value Fund Inc. [stock listing]

NCB – National Cooperative Bank

NCB – NCNB Corp. [stock listing]

NCC – National City Corp. [stock listing]

NCC – Network Control Center

NCCAM – National Center for Complementary and Alternative Medicine

NCCDPHP – National Center for Chronic Disease Prevention and Health Promotion

NCD – AT&T Capital Corp. [stock listing]

NCD – National Council on Disability

NCDC – National Climate Data Center

NCEH – National Center for Environmental Health

NCES – National Center for Education Statistics

NCF – AT&T Capital Corp. [stock listing]

NCGA – National Computer Graphics Association

NCH – NCH Corp. [stock listing]

NCHS – National Center for Health Statistics

NCHSTP – National Center for HIV, STD and TB Prevention

NCI – National Cancer Institute

NCI – Navigant Consulting Inc. [stock listing]

NCID – National Center for Infectious Diseases

NCIPC – National Center for Injury Prevention and Control

NCIS – Naval Criminal Investigative Service

NCJRS – National Criminal Justice Reference Service

NCLIS – National Commission on Libraries and Information Science

NCN – NCE Petrofund [stock listing]

NCO – Nuveen California Municipal Market Opportunity Fund Inc. [stock listing]

NCP – network control program

NCP – Nuveen California Performance Plus Municipal Fund Inc. [stock listing]

NCPC – National Capital Planning Commission

NCPGEN – network control program generation

NCR – NCR Corp. [stock listing]

NCRR – National Center for Research Resources

NCS – NCI Building Systems Inc. [stock listing]

NCSA – National Center for Supercomputing Applications

NCSC – National Computer Security Center

NCSL – National Conference of State Legislatures

NCTR – National Center for Toxicological Research

NCU – Nuveen California Premium Income Municipal Fund [stock listing]

NCUA – National Credit Union Administration

NCVHS – National Committee on Vital and Health Statistics

NCVS – National Crime Victimization Survey

NCX – Nova Chemicals Corp. [stock listing]

ND – North Dakota

NDB – National Discount Brokers Group Inc. [stock listing]

NDC – National Data Corp. [stock listing]

NDC – National Drug Code

NDDN – National Dry Deposition Network

NDE – Indymac Bancorp Inc. [stock listing]

NDIC – National Drug Intelligence Center

NDMS – National Disaster Medical System

NDN – 99 Cents Only Stores [stock listing]

NDSC – Network for the Detection of Stratospheric Change

NDTE – North Dakota Tracer Experiment

NDU – National Defense University

NE – CareerEngine Network Inc. [stock listing]

NE – Nebraska

NE – Niger

NE – Noble Drilling Corp. [stock listing]

NEA – National Endowment for the Arts

NEA – Nuclear Energy Agency

Neb. – Nebraska [standard newspaper abbreviation]

NEB – New England Business Service Inc. [stock listing]

NEC – National Electrical Commission

NEC – Nuclear Energy Commission

NEH – National Endowment for the Humanities

NEI – National Eye Institute

NEIC – National Earthquake Information Center

NEM – Newmont Mining Corp. [stock listing]

NEMA – National Electrical Manufacturers Association

NEMPR – Newmont Mining Corp. [stock listing]

NEP – Northeast Pennsylvania Financial Corp. [stock listing]

NER – Newcor Inc. [stock listing]

NERSC – National Energy Research Scientific Computing Center

NES – National Energy Strategy

NESC – National Environmental Satellite

NESDRES – National Environmental Data Referral Service

NET – North European Oil Royalty Trust [stock listing]

NETL – National Energy Technology Laboratory

NEU – Neuberger Berman Inc. [stock listing]

Nev. – Nevada [standard newspaper abbreviation]

NEV – Nuevo Energy Co. [stock listing]

NEW – Nvest L.P. [stock listing]

NEXRAD – next generation weather radar

NF – Norfolk Island

NFA – National Fire Academy

NFB – North Fork BanCorp. Inc. [stock listing]

NFC – Nuveen Connecticut Dividend Advantage Municipal Fund [stock listing]

NFF – Neff Corp. [stock listing]

NFG – National Fuel Gas Co. [stock listing]

NFI – Novaastar Financial Inc. [stock listing]

NFIB – National Federation of Independent Businesses

NFL – Nuveen Insured Florida Premium Income Municipal Fund [stock listing]

NFM – Nuveen Maryland Dividend Advantage Municipal Fund [stock listing]

NFO – NFO Worldwide Inc. [stock listing]

NFPA – National Fire Protection Agency

NFS – Nationwide Financial Services Inc. [stock listing]

NFS – network file system

NFX – Newfield Exploration Co. [stock listing]

NFZ – Nuveen Arizona Dividend Advantage Municipal Fund [stock listing]

NG – Nigeria

NGA – National Governors' Association

NGB – Nuveen Virginia Dividend Advantage Municipal Fund [stock listing]

NGDC – National Geophysical Data Center

NGF – Nations Government Income Term Trust 2004 Inc. [stock listing]

NGG – National Grid Group [stock listing]

NGH – Nabisco Group Hldg Corp [stock listing]

NGI – Nations Government Income Term Trust 2003 Inc. [stock listing]

NGO – nongovernmental organization

NGS – National Geographic Society

NGT – Eastern American Natural Gas Trust [stock listing]

NH – Naval Hospital

NH – New Hampshire

NHC – National HealthCare Corp. [stock listing]

NHGRI – National Human Genome Research Institute

NHI – National Health Investors Inc. [stock listing]

NHI – National Highway Institute

NHIC – National Health Information Center

NHL – Newhall Land & Farming Co. [stock listing]

NHLBI – National Heart, Lung and Blood Institute

NHP – Nationwide Health Properties Inc. [stock listing]

NHPRC – National Historical Publications and Records Commission

NHR – National Health Realty Inc. [stock listing]

NHRE – National Hail Research Experiment

NHT – Northolt Airport

NHTSA – National Highway Traffic Safety Administration

NHY – Norsk Hydro A.S. [stock listing]

NI – Nicaragua

NI – Nipsco Industries Inc. [stock listing]

NI – Northern Indiana Public Service Co. [stock listing]

NIA – National Institute on Aging

NIAA – National Institute on Alcohol Abuse and Alcoholism

NIAID – National Institute for Allergy and Infectious Diseases

NIAMS – National Institute of Arthritis and Musculoskeletal and Skin Diseases

NIC – National Institute of Corrections

NIC – network information center

NIC – network interface card

NIC – newly industrializing country

NIC – Nipsco Cap Mkts Inc. [stock listing]

NICHD – National Institute of Child Health and Human Development

NIDA – National Institute on Drug Abuse

NIDCD – National Institute on Deafness and Other Communication Disorders

NIDCR – National Institute of Dental and Craniofacial Research

NIDDK – National Institute of Diabetes and Digestive and Kidney Disease

NIDR – National Institute of Dental Research

NIDRR – National Institute on Disability and Rehabilitation Research

NIE – NBCI Auto Common Exchange [stock listing]

NIE – newly industrializing economy

NIEHS – National Institute of Environmental Health Sciences

NIF – Nuveen Premier Insured Municipal Income Fund Inc. [stock listing]

NIGMS – National Institute of General Medical Sciences

NIH – National Institute of Health

NIJ – National Institute of Justice

NIM – Nuveen Select Maturities Municipal Fund [stock listing]

NIMA – National Imagery and Mapping Agency

NIMBUS – network information management client-based user service

NIMH – National Institute of Mental Health

NINDS – National Institute of Neurological Disorders and Stroke

NINR – National Institute of Nursing Research

NIO – Nuveen Insured Municipal Opportunity Fund Inc. [stock listing]

NIOSH – National Institute for Occupational Safety and Health

NIP – network interface processor

NIPC – National Infrastructure Protection Center

NIPRB – Nisource Inc. [stock listing]

NIS – network information services

NIS – Nova Corp. [stock listing]

NISO – National Information Standards Organization

NIST – National Institute of Standards and Technology

NJ – New Jersey

NJP – NJ Eco Auth St Pens Fdg [stock listing]

NJR – New Jersey Resources Corp. [stock listing]

NKC – Newtek Capital Inc. [stock listing]

NKE – Nike Inc. [stock listing]

NKM – Merrill Lynch & Co. Inc. [stock listing]

NL – Netherlands

NL – NL Industries Inc. [stock listing]

NLAES – National Longitudinal Alcohol Epidemiologic Survey

NLC – Nalco Chemical Co. [stock listing]

NLC – National League of Cities

NLE – National Library of Education

NLEA – Nutrition Labeling and Education Act of 1990

NLI – NTL Inc. [stock listing]

NLM – National Library of Medicine

NLP – natural language processing

NLQ – near-letter quality

NLRB – National Labor Relations Board

NLS – network log-on system

NLY – Annaly Mortgage Management Inc. [stock listing]

nm – nautical mile

NM – New Mexico

NMA – Nuveen Municipal Advantage Fund Inc. [stock listing]

NMB – National Mediation Board

NMB – Nuveen Massachusetts Dividend Advantage Municipal Fund [stock listing]

NMC – National Meteorological Center

NMFS – National Marine Fisheries Service

NMGA – Neiman Marcus Groups Inc. [stock listing]

NMI – Nuveen Municipal Income Fund Inc. [stock listing]

NMK – Niagara Mohawk Holdings Inc. [stock listing]

NML – Merrill Lynch & Co. Inc. [stock listing]

NMN – Nematron Corp. [stock listing]

NMO – Nuveen Municipal Market Opportunity Fund Inc. [stock listing]

NMP – Nuveen Michigan Premium Income Municipal Fund Inc. [stock listing]

NMR – Nielsen Media Research Inc. [stock listing]

NMS – network management system

NMT – Nuveen Massachusetts Premium Income Municipal Fund [stock listing]

NMU – National Maritime Union

NMY – Nuveen Maryland Premium Income Municipal Fund [stock listing]

NNC – Nuveen North Carolina Premium Income Municipal Fund [stock listing]

NNF – Nuveen Insured New York Premium Income Municipal Fund Inc. [stock listing]

NNJ – Nuveen New Jersey Premium Income Municipal Fund Inc. [stock listing]

NNN – Commercial Net Lease Realty Inc. [stock listing]

NNP – Nuveen New York Performance Plus Municipal Fund Inc. [stock listing]

NNS – Newport News Shipblding Inc. [stock listing]

NNTP – network news transfer protocol

NNY – Nuveen New York Municipal Value Fund Inc. [stock listing]

NO – Norway

NOAA – National Oceanic and Atmospheric Administration

NOARL – Naval Ocean and Atmosphere Research Laboratory

NOC – Northrop Grumman Corp. [stock listing]

NOCPRB – Northrop Grumman Corp. [stock listing]

NOI – National Oilwell Inc. [stock listing]

NOK – Nokia Corp. [stock listing]

NOM – Nuveen Missouri Premium Income Municipal Fund [stock listing]

NOR – Northwestern Corp. [stock listing]

NORAD – North American Aerospace Defense Command

NOS – National Ocean Service

NOS – network operating system

NOSS – National Oceanic Satellite System

NOW – MAI Systems Corp. [stock listing]

NOW – National Organization for Women

NOX – Novavax Inc. [stock listing]

NP – National Power P.L.C. [stock listing]

NP – Nepal

NPC – National Petroleum Council

NPC – Nuveen Insured California Premium Income Municipal Fund Inc. [stock listing]

NPDB – National Practitioners Data Bank

NPF – Nuveen Premier Municipal Income Fund Inc. [stock listing]

NPG – Nuveen Georgia Premium Income Municipal Fund [stock listing]

NPI – Nuveen Premium Income Municipal Fund Inc. [stock listing]

NPIW – North Pacific Intermediate Water

NPK – National Presto Industries Inc. [stock listing]

NPP – Nuveen Performance Plus Municipal Fund Inc. [stock listing]

NPR – National Partnership for Reinventing Government

NPRC – National Personnel Records Center

NPRE – Inco Ltd. [stock listing]

NPS – National Park Service

NPS – Naval Postgraduate School

NPTO – National Petroleum Technology Office

NPTZ – North Pacific transition zone

NPV – Nuveen Virginia Premium Income Municipal Fund [stock listing]

NPW – NewPower Holdings Inc. [stock listing]

NQC – Nuveen California Investment Quality Municipal Fund Inc. [stock listing]

NQE – Salomon Smith Barney Holdings Inc. [stock listing]

NQF – Nuveen Florida Investment Quality Municipal Fund [stock listing]

NQH – Salomon Smith Barney Holdings Inc. [stock listing]

NQI – Nuveen Insured Quality Municipal Fund Inc. [stock listing]

NQJ – Nuveen New Jersey Investment Quality Municipal Fund Inc. [stock listing]

NQM – Nuveen Investment Quality Municipal Fund Inc. [stock listing]

NQN – Nuveen New York Investment Quality Municipal Fund Inc. [stock listing]

NQP – Nuveen Pennsylvania Investment Quality Municipal Fund [stock listing]

NQS – Nuveen Select Quality Municipal Fund Inc. [stock listing]

NQU – Nuveen Quality Income Municipal Fund Inc. [stock listing]

NR – Nauru

NR – Newpark Resources Inc. [stock listing]

NRB – Nuveen North Carolina Dividend Advantage Municipal Fund [stock listing]

NRC – National Research Council

NRC – Nuclear Regulatory Commission

NRDC – Natural Resources Defence Council

NRDP – National Rural Development Partnership

NREN – National Research and Education Network

NREVSS – National Respiratory and Enteric Virus Surveillance System

NRG – NRG Energy Inc. [stock listing]
NRI – Nationsrent Inc. [stock listing]
NRL – Naval Research Laboratory
NROSS – Navy Remote Ocean Sensing System
NRPC – National Railroad Passenger Corp. [informally known as AMTRAK]
NRT – Narita International Airport
NRT – Nortel Inversora S.A. [stock listing]
NRU – National Rural Utils Coop Fn [stock listing]
NRZ – NRG Energy Inc. [stock listing]
NS – National Steel Corp. [stock listing]
NSA – National Security Agency
NSB – National Science Board
NSC – National Science Council
NSC – National Security Council
NSC – National Space Council
NSC – Norfolk Southern Corp. [stock listing]
NSF – National Science Foundation, The
NSG – Nuclear Suppliers Group
NSGIC – National States Geographic Information Council
NSH – Nashua Corp. [stock listing]
NSI – National Svc Inds Inc. [stock listing]
NSIA – National Security Industrial Association
NSK – New Skies Satellites N.V. [stock listing]
NSM – National Semiconductor Corp. [stock listing]
NSO – nStor Technologies Inc. [stock listing]
NSRDB – National Solar Radiation Data Base
NSRDC – Naval Ship Research and Development Center
NSS – NS Group Inc. [stock listing]
NSSDC – National Space Science Data Center
NSSFC – National Severe Storms Forecast Center
NSSL – National Severe Storms Laboratory
NST – Nstar [stock listing]
NSTA – National Science Teachers Association
NSTC – National Science and Technology Council

NSTL – National Space Technology Laboratories
NSTS – National Space Transportation System
NSV – National Equipment Services Inc. [stock listing]
NT – Nortel Network Corp. [stock listing]
NTC – Nuveen Connecticut Premium Income Municipal Fund [stock listing]
NTG – NATCO Group Inc. [stock listing]
NTI – Northern Technologies International Corp. [stock listing]
NTIA – National Telecommunications and Information Administration
NTIS – National Technical Information Service
NTK – Nortek Inc. [stock listing]
NTL – Nortel Inversora S.A. [stock listing]
NTN – NTN Communications Inc. [stock listing]
NTS – Nevada Test Site
NTSB – National Transportation Safety Board
NTSC – National Television System Committee
NTT – Nippon Telegraph and Telephone Corp. [stock listing]
NTX – Nuveen Texas Quality Income Municipal Fund [stock listing]
NTZ – Industrie Natuzzi S.P.A [stock listing]
NU – Niue
NU – Northeast Utilities Systems [stock listing]
NUC – Naval Undersea Research and Development Center
NUC – Nuveen California Quality Income Municipal Fund Inc. [stock listing]
NUE – Nucoal Inc. [stock listing]
NUF – Nuveen Florida Quality Income Municipal Fund [stock listing]
NUI – NUI Corp. [stock listing]
NUM – Nuveen Michigan Quality Income Municipal Fund Inc. [stock listing]
NUN – Nuveen New York Quality Income Municipal Fund Inc. [stock listing]

NUO – Nuveen Ohio Quality Income Municipal Fund Inc. [stock listing]

NUS – Nu Skin Enterprises Inc. [stock listing]

NUT – Ml Macadamia Orchards L.P. [stock listing]

NUV – Nuveen Municipal Value Fund Inc. [stock listing]

NV – Nevada

NVB – Inco Ltd. [stock listing]

NVC – Nuveen California Select Quality Municipal Fund Inc. [stock listing]

NVH – National R V Hldgs Inc. [stock listing]

NVN – Nuveen New York Select Quality Municipal Fund Inc. [stock listing]

NVO – Novo Nordisk A/S [stock listing]

NVP – Nevada Power Co. [stock listing]

NVR – NVR Inc. [stock listing]

NVS – Novartis [stock listing]

NVSS – National Vital Statistics System

NWC – National War College

NWK – Network Equipment Technologies Inc. [stock listing]

NWL – Newell Rubbermaid Inc. [stock listing]

NWN – Northwest Natural Gas Co. [stock listing]

NWS – National Weather Service

NWS – News Corp. Ltd. [stock listing]

NWSEO – National Weather Service Employees Organization

NX – Quanex Corp. [stock listing]

NXC – Nuveen Insured California Select Tax-Free Income Portfolio [stock listing]

NXI – Nuveen Ohio Dividend Advantage Municipal Fund [stock listing]

NXJ – Nuveen New Jersey Dividend Advantage Municipal Fund [stock listing]

NXL – New Plan Excel Realty Trust Inc. [stock listing]

NXM – Nuveen Pennsylvania Dividend Advantage Municipal Fund [stock listing]

NXN – Nuveen Insured New York Select Tax-Free Income Portfolio [stock listing]

NXP – Nuveen Select Tax-Free Income Portfolio [stock listing]

NXS – Salomon Smith Barney Holding Inc. [stock listing]

NXY – Nexen Inc. [stock listing]

NXZ – Nuveen Dividend Advantage Municipal Fund 2 [stock listing]

NY – New York

NYE – Nycomed Amersham P.L.C. [stock listing]

NYM – Nymagic Inc. [stock listing]

NYT – New York Times Co. [stock listing]

NYU – New York University

NZ – New Zealand

NZ – NZ Corp. [stock listing]

NZT – Telecom New Zealand [stock listing]

O&C – operations and checkout

O – Realty Income [stock listing]

OA – office automation

OA – office of administration

OAIT – Office of American Indian Trust

OAK – Oakland International Airport

OALJ – Office of Administrative Law Judges

OAPEC – Organization of Arab Petroleum Exporting Countries

OAR – Office of AIDS Research

OAR – Office of Oceanic and Atmospheric Research

OAR – Ohio Art Co., The [stock listing]

OAS – Organization of American States

OASD – Office of the Assistant Secretary of Defense

OAT – Quaker Oats Co., The [stock listing]

OAU – Organization of African Unity

OBEMLA – Office of Bilingual Education and Minority Languages Affairs

OBI – Office of Business Innovations

OBJ – Queryobject System Corporation Com New [stock listing]

OBL – Office of Business Liaison

OC – Orion Capital Corp. [stock listing]

OCA – Office of Consumer Affairs

OCA – Orthodontic Centers of America Inc. [stock listing]

OCC – Office of the Comptroller of the Currency

OCD – Office of Community Development

OCI – Office of Criminal Investigation

OCN – Ocwen Financial Corp. [stock listing]

OCONUS – outside the continental United States

OCQ – Oneida Ltd. [stock listing]

OCR – Office of Civil Rights

OCR – Omnicare Inc. [stock listing]

OCR – optical character recognition

OCRD – Ocean Climate Research Division

OCRM – Office of Coastal Resource Management

OCS – Officer Candidate School

OCSE – Office of Child Support Enforcement

OD – optical disk

OD – overdose

ODA/ODIF – open document architecture/open document interchange

ODA – Overseas Development Administration

ODAS – Ocean Data Acquisition Systems, Aids and Devices

ODC – Office of Defense Corp.

ODC – Oil Dri Corp. of America [stock listing]

ODEP – Office of Disability Employment Policy

ODL – open document language

ODP – Office Depot Inc. [stock listing]

ODP – Office of Disease Prevention

ODS – optical data system

ODT – operational demonstration test

OE – operating expenses

OE – Orbital Engine Corp. Ltd. [stock listing]

OEA – Oea Inc. [stock listing]

OECD – Organization for Economic Cooperation and Development

OECS – Organization of Eastern Caribbean States

OEH – Orient-Express Hotels Ltd. [stock listing]

OEI – Ocean Energy Inc. [stock listing]

OEM – original equipment manufacturer

OEP – Office of Emergency Preparedness

OEP – Office of Environmental Policy

OERI – Office of Educational Research and Improvement

OES – order entry system

OESE – Office of Elementary and Secondary Education

OFA – Office of Family Assistance

OFAC – Office of Foreign Assets Control

OFC – Corporate Office Properties Trust [stock listing]

OFCCP – Office of Federal Contract Compliance Programs

OFDA – Office of U.S. Foreign Disaster Assistance

OFG – Oriental Financial Group Inc. [stock listing]

OFHEO – Office of Federal Housing Enterprise Oversight

OFI – operational flight instrumentation

OFM – Office of Financial Management

OFR – Office of the Federal Register

OG/A – Moog Inc. [stock listing]

OGE – Office of Government Ethics

OGE – OGE Energy Corp. [stock listing]

OGG – Kahului Airport

OH – Oakwood Homes Corp. [stock listing]

OH – Ohio

OHASIS – Office of Health and Safety Information System

OHB – Orleans Homebuilders Inc. [stock listing]

OHI – Omega Healthcare Investors Inc. [stock listing]

OHP – Oxford Health Plans Inc. [stock listing]

OHSE – Office of Health Systems Evaluation

OHTEX – Ocean Heat Transport Experiment

OI – optimum interpolation

OI – Owens Illinois Inc. [stock listing]

OIA – Morgan Stanley Dean Witter [stock listing]

OIC – Morgan Stanley Dean Witter [stock listing]

OIC – officer in charge

OIC – Organization of the Islamic Conference

OIG – Office of Inspector General

OIH – Merrill Lynch Market Oil Service HOLDRS [stock listing]

OII – Oceaneering International Inc. [stock listing]

OIIA – Office of Intergovernmental and Interagency Affairs

OIL – Triton Energy Ltd. [stock listing]

OIRM – Office of Information Resources Management

OIS – office information system

OIS – Oil State International Inc. [stock listing]

OJ – Orange Co Inc. [stock listing]

OJA – Ohio Power Co. [stock listing]

OJCS – Organization of the Joint Chiefs of Staff

OJJDP – Office of Juvenile Justice and Delinquency Prevention

OJP – Office of Justice Programs

OJT – on-the-job training

OK – Oklahoma

OK – Old Kent Financial Corp. [stock listing]

OKC – Will Rogers World Airport

OKE – Oneok Inc. [stock listing]

Okla. – Oklahoma [standard newspaper abbreviation]

OLMS – Office of Labor Management Standards

OLN – Olin Corp. [stock listing]

OLP – One Liberty Properties Inc. [stock listing]

OLPU – on-line personnel update

OLR – outgoing longwave radiation

OLS – operational linescan system

OLTP – on-line transaction processing

OLY – Olympic Cascade Financial Corp. [stock listing]

OM – Oman

OMA – Eppley Airfield

OMA – Oceanography and Marine Assessment

OMAR – Office of Medical Applications of Research

OMB – Office of Management and Budget

OMC – Office of Military Cooperation

OMC – Omnicom Group Inc. [stock listing]

OME – Omega Protein Corp. [stock listing]

OMG – OM Group Inc. [stock listing]

OMH – Office of Minority Health

OMI – Owens & Minor Inc. [stock listing]

OMM – Offshore Minerals Management Program

OMM – Omi Corp. [stock listing]

OMN – OMNOVA Solutions Inc. [stock listing]

OMS – Oppenheimer Multi Sector Income Trust [stock listing]

OMX – Officemax Inc. [stock listing]

ONBPRA – ONB Capital Trust I [stock listing]

ONDCP – Office of National Drug Control Policy

ONE – Bank One Corp. [stock listing]

ONR – Office of Naval Research

ONT – On2.com Inc. [stock listing]

ONT – Ontario International Airport

ONUSAL – United Nations Observer Mission in El Salvador

OO – Oakley Inc. [stock listing]

OOI – S&P Global 100 Index [stock listing]

OPA – Office of Public Affairs

OPAS – ophthalmolic production automated system

OPC/WS – QC Optics Inc. [stock listing]

OPC – Ocean Products Center

OPC – QC Optics Inc. [stock listing]

OPCW – Organization for the Prohibition of Chemical Weapons

OPDS – Operation Desert Shield/Storm

OPE – Office of Planning and Evaluation

OPE – Office of Postsecondary Education

OPEC – Organization of Petroleum Exporting Countries

OPI – Opinion Research Corp. [stock listing]

OPJ – Ohio Power Co. [stock listing]

OPM – Office of Personnel Management

OPRB – Realty Income TR [stock listing]

OPRC – Realty Income Corp. [stock listing]

OPRPRD – Santander Overseas Bank Inc. [stock listing]

OPT – OptiCare Health Systems Inc. [stock listing]

OR – Oregon

ORA – Office of Regulatory Affairs

ORACBA – Office of Risk Assessment and Cost-Benefit Analysis

ORB – Orbital Sciences Corp. [stock listing]

ORD – Chicago-O'Hare International Airport

Ore. – Oregon [standard newspaper abbreviation]

ORF – Norfolk International Airport

ORG – Organogenesis Inc. [stock listing]

ORHP – Office of Rural Health Policy

ORI – Old Republic International Corp. [stock listing]

ORISE – Oak Ridge Institute for Science and Education

ORK – Cork International Airport

ORMH – Office of Research on Minority Health

ORN – Orion Power Holdings Inc. [stock listing]

ORNL – Oak Ridge National Laboratory

ORP – Morgan Stanley Dean Witter & Co. [stock listing]

ORR – Office of Refugee Resettlement

ORSA – Operations Research Society of America

ORTA – Office of Research and Technology Applications

ORWH – Office of Research on Women's Health

ORY – Paris Orly Airport

OS – operating system

OS – Oregon Steel Mills Inc. [stock listing]

OSBP – Office of Small Business Programs

OSC – Ocean Science Committee

OSC – Office of Special Counsel

OSC – Office of Standards and Compliance

OSC – Operations Support Center

OSCE – Office of Child Support Enforcement

OSCE – Organization for Security and Cooperation in Europe

OSD – Office of the Secretary of Defense

OSDBU – Office of Small and Disadvantaged Business Utilization

OSDP – Operations System Development Program

OSE – open systems environment

OSERS – Office of Special Education and Rehabilitative Services

OSF – Office of Space Flight

OSF – Open Software Foundation

OSF – Operation Support Facility

OSG – Overseas Shipholding Group Inc. [stock listing]

OSH – Oshman's Sporting Goods Inc. [stock listing]

OSHA – Occupational Safety & Health Administration

OSI – Outback Steakhouse Inc. [stock listing]

OSM – Osmonics Inc. [stock listing]

OSS – Office of Space Science

OSS – Office of Strategic Services

OSS – open source software

OSSA – Office of Space Science and Applications

OST – Office of the Secretary of Transportation

OST – Austria Fund Inc., The [stock listing]

OSTA – Office of Space and Terrestrial Applications

OSTAC – Ocean Science and Technology Advisory Committee

OSTI – Office of Scientific and Technical Information

OSTP – Office of Science and Technology Policy

OSU – Osullivan Industries Holdings Inc. [stock listing]

OTA – Office of Technology Assessment

OTC – over-the-counter

OTE – Hellenic Telecommunication Organization S.A. [stock listing]

OTE – operational test environment

OTEC – ocean thermal energy conversion

OTI – Office of Technical Integration

OTIS – Office of Telecommunications and Information Systems

OTJ – Office of Tribal Justice

OTL – Octel Corp. [stock listing]

OTOH – on the other hand

OTR – OTR Express Inc. [stock listing]

OTS – off-the-shelf

OTSG – Office of the Surgeon General

OUI – Realty Income Corp. [stock listing]

OV – One Valley Bancorp of WV Inc. [stock listing]

OV – orbiter vehicle

OVAE – Office of Vocational and Adult Education

OVC – Office for Victims of Crime

OVH – Overhill Corp. [stock listing]

OWBO – Office of Women's Business Ownership

OWC – Owens Corning [stock listing]

OWCP – Office of Workers' Compensation Programs

OWH – Office on Women's Health

OXE – OEC Medical Systems Inc. [stock listing]

OXM – Oxford Industries Inc. [stock listing]

OXY – Occidental Petroleum Corp. [stock listing]

OY – optimum yield

P&L – profit and loss

P.L. – Public Law

p.m. – noon to midnight

P – Phillips Petroleum Co. [stock listing]

Pa. – Pennsylvania [standard newspaper abbreviation]

PA – Panama

PA – Pennsylvania

PA – Pimco Advisors [stock listing]

PA – Privacy Act

PA – public affairs

PAA – Plains All Amern Pipeline L [stock listing]

PAB – PAB Bankshares Inc. [stock listing]

PACE – Prelaunch Automatic Checkout Equipment

PACOM – Pacific Command

PAD – packet assembler/dissembler

PAD – Patient Administration Division

PAE – Peace Arch Entertainment Group Inc. [stock listing]

PAG – Pacific Gulf Properties Inc. [stock listing]

PAHO – Pan American Health Organization

PAI – Pacific American Income Shares Inc. [stock listing]

PAL – North American Palladium Ltd. [stock listing]

PAO – Palo Alto Airport of Santa Clara County

PAO – Public Affairs Office

PAO – public affairs officer

PAP – Asia Pulp & Paper [stock listing]

PAR – Coastalcast Corp. [stock listing]

PAR – patient accounting and reporting

PAS – public affairs specialist

PASBA – Patient Administration and Biostatistics Activity

PAX – Paxson Communications Corp. [stock listing]

PAYCOM – Payload Command Coordinator

PB – Panamerican Beverages Inc. [stock listing]

PBAC – Program Budget Advisory Committee

PBG – Pepsi Bottling Group Inc. [stock listing]

PBGC – Pension Benefit Guaranty Corp.

PBI – Palm Beach International Airport

PBI – Pitney Bowes Inc. [stock listing]

PBR – Petroleo Brasileiro-Petrobras [stock listing]

PBS – Public Broadcasting Service

PBT – Permian Basin Realty Trust [stock listing]

PBX – private branch exchange

PBY – Pep Boys Manny Moe & Jack [stock listing]

PC CARP – personal computer/cluster analysis and regression program

PC – Peace Corps

PC – personal computer

PC – politically correct

PC – professional corporation

PCA – Permanent Court of Arbitration

PCA – physical configuration audit

PCA – Putnam California Investment Grade Municipal Trust [stock listing]

PCAST – President's Council of Advisors on Science and Technology

PC-AT – personal computer/advanced technology

PCB – polychlorinated biphenyl

PCC – Panama Canal Commission

PCC – PMC Commercial Trust [stock listing]

PCD – PlanetCAD Inc. [stock listing]

PCF – Putnam High Income Convertible and Bond Fund [stock listing]

PCG – PG&E Corp. [stock listing]

PCGRIDS – personal computer gridded interactive display and diagnostic system

PCH – Potlatch Corp. [stock listing]

PCI – peripheral component interconnect

PCL – Plum Creek Timber Co. Inc. [stock listing]

PCM – Pimco Commercial Mortgage Securities Trust Inc. [stock listing]

PCMCIA – Personal Computer Memory Card International Association

PCMI – President's Council on Management Improvement

PCN – Pameco Corp. [stock listing]

PCP – Precision Castparts Corp. [stock listing]

PCQ – Pacificorp [stock listing]

PCR – Perini Corp. [stock listing]

PCS – permanent change of station

PCS – Sprint Corp. [stock listing]

PCSD – President's Council on Sustainable Development

PCT – Princeton Airport

PCT – Provident Capital Trust [stock listing]

PCU – Southern Peru Copper Corp. [stock listing]

PCV – Putnam Convertible Opportunities and Income Trust [stock listing]

PCW – Pacific Century Cyberworks Ltd. [stock listing]

PCX – Pacificorp [stock listing]

PC-XT – personal computer/extended technology

PCZ – Petro-Canada [stock listing]

PD – Phelps Dodge Corp. [stock listing]

PD – position description

PDA – personal digital assistant

PDA – public display of affection

PDC – Pacific Disaster Center

PDC – South Texas Drilling & Exploration Inc. [stock listing]

PDE – Pride Intl Inc. [stock listing]

PDG – Placer Dome Inc. [stock listing]

PDI – Putnam Dividend Income Fund [stock listing]

PDL/A – Presidential Realty Corp. [stock listing]

PDL – page description language

PDM – Pitt-Des Moines Inc. [stock listing]

PDM – program decision memorandum

PDMA – Prescription Drug Marketing Act

PDMP – project data management plan

PDP – program development plan

PDRS – payload deployment & retrieval system

PDRY – People's Democratic Republic of Yemen

PDS – Precision Drilling Corp. [stock listing]

PDT – John Hancock Patriot Premium Dividend Fund II [stock listing]

PDU – power distribution unit

PDX – Pediatrix Medical Group Inc. [stock listing]

PDX – Portland International Airport

P/E – price/earnings

PE – Peru

PE – Peco Energy Co. [stock listing]

PEC – Pharmacoeconomic Center

PEC – program element code

PECPRX – Penelec Capital Trust [stock listing]

PEF – S&P 500 Protected Equity Fd [stock listing]

PEG – Perugia International Airport

PEG – Public Service Enterprise Group Inc. [stock listing]

PEI – Pennsylvania Real Estate Investment Trust [stock listing]

PEN – Pacific Exchange Network

PEO – Petroleum & Resources Corp. [stock listing]

PEP – PepsiCo Inc. [stock listing]

PEQ – Potomac Edison Co. [stock listing]

PEQUOD – Pacific Equatorial Ocean Dynamics

PER – Perot Sys Corp. [stock listing]

PER – Perth, Western Australia, Airport

PERL – pratical extraction and reporting language

PERT – performance evaluation and review technique

PETA – Pacific Enterprises [stock listing]

PETA – People for the Ethical Treatment of Animals

PEX – PetroCorp Inc. [stock listing]

PF – French Polynesia

PFA – Alliance Forest Products Inc. [stock listing]

Pfc. – private first class

PFC – perfluorocarbon

PFD – Preferred Income Fund Inc. [stock listing]

PFE – Pfizer Inc. [stock listing]

PFGPR – Penncorp Financial Group Inc. [stock listing]

PFH – Cabco Tr For JC Penney Debs [stock listing]

PFI – Pelican Financial Inc. [stock listing]

PFO – Preferred Income Opportunity Fund Inc. [stock listing]

PFP – Partnership for Peace

PFP – Premier Farnell [stock listing]

PFX – Pilgrim America Capital Corp. [stock listing]

PG – Papua New Guinea

PG – parental guidance suggested [MPAA rating]

PG – Procter & Gamble Co. [stock listing]

PG-13 – parental guidance suggested for children under 13 [MPAA rating]

PGA – Personnel Group of America Inc. [stock listing]

PGB – Portland Gen Elec Co. [stock listing]

PGC – Peapack-Gladstone Financial Corp. [stock listing]

PGD – John Hancock Patriot Global Dividend Fund [stock listing]

PGE – Prime Group Realty Trust [stock listing]

PGF – Progressive Return Fund, Inc. [stock listing]

PGHM – Payload Ground Handling Mechanism

PGI – Polymer Group Inc. [stock listing]

PGL – Peoples Energy Corp. [stock listing]

PGM – Putnam Investment Grade Municipal Trust [stock listing]

PGN – Progress Energy Inc. [stock listing]

PGO – Archuleta County Airport/Stevens Field

PGO – Petroleum Geo-Services [stock listing]

PGOPRA – Petroleum Geo-Svcs AsaTrust I [stock listing]
PGP – Pretty Good Privacy
PGR – Progressive Corp. [stock listing]
PGT – Merrill Lynch & Co., Inc. [stock listing]
PGX – Perigueux Bassillac Airport
Ph.D. – doctor of philosophy
PH – Parker Hannifin Corp. [stock listing]
PH – Philippines
PHA – Pharmacia Corp. [stock listing]
PHA – Public Housing Agency
PHC – Peoples Holding Co., The [stock listing]
PHF – Newport News/Williamsburgh Airport
PHF – Pacholder High Yield Fund Inc. [stock listing]
PHG – Koninklijke Philips Electronics [stock listing]
PHI – Philippine Long Distance Telephone Co. [stock listing]
PHIGS – programmers hierarchical interactive graphics system
PHL – Philadelphia International Airport
PHM – Pulte Corp. [stock listing]
PHPPO – Public Health Practice Program Office
PHR – Philips International Realty Corp. [stock listing]
PHS – Public Health Service
PHT – Managed High Yield Fund [stock listing]
PHTN – Public Health Training Network
PHX – Phoenix Sky Harbor International Airport
PHX – Photoelectron Corp. [stock listing]
PHY – Prospect Street High Income Portfolio Inc. [stock listing]
PI – Pacific Islands
PI – Premdor Inc. [stock listing]
PI – principal investigator
PI – private investigator

PIA – Morgan Stanley Dean Witter [stock listing]
PIC – Pichin Corp. [stock listing]
PICA – Primary Inventory Control Activity
PICA – Proposal Instruction Compliance Audit
PIE – St. Petersburg-Clearwater International Airport
PIF – Insured Municipal Income Fund [stock listing]
PIH – Office of Public and Indian Housing
PII – Polaris Inds Inc. [stock listing]
PIK – Water Pik Technologies Inc. [stock listing]
PIM – Putnam Master Intermediate Income Trust [stock listing]
PIMRIS – Pacific Islands Marine Resources Information System
PIN – AMF Bowling Inc. [stock listing]
PIO – Pioneer Corp. Japan [stock listing]
PIO – programming input/output
PIO – public information officer
PIR – Pier 1 Imports Inc. [stock listing]
PIT – Pittsburgh International Airport
PK – Pakistan
PKD – Parker Drilling Co. [stock listing]
PKE – Park Electrochemical Corp. [stock listing]
PKF – Pakistan Investment Fund Inc. [stock listing]
PKG – Packaging Corp. of America [stock listing]
PKI – Perkinelmer Inc. [stock listing]
PKI – public key infrastructure
PKS – Six Flags Inc. [stock listing]
PKX – Pohang Iron & Steel Ltd. [stock listing]
PKY – Parkway Properties Inc. [stock listing]
PL/1 – Programming Language One
PL – Poland
PL – Propective Life Corp. [stock listing]
PLA – New Playboy Inc. [stock listing]
PLB – American Italian Pasta Co. [stock listing]
PLC – Manchester Airport

PLC – PLC Systems Inc. [stock listing]
PLD – Prologis [stock listing]
PLE – Pinnacle Bancshares, Inc. [stock listing]
PLEX – planning and execution
PLH – Pierce Leahy Corp. [stock listing]
PLI – PolyVision Corp. [stock listing]
PLL – Pall Corp. [stock listing]
PLL – Prescribed Load List
PLM – PLM International Inc. [stock listing]
PLO – Palestine Liberation Organization
PLP – Phosphate Resource Partners Ltd. [stock listing]
PLR/A – Plymouth Rubber Co. Inc. [stock listing]
PLS – Paracelsus Healthcare Corp. [stock listing]
PLT – Plantronics Inc. [stock listing]
PLX – Plains Resources Inc. [stock listing]
PLZ – Port Elizabeth Airport
PM – process manager
PM – project management
PM – Saint Pierre and Miquelon
PMBS – Property Management and Budgeting System
PMC – PMC Capital Inc. [stock listing]
PMCS – project management control system
PMD – Psychemedics Corp. [stock listing]
PME – Penton Media Inc. [stock listing]
PME – personnel management evaluation
PMH – Putnam Tax-Free Health Care Fund [stock listing]
PMI – Palma de Mallorca Airport, Balearic Islands
PMI – PMI Group Inc., The [stock listing]
PMIS – purchase management information system
PML – Plymouth Marine Laboratory
PMM – Putnam Managed Municipal Income Trust [stock listing]
PMN – Putnam New York Investment Grade Municipal Trust [stock listing]
PMO – Putnam Municipal Opportunities Trust [stock listing]

PMP – Performance Management Program
PMP – prevention, mitigation and preparedness
PMR – postmaster return
PMS – Policy Management Systems Corp. [stock listing]
PMSA – primary metropolitan statistical area
PMSS – project management support system
PMT – process management team
PMT – Putnam Master Income Trust [stock listing]
PN – Pitcairn Island
PNC – PNC Financial Services Group, The [stock listing]
PNG – Penn-America Group Inc. [stock listing]
PNK – Pinnacle Entmt Inc. [stock listing]
PNL – Pacific Northwest National Laboratory
PNM – Public Services Co. of New Mexico [stock listing]
PNN – PennEngineering [stock listing]
PNNA – Penn Engineering & Manufacturing Corp. [stock listing]
PNO – PANACO Inc. [stock listing]
PNP – Pan Pacific Retail Properties [stock listing]
PNR – Pentair Inc. [stock listing]
PNS – Pinnacle Data Systems Inc. [stock listing]
PNSN – Pacific Northwest Seismic Network
PNT – Pennsylvania Enterprises Inc. [stock listing]
PNU – Pharmacia & UpJohn Inc. [stock listing]
PNW – Pinnacle West Capital Corp. [stock listing]
PNY – Piedmont Natural Gas Co Inc. [stock listing]
PO – purchase order
POB – Philadelphia Pa Au Ind Dev P [stock listing]
POB – place of birth
POC – P&O Princess [stock listing]

POC – particulate organic carbon

POD – Payload Operations Director

POD – probability of detection

POG – Patina Oil & Gas Corp. [stock listing]

POI – Protection One Inc. [stock listing]

POL/ECO – Political/Economic Section

POL/LAB – Political and Labor Section

POL – PolyOne Corp. [stock listing]

POM – Potomac Electric Power Co. [stock listing]

POP – pay one price

POP – point of purchase

POP – point of presence

POP – Pope & Talbot Inc. [stock listing]

POP – Population Division

POP – post office protocol

POPMAIL – post office protocol mail

POS – point of sale

POSIX – portable operating system interface for computer

POST – power-on self-test

POT – Potash Corp. of Saskatchewan Inc. [stock listing]

POT – Program for Operational Trajectories

POTAD – Program for Operational Transport and Dispersion

POV – privately owned vehicle

POW-MIA – prisoner of war/missing in action

POW/MP – prisoner of war/missing personnel

PP – Prentiss Properties Trust [stock listing]

PPA – Premier Bancorp Inc. [stock listing]

PPBS – planning, programming and budget system

PPC – product and price comparison

PPD – Pre-Paid Legal Services Inc. [stock listing]

PPE – Park Place Entertainment Corp. [stock listing]

PPF – John Hancock Patriot Preferred Dividend Fund [stock listing]

PPG – PPG Industries Inc. [stock listing]

PPH – Merrill Lynch Pharmaceutical HOLDRS [stock listing]

PPK – Polyair Inter Pack Inc. [stock listing]

PPL – PP&L RES INC [stock listing]

PPM – Investment Grade Municipal Income Fund [stock listing]

ppm – pages per minute

ppm – parts per million

pmv – parts per million by volume

PPN – Morgan Stanley Dean Witter & Co [stock listing]

PPO – Pepsi Cola Puerto Rico Bottling Co. [stock listing]

PPO – preferred provider organization

PPP – Pogo Producing Co. [stock listing]

PPP – point-to-point protocol

PPR – Pilgrim America Prime Rate Trust [stock listing]

PPS – Post Properties Inc. [stock listing]

ppt – parts per trillion

PPT – Putnam Premier Income Trust [stock listing]

PPW – PacifiCorp [stock listing]

PR – Prices Communication Corp. [stock listing]

PR – Puerto Rico

PRB – Paso Robles Municipal Airport

PRB – Probex Corp. [stock listing]

PRC – postal rate commission

PRC – program review committee

PRD – Polaroid Corp. [stock listing]

PRD – presidential review directive

PRE – Partnerre Ltd. [stock listing]

PRH – Promus Hotel Corp. [stock listing]

PRI – Cox Communications Inc. New [stock listing]

PRK – Park National Corp. [stock listing]

PRL – Prolong International Corp. [stock listing]

PRM – Primedia Inc. [stock listing]

PRN – Puerto Rican Cem Inc. [stock listing]

PROM – programmable read-only memory

PROMAR – Program on the Promotion of Marine Sciences [UNESCO]

PRS – Pure Resources Inc. [stock listing]

PRT – Prime Retail Inc. [stock listing]
PRW – PracticeWorks Inc. [stock listing]
PRW – purchase request worksheet
PRX – Pharmaceutical Resources Inc. [stock listing]
PRZ – Prize Energy Corp. [stock listing]
PS – payload specialist
PS – postscript
PSA – principal staff assistant
PSA – Public Storage Inc. [stock listing]
PSAC – President's Science Advisory Council
PSAD – political/statistical area description
PSB – PS Business Parks Inc. [stock listing]
PSC – Philadelphia Suburban Corp. [stock listing]
PSD – Puget Energy Inc. [stock listing]
PSDP – professional skills development program
PSDPRC – Puget Sound Energy Inc. [stock listing]
PSF – program support facility
PSG – project support group
PSI – Porta Systems Corp. [stock listing]
psi – pounds per square inch
psia – pounds per square inch, absolute
psid – pounds per square inch, differential
psig – pounds per square inch, gauge
PSL/PSA – problem statement language/ problem statement analyzer
PSMSL – permanent service for mean sea level
PSN – packet-switched node
PSN – processing sequence number
PSO – Pearson P.L.C. [stock listing]
PSP – paralytic shellfish poisoning
PSPC – ROSAT Position Sensitive Proportional Counters
PSS – Payless Shoesource Inc. [stock listing]
PST – Pacific standard time
PSU – Pennsylvania State University
PSU – Plastic Surgery Co., The [stock listing]
PSU – primary sampling unit
PT – Portugal

PT – Portugal Telecom SGPS S.A. ADS [stock listing]
PTA – Penn Treat American Corp. [stock listing]
PTC – Par Technology Corp. [stock listing]
PTG – Paragon Technologies Inc. [stock listing]
PTM – Putnam Managed High Yield Trust [stock listing]
PTN – Palatin Technologies Inc. [stock listing]
PTO – Patent and Trademark Office
PTR – Petrochina Ltd. [stock listing]
PTT – Peak Trends Trust [stock listing]
PTV – Pactiv Corp. [stock listing]
PTX – Pillowtex Corp. [stock listing]
PTZ – Pulitzer Inc. [stock listing]
PUB – Publicis Groupe S.A. [stock listing]
PUK – Prudential P.L.C. [stock listing]
PV – Pfeiffer Vacuum Technology A.G. [stock listing]
PV – prime vendor
PVA – Penn Virginia Corp. [stock listing]
PVC – permanent virtual circuit
PVC – Planvista Corp. [stock listing]
PVC – polyvinyl chloride
PVD – Administradora de Fondos de Pensiones-Provida [stock listing]
PVH – Phillips Van Heusen Corp. [stock listing]
PVI – Panavision Inc. [stock listing]
PVI – prime vendor interface
PVN – Providian Financial Corp. [stock listing]
PVR – Puerto Vallarta International Airport
Pvt. – private
PW – Palau
PW – Pittsburgh & West Virginia Railroad [stock listing]
PWBA – Pension and Welfare Benefits Administration
PWD – Public Works Department
PWG – Powergen P.L.C. [stock listing]
PWN – Cash America International Inc. [stock listing]

PWR – Prepositioned War Reserve
PWR – Quanta Services Inc. [stock listing]
PWX – Providence and Worcester Railroad Co. [stock listing]
PX – Praxair Inc. [stock listing]
PXD – Pioneer Natural Resources Co. [stock listing]
PXP – Phoenix Investment Partners Ltd. [stock listing]
PXR – Paxar Corp. [stock listing]
PXT – Pxre Group Ltd. [stock listing]
PY – Paraguay
PY – Pechiney [stock listing]
PYM – Putnam High Yield Municipal Trust [stock listing]
PYR – PYR Energy Corp. [stock listing]
PYX – Playtex Products Inc. [stock listing]
PZA – Provena Foods Inc. [stock listing]
PZB – Pittston Co., The [stock listing]
PZL – Pennzoil-Quaker State Co. [stock listing]
PZN – Prison Realty Corp. [stock listing]
PZNPRA – Prison Realty Trust [stock listing]
Q – Qwest Communications Intl Inc. [stock listing]
QA – Qatar
QA – quality assurance
QACAS – quality assurance corrective action system
QC – quality control
QED – quod erat demonstrandum (which was to be demonstrated) [Latin]
QEPO – Quality Engineering Program Office
QFR – quarterly financial report
QMB – Quality Management Board
QPMP – quality project management process
QQQ – Nasdaq-100 Index Tracking Stock [stock listing]
QRAY – Raytech Corp. [stock listing]
QRDF – quick retrieval data file
QSC – Questcor Pharmaceuticals Inc. [stock listing]
R&A – request and authorization

R&D – research and development
R.I. – Rhode Island [standard newspaper abbreviation]
R – Ryder System Inc. [stock listing]
RA – Reckson Associates Realty Corp. [stock listing]
RAA – BlackRock California Investment Quality Municipal Trust Inc. [stock listing]
RAC – Rampart Capital Corp. [stock listing]
RAD – Rite Aid Corp. [stock listing]
RADAR – radio detecting and ranging
RADS – real-time analysis and display system
RAF – Royal Air Force
RAH – Ralcorp Holding Inc. [stock listing]
RAL – Ralston Purina Co. [stock listing]
RAM – random access memory
RAM – Royal Appliance Manufacturing Co. [stock listing]
RAMC – Walter Reed Army Medical Center
RAMIS – rapid access management information system
RAP – regional analysis and prediction
RAPIDS – Real-Time Automated Personnel Identification System
RAPS – resource analysis and planning system
RAS – RAIT Investment Trust [stock listing]
RAS – Royal Astronomical Society
RBA – Ritchie Bros Auctioneers Inc. [stock listing]
RBC – Regal-Beloit Corp. [stock listing]
RBK – Reebok International Ltd. [stock listing]
RBN – Robbins & Myers Inc. [stock listing]
RBRVS – resource-based relative-value scale
RBS – Rural Business-Cooperative Service
RBT – Morgan Stanley Group Inc. [stock listing]
RC – Grupo Radio Centro S.A. [stock listing]
RCC – regional census center
RCC – regional climate center
RCF – Rica Foods Inc. [stock listing]
RCG – eResource Capital Group Inc. [stock listing]

RCL – Royal Caribbean Cruises Ltd. [stock listing]

RCN – Rogers Wireless Communications Inc. [stock listing]

RCON – regional consular affairs officer

RCRA – Resource Conservation and Recovery Act

RCS – Rcm Strategic Global Government Fund, Inc. [stock listing]

RCZ – red blood cells

RD – Royal Dutch Petroleum Co. [stock listing]

RDA – Readers Digest Associates Inc. [stock listing]

RDA – relational database access

RDB – Readers Digest Association Inc. [stock listing]

RDB – relational database

RDBMS – relational database management system

RDC – Rowan Cos. Inc. [stock listing]

RDD – random digit dialing

RDD – required delivery date

RDDB – reportable diseases database

RDK – Ruddick Corp. [stock listing]

RDL – Riddell Sports Inc. [stock listing]

RDN – Radian Group Inc. [stock listing]

RDO – Rdo Equipment Co. [stock listing]

RDT – Readers Digest Automatic Com [stock listing]

RDU – Raleigh-Durham International Airport

RDY – Dr. Reddy's Laboratories Ltd. [stock listing]

RE – Everest Re Group Ltd. [stock listing]

re – regarding

RE – Reunion

REA – Rural Electrification Administration

Rear Adm. – rear admiral

rec – recreation

REF – Refac [stock listing]

REG – Regency Centers Corp. [stock listing]

REI – Reliant Energy Inc. [stock listing]

REL – Reliance Group Holdings Inc. [stock listing]

REOM – Regional Elected Officials Meeting

REP – representative

REP – Repsol Ypf S A [stock listing]

RES – Rpc Inc. [stock listing]

REV – Revlon Inc. [stock listing]

REX – research and experimentation

REY – Reynolds & Reynolds Co. [stock listing]

RF – radio frequency

RFA – BlackRock Florida Investment Quality Municipal Trust Inc., The [stock listing]

RFC – request for comment

RFC – River Forecast Center

RFDD – regional food and drug director

RFI – Cohen & Steers Total Return Realty Fund Inc. [stock listing]

RFI – radio frequency interference

RFP – request for proposal

RFQ – request for quotation

RFS – RFS Hotels Investors Inc. [stock listing]

RFT – request for technology

RG – Rogers Communication Inc. [stock listing]

RGA – Reinsurance Group of America Inc. [stock listing]

RGB – Barry RG Corp. [stock listing]

RGB – red, blue and green

RGL – Royce Focus Trust, Inc. [stock listing]

RGR – Sturm Ruger & Co. Inc. [stock listing]

RGS – Rochester Gas & Electric Corp. [stock listing]

RGX – Radiologix Inc. [stock listing]

Rh – Rhesus factor

RH – Rottlund Co. Inc., The [stock listing]

RHA – Rhodia [stock listing]

RHB – Rehabcare Group Inc. [stock listing]

RHD – RH Donnelley Corp. [stock listing]

RHH – Robertson Ceco Corp. [stock listing]

RHI – Half Robert International Inc. [stock listing]

RHS – Rural Housing Service

RHT – Richton International Corp. [stock listing]

RHUDO – Regional Housing and Urban Development Office

RI – Rhode Island

RI – Ruby Tuesday Inc. [stock listing]

RIA – radio immunoassay

RIC – Richmond International Airport

RIC – Richmont Mines Inc. [stock listing]

RID – routing identifier

RIDGE – Ridge Interdisciplinary Global Experiments

RIF – Cohen & Steers Realty Income Fund Inc. [stock listing]

RIF – reduction in force

RIG – Transocean Sedco Forex Inc. [stock listing]

RIL – Garfield County Regional Airport

RIM – Regional Indian Meeting

RIM – retail inventory management

RIN – regulation identifier number

RIP – requiescat in pace (rest in peace) [Latin]

RIP – routing information protocol

RIS – retail inventory survey

RISC – reduced instruction set computer

RISD – Rhode Island School of Design

RIT – Rightchoice Managed Care Inc. [stock listing]

RIV – Riviera Holdings Corp. [stock listing]

RJE – remote job entry

RJF – Raymond James Financial Inc. [stock listing]

RJI – Reeds Jewelers Inc. [stock listing]

RJR – RJ Reynolds Tobacco Holdings Inc. [stock listing]

RKT – Rock Tenn Co. [stock listing]

RKY – Coors Adolph Corp. [stock listing]

RL – Polo Ralph Lauren Corp. [stock listing]

RLC – Rollins Truck Leasing Corp. [stock listing]

RLI – RLI Corp. [stock listing]

RMA – Risk Management Agency

RMA – Rubber Manufacturers Association

RMD – Resmed Inc. [stock listing]

RME – Morgan Stanley Dean Witter & Co. [stock listing]

RMF – resource measurement facility

RMG – Rainbow Media Group [stock listing]

RMI – Republic of the Marshall Islands

RMI – Rotonics Manufacturing Inc. [stock listing]

RML – Russell Corp [stock listing]

RMO – Resource Management Office

RMP – reliability management program

RMS – remote manipulator system

RMS – resource management system

RMS – root-mean-square

RMY – Delco Remy International [stock listing]

RNE – Morgan Stanley Dean Witter Eastern Europe Fund Inc. [stock listing]

RNJ – BlackRock New Jersey Investment Quality Municipal Trust Inc. [stock listing]

RNO – Reno Cannon International Airport

RNR – Renaissancere Hldgs Ltd. [stock listing]

RNS – Public Steers Tr [stock listing]

RNT – Aaron Rents Inc. [stock listing]

RNY – BlackRock New York Investment Quality Municipal Trust Inc., The [stock listing]

RO – Regional office

RO – Romania

ROC – R.O.C. Taiwan Fund, The [stock listing]

ROCAP – regional officer for Central American programs

ROFL – rolling on floor laughing

ROG – Rogers Corp. [stock listing]

ROH – Rohm & Haas Co. [stock listing]

ROI – return on investment

ROK – Rockwell International Corp. [stock listing]

ROL – Rollins Inc. [stock listing]

ROM – read-only memory

ROMPR – Rio Algom Ltd. [stock listing]

ROP – Roper Industries Inc. [stock listing]

ROS – Rostelecom Long Distance & I [stock listing]

ROSAT – Roentgen Satellite

ROTC – Reserve Officers' Training Corps

ROTFL – rolling on the floor laughing

ROU – Rouge Industries Inc. [stock listing]

ROV – Rayovac Corp. [stock listing]

ROW – Rowe Cos. [stock listing]

ROY – Royce Micro-Cap Trust Inc. [stock listing]

RP – Rhone-Poulenc S.A. [stock listing]

RPH – Morgan Stanley Dean Witter & Co. [stock listing]

RPI – Roberts Realty Investors Inc. [stock listing]

RPIE – real property installed equipment

RPJ – Morgan Stanley Dean Witter & Co. [stock listing]

rpm – revolutions per minute

RPM – Rpm Inc. [stock listing]

RPN – Morgan Stanley Dean Witter & Co. [stock listing]

RPP – Stonehaven Realty Trust [stock listing]

RPSO – regional procurement and support office

rps – revolutions per second

RPT – Ramco Gershenson Properties Trust [stock listing]

RPWS – Rhone-Poulenc S.A. [stock listing]

RPX – Morgan Stanley Dean Witter & Co. [stock listing]

RQU – Morgan Stanley Dean Witter & Co. [stock listing]

RRB – Railroad Retirement Board

RRC – Range Resources Corp. [stock listing]

RRDI – Relief, Reconstruction and Development Initiatives

RRS – readiness reporting system

RS – Reliance Steel & Alum Co. [stock listing]

RS – requirements statement

RSA – Rehabilitation Services Administration

RSA – Royal & Sun Alliance Insurance Group P.L.C. [stock listing]

RSB – Salomon Smith Barney Holdings Inc. [stock listing]

RSC – Rex Stores Corp. [stock listing]

RSE – Rouse Co. [stock listing]

RSG – Republic Services Inc. [stock listing]

RSH – RadioShack Corp. [stock listing]

RSHMI – Russian Hydrometeorological Institute

RSM – Merrill Lynch & Co. Inc. [stock listing]

RSO – regional security officer

RSPA – Research and Special Programs Administration

RSSA – Resources Support Services Agreement

RST – Boca Resorts Inc. [stock listing]

RSVP – *répondez s'il vous plaît* (please reply) [French]

RSW – Southwest Florida International Airport

RSY/WS – Merrill Lynch & Co. Inc. [stock listing]

RT – Ryerson Tull Inc. [stock listing]

RTB – Rural Telephone Bank

RTB – Telecomunicacoes Brasileiras [stock listing]

RTC – real time clock

RTC – Riviera Tool Co. [stock listing]

RTE – remote terminal emulator

RTF – rich text format

RTI – real-time interface

RTI – RTI International Metals Inc. [stock listing]

RTK – Rentech Inc. [stock listing]

RTP – Rio Tinto P.L.C. [stock listing]

RTR – Automatic Com Exchng Sec Tri [stock listing]

RTX – RateXchange Corp. [stock listing]

RTY – Security Capital U.S. Realty [stock listing]

RU – Russian Federation

RUK – Reed Elsevier P.L.C. [stock listing]

RUN – Reunion Industries Inc. [stock listing]

RUS – Rural Utilities Service

RUS – Russ Berrie & Co. Inc. [stock listing]

RVT – Royce Value Trust Inc. [stock listing]

RW – Rwanda

RWR – streetTRACKS Wilshire REIT Index Fund [stock listing]

RWT – Redwood Trust Inc. [stock listing]

RWTPRB – Redwood Tr Inc. [stock listing]

RWY – Rent-Way Inc. [stock listing]

RX – Ims Health Inc. [stock listing]

RY – Royal Bk Cda Montreal Que [stock listing]

RYD – Decs Tr Ii [stock listing]

RYG – Royal Group Technologies Ltd. [stock listing]

RYL – Ryland Group Inc. [stock listing]

RYN – Rayonier Inc. [stock listing]

RYO – Morgan Stanley Dean Witter & Co. [stock listing]

RZT – Resortquest International Inc. [stock listing]

S.C. – South Carolina [standard newspaper abbreviation]

S.D. – South Dakota [standard newspaper abbreviation]

S – Sears Roebuck & Co. [stock listing]

SA – Saudi Arabia

SA – Stage II Apparel Corp. [stock listing]

SA – system administration

SAA – systems application architecture

SAARC – South Asian Association for Regional Cooperation

SAB – Grupo Casa Saba S.A. de C.V. [stock listing]

SAC – Small Agency Council

SAC – special analysis center

SAC – Strategic Air Command

SAE – Super-Sol Ltd. [stock listing]

SAF – Scudder New Asia Fund Inc. [stock listing]

SAFMLS – Society of Armed Forces Medical Laboratory Scientists

SAH – Sonic Automotive Inc. [stock listing]

SAI – Security Associates International Inc. [stock listing]

SAJ – St. Joseph Light & Power Co. [stock listing]

SAL – Salisbury Bancorp Inc. [stock listing]

SAM – Boston Beer Co. [stock listing]

SAM – Society for Advancement of Management

SAM – system activity manager

SAMHSA – Substance Abuse and Mental Health Services Administration

SAN – Banco Santiago [stock listing]

SAN – San Diego International Airport-Lindberg

SAP – SAP A.G. [stock listing]

SAR – search and rescue

SAS – statistical analysis system

SASC – Senate Armed Services Committee

SASE – self-addressed stamped envelope

SAT – Asia Satellite Telecommunications Holdings Ltd. [stock listing]

SAT – San Antonio International Airport

SAT – Scholastic Assessment Test

SAV – Savannah International Airport

SB – Solomon Islands

SBA – Santa Barbara Municipal Airport

SBA – Small Business Administration

SBB – Sussex Bancorp [stock listing]

SBC – SBC Communication Inc. [stock listing]

SBF – Salomon Brothers Fund Inc., The [stock listing]

SBG – Salomon Brothers 2008 Worldwide Dollar Government Term Trust Inc. [stock listing]

SBI – Smith Barney Intermediate Municipal Fund Inc. [stock listing]

SBKA – Spectrum BanCorp. Inc. [stock listing]

SBKB – Spectrum Capital Trust [stock listing]

SBL – Symbol Technologies Inc. [stock listing]

SBN – Michiana Regional Transportation Center

SBNA – Southern BancShares (N.C.) Inc. [stock listing]

SBP – San Luis Obispo County Airport-McChesney

SBP – Santander Bancorp [stock listing]

SBR – Sabine Royalty Trust [stock listing]

SBS – Steamboat Springs/Bob Adams Field Airport

SBW – Salomon Brothers Worldwide Income Fund Inc. [stock listing]

SC – Seychelles

SC – Shell Trans & Trading P.L.C. [stock listing]

SC – South Carolina

SC – Space Council

SCB – Community Bankshares Inc. [stock listing]

SCC – Security Capital Corp. [stock listing]

SCDD – Subcommittee on Cultural and Demographic Data

SCF – Save the Children Federation

SCG – Scana Corp. [stock listing]

SCH – Schwab Charles Corp. [stock listing]

SCI – SCI Systems Inc. [stock listing]

sci – science-oriented newsgroups

SCL – Stepan Co. [stock listing]

SCM – Swisscom A.G. [stock listing]

SCO – Scor US Corp. [stock listing]

SCOPE – San Clemente Ocean Probing Experiment

SCP – Scope Industries [stock listing]

SCR – Shipboard Census Report

SCRA – Sea Containers Ltd. [stock listing]

SCS – Soil Conservation Service

SCS – Steelcase Inc. [stock listing]

SCSI – small computer system interface

SCUBA – self-contained underwater breathing apparatus

SCVA – Scania Aktiebolag [stock listing]

SCX – Starrett LS Co. [stock listing]

SCY – Sports Club Co. Inc., The [stock listing]

SCZ – Security Capital Group Inc. [stock listing]

SD – school district

SD – secretary of defense

SD – South Dakota

SD – Sudan

SDA – Sadia S.A. [stock listing]

SDC – Santa Fe Intl Corp. [stock listing]

SDF – Standiford Field Airport

SDFS – Safe and Drug-Free Schools

SDH – Sodexho Marriott Services Inc. [stock listing]

SDI – Strategic Defense Initiative

SDLC – Synchronous Data Link Control

SDOA – San Diego Gas & Electric Co. [stock listing]

SDP – Sunsource Inc. [stock listing]

SDRAM – synchronous dynamic random access memory

SDS – Sungard Data Systems Inc. [stock listing]

SDSL – synchronous digital subscriber line

SDTS – spatial data transfer standard

SDW – Southdown Inc. [stock listing]

SDWIS – Safe Drinking Water Information System

SE – 7-Eleven Inc. [stock listing]

SE – Sweden

SE – systems engineer

SEA – Bio-Aqua Systems [stock listing]

SEA – Seattle-Tacoma International Airport

SEB – Seaboard Corp. [stock listing]

SEC DEL – Secretary of Delegation

SEC – Securities and Exchange Commission

SEC – Speciality Equipment Cos. Inc. [stock listing]

SED – systems engineering development

SEDF – sample edited detail file

SEE – Sealed Air Corp. [stock listing]

SEEC – standard expense element code

SEEPRA – Sealed Air Corp. New [stock listing]

SEF – Sebring Florida Regional Airport

SEFCAR – Southeast Florida and Caribbean Recruitment

SEG – Seagate Technology Inc. [stock listing]

SEH – Spartech Corp. [stock listing]

SEI – Seitel Inc. [stock listing]

SEI – Software Engineering Institute

SEL – Kimpo International Airport

SEL – Seligman Select Municipal Fund Inc. [stock listing]

SEM – General Semiconductor Inc. [stock listing]

SEM – scanning electron microscope

SEN – Semco Energy Inc. [stock listing]

SEO – Stora Enso Corp. [stock listing]

SERC – Smithsonian Environmental Research Center

SERF – solar electromagnetic radiation flux

SERV HQ – service headquarters

SES – Senior Executive Service

SESPA – Scientists and Engineers for Social and Political Action

SETAC – systems engineering and technical assistance contractor

SEUA – special economic urban area

SEV – Seven Seas Petroleum Inc. [stock listing]

SF – standard form

SF – Stifel Financial Corp. [stock listing]

SFA – Scientific Atlanta Inc. [stock listing]

SFC/WS – SFBC International Inc. [stock listing]

SFC – SFBC International Inc. [stock listing]

SFC – Space Forecast Center

SFD – Smithfield Foods Inc. [stock listing]

SFE – Safeguard Scientifics Inc. [stock listing]

SFF – Santa Fe Energy Trust [stock listing]

SFG – Stancorp Financial Group Inc. [stock listing]

SFI – iStar Financial Inc. [stock listing]

SFM – supply and financial management

SFMR – stepped frequency microwave radiometer

SFN – Spherion Corp. [stock listing]

SFO – San Francisco International Airport

SFOSRC – South Florida Oil Spill Research Center

SFP – Salton Inc. [stock listing]

SFR – summary functional requirement

SFRY – Socialist Federal Republic of Yugoslavia

SFSC – Southeast Fisheries Science Center

SFSS – satellite field service station

SFT – Stratesec Inc. [stock listing]

SFY – Swift Energy Co. [stock listing]

SG – Singapore

SG – surgeon general

SGA – Saga Communications Inc. [stock listing]

SGAC – State Government Affairs Council

SGB – Southwest Georgia Financial Corp. [stock listing]

SGC – Superior Uniform Group Inc. [stock listing]

SGF – Singapore Fund Inc., The [stock listing]

SGH – Star Gas Partners L.P. [stock listing]

SGI – Silicon Graphics Inc. [stock listing]

SGK – Schawk Inc. [stock listing]

SGL – Strategic Global Income Fund Inc. [stock listing]

SGLI – Servicemembers' Group Life Insurance

SGM – Scientific Games Corp [stock listing]

SGML – standard generalized markup language

SGP – Schering Plough Corp. [stock listing]

SGR – Shaw Group Inc. [stock listing]

SGRAM – synchronous graphics random access memory

Sgt. 1st Class – sergeant first class

Sgt. Maj. of the Army – sergeant major of the Army

Sgt. Maj. of the Marine Corp. – sergeant major of the Marine Corps

Sgt. Maj. – sergeant major

Sgt. – sergeant

SGT – Sames Corp. [stock listing]

SGU – Star Gas Partners LP [stock listing]

SGY – Stone Energy Corp. [stock listing]

SH – Saint Helena

SH – Shandong Huaneng Power Development [stock listing]

SH – Southern Hemisphere

SHAPE – Supreme Headquarters Allied Powers Europe

SHF – Schuff Steel Co. [stock listing]

SHF – super-high frequency

SHI – Sinopec Shanghai Petrochemical Co. Ltd. [stock listing]

SHM – Sheffield Pharmaceuticals Inc. [stock listing]

SHQ – Brunswick County Airport

SHR – Schering A.G. [stock listing]

SHS – Sauer-Danfoss Inc. [stock listing]

S-HTTP – secure hyper text transfer protocol

SHU – Shurgard Storage Centers Inc. [stock listing]

SHW – Sherwin Williams Co. [stock listing]

SHX – Shaw Industries Inc. [stock listing]

SI – Siemens A.G. [stock listing]

SI – Slovenia

SI – Smithsonian Institution

SIB – Staten Island Bancorp Inc. [stock listing]

SIC – standard industrial classification

SICC – secondary inventory control center

SID – Companhia Siderurgica Nacional [stock listing]

SIE – Sierra Health Services Inc. [stock listing]

SIES – Office of Strategic Industries and Economic Security

SIF – SIFCO Industries Inc. [stock listing]

SIH – Sun International Hotels Ltd. [stock listing]

SII – Smith International Inc. [stock listing]

SIL – Apex Silver Mines Ltd. [stock listing]

SIM – Grupo Simec S.A. de CV [stock listing]

SIMA – systems integration management activity

SIMM – single in-line memory module

SIN – Singapore Changi International Airport

SIO – Scripps Institution of Oceanography

SIP – standard interface panel

SIZ – Sizeler Property Investors Inc. [stock listing]

SJ – Svalbard and Jan Mayen Islands

SJC – San Jose International Airport

SJH – Stelmar Shipping Ltd. [stock listing]

SJI – South Jersey Industries Inc. [stock listing]

SJM – J.M. Smucker Co. [stock listing]

SJR – Shaw Communications Inc. [stock listing]

SJT – San Juan Basin Royalty Trust [stock listing]

SJW – SJW Corp. [stock listing]

SK – Slovak Republic

SKE – Spinnaker Exploration Co. [stock listing]

SKI – American Skiing Co. [stock listing]

SKK – Spinnaker Industries Inc. [stock listing]

SKM – Sk Telecom Ltd. [stock listing]

SKO – Shopko Stores Inc. [stock listing]

SKP – Scpie Holdings Inc. [stock listing]

SKS – Saks Inc. [stock listing]

SKT – Tanger Factory Outlet Centers Inc. [stock listing]

SKTPRA – Tanger Factory Outlet Ctrs [stock listing]

SKX – Skechers USA Inc. [stock listing]

SKY – Skyline Corp. [stock listing]

SL – Sierra Leone

SL – SL Industries Inc. [stock listing]

SL – Spacelab

SLA – American Select Portfolio Inc. [stock listing]

SLB – Schlumberger Ltd. [stock listing]

SLC – Salt Lake City International Airport

SLC – SunLife Financial Services [stock listing]

SLE – Sara Lee Corp. [stock listing]

SLG – Sl Green Realty Corp. [stock listing]

SLI – Sli Inc. [stock listing]

SLIP – serial line Internet protocol

SLM – USA Ed Inc. [stock listing]

SLN – Salina Municipal Airport

SLP – sea level pressure

SLR – Solectron Corp. [stock listing]

SLS – Selas Corp. of America [stock listing]

SLSDC – Saint Lawrence Seaway Development Corp.

SLT – Silverline Technologies Ltd. [stock listing]

SM – San Marino

SM – Sulzer Medica [stock listing]

SMC/A – Smith (A.O.) Corp. [stock listing]

SMD – Singing Machine Co. Inc., The [stock listing]

SMD – Sunrise Medical Inc. [stock listing]

SMDA – Safe Medical Devices Act

SME – Merrill Lynch & Co. Inc. [stock listing]

SMF – Sacramento Executive Airport

SMF – Smart & Final Inc. [stock listing]

SMF – System Measurement Facility

SMG – Scotts Co. [stock listing]

SMH – Merrill Lynch Semiconductor HOLDRS [stock listing]

SMI – Springs Industries Inc. [stock listing]

SMO – Science Management Office

SMOBE – Survey of Minority-Owned Business Enterprises

SMP – Standard Motor Products Inc. [stock listing]

SMS – Shuttle Mission Simulator

SMS – synchronous meteorological satellite

SMT – Summit Properties Inc. [stock listing]

SMTP – simple mail transfer protocol

SMU – Simula Inc. [stock listing]

SMVA – Smedvig Asa [stock listing]

SMX – Santa Maria Public Airport

SN – Senegal

SNA – John Wayne Airport

SNA – Snap On Inc. [stock listing]

SNA – Systems Network Architecture

SNAFU – situation normal all fouled up (polite)

SNAME – Society of Naval Architects and Marine Engineers

SNAP – Shipboard Nontactical Automated Data Processing Program

SNB – Sunburst Hospitality Corp. [stock listing]

SNE – Sony Corp. [stock listing]

SNF – Spain Fund Inc., The [stock listing]

SNMP – simple network management protocol

SNMP – small network management packet

SNN – Smith & Nephew P.L.C. [stock listing]

SNP – China Petroleum & Chemical Corp. [stock listing]

SNR – Sunair Electronics Inc. [stock listing]

SNS – Consolidated Products Inc. [stock listing]

SNV – Synovus Financial Corp. [stock listing]

SO – Somalia

SO – Southern Co. [stock listing]

SOA – Southern Africa Fund Inc., The [stock listing]

soc – discussion of cultures or social groups

SOC – Sunbeam Corp. [stock listing]

SOF – Special Operations Forces

SOHF – sense of humor failure

SOHO – small office, home office

SoHo – south of Houston Street [New York]

Soho – south of Oxford Street [London]

SOI – Solutia Inc. [stock listing]

SOL – Sola International Inc. [stock listing]

SOLRAD – solar radiation

SON – Sonoco Products Co. [stock listing]

SONAR – sound navigation and ranging

SOON – solar observing optical network

SOP – standard operating procedure

SOPS – Select Committee on Ocean Policy

SOR – Source Capital Inc. [stock listing]

SOS – Storage Computer Corp. [stock listing]

SOUTHCOM – Southern Command

SP – Specialty Laboratories Inc. [stock listing]

SPA – Software Publishers Association

SPA – Sparton Corp. [stock listing]

SPACIFICS – Security Pacific Merchant Banking Group Network

SPAD – Shared Patient Administration

SPADE – Stratospheric Photochemistry, Aerosols and Dynamics Expedition

SPARC – scaleable processor architecture

Spc. – specialist

SPC – St. Paul Cos. [stock listing]

SPC – statistical process control

SPCOOR – Strategic Planning Council on Organizational Resources

SPCZ – South Pacific Convergence Zone

SPD – Standard Products Co. [stock listing]

SPECmark – Standard Performance Evaluation Corporation

SPECS – specifications

SPF – South Pacific Forum

SPF – Standard Pacific Corp. [stock listing]

SPF – sun protection factor

SPG – Simon Property Group Inc. [stock listing]

SPH – Suburban Propane Partners L.P. [stock listing]

SPI – Scottish Power P.L.C. [stock listing]

SPJ – Society of Professional Journalists

SPK – Spieker Properties Inc. [stock listing]

SPL – Amsterdam Airport

SPM – suspended particulate matter

SPM – systems product management

SPMS – standard personnel management system

SPN – shared processing network

SPO – Sonicport Inc. [stock listing]

SPP – Sappi Ltd. [stock listing]

SPR – Sterling Capital Corp. [stock listing]

SPSS – Statistical Package for the Social Sciences

SPU – Split Airport

SPW – SPX Corp. [stock listing]

SPY – SPDR Trust Series I [stock listing]

sq km – square kilometer

sq mi – square mile

SQAA – Sequa Corp. [stock listing]

SQF – Seligman Quality Municipal Fund Inc. [stock listing]

SQL – San Carlos Airport

SQL – structured query language

SQM – Socieda Quimica Min de Chile [stock listing]

Sr. – senior

SR – Standard Register [stock listing]

SR – Suriname

SRA – scanning radar altimeter

SRA – Serono [stock listing]

SRA – Systems Research and Applications Corp.

SRAM – static random access memory

SRE – Sempra Energy [stock listing]

SRF – Sears Roebuck Accep Corp. [stock listing]

SRI – Stoneridge Inc. [stock listing]

SRK – Seracare Inc. [stock listing]

SRM – Sensormatic Electronics Corp. [stock listing]

SRN – Southern Banc Co. Inc., The [stock listing]

SRO – Spigadoro Inc. [stock listing]

SRP – Sierra Pacific Resources New [stock listing]

SRQ – Sarasota/Bradenton International Airport

SRR – Stride Rite Corp. [stock listing]

SRS – ARV Assisted Living Inc. [stock listing]

SRT – Startek Inc. [stock listing]

SRV – Service Corp. International [stock listing]

SRW – Smith Charles E Residential Realty Inc. [stock listing]

SS – secret service

SS – system specification

SSA – Social Security Administration

SSA – Source Selection Authority

SSAN – Social Security account number

SSB – Salomon Smith Barney Holdings Inc. [stock listing]

SSC – Stennis Space Center

SSD – Simpson Mfg Inc. [stock listing]

SSI – Sunstone Hotel Investors Inc. [stock listing]

SSI – Supplemental Security Income Program

SSL – secure socket layer

SSMC – Silver Spring Metropolitan Complex

SSN – Social Security number

SSN – Sonus Corp. [stock listing]

SSP – E.W. Scripps Co., The [stock listing]

SSR – SSBH Cap I [stock listing]

SSS – Selective Service System
SSS – Sovran Self Storage Inc. [stock listing]
SST – sea-surface temperature
SSW – Sterling Software Inc. [stock listing]
ST – stratosphere-troposphere
ST – STS Technologies Inc. [stock listing]
STA – Science and Technology Agency
STA – shuttle training aircraft
STACS – Subtropical Atlantic Climate Studies
Staff Sgt. – staff sergeant
START – Strategic Arms Reduction Treaty
STAT-ID – statistic identifier
STAWRS – Simplified Tax and Wage
   Reporting System
STB – State Bancorp Inc. [stock listing]
STC – Security Trade Control
STC – Stewart Information Services Corp.
   [stock listing]
STD – Banco Santander Central Hispano S.A.
   [stock listing]
STD – sexually transmitted disease
STE – Steris Corp. [stock listing]
STEP – Stratosphere-Troposphere Exchange
   Project
STG – Stonepath Group Inc. [stock listing]
STI – Standard Technology Inc.
STI – Suntrust Banks Inc. [stock listing]
STJ – St. Jude Medical Inc. [stock listing]
STK – StorageTek Corp. [stock listing]
STL – Lambert-St. Louis International Airport
STL – Sterling Bancorp [stock listing]
STLDD – software top-level design document
STM – STmicroelectronics NV [stock listing]
STN – Stansted Airport
STN – Station Casinos Inc. [stock listing]
STOCSS – SETAC (Society of Environmental
   Toxicology and Chemistry) Task Order Cost
   Sheet Summary
STOPRE – Stone Container Corp. [stock
   listing]
STP – shielded twisted pair
STR – Questar Corp. [stock listing]
STS – Supreme Industries Inc. [stock listing]

STT – State Street Corp. [stock listing]
STU – Student Loan Corp. [stock listing]
STW – Standard Commercial Corp. [stock
   listing]
STZ – Constellation Brands Inc. [stock listing]
SU – single-unit company
SU – Soviet Union
SU – Suncor Energy Inc. [stock listing]
SUA – Abbey National P.L.C. [stock listing]
SUB – Summit Bank Corp. [stock listing]
SUD – Abbey National P.L.C. [stock listing]
SuDoc – superintendent of documents
SUG – Southern Union Co. [stock listing]
SUI – Sun Communities Inc. [stock listing]
SUN – Sunoco Inc. [stock listing]
SUP – Superior Industries International Inc.
   [stock listing]
SUPRA – Suncor Energy Inc. [stock listing]
SUR – CNA Surety Corp. [stock listing]
SUS – Storage USA Inc. [stock listing]
SUT – Superior Telecom Inc. [stock listing]
SV – El Salvador
SV – Stilwell Financial [stock listing]
SVCPR – Stokely Van Camp Inc. [stock listing]
SVGA – super video graphics adapter
SVI – SVI Solutions Inc. [stock listing]
SVM – Servicemaster Co. [stock listing]
SVR – Silverleaf Resorts Inc. [stock listing]
SVT – Servotronics Inc. [stock listing]
SVU – Supervalu Inc. [stock listing]
SW – Stone & Webster Inc. [stock listing]
SWAK – sealed with a kiss
SWALK – sealed with a loving kiss
SWAT – Special Weapons and Tactics
SWATH – small waterplane area twin hull
SWC – Stillwater Mining Co. [stock listing]
SWH – Merrill Lynch Software HOLDRS
   [stock listing]
SWISH – Simple Web Indexing System for
   Humans
SWK – Stanley Works [stock listing]
SWM – Schweitzer Mauduit International Inc.
   [stock listing]

SWN – Southwestern Energy Co. [stock listing]

SWS – Southwest Securities Group Inc. [stock listing]

SWW – Sitel Corp. [stock listing]

SWX – Southwest Gas Corp. [stock listing]

SWXPRA – Southwest Gas Cap I [stock listing]

SWY – Safeway Inc. [stock listing]

SWZ – Swiss Helvetia Fund Inc., The [stock listing]

SXI – Standex International Corp. [stock listing]

SXRP – Stellar X-ray polarimeter

SXT – Sensient Technologies Corp. [stock listing]

SY – Syria

SYD – Sybron Dental Specialties [stock listing]

SYI – S.Y. Bancorp Inc. [stock listing]

SYK – Stryker Corp. [stock listing]

SYM – Syms Corp. [stock listing]

SYSGEN – system generation

SYT – Syngenta AG [stock listing]

SYX – Systemax Inc. [stock listing]

SYY – SYSCO Corp. [stock listing]

SZ – Sizzler International Inc. [stock listing]

SZ – Swaziland

SZA – Suiza Foods Corp. [stock listing]

SZB – SouthFirst Bancshares Inc. [stock listing]

T – AT&T Corp. [stock listing]

TA – technology administration

TAA – Trade Adjustment Assistance

TAC – Tandycrafts Inc. [stock listing]

TAC – terminal access controller

TACAN – Tactical Air Navigation

TAEM – terminal area energy management

TAG – Tag-It Pacific Inc. [stock listing]

TAI – Transamerica Income Shares Inc. [stock listing]

TAM – Tubos de Acero de Mexico S.A. [stock listing]

TAMC – Tripler Army Medical Center

TAMMIS – Theater Army Medical Management Information System

TAMU – Texas A&M University

TAPS – Trans-Alaskan Pipeline

TARFOX – Tropospheric Aerosol Radiative Forcing Observational Experiment

TASC – Transportation Administrative Service Center

TAZ – transportation analysis zone

TBA – TBA Entertainment Corp. [stock listing]

TBA – to be announced

TBC – Tasty Baking Co. [stock listing]

TBD – to be determined

TBH – Telebras HOLDRS [stock listing]

TBL – Timberland Co. [stock listing]

TBP – Tab Products Co. [stock listing]

TBW – TB Woods Corp. [stock listing]

TBY – Toby Enterprises Inc. [stock listing]

TC – Thai Capital Fund, Inc., The [stock listing]

TC – Turks and Caicos Islands

TCB – TCF Financial Corp. [stock listing]

TCB – trusted computing base

TCC – Trammell Crow Co. [stock listing]

TCH – Templeton China World Fund Inc. [stock listing]

TCI – Transcontinental Realty Investors Inc. [stock listing]

TCLPR – Transcontinental Realty Investors Inc. [stock listing]

TCM – TyCom Ltd. [stock listing]

TCO – Tauban Centers Inc. [stock listing]

TCO – telecommunications office

TCOPRA – Taubman Ctrs Inc. [stock listing]

TCP – transmission control protocol

TCP/IP – transmission control protocol/Internet protocol

TCR – Cornerstone Realty Income Trust Inc. [stock listing]

TCT – Town & Country Trust [stock listing]

TCZ – Salomon Smith Barney Holdings Inc. [stock listing]

TD – Chad

TD – technical documentation

TD – Toronto-Dominion Bank [stock listing]

TDA – table of distribution and allowances

TDA – Trade and Development Agency

TDD – technical development division

TDE – touchtone data entry

TDF – Templeton Dragon Fund Inc. [stock listing]

TDH – Salomon Smith Barney Holdings Inc. [stock listing]

TDI – Twin Disc Inc. [stock listing]

TDK – TDK Corp. [stock listing]

TDM – time-division multiplexer

TDR – Tricom [stock listing]

TDRS – Tracking and Data Relay Satellite

TDS – Telephone and Data Systems Inc. [stock listing]

TDW – Tidewater Inc. [stock listing]

TDWR – Terminal Doppler Weather Radar

TDY – Teledyne Technologies Inc. [stock listing]

TDY – temporary duty

TE – Teco Energy Inc. [stock listing]

TEA – Templeton Emerging Markets Appreciation Fund Inc. [stock listing]

TEB – Teterboro Airport

TEC – ATEC Group Inc. [stock listing]

TEC – Commercial Intertech Corp. [stock listing]

Tech. Sgt. – technical sergeant

TEDA – Toledo Edison Co. [stock listing]

TEE – National Golf Properties Inc. [stock listing]

TEF – Telefonica S.A. [stock listing]

TEGPRA – TXU Europe [stock listing]

TEI – Templeton Emerging Markets Income Fund Inc. [stock listing]

TEK – Tektronix Inc. [stock listing]

TELSAR – tracking and evolution of solar active regions

TEM – transmission electron microscope

TEMP – Test and Evaluation Master Plan

TEN – Tenneco Automotive Inc. [stock listing]

Tenn. – Tennessee [standard newspaper abbreviation]

TEO – Telecom Argentina [stock listing]

TEP – Technical Evaluation Plan

TEPRT – Teco Energy Inc. [stock listing]

TER – Teradyne Inc. [stock listing]

TEW – Transport of Equatorial Waters

TEX – Telluride Regional Airport

TEX – Terex Corp. [stock listing]

TF – French Southern and Antarctic Territories

TFA – Morgan Stanley Dean Witter [stock listing]

TFA – transparent file access

TFB – Morgan Stanley Dean Witter [stock listing]

TFC – Morgan Stanley Dean Witter [stock listing]

TFD – Transamerica Fin Corp. [stock listing]

TFF – Technology Flavors & Fragrances Inc. [stock listing]

TFG – Thackeray Corp. Inc. [stock listing]

TFG – Thermo Fibergen Inc. [stock listing]

TFH – Transfinancial Holdings Inc. [stock listing]

TFN – Transnational Financial Network Inc. [stock listing]

TFP – therapeutic feeding program

TFR – Tefron Ltd. [stock listing]

TFS – Three-Five Systems Inc. [stock listing]

TFT – Thermo Fibertek Inc. [stock listing]

TFU – telephone follow-up

TFW – tactical fighter wing

TFX – Teleflex Inc. [stock listing]

TG – Togo

TG – Tredegar Corp. [stock listing]

TGC – Tengasco Inc. [stock listing]

TGG – Templeton Global Governments Income Trust [stock listing]

TGH – Trigon Healthcare Inc. [stock listing]

TGI – Triumph Group Inc. [stock listing]

TGP – Georgia Pacific Corp. [stock listing]

TGS – Transportadora de Gas del Sur [stock listing]

TGT – Target Corp. [stock listing]

TGX – Theragenics Corp. [stock listing]

TH – Merrill Lynch Utilities HOLDRS [stock listing]

TH – Thailand

THC – Tenet Healthcare Corp. [stock listing]

THF – Berlin Tempelhof Airport

THIR – Temperature Humidity Infrared Radiometer

THM – Thermwood Corp. [stock listing]

THN – Salomon Smith Barney Holdings Inc. [stock listing]

THO – Thor Industries Inc. [stock listing]

THT – Todhunter International Inc. [stock listing]

THV – Thermoview Industries Inc. [stock listing]

THX – Houston Exploration Co., The [stock listing]

TIA – Telecom Italia Spa [stock listing]

TIA – Telecommunications Industry Association

TIA – thanks in advance

TIC – Trade Information Center

TIE – Titanium Metals Corp. [stock listing]

TIF – Tiffany & Co. [stock listing]

TIGER – topologically integrated geographic encoding and referencing

TIGER-CTSI – TIGER-Census Tract Street Index

TII – Thomas Industries Inc. [stock listing]

TIM – technical integration manager

TIMPL – technical implementation management

TIN – Temple-Inland Inc. [stock listing]

TIR – China Tire Holding Ltd. [stock listing]

TIR – technical integration repository

TIROS – television infrared observational satellite

TIUS – truck inventory and use survey

TJ – Tajikistan

TJSA – Tribal Jurisdiction Statistical Area

TJX – TJX Cos. Inc. [stock listing]

TK – Teekay Shipping Corp. [stock listing]

TK – Tokelau

TKA – Telekom Austria A.G. [stock listing]

TKC – Turkcell A.S. [stock listing]

TKE – turbulent kinetic energy

TKF – Turkish Investment Fund Inc., The [stock listing]

TKM – Merrill Lynch & Co. Inc. [stock listing]

TKR – Timken Co. [stock listing]

TKS – Tomkins P.L.C. [stock listing]

TLB – Talbots Inc. [stock listing]

TLD – Tele Danmark A.S. [stock listing]

TLF – Leather Factory Inc., The [stock listing]

TLH – Tallahassee Regional Airport

TLI – Travelers Corporate Loan Fund Inc. [stock listing]

TLK – Pt Telekomunikiasi Indonesia [stock listing]

TLL – Tallinn Yulemiste [Estonia]

TLL – Teletouch Communications Inc. [stock listing]

TLM – Talisman Energy Inc. [stock listing]

TLS – Telstra Ltd. [stock listing]

TLX – Trans-Lux Corp. [stock listing]

TM – Toyota Motor Corp. [stock listing]

TM – Turkmenistan

TMA – Thornburg Mortgage Inc. [stock listing]

TMAP – thermal modeling and analysis program

TME – Tribune Co. [stock listing]

TMG – TransMontaigne Inc. [stock listing]

TMI – Team Inc. [stock listing]

TMIS – theater medical information system

TMIS – travel management information system

TMK – Torchmark Corp. [stock listing]

TMN – Transmedia Network [stock listing]

TMN – Transmedia Networks Inc. [stock listing]

TMO – Table Mountain Observatory

TMO – Technologies Management Office
TMO – Thermo Electron Corp. [stock listing]
TMP – technical management plan
TMP – TompkinsTrustco Inc. [stock listing]
TMPS – Tri-Service Micro Pharmacy System
TMR – Merdian Resource Corp. [stock listing]
TMRP – Tropical Meteorology Research Programme
TMS – Thomson Multimedia [stock listing]
TMSO – Telecommunications Management Service Organization
TMT – TCW/DW Term Trust 2003 [stock listing]
TMY – Salomon Smith Barney Holdings Inc. [stock listing]
TN – Tennessee
TN – Tunisia
TNB – Thomas & Betts Corp. [stock listing]
TNC – Tennant Co. [stock listing]
TNH – Terra Nitrogen Co. L.P. [stock listing]
TNL – Technitrol Inc. [stock listing]
TNM – Nelson Thomas Inc. [stock listing]
TNMB – Nelson Thomas Inc. [stock listing]
TNO – True North Communication Inc. [stock listing]
TNR – Tenera Inc. [stock listing]
TNT – AO Tatneft [stock listing]
TO – task order
TO – Tech/Ops Sevcon Inc. [stock listing]
TO – Tonga
TOA – Terre Ocean Atmosphere
TOA – Transportation Operating Agency
TOD – time of delivery
TOD – Todd Shipyards Corp. [stock listing]
TOE – Salomon Smith Barney Holdings Inc. [stock listing]
TOE – table of organization and equipment
TOF – Tofutti Brands Inc. [stock listing]
TOL – Toll Brothers Inc. [stock listing]
TOM – Tommy Hilfiger Corp. [stock listing]
TOMS – total ozone mapping spectrophotometer
TOO – TOO INC. [stock listing]

TOPS – Total Ocean Profiling System
TOS – Tosco Corp. [stock listing]
TOT – Total Fina Elf S.A. [stock listing]
TOX – Medtox Scientific Inc. [stock listing]
TOY – Toys R US Inc. [stock listing]
TP – East Timor
TPA – Tampa International Airport
TPAD – trunnion pin acquisition device
TPC/AR – third party collection/accounts receivable
TPC – third party collection
TPD – technical products division
TPG – TNT Post Group [stock listing]
TPL – Texas Pacific Land Trust [stock listing]
TPN – TPN Holdings P.L.C. [stock listing]
TPOCS – third-party outpatient collection system
TPP – Teppco Partners L.P. [stock listing]
TPR – Transpro Inc. [stock listing]
TPS – thermal protection system
TPS – trans-Pacific sections
TPS – tri-service pharmacy system
TPTMS – tropical Pacific thermal monitoring system
TPV – taxable property value
TPY – Tipperary Corp. [stock listing]
TQ – Cash Technologies Inc. [stock listing]
TQM – total quality management
TR – Tootsie Roll Industries Inc. [stock listing]
TR – Turkey
TRA – technical resource acquisition
TRA – Terra Industries Inc. [stock listing]
TRACIR – tracking air with circularly polarized radar
TRANSCOM – Transportation Command
TRB – Transportation Research Board
TRB – Tribune Co. [stock listing]
TRC – Tejon Ranch Co. [stock listing]
TRD – Tribune Co. [stock listing]
TRE – Tremont Corp. [stock listing]
TRF – Templeton Russia Fund Inc. [stock listing]

TRH – Trans Atlantic Holdings Inc. [stock listing]

TRI – Triad Hospitals Inc. [stock listing]

TRIRAD – tri-service radiology information system

TRK – Speedway Motorsports Inc. [stock listing]

TRM – TCW/DW Term Trust 2002 [stock listing]

TRM – technical reference model

TRN – Trinity Industries Inc. [stock listing]

TROPIC HEAT – Tropical Pacific Upper Ocean Heat and Mass Budgets

TRP – Transcanada Pipelines Ltd. [stock listing]

TRR – TRC Cos. Inc. [stock listing]

Trrn – terrain

TRT – Trio-Tech International [stock listing]

TRU – Torch Energy Royalty Trust [stock listing]

TRV – Thousand Trails Inc. [stock listing]

TRW – TRW Inc. [stock listing]

TRY – Triarc Cos. Inc. [stock listing]

TSA – Sports Authority Inc. [stock listing]

TSC – Stephan Co., The [stock listing]

TSC – Transportation Systems Center

TSG – Sabre Group Inc. [stock listing]

TSH – Teche Holding Co. [stock listing]

TSI – Transportation Safety Institute

TSM – Tail Service Mast

TSM – Taiwan Semiconductor Mfg Co. [stock listing]

TSM – technical system manager

TSN – Tyson Foods Inc. [stock listing]

TSO – Tesoro Petroleum Corp. [stock listing]

TSO – time sharing option

TSP – telecommunications support plan

TSP – thrift savings plan

TSS – Total System Services Inc. [stock listing]

TSSG – technical support services group

TT – Transtechnology Corp. [stock listing]

TT – Trinidad and Tobago

TTA – Take To Auction.com Inc. [stock listing]

TTC – Toro Co. [stock listing]

TTF – Thai Fund Inc., The [stock listing]

TTFN – ta ta for now

TTG – Tutogen Medical Inc. [stock listing]

TTH – Merrill Lynch Telecom HOLDRS [stock listing]

TTI – Tetra Technologies Inc. [stock listing]

TTMA – Truck Trailer Manufacturers Association

TTN – Titan Corp. [stock listing]

TTP – Titan Pharmaceuticals Inc. [stock listing]

TTV – Cabletel Communications Corp. [stock listing]

TTY – Teletype

TU – TELUS Corp. [stock listing]

TUC – Mac-Gray Corp. [stock listing]

TUG – Maritrans Inc. [stock listing]

TUI – Transportation Components Inc. [stock listing]

TUL – Tulsa International Airport

TUP – Tupperware Corp. [stock listing]

TUS – Tucson International Airport

TUX – Tuxis Corp. [stock listing]

TV – Grupo Televisa S.A. [stock listing]

TV – Tuvalu

TVE – Tennessee Valley Authority [stock listing]

TVF – Templeton Vietnam and Southeast Asia Fund Inc. [stock listing]

TVX – TVX Gold Inc. [stock listing]

TW – Taiwan

TWE – TD Waterhouse Group Inc. [stock listing]

TWH – Transworld HealthCare Inc. [stock listing]

TWI – Titan International Inc. [stock listing]

TWK – Trenwick Group Ltd. [stock listing]

TWN – Taiwan Fund Inc., The [stock listing]

TWP – Trex Inc. [stock listing]

TWP – Tropical Western Pacific

TWR – Tower Automotive Inc. [stock listing]

TWW – Terremark Worldwide Inc. [stock listing]

TWX – Time Warner Inc. [stock listing]

TX – Texaco Inc. [stock listing]

TX – Texas

TXA – Tribune Co. [stock listing]

TXB – Texas Biotechnology Corp. [stock listing]

TXI – Texas Industries [stock listing]

TXL – Berlin Tegel Airport

TXN – Texas Instruments Inc. [stock listing]

TXT – Textron Inc. [stock listing]

TXU – Texas Utilities Co. [stock listing]

TY – Tri-Continental Corp. [stock listing]

TYC – Tyco Intl Ltd. New [stock listing]

TYL – Tyler Technologies Inc. [stock listing]

TYS – McGhee Tyson Airport

TYW – Taiwan Equity Fund Inc., The [stock listing]

TZ – Essex Bancorp Inc. [stock listing]

TZ – Tanzania

TZA – TV Azteca S.A. [stock listing]

TZH – Trizec Hahn Corp. [stock listing]

U.N. – United Nations

U.S.A. – United States of America

U.S.C. – United States Code

U – US Airways Group Inc. [stock listing]

UA – Ukraine

UA – urbanized area

UAA – undeliverable as addressed

UAE – United Arab Emirates

UAG – United Auto Group Inc. [stock listing]

UAL – UAL Corp. [stock listing]

UAM – United Asset Management Corp. [stock listing]

UAX – USURF America Inc. [stock listing]

UB – UnionBanCal Corp. [stock listing]

UBH – U.S.B. Holding Co. Inc. [stock listing]

UBI – Ubrandit.com [stock listing]

UBP – Urstadt Biddle Properties Inc. [stock listing]

UBS – UBS A.G. [stock listing]

UC – University of California

UCA – uniform chart of accounts

UCAPERS – uniform chart of accounts personnel system

UCAR – University Corporation for Atmospheric Research

UCI – Uici [stock listing]

UCI – user class identifier

UCL – Unocal Corp [stock listing]

UCO – Universal Compression Holdings Inc. [stock listing]

UCP – UniCapital Corp. [stock listing]

UCR – Ucar International Inc. [stock listing]

UCSD – University of California at San Diego

UCU – Utilicorp United Inc. [stock listing]

UDA – user-defined area

UDAPS – uniform data automation processing system

UDI – United Dominion Industries Ltd. [stock listing]

UDL – Shamrock Logistic L.P. [stock listing]

UDM – United Dominion Realty Trust Inc. [stock listing]

UDS – Ultramar Diamond Shamrock Corp. [stock listing]

UEMOA – Union Economique et Monetaire Ouest Africaine

UFI – Unifi Inc. [stock listing]

UFS – U.S. Foodservice [stock listing]

UG – Uganda

UG – United-Guardian Inc. [stock listing]

UGI – UGI Corp. [stock listing]

UGS – Unigraphics Solutions Inc. [stock listing]

UH – University of Hawaii

UHF – ultra-high frequency

UHGA – U.S. Home & Garden Inc. [stock listing]

UHS – Universal Health Services Inc. [stock listing]

UHT – Universal Health Realty Income Trust [stock listing]

UIC – unit identification code

UIC – United Industries Corp. [stock listing]

UIF – Uslife Income Fund Inc. [stock listing]

UIL – UIL Holding Corp. [stock listing]

UIS – Unisys Corp. [stock listing]

UISPRA – Unisys Corp. [stock listing]

UJNR – United States-Japan Cooperative Program in Natural Resources

UK – Union Carbide Corp. [stock listing]

UK – United Kingdom

UKIPC – United Kingdom Information Processing Center

UL – Unilever P.L.C. [stock listing]

ULANA – Unified Local Area Network Architecture

ULSI – Ultra Large Scale Integration

UM – Merrill Lynch & Co. Inc. [stock listing]

UM – University of Miami

UMC – United Microelectronics Corp [stock listing]

UMERS – uniform medical expense reporting system

UMG – MediaOne Group Inc. [stock listing]

UMH – United Mobile Homes Inc. [stock listing]

UMP – Upper Mantle Project

UMX – MediaOne Group Inc. [stock listing]

UN – Unilever N.V. [stock listing]

UNA – Unova Inc. [stock listing]

UNAMIR – United Nations Assistance Mission for Rwanda

UNAMSIL – United Nations Mission in Sierra Leone

UNAVEM III – United Nations Angola Verification Mission III

UNB – Union Bankshares Inc. [stock listing]

UNCED – United Nations Conference on Environment and Development

UNCLOS – United Nations Conference on the Law of the Sea

UNCRO – United Nations Confidence Restoration Operation in Croatia

UNCSTD – United Nations Conference for Science and Technology for Development

UNCTAD – United Nations Conference on Trade and Development

UND – Unumprovident Corp. [stock listing]

UNDOF – United Nations Disengagement Observer Force

UNDP – United Nations Development Program

UNDTCD – United Nations Department of Technical Cooperation for Development

UNEP – United Nations Environment Program

UNESCO – United Nations Educational, Scientific and Cultural Organization

UNF – Unifirst Corp. [stock listing]

UNFICYP – United Nations Peacekeeping Force in Cyprus

UNFPA – United Nations Fund for Population Activities

UNFPA – United Nations Population Fund

UNGA – United Nations General Assembly

UNH – UnitedHealth Group Inc. [stock listing]

UNHCR – United Nations High Commissioner for Refugees

UNI – Uni-Marts Inc. [stock listing]

UNI – user to network interface

UNICEF – United Nations Children's Emergency Fund

UNICOR – Federal Prison Industries Inc.

UNIDO – United Nations Industrial Development Organization

UNIENET – United Nations International Emergency Network

UNIFIL – United Nations Interim Force in Lebanon

UNIKOM – United Nations Iraq-Kuwait Observation Mission

UNIPAC – UNICEF Packing and Assembly Center

UNISYS – Unisys Corp.

UNISYS – United Information Systems

UNITAR – United Nations Institute for Training and Research

UNIVAC – universal automatic computer

UNM – UnumProvident Corp. [stock listing]

UNMIBH – United Nations Mission in Bosnia and Herzegovina

UNMIH – United Nations Mission in Haiti

UNMIK – United Nations Interim Administration Mission in Kosovo

UNMOGIP – United Nations Military Observer Group in India and Pakistan

UNMOP – United Nations Mission of Observers in Prevlaka

UNMOT – United Nations Mission of Observers in Tajikistan

UNMOVIC – United Nations Monitoring and Verification Commission

UNO – UNO Restaurant Corp. [stock listing]

UNOLS – University-National Oceanographic Laboratory System

UNOMIG – United Nations Observer Mission in Georgia

UNOMIL – United Nations Observer Mission in Liberia

UNOMOZ – United Nations Operation in Mozambique

UNOMSIL – United Nations Mission of Observers in Sierra Leone

UNOMUR – United Nations Observer Mission Uganda-Rwanda

UNOSOM II – United Nations Operation in Somalia II

UNP – Union Pacific Corp. [stock listing]

UNPREDEP – United Nations Preventive Deployment Force

UNPROFOR – United Nations Protection Force

UNR – Supermercados Unimarc S.A. [stock listing]

UNRISD – United Nations Research Institute for Social Development

UNRWA – United Nations Relief and Works Agency for Palestine Refugees in the Near East

UNS – UniSource Energy Corp. [stock listing]

UNSC – United Nations Statistical Commission

UNSCOM – United Nations Special Commission for the Elimination of Iraq's Weapons of Mass Destruction

UNSMIH – United Nations Support Mission in Haiti

UNT – Unit Corp. [stock listing]

UNTAC – United Nations Transitional Authority in Cambodia

UNTAES – United Nations Transitional Administration in Eastern Slavonia, Baranja and Western Sirmium

UNTAET – United Nations Transitional Administration in East Timor

UNTSO – United Nations Truce Supervision Organization

UNU – United Nations University

UP&B – Unified Programming and Budgeting

UPC – Union Planters Corp. [stock listing]

UPC – universal product code

UPI – United Press International

UPK – United Park City Mines Co. [stock listing]

UPL – Ultra Petroleum Corp. [stock listing]

UPM – Upm-Kymmene Corp. [stock listing]

UPS – uninterruptible power supply

UPS – United Parcel Service

UPS – United Parcel Service Inc. [stock listing]

UPU – Universal Postal Union

UQM – UQM Technologies Inc. [stock listing]

UR – utilization review

URB – Urban Shopping Centers Inc. [stock listing]

URDB – user requirements database

URE – usual residence elsewhere

URI – United Rental Inc. [stock listing]

URI – University of Rhode Island

URISA – Urban and Regional Information System Association

URL – uniform resource locator

URS – URS Corp. [stock listing]

URSI – International Union of Radio Science

US/GCRP – United States Global Change Research Program

USA – Liberty All-Star Equity Fund [stock listing]

USA – United States Army

USACE – United States Army Corps of Engineers

USACOE – United States Army Corps of Engineers

USACOM – United States Atlantic Command

USAF – United States Air Force

USAFA – United States Air Force Academy

USAFE – United States Air Force European Command

USAFH – United States Air Force Hospital

USAID – United States Agency for International Development

USAMMA – United States Army Medical Materiel Management Activity

USAREUR – United States Army Europe

USB – universal serial bus

USB – US Bancorp [stock listing]

USC – US Can Corp. [stock listing]

USCCR – United States Commission on Civil Rights

USCENTCOM – United States Central Command

USCG – United States Coast Guard

USCINCEUR – United States Commander-In-Chief European Command

USCS – United States Customs Service

USCSOI – United States Customs Service Office of Investigation

USDA – United States Department of Agriculture

USDOC – United States Department of Commerce

USEU – United States Mission to the European Union

USEUCOM – United States European Command

USEUCOMJMRO – USEUCOM Joint Medical Regulating Office

USFA – United States Fire Administration

USFS – United States Forest Service

USFWS – United States Fish and Wildlife Service

USG – United States Government

USG – USG Corp. [stock listing]

USGS – United States Geological Survey

USI – US Industries Inc. [stock listing]

USIA – United States Information Agency

USINT – United States Interests Section

USIP – United States Institute of Peace

USIS – United States Information Service

USITC – United States International Trade Commission

USL – U.S. Liquids Inc. [stock listing]

USLO – United States Liaison Office

USM – United States Cellular Corp. [stock listing]

USMC – United States Marine Corps

USN – United States Navy

USNATO – United States Mission to the North Atlantic Treaty Organization

USNAVHOSP – United States Naval Hospital

USNCB – United States National Central Bureau of INTERPOL

USNS – United States Naval Ship

USOAS – United States Mission to the Organization of American States

USOECD – United States Mission to the Organization for Economic Cooperation and Development

USP – United States Pharmacopeia

USPACOM – United States Pacific Command

USPHS – Public Health Service

USPS – United States Postal Service

USS – United States ship

USSR – Union of Soviet Socialist Republics

UST – UST Inc. [stock listing]

USTF – Uniformed Services Treatment Facility

USTR – United States Trade Representative

USTR – United States Trade Representative

USTRANSCOM – United States Transportation Command

USU – USEC Inc. [stock listing]

USUHS – Uniformed Services University for Health Sciences

USUN – United States Mission to the United Nations

USV – United States Restaurant Properties Inc. [stock listing]

UT – unorganized territory

UT – Utah

UTC – U.S. Trust Corp. [stock listing]

UTI – UTI Energy Corp. [stock listing]

UTL – UNITIL Corp. [stock listing]

UTN – Upington South Africa – Municipal Airport

UTP – unshielded twisted pair

UTX – United Technologies Corp. [stock listing]

UU – United Utils P.L.C. [stock listing]

UV – ultraviolet

UV-B – ultraviolet-biological

UVM – University of Vermont

UVN – Univision Communications Inc. [stock listing]

UVV – Universal Corp. [stock listing]

UW – University of Washington

UWR – United Water Resources Inc. [stock listing]

UWW – Unisource Worldwide Inc. [stock listing]

UXL – Laidlaw One Inc. [stock listing]

UXP – United States Exploration Inc. [stock listing]

UY – Uruguay

UZ – Uzbekistan

V&V – verification and validation

V – Vivendi Universal [stock listing]

Va. – Virginia [standard newspaper abbreviation]

VA/DHCP – Department of Veterans Affairs Decentralized Hospital

VA – Department of Veteran Affairs

VA – Vatican City

VA – Virginia

VAERS – Vaccine Adverse Event Reporting System

VAI – Savia S.A. [stock listing]

VAL – Valspar Corp., The [stock listing]

VAMC – Veterans Affairs Medical Center

VAN – value added network

VAN – virtual area network

VAP – Van Kampen Advantage Pennsylvania Municipal Income Trust [stock listing]

VAR – value-added reseller

VAR – Varian Madical Systems Inc. [stock listing]

VAS – VISSR atmospheric sounder

VAT – value-added tax

VAX – virtual address extension

VAZ – Voyageur Arizona Municipal Income Fund Inc. [stock listing]

VBA – Veterans Benefits Administration

VBF – Van Kampen Bond Fund [stock listing]

VC – Saint Vincent and the Grenadines

VC – vice consul

VC – Visteon Corp. [stock listing]

VCD – Value City Department Stores Inc. [stock listing]

VCF – Voyageur Colorado Insured Municipal Income Fund Inc. [stock listing]

VCI – Valassis Communications [stock listing]

VCN – visual communications network

VCP – Voluntary Cooperation Program

VCP – Votorantim Celulose e Papel [stock listing]

VCR – Sensory Science Corp. [stock listing]

VCV – Van Kampen California Value Municipal Income Trust [stock listing]

VDT – video display terminal

VDUC – VAS Data Utilization Center

V-E Day – Victory in Europe Day

VE – Venezuela

VEA – Virginia Electric & Power Co. [stock listing]

VES – Vestaur Securities Inc. [stock listing]

VESA – Video Electronic Standards Association

VETS – Veterans' Employment and Training Service

VF – voice frequency

VFC – VF Corp. [stock listing]

VFEP – voice front-end processor

VFL – Voyageur Florida Insured Municipal Income Fund [stock listing]

VFM – Van Kampen Florida Quality Municipal Trust [stock listing]

VFW – Veterans of Foreign Wars

VG – Viasystems Group Inc. [stock listing]

VG – British Virgin Islands

VGA – video graphics array

VGLI – Veterans' Group Life Insurance

VGM – Van Kampen Trust for Investment Grade Municipals [stock listing]

VGR – Vector Group Ltd. [stock listing]

VGZ – Vista Gold Corp. [stock listing]

VHA – Veterans Health Administration

VHF – very high frequency

VHI – Valhi Inc. [stock listing]

VI – Virgin Islands of the United States

VIA – Viacom Inc. [stock listing]

VIC – Van Kampen Trust for Investment Grade California Municipals [stock listing]

Vice Adm. – vice admiral

VIE – Schwechat Airport

VIG – Van Kampen Investment Grade Municipal Trust [stock listing]

VII – Vicon Industries Inc. [stock listing]

VIM – Van Kampen Trust for Insured Municipals [stock listing]

VIM – vendor independent messaging

VIN – Van Kampen Income Trust [stock listing]

VIN – vendor identification number

VIP – Open Jt Stk Co-Vimpelcommuni [stock listing]

VIR – Virco Manufacturing Corp. [stock listing]

VIS – VSI Holdings Inc. [stock listing]

VISSR – visible-infrared spin-scan radiometer

VISTA – Volunteers in Service to America

VIT – Van Kampen High Income Trust [stock listing]

VITA – Volunteers in Technical Assistance

V-J Day – Victory over Japan Day

VJV – Van Kampen New Jersey Value Municipal Income Trust [stock listing]

VKA – Van Kampen Advantage Municipal Income Trust [stock listing]

VKC – Van Kampen American Capital California Municipal Trust [stock listing]

VKI – Van Kampen Advantage Municipal Income Trust [stock listing]

VKL – Van Kampen Select Sector Municipal Trust [stock listing]

VKO – Moscow International Airport

VKQ – Van Kampen Municipal Trust [stock listing]

VKS – Van Kampen Strategic Sector Municipal Trust [stock listing]

VKV – Van Kampen Value Municipal Income Trust [stock listing]

VL – Vlasic Foods International Inc. [stock listing]

VLBI – very long baseline interferometry

VLF – very-low frequency

VLG – Valley National Gases Inc. [stock listing]

VLO – Valero Energy Corp. [stock listing]

VLSI – very large-scale integration

VLY – Valley National Bancorp [stock listing]

VM/WS/A – Cel-Sci Corp. [stock listing]

VM – virtual memory

VMC – Vermont Monitoring Cooperative

VMC – Vulcan Materials Co. [stock listing]

VMN – Voyageur Minnesota Municipal Income Fund Inc. [stock listing]

VMO – Van Kampen Municipal Opportunity Trust [stock listing]

VMS – virtual memory system

VMT – Van Kampen Municipal Income Trust [stock listing]

VMV – Van Kampen Massachusetts Value Municipal Income Trust [stock listing]

VN – Vietnam

VNM – Van Kampen New York Quality Municipal Trust [stock listing]

VNO – Vornado Realty Trust [stock listing]

VNODC – Vietnamese National Oceanographic Data Center

VNT – Compania Anonima Nacional Telefonos de Venezuela [stock listing]

VNV – Van Kampen New York Value Municipal Income Trust [stock listing]

VO – verifying officer

VOA – Voice of America

VOC – volatile organic compound

VOD – Vodafone Group P.L.C. [stock listing]

VOF – Van Kampen Florida Municipal Opportunity Trust [stock listing]

VOL – Volt Information Sciences Inc. [stock listing]

VOLAGS – voluntary agencies

VOO – Vornado Operating Co. [stock listing]

VOQ – Van Kampen Ohio Quality Municipal Trust [stock listing]

VOV – Van Kampen Ohio Value Municipal Income Trust [stock listing]

VPA – Virginia Electric & Power Co. [stock listing]

VPF – vertical processing facility

VPI – Vintage Petroleum Inc. [stock listing]

VPQ – Van Kampen Pennsylvania Quality Municipal Trust [stock listing]

VPS – Vermont Pure Holdings Ltd. [stock listing]

VPV – Van Kampen Pennsylvania Value Municipal Income Trust [stock listing]

VQC – Van Kampen California Quality Municipal Trust [stock listing]

VR – virtual reality

VRA – Viragen Inc. [stock listing]

VRAM – video random access memory

VRB – variable rate billing

VRC – Varco International Inc. [stock listing]

VRE – voice recognition entry

VRI – Vector Research Inc.

VS – virtual storage

VSADMS – Veterinary Services Automated Data Management System

VSAM – virtual sequential access method

VSAM – virtual storage access method

VSAT – very small aperture terminal

VSE – virtual system environment

VSF – Vita Food Products Inc. [stock listing]

VSG – viscous semigeostrophic

VSH – Vishay Intertechnology Inc. [stock listing]

VSL – Videsh Sanchar Nigam Ltd. [stock listing]

VSR – Versar Inc. [stock listing]

Vt. – Vermont [standard newspaper abbreviation]

VT – Vermont

VTA – Vesta Insurance Group Inc. [stock listing]

VTAM – Virtual Telecommunications Access Method

VTC – Voicenet Inc. [stock listing]

VTD – voting district

VTF – Van Kampen Trust for Investment Grade Florida Municipals [stock listing]

VTJ – Van Kampen Trust for Investment Grade New Jersey Muncipals [stock listing]

VTN – Van Kampen Trust for Investment Grade New York Municipals [stock listing]

VTO – Vitro [stock listing]

VTP – Van Kampen Trust for Investment Grade Pennsylvania Municpals [stock listing]

VTR – Ventas Inc. [stock listing]

VTS – Veritas DGC Inc. [stock listing]

VU – Vanuatu

VUL – Vulcan International Corp. [stock listing]

VUP – VAX units of performance

VV – vertical visibility

VVC – Vectren Corp. [stock listing]

VVI – Viad Corp. [stock listing]

VVN – Vitran Corp. Inc. [stock listing]

VVR – Van Kampen Senior Income Trust [stock listing]

VZ – Verizon Communications [stock listing]

W. Va. – West Virginia [standard newspaper abbreviation]

W – Westvaco Corp. [stock listing]

W3C – World Wide Web Consortium

WA – Washington

WAB – Wabtec Corporate [stock listing]

WAC – Warnaco Group Inc. [stock listing]

WADB – West African Development Bank

WAEMU – West African Economic and Monetary Union

WAFC – World Area Forecast Center

WAFR – World Appraisal of Fishery Resources

WAFS – World Area Forecast System

WAG – Walgreen Co. [stock listing]

WAH – Web application hosting

WAIS – wide area information server

WAK – Wackenhut Corp. [stock listing]

WAMEX – West African Monsoon Experiment

WAN – wide area network

WAP – wireless application protocol

WAPA – Western Area Power Administration

WAPOR – World Association for Public Opinion Research

WARFS – Water Resources Forecasting System

Wash. – Washington State [standard newspaper abbreviation]

WASH – Water and Sanitation for Health Project

WAT – Waters Corp. [stock listing]

WATOX – Western Atlantic Ocean Experiment

WATS – wide-area telephone system

WAVES – Women Accepted for Volunteer Emergency Service

WB – Wachovia Corp. [stock listing]

WB – Women's Bureau

WB – World Bank

WBB – Del Webb Corp. [stock listing]

WBK – Westpac Banking Corp. [stock listing]

WBM – whole blood modified

WBS – work breakdown structure

WBZ – whole blood

WCC – CDW Holding Corp. [stock listing]

WCDMP – World Climate and Data Monitoring Program

WCDP – World Climate Data Program

WCG – Williams Communications Group Inc. [stock listing]

WCIP – World Climate Impact Studies Program

WCL – World Confederation of Labor

WCMC – World Conservation Monitoring Center

WCO – World Customs Organization

WCP – World Climate Program

WCRP – World Climate Research Program

WCS – Wallace Computer Services Inc. [stock listing]

WCS – waste collection system

WCSMP – World Climate System Monitoring Program

WDC – Western Digital Corp. [stock listing]

WDC – World Data Center

WDCGG – World Data Center for Greenhouse Gases

WDDES – World Digital Database for Environmental Sciences

WDR – Weddell & Reed Financial Inc. [stock listing]

WDSS – Warning Decision Support System

WE – Westcoast Energy Inc. [stock listing]

WEA – Westfield America Inc. [stock listing]

WEAC – Winchester Engineering and Analytical Center

WEB – Webco Industries Inc. [stock listing]

WEC – Wisconsin Energy Corp. [stock listing]

WECAFC – Western Central Atlantic Fishery Commission

WEG – Williams Energy Partners L.P. [stock listing]

WEH – Westcoast Hospitality Corp. [stock listing]

WEL – Boots and Coots International Well Control Inc. [stock listing]

WEN – Wendys International Inc. [stock listing]

WEPOCS – Western Equatorial Pacific Ocean Climate Studies

WES – Waterways Experiment Station

WES – Westcorp [stock listing]

WESTRAX – Western Tropical Atlantic Experiment

WEU – Western European Union

WEX – Winland Electronics Inc. [stock listing]

WF – Wallis and Futuna Islands

WFC – Norwest Corp. [stock listing]

WFC – World Food Council

WFI – Winton Financial Corp. [stock listing]

WFO – Weather Forecast Office

WFP – World Food Program

WFR – Memc Electronic Materials Inc. [stock listing]

WFT – Weatherford International Inc. [stock listing]

WFTU – World Federation of Trade Unions

WG – Willbros Group Inc. [stock listing]

WGA – Wells-Gardner Electronics Corp. [stock listing]

WGCCD – Working Group on Climate Change Detection

WGCOM – Working Group on the Commercialization of Meteorological and Hydrological Services

WGI – within grade increase

WGL – Washington Gas Light Co. [stock listing]

WGO – Winnebago Industries Inc. [stock listing]

WGR – Western Gas Res Inc. [stock listing]

WGRF – Working Group on Radiation Fluxes

WGSAT – Working Group on Satellites

WGSI – Working Group on Sea Ice

WH – Whitman Corp. [stock listing]

WHC – Wackenhut Corp. [stock listing]

WHD – wage and hour division

WHI – Washington Homes Inc. [stock listing]

WHO – World Health Organization

WHOI – Woods Hole Oceanographic Institution

WHP – WOCE Hydrographic Program

WHPO – WOCE Hydrographic Program Office

WHR – Whirlpool Corp. [stock listing]

WHS – Washington Headquarters Services

WHS – wholesale trade survey

WHUHE – whole household usual home elsewhere

WHX – WHX Corp. [stock listing]

WHYCOS – World Hydrological Cycle Observing System

WI – Westminster Capital Inc. [stock listing]

WI – Wisconsin

WIA – weather-impacted airspace

WIC – Wicor Inc. [stock listing]

WIC – women, infants and children

WIMP – Windward Island Passages Monitoring Program

WIN – Winn Dixie Stores Inc. [stock listing]

WIPO – World Intellectual Property Organization

Wis. – Wisconsin [standard newspaper abbreviation]

WIS – Wisconsin Power & Light Co. [stock listing]

WISP – Winter Icing and Storms Project

WISPIT – WISP Instrument Test

WISQARS – Web-based Injury Statistics Query and Reporting System

WIT – Wipro Ltd. [stock listing]

WIX – Whitman Education Group Inc. [stock listing]

WKS – Weeks Corp. [stock listing]

WL – Wilmington Trust Corp. [stock listing]

WLA – Warner Lambert Co. [stock listing]

WLB – Westmoreland Coal Co. [stock listing]

WLC – Wellco Enterprises Inc. [stock listing]

WLK – Waterlink Inc. [stock listing]

WLL – Willamette Industries Inc. [stock listing]

WLM – Wellman Inc. [stock listing]

WLOC – Wang Loal Office Connection

WLP – Wellpoint Health Networks Inc. [stock listing]

WLS – William Lyon Homes [stock listing]

WLT – Walter Industries Inc. [stock listing]

WLV – Wolverine Tube Inc. [stock listing]

WM – Washington Mutual Inc. [stock listing]

WMB – Williams Cos. Inc. [stock listing]

WMC – WMC Ltd. [stock listing]

WMH – Merrill Lynch Wireless HOLDRS [stock listing]

WMI – Waste Management Inc. [stock listing]

WMK – Weis Markets Inc. [stock listing]

WMO – Wausau Mosinee Paper Mills Corp. [stock listing]

WMO – World Meteorological Organization

WMS – WMS Industries Inc. [stock listing]

WMT – Wal Mart Stores Inc. [stock listing]

WN – Wynns International Inc. [stock listing]

WNC – Wabash National Corp. [stock listing]

WND – Windmere Durable Holdings Inc. [stock listing]

WNET – Women's Network for Entrepreneurial Training

WNG – Washington Group International Inc. [stock listing]

WNI – Weider Nutrition International Inc. [stock listing]

WO3DC – World Ozone Data Center

WOB – women-owned businesses

WOC – Wilshire Oil Co. of Texas [stock listing]

WOCE – World Ocean Circulation Experiment

WOCE-SSG – WOCE Scientific Steering Group

WODC – World Ozone Data Center

WON – Westwood One Inc. [stock listing]

WOR – Worthington Inds. Inc. [stock listing]

WORM – write once, read many

WOW – World Ocean Watch

WP – Warsaw Pact

WP – word processing

WPC – WP Carey & Co. L.L.C. [stock listing]

WPDN – Wind Profiler Demonstration Network

WPFCC – Western Pacific Fisheries Consultative Committee

WPI – Watson Pharmaceuticals Inc. [stock listing]

WPL – W.P. Stewart & Co. Ltd. [stock listing]

WPL – wave propagation laboratory

WPO – Washington Post Co. [stock listing]

WPS – WPS Resources Corp. [stock listing]

WPZ – WorldPages.com, Inc. [stock listing]

WQP – West Penn Pwr Co. [stock listing]

WR – Western Res Inc. [stock listing]

WRC – Westport Resources Corp. [stock listing]

WRE – Washington Real Estate Investment [stock listing]

WRI – Weingarten Realty Investors [stock listing]

WRIPS – Wave Rider Information Processing System

WRM – war reserve matériel

WRO – Woronoco Bancorp Inc. [stock listing]

WRP – Wellsford Real Properties Inc. [stock listing]

WRT – with respect to

WS – Biovail Corp. [stock listing]

WS – Samoa

WS – Weirton Steel Corp. [stock listing]

WSB – Washington Savings Bank F.S.B., The [stock listing]

WSC – Wesco Financial Corp. [stock listing]

WSM – Weapons System Management

WSM – wheat soya milk

WSM – Williams Sonoma Inc. [stock listing]

WSMC – Western Space & Missile Center

WSMR – White Sands Missile Range

WSN – Wang System Network

WSO/B – Watsco Inc. [stock listing]

WSO – Watsco Inc. [stock listing

WSPPR – West Penn Power Co. [stock listing]

WSR – weather surveillance radar

WSSH – White Sands Space Harbor

WST – West Pharmaceutical Services Inc. [stock listing]

WTM – White Mount Ins Grp Ltd. Berm [stock listing]

WTO – World Trade Organization

WTO – World Tourism Organization

WTS – Watts Industries Inc. [stock listing]

WTS – wholesale trade survey

WTT – Wireless Telecom Group Inc. [stock listing]

WTU – Williams Coal Seam Gas Royalty Trust [stock listing]

WTX – World Tex Inc. [stock listing]

WV – West Virginia

WVQ – Monongahela Pwr Co. [stock listing]

WVRD – World Vision Relief and Development Inc.

WW – Watson Wyatt & Co. Holdings [stock listing]

WWF – World Wildlife Fund

WWF – World Wrestling Federation Entertainment Inc. [stock listing]

WWMCCS – World-Wide Military Command and Control System

WWNWS – World-Wide Navigational Warning Service

WWW or 3W – World Wide Web

WWW – Wolverine World Wide Inc. [stock listing]

WWW – World Weather Watch

WWY – Wrigley William Jr Co. [stock listing]

WXH – Winston Hotels Inc. [stock listing]

WXS – Westpoint Stevens Inc. [stock listing]

WY – Weyerhaeuser Co. [stock listing]

WY – Wyoming

WYN – Wyndham International Inc. [stock listing]

Wyo. – Wyoming [standard newspaper abbreviation]

WYSIWYG – what you see is what you get

WZR – Wiser Oil Co. [stock listing]

X – USX Corp. [stock listing]

XA – Office of External Affairs

XAA – American Municipal Income Portfolio Inc. [stock listing]

XCP – expendable current profiler

XEL – Xcel Energy Inc. [stock listing]

XFDL – extensible forms description language

XIMAGE – image analysis program in XANADU

XLA – Xcelera Inc. [stock listing]

XLB – Select Sector SPDR Fund–Basic Industries [stock listing]

XLE – Select Sector SPDR Fund-Energy Select Sector [stock listing]

XLF – Select Sector SPDR Fund-Financial [stock listing]

XLG – Excel Legacy Corp. [stock listing]

XLI – Select Sector SPDR Fund-Industrial [stock listing]

XLK – Select Sector SPDR Fund-Technology [stock listing]

XLP – Select Sector SPDR Fund-Consumer Staples [stock listing]

XLU – Select Sector SPDR Fund-Utilities [stock listing]

XLV – Select Sector SPDR Fund-Consumer Services [stock listing]

XLY – Select Sector SPDR Fund-Cyclical/Transportation [stock listing]

XML – extensible markup language

XMM – Cross Media Marketing Corp. [stock listing]

XMM – X-ray multi-mirror mission

XOM – Exxon Mobil Corp. [stock listing]

XOS – Salomon Smith Barney Holdings Inc. [stock listing]

XRF – X-ray fluorescence

XRX – Xerox Corp. [stock listing]

XSB – Salomon Smith Barney Holding Inc. [stock listing]

XT – extended technology

XTO – Cross Timbers Oil Co. [stock listing]

XTR – XTRA Corp. [stock listing]

XTS – SBC Communications Inc. [stock listing]

XVF – Mediaone Group Inc. [stock listing]

XWC – World Wireless Communications Inc. [stock listing]

XWM – Washington Mutual Inc. [stock listing]

XZL – Select Therapeutics Inc. [stock listing]

Y – Alleghany Corporation [stock listing]

YAR – Yemen Arab Republic

YCC – Yankee Candle Inc. [stock listing]

YCD – Nanaimo Airport

YDT – Boundary Bay Airport

YE – Yemen

YEG – Edmonton International Airport

YFM – Big City Radio Inc. [stock listing]

YKF – Waterloo Guelph Regional Airport

YLD – Morgan Stanley Dean Witter [stock listing]

YLF – International Airline Support Group Inc. [stock listing]

YLH – Morgan Stanley Dean Witter [stock listing]

YLT – Morgan Stanley Dean Witter [stock listing]

YMCA – Young Men's Christian Association

YOW – Macdonald-Cartier International Airport

YPF – YPF [stock listing]

YRK – York International Corp. [stock listing]

YTD – year to date

YU – Yugoslavia

YUM – Tricon Global [stock listing]

YVR – Vancouver International Airport

YWCA – Young Women's Christian Association

YWIA – your welcome in advance

YXU – London Airport

YYB – North Bay Airport

YYC – Calgary International Airport

YYJ – Victoria International Airport

YYZ – Lester B. Pearson International Airport

YZC – Yanzhou Coal Mng Co. Ltd. [stock listing]

Z – Venator Group Inc. [stock listing]

ZA – South Africa

ZAIPC – Zaragoza, Spain, Information Processing Center

ZAP – Zapata Corp. [stock listing]

ZC – Zangger Committee

ZCO – Ziegler Cos. Inc., The [stock listing]

ZD – zero defects

ZF – Zweig Fund Inc., The [stock listing]

ZIF – Zenix Income Fund Inc. [stock listing]

ZIP code – Zone Improvement Plan code

ZLC – Zale Corp. [stock listing]

ZM – Zambia

ZMX – Zemex Corp. [stock listing]

ZNH – China Southern Airlines Co. Ltd. [stock listing]

ZNT – Zenith National Insurance Corp. [stock listing]

ZQK – Quiksilver Inc. [stock listing]

ZR – Zaire

ZRH – Zurich-Kloten Airport

ZTR – Zweig Total Return Fund Inc., The [stock listing]

ZW – Zimbabwe

Colleges and Universities

Abilene Christian University
Abraham Baldwin Agricultural College
Academy of Art College
Adams State College
Adelphi University
Adirondack Community College
Adrian College
Agnes Scott College
Aiken Technical College
Aims Community College
Air Force Institute of Technology
Air University
Alabama A&M (Agricultural and Mechanical) University
Alabama Aviation and Technical
Alabama Southern Community College
Alabama State University
Alamance Community College
Alamo Community College District
Alaska Pacific University
Albany State University
Albertson College of Idaho
Albion College
Albright College
Albuquerque Technical Vocational Institute
Alcorn State University
Alderson-Broaddus College

Alexandria Technical College
Alfred University
Allan Hancock College
Allegany College of Maryland
Allegheny College
Allen College
Allen County Community College
Allen University
Allentown College
Alma College
Alpena Community College
Alvernia College
Alverno College
Alvin Community College
Amarillo Community College
Ambassador University
Amber University
American Bible College and Seminary
American Coastline University
American College, The
American Conservatory of Music, The
American Global University
American Graduate School of International Management
American Institute for Computer Sciences
American Institute of Business
American InterContinental University

American International College
American Military University
American River College
American Schools of Professional Psychology
American University
American University of Hawaii
Amherst College
Anderson College
Anderson University
Andon College
Andrew Jackson University
Andrews University
Angelo State University
Anna Maria College
Anne Arundel Community College
Anoka-Hennepin Technical College
Anoka-Ramsey Community College
Anson Community College
Antelope Valley College
Antioch New England Graduate School
Antioch University
Antioch University Los Angeles
Antioch University Santa Barbara
Antioch University Seattle
Apache University
Apollo College
Appalachian School of Law
Appalachian State University
Aquinas College
Arapahoe Community College
Arcadia University
Arizona International College
Arizona State University
Arizona State University West
Arizona Western College
Arkansas State University
Arkansas Tech University
Armstrong State University
Art Center College of Design
Art Institute of Phoenix, The
Art Institute of Seattle, The
Art Institute of Washington, The
Asbury College

Asheville-Buncombe Technical Community
  College
Ashland Community College
Ashland University
Asnuntuck Community College
Assumption College
Athena University
Athens Area Technical Institute
Athens State College
Atlantic Community College
Atlantic Union College
Auburn University
Auburn University, Montgomery
Audrey Cohen College
Augsburg College
Augusta State University
Augusta Technical Institute
Augustana College [IL]
Augustana College [SD]
Aurora University
Austin College
Austin Community College
Austin Peay State University
Averett College
Avila College
Azusa Pacific University
Babson College
Bainbridge College
Baker College
Baker University
Bakersfield College
Baldwin-Wallace College
Ball State University
Baltimore City Community College
Baltimore Hebrew University
Bank Street College of Education
Barclay College
Bard College
Barnard College
Barrington University
Barry University
Barstow Community College
Bartlesville Wesleyan College

Barton County Community College
Bastyr University
Bates College
Baton Rouge Community College
Bauder College
Bay de Noc Community College
Bay Mills Community College
Bay Path College
Bay State College
Baylor College of Dentistry
Baylor College of Medicine
Baylor University
Beaufort County Community College
Beaver College [now Arcadia Univeristy]
Belhaven College
Bellarmine College
Belleville Area Community College
Bellevue Community College
Bellevue University
Bellingham Technical College
Belmont Abbey College
Belmont University
Beloit College
Bemidji State Univeristy
Benedict College
Benedictine College
Benedictine University
Bennett College
Bennington College
Bentley College
Berea College
Bergen County College
Berkeley College
Berklee College of Music
Berks Technical Institute
Berkshire Community College
Bernadean University
Berry College
Bethany Bible College
Bethany College [CA]
Bethany College [KS]
Bethany College [WV]
Bethel College [IN]

Bethel College [KS]
Bethel College [TN]
Bethel College and Seminary [MN]
Bethune-Cookman College
Bevill State Community College
Bienville University
Big Bend Community College
Biola University
Birmingham-Southern College
Bishop State Community College
Bismarck State College
Black Hawk College
Black Hills State University
Blackburn College
Blackhawk Technical College
Bladen Community College
Blair College
Blinn College
Bloomsburg University
Blue Ridge Community College
Bluefield State Community and Technical
  College
Bluffton College
Bob Jones University
Boise State University
Borough of Manhattan Community College
Bossier Parish Community College
Boston Architectural Center, The
Boston College
Boston University
Bowdoin College
Bowie State University
Bowling Green Community College of
  Western Kentucky University
Bowling Green State University
Bradford College
Bradley University
Brandeis University
Brazosport College
Brenau University
Brevard Community College
Brewton-Parker College
Briarcliffe College

Bridgewater State College

Brigham Young University

Bristol Community College

Bronx Community College

Brookdale Community College

Brooklyn College

Brooklyn Law School

Broome Community College

Broward Community College

Brown University

Brunswick Community College

Bryant College

Bryn Mawr College

Bucknell University

Bucks County Community College

Buena Vista University

Bunker Hill Community College

Burlington County College

Butler County Community College

Butler University

Butte College

C.R. Drew University of Medicine and Science

Cabrillo College

Caldwell College

California Baptist University

California Coast University

California College for Health Sciences

California College of Podiatric Medicine

California Institute for Human Science

California Institute of Integral Studies

California Institute of Technology

California Institute of the Arts

California Lutheran University

California Maritime Academy, The

California Pacific University

California Polytechnic State University, San Luis Obispo

California School of Professional Psychology

California State Polytechnic University, Pomona

California State University, Bakersfield

California State University, Channel Islands

California State University, Chico

California State University, Dominguez Hills

California State University, Fresno

California State University, Fullerton

California State University, Hayward

California State University, Long Beach

California State University, Los Angeles

California State University, Monterey

California State University, Northridge

California State University, Sacramento

California State University, San Bernardino

California State University, San Marcos

California State University, Stanislaus

California University of Pennsylvania

Calumet College of St. Joseph

Calvin College

Cambria County Area Community College

Cambridge College

Camden County College

Cameron University

Campbell University

Campbellsville College

Canisius College

Cankdeska Cikana Community College

Canyon College

Cape Cod Community College

Cape Fear Community College

Capella University

Capital Community-Technical College

Capital University

Capitol City Careers

Capitol City Trade and Technical School

Capitol College

Cardinal Stritch University

Carl Albert State College

Carl Sandburg College

Carleton College

Carlow College

Carnegie Institution of Washington

Carnegie Mellon University

Carroll College [MT]

Carroll College [WI]

Carroll Community College

Carroll Technical Institute

Carson-Newman College
Carteret Community College
Carthage College
Cascadia Community College
Case Western Reserve University
Casper College
Castleton State College
Catawba College
Catawba Valley Community College
Catholic University of America, The
Catonsville Community College
Cayuga Community College
Cazenovia College
Cecil Community College
Cedar Crest College
Cedar Valley College
Cedarville College
Centenary College of Louisiana
Centenary College of New Jersey
Central Arizona College
Central Carolina Community College
Central Carolina Technical College
Central Community College
Central Connecticut State University
Central Florida Community College
Central Lakes Community College
Central Maine Technical College
Central Methodist College
Central Michigan University
Central Missouri State University
Central Ohio Technical College
Central Oregon Community College
Central Piedmont Community College
Central State University
Central Texas College
Central Virginia Community College
Central Washington University
Central Wyoming College
Centralia College
Centre College
Century College
Cerritos College
Cerro Coso Community College

Chabot College
Chadron State College
Chadwick University
Chaffey College
Chaminade University of Honolulu, Hawaii
Champlain College
Chandler Gilbert Community College
Chapman University
Charles County Community College
Charles R. Drew University of Medicine and
  Science
Charleston Southern University
Charter Oak State College
Chatham College
Chattahoochee Technical Institute
Chattahoochee Valley Community College
Chattanooga State Technical Community
  College
Chemeketa Community College
Chesapeake College
Cheyney University of Pennsylvania
Chicago School of Professional Psychology
Chicago State University
Chicago-Kent College of Law
Chippewa Valley Technical College
Chowan College
Christendom College
Christian Bible College and Seminary
Christian Brothers University
Christopher Newport University
Cincinnati State
Cisco Junior College
Citadel, The
Citrus College
City College of San Francisco
City Colleges of Chicago
City University of Los Angeles
City University of New York
City University, Bellevue Washington
Clackamas Community College
Claflin College
Claremont Graduate University
Claremont McKenna College

Clarion University
Clark Atlanta University
Clark College
Clark State Community College
Clark University
Clarke College
Clarkson University
Clatsop Community College
Clayton College and State University
Clayton College of Natural Health
Clear Creek Baptist Bible College
Cleary College
Clemson University
Cleveland Chiropractic College
Cleveland Community College
Cleveland Institute of Art
Cleveland Institute of Music
Cleveland State Community College
Cleveland State University
Clinch Valley College
Clinton Community College
Cloud County Community College
Clover Park Technical College
Clovis Community College
Coast Community College District
Coastal Bend College
Coastal Carolina Community College
Coastal Carolina University
Coastal Georgia Community College
Coastline Community College
Cochise Community College
Coconino Community College
Coe College
Coffeyville Community College
Cogswell Polytechnical College
Coker College
Colby College
Colby Community College
Colby-Sawyer College
Coleman College
Colgate University
College Misericordia
College of Aeronautics

College of Alameda
College of Charleston
College of DuPage
College of Eastern Utah
College of Insurance, The
College of Lake County
College of Marin
College of Metaphysical Studies, The
College of Mount Saint Joseph
College of New Jersey, The
College of New Rochelle
College of Notre Dame [CA]
College of Notre Dame of Maryland
College of Saint Benedict
College of Saint Catherine
College of Saint Elizabeth
College of Saint Mary
College of Saint Rose, The
College of Saint Scholastica
College of Saint Thomas More, The
College of San Mateo
College of Santa Fe, The
College of Southern Idaho
College of Southern Maryland
College of the Albemarle
College of the Atlantic
College of the Canyons
College of the Desert
College of the Holy Cross
College of the Mainland
College of the Menominee Nation
College of the Ozarks
College of the Redwoods
College of the Sequoias
College of the Siskiyous
College of William and Mary
College of Wooster, The
Collin County Community College
Colorado Aero Tech
Colorado Christian University
Colorado College
Colorado Community College and
   Occupational Educational System

Colorado Mountain College
Colorado Northwestern Community College
Colorado School of Mines
Colorado State University
Colorado Technical University
Columbia Basin College
Columbia College
Columbia Community College
Columbia Gorge Community College
Columbia International University
Columbia Southern University
Columbia State Community College
Columbia Union College
Columbia University
Columbia-Greene Community College
Columbus State Community College
Columbus State University
Columbus Technical Institute
Community and Technical College
Community College of Allegheny County
Community College of Aurora
Community College of Baltimore County
Community College of Beaver County
Community College of Denver
Community College of Philadelphia
Community College of Rhode Island
Community College of Southern Nevada
Community College of the Air Force
Community College of Vermont
Community Colleges of Spokane
Compton Community College
Concord College
Concordia College [AL]
Concordia College [MI]
Concordia College [MN]
Concordia College [NE]
Concordia College [NY]
Concordia College [TX]
Concordia University [CA]
Concordia University [IL]
Concordia University [OR]
Concordia University [WI]
Connecticut College

Connecticut Community-Technical Colleges
Conners State College
Contra Costa College
Converse College
Cooper Union for the Advancement of Science and Art
Coosa Valley Technical Institute
Copiah Lincoln Community College
Copper Mountain Community College District
Coppin State College
Cornell College, Iowa
Cornell University
Cornerstone University
Corning Community College
Cornish College of the Arts
Cossatot Technical College
Cosumnes River College
Cottey College
County College of Morris
Covenant College
Crafton Hills College
Craven Community College
Creighton University
Crichton College
Crowder College
Crowley's Ridge College
Crown College
Cuesta College
Culver-Stockton College
Cumberland County College
Cumberland University
Curry College
Cuyahoga Community College
Cuyamaca Community College District
Cypress College
Dabney S. Lancaster Community College
Daemen College
Dakota County Technical College
Dakota State University
Dakota Wesleyan University
Dallas Baptist University
Dallas County Community College District
Dallas Theological Seminary

Dalton State College
Dana College
Daniel Webster College
Danville Area Community College
Danville Community College
Dartmouth College
Darton College
Davenport College
David Lipscomb University
Davidson College
Davidson County Community College
Davis and Elkins College
Dawson College
Daytona Beach Community College
De Anza College
Dean College
Deep Springs College
Defiance College
Dekalb Technical Institute
Del Mar College
Delaware County Community College
Delaware State University
Delaware Technical and Community
Delaware Valley College
Delgado Community College
Delta College
Delta State University
Denison University
Denver Seminary
DePaul University
DePauw University
Des Moines Area Community College
Devry Institute of Technology
Dickinson College
Dickinson State University
Dillard University
Doane College
Dodge City Community College
Dominican College
Dominican College of San Rafael
Dominican University
Dominion College
Don Bosco Technical Institute

Dona Ana Branch Community College
Donnelly College
Dordt College
Dowling College
Drake University
Draughons Junior College
Drew University
Drexel University
Drury College
Duke University
Dundalk Community College
Duquesne University
Durham Technical Community College
Dutchess Community College
Dyersburg State Community College
D'Youville College
Earlham College
East Carolina University
East Central College
East Central University
East Georgia College
East Los Angeles College
East Mississippi Community College
East Stroudsburg State University
East Tennessee State University
East Texas Baptist University
Eastern Arizona College
Eastern College
Eastern Connecticut State University
Eastern Idaho Technical College
Eastern Illinois University
Eastern Iowa Community College
    District
Eastern Kentucky University
Eastern Maine Technical College
Eastern Mennonite University
Eastern Michigan University
Eastern Nazarene College
Eastern New Mexico University
Eastern Oklahoma State College
Eastern Oregon State College
Eastern Oregon University
Eastern Washington University

Eastern West Virginia Community and Technical College
Eastern Wyoming College
Eastfield College
Eckerd College
Edgecombe Community College
Edgewood College
Edinboro University of Pennsylvania
Edison Community College
Edmonds Community College
Edward Waters College
El Camino College
El Centro Community College
El Paso Community College
Elgin Community College
Elizabeth City State University
Elizabethtown College
Elmhurst College
Elmira College
Elms College
Elon College
Embry-Riddle Aeronautical University
Emerson College
Emmanuel College
Emmaus Bible College
Emory University
Empire State College
Emporia State University
Endicott College
Enterprise State Junior College
Erie Community College
Erskine College
Essex Community College
Essex County College
Estrella Mountain Community College
Eureka College
Evangel University
Everett Community College
Evergreen State College
Evergreen Valley College
Fairfield University
Fairleigh Dickinson University
Fairmont State College

Faith Baptist Bible College
Faulkner University
Fayetteville State University
Fayetteville Technical Community College
Feather River College
Felician College
Fergus Falls Community College
Ferris State University
Ferrum College
Fielding Institute
Finch University of Health Sciences
Fisher College
Fisk University
Fitchburg State College
Flagler College
Flathead Valley Community College
Florence-Darlington Technical College
Florida A&M University
Florida Atlantic University
Florida Baptist Theological College
Florida Community College at Jacksonville
Florida Gulf Coast University
Florida Institute of Technology
Florida International University
Florida Keys Community College
Florida Memorial College
Florida Metropolitan University
Florida National College
Florida Southern University
Florida State University
Floyd College
Fond du Lac Tribal and Community College
Fontbonne College
Foothill College
Fordham University
Forsyth Technical Community College
Fort Belknap College
Fort Hays State University
Fort Lewis College
Fort Scott Community College
Fort Valley State University
Fox Valley Technical College
Framingham State College

Francis Marion University
Franciscan University of Steubenville
Frank Phillips College
Franklin and Marshall College
Franklin College
Franklin Pierce College
Franklin Pierce Law Center
Franklin University
Frederick Community College
Freed-Hardeman University
Fresno Pacific College
Friends University
Front Range Community College
Frontier Community College
Frostburg State University
Fuller Theological Seminary
Fullerton College
Fulton-Montgomery Community College
Furman University
Gadsden State Community College
Gainesville College
Gallaudet University
Galveston College
Gannon University
Garden City Community College
Gardner-Webb University
Garland County Community College
Garrett Community College
Gaston College
Gateway Community College
Gateway Community-Technical College
Gateway Technical College
Gavilan Community College
Genesee Community College
Geneva College
George C. Wallace State Community College
George Fox University
George Mason University
George Washington University
Georgetown College
Georgetown University
Georgia College and State University
Georgia Institute of Technology

Georgia Military College
Georgia Perimeter College
Georgia Southern University
Georgia Southwestern State University
Georgia State University
Georgian Court College
Germanna Community College
Gettysburg College
Glen Oaks Community College
Glendale Community College
Glenville State College
Globe Institute of Technology
Gloucester County College
GMC (Georgia Military College) Community
  College
Goddard College
Gogebic Community College
Golden Gate University
Golden West College
Goldey-Beacom College
Gonzaga University
Gooding Institute of Nurse Anesthesia
Goodwin College
Gordon College
Gordon-Conwell Theological Seminary
Goshen College
Goucher College
Governors State University
Grace College
Grace University
Graceland College
Graduate Center, City University of New
  York, The
Grambling State University
Grand Canyon University
Grand Rapids Community College
Grand Valley State University
Grand View College
Grays Harbor Community College
Grayson County College
Green Mountain College
Green River Community College
Greenfield Community College

Greenleaf University
Greensboro College
Greenville Technical College
Greenwich University
Griffin Technical Institute
Grinnell College
Grossmont-Cuyamaca Community College District
Grove City College
Guam Community College
Guilford College
Guilford Technical Community College
Gulf Coast Community College
Gustavus Adolphus College, St. Peter, Minnesota
Gwinnett Technical Institute
Gwynedd-Mercy College
Hagerstown Business College
Hagerstown Community College
Halifax Community College
Hamilton College
Hamilton University
Hamline University
Hampden-Sydney College
Hampshire College
Hampton University
Hannibal-LaGrange College
Hanover College
Harcum College
Harding University
Hardin-Simmons University
Harford Community College
Harold Washington College
Harper Community College
Harrington Institute of Interior Design
Harrisburg Area Community
Harris-Stowe State College
Harry M. Ayers State Technical College
Hartnell Community College
Hartwick College
Harvard University
Harvey Mudd College
Haskell Indian Nations University

Hastings College
Haverford College
Hawaii Community College
Hawaii Pacific University
Hawkeye Community College
Haywood Community College
Heartland Community College
Hebrew College
Heidelberg College
Henderson State Univerisity
Hendrix College
Henry Cogswell College
Henry Ford Community College
Heritage College
Herkimer County Community College
Herzing College
Hesser College
Hesston College
Hibbing Community College
High Point University
Highland Community College
Hill College
Hillsborough Community College
Hillsdale College
Hinds Community College
Hiram College
Hobart and William Smith Colleges
Hocking College
Hofstra University
Hollins University
Holmes Community College
Holy Cross College
Holy Family College
Honolulu Community College
Hood College
Hope College
Horry-Georgetown Technical College
Hostos Community College
Houghton College
Housatonic Community-Technical College
Houston Baptist University
Houston Community College Southwest
Houston Community College System

Howard Community College
Howard County Junior College District
Howard Payne University
Howard University
Hudson County Community College
Hudson Valley Community College
Humboldt State University
Hunter College
Huntingdon College
Huntington College
Huron University
Husson College
Huston-Tillotson College
Hutchinson Community College
ICM School of Business and Medical Careers
Idaho State University
Ilisagvik Community College
Illinois Central College
Illinois College
Illinois Community College Board
Illinois Institute of Technology
Illinois State University
Illinois Valley Community College
Illinois Wesleyan University
Immaculata College
Imperial Valley College
Independence Community College
Indian Hills Community College
Indian River Community College
Indiana Institute of Technology
Indiana State University
Indiana University
Indiana University at South Bend
Indiana University Northwest
Indiana University of Pennsylvania
Indiana University Southeast
Indiana Wesleyan University
Institute for Christian Works
Institute for Extended Learning
Institute of Paper Science and Technology
International College
International Fine Arts College
International Reform University

Inver Hills Community College
Iona College
Iowa Central Community College
Iowa Lakes Community College
Iowa State University
Iowa Valley Community College District
Iowa Wesleyan College
Iowa Western Community College
Irvine Valley College
Itasca Community College
Itawamba Community College
Ithaca College
Ivy Tech State College
J. Sargeant Reynolds Community College
Jackson Community College
Jackson State Community College
Jackson State University
Jacksonville State University
Jacksonville University
James H. Faulkner State Community College
James Madison University
Jamestown College
Jamestown Community College
Jarvis Christian College
Jefferson College
Jefferson Community College
Jefferson Davis Community College
Jefferson State Community College
Jewish Theological Seminary
John A. Gupton College
John A. Logan College
John Brown University
John C. Calhoun State Community College
John Carroll University
John F. Kennedy University
John Jay College of Criminal Justice
John Tyler Community College
John Wood Community College
Johns Hopkins University, The
Johnson and Wales University
Johnson Bible College
Johnson C. Smith University
Johnson County Community College

Johnston Community College
Joint Military Intelligence College
Joliet Junior College
Jones College
Jones County Junior College
Jones International University
Judson College [AL]
Judson College [IL]
Julliard School, The
Juniata College
Kalamazoo College
Kalamazoo Valley Community College
Kankakee Community College
Kansas City Kansas Community College
Kansas Newman College
Kansas State University
Kansas Wesleyan University
Kapiolani Community College
Kaskaskia College
Kauai Community College
Kean University
Keck Graduate Institute
Keene State College
Keiser College of Technology
Kellogg Community College
Kenai Peninsula College
Kennebec Valley Technical College
Kennedy-King College
Kennedy-Western University
Kennesaw State University
Kent State University
Kentucky Christian College
Kentucky State University
Kentucky Wesleyan College
Kenyon College
Kern Community College District
Kettering University
Keuka College
Keystone Junior College
Kilgore College
King College
King's College
Kingsborough Community College

Kingwood College
Kirkwood Community College
Kirtland Community College
Kishwaukee College
Klamath Community College
Knox College
Knox Theological Seminary
Kutztown University of Pennsylvania
La Roche College
La Salle University
La Sierra University
Labette Community College
Lafayette College
LaGrange College
LaGuardia Community College
Lake City Community College
Lake Erie College
Lake Forest College
Lake Land College
Lake Michigan College
Lake Superior College
Lake Superior State University
Lake Tahoe Community College
Lake Washington Technical College
Lakeland College
Lakeland Community College
Lakeshore Technical College
Lake-Sumter Community College
Lamar Community College
Lamar University
Lambuth University
Lander University
Landmark College
Lane Community College
Laney College
Langston University
Lansing Community College
Laramie County Community College
Laredo Community College
Las Positas Community College
Lassen College
Lawrence Technological University
Lawrence University

Lawson State Community College
Le Moyne College
Lebanon College
Lebanon Valley College
Lee College
Lee University
Lees-McRae College
Leeward Community College
Lehigh Carbon Community College
Lehigh Univervsity
LeMoyne-Owen College
Lenoir Community College
Lenoir-Rhyne College
Lenox Institute of Water Technology
Lesley College
LeTourneau University
Lewis & Clark College
Lewis University
Lexington Community College
Liberty University
Lima Technical College
Limestone College
Lincoln College
Lincoln Land Community College
Lincoln Memorial University
Lincoln School of Commerce
Lincoln Trail College
Lincoln University [CA]
Lincoln University [MI]
Lincoln University of Pennsylvania
Lindenwood College
Lindsey Wilson College
Linfield College
Linn State Technical College
Linn-Benton Community College
Lipscomb University
Little Priest Tribal College
Lock Haven University
Logan College of Chiropractic
Loma Linda University
Lon Morris College
Long Beach City College
Long Island University

Long Technical College
Longview Community College
Longwood College
Lorain County Community College
Loras College
Lord Fairfax Community College
Los Angeles City College
Los Angeles College of Chiropractic
Los Angeles Community Colleges
Los Angeles Mission College
Los Angeles Pierce College
Los Angeles Trade-Technical College
Los Angeles Valley College
Los Rios Community College District
Louisburg College
Louisiana Baptist Universty
Louisiana College
Louisiana State University at Alexandria
Louisiana State University at Baton Rouge
Louisiana State University at Eunice
Louisiana State University at Shreveport
Louisiana State University Health Sciences
  Center
Louisiana Tech University
Louisville Technical Institute
Lower Columbia College
Loyola College
Loyola Marymount University
Loyola University [IL]
Loyola University [LA]
Lubbock Christian University
Lurleen B. Wallace State Junior College
Luther College
Luther Seminary
Lutheran Bible Institute
Luzerne County Community College
Lycoming College
Lyme Academy of Fine Arts
Lynchburg College
Lyndon State College
Lynn University
Lyon College
Macalester College

Macarthur State Technical College
MacMurray College
Macomb Community College
Macon State College
Macon Technical Institute
Madison Area Technical College
Madonna University
Maharishi University of Management
Maine College of Art
Maine Maritime Academy
Malcolm X College
Malone College
Manatee Community College
Manchester College
Manchester Community-Technical College
Manhattan College
Mankato State University
Manor Junior College
Mansfield University
Marian College
Maric College
Marietta College
Marion Technical College
Marist College
Marlboro College
Marquette University
Mars Hill College
Marshall Community and Technical College
Marshall University
Martin Community College
Mary Baldwin College
Mary Washington College
Maryland Institute, College of Art
Marylhurst University
Marymount College
Marymount Manhattan College
Marymount University
Maryville College
Maryville University of Saint Louis
Marywood University
Massachusetts Bay Community College
Massachusetts College of Art
Massachusetts College of Liberal Arts

Massachusetts College of Pharmacy and Allied
    Health Sciences
Massachusetts Communications College
Massachusetts Institute of Technology
Massachusetts Maritime Academy
Massasoit Community College
Master's College, The
Maui Community College
Mayland Community College
Mayo Foundation, The
Mayville State University
McDowell Technical Community College
McGregor School of Antioch University, The
McHenry County College
McLennan Community College
McMurry University
McNeese State University
McPherson College
Medical College of Georgia
Medical College of Ohio
Medical College of Pennsylvania and
    Hahnemann University
Medical College of Wisconsin
Medical University of South Carolina
Meharry Medical College
Mendocino College
Menlo College
Merced College
Mercer County Community College
Mercer University
Mercy College
Mercy College of Health Sciences
Mercyhurst College
Meredith College
Meridian Commmunity College
Merrimack College
Merritt College
Mesa Community College
Mesa State College
Mesa Technical College
Messiah College
Methodist College
Metropolitan College

Metropolitan Community College [NE]
Metropolitan Community Colleges [MO]
Metropolitan State College of Denver
Metropolitan State University
Miami Christian University
Miami University of Ohio
Miami-Dade Community College
Michigan State University
Michigan Technological University
Mid Michigan Community College
Mid State Technical College
Mid-America Nazarene University
Middle Georgia College
Middle Tennessee State University
Middlebury College
Middlesex Community College
Middlesex Community-Technical College
Middlesex County College
Midland College
Midlands Technical College
Mid-South Community College
Midwestern Baptist College
Midwestern State University
Millersville University
Milligan College
Millikin University
Mills College
Millsaps College
Milwaukee Area Technical College
Milwaukee School of Engineering
Mineral Area College
Minneapolis College of Art and Design
Minneapolis Community and Technical College
Minot State University
MiraCosta College
Mission College
Mississippi College
Mississippi County Community College
Mississippi Delta Community College
Mississippi State University
Mississippi University for Women
Mississippi Valley State University
Missouri Baptist College

Missouri College
Missouri Southern State College
Missouri Tech
Missouri Valley College
Missouri Western State College
Mitchell Community College
Mitchell Technical Institute
Moberly Area Community College
Modern Technology College
Modesto Junior College
Mohave Community College
Mohawk Valley Community College
Molloy College
Monmouth College [IL]
Monmouth University [NJ]
Monroe College
Monroe Community College
Montana State University at Billings
Montana State University at Bozeman
Montana State University at Northern
  Havre
Montana State University College of
  Technology, Great Falls
Montcalm Community College
Montclair State University
Monterey Institute of International Studies
Monterey Peninsula College
Montgomery College
Montgomery Community College
Montgomery County Community College
Montreat College
Moorhead State University
Moorpark College
Moraine Valley Community College
Moravian College
Morehead State University
Morehouse College
Morehouse School of Medicine
Morgan Community College
Morgan State University
Morningside College
Morris Brown College
Morris College

Morrison Institute of Technology
Morton College
Motlow State Community College
Mott Community College
Mount Aloysius College
Mount Holyoke College
Mount Ida College
Mount Marty College
Mount Mary College
Mount Mercy College
Mount Olive College
Mount Senario College
Mount St. Clare College
Mount St. Mary's College and Seminary [MD]
Mount St. Mary's College [CA]
Mount Union College
Mount Vernon Nazarene College
Mount Wachusett Community College
Mountain Empire Community College
Mountain View College
Mountain West Hebrew University
Mt. Hood Community College
Mt. San Antonio College
Mt. San Jacinto Community College
Mt. Sierra College
Muhlenberg College
Murray State College
Murray State University
Muscatine Community College
Muskegon Community College
Muskingum College
Napa Valley College
Naropa Institute, The
Nash Community College
Nashville State Technical Institute
Nassau Community College
National American University
National Defense University
National Graduate School, The
National Technological University
National University
National-Louis University

Naugatuck Valley Community Technical College
Naval Postgraduate School, The
Navarro College
Nazarene Bible College
Nazareth College
Nebraska College of Business
Nebraska Wesleyan University
Neosho County Community College
Neumann College
New Brunswick Theological Seminary
New England College of Optometry
New England Conservatory of Music
New England Institute of Technology
New Hampshire College
New Hampshire Community Technical College at Berlin
New Hampshire Community Technical College at Claremont
New Hampshire Community Technical College at Nashua
New Hampshire Community Technical College at Laconia
New Hampshire Community Technical College at Manchester
New Hampshire Community Technical College at Stratham
New Hampshire Community Technical College at System
New Hampshire Technical Institute
New Jersey City University
New Jersey Institute of Technology
New Mexico Highlands University
New Mexico Institute of Mining and Technology
New Mexico Junior College
New Mexico Military Institute
New Mexico State University
New Mexico State University-Alamogordo
New River Community College
New School University
New York Academy of Art
New York Institute of Technology

New York Law School
New York University
Newberry College
Newbury College
Newport University
Niagara University
Nicholls State University
Nichols College
Nicolet Area Technical College
Norfolk State University
Normandale Community College
North Arkansas College
North Carolina Agricultural and Technical
  State University
North Carolina Central University
North Carolina Community College System
North Carolina State University
North Carolina Wesleyan College
North Central College
North Central Community College
North Central Michigan College
North Central Technical College
North Central Texas College
North Central University
North Country Community College
North Dakota State College of Science
North Dakota State University-Bottineau
North Dakota State University-Fargo
North Dakota University System
North Florida Community College
North Georgia College
North Georgia Technical Institute
North Greenville College
North Harris College
North Harris Montgomery Community
  College District
North Hennepin Community College
North Idaho College
North Iowa Area Community College
North Lake
North Metro Tech
North Park University
North Seattle Community College

North Shore Community College
Northeast Alabama Community College
Northeast Community College
Northeast Iowa Community College
Northeast Mississippi Community College
Northeast State Technical Community College
Northeast Texas Community College
Northeast Wisconsin Technical College
Northeastern Illinois University
Northeastern Junior College
Northeastern Oklahoma A&M College
Northeastern State University
Northeastern University
Northern Arizona University
Northern Essex Community College
Northern Illinois University
Northern Kentucky University
Northern Maine Technical College
Northern Michigan University
Northern State University
Northern Virginia Community College
Northern Wyoming Community College
  District-Sheridan College
Northlake College
Northland College
Northland Community and Technical College
Northland Pioneer College
Northwest Arkansas Community College
Northwest Christian College
Northwest College
Northwest Iowa Community College
Northwest Mississippi Community College
Northwest Missouri State University
Northwest Nazarene College
Northwest Pennsylvania Technical Institute
Northwest State Community College
Northwest Technical College
Northwest Vista College
Northwestern Business College
Northwestern College [IA]
Northwestern College [MN]
Northwestern Community-Technical College
Northwestern Michigan College

Northwestern Oklahoma State University
Northwestern State University, Louisiana
Northwestern Technical Institute
Northwestern University
Northwest-Shoals Community College
Northwood University
Norwalk Community-Technical College
Norwich University
Notre Dame College of Ohio
Nova Southeastern University
Nunez Community College
Nyack College
Oakland Community College
Oakland University
Oakton Community College
Oakwood College
Oberlin College
Occidental College
Ocean County College
Odessa College
Ogeechee Technical Institute
Oglethorpe University
Ohio Dominican College
Ohio Institute of Photography & Technology
Ohio Northern University
Ohio State University, The
Ohio University
Ohio Valley College
Ohio Wesleyan University
Ohlone College
Okaloosa-Walton Community College
Oklahoma Baptist University
Oklahoma Christian University
Oklahoma City Community College
Oklahoma City University
Oklahoma Panhandle State University
Oklahoma State University
Old Dominion University
Olive Harvey College
Olivet College
Olivet Nazarene University
Olympic College
Onondaga Community College

Open University, The
Oral Roberts University
Orange Coast College
Orange County Community College
Orangeburg Calhoun Technical College
Oregon Coast Community College
Oregon Community College Association
Oregon Graduate Institute of Science and
    Technology
Oregon Health Sciences University
Oregon Institute of Technology
Oregon State University
Otero Junior College
Ottawa University
Otterbein College
Ouachita Baptist University
Ouachita Technical College
Our Lady of Holy Cross College
Our Lady of the Lake University
Owens Community College
Owensboro Community College
Oxnard College
Ozark Technical Community College
Ozarka Technical College
Pace University
Pacific Lutheran University
Pacific Northwest College of Art
Pacific States University
Pacific Union College
Pacific University
Paducah Community College
Paine College
Palm Beach Atlantic College
Palm Beach Community College
Palmer College of Chiropractic
Palo Alto College
Palomar College
Pamlico Community College
Panola College
Paradise Valley Community College
Paris Junior College
Park University
Parkland College

Parks College
Parsons School of Design
Pasadena City College
Pasco Hernando Community College
Passaic County Community College
Patrick Henry College
Patrick Henry Community College
Patten College
Paul D. Camp Community College
Paul Quinn College
Paul Smith's College
Pear River Community College
Pellissippi State Technical Community College
Peninsula College
Penn Valley Community College
Pennsylvania College of Technology
Pennsylvania State University
Pennsylvania State University at Altoona
Pennsylvania Virtual Community College
 Consortium
Pepperdine University
Peralta Community College District
Peru State College
Pfeiffer University
Philadelphia University
Philander Smith College
Phillips University
Phoenix College
Pickering University
Piedmont College
Piedmont Community College
Piedmont Technical College
Piedmont Virginia Community College
Pierce College
Pikes Peak Community College
Pima Community College
Pine Manor College
Pine Technical College
Pitt Community College
Pittsburg State University
Pitzer College
Plymouth State College
Point Loma Nazarene College

Point Park College
Polk Community College
Polytechnic University of New York
Polytechnic University of Puerto Rico
Pomona College
Porterville College
Portland Community College
Portland State University
Potomac College
Prairie State College
Prairie View A&M University
Pratt Community College
Pratt Institute
Presbyterian College
Prescott College
Preston University
Prince George's Community College
Prince William Sound Community College
Princeton University
Principia College
Providence College
Pueblo Community College
Pulaski Technical College
Purdue University
Queens College
Queensborough Community College
Quest College
Quincy College
Quincy University
Quinebaug Valley Community-Technical
 College
Quinnipiac College
Quinsigamond Community College
Radford University
Rainy River Community College
Ramapo College of New Jersey
Rancho Santiago Community College
 District
Randolph Community College
Randolph-Macon College
Randolph-Macon Woman's College
Rappahannock Community College
Raritan Valley Community College

Reading Area Community College
Red Rocks Community College
Redlands Community College
Reed College
Reedley College
Regent University
Regents College
Regis College
Regis University
Reinhardt College
Rend Lake College
Rensselaer Polytechnic Institute
Renton Technical College
Rhode Island College
Rhode Island Community College
Rhode Island School of Design
Rhodes College
Rice University
Rich Mountain Community College
Richard J. Daley College
Richard Stockton University
Richland Community College
Richmond Community College
Ricks College
Rider University
Ridgewater College
Ringling School of Art and Design
Rio Grande Community College
Rio Hondo College
Rio Salado Community College
Ripon College
River Parishes Community College
Riverland Community College
Riverside Community College
Rivier College
Roane State Community College
Roanoke College
Roanoke-Chowan Community College
Robert Morris College [IL]
Robert Morris College [PA]
Roberts Wesleyan College
Robeson Community College
Rochester Business Institute

Rochester College
Rochester Community and Technical College
Rochester Institute of Technology
Rock Valley College
Rockefeller University, The
Rockford College
Rockhurst College
Rockingham Community College
Rockland Community College
Rocky Mountain College
Roger Williams University
Rogers State University
Rogue Community College
Rollins College
Roosevelt University
Rose State College
Rose-Hulman Institute of Technology
Rosemont College
Rowan University
Rowan-Cabarrus Community College
Rudolf Steiner College
Rush University
Russell Sage College
Rust College
Rutgers University
Sacramento City College
Sacred Heart University
Sacred Heart University, Puerto Rico
Saddleback College
Sage Colleges, The
Saginaw Valley State University
Saint Ambrose University
Saint Andrews Presbyterian College
Saint Anselm College
Saint Augustine's College
Saint Bonaventure University
Saint Cloud State University
Saint Edwards University
Saint Francis College [IN]
Saint Francis College [NY]
Saint Francis College [PA]
Saint John Fisher College

Saint John's College
Saint John's University [MN]
Saint John's University [NY]
Saint Joseph College
Saint Joseph's College
Saint Joseph's College of Maine
Saint Joseph's University
Saint Lawrence University
Saint Leo College
Saint Louis University
Saint Martin's College
Saint Mary College
Saint Mary-of-the-Woods College
Saint Mary's College
Saint Mary's College of California
Saint Mary's College of Maryland
Saint Mary's University of Minnesota
Saint Mary's University of San Antonio
Saint Meinrad's School of Theology
Saint Michael's College
Saint Norbert College
Saint Olaf College
Saint Paul's College
Saint Peter's College
Saint Rose College
Saint Thomas Aquinas College
Saint Thomas University
Saint Vincent College
Saint Xavier University
Salem College
Salem Community College
Salem State College
Salisbury State University
Salk Institute for Biological Studies, The
Salt Lake Community College
Salve Regina University
Sam Houston State University
Samford University
Sampson Community College
Samuel Merritt College
San Antonio College
San Antonio College of Medical and Dental
   Assistants

San Bernardino Valley College
San Diego City College
San Diego Community College District
San Diego State University
San Francisco Law School
San Francisco State University
San Jacinto College District
San Joaquin Delta College
San Jose City College
San Jose State University
San Jose/Evergreen Community College
   District
San Juan College
San Luis Obispo Community College District
Sandhills Community College
Santa Ana College
Santa Barbara Business College-Bakersfield
Santa Barbara City College
Santa Clara University
Santa Fe Community College
Santa Monica Community College
Santa Rosa Junior College
Santiago Canyon College
Sarah Lawrence College
Saratoga University School of Law
Sauk Valley Community College
Savannah College of Art and Design
Savannah State University
Schenectady County Community College
Schiller International University
School for International Training
School of Islamic and Social Sciences
School of the Art Institute of Chicago
School of the Museum of Fine Arts, Boston
School of the Visual Arts
Schoolcraft College
Schreiner College
Schuylkill Institute of Business and Technology
Scottsdale Community College
Scripps College
Scripps Research Institute, The
Seattle Central Community College
Seattle Community College District

Seattle Pacific University
Seattle University
Seattle Vocational Institute
Seminole Community College
Seminole State College
Seton Hall University
Seton Hill College
Seward County Community College
Shasta Bible College
Shasta College
Shaw University
Shawnee Community College
Shawnee State University
Shelby State Community College
Sheldon Jackson College
Shelton State Community College
Shenandoah University
Shepherd College
Shepherd College-South Branch
Sheridan College
Sherman College of Straight Chiropractic
Shimer College
Shippensburg University of Pennsylvania
Shoreline Community College
Shorter College
Siena College
Siena Heights University
Sierra College
Silicon Valley College
Silver Lake College
Simmons College
Simon's Rock College
Simpson College [IA]
Simpson College [CA]
Sinclair Community College
Sisseton Wahpeton Community College
Skagit Valley College
Skidmore College
Slippery Rock University
Smith Chapel Bible College
Smith College
Snead State Community College
Snow College

Soka University of America
Solano Community College
Somerset Community College
Sonoma State University
South Arkansas Community College
South Carolina State University
South Central Technical College
South Dakota School of Mines and Technology
South Dakota State University
South Florida Community College
South Georgia College
South Louisiana Community College
South Mountain Community College
South Orange County Community College
South Pacific University
South Plains College
South Puget Sound Community College
South Seattle Community College
South Suburban College
South Texas College of Law
South Texas Community College
Southampton College
Southeast Arkansas Technical College
Southeast College of Technology
Southeast Community College
Southeast Missouri State University
Southeast Technical Institute
Southeastern Community College
Southeastern Illinois College
Southeastern Louisiana University
Southeastern Oklahoma State University
Southeastern University
Southern Adventist University
Southern Arkansas University
Southern California University of Professional
  Studies
Southern Connecticut State University
Southern Illinois University at Carbondale
Southern Illinois University at Edwardsville
Southern Maine Technical College
Southern Methodist University
Southern Nazarene University
Southern Oregon State College

Southern Polytechnic State Univerisity
Southern State Community College
Southern Union State Community College
Southern University, Baton Rouge
Southern University, New Orleans
Southern University, Shreveport-Bossier City
Southern Utah University
Southern Vermont College
Southern Virginia College
Southern Wesleyan University
Southern West Virginia Community and
   Technical College
Southside Virginia Community College
Southwest Baptist University
Southwest Bible College and Seminary
Southwest Florida College
Southwest Missouri State University
Southwest Missouri State University-West
   Plains
Southwest School of Electronics
Southwest State University
Southwest Tennessee Community College
Southwest Texas State University
Southwest Wisconsin Technical College
Southwestern Adventist University
Southwestern Assemblies of God University
Southwestern College
Southwestern Community College
Southwestern Indian Polytechnic Institute
Southwestern Michigan College
Southwestern Oklahoma State University
Southwestern Oregon Community College
Southwestern University
Southwestern University School of Law
Spalding University
Sparks State Technical College
Spartanburg Methodist College
Spartanburg Technical College
Spelman College
Spencerian College-Lexington
Spencerian College-Louisville
Spokane Community College
Spokane Falls Community College

Spoon River College
Spring Arbor College
Spring Hill College
Springfield College
Springfield Technical Community College
St. Charles County Community College
St. Clair County Community College
St. Cloud Technical College
St. George's University
St. Gregory's University
St. Johns River Community College
St. Louis Community College
St. Paul Technical College
St. Petersburg Junior College
St. Philip's College
Stamford International College
Stanford University
Stanly Community College
Stark State College of Technology
State Center Community College District
State Technical Institute at Memphis
State University of New York at Albany
State University of New York at
   Binghamton
State University of New York at Buffalo
State University of New York at Stony
   Brook
State University of New York College at
   Brockport
State University of New York College at
   Buffalo
State University of New York College at
   Cortland
State University of New York College at
   Farmingdale
State University of New York College at
   Fredonia
State University of New York College at
   Geneseo
State University of New York College at New
   Paltz
State University of New York College at
   Oneonta

State University of New York College at
Oswego

State University of New York College at
Plattsburgh

State University of New York College at
Potsdam

State University of New York College at
Purchase

State University of New York College Maritime
College at Fort Schuyler

State University of New York College of
Agriculture and Technology, Cobleskill

State University of New York College of
Agriculture and Technology, Morrisville

State University of New York College of
Environmental Science and Forestry

State University of New York College of
Technology at Alfred

State University of New York Institute of
Technology at Alfred

State University of New York Institute of
Technology at Canton

State University of New York Institute of
Technology at Delhi

State University of New York Institute of
Technology at Utica/Rome

State University of West Georgia

Stefan University, The

Stephen F. Austin State University

Stephens College

Sterling College

Stetson University

Stevens Institute of Technology

Stillman College

Stonehill College

Stratford College

Strayer University

Suffolk Community College

Suffolk University

Sul Ross State University

Sullivan County Community College

Sullivan University

Summit University of Louisiana

Surry Community College

Susquehanna University

Sussex County Community College

Swarthmore College

Sweet Briar College

Syracuse University

Tabor College

Tacoma Community College

Taft College

Talladega College

Tallahassee Community College

Tarleton State University

Tarrant Count Junior College

Taylor University

Technical Career Institute

Technical College of the Lowcountry

Teikyo Marycrest University

Teikyo Post University

Temple College

Temple University

Tennessee State University

Tennessee Technological University

Terra Community College

Texarkana Community College

Texas A&M International University

Texas A&M University

Texas A&M University-Commerce

Texas A&M University-Corpus Christi

Texas A&M University-Kingsville

Texas A&M University-Texarkana

Texas Christian University

Texas Lutheran University

Texas Southern University

Texas State Technical College

Texas Tech University

Texas Wesleyan University

Texas Women's University

Thaddeus Stevens College of Technology

Thiel College

Thomas Aquinas College

Thomas College

Thomas Cooley Law School

Thomas Edison State College

Thomas Jefferson University
Thomas More College
Thomas Nelson Community College
Thompson Institute
Three Rivers Community College
Three Rivers Community-Technical College
Tidewater Community College
Tillamook Bay Community College
Toccoa Falls College
Tomball College
Tompkins Cortland Community College
Tougaloo College
Touro College
Towson University
TransPacific Hawaii College
Transylvania University
Treasure Valley Community College
Trevecca Nazarene University
Tri-County Community College
Trident Technical College
Trinidad State Junior College
Trinity Baptist College
Trinity Christian College
Trinity College [CT]
Trinity College [DC]
Trinity College of Florida
Trinity College of Vermont
Trinity International University
Trinity University
Trinity Valley Community College
Tri-State University
Triton College
Trocaire College
Troy State University
Truckee Meadows Community College
Truman College
Truman State University
Tufts University
Tulane University
Tulsa Community College
Tunxis Community-Technical College
Turtle Mountain Community
Tusculum College

Tuskegee University
Tyler Junior Community College
Ulster County Community College
Umpqua Community College
Union College
Union County College
Union Institute, The
Union Theological Seminary
Union University
United States Air Force Academy
United States Coast Guard Academy
United States International University
United States Merchant Marine Academy
United States Military Academy
United States Naval Academy
United States Open University
United States Sports Academy
Unity College
University College of Bangor
University of Advancing Computer Technology
University of Akron
University of Alabama
University of Alabama at Birmingham
University of Alabama in Huntsville
University of Alaska Anchorage
University of Alaska Fairbanks
University of Alaska Southeast
University of Arizona
University of Arkansas at Little Rock
University of Arkansas at Monticello
University of Arkansas at Pine Bluff
University of Arkansas Community College
  at Batesville
University of Arkansas Community College
  at Hope
University of Arkansas, Fayetteville
University of Baltimore
University of Bridgeport
University of California, Berkeley
University of California, Davis
University of California, Hastings College
  of Law
University of California, Irvine

University of California, Los Angeles
University of California, Merced
University of California, Riverside
University of California, San Diego
University of California, San Francisco
University of California, Santa Barbara
University of California, Santa Cruz
University of Central Arkansas
University of Central Florida
University of Central Oklahoma
University of Charleston
University of Chicago
University of Cincinnati
University of Colorado
University of Colorado, Colorado Springs
University of Colorado, Denver
University of Connecticut
University of Dallas
University of Dayton
University of Delaware
University of Denver
University of Detroit Mercy
University of Dubuque
University of Evansville
University of Findlay
University of Florida
University of Georgia
University of Guam
University of Hartford
University of Hawaii
University of Hawaii, Hilo
University of Hawaii, West Oahu
University of Health Sciences College of
  Osteopathic Medicine
University of Houston
University of Houston at Clear Lake
University of Houston at Downtown
University of Houston at Victoria
University of Idaho
University of Illinois at Chicago
University of Illinois at Springfield
University of Illinois at Urbana-Champaign
University of Indianapolis

University of Iowa
University of Judaism
University of Kansas
University of Kansas Medical Center
University of Kentucky
University of La Vernee
University of Louisiana at Lafayette
University of Louisiana at Monroe
University of Louisville
University of Maine
University of Maine at Fort Kent
University of Maine at Presque Isle
University of Maine System
University of Mary Hardin-Baylor
University of Maryland at Baltimore
University of Maryland at College Park
University of Maryland Baltimore County
University of Maryland Eastern Shore
University of Maryland University College
University of Massachusetts at Amherst
University of Massachusetts at Boston
University of Massachusetts at Dartmouth
University of Massachusetts at Lowell
University of Medicine and Dentistry of New
  Jersey
University of Memphis
University of Miami
University of Michigan-Ann Arbor
University of Michigan-Dearborn
University of Michigan-Flint
University of Minnesota-Crookston
University of Minnesota-Duluth
University of Minnesota-Morris
University of Minnesota-Twin Cities
University of Mississippi
University of Missouri-Columbia
University of Missouri-Kansas City
University of Missouri-Rolla
University of Missouri-Saint Louis
University of Montana, Missoula
University of Montevallo
University of Natural Medicine
University of Nebraska, Kearney

University of Nebraska, Lincoln
University of Nebraska, Omaha
University of Nevada Las Vegas
University of Nevada Reno
University of New England
University of New Hampshire, Durham
University of New Haven
University of New Mexico
University of New Mexico at Gallup
University of New Mexico at Valencia Campus
University of New Orleans
University of Newport
University of North Alabama
University of North Carolina at Asheville
University of North Carolina at Chapel Hill
University of North Carolina at Charlotte
University of North Carolina at Greensboro
University of North Carolina at Pembroke
University of North Carolina at
  Wilmington
University of North Dakota
University of North Florida
University of North Texas
University of Northern Colorado
University of Northern Iowa
University of Northern Washington
University of Notre Dame
University of Oklahoma
University of Oregon
University of Orlando
University of Osteopathic Medicine and Health
  Science
University of Pennsylvania
University of Phoenix
University of Pittsburgh
University of Pittsburgh at Bradford
University of Pittsburgh at Greensburg
University of Pittsburgh at Johnstown
University of Portland
University of Puerto Rico
University of Puerto Rico, Mayaguez
University of Puerto Rico, Rio Piedras
University of Puget Sound

University of Redlands
University of Rhode Island
University of Richmond
University of Rio Grande
University of Rochester
University of Saint Francis
University of Saint Thomas [MN]
University of Saint Thomas [TX]
University of San Diego
University of San Francisco
University of Sararsota
University of Science and Arts of Oklahoma
University of Scranton
University of Sioux Falls
University of South Alabama
University of South Carolina
University of South Carolina, Aiken
University of South Carolina, Spartanburg
University of South Dakota
University of South Florida
University of Southern California
University of Southern Colorado
University of Southern Indiana
University of Southern Maine
University of Southern Mississippi
University of St. Francis
University of Tampa
University of Tennessee, Chattanooga
University of Tennessee, Knoxville
University of Tennessee, Martin
University of Tennessee, Memphis
University of Texas at Arlington
University of Texas at Austin
University of Texas at Brownsville
University of Texas at Dallas
University of Texas at El Paso
University of Texas at San Antonio
University of Texas at Tyler
University of Texas Health Center at Tyler
University of Texas Health Science Center at
  Houston
University of Texas Health Science Center at
  San Antonio

University of Texas Medical Branch
University of Texas of the Permian Basin
University of Texas Southwestern Medical
  Center
University of Texas-Pan American
University of the Arts
University of the District of Columbia
University of the Incarnate Word
University of the Ozarks
University of the Pacific
University of the Sciences in Philadelphia
University of the South
University of the Virgin Islands
University of Toledo
University of Tulsa
University of Utah
University of Vermont
University of Virginia
University of Washington
University of West Alabama
University of West Florida
University of Wisconsin-Eau Claire
University of Wisconsin-Green Bay
University of Wisconsin-La Crosse
University of Wisconsin-Madison
University of Wisconsin-Milwaukee
University of Wisconsin-Oshkosh
University of Wisconsin-Parkside
University of Wisconsin-Platteville
University of Wisconsin-River Falls
University of Wisconsin-Stevens Point
University of Wisconsin-Stout
University of Wisconsin-Superior
University of Wisconsin-Whitewater
University of Wyoming
University System of Maryland
Upper Iowa University
Urban College of Boston, The
Ursinus College
Ursuline College
Utah State University
Utah Valley State College
Utica College

Valdosta State University
Valencia Community College
Valley City State University
Valparaiso University
Vance-Granville Community College
Vanderbilt University
Vanguard University
Vassar College
Vennard College
Ventura College
Vermont Technical College
Vernon Regional Junior College
Victor Valley Community College
Victoria College
Villa Julie College
Villanova University
Vincennes University
Virginia College
Virginia Commonwealth University
Virginia Community College System
Virginia Highlands Community College
Virginia Intermont College
Virginia Military Institute
Virginia Polytechnic Institute and State
  Univeristy
Virginia State University
Virginia Union University
Virginia Wesleyan College
Virginia Western Community College
Vista College
Viterbo College
Volunteer State Community College
Voorhees College
Wabash College
Wagner College
Wake Forest University
Walden University
Waldorf College
Walla Walla College
Walla Walla Community College
Walsh University
Walters State Community College
Warner Pacific College

Warren County Community College
Warren Wilson College
Wartburg College
Washburn University
Washington & Jefferson College
Washington and Lee University
Washington College
Washington County Technical College
Washington State Community College
Washington State University
Washington University in Saint Louis
Washtenaw Community College
Waubonsee Community College
Waukesha County Technical College
Waycross College
Wayland Baptist University
Wayne Community College
Wayne County Community College
Wayne State College
Wayne State University
Weatherford College
Webb Institute
Weber State University
Webster University
Wellesley College
Wells College
Wenatchee Valley College
Wentworth Institute of Technology
Wentworth Military Academy and Junior
  College
Wesley College
Wesleyan College
Wesleyan University
West Chester University of Pennsylvania
West Coast University
West Georgia Technical College
West Hills Community College District
West Liberty State College
West Los Angeles College
West Shore Community College
West Texas A&M University
West Valley-Mission Community College
  District

West Valley College
West Virginia Institute of Technology
West Virginia Northern Community College
West Virginia State College
West Virginia University
West Virginia University Parkersburg
West Virginia Wesleyan College
Westark College
Westchester Community College
Western Baptist College
Western Business College
Western Carolina University
Western Connecticut State University
Western Governors University
Western Illinois University
Western International University
Western Iowa Tech Community College
Western Kentucky University
Western Maryland College
Western Michigan University
Western Montana College
Western Nebraska Community College
Western Nevada Community College
Western New England College
Western New Mexico University
Western Oregon University
Western Piedmont Community College
Western State College
Western State University College of Law
Western States Chiropractic College
Western Technical Institute
Western Texas College
Western University of Health Sciences
Western Washington University
Western Wisconsin Technical College
Western Wyoming Community College
Westfield State College
Westminster College [MI]
Westminster College [PA]
Westminster College [UT]
Westminster Theological Seminary
Westminster Theological Seminary in
  California

Westmont College
Westmoreland County Community College
Westwood College of Technology
Whatcom Community College
Wheaton College
Wheeling Jesuit University
Whitman College
Whittier College
Whitworth College
Wichita Area Technical College
Wichita State University
Widener University
Wilberforce University
Wilbur Wright College
Wilkes Community College
Wilkes University
Willamette University
William Howard Taft University
William Jewell College
William Mitchell College of Law
William Paterson University
William Penn College
William Rainey Harper College
William Woods University
Williams Baptist College
Williams College
Williamsburg Technical College
Wilmington College, New Castle Delaware
Wilmington College, Wilmington Ohio
Wilson College
Wilson Technical Community College
Windward Community College
Wingate University
Winona State University
Winston-Salem State University
Winthrop University
Wisconsin Indianhead Technical College
Wisconsin Lutheran College
Wisconsin Technical College System
Wittenberg University
Wofford College
Woodbury University
Woodland Community College

Woods Hole Oceanographic Institution
Worcester Polytechnic Institute
Worcester State College
Wor-Wic Community College
Wright State University
Xavier University of Louisiana
Xavier University [OH]
Yakima Valley Community College
Yale University
Yavapai Community College
Yellowstone Baptist College
Yeshiva University
York College
York College of Pennsylvania
York County Technical College
York Technical College
Yosemite Community College District
Youngstown State University
Yuba Community College District

3

Companies, Nonprofits and Products

1-2-3 [product]
3 IN 1 [product]
3 Musketeers [product]
3Com [company]
3M [company]
4 Kids Entertainment Inc. [company]
5 O'Clock Computers [product]
7-Eleven Inc. [company]
7UP (7 UP; Seven-Up) [product]
9-Lives [product]
15th St. Fisheries [company]
17 Mile Drive [product]
18 Hour [product]
20 Mule Team [product]
20th Century Fox [company]
21st Century Insurance Group [company]
76 [product]
84 Lumber [company]
99 Cents Only Stores [company]
100 Pipers Scotch [product]
409 [product]
1800flowers.com [company]
A&P [company]
A and D [product]
A.1. [product]
A.G. Edwards Inc. [company]
A.H. Belo Corp. [company]

A.O. Smith Corp. [company]
A/S Eksportfinans Norway [company]
AAA [auto club] [company]
AAdvantage [product]
aafes.com [company]
AAirpass [product]
AAR Corp. [company]
Aaron Rents Inc. [company]
Abacus Computer Services [company]
ABB Ltd. [company]
Abbey National P.L.C. [company]
Abbott Laboratories [company]
ABC [company]
abcdistributing.com [company]
Abdomenizer [product]
Abdon Callais Offshore [company]
Abell Foundation Inc., The [nonprofit]
Abell-Hanger Foundation [nonprofit]
Abercrombie & Fitch [company]
Abington Foundation [nonprofit]
Abitibi-Consolidated Inc. [company]
Able Trust, The [nonprofit]
Ableauctions.Com Inc. [company]
Ablest Inc. [company]
ABM Industries Inc. [company]
ABN AMRO Capital Funding Trust [company]
Abney Foundation, The [nonprofit]

Above The Crowd [product]
Above The Rim [product]
Abraxas Petroleum Corp. [company]
Abreu Foundation, Francis L., The [nonprofit]
AC [product]
Academy [product]
Acadia Realty Trust [company]
Acadiana Bancshares Inc.[company]
Accenture [company]
Acceptance Insurance Cos. [company]
Access Direct Telemarket [company]
Access Pharmaceuticals Inc. [company]
Acco [company & product]
Accord Human Resources [company]
Accredited Home Lenders [company]
Accu Treat [product]
Accupril [product]
Accuship.com [company]
Accutane [product]
Ace [product]
Ace Hardware [company]
ACE Ltd. [company]
Achelis Foundation, The [nonprofit]
Ackerley Group Inc. [company]
Ackerman Foundation, Thomas C., The
   [nonprofit]
ACM Inc. [company]
Acme United Corp. [company]
Acorn Foundation, The [nonprofit]
Acoustic Wave [product]
Acrilan [product]
Acrobat [product]
Acrylite [product]
Acs Inc. [company]
ACS International Resources [company]
ACT Manufacturing Inc. [company]
Actibath [product]
Actifed [product]
Actigall [product]
ActionBac [product]
ActionPacker [product]
Actuant Corp. [company]
Adalat CC [product]

Adams Express Co. [company]
Adams Resources & Energy, Inc. [company]
Adderall [product]
Adecco S.A. [company]
Adelphia Communications Corp. [company]
Adexa [product]
Adidas [company & product]
Adiprene [product]
AdMasters [company]
Administaff Inc. [company]
Administradora de Fondos de Pensiones-
   Provida [company]
Admiral [product]
Adobe [company & product]
Adobe Systems [company]
Adolph Coors Co. [company]
Adrenalin [product]
Advanced Automation Technologies [company]
Advanced Composites Technology [company]
Advanced Financial Solutions [company]
Advanced Magnetics Inc. [company]
Advanced Marketing Services Inc. [company]
Advanced Micro Devices Inc. [company]
Advanced Modular Power Systems [company]
Advanced Photonix Inc. [company]
Advanced Semiconductor Engineering Inc.
   [company]
Advanced System Integration [company]
Advanced Systems Design [company]
Advantage Credit International [company]
Advantage Marketing Systems Inc. [company]
Advantica Restaurant Group Inc. [company]
Advest Group Inc. [company]
Advil [product]
Advo Inc. [company]
Aegis Realty Inc. [company]
Aegis Software [company]
AEGON N.V. [company]
Aer Lingus [company]
AeroCentury Corp. [company]
Aeroshell [product]
Aerosonic Corp. [company]
AES Corp., The [company]

AES Trust III [company]
Aetna Inc. [company]
Affiliated Computer Services Inc. [company]
Affiliated Managers Group [company]
AFLAC Inc. [company]
AFL-CIO [nonprofit]
Afrin [product]
AFTA [company & product]
After Eight [product]
After Thoughts [product]
AGCO Corp. [company]
Agere Systems Inc. [company]
Agfa [company & product]
Agilent Technologies Inc. [company]
Agnico-Eagle Mines Limited [company]
Agree [product]
Agree Realty Corp. [company]
Agribrands International Inc. [company]
Agrium Inc. [company]
AGS [company]
Agway Inc. [company]
Ahead Headgear [product]
Ahold [product]
Ahold USA [product]
Ahrens Foundation, Claude W. and Dolly, The
    [nonprofit]
AI Signal Research [company]
Aid Association for Lutherans [nonprofit]
AIG [company]
AIMGlobal Technologies Co. Inc. [company]
AIMS Logistics [company]
Air Jordan [company]
Air Line Pilots Association [nonprofit]
Air Products and Chemicals Inc. [company]
Airborne Freight Corp. [company]
Airborne Inc. [company]
Airbus [company]
AirFlex [product]
Airgas Inc. [company]
Airgas On-line [company]
Airlease Ltd. [company]
Airmax [company]
Airnet Systems Inc. [company]

Airopak [company & product]
Air-Pillo [product]
AirTran Holdings Inc. [company]
Airwalk [product]
AIU [company]
Ajax [product]
Ak Steel Holding Corp. [company]
Akerman, Senterfitt & Eidson [company]
Akili Systems Group [company]
Al Pharma Inc. [company]
Alabama Power Co. [company]
Alamo Group Inc. [company]
Alaris Medical Inc. [company]
Alaska Air Group Inc. [company]
Alaskan Automotive Distributing [company]
Albemarle Corp. [company]
Alberta Energy Co. Ltd. [company]
Alberto Culver Co. [company]
Albertson Foundation, J.A. and Kathryn, The
    [nonprofit]
Albertson's Inc. [company]
Albin Engineering Services [company]
Albuterol [product]
Alcan [company]
Alcan Inc. [company]
Alcatel [company]
Alcoa, Inc. [company]
Alcoholic Beverage Medical Research
    Foundation, The [nonprofit]
Alesse [product]
Aleve [product]
Alexanders Inc. [company]
Alexandria Real Estate Equities Inc. [company]
Alfa Romeo [company & product]
Alfred Dunhill [company & product]
Algoma Steel [company]
Alico [company]
Alka-Seltzer [product]
All Star [product]
All-American Term Trust Inc. [company]
All-Bran [product]
All-Clad [product]
Alleghany Corp. [company]

Allegheny Technologies Inc. [company]

Allegiant Bancorp Inc. [company]

Allegra [product]

Allegra-D [product]

Allen [product]

Allen Charitable Foundation, Paul G., The [nonprofit]

Allen Forest Protection Foundation, Paul G., The [nonprofit]

Allen Foundation for Medical Research, Paul G., The [nonprofit]

Allen Foundation for the Arts, Paul G., The [nonprofit]

Allen Foundation Inc.. The [nonprofit]

Allen Telecommunication Inc. [company]

Allen Virtual Education Foundation, Paul G., The [nonprofit]

Allengheny Energy Inc. [company]

Allerest [product]

Allergan Inc. [company]

Allete [company]

Allfirst Financial Inc. [company]

Allgauer's [company]

Alliance All-Market Advantage Fund Inc. [company & product]

Alliance Bancorp of New England Inc. [company]

Alliance Capital Management L.P. [company]

Alliance Consulting [company]

Alliance Forest Products Inc. [company]

Alliance Healthcare Foundation [company]

Alliance of Professionals & Consultants [company]

Alliance World Dollar Government Fund [company]

Alliant Energy Corp. [company]

Alliant Techsystems Inc. [company]

Allianz AG [company]

Allied Group [company]

Allied Holdings Inc. [company]

Allied Irish Banks P.L.C. [company]

Allied Research Corp. [company]

Allied Waste Industries Inc. [company]

AlliedSignal [company]

Allink [company]

Allmerica Financial Corp. [company]

Allmerica Securities Trust [company]

Allopurinol [product]

Allou Health & Beauty Care Inc. [company]

alloy.com [company]

Allstate Corp., The [company]

Alltel Corp. [company]

Alltrista Corp. [company]

Almaden [product]

Alogent [product]

Alpert Foundation, Herb, The [company]

Alpha Data [company]

Alpha Pro Tech Ltd. [company]

Alpha Telcom [company]

Alphagan [product]

AlphaSoft Services [company]

Alpine [product]

Alpine Group Inc., The [company]

Alprazolam [product]

Alstom [company]

Alston & Bird [law firm] [company]

Alta Resources [company]

Altace [company]

AltaVista [company]

Alteon Inc. [company]

Altera Corp. [company]

Alterra Healthcare Corp. [company]

Altheimer & Gray [company]

Altman Foundation, Jenifer, The [nonprofit]

Altoids [product]

ALZA Corp. [company]

Alzheimer's Association [nonprofit]

Amaryl [company]

Amateur Athletic Foundation of Los Angeles, The, [nonprofit]

Amazon Foundation [nonprofit]

Amazon.Com Inc. [company]

AMB Property Corp. [company]

Ambac Financial Group Inc. [company]

Ambrosia [product]

Ambush [product]

AMC Computer [company]
AMC Entertainment Inc. [company]
Amcast Industrial Corp. [company]
Amcol International Corp. [company]
AMCON Distributing Co. [company]
Amdocs Ltd. [company]
Amerada Hess Corp. [company]
Amerco [company]
Ameren Corp. [company]
America First Mortgage Investments Inc.
  [company]
America Online Inc. [company]
America West Airlines Inc. [company]
America West Holding Corp. [company]
America/Center Café [company]
America's Second Harvest [nonprofit]
American AAdvantage Funds [company &
  product]
American Axle & Manufacturing Holdings Inc.
  [company]
American Bank of Connecticut [company]
American Bible Society [nonprofit]
American Biltrite Inc. [company]
American Business Products Inc. [company]
American Cafe [company]
American Cancer Society [nonprofit]
American Classic [product]
American Coin Merchandising Inc.
  [company]
American Diabetes Association [nonprofit]
American Eagle [company]
American Electric Power Co. Inc. [company]
American Express (AmEx) [company]
American Express Co. [company]
American Family Mutual Insurance Co.
  [company]
American Financial Group Inc. [company]
American General Capital L.L.C. [company]
American General Corp. [company]
American Greetings Corp. [company]
American Health Properties Inc. [company]
American Heart Association [nonprofit]
American Home Products Corp. [company]

American Income Fund Inc. [company &
  product]
American Industrial Properties REIT
  [company & product]
American Insured Mortgage Investors
  [company]
American International Group Inc. [company]
American Israeli Paper Mills Ltd. [company]
American Italian Pasta Co. [company]
American Land Lease Inc. [company]
American League [company]
American Lung Association [nonprofit]
American Management Systems Inc. [company]
American Manufacturing and Machine
  [company]
American Medical Security Group Inc.
  [company]
American Mortgage Acceptance Co. [company]
American Municipal Income Portfolio Inc.
  [company]
American Municipal Term Trust Inc.
  [com-pany]
American Museum of Natural History
  [nonprofit]
American National Can Group Inc. [company]
American National Insurance Co. [company]
American Park Network [company]
American Power Conversion Corp. [company]
American Precision Industries Inc. [company]
American Psych Systems [company]
American Realty Investors Inc. [company]
American Red Cross [nonprofit]
American Residential Investment Trust Inc.
  [company]
American Retirement Corp. [company]
American Safety Insurance Group Ltd.
  [company]
American Science and Engineering Inc.
  [company]
American Select Portfolio Inc. [company]
American Shared Hospital Services [company]
American Standard Cos. Inc. [company]
American States Water Co. [company]

American Strategic Income Portfolio Inc. [company]

American Technical Ceramics Corp. [company]

American Tower Corp. [company]

American Vanguard Corp. [company]

American Water Works Co. Inc. [company]

America's Media Marketing [company]

Americredit Corp. [company]

Amerigas Partners L.P. [company]

Amerind Foundation Inc., The [nonprofit]

AmeriSource Health Corp. [company]

Ameritech [company]

AmeriVest Properties Inc. [company]

Ameron Internation Corp. [company]

Amerus Group Co. [company]

Amerus Life Holdings Inc. [company]

Ames Department Stores Inc. [company]

Ametek Inc. [company]

AMF Bowling Inc. [company]

Amgen Inc. [company]

Amica Mutual Insurance Co. [company]

Amitriptyline [product]

Amkor Technology Inc. [company]

AMLI Residential Properties Trust [company]

Amoco [company]

Amoxicillin [product]

Amoxil [product]

AMP [company]

AMPCO Pittsburgh Corp. [company]

Ampex Corp. [company]

Amphenol Corp. [company]

AMR Corp. [company]

AMREP Corp. [company]

Amsouth BanCorp. [company]

Amtrak [company]

Amtran Inc. [company]

AMVESCAP P.L.C. [company]

Amway [company]

Amwest Insurance Group Inc. [company]

AMX International [company]

Amy Foundation [company]

Anacin [product]

Anacon [company]

Anadarko Petroleum Corp. [company]

Anafranil [product]

Analog Devices Inc. [company]

Anandron [company]

Anchor [product]

ANCO [company]

Andersen Foundation, Hugh J., The [nonprofit]

André [product]

Andrea Electronics Corp. [company]

Andrews & Kurth [company]

andysauctions.com [company]

andysgarage.com [company]

Angel Sales [company]

Angelica Corp. [company]

Angelica Foundation [nonprofit]

Angels on Track Foundation, The [nonprofit]

Anglamol [product]

Anglogold Ltd. [company]

Angus Barn, The [company]

Anheuser-Busch Cos. Inc. [company]

Animaniacs [product]

Annaly Mortgage Management Inc. [company]

Anne Klein [company & product]

Anne Klein II [product]

Annenberg Foundation, The [nonprofit]

AnnTaylor [company & product]

AnnTaylor Stores Corp. [product]

Ansaid [product]

ANSO [product]

Answer [product]

Ant Farm [product]

Antex Biologics Inc. [company]

Anthem Insurance Cos. Inc. [company]

Anthony's Pier 4 [company]

Anthracite Capital Inc. [company]

Antibacterial Plus [product]

Anusol [product]

Anvil [product]

Anworth Asset Mortgage Corp. [company]

AO Tatneft [company]

AOL Time Warner Inc. [company]

aol.com [company]

Aon Corp. [company]

Apache Corp. [company]
Apartment Investment & Management Co. [company]
APB Energy [company]
Apex Mortgage Capital Inc. [company]
Apex Municipal Fund Inc. [company]
Apex Silver Mines Limited [company]
APG [product]
Apogent Technologies Inc. [company]
Apollo Design Technology [company]
Apollo Management L.P. [company]
Appalachian Power Co. [company]
Apple [company]
Apple Computer Inc. [company]
Apple Jacks [product]
apple.com [company]
Applera [company]
Applera Corp. [company]
Application Objects [company]
Applied Card Systems [company]
Applied Graphics Technologies Inc. [company]
Applied Industrial Technologies Inc. [company]
Applied Materials Inc. [company]
Applied Power [company]
Apria Healthcare Group Inc. [company]
Aprica [product]
AptarGroup Inc. [company]
APW Ltd. [company]
Aqua Net [product]
Aqua Velva [product]
AquaCell Technologies Inc. [company]
Aquacoat [product]
Aquadag [product]
Aquaflex [product]
Aquafresh [product]
Aqua-Lung [product]
Aquascape Designs [company]
Aquateric [product]
Aquila Inc. [company]
Aracruz Celulose [company]
Araldite [company]
ARAMARK Corp. [company]
Arbitron Inc. [company]

Arby's [company]
Arca Foundation, The [nonprofit]
Arcadia Financial Ltd. [company]
arcamax.com [company]
Arch Chemical Inc. [company]
Arch Coal Inc [company]
Archer Daniels Midland Co. [company]
Archie [product]
Archstone Communities Trust [company]
Archstone Foundation, The [nonprofit]
ARCO [company]
Arcus Foundation [nonprofit]
Arden Realty Inc. [company]
Arena & Co. [company]
Arent Fox Kintner Plotkin & Kahn [company]
Argentina Fund Inc., The [company]
ARGO [product]
Argo Bancorp Inc. [company]
Argosy Gaming Co. [company]
Arguss Communications Inc. [company]
Aricept [company]
Aris [product]
Arizona Land Income Corp. [company]
Arkansas Best Corp. [company]
Arm & Hammer [company]
Armco Inc. [company]
Armoc Inc. [company]
Armor All [product]
Armor Holdings Inc. [company]
Armstrong Foundation, Ethel Louise, The [nonprofit]
Armstrong Holdings Inc. [company]
Armstrong World Industries Inc. [company]
Arnold & Porter [company]
Arrhythmia Research Technology Inc. [company]
Arrid [product]
Arrow [company & product]
Arrow Electronics Inc. [company]
Arsalyn Foundation [nonprofit]
Art Institute of Chicago, The [nonprofit]
Arter & Hadden [company]
Arthritis Foundation [nonprofit]

Arthrotec [product]
Arthur J. Gallagher & Co. [company]
Artis & Associates [company]
Aruba Beach Café [company]
ARV Assisted Living Inc. [company]
Arvin Industries Inc. [company]
AS/400 [product]
Asa Ltd. [company]
ASAP [company]
Ascend HR Solutions [company]
Ascent Computing Group [company]
Ashanti Goldfields Co. Ltd. [company]
ashford.com [company]
Ashland Inc. [company]
Asia Pacific Fund Inc., The [nonprofit]
Asia Pacific Resources International Holding
　Ltd. [company]
Asia Pacific Wire & Cable [company]
Asia Satellite Telecommunications Holdings
　Limited [company]
Asian Garden [company]
ASK Data Communications [company]
Ask Jeeves Inc. [company]
Aspercreme [product]
Assisted Living Concepts Inc. [company]
Associated Estates Realty Corp. [company]
Associates First Capital Corp. [company]
Assured Stock Program [company]
Asterite [product]
Aston Martin [company & product]
Astoria Financial Corp. [company]
AstraZeneca Group P.L.C. [company]
AstroTurf [product]
AT [product]
AT Plastics Inc. [company]
AT&T [company]
AT&T Capital Corp. [company]
AT&T Corp. [company]
Atari [company]
ATEC Group Inc. [company]
Atenolol [product]
Athalon [product]
Athletic X-Press [product]

Atichison Casting Corp. [company]
Atlanta Fish Market [company]
Atlanta Foundation, The [company]
Atlantic Corporate Interiors [company]
Atlantic Premium Brands Ltd. [company]
Atlantic Richfield Co. [company]
Atlantic Tele-Network Inc. [company]
Atlantic.Net [company]
Atlantis Plastics Inc. [company]
Atlas [product]
Atlas Air Worldwide [company]
Atlas Pipeline Partners L.P. [company]
Atmel [company]
Atmos Energy Corp. [company]
ATP Oil & Gas [company]
Atrovent [company]
ATSI Communications Inc. [company]
Atwood Oceanics Inc. [company]
ATX Forms [company]
Audi [company & product]
Audio Visual Services Corp. [company]
Audio-Animatronics [company & product]
Audiovox Corp. [company]
Augmentin [company]
Aunt Jemima [product]
Aureomycin [product]
Aurora Foods Inc. [company]
Aurora Pink [company]
Austin-Bailey Health and Wellness [product]
Australia and New Zealand Banking Group
　Ltd. [company]
Austria Fund Inc., The [company]
Authoria [company]
Auto Check [company]
Auto Color [product]
Auto Syringe [product]
Autoharp [product]
Autolite [company]
Autoliv Inc. [company]
Automatic Data Processing Inc. [company]
AutoNation Inc. [company]
Auto-Owners Insurance Co. [company]
Autophoretic [product]

Auto-Train Corp. [company]
AutoZone [company]
AutoZone Inc. [company]
Avalon Holdings Corp. [company]
Avalonbay Communities Inc. [company]
AVANIR Pharmaceuticals [company]
Avapro [company]
Avaya Inc. [company]
Aveeno [company & product]
Aventis S.A. [company]
Avenue A Inc. [company]
Avery Dennison Corp. [company]
Avesta Computer Services [company]
Avia [product]
Aviall Inc. [company]
Avicel [product]
Avis Rent A Car Inc. [company]
Avista Corp. [company]
Avitar Inc. [company]
Avnet Inc. [company]
Avocet Capital Management L.P. [company]
Avon Products Inc. [company]
Avx Corp. [company]
Axid [company]
AXS-One Inc. [company]
Azco Mining Inc. [company]
Azmacort [company]
Aztar Corp. [company]
Azurix Corp. [company]
Azz Inc. [company]
B&B Technologies [company]
B+H Ocean Carriers Ltd. [company]
Babcock & Wilcox [company]
Babcock Foundation Inc., Mary Reynolds [nonprofit]
Baby Alive [product]
Baby Magic [product]
Baby Ruth [product]
babycenter.com [company]
BabyGap [company]
Baby-Sitters Club, The [company]
Bac*Os bacon [product]
Bacardi Baccarat [product]

BACOU USA Inc. [company]
Bactroban [product]
Bader Foundation Inc., Helen, The [nonprofit]
Badger Meter, Inc. [company]
Baggies [product]
Bagnoud Foundation, Francois-Xavier, The [nonprofit]
Baileys [product]
Bairnco Corp. [company]
Bake-Off [product]
Baker & Daniels [company]
Baker & Hostetler [company]
Baker & McKenzie [company]
Baker Hughes Inc. [company]
Baker's Choice [product]
Balanced Care Corp. [company]
Balchem Corp. [company]
Baldor Electric Co. [company]
Baldwin Technology Co. Inc. [company]
Ball Corp. [company]
Ball Park [product]
Ballantine's Scotch [product]
Ballantyne Omaha Inc. [company]
Ballard Spahr Andrews & Ingersoll [company]
Ballatore [product]
Bally Total Fitness Holding Corp. [company]
Balm Barr [product]
Ban [product]
Ban Lon [product]
Banana Republic [company]
bananarepublic.com [company]
Banco Rio de la Plata S.A. [company]
Banco Santander de Puerto Rico [company]
Banco Santander-Chile [company]
Banco Santiago [company]
Banco Wiese Surameris [company]
BanColombia S.A. [company]
Bancroft Convertible Fund Inc. [company]
BancWest Corp. [company]
Bandag [company]
Bandag Inc. [company]
Band-Aid [product]
Bang & Olufsen [company]

Bangor Hydro Electric Co. [company]
Bank of America Corp. [company]
Bank of Montreal [company]
Bank of New York Co. Inc., The [company]
Bank of Texas N.A. [company]
Bank of Tokyo Mitsubishi Ltd. [company]
Bank One Corp. [company]
Bank United Corp. [company]
Bank UTD Houston Texas [company]
Bankatlantic [company]
Banknorth Group [company]
Banners [company]
Banta Corp. [company]
Baptist Community Ministries of New Orleans [nonprofit]
Bar Harbor Bankshares Inc. [company]
Barbie [product]
Barcalounger [product]
BarCharts [product]
Barclays [company]
Barclays P.L.C. [company]
Barnes & Noble Inc. [company]
Barnes & Thornburg [company]
Barnes Group Inc. [company]
Barnwell Industries Inc. [company]
Barr Laboratories Inc. [company]
Barrett Resources Corp. [company]
Barrick Gold Corp. [company]
Barrister Global Services Network Inc. [company]
Barry R G Corp. [company]
Barth Foundation, William E., The [company]
Bartles & Jaymes [company]
Bartol Foundation, Stockton Rush, The [nonprofit]
Barton & Guestier [company]
BASE Consulting Group [company]
BASF [company]
Baskin-Robbins [company]
Bass [company]
Bass Foundation, Lee and Ramona, The [nonprofit]
Bass P.L.C. [company]

Batman [product]
Battle Mountain Gold Co. [company]
Bausch & Lomb Inc. [company]
Baxter International Inc. [company]
Bay State Bancorp [company]
BayCorp Holdings Ltd. [company]
Bayer [company & product]
Bayer Institute for Health Care Communication, The [nonprofit]
Bayou Steel Corp. [company]
Bayport Foundation, The [company]
BB&T Corp. [company]
BBDO Worldwide [company]
Beacon [product]
Beaird Foundation, Charles T., The [nonprofit]
Beanie Babies [product]
Beano [product]
Bears Stearns & Co. Inc. [product]
Beaulieu [product]
BeaverHome.com [company]
Beazer Homes USA, Inc. [company]
Beckman Coulter Inc. [company]
Beckman Foundation, Arnold and Mabel, The [nonprofit]
Beck's [product]
Becton, Dickinson and Co. [company]
Bed Bath & Beyond Inc. [company]
Bedford Property Investors Inc. [company]
Beech-Nut [company & product]
Beefaroni [product]
Beefeater [product]
Beetle [product]
BEI Technologies [company]
Beijing Yanhua Petrochemical [company]
Beim Foundation, The [nonprofit]
Belco Oil & Gas Corp. [company]
Belden Inc. [company]
Belk Inc. [company]
Belks [company]
Bell [company]
Bell & Howell Co. [company]
Bell Atlantic Corp. [company]
Bell Foundation, James Ford, The [nonprofit]

Bell Industries Inc. [company]
Bell Microproducts Inc. [company]
BellSouth Corp. [company]
Belz Richard [company]
Bema Gold Corp. [company]
Bemis Co. Inc. [company]
Ben & Jerry's [company]
Ben Benson's Steakhouse [company]
Benadryl [product]
Bench Top [product]
Benchmark Electronics Inc. [company]
Bendix [company]
Benedum Foundation, Claude Worthington, The [nonprofit]
Benetton [company]
Benetton Group S.P.A. [company]
Ben-Gay [product]
Benson & Hedges [product]
Bentley [company & product]
Bentley Pharmaceuticals Inc. [company]
Benton Foundation, The [nonprofit]
Benton Oil & Gas Co. [company]
Benylin [product]
Beretta [product]
Bergdorf Goodman [company]
Bergen Brunswig Corp. [company]
Berger Foundation, H.N. & Frances, The [nonprofit]
Bergstrom Capital Corp. [company]
Berkshire Hathaway Inc. [company]
Berkshire Hills Bancorp Inc. [company]
Berlitz International Inc. [company]
Bern's Steak House [company]
Bernsen Foundation, Grace and Franklin, The [nonprofit]
Berry Petroleum Co. [company]
Best Buy Co. Inc. [company]
Best Computer Supplies [company]
Best Foods [company]
Best of Times, The [company]
Bestfoods [company]
Betah Associates [company]
Bethlehem Steel Corp. [company]

Better Homes and Families [company & product]
Better Homes and Gardens [company & product]
Betty Crocker [company]
Beveridge Foundation Inc., Frank Stanley, The [nonprofit]
Beverly Enterprises Inc. [company]
Bexil Corp. [company]
beyond.com [company]
BFGoodrich [company]
BFGoodrich Co., The [company]
BHC Communications Inc. [company]
Bianchi [product]
Biaxin [product]
Bic [product]
Big Boy [product]
Big Brothers Big Sisters of America [nonprofit]
Big City Radio Inc. [company]
Big Gulp [product]
Big Mac [product]
Big Red [product]
Big Wheel [product]
bigstar.com [company]
Billy Graham Evangelistic Association [nonprofit]
Billy The Kid [product]
Bindley Western Industries Inc. [company]
Bingham Foundation, William, The [nonprofit]
Binker International Inc. [company]
Bio-Aqua Systems [company]
BioLabs Inc. [company]
Biomatrix Inc. [company]
Bionova Holding Corp. [company]
Bio-Rad Laboratories Inc. [company]
BioTime Inc. [company]
Birkenstock [product]
Birmingham Foundation [nonprofit]
Birmingham Steel Corp. [company]
Birmingham Utilities, Inc. [company]
Bisquick [product]
Bissell [company & product]
Bit-O-Honey [product]

Bituthene [product]
Bizstrata [product]
BJ Services Co. [company]
BJ's Wholesale Club [company]
BJ's Wholesale Club, Inc. [company]
BL Cos. [company]
Black and Decker Corp. [company]
Black Gold [company]
Black Hills Corp. [company]
Blackglama [product]
BlackHawk Information Services [company]
Blackrock Inc. [company]
Blackwell Sanders Peper Martin [company]
Blain Olsen White Gurr Advertising [company]
Blair Corp. [company]
Blakemore Foundation, The [nonprofit]
Blanch E.W. Holdings Inc. [company]
Blandin Foundation, The [company]
Blank Family Foundation, Arthur M., The
  [nonprofit]
Blank Rome Comisky & McCauley [company]
Blimpie International Inc. [company]
Blockbuster Inc. [company]
Blockbuster Video [company]
Blonder Tongue Laboratories Inc. [company]
Bloomingdale's [company]
Blossom Hill [product]
Blount International Inc. [company]
Blow Pop [product]
Blowitz-Ridgeway Foundation, The [nonprofit]
Blue Chip Value Fund Inc. [company]
Blue Creek [product]
Blue Cross [nonprofit]
Blue Ocean Software [company]
Blue Ribbon [product]
Blue Square-Israel Ltd. [company]
Blue's Clues [product]
Bluegreen Corp. [company]
Blyth Industries Inc. [company]
BMC Industries Inc. [company]
BMC Software [company]
BMC Software Inc. [company]
bmgmusicservice.com [company]

BMS [company]
BMW [company & product]
BNP Residential Properties Inc. [company]
BNS Co. [company]
Boardwalk Equities Inc. [company]
Bob Chinn's Crabhouse [company]
Bobcat [company & product]
Boc Group P.L.C. [company]
Boca Resorts Inc. [company]
Bodman Foundation, The [nonprofit]
Body Shop, The [company]
BOE [company & product]
Boeing [company]
Boeing Co., The [company]
Boeing Corp. [company]
Boettcher Foundation, The [nonprofit]
Boggle [product]
Bogliasco Foundation Inc., The [company]
Bohnett Foundation, David, The
  [nonprofit]
Boise Cascade Corp. [company]
Boks [product]
Bolla [product]
Bolt Technology Corp. [company]
Bolta [company & product]
Bombay Co. Inc. [company]
Bon Bons [product]
Bonderite [company]
Bone's [company]
Bonner Foundation, Corella & Bertram F., The
  [nonprofit]
Boo Berry [product]
Boogie [product]
Book-of-the-Month Club [company]
Books in Print [company]
Books on Tape [company]
booktech.com Inc. [company]
Boone's Farm [company & product]
Boots and Coots International Well Control,
  Inc. [company]
Borden [company]
Borden Chemicals and Plastics Ltd. P.
  [company]

Borden Foundation, Mary Owen, The [nonprofit]
Borden Inc. and Affiliates [company]
Borders Group Inc. [company]
borders.com [company]
Borgwagner Inc. [company]
Borland [company]
Bostik [company]
Boston Beer Co. [company]
Boston Celtics Ltd. P. [company]
Boston Properties Inc. [company]
Boston Scientific Corp. [company]
Boston Symphony Orchestra [nonprofit]
Boston Whaler [company & product]
BostonFed Bancorp Inc. [company]
Botany [company & product]
Bothin Foundation, The [nonprofit]
BOTOX [product]
Bottle Master [product]
Boulder Total Return Fund Inc. [company]
Boundless Corp. [company]
Bouygues Offshore [company]
Bowater [company]
Bowater Inc. [company]
Bowl America Inc. [company]
Bowman Consulting Group [company]
Bowne & Co. Inc. [company]
Bowne Foundation Inc., Robert, The [nonprofit]
Boy Scouts of America [nonprofit]
Boyd Collection Ltd. [company]
Boyd Gaming Corp. [company]
Boykin Lodging Co. [company]
Boys & Girls Clubs of America [nonprofit]
BP [company]
BP Amoco P.L.C. [company]
BP Prudhoe Bay Royalty Trust [company]
Bracewell & Patterson [company]
Brackett Foundation, The [nonprofit]
Bradlees [company]
Bradley Foundation Inc., Lynde and Harry, The [nonprofit]
Bradley Real Estate Inc. [company]

Brady Corp. [company]
Brainerd Foundation, The [nonprofit]
Bran Buds [product]
Bran'nola [product]
Branan Foundation, Mary Allen Lindsey, The [nonprofit]
Brand Central [product]
Brandywine Realty Trust [company]
Brascan Corp. [company]
Brasil Telecom Participacoes [company]
Braun [company & product]
Brazilian Equity Fund Inc., The [company]
BRE Properties Inc. [company]
Breakfast of Champions [product]
Breathalyzer [product]
Breeze Software Pty. Ltd. [company]
Bremer Foundation, Otto, The [nonprofit]
Brennan's [company]
Brennan's of Houston [company]
Brentwood Foundation [nonprofit]
Breyers [company]
Bridgestone [company]
Briggs & Stratton Corp. [company]
Bright & Early [product]
Brightpoint [company]
Brilliance China Automotive Holdings Ltd. [company]
Brilliant Digital Entertainment Inc. [company]
Brillo [product]
Brinker International Inc. [company]
Bristol-Myers Squibb Co. [company]
Brite [product]
British Airways P.L.C. [company]
British American Tobacco Industries P.L.C. [company]
British Energy P.L.C. [company]
British Sky Broadcasting Group [company]
British Steel P.L.C. [company]
British Telecommunications P.L.C. [company]
Broad Foundation, The [nonprofit]
Broadway Deli [company]
Broadway Stores Inc. [company]
Broadwing Inc. [company]

Brobeck Phleger & Harrison [company]

Broken Hill Proprietary Ltd. [company]

Bromo-Seltzer [product]

Brookdale Foundation, The [company]

Brooks [company & product]

Brooks Brothers [company]

Brother's Brother Foundation, The [nonprofit]

Brown & Brown Insurance [company]

Brown & Wood [company]

Brown Cow [product]

Brown Forman Corp. [company]

Brown Foundation, George Warren, The [nonprofit]

Brown Foundation Inc., James Graham, The [nonprofit]

Brown Shoe Co. Inc. [company]

Brown-Forman Corp. [company]

Brownie [product]

BRT Realty Trust. [company]

Bruner Foundation Inc. [company]

Brunswick Bancorp. [company]

Brunswick Corp. [company]

Brush Wellman Inc. [company]

Brut [product]

Bryan Cave [company]

Bryant Park Grill [company]

Brylcreem [company]

BSCH Finance Ltd. [company]

Bub City Crabshack & Bar B.Q. [company]

Bubble Yum [product]

Bubblicious [product]

Buchanan Associates [company]

Buchanan Ingersoll [company]

Buck [company]

Buck Foundation, Frank H. and Eva B., The [nonprofit]

Buckeye Partners L.P.

Buckeye Technologies Inc. [company]

Buckle Inc., The [company]

Bud [product]

Bud Light [product]

Budget Group Inc. [company]

Budweiser [product]

Bugles [product]

Bugs Bunny [product]

Buick [product]

Bulb Booster [product]

Bullet [product]

Bullitt Foundation, The [nonprofit]

Bundtbaking [product]

Bunzl P.L.C. [company]

Burberry [company & product]

Burger King [company]

Burlington Coat Factory Warehouse Corp. [company]

Burlington Industries Inc. [company]

Burlington Northern Santa Fe Corp. [company]

Burlington Resources Inc. [company]

Burnham Charitable Trust, Margaret E., The [nonprofit]

Burnham Pacific Properties Inc. [company]

Burroughs [company]

Burroughs Wellcome Fund [company]

Busch [company & product]

Busch Gardens [company]

Bush Boake Allen Inc. [company]

Bush Charitable Foundation Inc., Edyth, The [nonprofit]

Bush Foundation, The [nonprofit]

Bush Industries Inc. [company]

Bushnell [company & product]

Bushwacker [product]

BuSpar [product]

Buss [company & product]

Buster Brown Co. [company]

Busy [product]

Butler [company & product]

Butler Manufacturing Inc. [company]

Butterfly [company]

buy.com [company]

BV [product]

BVD [company & product]

Bway Corp. [company]

BYTE [company & product]

C&C Concrete Pumping [company]

C&D Technologies Inc. [company]
C.H. Robinson Worldwide Inc. [company]
C.A.W. Foundation The, [nonprofit]
Cabbage Patch Kids [product]
cabelas.com [company]
Cable & Wireless P.L.C. [company]
Cable Design Technologies Corp. [company]
Cabletel Communications Corp. [company]
Cabletron Systems Inc. [company]
Cablevision Systems Corp. [company]
Cabot Corp. [company]
Cabot Industries Trust [company]
Cabot Oil & Gas Corp. [company]
Cacharel [company]
Cadapult Graphic Systems Inc. [company]
Cadbury Schweppes Del L.P. [company]
Cadbury Schweppes P.L.C. [company]
Cadence Design Systems Inc. [company]
Cadillac [product]
Cadwalader, Wickersham & Taft [company]
Cafritz Foundation, Morris and Gwendolyn, The [nonprofit]
Cagle's Inc. [company]
Cahill Gordon & Reindel [company]
Caladryl [product]
Calder Foundation, Louis, The [nonprofit]
Calence [company]
Calgon [company & product]
Calgon Carbon Corp. [company]
California Cooler [product]
California Endowment, The [nonprofit]
California Federal Bank, A Federal Savings Bank [company]
California Masonic Foundation [nonprofit]
California Raisins, The [product]
California Water Services Group [company]
California Wellness Foundation, The [nonprofit]
Call Henry [company & product]
Callaway Golf Co. [company]
Callon Petroleum Co. [company]
Calpine Corp. [company]
Calton, Inc. [company]

Cambex Corp. [company]
Cambior Inc. [company]
Cambridge [company & product]
Camden National Corp. [company]
Camden Properties Trust [company]
Cameco Corp. [company]
Camel [product]
cameraworld.com [company]
Campbell Foundation, The [company]
Campbell Resources Inc. [company]
Campbell Soup Co. [company]
Campbell's [company & product]
CampBook [company]
Campfire [product]
Campho-Phenique [product]
Campus Crusade for Christ [nonprofit]
Canada Life Financial Corp. [company]
Canadian 88 Energy Corp. [company]
Canadian Imperial Bank of Commerce [company]
Canadian Mist [product]
Canadian National Railway Co. [company]
Canadian Natural Resources, Ltd. [company]
Canadian Pacific Ltd. [company]
Canandaigua Brands Inc. [company]
Candy Land [product]
Cannon Express Inc. [company]
Canon Inc. [company]
Cantor Foundation, Iris & B. Gerald, The [nonprofit]
CANUSAMEX [company]
Canwest Global Communications Corp. [company]
Canyon Research [company]
Canyon Resources Corp. [company]
Canyon River Blues [product]
Capella Education [company]
Capezio [company & product]
Capital Alliance Income Trust Ltd. [company]
Capital One Finanacial Corp. [company]
Capital Pacific Holdings Inc. [company]
Capital Properties Inc. [company]
Capital Re L.L.C. [company]

Capital Senior Living Corp. [company]
Capital Trust Inc. [company]
Cap'n Crunch [product]
Capoten [product]
Capri [product]
Capron [product]
Capstead Mortgage Corp. [company]
Captain Morgan [product]
Captain Planet Foundation Inc. [nonprofit]
Capture [product]
Caravan [product]
Carbo Ceramics Inc. [company]
Carbon Energy Corp. [company]
Cardinal [product]
Cardinal Health Inc. [company]
Cardiotech International Inc. [company]
Cardizem [product]
Cardizem CD [product]
CARE USA [company]
CareerEngine Network Inc. [company]
CareerXroads [company]
Carefree [product]
Caremark Rx Inc. [product]
Careside Inc. [product]
CarEth Foundation, The [nonprofit]
Car-Freshener [product]
Carisoprodol [product]
Carlisle Cos. Inc. [company]
Carlisle Foundation, The [nonprofit]
Carlson Wagonlit Travel [company]
Carlton Communications P.L.C. [company]
Carlyle Grand Café [company]
Carmel Container Systems Ltd. [company]
Carmike Cinemas Inc. [company]
Carnation [company & product]
Carnegie Corp. of New York [nonprofit]
Carnegie Endowment for International Peace [nonprofit]
Carnegie Foundation for the Advancement of Teaching, The [nonprofit]
Carnegie Hero Fund Commission [nonprofit]
Carnelian Room, The [company]
Carnival [company]

Carnival Corp. [company]
Carolina Holdings [company]
Carolina Power & Light Co. [company]
Carousel [product]
Carpenter Technology Corp. [company]
Carpet Science [product]
Carr Fund, Kristen Ann, The [nonprofit]
CarrAmerica Realty Corp. [company]
Carrefour S.A. [company]
Carrera [company & product]
Carriage Services Inc. [company]
Carrier [company]
Carsan Engineering [company]
Carte Blanche [company]
Carter Wallace Inc. [company]
Carter's Little Pills [product]
Carthage Foundation, The [nonprofit]
Cartier [company]
Cartwheel Books [company]
Carver Bancorp Inc. [company]
Carver Charitable Trust, Roy J., The [nonprofit]
Cary Charitable Trust, Mary Flagler, The [nonprofit]
Casa Bonita [company]
Cascade Corp. [company]
Cascade Natural Gas Corp. [company]
Case Corp. [company]
Casey Family Program, The [nonprofit]
Casey Foundation, Annie E., The [nonprofit]
Casey's General Stores Inc. [company]
Cash America International Inc. [company]
Cash Technologies Inc. [company]
Cashmere Bouquet [product]
Castle (A.M.) & Co. [company]
Castle Convertible Fund Inc. [company]
Castle Foundation, Harold K. L., The [nonprofit]
Castle Foundation, Samuel N. and Mary [nonprofit]
Casual Corner [company]
Cat [product]
Cat Chow [product]
Cataflam [company]

Catalina Lighting Inc. [company]
Catalina Marketing Corp. [company]
Catapult [product]
Catapult Systems [company]
Catellus Development Corp. [company]
Caterpillar [company & product]
Caterpillar Inc. [company]
Catholic Charities USA [nonprofit]
Catholic Relief Services [nonprofit]
CAV [product]
Cavalier Homes Inc. [company]
Cavanaugh [company]
CB Richard Ellis Services Inc. [company]
CBL & Associates Properties Inc. [company]
CBRL Group [company]
CBS [company]
CBS Corp. [company]
cdnow.com [company]
cdw.com [company]
CE Franklin Ltd. [company]
Cedar Fair LP [company]
Cefizox [product]
Ceftin [product]
Cefzil [product]
Celanese [company]
Celanese A.G. [company]
Celcor [product]
Celebrex [product]
Celeste [product]
Celestica Inc. [company]
Celexa [company]
CellStar Corp. [company]
Celltech Group P.L.C. [company]
Cel-Sci Corp. [company]
Celsion Corp. [company]
Cemex Inc. [company]
Cendant Corp. [company]
Cenex Harvest States Cooperatives [company]
Center Trust Inc. [company]
Centerpoint Properties Trust [company]
Centex Construction Products Inc. [company]
Centex Corp. [company]
Central & South West Corp. [company]

Central European Equity Fund Inc., The
  [nonprofit]
Central Fund of Canada Ltd. [company]
Central Garden & Pet Co. [company]
Central Hudson Gas & Electric Corp.
  [company]
Central Maine Power Co. [company]
Central Parking Corp. [company]
Central Securities Corp. [company]
Central Vermont Public Service Corp.
  [company]
Centrax [product]
Centris Group Inc. [company]
Centrum [vitamin] [product]
Centura Banks Inc. [company]
Century 21 [company]
Century Foundation, The [nonprofit]
Century Telephone Enterprises Inc. [company]
CenturyTel, Inc. [company]
Cepacol [product]
Cepastat [product]
Cephalexin [product]
Ceridian Corp. [company]
Certified Associates [company]
Certs [product]
Cerulean Technology [company]
Cessna [company & product]
CET Environmental Services Inc. [company]
CH2M Hill Cos. Ltd. [company]
Chad Therapeutics Inc. [company]
Chadbourne & Parke [company]
Champion [company]
Champion Enterprises Inc. [company]
Champion International Corp. [company]
Championship Auto Racing Teams Inc.
  [company]
Champlin Foundations, The [company]
Chanel [company & product]
Channeling [product]
Chap Stick [product]
Chapman [product]
Charge [product]
Charger [product]

Charles of the Ritz [product]
Charming Shoppes [company]
Charming Shoppes Inc. [company]
Chart House Enterprises Inc. [company]
Chart Industries Inc. [company]
Charter Communications Inc. [company]
Charter Municipal Mortgage Acceptance Co.
  [company]
Chartwell Dividend and Income Fund Inc.
  [company]
Chartwell Re Corp. [company]
Chase Corp. [company]
Chase Industries Inc. [company]
Chase Manhattan Corp. [company]
Chateau Communities Inc. [company]
Chateau Restaurant of Waltham, The [company]
Checker [company]
Checkpoint Systems Inc. [company]
Chedarella [product]
Chee•tos [product]
Cheerios [product]
Cheez Doodles [product]
Cheez Whiz [product]
Cheez-It [product]
Chef Boyardee [product]
Chelsea Property Group Inc. [company]
Chemfirst Inc. [company]
Cheniere Energy Inc. [company]
Chequemate International Inc. [company]
Cherokee Information Services [company]
Cherry Garcia [product]
Chesapeake Energy Corp. [company]
Chesapeake Utilities Corp. [company]
Chevrolet [company & product]
Chevron [company]
Chevron Corp. [company]
Chevy [nickname for Chevrolet] [company &
  product]
Chia Pet [product]
Chiang Ching-Kuo Foundation for
  International Scholarly Exchange, The
  [nonprofit]
Chic By His Inc. [company]

Chicago Bridge & Iron Co. [company]
Chicken McNuggets [product]
Chiclets [product]
Chico's FAS Inc. [company]
Chieftain International Inc. [company]
Chiesman Foundation for Democracy Inc.
  [company]
Chiles Offshore Inc. [company]
China Eastern Airlines Corp. Ltd. [company]
China Fund Inc., The [company]
China Grill Miami Beach [company]
China Grill New York [company]
China Mobile [company]
China Petroleum & Chemical Corp.
China Southern Airlines Co. Ltd. [company]
China Tire Holding Ltd. [company]
China Unicom Ltd. [company]
China Yuchai International Ltd. [company]
Chippendales [company & product]
Chipwich [product]
Chiquita [company]
Chiquita Brands International Inc. [company]
Chittenden Corp. [company]
Chivas Regal Scotch [product]
Chloé [product]
Chloraseptic [product]
Chloromycetin [product]
Chlor-Trimeton [product]
Chock full o' Nuts [product]
Choc-ola [product]
Chocolate Cow [product]
Choice Hotels International Inc. [company]
Choicepoint Inc. [company]
Chris Craft Industries Inc. [company]
Chris-Craft [company]
Christensen Fund, The [nonprofit]
Christian and Missionary Alliance, The
  [nonprofit]
Christian Brothers, The [nonprofit]
Christian Children's Fund [nonprofit]
Christian Dior [company & product]
Christian Science Monitor, The [company]
Chromcraft Revington Inc. [company]

CHS Electronics Inc. [company]
Chubb Corp. [company]
Chuck E. Cheese [company]
Chuck Taylor [company]
Chunky [product]
Chunky Monkey [product]
Church & Dwight Co. Inc. [company]
Chyron Corp. [company]
Ciba Specialty Chemicals Holding, Inc.
  [company]
Cibachrome [product]
CIBER Inc. [company]
CIGNA Corp. [company]
Cigna High Income Shares [company]
Cigna Investment Securities Inc. [company]
CIM High Yield Securities [company]
Cinch Sak [product]
Cincinnati Financial Corp. [company]
Cincinnati Gas & Electric Co. [company]
Cinemax [product]
Cineplex [company & product]
Cinergy Corp. [company]
Cinn*A*Burst [product]
Cinnamon Toast Crunch [product]
Cintas Corp. [company]
CINTAS Foundation, The [nonprofit]
Cinzano [product]
Cipro [company & product]
Circor International Inc. [company]
Circuit City [company]
Circuit City Stores Inc. [company]
Cisco Systems Inc. [company]
CIT Group Inc. [company]
Citadel Holding Corp. [company]
Citibank [company]
Citicorp [company]
Citigroup Inc. [company]
Citizens Holding Co. [company]
Citizens Inc. [company]
Citizens Utilities Co. [company]
Citizens' Scholarship Foundation of America,
  The [nonprofit]
Citroën [company & product]

City National Corp. [company]
City of Hope [nonprofit]
CK One [product]
CK Witco Corp. [company]
CKE Restaurants Inc. [company]
Claiborne Liz Inc. [company]
Claire's Stores [company]
Claire's Stores Inc. [company]
Clamato [product]
Clarcor Inc. [company]
Clarins [company & product]
Clarion Commercial Holdings Inc. [company]
Claritin [product]
Claritin D 12HR [product]
Claritin D 24HR [product]
Claritin Reditabs [product]
Clark Foundation, Edna McConnell, The
  [nonprofit]
Clark Foundation, Inc., Robert Sterling, The
  [nonprofit]
Clark USA [company]
Clarkston-Potomac Group [company]
Classic [product]
Classic Black [product]
Classic Car Wash [company]
Classic Sport Cos. [company]
Classico [product]
Claymation [company]
Clayton Homes Inc. [company]
Clear Channel Communications Inc. [company]
Clear Eyes [product]
Clearasil [product]
ClearTint [product]
Cleary, Gottlieb, Steen & Hamilton [company]
Cleco Corp. [company]
Clemente Strategic Value Fund Inc. [company]
Cleveland Cliffs Inc. [company]
Cleveland Medical Devices [company]
Clicquot-Club [product]
Clif Bar [company]
Cliff House [company]
Cliff's Notes [product]
Clifford Chance [company]

Clifford ChanceRogers & Wells [company]
Climara [product]
Cling Free [product]
Clinique [company & product]
Clipper Ship Foundation Inc. [nonprofit]
Clonazepam [product]
Clonidine [product]
Clorets [product]
Clorox [product]
Clorox Co., The [company]
Close-Up [product]
Cloud Foundation, The [nonprofit]
Club, The [product]
Clyde's of Chevy Chase [company]
Clyde's of Reston [company]
Clyde's of Tysons Corner [company]
Clydesdale [product]
C-MAC Industries Inc. [company]
CMG Mortgage Insurance [company]
CMI Corp. [company]
CMS Energy Corp. [company]
CNA Financial Corp. [company]
CNA Income Shares Inc. [company]
CNA Surety Corp. [company]
CNB Bancshares Inc. [company]
cnet.com [company]
CNF Transportation Inc. [company]
CNH Global NV [company]
CNN [company]
CNOOC [company]
Coach [company & product]
Coach Inc. [company]
Coachmen Industries Inc. [company]
Coalition America [nonprofit]
Coast Distribution System Inc., The [company]
Coastal Corp., The [company]
Coastalcast Corp. [company]
Cobalt Corp. [company]
CoBiz Inc. [company]
Cobra [product]
Coca-Cola [company & product]
Coca-Cola Co., The [company]
Coca-Cola Enterprises Inc. [company]

Cocktails for Two [product]
Coco [product]
Cocoa Classics [company]
Cocoa Krispies [product]
Cocoa Puffs [product]
CodeSoft International [company]
Coeur d'Alene Mines Corp. [company]
Cognitronics Corp. [company]
Cohen & Steers Realty Income Fund Inc. [company]
Cointreau [company]
Coke [product]
Cold Generator [product]
Cold Metal Products Inc. [company]
Cold Spring Harbor Laboratory [company]
coldwatercreek.com [company]
Cole National [company]
Cole National Corp. [company]
Cole, Kenneth Productions Inc. [company]
Coleman [company & product]
Coleman Foundation Inc., The [company]
Coles Myer Ltd. [company]
Colgate-Palmolive Co. [company]
CollegeLink.com Inc. [company]
Collegiate Pacific Inc. [company]
Collins & Aikman Corp. [company]
Colonial Bancgroup Inc. [company]
Colonial Municipal Income Trust [company]
Colonial Properties Trust [company]
Colonial Williamsburg Foundation, The [nonprofit]
Colorado Trust, The [nonprofit]
Colorforms [product]
ColorPro [product]
Columbia Energy Group [company]
Columbia Foundation, The [nonprofit]
Columbia Laboratories Inc. [company]
Columbia/HCA Healthcare Corp. [company]
columbiahouse.com [company]
Columbus Southern Power Co. [company]
Combat [product]
Combivent [product]
Comcast Corp. [company]

Comdial Corp. [company]
Comdisco Inc. [company]
Comeco Corp. [company]
Comed Financing [company]
Comerica Inc. [company]
COMFORCE Corp. [company]
Comfort Systems USA Inc. [company]
Cominco Ltd. [company]
Command [product]
Commander's Palace [company]
Commerce Bancorp Inc. [company]
Commerce Group Inc. [company]
Commercial Federal Corp. [company]
Commercial Intertech Corp. [company]
Commercial Metals Co. [company]
Commercial Net Lease Realty Inc. [company]
Commodore Applied Technologies Inc.
  [company]
Common Sense [product]
Commonweal Foundation Inc. [company]
Commonwealth Edison Co. [company]
Commonwealth Fund, The [company]
Commonwealth General L.L.C. [company]
Commscope Inc. [company]
Community Bank Systems Inc. [company]
Community Banks Inc. [company]
Community Bankshares Inc. [company]
Community Capital Corp. [company]
Community Health Systems Inc. [company]
Community Technology Foundation of
  California [company]
Comnet International [company]
Companhia Cerve Jaria Brahma [company]
Companhia de Bebidas das Americas [company]
Companhia Paranaense de Energia-COPEL
  [company]
Companhia Siderurgica Nacional [company]
Companhia Vale Rio do Doce [company]
Compania Anonima Nacional Telefonos de
  Venezuela [company]
Compania de Telecomunicaciones De Chile
  S.A. [company]
Compaq [company & product]

Compaq Computer Corp. [company]
compaq.com [company]
Compass [product]
Compass Bancshares Inc. [company]
Competitive Technologies Inc. [company]
compgeeks.com [company]
Complete [product]
Compri Consulting [company]
Compton Foundation Inc., The [nonprofit]
CompUSA [company]
CompUSA Inc. [company]
compusa.com [company]
Computech Resources [company]
Computer & Hi-Tech Management [company]
Computer Associates International Inc.
  [company]
Computer Consultants of America [company]
Computer Enterprises [company]
Computer Sciences Corp. [company]
Computer Sciences Corp. [company]
Computer Task Group Inc. [company]
Computerized Thermal Imaging Inc. [company]
Computrac Inc. [company]
Compuware Corp. [company]
CompX International Inc. [company]
Comstock Resources Inc. [company]
Comverse Technology [company]
ConAgra [company]
ConAgra Foods Inc. [company]
Concord EFS Inc. [company]
Cone Mills Corp. [company]
Conectiv [product]
Conectiv Inc. [company]
Conexant Systems Inc. [company]
Confluence Technologies [company]
Congoleum [company]
Congoleum Corp. [company]
Connelly Foundation, The [nonprofit]
Connie [footwear] [product]
Conoco [company]
Conoco Inc. [company]
CONS [company]
Conseco Inc. [company]

Conservation, Food & Health Foundation Inc. [company]
Consoilidated Graphics Inc. [company]
Consol Energy Inc.
Consolidated Delivery & Logistics Inc. [company]
Consolidated Edison Co. of New York Inc. [company]
Consolidated Edison Inc. [company]
Consolidated Freightways [company]
Consolidated Natural Gas Co. [company]
Consolidated Products Inc. [company]
Consolidated Stores [company]
Consolidated Stores Corp. [company]
Consolidated-Tomoka Land Co. [company]
Consorcio G Grupo Dina [company]
Consorcio G Grupo Dina Sa Cv [company]
Constellation Brands Inc. [company]
Constellation Energy Group Inc. [company]
Consumers Energy Co. [company]
Contac [product]
Con-Tact [product]
Contango Oil & Gas Co. [company]
Contel [product]
Contifinancial Corp. [company]
Continental Airlines Inc. [company]
Continental Materials Corp. [company]
Continucare Corp. [company]
Controladora Comml Mexicana [company]
Contuss-XT [product]
Convergys Corp. [company]
Converse [product]
Converted [product]
Convertible [product]
Cooker Restaurant Corp. [company]
Cool Ranch [product]
Cool Whip [product]
Coolerator [product]
Cooley Godward [product]
CoolMax [product]
Coombs Corporate Media [company]
Cooper [company]
Cooper Cameron Corp. [company]

Cooper Cos. Inc., The [company]
Cooper Foundation, The [nonprofit]
Cooper Industries Inc. [company]
Cooper Institute for Advanced Studies in Medicine and the Humanities, The [nonprofit]
Cooper Tire & Rubber Co. [company]
Cooperative Resource Services [company]
Coors [company & product]
Coors, Adolph Corp. [company]
Copland Fund for Music Inc., Aaron, The [nonprofit]
Coppertone [product]
Corbase [product]
Corbin Russwin [company]
Cordant Technologies Inc. [company]
Cordiant Communications Group [company]
Cordon Rouge [product]
Core laboratories [company]
Core Materials Corp. [company]
Corelle [product]
Core-Mark International Inc. [company]
Corex [product]
Coricidin [product]
Corman Foundation Inc. [company]
Corn Pops [product]
Corn Products International Inc. [company]
Cornell Cos. Inc. [company]
Cornerstone Bancorp Inc. [company]
Cornerstone Propane Partnership L.P. [company]
Cornerstone Properties Inc. [company]
Cornerstone Realty Income Trust Inc. [company]
Cornerstone Strategic Return [company]
Corning Inc. [company]
Corning Ware [product]
Corporate High Yield Fund, Inc. [company]
Corporate Office Properties Trust [company]
Correctional Properties Trust [company]
Corrections Corp. of America [company]
Correctol [product]
CorrFlex Graphics L.L.C. [company]

Corrpro Cos. Inc. [company]
Corsearch [product]
Cort Trust for Countrywide Capital [company]
Cor-Ten [product]
Cortisporin [product]
Cortone [product]
Corus Entertainment Inc. [company]
Corvette [company & product]
COSMOS [product]
Costco [product]
Costco Wholesale Corp. [company]
Cotelligent Inc. [company]
Coudert Brothers [company]
Coumadin [product]
Count Chocula [product]
Counter Culture Coffee [product]
Country Home [product]
Country Morning [product]
Countrywide Credit Industries Inc. [company]
Court Square Data Group [company]
Courvoisier [product]
Cousins Properties Inc. [company]
Covance Inc. [company]
Covanta Energy Corp. [company]
Covenant House [nonprofit]
Coventry Health Care Inc. [company]
Covington & Burling [company]
Covitol [nonprofit]
Cowell Foundation, S. H., The [nonprofit]
Cox Charitable Trust, Jessie B. [company]
Cox Communication Inc. [company]
Cox Radio Inc. [company]
Cozaar [product]
Cozen and O'Connor [company]
CP Internet [product]
CPI Aerostructures Inc. [company]
Crack'N Peel [product]
Cracker Jack [product]
Cracklin' Oat Bran [product]
Craftmatic [product]
Craftsman [product]
Craftways [product]
Craig Corp. [company]

Craig, Jenny Inc. [company]
Crail-Johnson Foundation, The [nonprofit]
Craisins [product]
Crane Co. [company]
Crash Dummies [product]
Crate & Barrel [company]
Cravath, Swaine & Moore [company]
Crawford & Co. [company]
Crayola [product]
Cream of Wheat [product]
Creamy Deluxe [product]
CreataCard [product]
Creative Civilization [product]
Creative Computer Applications Inc. [company]
Creative Technology [company]
Credicorp Ltd. [company]
Credit Store Inc., The [company]
Credit Suisse First Boston [company]
Cremora [product]
Crescent [product]
Crescent Breakfast [product]
Crescent Real Estate Equities Co. [company]
Creslan [product]
Crest [product]
Crestline Capital Corp. [company]
Criimi MAE Inc. [company]
Crimson Consulting Group [company]
Crisco [product]
Crispers! [product]
Crispix [product]
Crispy Critters [product]
Cristal Champagne [product]
Cristaler\'edas de Chile [product]
Crock-Pot [product]
Crompton Corp. [company]
Crosby, Heafey, Roach & May [company]
Cross (A.T.) Co. [company]
Cross [product]
Cross Media Marketing Corp. [company]
Cross Timbers Oil Co. [company]
Cross Timbers Royalty Trust [company]
Cross Townsend [company]
CrossLink [product]

Crotched Mountain Foundation, The [nonprofit]
Croutettes [product]
Crown Castle International Corp. [company]
Crown Central Petroleum Corp. [company]
Crown Cork & Seal Co. Inc. [company]
Crown Cork & Seal Inc. [company]
Crown Crafts Inc. [company]
Crown Pac Partners L.P. [company]
Crown Products [product]
Crown Royal Canadian [company]
Crowne Plaza [company]
Cruvinet [product]
CryoLife Inc. [company]
CRYO-QUICK [product]
Cryovac [product]
Crystal Clean [product]
Crystal Color [product]
Crystal White [product]
Crystallex International Corp. [company]
CSK Auto [company]
CSK Auto Corp. [company]
C-SPAN [company]
Css Industries Inc. [company]
CSX Corp. [company]
CTS Corp. [company]
CTX [company]
Cubic Corp. [company]
Cue Data Services [company]
Cuisinart [product]
Cullen/Frost Bankers Inc. [company]
Culp Inc. [company]
Cummings Foundation, Inc. Nathan, The [nonprofit]
Cummins Engine Co., Inc. [company]
CUNA Mutual Group [company]
Cup-a-Soup [product]
Curad [product]
Cure 81 [product]
Curity [product]
Current Income Shares, Inc. [company]
Curtiss Wright Corp. [company]
CUShopper [product]

Custom Gard [product]
Custom Royale [product]
Custom Staffing [company]
Cutler-Hammer [product]
Cut-Rite [product]
CVB Financial Corp. [company]
CVF Corp. [company]
CVS [company]
CVS Automatic Common Exhange Security [company]
CVS Corp. [company]
Cyber Dialogue [product]
cyberrebate.com [company]
CyberStaff America [company]
Cybex [product]
Cybex International Inc. [company]
Cycle [product]
Cyclobenzaprine [product]
Cyclone [product]
Cycrin [product]
Cypress Food Distributors [company]
Cypress Semiconductor Corp. [company]
Cystic Fibrosis Foundation, The [nonprofit]
Cytec Industries Inc. [company]
Cytomation [product]
D & K Healthcare Resources Inc. [company]
D.R. Horton [company]
Dacron [product]
Dade Behring Inc. [company]
Daffy Duck [product]
Dag [product]
Daimler Benz A.G. [company]
DaimlerChrysler A.G. [company]
Dain Rauscher Corp. [company]
Dairy Ease [product]
Dairy Mart Convenience Stores Inc. [company]
Dairypak [product]
Dakota [product]
Dal Tile International Inc. [company]
Dallas Semiconductor Corp. [company]
Dalmane [product]
Dan River Inc. [company]
Dana Corp. [company]

Dana Farber Cancer Institute [nonprofit]
Dana Foundation Inc., Charles A., The [nonprofit]
Danaher Corp. [company]
Daniels Foundation, Lucy, The [nonprofit]
Danielson Holding Corp. [company]
Dannon [company & product]
Dansk [product]
Danskin [product]
Dansko [product]
Darden Restaurants Inc. [company]
Darling International Inc. [company]
Dataforce [product]
Datamatics Consultants [company]
Datapro [product]
DataSource [product]
Datazed Software Services [company]
Dave & Busters Inc. [company]
Davidson Foundation, The [nonprofit]
Davis Foundations, Arthur Vining, The [nonprofit]
Davis Polk & Wardwell [company]
Davis Wright Tremaine [company]
Davita Inc. [company]
Daxor Corp. [company]
Day & Night [product]
Day, Berry & Howard [company]
Day-Glo [product]
Daypro [product]
DayQuil [product]
Day-Timer [product]
Dayton [product]
Dayton Mining Corp. [company]
Dayton Superior Corp. [company]
DB2 [product]
Dbt Online Inc. [company]
DC Group [company]
DCH Technology, Inc. [company]
d-Con [product]
Deal-A-Meal [product]
Dean Foods Co. [company]
Dean Foods Inc. [company]
Debevoise & Plimpton [company]

Dechert Price & Rhoads [company]
Decision Point Systems [company]
Decker Foundation, Dr. G. Clifford & Florence B., The [nonprofit]
Decora [product]
Decorator Industries Inc. [company]
Deere & Co. [company]
Deerfield.com [company]
Defend [product]
Dekko Foundation Inc., The [nonprofit]
Del Frisco's Double Eagle Steak House [company]
Del Laboratories Inc. [company]
Del Monte [company]
Del Monte Foods Co. [company]
Del Webb Corp. [company]
Delano Foundation Inc., Barbara, The [nonprofit]
Delaware Group Dividend & Income Fund Inc. [company]
Delaware Group Global Dividend and Income Fund Inc. [company]
Delaware Heart Institute [nonprofit]
Delco [company]
Delco Remy International [company]
Delhaize America Inc. [company]
Delhaize Group [company]
delias.com [company]
Dell Computer Corp. [company]
dell.com [company]
Delmas Foundation, Gladys Krieble, The [nonprofit]
Delo [product]
DeLonghi [company & product]
Delphi Automotive Systems Corp. [company]
Delphi Financial Group Inc. [company]
Delta Air Lines [company]
Delta Air Lines Inc. [company]
Delta and Pine Land Co. [company]
Delta Apparel Inc. [company]
Delta Financial Corp. [company]
Delta Woodside Industries Inc. [company]
Deltic Timber Corp. [company]

Deluxe Corp. [company]
Demerol [product]
DeMoulas [product]
Demulen [product]
Denbury Resources Inc. [company]
Denny's [company]
Dentagard [product]
Dental Select [product]
Dentyne [product]
Depakote [product]
Department 56 Inc. [company]
Depend [product]
DepoMed Inc. [company]
Depo-Provera [product]
Desenex [product]
Desitin [product]
DeskJet [product]
DeskManager [product]
DeskScan [product]
DeskTalk Systems [company & product]
DeskWriter [product]
Desogen [product]
Destiny Group [company]
Detroit Diesel Corp. [company]
Detroit Edison Co. [company]
Detrol [product]
Deutsche Bank A.G. [company]
Deutsche Telekom A.G. [company]
Developers Diversified Realty Corp. [company]
Devil Dogs [product]
Devon Energy Corp. [company]
Devonsheer [product]
Devry, Inc. [company]
DeWALT [company]
Dewar's Scotch [product]
DeWolfe Cos. Inc., The [company]
Dexedrine [product]
Dexter Corp. [company]
DFS Group [company]
DHL [product]
Di Giorgio Corp. [company]
di Rosa Foundation, Rene & Veronica, The [nonprofit]

Dia Met Minerals Ltd. [company]
Diagnostic Products Corp. [company]
Dial [product]
Dial Corp., The [company]
Dialog [product]
Diamond [product]
Diamond Crystalsalt [product]
Diamond Offshore Drilling Inc. [company]
Diaparene [product]
Diaper Genie [product]
DiaSys Corp. [company]
Diazepam [product]
Dickson Concepts [company]
Dickstein Shapiro Morin & Oshinsky [company]
Dictaphone [product]
Diebold, Inc. [company]
DieHard [product]
Diet-Rite [product]
Diflucan [product]
Di-Gel [product]
Digest, The [product]
Digital [company]
Digital Photo Imaging [product]
Digital Power Corp. [company]
Dilantin (phenytoin) [product]
Dilaudid [product]
Dillard's [company]
Dillards Inc. [company]
Dime Bancorp Inc. [company]
Dimetapp [product]
Dimon Inc. [company]
DIMON Inc. [company]
Diners Club [company]
Dingwall Foundation, William Orr, The [nonprofit]
Dinty Moore [product]
Dior [company & product]
Diovan [product]
Dippity-Do [product]
Direct/Reflecting [product]
Disabled American Veterans [nonprofit]
Discman [product]

Discount Auto Parts Inc. [company]
Discovery Channel [company]
Discovery.com [company]
Disney Walt Co. Walt Disney Internet Group [company]
disney.com [company]
Disneyland [product]
Disposall [product]
Dive! Las Vegas [product]
Diversified Communications Group [company]
Diversified Computer Consultants [company]
Diversified Corporate Resources Inc. [company]
Dixie [product]
Dixon Ticonderoga Co. [company]
DJ & T Foundation, The [nonprofit]
Dlt Solutions [company]
Do Right Foundation, The [nonprofit]
Dock's Oyster Bar and Seafood Grill [company]
Dodge [company & product]
Dodge Foundation, Inc., Geraldine R., The [nonprofit]
Dog Chow [product]
Dolby [product]
Dolby Surround [product]
Dolce & Gabbana [company & product]
Dole [product]
Dole Food Co. Inc. [company]
Dollar General [company]
Dollar General Corp. [company]
Dollar Thrifty Automotive Group Inc. [company]
Dollar Tree Stores, Inc. [company]
Dom Pérignon [product]
domestications.com [company]
Dominion Resources Black Warrior Trust [company]
Dominion Resources Capital Trust II [company]
Dominion Resources Inc. [company]
Domino's Pizza [company]
Domtar Inc. [company]
Donaldson Co Inc. [company]

Doncasters P.L.C. [company]
Donna Karan [company & product]
Donna Karan International Inc. [company]
Donnelley Foundation, Gaylord and Dorothy, The [nonprofit]
Donnelly Corp. [company]
Donner Foundation Inc., William H., The [nonprofit]
Donzi [product]
Dopp Kit [product]
Doral [product]
Doral Dental USA [product]
Doritos [product]
Dorot Foundation, The [nonprofit]
Dot Hill Systems Corp. [company]
Doublemint [product]
DoubleStar [product]
Dove Data Products [product]
DoveBar [product]
Dover Corp. [company]
Dover Downs Entertainment Inc. [company]
Dow Chemical Co. [company]
Dow Chemical Co., The [company]
Dow Jones & Co. [company]
Dow Jones & Co. Inc. [company]
Down Under Construction [company]
Downey Financial Corp. [company]
Downing Foundation, J.C., The [nonprofit]
DPL Inc. [company]
DQE Inc. [company]
Dr Pepper [product]
Dr. Brown's [product]
Dr. Denton's [product]
Dr. Martens [product]
Dr. Reddy's Laboratories Ltd. [company]
Dr. Scholl's [product]
Drachen Foundation, The [nonprofit]
Dracon [product]
Draftmaster [product]
DraftPro [product]
Dragnet [product]
Drake's [company]
Dralon [product]

Dramamine [product]
Drambuie [product]
Drano [product]
Dream Vacation [product]
Dresdner Bank A.G. [company]
Dress Barn [company]
Drew Industries Inc. [company]
Dreyfus Foundation Inc., Camille and Henry, The [nonprofit]
Dreyfus Municipal Income, Inc. [company]
Dril-Kwick [product]
Dril-Quip, Inc. [company]
Drinker Biddle & Reath [company]
Dristan [product]
Driver-Harris Co. [company]
Drixoral [product]
Drown Foundation, Joseph, The [nonprofit]
DRS Technologies Inc. [company]
Drucker Foundation for Nonprofit Management Inc., Peter F., The [nonprofit]
drugstore.com [company]
Drumstick [product]
Dryclean USA Inc. [company]
Drygas [product]
DSP Communications Inc. [company]
DST Systems Inc. [company]
DTE Energy Co. [company]
Dual [product]
Duane Reade Inc. [company]
Duane, Morris & Heckscher [company]
Ducati Motor Holding S.P.A. [company]
Duck [product]
Duck Head Apparel Co. Inc. [company]
Ducks Unlimited [nonprofit]
Ducommun Inc. [company]
Dudley Foundation, The [nonprofit]
Duff & Phelps Utilities Income Inc. [company]
Duke Charitable Foundation, Doris, The [nonprofit]
Duke Endowment, The [nonprofit]
Duke Energy Corp. [company]
Duke Nukem [product]
Duke Realty Investments Inc. [company]

Duke-Weeks Realty Corp. [company]
Dulux [product]
Dumpster [product]
Dun & Bradstreet Corp. [company]
Dune [product]
Dungeons & Dragons [product]
Dunkin' Donuts [company]
Duodozen [product]
Duplo [product]
DuPont [company]
Du Pont E.I. Nemours & Co. [company]
Du Pont Fund, Jessie Ball, The [company]
Dura Automotive Systems Inc. [company]
Dura Cushion [product]
Duracell [product]
Dura-Flex [product]
Dura-Max [product]
DuraSoft [product]
Durfee Foundation, The [nonprofit]
DUROCK [product]
Dustbuster [product]
Dutch Masters [product]
DVI Inc. [company]
DVITS [product]
Dycom Industries Inc. [company]
Dyerburg Corp. [company]
Dykema & Gossett [company]
Dymoembossing [product]
Dyna*Kids [product]
Dyna-Band [product]
Dynalink Systems [company]
Dynamex Inc. [company]
Dynamic [product]
Dynamic Resources [company]
DynCorp. [company]
Dynegy Inc. [company]
Dyson Foundation, The [nonprofit]
E&J [company]
ECC International Corp. [company]
E! Entertainment Television (E!) [company]
E*Trade Group Inc. [company]
E.W. Scripps Co., The [company]

Eagle [snacks] [product]
Eagle [tires] [product]
Eagle Bancshares Inc. [company]
Eagle Sky Foundation Inc., The [company]
Eagle Wireless International Inc. [company]
Eames [product]
Earl Scheib Inc. [company]
Earth [product]
Earthgrains Co., The [company]
eastbay.com [company]
Eastern American Natural Gas Trust [company]
Eastern Co., The [company]
Eastern Enterprises [company]
Eastern Utilities Associates [company]
Eastgroup Properties Inc. [company]
Eastman Chemical Co. [company]
Eastman Kodak Co. [Kodak] [company]
Easy Living [product]
Easy Spirit [product]
Easy-Bake [product]
Easy-Off [product]
Easyriders Inc. [company]
Eaton [car parts] [product]
Eaton Corp. [company]
Eaton Vance Corp. [company]
eBay Inc. [company]
EBC Computers [company]
ebworld.com [company]
Echo Bay Mines Ltd. [company]
Echoing Green Foundation [nonprofit]
Echostar Communications Corp. [company]
Eckert Seamans Cherin & Mellott [company]
Ecocrete [product]
Ecolab Inc. [company]
Ecology and Environment, Inc. [company]
ecost.com [company]
eCybersuite [company]
Edah Inc. [company]
eddiebauer.com [company]
Edensoy [product]
e-dentist.com Inc. [company]
Edge [product]
Edgewise Media Services [company]

EDI*Net [company]
Edison [lighting fixtures] [product]
Edison International [company]
Educational Foundation for America, The [nonprofit]
Edwards & Angell [company]
Edwards A.G. Inc. [company]
Edwards Foundation, O.P. & W.E., The [nonprofit]
Edwards Lifesciences Corp. [company]
EEX Corp. [company]
EFC Bancorp Inc. [company]
Efferdent [product]
Effexor XR [product]
Efidac/24 [product]
Egghead.com [company]
Eggo [product]
EIX Trust [company]
Ektachrome [product]
El Paso Corp. [company]
El Paso Electric Co. [company]
El Paso Energy Corp. [company]
El Paso Tennessee Pipeline Co. [company]
El Pomar Foundation [company]
eLabor.com [company]
Elan Corp. P.L.C. [company]
Elder Trust [company]
Elecsys Corp. [company]
Electric City Corp. [company]
Electricidade De Portugal [company]
Electrolux [product]
Electronic Arts Inc. [company]
Electronic Data Systems Corp. [company]
Electronic Technologies [company]
Electronics Boutique [company]
Elevators [products]
Eli Lilly & Co. [company]
Elite Pharmaceuticals, Inc. [company]
Elite Systems [company]
Ellesse [product]
Ellison Medical Foundation, The [nonprofit]
Ellsworth Convertible Growth and Income Fund, Inc. [company]

Elmer's [product]
Elu [product]
eMagin Corp. [company]
Emanuel Ungaro [company]
Embassy Suites [company]
EMC Corp. [company]
Emcor Group Inc. [company]
e-Medsoft.com [company]
Emerging Markets Floating Rate Fund Inc,
  The [company]
Emerging Markets Income Fund Inc.
  [company]
Emerging Markets Telecommunications Fund
  Inc., The [company]
Emeritus Corp. [company]
Emerson [company & product]
Emerson Electric Co. [company]
Emerson Radio Corp. [company]
Emhart [company & product]
EMI Group P.L.C. [company]
EMLA [product]
Empire District Electric Co. [company]
Empire Resources Inc. [company]
Empirin [product]
Encal Energy Ltd. [company]
Encompass Services Corp. [company]
Encore Acquisition Corp. [company]
Encore Software [company]
Endorex Corp. [company]
Energen Corp. [company]
Energizer [product]
Energizer Holdings Inc. [company]
Energol [product]
Energy East Corp. [company]
Energy Foundation [nonprofit]
Energy Wave [product]
EnergyNorth Inc. [company]
Enerplus Resources Fund [company]
Enersis S.A. [company]
Enesco Group Inc. [company]
Engelhard Corp. [company]
Engex, Inc. [company]
Engineering Diagnostics [company]

Engineering Information Foundation
  [company]
Engineering Solid Solutions [company]
England Family Foundation Inc., Lois &
  Richard, The [nonprofit]
Enhance Financial Services Group Inc.
  [company]
Eni S.P.A. [company]
Eniro A.B. [company]
Ennis Business Forms Inc. [company]
Enodis P.L.C. [company]
Enrich [product]
Enron [company]
Enron Corp. [company]
Enscicon [company]
Ensco International Inc. [company]
Enserch Corp. [company]
Enskilda Securities A.B. [company]
Ensure [product]
Entenmann's [company & product]
Enterbank Holdings, Inc. [company]
Entercom Communications Corp. [company]
Entergy Corp. [company]
Enterprise Development Services [company]
Enterprise Oil P.L.C. [company]
Enterprises Products Partners L.P. [company]
Entertainment Properties Trust [company]
Entrade Inc. [company]
Entravision Communication Corp. [company]
Entreport Corp. [company]
Entrust Technologies Inc. [company]
Environmental Elements Corp. [company]
Environmental Safeguards Inc. [company]
Environmental Tectonics Corp. [company]
Environmental Trust, The [company]
Envision [company]
Enzo Biochem Inc. [company]
EOG Resources Inc. [company]
Eott Energy Partners L.P. [company]
EPartners [company]
Epcos A.G. [company]
Epcot [company]
Epibond [product]

EpicEdge Inc. [company]
Epon [product]
Eponex [product]
Epson [company]
Epstein Becker & Green [company]
Equal [product]
Equant N.V. [company]
Equidyne Corp. [company]
Equifax Inc. [company]
Equilasers [product]
Equitable Resources [company]
Equitable Resources Inc. [company]
Equity [computers] [product]
Equity Income Fund, First Exchange Series
    [company]
Equity Inns Inc. [company]
Equity Office Properties Trust [company]
Equity One Inc. [company]
Equity Residential Properties Trust [company]
Erector [product]
eResource Capital Group Inc. [company]
Erie Insurance Group [company]
Ernest & Julio Gallo [company]
Ery-Tab [product]
Erythrocin [product]
Escal-Aire [product]
Esco Techologies Inc. [company]
Espirito Santo Overseas Ltd. [company]
ESPN [company]
Esprit [product]
Esquel Group Foundation, Inc. [company]
Esselte [product]
Essex [product]
Essex Bancorp Inc. [company]
Essex Property Trust Inc. [company]
Estate [product]
Estée Lauder [company & product]
Estee Lauder Cos. Inc. [company]
Esterline Technologies Corp. [company]
Estrace [company]
Estraderm [product]
ETA Engineering Consultants [company]
Etch A Sketch [product]

Ethan Allen [company & product]
Ethan Allen Interiors Inc. [company]
Ethyl Corp. [company]
E'town Corp. [company]
etoys.com [company]
ETS [company & product]
ETZ Lavuad Ltd. [company]
Eudora [product]
Europe Fund Inc. [company]
European Warrant Fund Inc., The
    [company]
EuroSoft [product]
Eurotech Ltd. [product]
Evan-Picone [product]
Evans Foundation Inc., Lettie Pate, The
    [company]
Evenflo [product]
Eveready [product]
Evergreen Resources Inc. [company]
Everlast [product]
Eversoft [product]
Everstart [product]
Evian [product]
Evinrude [product]
Evista [product]
Evista [product]
Examen [product]
Excedrin [product]
Excel Legacy Corp. [company]
Excel Maritime Carriers Ltd. [company]
Excell Global Services [company]
Excide Corp. [company]
Excite [on-line service] [company]
Excite@Home [company]
Exelon Corp. [company]
Exercycle [product]
Exerflex [product]
Exersole [product]
Exide Corp. [company]
Exiss Aluminum Trailers [product]
Ex-Lax [product]
EXP Pharmaceutical Waste Management
    [company]

Expeditors International of Washington Inc. [company]

Experimental and Applied Sciences [company]

Expert Eyes [product]

Express Mail [product]

Express Scripts Inc. [company]

Express.com [company]

Express-Med [company]

ExpressPay [company]

Extended Stay America Inc. [company]

Extendicare Inc. [company]

Extra [product]

Extra Value Meal [product]

ExtravaganZZa, The [company & product]

EXX Inc. [company]

Exxon [company]

Exxon Mobil Corp. [company]

E-Z-EM Inc. [company]

F & M National Corp. [company]

Fa [product]

FAB Industries Inc. [company]

Fabergé [company & product]

Factset Research Systems Inc. [company]

Faegre & Benson [company]

Fahnestock Viner Holdings Inc. [company]

Fahrenheit [product]

Fair Isaac & Co. Inc. [company]

Fairchild Semiconductor International Inc. [company]

Fairfield Communities Inc. [company]

Falcon Products Inc. [company]

Fales Foundation Trust, The [nonprofit]

Falmouth Bancorp, Inc. [company]

Family Dollar Stores [company]

Family Dollar Stores Inc. [company]

Family Planning International Assistance [nonprofit]

Famous Footwear [company]

Fanggs [product]

Fannie Mae [nickname for Federal National Mortgage Association] [company]

Fansteel Inc. [company]

Fanta [product]

Fantastik [product]

FAO Schwarz [company]

Farm Family Holding Inc. [company]

Farm Plan [company]

Farmland Industries, Inc. [company]

Farmstead Telephone Group Inc. [company]

Fassino Foundation [nonprofit]

Father Flanagan's Boys' Town [nonprofit]

Favor [product]

FaxWatch Strategic Information Services [company]

FBL Financial Group Inc. [company]

FBR Asset Investment Corp. [company]

FDX Corp. [company]

Fedders Corp. [company]

Federal Express (also FedEx) [company]

Federal Home Mortgage Corp. [official name of Freddie Mac] [company]

Federal National Mortgage Association [official name of Fannie Mae] [company]

Federal Realty Investment Trust [company]

Federal Signal Corp. [company]

Federal-Mogul Corp. [company]

Federated Department Stores, Inc. [company]

Federated Investors Inc. [company]

FedEx Corp. [company]

Feed the Children [nonprofit]

Feel Good for Life [company]

Feen-a-mint [product]

FelCor Lodging Trust Inc. [company]

Fels Fund, Samuel S, The [nonprofit]

Fenwick & West [company]

Ferrari [product]

Ferrellgas Partners L.P. [company]

Ferro Corp. [company]

Fetzer California [company]

Fetzer Institute [nonprofit]

FFP Marketing Co. Inc. [company]

FFP Partners L.P. [company]

FHL Foundation Inc. [company]

Fiat S.P.A. [company]

Fiber Plus [product]

Fiberglas [product]

Fibermark Inc. [company]
Fiberworks [company]
Fidelity BancShares Inc. [company]
Fidelity Investments Charitable Gift Fund
  [company]
Fidelity National Financial Inc.
  [company]
Field of Dreams [company]
Fields Pond Foundation Inc. [company]
Fifth Third Bancorp [company]
Fig Newtons [product]
Figurines [product]
Fila [company & product]
Filene's [company]
Filene's Basement [company]
Filet-O-Fish [product]
Film Foundation Inc., The [nonprofit]
Filofax [product]
Fimo [product]
Financial Federal Corp. [company]
Financial Security Assurance Holdings Ltd.
  [company]
Financial Technologies [company]
Find an NYSE Listed Co. [company]
Fin-Fan [product]
fingerhut.com [company]
Finish Line [company & product]
Finlay Enterprises [company]
Finnegan Henderson Farabow Garrett &
  Dunner [company]
Finova Finance Trust [company]
Finova Group Inc. [company]
Fiorellos [company]
Firehawk [company & product]
Firestone [company]
First American Corp., The [company]
First American Financial Corp. [company]
First American Health Concepts Inc.
  [company]
First Banks America Inc. [company]
First City Bank [company]
First Commonwealth Financial Corp.
  [company]

First Commonwealth Fund Inc. [company]
First Data Corp. [company]
First Edge Sornson [company]
First Financial Fund Inc. [company]
First Foods [company]
First Fruit Inc. [company]
First Industries Realty Trust Inc. [company]
First Israel Fund Inc., The [company]
First National of Nebraska Inc. [company]
First Philippine Fund Inc., The [company]
First Republic Bank [company]
First Residential Mortgage Network [company]
First Response [product]
First Tennessee National Corp. [company]
First Things First [company]
First Union Corp. [company]
First Union Real Estate Equity & Mortgage
  Investment [company]
First Virginia Banks Inc. [company]
First Washington Realty Trust Inc. [company]
First West Virginia Bancorp Inc. [company]
Firstar Corp. [company]
firstauction.com [company]
FirstEnergy Corp. [company]
Firstfed Financial Corp. [company]
Firstier Bancorp Inc. [company]
FirstPro [company]
Fiserv Inc. [company]
Fisher Scientific International Inc. [company]
Fisher-Price [company]
Fisons [company]
Fitzpatrick Foundation, The [nonprofit]
Five Alive [product]
Flagyl [product]
Flair [product]
Flanigan's Enterprises Inc. [company]
Flash Electronics [company]
Fleet Financial Group Inc. [company]
FleetBoston Financial Corp. [company]
Fleetwood Enterprises Inc. [company]
Fleischmann's [company & product]
Fleming Cos. Inc. [company]
Fleming Retail [company]

Fletcher Building Ltd. [company]
Fletcher Challenge Energy Division [company]
Fletcher Challenge Ltd. [company]
Fletcher Challenge Ltd. [company]
Flexeril [product]
Flexible Flyer [product]
Flexzone [product]
Flinn Foundation, The [nonprofit]
Flomax [product]
Flonase [product]
Flooring America [company]
Florida East Coast Industries Inc. [company]
Florida Progress Corp. [company]
Florida Public Utilities Co. [company]
Florida Rock Industries Inc. [company]
Flovent [product]
Flowers Industries Inc. [company]
Flowserve Corp. [company]
Fluon [product]
Fluor Corp. [company]
Fluorigard [product]
Flying Horse, The [company]
FMC Corp. [company]
Foamaster [product]
Foamex International Inc. [company]
Foamglas [product]
Foamy [product]
Focus on the Family [nonprofit]
fogdog.com [company]
Foley & Lardner [company]
Folgers [product]
Food for the Poor [nonprofit]
Foodarama Supermarkets Inc. [company]
Foot Locker [company]
Footaction [company]
footlocker.com [company]
Footstar [company]
Footstar Inc. [company]
Ford Family Foundation, The [nonprofit]
Ford Foundation, Edward E., The [nonprofit]
Ford Foundation, The [nonprofit]
Ford Motor Co. [company]

Fordham Foundation, Thomas B., The [nonprofit]
Forest City Enterprises Inc. [company]
Forest Oil Corp. [company]
Formica [product]
Formula 409 [product]
Fort Dearborn Income Securities Inc. [company]
Fort James Corp. [company]
Fortis Securities Inc. [company]
Fortune 500 Index Tracking Stock [company]
Fortune Brands Inc. [company]
Fortune e-50 Index Tracking Stock [company]
Fosamax [product]
Foster Wheeler Corp. [company]
Foster's [product]
Fotomat [company]
Foundation for Child Development [nonprofit]
Foundation for College Christian Leaders, The [nonprofit]
Foundation for Hellenic Culture Inc., The [nonprofit]
Foundation for Microbiology [nonprofit]
Foundation for Middle East Peace [nonprofit]
Foundation for Seacoast Health [nonprofit]
Foundation for the Advancement of MesoAmerican Studies Inc. [nonprofit]
Foundation for the Future [nonprofit]
Foundation Health System Inc. [nonprofit]
Foundation of Faith [nonprofit]
Four Seasons Hotels Inc. [company]
Four Seasons, The [company]
Fourjay Foundation, The [nonprofit]
Fowler Memorial Foundation [nonprofit]
FOX [company]
Fox Entertainment Group, Inc. [company]
Fox, Rothschild, O'Brien & Frankel [company]
FoxPro [company]
FPL Group Inc. [company]
France Growth Fund Inc., The [company]
France Telecom [company]
Franchise Finance Corp. of America [company]
Franco-American [company]

Frangelico [product]
Franken Berry [product]
Frankenmuth Bavarian Inn [product]
Franklin American Mortgage [company]
Franklin Capital Corp. [company]
Franklin Covey Co. [company]
Franklin Electronic Publishers Inc. [company]
Franklin Multi-Income Trust [company]
Franklin Resources Inc. [company]
Franklin Telecommunications Corp. [company]
Franklin Templeton Investments [company]
Franklin Universal Trust [company]
Frappuccino [product]
Fred Hutchinson Cancer Research Center
   [nonprofit]
Freddie Mac [nickname for Federal Home
   Mortgage Corp.] [company]
Freedent [product]
Freedom Forum Inc. [nonprofit]
Freelance Graphics [company]
FreeLife International [company]
Freeman Spogli & Co. [company]
Freeport-McMoRan Copper & Gold, Inc.
   [company]
Fremont General Corp. [company]
French's [company & product]
Freon [product]
Frequency Electronics Inc. [company]
Fresca [product]
Fresh Del Monte Produce Inc. [company]
Fresh Step [product]
Fresh-Trak [company]
Frey Foundation, The [nonprofit]
Frialator [company & product]
Friede Goldman International Inc. [company]
Friedman Industries Inc. [company]
Friedman-Klarreich Family Foundation, The
   [nonprofit]
Friendly Ice Cream Corp. [company]
Frigidaire [company & product]
Frisbee [product]
Frisch's Restaurants Inc. [company]
Frist Foundation, The [nonprofit]

Frito-Lay [Frito-Lay's, Frito Lay] [company]
Fritz Cos. Inc. [company]
Frontier Adjusters of America Inc. [company]
Frontier Insurance Group Inc. [company]
Frontier Oil Corp. [company]
Frontline Communications Corp. [company]
FrontPage [product]
Froot Loops [product]
Frost Bank [company]
Frosted Mini-Wheats [product]
Frozfruit [product]
Fruit & Fibre [product]
Fruit Of The Loom [company & product]
Fruit Roll-Ups [product]
Fruitful Bran [product]
Fruitopia [product]
Frusen Glädjé [product]
Fry Baby [product]
Fry Foundation, Lloyd A., The [nonprofit]
FryDaddy [product]
FTD [company]
FTI Consulting Inc. [company]
Fudgsicle [product]
Fulbright & Jaworski [company]
Fuld Health Trust, Helene, The [nonprofit]
Full Line Distributors, Inc. [company]
Fuller [company]
Fuller Foundation Inc., The [nonprofit]
Fulton's Crab House [company]
Fun Pak [product]
Fund for Astrophysical Research [nonprofit]
Fund for Nonviolence [nonprofit]
Fund for the City of New York Inc. [nonprofit]
Funyunsonion [product]
Furniture Brands International Inc. [company]
furniture.com [company]
Furon Co. [company]
Furosemide [product]
Furrow, The [company]
Furr's Restaurant Group Inc. [company]
Futura [product]
Future [product]
G&L Realty Corp. [company]

G&P Charitable Foundation Inc., The [nonprofit]
G.A. Sullivan [company]
G.I. Joe [product]
GA Financial Inc. [company]
Gabelli Convertible Securities Fund Inc., The [nonprofit]
Gabelli Equity Trust Inc., The [company]
Gabelli Global Multimedia Trust Inc., The [company]
Gabelli Utility Trust, The [company]
Gables Residential Trust [company]
Gaines [company & product]
Gainsco Inc. [company]
Galaxy Nutritional Foods Inc. [company]
Galey & Lord Inc. [company]
Galileo International Inc. [company]
Gallagher's Steak House [company]
Gallaher Group P.L.C. [company]
Gallo [company]
Gallup Poll, The [company & product]
Game Boy [product]
Game of Life [product]
Gannett Co. Inc. [company]
Gant [product]
Gap [clothing] [company]
Gap Inc. [company]
Gap Inc., The [company]
Gap Kids [company]
Gap, The [company]
gap.com [company]
Gardner Denver Inc. [company]
Gardner, Carton & Douglas [company]
Gart Sports [company]
Gartner Inc. [company]
Gates Family Foundation, The [nonprofit]
Gates Foundation, Bill and Melinda, The [nonprofit]
Gateway Inc. [company]
gateway.com [company]
Gatorade [product]
Gatx Corp. [company]
Gauloises [product]

Gaylord Container Corp. [company]
Gaylord Entertainment Co. [company]
GB Holdings Inc. [company]
GBI Capital Management Corp. [company]
GC Cos. Inc. [company]
GDI Infotech [company]
GelBond [product]
Gellert Foundation, Carl Gellert and Celia Berta, The [nonprofit]
GelStar [product]
Gemfibrozil [product]
Gemini [company & product]
GenAmerica Corp. [company]
Gencorp Inc. [company]
Genentech Inc. [company]
Gener S.A. [company]
General American Investors Co. Inc. [company]
General Cable Corp. [company]
General Chemical Group Inc. [company]
General Cigar Holdings Inc. [company]
General Datacomm Industries Inc. [company]
General Dynamics Corp. [company]
General Electric (GE) [company]
General Electric Co. [company]
General Employment Enterprises Inc. [company]
General Growth Properties Inc. [company]
General Mills Inc. [company]
General Motors Acceptance Corp. [company]
General Motors Corp. [company]
General Semiconductor Inc. [company]
General Service Foundation, The [nonprofit]
Genesco Inc. [company]
Genesco Retail[company]
Genesis Communications International [company]
Genesis Energy L.P. [company]
Genesis Health Ventures Inc. [company]
Genesis Worldwide Inc. [company]
Genetronics Biomedical Ltd. [company]
GenRad Inc. [company]
GenStar Therapeutics Corp. [company]
Gentek Inc. [company]

Gentiva Health Services [company]
Gentle Touch [product]
Genuine Parts Co. [company]
Geo [product]
George Family Foundation, The [nonprofit]
George Foundation, The [nonprofit]
Georges Marciano [company & product]
Georgia Gulf Corp. [company]
Georgia Pacific Corp. [company]
Georgia Power Capital L.P. [company]
Georgia Power Co. [company]
Georgia-Pacific [company]
Georgia-Pacific Corp. [company]
Gerber [company]
Gerber Childrenswear Inc. [company]
Gerber Foundation, The [nonprofit]
Gerber Scientific Inc. [company]
Gerbode Foundation, Wallace Alexander Getty
   Trust, J. Paul, The [nonprofit]
Geritol [product]
Germany Fund Inc., The [company]
Get A Piece of the Rock [product]
Getaway [company]
Getty Realty Corp. [company]
Giant Eagle [company]
Giant Industries Inc. [company]
Gibson Foundation, Addison H., The
   [nonprofit]
Gibson, Dunn [product]
Gibsons [product]
Gifts in Kind International [company]
GigaMedia Ltd. [company]
Gilbert [company & product]
Gildan Activewear Inc. [company]
Gill Foundation, The [company]
Gillette [company]
Gillette Co., The [company]
Gilmore Foundation, Irving S., The [nonprofit]
Gilsonite [product]
Ginsu [product]
Giorgio Armani [company & product]
Girl Scouts of the USA [nonprofit]
Girling [company & product]

Girls Inc. [nonprofit]
Glacier Water Services Inc. [company]
GLAD [product]
Glade [product]
Gladstone's 4 Fish [company]
Glamis Gold Ltd. [company]
Glare [product]
Glaser Family Foundation [nonprofit]
Glass Mates [product]
GlaxoSmithKline P.L.C. [company]
Glazer Family Foundation, The [nonprofit]
Gleason Corp. [company]
Glenborough Realty Trust Inc. [company]
Glenlivet, The [company]
Glenn Foundation for Medical Research Inc.,
   Paul F., The [nonprofit]
Glimcher Realty Trust [company]
Global Consultants [company]
Global Crossing Ltd. [company]
Global Election Systems Inc. [company]
Global Environmental Project Institute Inc.
   [company]
Global High Income Dollar Fund Inc.
   [company]
Global Income Fund Inc. [company]
Global Industries Technologies Inc. [company]
Global Light Telecommunications Inc.
   [company]
Global Marine Inc. [company]
Global Partners Income Fund Inc. [company]
Global Payments Inc. [company]
Global Tech Appliances Inc. [company]
Global Technovations Inc. [company]
Global Telesystems Group Inc. [company]
Global Vacation Group Inc. [company]
Glock [company]
Glucophage [product]
Glucotrol XL [product]
Glyburide [product]
Glyphix Studio [company]
GM [company]
GMAC [company]
GMC [company]

GNS [company]
Godiva [company & product]
Godzilla [product]
Go-e-biz.com [company]
Going to the Game! [product]
Goizueta Foundation, The [nonprofit]
Gold Kist [company]
Gold Medal [company & product]
Gold Medallion [product]
Gold Top [product]
Goldcorp Inc. [company]
Golden Grahams [product]
Golden Rule Foundation Inc., The [nonprofit]
Golden State Bancorp Inc. [company]
Golden West Financial Corp. [company]
Goldfield Corp. The [company]
Goldfish [product]
Goldman Environmental Foundation, The
   [nonprofit]
Goldman Fund, Richard & Rhoda, The
   [nonprofit]
Goldman Sachs Group Inc. [company]
Golf Trust of America Inc. [company]
Goobers [product]
Good & Plenty [product]
Good Guys [company]
Good Housekeeping Seal of Approval
   [product]
Good Humor [company & product]
Goodrich BF Co. [company]
Goodrich Petroleum Corp. [company]
Goodwill Industries International Inc.
   [company]
Goodwin, Procter & Hoar [company]
Goody's [company]
Goody's Family Clothing Inc. [company]
Goodyear [company]
Goodyear Tire & Rubber Co. [company]
Goodyear Tire & Rubber Co. and Subsidiaries,
   The [company]
Gordon's [company]
Gore-Tex [product]
Gorham [company & product]

Gorman-Rupp Co., The [company]
Got Milk? [slogan]
Gotham Bar & Grill [company]
Gottschalks Inc. [company]
Gouverneur Bancorp Inc. [company]
GP Strategies Corp. [company]
GPU [company]
GPU Inc. [company]
Grable Foundation [company]
Graco Inc. [company]
Graduate Record Examinations [also GRE]
   [product]
Graduates [product]
Graham Corp. [company]
Graham Foundation for the Advanced Studies
   in the Fine Arts, The [nonprofit]
Grainger W. W. Inc. [company]
Grand Concourse [company]
Grand Marnier [product]
Grand Met Del L.P. [company]
Grand Ole Opry [company]
Grand Union [company]
Grand Union Co., The [company]
GrandMa's [product]
Granite Construction Inc. [company]
Granite Systems [company]
Grant Foundation, William T., The [nonprofit]
Grant Prideco Inc. [company]
Grape-Nuts [product]
Graphics Packaging Corp. [company]
Grass Foundation, The [nonprofit]
Graustein Memorial Fund, William Casper,
   The [nonprofit]
GravyMaster [product]
Gray, Cary, Ware & Freidenrich [company]
Gray Communications Systems Inc. [company]
Graybar Electric Co. Inc. [company]
GRC International Inc. [company]
Great American Financial Resources Inc.
   [company]
Great Atlantic & Pacific Tea Co Inc. [company]
Great Expectations [company]
Great Lakes Chemical Corp. [company]

Great Lakes REIT Inc. [company]
Great Lash [product]
Great Northern Iron Ore Properties [company]
Great Outdoors [product]
Great Start [product]
Greater China Fund Inc., The [company]
Great-West Life Assurance Co., The [company]
Green Giant [product]
Green Mountain Fund Inc. [company]
Green Mountain Power Corp. [company]
Greenberg, Traurig, Kirkpatrick & Lockhart [company]
Greenbriar Corp. [company]
Greenbrier Cos. Inc. [company]
Greenleaf Landscape Systems & Services [company]
Greenpoint Financial Corp. [company]
Greenwall Foundation, The [nonprofit]
Greenwich Street California Municipal Fund Inc. [company]
Grey Global [company]
Grey Wolf Inc. [company]
Greyhound [company]
Griffon Corp. [company]
Gripco [company & product]
Gristede's Foods Inc. [company]
Grotto Foundation Inc., The [nonprofit]
Group 1 Automotive Inc. [company]
Groupe Danone [company]
Grubb & Ellis Co. [company]
Grupo Elektra [company]
Grupo Imsa S.A. [company]
Grupo Radio Centro S.A. [company]
Grupo Simec S.A. de C.V. [company]
Grupo Televisa S.A. [company]
Grupo Tribasa S.A. [company]
GSE Systems Inc. [company]
GTE [company]
GTE Corp. [company]
Gtech Holdings Corp. [company]
GTI [company]
GTR Group Inc. [company]

Guangshen Railway Ltd. [company]
Guardian Life Insurance Co. of America [company]
Gucci [company & product]
Gucci Group N.V. [company]
Guess? [company & product]
Guest Supply Inc. [company]
Guggenheim Foundation, Harry Frank, The [nonprofit]
Guggenheim Memorial Foundation, John Simon, The [nonprofit]
Guidant Corp. [company]
Guinness [company & product]
Guitar Center [company]
Gulf [company]
Gumbiner Foundation, Josephine S., The [nonprofit]
Gund Foundation, George, The [nonprofit]
Gunk Foundation, The [nonprofit]
GWI Software [company]
Gyne-Lotrimin [product]
H&Q Healthcare Investors [company]
H&Q Life Sciences Investors [company]
H&R Block Inc. [company]
H.B. Fuller Co. [company]
H.E.B. [company]
H.J. Heinz Co. [company]
H2OH! [product]
Häagen-Dazs [product]
Haas Fund, Walter and Elise, The [nonprofit]
Habitat for Humanity International [nonprofit]
Habitrol [product]
Hacky Sack [product]
Hadassah Medical Relief Association [nonprofit]
Hadco Corp. [company]
Haemonetics Corp. [company]
Hagen Family Foundation, The [nonprofit]
Halcion [product]
Halcyon Hill Foundation [product]
Haldol [product]
Hale & Dorr [company]
Half Robert International Inc. [company]

Halifax Corp. [company]
Halliburton Co. [company]
Hallmark [company]
Hallmark Financial Services Inc. [company]
Halls [company & product]
Hall-Voyer Foundation, The [nonprofit]
Hallwood Group Inc. [company]
Hallwood Realty Partners L.P. [company]
Halo [company & product]
Halo Industries Inc. [company]
Halon [company & product]
Hambrecht & Quist Group [company]
Hamburger Helper [product]
Hamel Group [company]
Hampton Industries Inc. [company]
Hampton Inn [company]
Hancock Fabrics Inc. [company]
Hancock Foundation, Luke B., The [nonprofit]
Handi Wipes [product]
Handi-Pak [product]
Handi-Wrap [product]
Handleman Co. [product]
Handsaver [product]
Handycam [product]
Hanes [company & product]
Hanger Orthopedic Groups Inc. [company]
Hannaford Bros. Co. [company]
Hanover Capital Mortgage Holdings Inc.
 [company]
Hanover Compressor Co. [company]
Hanover Direct [company]
Hanover Direct Inc. [company]
Hanson P.L.C. [company]
Happy Meal [product]
Happy Strips [product]
harborfreight.com [product]
Harcourt General Inc. [company]
Hard Drives Northwest [company]
Hard Rock Cafe [company]
Hardee's [company]
Hardin Foundation, Phil, The [nonprofit]
Hardwick [appliances] [company]
Harken Energy Corp. [company]

Harlequin [company]
Harley-Davidson (also Harley) [product]
Harley-Davidson Cafe [company]
Harley-Davidson Inc. [company]
Harleysville Mutual Insurance Co. [company]
Harman International Industries Inc.
 [company]
Harnischfeger Industries [company]
Harold's Stores, Inc. [company]
Harp [company & product]
Harrah's [company]
Harrahs Entertainment Inc. [company]
Harris [company]
Harris Corp. [company]
Harris Ranch Restaurant [company]
Harris, Shriver & Jacobson [company]
Harris-Teeter [company]
Harry Caray's [company]
harryanddavid.com [company]
Harsco Corp. [company]
Hart Schaffner & Marx [company]
Harte Hanks Inc. [company]
Hartex Property Group [company]
Hartford [company]
Hartford Courant Foundation, The [nonprofit]
Hartford Financial Services Group Inc.
 [company]
Hartford Foundation Inc., John A., The
 [nonprofit]
Hartford Life Inc. [company]
Hartmann [company]
Hartmarx Corp. [company]
Har-Tru [product]
Harveys Bristol Cream [product]
Hasbro Inc. [company]
Hasselblad [company]
Hastings Manufacturing Co. [company]
Hatteras Income Securities Inc. [company]
Havahart [company & product]
Have it your way [slogan]
Haverty Furniture Cos. Inc. [company]
Havoline [product]
Hawaiian Airlines Inc. [company]

Hewlett Foundation, William and Flora, The [nonprofit]
Hewlett-Packard [company]
Hewlett-Packard Co. [company]
Hexcel Corp. [company]
Hibernia Corp. [company]
Hi-C [product]
Hickey-Freeman [company]
Hidden Valley Ranch [product]
Hide-A-Bed [company]
High Income Opportunity Fund, Inc. [company]
High Yield Income Fund Inc., The [company]
High Yield Plus Fund Inc., The [company]
Highlands Insurances Group Inc. [company]
HighMark [company]
Hilb, Rogal & Hamilton Co. [company]
Hi-Liter [product]
Hillenbrand Industries Inc. [company]
Hilles Fund, Allen, The [company]
Hilton Foundation, Conrad N., The [nonprofit]
Hilton Group P.L.C. [company]
Hilton Hotels Corp. [company]
Hinshaw & Culbertson [company]
Hi-Shear Technology Corp. [company]
Hispanic Broadcasting Corp. [company]
History Book Club, The [company]
Hitachi [company]
Hitachi Ltd. [company]
HLM Design Inc. [company]
HMG/Courtland Properties Inc. [company]
Ho Hos [product]
Hobart [company]
Hobby Lobby [company]
Hobie Cat [company & product]
Hoblitzelle Foundation, The [nonprofit]
Hogan & Hartson [company]
Hoglund Foundation, The [nonprofit]
Holiday Inn [company]
Holland & Knight [company]
Hollinger International Inc. [company]
Hollofil [product]
Holly Corp. [company]

Holly Hobbie [product]
Hollywood Casino Corp. [company]
Home Cookin' [product]
Home Depot, The [company]
Home Depot Inc., The [company]
Home Properties of New York Inc. [company]
Home Security International Inc. [company]
Home Shopping Network [company]
HomeBase [company]
HomeBase Inc. [company]
Homefed Corp. [company]
homegrocer.com [company]
Homeowners' Do-It-Yourself [product]
HomePlace of America [company]
Homestake Mining Co. [company]
Homestead Village Inc. [company]
Hometown Pride Awards [product]
Hon Industries Inc. [company]
Honda Motors Inc. [company]
Honey Baked Ham [product]
Honeywell International Inc. [company]
Hooper Holmes, Inc. [company]
Hooters [company]
Hoover [company]
Horace Mann Educators Corp. [company]
Horizon [spas] [product]
Horizon Foundation, The [nonprofit]
Horizon Medical Products Inc. [company]
Horizon Pharmacies Inc. [company]
Hormel [company]
Hormel Foods Corp. [company]
Hospitality Properties Trust [company]
Hospitality Solutions International [company]
Host Marriott Corp. [company]
Host Marriott Services Corp. [company]
Hostess [company & product]
Hot Wheels [company & product]
Hot Wings [product]
HotBot [company]
Hotelworks.com Inc. [company]
Hotmail [product]
Hotpoint [company]
Houghton Mifflin Co. [company]

Hound Dog Products [company]
Household Capital Trust [company]
Household International Inc. [company]
Houston Endowment Inc. [company]
Houston Exploration Co., The [company]
Houston Nutrition [company]
Hovnanian Enterprises Inc. [company]
Howard Johnson [company]
Howell Corp. [company]
Howmet International Inc. [company]
Howrey, Simon [company]
hp.com [company]
HPSC Inc. [company]
HS Resources Inc. [company]
HSB Group, Inc. [company]
HSBC Holding P.L.C. [company]
hsn.com [company]
HSU Development [company]
HTC Global Services [company]
HTH [company]
Huaneng Power International Inc. [company]
Hub Group Distribution Services [company]
Hub Group Inc. [company]
Hubba Bubba [product]
Hubbard Health Care [company]
Hubbell Inc. [company]
Hudson [company]
Hudson United Bancorp [company]
Huffy Corp. [company]
Huggies [product]
Hughes Electronics Corp. [company]
Hughes Hubbard Reed [company]
Hughes Supply, Inc. [company]
Hugoton Royalty Trust [company]
Hula-Hoop [product]
Humana Inc. [company]
Humvee [product]
Hungarian Telephone & Cable Corp.
  [company]
Hungry-Man [product]
Hunt Corp. [company]
Hunt's [company]
Huntco Inc. [company]

Hunter's Hope Foundation Inc. [nonprofit]
Huntington Bancshares Inc. [company]
Hunton & Williams [company]
Huntway Refining Co. [company]
Hush Puppies [product]
Hussmann International Inc. [company]
Hut Foundation [nonprofit]
Huttig Building Products Inc. [company]
Hutton Foundation [nonprofit]
Hyatt [company]
Hyde and Watson Foundation, The [nonprofit]
Hydraloe [product]
Hydrochlorothiazide [product]
Hydrocodone w/APAP [product]
Hydrocortone [product]
Hy-Gard [product]
Hyjet [product]
Hyland Software [company]
Hypercom Corp. [company]
HyperEdge [company]
Hyperion Total Return Fund Inc., The
  [company]
HypoVereinsbank A.G. [company]
Hytrin [product]
Hyundai Engineering & Construction Co.
  [company]
Hy-Vee [product]
Hyzaar [product]
I.C.H. Corp. [company]
i2 Foundation, The [nonprofit]
IASIS Healthcare Corp. [company]
iBASEt [company]
IBC [company]
IBEAR [company]
IBM [company]
IBP Inc. [company]
ICI [company]
ICICI Bank Ltd. [company]
ICN Pharmaceuticals Inc. [company]
Icon Mechanical Construction and Engineering
  [company]
Idacorp Inc. [company]
Identix Inc. [company]

Idex Corp. [company]
IDT Corp. [company]
IEM [company]
IES Utilities Inc. [company]
IGI Inc. [company]
Igloo [company]
Ihop Corp. [company]
IKEA [company]
IKON Office Solution Inc. [company]
Illinois Tool Works Inc. [company]
ILX Resorts Inc. [company]
Image Process Design [company]
Imagecom [company]
ImageWare Systems Inc. [company]
Imagio [company]
Imation Corp. [company]
IMAX [company]
IMC Global Inc. [company]
Imco Recycling Inc. [company]
Imdur [product]
Imitrex [product]
Immune Response [product]
Immunopure [product]
Imodium [product]
Impac Mortgage Holdings, Inc. [company]
Imperial Bancorp [company]
Imperial Chem Inds P.L.C. [company]
Imperial Oil Ltd. [company]
Imperial Parking Corp. [company]
Imperial Sugar Co. [company]
Imperial Tobacco Group P.L.C. [company]
Implant Sciences Corp. [company]
Improv [company]
Impulse Group [company]
IN/MAX [company]
InaCom Corp. [company]
INCO [company]
Income Opportunities Fund 1999 Inc.
  [company]
Income Opportunity Realty Trust [company]
Inco-Weld [company]
Independent Bankshares Inc. [company]
Inderal [product]

India Fund Inc. [company]
India Growth Fund Inc., The [company]
Indiana Energy Inc. [company]
Indiana Michigan Power Co. [company]
Indicator [product]
Indigo Investment Systems [company]
Indonesian Satelite Corp. [company]
Indus [company]
Industrial Data Systems Corp. [company]
Industrial Distribution Group Inc. [company]
Indymac Bancorp Inc. [company]
Infineon Technologies A.G. [company]
Infinity Broadcasting Corp. [company]
Infinity Contractors [company]
Infinity Software Development [company]
Inflate-All [product]
Info Technologies [company]
Infonet Services Corp. [company]
InfoNXX [company]
Informatica [company]
Information Holdings Inc. [company]
Inforonics [company]
InfoSphere [company]
Infrasoft [company]
ING Capital Funding Trust [company]
Ingersoll-Rand Co. [company]
Inglenook [company]
Ingles Markets Inc. [company]
Ingram Micro Inc. [company]
Inline [product]
Innkeepers USA Trust [company]
Innogy Holdings P.L.C. [company]
InnSuites Hospitality Trust [company]
Inocor [product]
Input Output Inc. [company]
Insight Enterprises Inc. [company]
Insignia Financial Group Inc. [company]
InSite Vision Inc. [company]
Inspired Design [product]
Instagreen [product]
InstallShield Software [product]
Instamatic [product]
Insteel Industries Inc. [company]

Institute of Current World Affairs Inc. [company]

Institute of Mental Hygiene of the City of New Orleans [nonprofit]

Institute of Turkish Studies Inc. [nonprofit]

Insured Municipal Income Fund [company]

Intal [company]

Integra Inc. [company]

Integral Technologies [company]

Integrated Electrical Services Inc. [company]

Integrated Health Services Inc. [company]

Integro [company]

Intel Corp. [company]

Intel Inside [product]

Intelli-Check, Inc. [company]

Intelligent Controls, Inc. [company]

Intelligent Systems Corp. [company]

IntelliNet [company]

Intellipath [company]

Intellisol International [company]

InteQ [company]

Interface [company]

Interface Software [company]

Intergrated Electrical Services Inc. [company]

Interim Services Inc. [company]

Interlott Technologies Inc. [company]

Intermagnetics General Corp. [company]

International [trucks] [company & product]

International Airline Support Group Inc. [company]

International Aluminum Corp. [company]

International Business Machines Corp. [IBM] [company]

International Flavors & Fragrances Inc. [company]

International Game Technology [company]

International Inventory Management [company]

International Multifoods Corp. [company]

International Nickel [company]

International Paper Co. [company]

International Power P.L.C. [company]

International Rectifier Corp. [company]

International Remote Imaging Systems Inc. [company]

International Shipholding Corp. [company]

International Specialty Products Inc. [company]

internationalmale.com [company]

INTERPLAK [product]

Interpool Inc. [company]

Interpublic Group of Cos. Inc. [company]

Interstate Bakeries Corp. [company]

Interstate General Co. L.P. [company]

InterSystems Inc. [company]

Intertan Inc. [company]

Intertape Polymer Group [company]

Intimate Brands [company]

Intimate Brands Inc. [company]

International Aid [company]

Intrawest Corp. [company]

INTRUST Capital Trust [company]

Invacare Corp. [company]

Inverness Medical Technology Inc. [company]

Invesco Global Health Sciences Fund [company]

Investment Co. Institute [nonprofit]

Investment Grade Municipal Income Fund [company]

Investment Technology Group Inc. [company]

Investors Capital Holdings Ltd. [company]

Iomed Inc. [company]

Iomega Corp. [company]

Ionics Inc. [company]

Ipalco Enterprises Inc. [company]

iParty Corp. [company]

IPI Inc. [company]

Ipsco Inc. [company]

IQ Group [company]

IQ Systems [company]

iqvc.com [company]

IRI International Corp. [company]

Irish Investment Fund Inc., The [company]

Irish Mist [product]

Irish Spring [product]

Iron Mountain Inc. [company]

Jenn-Air [company & product]

Jenner & Block [company]

Jennings Foundation, Martha Holden, The [nonprofit]

Jergens [company & product]

Jerky Treats [product]

Jerome Foundation, The [nonprofit]

Jersey Central Power & Light Co. [company]

Jet Ski [product]

JetPaper [company & product]

Jetta [product]

Jewish Board of Family & Children's Services [nonprofit]

Jewish Foundation for Education of Women [nonprofit]

Jewish Healthcare Foundation [nonprofit]

Jheri Redding [company]

Jiffy [product]

Jiffy Pop [product]

Jim Beam [product]

Jimmy Dean [product]

Jimmy's Harborside [company]

Jinpan International Ltd. [company]

JLG Industries Inc. [company]

JLK Direct Distribution Inc. [company]

Jo Ann Stores, Inc. [company]

Jo-Ann Stores [company]

Jo-Ann Stores Inc. [company]

JobOptions.com [company]

Jockey [company]

Joe's Stone Crab [company]

Jogbra [product]

John Deere [company & product]

John Edward [company]

John H. Harland Co. [company]

John Hancock Bank and Thrift Opportunity Fund [company]

John Hancock Financial Services [company]

John Hancock Financial Services Inc. [company]

John Keeler & Co. [company]

John Q. Hammons Hotels Inc. [company]

Johnnie Walker Scotch [product]

Johns-Manville Corp. [company]

Johnson & Johnson [company]

Johnson & Michaels [company]

Johnson [company & product]

Johnson Foundation Inc., The [company]

Johnson Foundation, Helen K. and Arthur E., The [nonprofit]

Johnson Foundation, Robert Wood, The [nonprofit]

Johnson Foundation, Walter S., The [nonprofit]

Johnson's [floor care] [company & product]

Johnson's [shampoo] [company & product]

Johnston Industries Inc. [company]

Jolt [product]

JoMiJo Foundation, The [nonprofit]

Jones Foundation Inc., W. Alton, The [nonprofit]

Jones Foundation, Daisy Marquis, The [nonprofit]

Jones Lang Lasalle Inc. [company]

Jones, Day, Reavis & Pogue [company]

Jordache [company]

Jostens Inc. [company]

Joukowsky Family Foundation, The [nonprofit]

Joule Inc. [company]

Journal Register Co. [company]

Jox [product]

Joyce Foundation, The [nonprofit]

JP Realty Inc. [company]

Juicy Fruit [product]

Jujyfruits [product]

Jumbo Jack [product]

JumboTron [product]

Junior Mints [product]

Junior Achievement [company]

Junior Scholastic [company]

Juno Internet [company]

Just Right [product]

Justice Fund, The [nonprofit]

Juvenile Diabetes Foundation International, The [nonprofit]

Juxtamark [company]

KN Energy Inc. [company]
K.C. Masterpiece [company]
K2 Inc. [company]
K2r [product]
Kahlúa [product]
Kahn's [company & product]
Kaiser Aluminum Corp. [company]
Kaiser Engineers [product]
Kaiser Family Foundation, Henry J., The
  [nonprofit]
Kal Kan [product]
Kaliber [product]
Kaneb Pipeline Partners L.P. [company]
Kankakee Bancorp, Inc. [company]
Kansas City Power & Light Co. [company]
Kansas City Southern Industies Inc. [company]
Kansas Health Foundation, The [nonprofit]
Kaopectate [product]
Kapor Foundation, Mitchell, The [nonprofit]
Karate [product]
Karl Lagerfeld [company]
Karma Foundation, The [nonprofit]
Karmann [company]
Karo [product]
Katten Muchin Zavis [company]
Katy Inds Inc. [company]
Kauffman Foundation, Ewing Marion, The
  [nonprofit]
Kaufman & Broad Home Corp. [company]
Kawabe Memorial Fund, The [nonprofit]
Kay-Bee Toy Stores [company]
Kaydon Corp. [company]
Kaye, Scholer, Fierman, Hays & Handler
  [company]
Kazanjian Economics Foundation Inc., Calvin
  K., The [nonprofit]
KB Home [company]
K-B Toys [company]
KBK Capital Corp. [company]
kbkids.com [company]
KC Industries [company]
KCS Energy Inc. [company]
K-Dur [product]

Keane Inc. [company]
Keds [company]
Keebler Foods Co. [company]
Keepsake [company & product]
Keithley Instruments Inc. [company]
Kelley Drye & Warren [company]
Kellogg Co. [company]
Kellogg Foundation, W.K., The [nonprofit]
Kellogg's [product]
Kellwood Co. [company]
Kelly Services Inc. [company]
Kelly's Roast Beef of Saugus [company]
Kelmax Equipment [company]
Kelox [company]
Kelvinator [product]
Kemet Corp. [company]
Kemper High Income Trust [company]
Kemper Intermediate Government Trust
  [company]
Kempore [company]
Kendall [company]
Kendall Foundation, Henry P., The [nonprofit]
Ken-L Ration [product]
Kenmore [product]
Kennametal Inc. [company]
Kennedy Jr. Foundation, Joseph P., The
  [nonprofit]
Kent Electronics Corp. [company]
Kentucky First Bancorp Inc. [company]
Kentucky Foundation for Women Inc.
  [company]
Kentucky Fried Chicken (KFC) [company]
Kentucky Power Co. [company]
Kerr Mcgee Corp. [company]
Kettering Family Foundation, The [nonprofit]
Kettering Foundation, Charles F., The
  [nonprofit]
Kevlar [product]
Kewpie [product]
Key Energy Services Inc. [company]
Key Production Co. Inc. [company]
Key Transportation Services [company]
Key3Media Group Inc. [company]

KeyCorp [company]
Keyspan Corp. [company]
Keystone Consolidated Industries Inc.
  [company]
Keystone Property Trust [company]
Keystone RV [company]
KFX Inc. [company]
KGRO [company]
Kibbles 'n Bits [product]
Kid Stuff [company & product]
Kids "R" Us [company]
Kids & More [company]
Kids Foot Locker [company]
Kids Mart [company]
KidVantage [company]
Kiferbaum Construction [company]
Kilpatrick Stockton [company]
Kilroy Realty Corp. [company]
Kimball Foundation, Sara H. and William R.,
  The [nonprofit]
Kimberly-Clark Corp. [company]
Kimco Realty Corp. [company]
Kimmel Foundation, Sidney, The [nonprofit]
Kimsey Foundation, The [nonprofit]
Kinam Gold Inc. [company]
Kinark Corp. [company]
Kinder Morgan Energy Partners L.P.
  [company]
Kinder Morgan, Inc. [company]
King & Spalding [company]
King Family Foundation Inc., Charles and
  Lucille [company]
King Pharmaceuticals Inc. [company]
King Power International Group Co., Ltd.
  [company]
King World Productions Inc. [company]
Kingsford [company & product]
Kinko's [company]
Kinney [company]
Kinross Gold Corp. [company]
Kirby Corp. [company]
Kirby Foundation, F.M., The [nonprofit]
Kirk Stieff [company]

Kirkland & Ellis [company]
Kirkwood Family Foundation, The [nonprofit]
Kirsch [company]
Kit Kat [product]
Kit Manufacturing Co. [company]
Kitchen Bouquet [product]
KitchenAid [company & product]
Kitten Chow [product]
Kitty Litter [product]
Kiwi [company]
Kix [product]
K-Kote [product]
Kla-Tencor Corp. [company]
Klear [product]
Kleenex [product]
Kleinwort Benson Australian Income Fund Inc.
  [company]
Kliegl [product]
Klingenstein Third Generation Foundation,
  The [nonprofit]
KLM Royal Dutch Airlines [company]
Klor-Con [company]
Kmart [company]
Kmart Corp. [company]
Knight Foundation, John S. and James L., The
  [nonprofit]
Knight Ridder Inc. [company]
Knight Trading Group Inc. [company]
Knights of Columbus [nonprofit]
Knoll [company]
Knoll Inc. [company]
Knorr [company]
Knott Foundation, Marion I. & Henry J., The
  [nonprofit]
Knowing [product]
Kodak (Eastman Kodak Co.) [company]
Koger Equity Inc. [company]
Kohl's [company]
Kohl's Corp. [company]
Koinonia Foundation, The [nonprofit]
Kongsgaard-Goldman Foundation, The
  [nonprofit]
Konica [company]

Koninklijke Philips Electronics [company]
Konover Property Trust Inc. [company]
Kool [product]
Kool-Aid [product]
Koor Industries [company]
Kopp Family Foundation, The [nonprofit]
Korea Equity Fund Inc. [company]
Korea Fund Inc., The [company]
Korea Telecom [company]
Korean Investment Fund Inc. [company]
Ko-Rec-Type [product]
Koret Foundation, The [nonprofit]
Korn Ferry International [company]
Kotex [product]
Kouros [product]
Kowloon, Saugus [company]
Kraft [product]
Kramer Levin Naftalis & Frankel [company]
Kramont Realty Trust [company]
Krause's Furniture Inc. [company]
Krazy Glue [product]
Kresge Foundation, The [nonprofit]
K-Resin [product]
Kress Foundation, Samuel H. [nonprofit]
Krispy Kreme [company]
Krogen Co. [company]
Kroger [company]
Kroger Co., The [company]
Kromekote [product]
Kronkosky Charitable Foundation, The
  [nonprofit]
KRUG [company]
Krug International Corp. [company]
Krunchers! [product]
K-Swiss [company & product]
Kubota Ltd. [company]
Kulas Foundation, The [nonprofit]
KV Pharmaceutical Co. [company]
KWiK'N EZ [product]
Kwikset [product]
K-Y [product]
Kyocera Corp. [company]
L3 Communication Holdings Inc. [company]

L.A. Gear [product]
L.L. Bean [company]
L'eggs [product]
L'Oréal [company]
L-3 Communications [company]
La Choy [company & product]
La Corona [company & product]
LaBarge Inc. [company]
Labatt's [company & product]
Labor Realty Inc. [company]
Laboratorio Chile S.A. [company]
Laboratory Corp. of America Holdings
  [company]
Laboratory Management Systems [company]
Labranche & Co. Inc. [company]
Lachman Foundation, Ronald and Mary Ann,
  The [nonprofit]
Laclede Gas Co. [company]
Lacoste [company & product]
Lactaid [product]
Ladies' Home Journal [product]
Lady Foot Locker [company]
Lady Speed Dry [product]
Lady Speed Stick [product]
Lady's Choice [product]
LaFetra Private Operating Foundation, The
  [nonprofit]
Lafrage Corp. [company]
Laidlaw Global Corp. [company]
Laidlaw One Inc. [company]
Laird Norton Endowment Foundation, The
  [nonprofit]
Lakehead Pipeline Partners [company]
Lakeshore Staffing [company]
Lalique [product]
Lalor Foundation, The [nonprofit]
Lam Research Corp. [company]
Lamborghini [company & product]
Lamisil [product]
Lamson & Sessions Co. [company]
Lan Chile S.A. [company]
LanTimes [company]
Lancer Corp. [company]

Lancers [product]

Lancôme [product]

Land Cruiser [product]

Land O Lakes [product]

Land Rover [product]

Landamerica Financial Group Inc. [company]

Landauer Inc. [company]

Landry's Seafood Restaraunts Inc. [company]

Lands' End [company]

Lands' End Inc. [company]

landsend.com [company]

Landstar System Inc. [company]

Lane Bryant [company]

lanebryant.com [company]

Langeloth Foundation, Jacob and Valeria, The [nonprofit]

Lanier [company]

Lanier Worldwide Inc. [company]

Lannan Foundation, The [nonprofit]

Lanoxin [product]

Lante Corp. [company]

Lark [company & product]

LaRue Trust, George A. and Dolly F., The [nonprofit]

Lasalle Hotel Properties [company]

Laser Mortgage Management Inc. [company]

Laser Technology Inc. [company]

LaserJet [product]

LaserWriter [product]

Lasker Foundation, Inc., Albert & Mary, The [nonprofit]

Lasmo P.L.C. [company]

Lassale [company]

Latham & Watkins [company]

Latin America Equity Fund Inc., The [nonprofit]

Latin American Discovery Fund Inc., The [nonprofit]

Laundromat [company]

Lava [product]

Laxmi Group [company]

Lay's [company]

Lazare Kaplan International Inc. [company]

La-Z-Boy [company & product]

La-Z-Boy Inc. [company]

LC-65 [company]

LCA Group Inc. [company]

LCM Internet Growth [company]

Le Bernardin [company]

Le Menu [product]

Le Sportsac [product]

Lean Cuisine [company]

Leaps & Bounds [product]

Lear Corp. [company]

Learjet [product]

Leather Factory Inc., The [company]

LeBoeuf, Lamb, Greene & MacRae [company]

Lectric Shave [product]

Lectro-Salt [product]

Lee [company]

Lee Enterprises Inc. [company]

Leerink Swann [product]

Leeway Foundation, The [nonprofit]

LEF Foundation, The [nonprofit]

Legg Mason Inc. [company]

Leggett & Platt Inc. [company]

LEGO [product]

Lehman ABS Corp. [company]

Lehman Brothers Holdings Capital [company]

Lehman Brothers Holdings Inc. [company]

Leisure [product]

Lender Express [company]

Lenel Systems International [company]

Lennar Corp. [company]

Lennox International Inc. [company]

Lenox [product]

Lens Plus [company]

LensCrafters [company]

Lenskeeper [company]

Lescol [company]

Lestoil [product]

Let's Find Out [product]

Leucadia National Corp. [company]

Leukemia & Lymphoma Society [nonprofit]

Leukeran [product]

Levaquin [product]

Levasole [product]
Levi's [company & product]
Leviathan Gas Pipeline Partners L.P. [company]
Levitz [company]
Levolor [company]
Levothroid [product]
Levoxyl [product]
Lewis, D'Amato, Brisbois & Bisgaard [company]
Lexan [product]
Lexington Corporate Properties Trust [company]
Lexis [product]
LexJet [product]
Lexmark International Group Inc. [company]
Lexmark International Inc. [company]
LG&E Energy Corp. [company]
LHJ [company]
Libbey Inc. [company]
Libby's [company]
Liberate Tecnologies [company]
Liberte Investors Inc. [company]
Liberty Ale [product]
Liberty All-Star Growth Fund Inc. [company]
Liberty Corp. [company]
Liberty Financial Cos. Inc. [company]
Liberty Mutual Insurance Group [company]
Liberty Property Trust [company]
Libra Foundation, The [nonprofit]
Librium [product]
Life Savers (also LifeSavers) [product]
Life Stride [product]
Lifebridge Foundation Inc., The [nonprofit]
Lifecodes [product]
Lifecycle [product]
Lifepoint Inc. [company]
Lifestream Technologies Inc. [company]
Light & Lean [product]
Light 'N Juicy [product]
Light n' Lively [product]
Lillian Vernon Corp. [company]
lillianvernon.com [company]

Limited [company]
Limited Inc. [company]
Limited Inc., The [company]
Lincoln Center for the Performing Arts [nonprofit]
Lincoln Logs [product]
Lincoln National Capital III [company]
Lincoln National Convertible Securities Fund Inc. [company]
Lincoln National Corp. [company]
Lincoln National Income Fund Inc. [company]
Lindsay Manufacturing Co. [company]
Lindsay Student Aid Fund, Franklin, The [nonprofit]
Lindsay Trust, Agnes M., The [nonprofit]
Line 6 [product]
Linens 'n Things [company]
Linksys [company]
Lions Gate Entertainment Corp. [company]
Lipitor [product]
Lipton [company]
Liquid Paper [product]
Liquid-Plumr [product]
Liquifilm [product]
Liquore Galliano [company]
Lisa Adelle Design [company]
Lisn [company]
List Foundation Inc., Albert A., The [nonprofit]
Listerine [product]
Listserv [product]
Lithia Motors Inc. [company]
Little Caesar [company]
Little Charlie's Pizza [company]
Little Debbie [company]
Little League Baseball [company]
Little Sizzlers [company]
Little Tikes [product]
Littler Mendelson [company]
Litton Industries Inc. [company]
Living [product]
Livingston Cellars [company]
LIX [product]

Liz Claiborne [company]
LL&E Royalty Trust [company]
llbean.com [company]
Lloyd Foundation, John M., The [nonprofit]
Lo/Ovral [product]
Loafer [product]
Lobster House, The [company]
LocalNet [company]
Locke Foundation, John, The [nonprofit]
Locke Liddell & Sapp [company]
Lockheed Martin Corp. [company]
Loctite [product]
Locus Telecommunications [company]
Lodgian Inc. [company]
Loestrin [product]
Loews Cineplex Entertainment Corp.
   [company]
Loews Corp. [company]
Logical Choice Technologies [company]
Logical Net [company]
Lomar [product]
Lomotil [product]
Lone Star Technologies Inc. [company]
Longs Drug Stores [company]
Longs Drug Stores Corp. [company]
Longview Fibre Co. [company]
Longview Foundation, The [nonprofit]
Looney Tunes [product]
Loose Trust, Carrie J., The [nonprofit]
Loose Trust, Harry Wilson, The [nonprofit]
Lopressor [product]
Loral Space & Communications Ltd.
   [company]
Lorazepam [product]
Lord, Bissell & Brook [company]
Lorus [company & product]
Lo-Salt [product]
Lotensin [product]
Lotrel [product]
Lotrisone [product]
Lotus [company & product]
Lotus Notes [product]
Louis Dreyfus Natural Gas Corp. [company]

Louis Tambellini's [company]
Louis Vuitton [company]
Louis Vuitton S.A. [company]
Louisiana-Pacific Corp. [company]
Love My Carpet [product]
Lowe [company]
Lowe Foundation, Edward, The [nonprofit]
Lowe's [company]
Löwenbräu [product]
Lowe's Cos. Inc. [company]
LSI Logic Corp. [company]
LSI Temporaries of Omaha [company]
LTC Properties Inc. [company]
LTD Financial Services [company]
ltdcommodities.com [company]
LTV Corp. [company]
Lubrizol [company & product]
Lubrizol Corp., The [product]
Luby's Inc. [company]
Lucas Educational Foundation, George, The
   [nonprofit]
Luce Foundation, Inc., Henry, The [nonprofit]
Lucent Technologies [company]
Lucent Technologies Inc. [company]
Lucite [product]
Lucky Charms [product]
Lucky Strike [product]
Lucrum [company]
Ludwick Family Foundation, The
   [nonprofit]
Lumber Liquidators [company]
Luminal [product]
Luminex Corp. [company]
Lumirror [product]
Lumpkin Foundation, The [nonprofit]
Lunchables [product]
Lurex [product]
Lutheran Services in America [nonprofit]
Luvs [product]
Luxottica Group [company]
LVMH Moët Hennessy Louis Vuitton S.A.
   [company]
Lyanier Worldwide Inc. [company]

Lycos [company]
Lycra [product]
Lynch Corp. [company]
Lynch Interactive Corp. [company]
Lyndhurst Foundation, The [nonprofit]
Lynk Systems [company]
Lynn Charitable Foundation, Nancy L., The
　[nonprofit]
Lyondell Chemical Co. [company]
Lysol [product]
M&F Worldwide Corp. [company]
M&M's [product]
M&T Bank Corp. [company]
Maalox [product]
Mac [Macintosh] [product]
MacArthur Foundation, John D. and Catherine
　T., The [nonprofit]
macconnection.com [company]
Macdermid Inc. [company]
MacDonnell Foundation, The [nonprofit]
Mace [product]
Macerich Co. [company]
Mac-Gray Corp. [company]
Macintosh [Mac] [product]
Mack [company & product]
Mack Cali Realty Corp. [company]
Maclellan Foundation, Inc., The [nonprofit]
macmall.com [company]
Macor [company]
Macrobid [company]
Macromelt [product]
Macy, Jr., Foundation, Josiah, The [nonprofit]
Macy's [company]
maczone.com [company]
Maddie's Fund [nonprofit]
Madeco S.A. [company]
Magellan Health Services Inc. [company]
Magic 8 Ball [product]
Magic Chef [company & product]
Magic Kingdom [product]
Magic Marker [product]
Magic School Bus, The [product]
Maglite [product]

Magna [product]
Magna Doodle [product]
Magna International Inc. [company]
Magnetex Inc. [company]
Magnum [product]
Magnum Hunter Resources Inc. [company]
Magyar Tavkozlesi Rt [company]
MAI Systems Corp. [company]
Maidenform [product]
Mailgram [product]
Mail-Well Inc. [company]
Main Medical [company]
Main Street Bancorp Inc. [company]
Maine Public Service Co. [company]
Mainframe [company]
Mainline Information Systems [company]
Major League Baseball [company]
Maker's Mark [company]
Malan Realty Investors Inc. [company]
Malaysia Fund Inc., The [company]
Mallinckrodt Inc., New [company]
Mallomars [product]
Maloney & Porcelli [company]
Man Next Door, The [company]
Managed High Income Portfolio Inc.
　[company]
Managed High Yield Plus Fund Inc. [company]
Managed Municipals Portfolio Inc. [company]
ManagedOps.com [company]
Manatt, Phelps & Phillips [company]
Mandalay Resort Group [company]
Manhattan Ocean Club [company]
Manitou Foundation Inc. [company]
Manitowoc Co. Inc. [company]
Manor Care Inc. [company]
Manor, The [company]
Manpower Inc. [company]
Manufactured Home Communities Inc.
　[company]
Manufacturers' Services Ltd. [company]
Manulife Financial Corp. [company]
Map International [company]
Mapper [product]

Maus Haus [product]
Mavesa S.A. [company]
Max Factor [company]
Maxim Group Inc. [company]
Maximum [clothing] [company]
Maximus Inc. [company]
Maxtor Corp. [company]
Maxwell Foundation, Edmund F., The [nonprofit]
Maxx Petroleum Ltd. [company]
Maxxam Inc. [company]
May Department Stores Co., The [company]
May Department Stores [company]
Maybelline [company]
Mayday Fund [company]
Mayer, Brown & Platt [company]
MaynStream [company & product]
Mayo Clinic [nonprofit]
Mayor's Jewelers Inc. [company]
Maytag [company]
Maytag Corp. [company]
Mazola [company & product]
MBIA Inc. [company]
MBNA Corp. [company]
MC Shipping Inc. [company]
MC2 [company]
MCA [company]
MCB Financial Corp. [company]
McBeath Foundation, Faye, The [nonprofit]
McCarter & English [company]
McCarthy Family Foundation, The [nonprofit]
McChicken [product]
McClatchy Co., The [company]
McConnell Clark Foundation, Edna, The [nonprofit]
McCormick & Co. Inc. [company]
McCormick & Kuleto's Seafood [company]
McCormick Tribune Foundation, Robert R., The [nonprofit]
McCoy [company & product]
McCune Charitable Foundation, The [nonprofit]

McCutchen, Doyle, Brown & Enersen [company]
Mcdermott International Inc. [company]
McDermott, Will & Emery [company]
McDonald's [company]
McDonald's Corp. [company]
McDonnell Foundation, James S., The [nonprofit]
McEachern Charitable Trust, D.V. and Ida J., The [nonprofit]
McElroy Trust, R.J., The [nonprofit]
McGowan Charitable Fund, William G., The [nonprofit]
McGraw-Hill Cos. Inc., The [company]
McGregor [company]
McGregor Fund [company]
MCI WorldCom Inc. [company]
McKee Foundation, Robert E. and Evelyn, The [nonprofit]
McKenna & Cuneo [company]
McKesson HBOC Inc. [company]
McKibben Communications [company]
McKnight Endowment Fund for Neuroscience, The [nonprofit]
McKnight Foundation, The [nonprofit]
McLeodUSA, Inc. [company]
Mcmoran Exploration Co. [company]
MCN Energy Group Inc. [company]
McNeil Technologies [company]
McRae Industries Inc. [company]
Mcwhorter Technologies Inc. [company]
MDP [company]
MDU Resources Group Inc. [company]
M-E Cos. [company]
Mead [company & product]
Mead Corp., The [company]
Meadowbrook Insurance Group Inc. [company]
Meadows Foundation, Inc. [company]
Meals-On-Wheels [company]
Measurement Specialties Inc. [company]
Meat Lover's [product]
Meaty Bone [product]
Medalist [product]

Metropolitan Opera Association [nonprofit]

MET-Rx [company]

Metso Corp. [company]

Mettler Toledo International Inc. [company]

Metton [company]

Mevacor [product]

Mexico Equity and Income Fund Inc., The [company]

Mexico Fund Inc., The [company]

Meyer Foundation, Eugene and Agnes E., The [nonprofit]

Meyer Memorial Trust [company]

Meyers Foundation, Allen H. and Nydia, The [nonprofit]

MFS [company]

MGI Properties [company]

MGM Grand Inc. [company]

MHF Logistical Solutions [company]

MHSS Enterprises [company]

Miacalcin [product]

MIC [company]

Michael Anthony Jewelers Inc. [company]

Michael Best & Friedrich [company]

Michaels Stores Inc. [company]

Michelin [company]

Michelob [company & product]

Michelson Foundation, The [nonprofit]

Micro Channel [company & product]

Micro Scan [company & product]

Micro Source [company & product]

Micro/Pettor [company]

MicroAge Inc. [company]

Microballoons [company]

Microfinancial Inc. [company]

Micron Technology Inc. [company]

Micro-Sipe [product]

Microsoft [company]

Microsoft Corp. [company]

microsoft.com [company]

microwarehouse.com [company]

Mid America Apartment Communities Inc. [company]

Mid Atlantic Medical Services Inc. [company]

Mid Atlantic Realty Trust [company]

Mid Penn Bancorp [company]

MidAmerican Energy Holdings Co. [company]

Midas [company]

Midas Group Inc. [company]

Midcoast Energy Resources Inc. [company]

Midol [product]

MidSouth Bancorp [company]

Midway Games Inc. [company]

Midwest Banc Holdings Inc. [company]

Midwest Express Holdings Inc. [company]

Midwest Living [product]

MIIX Group Inc., The [company]

Mikasa Inc. [company]

Mike's American Grill [company]

Milbank Memorial Fund [company]

Milbank, Tweed, Hadley & McCloy [company]

Milestone Scientific Inc. [company]

Milk Duds [product]

Milka [product]

Milk-Bone [product]

Milken Family Foundation, The [nonprofit]

Milky Way [product]

Millennium Chemicals Inc. [company]

Miller [company & product]

Miller Foundation, The [nonprofit]

Miller Industries Inc. [company]

Miller Paper [company]

Miller, Canfield, Paddock & Stone [company]

Milliken [company]

Millionaire [product]

Millipore Corp. [company]

Millrose Brewery Co. [company]

Mills Corp. [company]

Mine Safety Appliances Co. [company]

Minerals Technologies Inc. [company]

Minnesota Life Insurance Co. [company]

Minnesota Masonic Foundation Inc. [company]

Minnesota Mining & Manufacturing Co. [company]

Minnesota Municipal Income Portfolio Inc. [company]

Minnesota Municipal Term Trust Inc. [company]

Minnesota Power Inc. [company]

Mintz, Levin, Cohn, Ferris, Glovsky & Popeo [company]

Minute [rice] [product]

Minute Maid [product]

Minwax [product]

Miracle-Gro [product]

Mirant Corp. [company]

Mirror [product]

MI Schottenstein Homes Inc. [company]

Mission Cap L.P. [company]

Mission West Properties Inc. [company]

Mississippi Chemical Corp. [company]

Mississippi Power Co. [company]

Mister Softee [product]

Mitchell Energy and Development Corp. [company]

Mitel Corp. [company]

Mitsubishi Tokyo Financial Group Inc. [company]

Mixmaster [product]

ML Macadamia Orchards L.P. [company]

MMI Products Inc. [company]

Mobile Storage Group [company]

Mobile Telesystems Inc. [company]

Modern Technology Solutions [company]

Modis Professional Services Inc. [company]

Mod-Podge [product]

Moët & Chandon [company]

Moffitt & L.Q. Moffitt Foundation, L.R., The [nonprofit]

Mohawk Industries Inc. [company]

Moistrite [product]

Moisture Block [product]

Moisture Whip [product]

Molecular Biosystems Inc. [company]

Molex Inc. [company]

Molly [product]

Molson [company & product]

Monaco Coach Corp. [company]

Monell Foundation, Ambrose, The [nonprofit]

Monet [product]

Monitronics International [company]

Monokote [product]

Monongahela Power Co. [company]

Monopoly [product]

Monopril [product]

Montana Power Co. [company]

Montblanc [product]

Monte Cristo [product]

Monterey Jack's [product]

Monterey Vineyard, The [company]

Montgomery Inn [company]

Montgomery Inn at the Boathouse [company]

Montgomery Street Income Securities Inc. [company]

Montgomery Ward [company]

Mony Group Inc. [company]

Moody Bible Institute of Chicago [nonprofit]

Moodys Corp. [company]

Moog Inc. [company]

Moon Pie [product]

Moore Corp. Ltd. [company]

Moore Medical Corp. [company]

Mop & Glo [product]

Mopar [company & product]

More [product]

more.com [company]

Morehead Foundation, John Motley, The [nonprofit]

Morgan Foundation, Burton D., The [nonprofit]

Morgan Grenfell Smallcap Fund Inc. [company]

Morgan Group Inc., The [company]

Morgan Keegan Inc. [company]

Morgan Stanley Dean Witter & Co. [company]

Morgan, Lewis, & Bockius [company]

Morrison & Foerster [company]

Morrison Management Specialists Inc. [company]

Morton's Restaurant Group, Inc. [company]

Most Like Mother [product]

Most Trusted Name, The [product]

Motel 6 [company]
Motivepower Industries Inc. [company]
Motorola [company]
Motorola Inc. [company]
Motrin [product]
Mott Foundation, Charles Stewart, The [nonprofit]
Mountain Dew [product]
Moussy [product]
Mr. B's Bistro [company]
Mr. Bubble [product]
Mr. Clean [product]
Mr. Coffee [product]
Mr. Goodwrench (also Goodwrench) [product]
Mr. Muscle [product]
Mr. Peanut [product]
Mr. Pibb [product]
Mr. Potato Head [product]
Mrs. Fields [product]
Mrs. Paul's [product]
Mrs. Richardson's [product]
Mrs. Smith's [product]
MSC Industries Direct Co Inc. [company]
Msc.Software Corp. [company]
MS-DOS [product]
MSMS Foundation, The [nonprofit]
msn.com [company]
MSS Group [company]
MTI Home Video [company]
MTV [company]
Mueller Inds Inc. [company]
Mueslix [product]
MultiMate [product]
Munchos [product]
Muniassets Fund, Inc. [company]
Munich Re A.G. [company]
Municipal Advantage Fund Inc. [company]
Municipal High Income Fund Inc. [company]
Municipal Partners Fund Inc. [company]
MuniEnhanced Fund Inc. [company]
MuniHoldings Fund Inc. [company]
MuniMae [company]
MuniYield Insured Fund Inc. [company]

Murine [product]
Murphy Foundation, John P., The [nonprofit]
Murphy Oil Corp. [company]
Muscular Dystrophy Association [company]
Museum of Fine Arts, Boston [nonprofit]
Museum of Fine Arts, Houston [nonprofit]
Museum of Modern Art, The [nonprofit]
Musicians Foundation Inc. [nonprofit]
Musicland [company]
Musicland Stores Corp. [company]
Musser Fund [company]
Must See TV [slogan/product]
Mustard Seed Foundation, The [nonprofit]
Mutual of Omaha Insurance Cos. [company]
Mutual Risk Mangement Ltd. [company]
Muzak [product]
My Little Pony [product]
Myers's [company]
Mylan Laboratories Inc. [company]
Mylanta [product]
Mylar [product]
My-T-Fine [product]
Nabisco [company]
Nabisco Group Holdings Corp. [company]
Nabors Industries Inc. [company]
NACCO Industries Inc. [company]
Nair [product]
Nakamichi Foundation, E., The [nonprofit]
NALCO [company]
Nalco Chemical Co. [company]
Naprosyn [product]
Nash Finch Co. [company]
Nashua Corp. [company]
Nasonex [product]
NATCO Group Inc. [company]
National Academy of Education, The [nonprofit]
National Association of Chain Drug Stores Education Foundation Inc. [nonprofit]
National Australia Bank Ltd. [company]
National Bancshares Corp. of Texas [company]
National Bank of Greece S.A. [company]

National Basketball Association (NBA)
 [company]
National Benevolent Association [company]
National Beverage Corp. [company]
National City Corp. [company]
National Commerce BanCorp. [company]
National Council of YMCAs, The [nonprofit]
National Data Corp. [company]
National Discount Brokers Group Inc.
 [company]
National Easter Seal Society, The [nonprofit]
National Equipment Services Inc. [company]
National Football League (NFL) [company]
National Fuel Gas Co. [company]
National Gallery of Art [nonprofit]
National Golf Properties Inc. [company]
National Grid Group [company]
National Health Investors Inc. [company]
National Health Realty Inc. [company]
National HealthCare Corp. [company]
National Health care Resources [company]
National Hockey League (NHL) [company]
National Jewish Medical and Research Center
 [nonprofit]
National Mental Health Association
 [nonprofit]
National Multiple Sclerosis Society
 [nonprofit]
National Oilwell Inc. [company]
National Power P.L.C. [company]
National Presto Industries Inc. [company]
National Processing Inc. [company]
National Semiconductor Corp. [company]
National Service Industries Inc. [company]
National Steel Corp. [company]
National Video Resources Inc. [company]
National Westminister Bank P.L.C. [company]
National Wildlife Federation [nonprofit]
National Association for the Exchange of
 Industrial Resources [nonprofit]
NationLink Wireless [company]
Nations Balanced Target Maturity Fund Inc.
 [company]

Nations Government Income Term Trust 2003
 Inc. [company]
Nations Government Income Term Trust 2004
 Inc. [company]
Nationsrent Inc. [company]
Nationwide [company]
Nationwide Financial Services Inc. [company]
Nationwide Health Properties Inc. [company]
Nationwide Insurance Enterprise [company]
Native American Systems [company]
Naturalizer [product]
Nature Conservancy, The [nonprofit]
Nature Valley [product]
Naugahyde [product]
Nautilus [product]
Naval Jelly [product]
Navigant Consulting Inc. [company]
Navigator Systems [company]
Navistar [company & product]
Navistar International Corp. [company]
NBC [company]
NBC Capital Corp. [company]
NBCI Automatic Common Exchange
 [company]
NCE Petrofund [company]
NCH Corp. [company]
NCI Building Systems Inc. [company]
NCNB Corp. [company]
NCR Corp. [company]
Nebco Evans Holding Co. [company]
Necco [product]
Necon [product]
Need-A-Service? [company]
Needmor Fund, The [nonprofit]
Neff Corp. [company]
Neighborhood Centers [nonprofit]
Neiman Marcus [company]
Neiman Marcus Group Inc., The [company]
Neiman Marcus Group [company]
Nelson Mullins Riley & Scarborough
 [company]
Nelson Thomas Inc. [company]
Nematron Corp. [company]

Nembutal [product]
Nemours Foundation, The [nonprofit]
Neolite [company]
Neomycin/Polymx/HC [product]
Neon [product]
Neosporin [product]
Neo-Synephrine [product]
Nerf [product]
Nescafé [product]
Nestea [product]
Nestlé [product]
Net.world [company]
NET/MASTER [product]
NetForce Technologies [company]
netmarket.com [company]
Netscape [company & product]
Netscape Navigator [product]
NetWare [company]
NetWindow [company]
Network Associates Inc. [company]
Network DataMover [product]
Network Equipment Technologies Inc.
   [company]
Network Hardware Resale [company]
Network One [company]
Neuberger Berman Inc. [company]
Neurontin [product]
Neutrogena [product]
Nevada Power Co. [company]
New America High Income Fund Inc., The
   [product]
New Century Energies Inc. [company]
New Corp. Ltd. [company]
New England Biolabs Foundation, The
   [nonprofit]
New England Business Service Inc. [company]
New Germany Fund Inc., The [company]
New Jersey Resources Corp. [company]
New Plan Excel Realty Trust Inc. [company]
New Playboy Inc. [company]
New Skies Satellites N.V. [company]
New South Bancshares Inc. [company]
New York Foundation, The [nonprofit]

New York Foundation for Architecture Inc.
   [nonprofit]
New York Life Insurance Co. [company]
New York Times Co., The [company]
New Age Systems [company]
Newcor Inc. [company]
Newell Rubbermaid Inc. [company]
Newfield Exploration Co. [company]
Newhall Ld & Farming Co. [company]
Newman's Own [product]
Newmont Mining Corp. [company]
Newpark Resources Inc. [company]
Newport News Shipbuilding Inc. [company]
newport-news.com [company]
NewPower Holdings Inc. [company]
News Corp. Ltd. [company]
Newscorp Overseas Ltd. [company]
Newtek Capital Inc. [company]
Newton [product]
Newton Resource Group [company]
Nexen Inc. [company]
Nexis [company & product]
NeXT [product]
Next Dimension Studios [company]
Nextel Communications Inc. [company]
NFO Worldwide Inc. [company]
NGB [company]
NGTS [company]
Niagara [starch] [product]
Niagara Mohawk Holdings Inc. [company]
Niagara Mohawk Power Corp. [company]
Niblets [product]
Nicad [product]
Nicoderm [product]
Nicor Inc. [product]
Nicorette [product]
Nicotrol [product]
Nielsen Media Research Inc. [company]
Night Hawk [company]
Nike [company]
Nike Inc. [company]
Nikon [company]
Nimonic [company]

Nine West [company]
Nintendo [company]
Nippon Telegraph and Telephone Corp. [company]
NIPSCO (Northern Indiana Public Service Co.) [company]
Nipsco Industries Inc. [company]
NiSource Inc. [company]
Nissan [company]
Nitrostat [product]
Nixon Peabody [company]
NL Industries Inc. [company]
NLX [company]
No More Tears [product]
No. 5 [product]
Noble Affiliates Inc. [company]
Noble Drilling Corp. [company]
Noble Foundation, Samuel Roberts, The [nonprofit]
No-Doz (also NoDoz) [product]
Nokia Corp. [company]
Nokomis Foundation, The [nonprofit]
Nomex [product]
Noodle Roni [product]
Norcross Wildlife Foundation Inc. [nonprofit]
Nord Family Foundation, The [nonprofit]
Nordic American Tanker Shipping Ltd. [company]
NordicTrack [product]
Nordstrom [company]
Nordstrom Inc. [company]
nordstrom.com [company]
Norfolk Southern Corp. [company]
Norge [company]
Norman Foundation, The [nonprofit]
Norplant [product]
Norris Foundation, Kenneth T. and Eileen L., The [nonprofit]
Norsk Hydro A.S. [company]
Nortek Inc. [company]
Nortel Inversora S.A. [company]
Nortel Network Corp. [company]
North American Palladium Ltd. [company]

North American Precast [company]
North European Oil Royalty Trust [company]
North Fork BanCorp. Inc. [company]
North Highland [company]
North Shore Networking [company]
Northeast Bancorp [company]
Northeast Pennsylvania Financial Corp. [company]
Northeast Utilities [company]
Northeast Utilities Systems [company]
Northern Border Partners L.P. [company]
Northern Reflections [company]
Northern Technologies International Corp. [company]
Northernaire [company & product]
Northrop Grumman Corp. [company]
Northwest Airlines Corp. [company]
Northwest Area Foundation, The [nonprofit]
Northwest Fund for the Environment, The [nonprofit]
Northwest Health Foundation, The [nonprofit]
Northwest Natural Gas Co. [company]
Northwestern Corp. [company]
Northwestern Mutual Life Insurance Co. [company]
northwestexpress.com [company]
Norvasc [product]
Norwest Corp. [company]
NoSalt [product]
Nova Chemicals Corp. [company]
Nova Corp. [company]
Novaastar Financial Inc. [company]
Novahistine [product]
Novartis [company]
NovaSoft Information Technology [company]
Novatel Wireless [company]
Novavax, Inc. [company]
Noveen New York Municipal Value Fund Inc. [company]
Novell [company]
Novocain [product]
NovolinPen [product]
Now [product]

Noxzema [product]
Noyes Foundation Inc., Jessie Smith, The [nonprofit]
NRG Energy Inc. [company]
NS Group Inc. [company]
NSA [company]
NSTAR [company]
nStor Technologies Inc. [company]
NTL Inc. [company]
NTN Communications Inc. [company]
NTT DoCoMo [company]
Nu Skin [product]
Nu Skin Enterprises Inc. [company]
Nubain [product]
Nucoal Inc. [company]
Nucor Corp. [company]
Nuevo Energy Co. [company]
Nuevo Grupo [company]
NUI Corp. [company]
Nuk [product]
Numerical Technologies [company]
Numorphan [product]
Nuprin [product]
Nut & Honey Crunch [product]
Nutella Hazelnut [product]
NutraSweet [product]
Nutri-Grain [product]
Nuveen Arizona Dividend Advantage Municipal Fund [company]
Nuveen John Co. [company]
NuWare Technology [company]
NVP Capital I [company]
NVR Inc. [company]
Nycomed Amersham P.L.C. [company]
Nymagic Inc. [company]
NYNEX [company]
NyQuil [product]
o.b. [product]
O'Brien [company]
O'Doul's [product]
O'Reilly Automotive [company]
Oakley Inc. [company]
Oakwood Homes Corp. [company]

Occasion Gallerie from Blue Mountain Arts, The [nonprofit]
Occidental Petroleum Corp. [company]
Ocean Energy Inc. [company]
Ocean Pacific (OP) [company]
Ocean Spray [product]
Ocean Star [product]
Oceaneering International Inc. [company]
Octamine [company]
Octel Corp. [company]
OcuClear [product]
Ocwen Financial Corp. [company]
OEA Inc. [company]
OEC Medical Systems Inc. [company]
Off! [product]
Office Depot [company]
Office Depot Inc. [company]
officedepot.com [company]
OfficeMax [company]
OfficeMax Inc. [company]
officemax.com [company]
OFIS [company & product]
OGE Energy Corp. [company]
Ogilvie [product]
Oh Henry! [product]
Ohio Art Co., The [nonprofit]
Ohio Casualty Corp. [company]
Ohio Edison Co. [company]
Ohio Power Co. [company]
Oil Dri Corp. of America [company]
Oil State International Inc. [company]
OILSCAN [company]
Old Ebbitt Grill/Ebbitt Express [company]
Old Forester [product]
Old Grand-Dad [product]
Old Kent Financial Corp. [company]
Old Navy [company]
Old Original Bookbinders [company]
Old Republic International Corp. [company]
Old Spice [product]
oldnavy.com [company]
Oldsmobile [company & product]
Olean [product]

Oster [company & product]
Osullivan Industries Holdings Inc. [company]
Otis [company & product]
OTR Express Inc. [company]
Ottinger Foundation, The [nonprofit]
Ouija [product]
Outback Steakhouse [company]
Outback Steakhouse Inc. [company]
outpost.com [company]
Outsource Receivable Services [company]
Overhill Corp. [company]
Overseas Shipholding Group Inc. [company]
overstock.com [company]
Owens & Minor Inc. [company]
Owens Corning [company]
Owens Illinois Inc. [company]
Owens-Illinois Inc. [company]
Oxford [stationery supplies] [product]
Oxford Health Plans Inc. [company]
Oxford Industries Inc. [company]
Oxycodone [product]
Oxycontin [product]
Oyster Bar at Grand Central Station [company]
P&O Princess [company]
P.A.M. [product]
P.H. Glatfelter Co. [company]
P3 [product]
PAB Bankshares Inc. [company]
Pabst [company]
Paccar Inc. [company]
PACE [company]
Pacholder High Yield Fund Inc. [company]
Pacific American Income Shares Inc. [company]
Pacific Century Cyberworks Ltd. [company]
Pacific Century Financial Corp. [company]
Pacific Enterprises [company]
Pacific Gas & Electric Co. [company]
Pacific Gulf Properties Inc. [company]
Pacific Life Insurance Co. [company]
Pacific Northwest Foundation, The [nonprofit]
Pacific Pioneer Fund [company]
Pacific Trade International [company]
PacifiCare Health Systems Inc. [company]

Pacificorp [company]
Packaged Ice Inc. [company]
Packaging Corp. of America [company]
Packard Foundation, David and Lucile, The [nonprofit]
Pactel [company]
Pactiv Corp. [company]
Pac-Van [company]
PADI Foundation, The [nonprofit]
PageMarq [company]
Paine Webber Group Inc. [company]
PaintJet [product]
Pakistan Investment Fund Inc. [company]
Paladin Data Systems [company]
PALASM [company]
Palatin Technologies Inc. [company]
Palisade [company]
Pall Corp. [company]
Pall Mall [product]
Palm Beach [product]
Pameco Corp. [company]
Pampers [product]
PAN Communications [company]
Pan Pacific Retail Properties [company]
Panache Designs [company]
PANACO Inc. [company]
Panamerican Beverages Inc. [company]
Panavision Inc. [company]
Pan-Cake [product]
Pantry Inc., The [company]
Pantry, The [company]
Paper Mate [company]
Pappagallo [company & product]
Par Technology Corp. [company]
Paracelsus Healthcare Corp. [company]
Paragon [product]
Paragon Technologies Inc. [company]
Paralyzed Veterans of America [nonprofit]
Paramount Technologies [company]
Para-Sail [product]
Park Avenue Café [company]
Park Electrochemical Corp. [company]
Park National Corp. [company]

Park Place Entertainment Corp. [company]
Parke-Davis [company]
Parker [pens] [company & product]
Parker Drilling Co. [company]
Parker Foundation, The [nonprofit]
Parker Hannifin Corp. [company]
Parker's [company]
Parker-Kalon [company & product]
Parkway Properties Inc. [company]
Parson Group [company]
Partnerre Ltd. [company]
Party Ball [product]
Passat [product]
Passport [product]
Pasta Accents [product]
Pathmark [product]
Pathways [product]
Patina Oil & Gas Corp. [company]
Patrina Foundation, The [nonprofit]
Patterns [product]
Patterson Foundation, Aliciad, The [nonprofit]
Patton Bogg [company]
Paul, Weiss, Rifkind, Wharton & Garrison
   [company]
Paxar Corp. [company]
Paxil [product]
Paxon [product]
Paxson Communications Corp. [company]
Paychex Inc. [company]
PayDay [product]
Payless Cashways [company]
Payless Cashways Inc. [company]
Payless ShoeSource [company]
Payless ShoeSource Inc. [company]
PayMaxx [company]
PB Systems [company]
PC Connection Inc. [company]
PC GlassBlock [product]
PC Productivity [company]
pcconnection.com [company]
PCI Services [company]
pcmall.com [company]
PCPOWER [company]

pczone.com [company]
PDF Solutions [company]
Peace Arch Entertainment Group Inc.
   [company]
Peak 1 [company & product]
Peak Trends Trust [company]
Peapack-Gladstone Financial Corp. [company]
peapod.com [company]
Pearl Drops [product]
Pearson P.L.C. [company]
Pebble Beach [company & product]
Pec Isreal Economic Corp. [company]
Pechiney [company]
Peco Energy Capital L.P. [company]
PECO Energy Co. [company]
Pedialyte [product]
Pediatrix Medical Group Inc. [company]
Pedigree [product]
Peds [product]
Pegasus [product]
Pegasus Foundation, The [nonprofit]
Pelican Financial Inc. [company]
Pemstar [company]
Pendaflex [product]
Penelec Capital Trust [company]
Penicillin VK [product]
Penn [company & product]
Penn Engineering & Manufacturing Corp.
   [company]
Penn Foundation, William, The [nonprofit]
Penn Mutual Life Insurance Co. [company]
Penn National Gaming Inc. [company]
Penn Traffic [company]
Penn Traffic Co., The [company]
Penn Treat American Corp. [company]
Penn Virginia Corp. [company]
Penn-America Group Inc. [company]
Penncorp Financial Group Inc. [company]
PennEngineering [company]
Pennsylvania Enterprises Inc. [company]
Pennsylvania Real Estate Investment Trust
   [company]
Pennzoil [company & product]

Pennzoil-Quaker State Co. [company]
Pentacon Inc. [company]
Pentair Inc. [company]
Pentaspan [company]
Pentium [product]
Penton Media Inc. [company]
Peoples Energy Corp. [company]
Peoples Holding Co., The [company]
PeopleSoft Inc. [company]
Pep Boys [company]
Pepcid [product]
Pepe [product]
Pepe Lopez [product]
Pepper Hamilton [company]
Pepperidge Farm [company & product]
Pepsi [company & product]
Pepsi Bottling Group Inc. [company]
Pepsi Cola Puerto Rico Bottling Co. [company]
PepsiCo Inc. [company]
Pepto-Bismol [product]
Percocet [product]
Percodan [product]
Performance Food Group Co. [company]
Perini Corp. [company]
PerkinElmer Inc. [company]
Permalens [product]
Perma-Prest [product]
Permian Basin Realty Trust [company]
Perrier [company & product]
Perrier-Jouet [company]
Persil [company]
Personal Pan Pizza [product]
Personnel Group of America Inc. [company]
Persuasive Presentations [company]
Petco Animal Supplies [company]
Peter Kiewit Sons [company]
Peter Luger Steakhouse [company]
Peter Pan [product]
Peterbilt [company & product]
Pete's Wicked Ale [product]
petopia.com [company]
Petra polyester [product]
Petro-Canada [company]

Petrochina Ltd. [company]
PetroCorp Inc. [company]
Petroleo Brasilero S.A.-Petrobras [company]
Petroleos de Venezuela [company]
Petroleum & Resources Corp. [company]
pets.com [company]
PetsMart Inc. [company]
petsmart.com [company]
petstore.com [company]
Peugeot [company & product]
Pew Charitable Trusts, The [nonprofit]
PEZ [product]
Pfeiffer Research Foundation, Gustavus and
    Louise, The [nonprofit]
Pfizer Inc. [company]
PG&E Corp. [company]
PGR Media [company]
Pharmaceutical Resources Inc. [company]
Pharmacia & Upjohn Inc. [company]
Pharmacia Corp. [company]
Pharmaseal [company & product]
Phar-Mor Inc. [company]
Phelps Dodge Corp. [company]
Phelps Dunbar [company]
Philadelphia Suburban Corp. [company]
Philip Morris [company]
Philip Morris Cos. Inc. [company]
Philippine Long Distance Telephone Co.
    [company]
Philips International Realty Corp. [company]
Phillips 66 Cap I [company]
Phillips Flagship [company]
Phillips Foundation, Ellis L., The [nonprofit]
Phillips Foundation, Louie M. & Betty M., The
    [nonprofit]
Phillips Harborplace [company]
Phillips Petroleum Co. [company]
Phillips Pozidriv [product]
Phillips Van Heusen Corp. [company]
Phillips' Milk of Magnesia [product]
Phillips-Van Heusen Corp. [company]
Phoenix Home Life Mutual Insurance
    [company]

Phoenix Investment Partners Ltd. [company]
Phoenix Management [company]
PhoneSmart [company]
Phosphate Resource Partners Ltd. [company]
Photobrown Extra [company]
Photoelectron Corp. [company]
Photomer [product]
Photoshop [product]
Physicians Formula [product]
Pichin Corp. [company]
Pick Up [product]
Pickett & Hatcher Educational Fund Inc.
   [company]
Pick-Me-Up [product]
Piedmont Natural Gas Co. Inc. [company]
Pier 1 Imports Inc. [company]
Pierce [product]
Pierce Leahy Corp. [company]
Piggly Wiggly [product]
Pilates [company & product]
Pilgrim America Capital Corp. [company]
Pilgrim America Prime Rate Trust [company]
Pilgrim's Pride Corp. [company]
Pillowtex Corp. [company]
Pillsbury [company]
Pillsbury Madison & Sutro [company]
Pimco Advisors [company]
Pimco Commercial Mortgage Securities Trust
   Inc. [company]
Pimm's [product]
Pinch Scotch [product]
Pine Action [product]
Pine Bros. [product]
Pine-Sol [product]
Ping-Pong [product]
Pinnacle Bancshares Inc. [company]
Pinnacle Data Systems Inc. [company]
Pinnacle West Capital Corp. [company]
Pioneer Corp. Japan [company]
Pioneer Interest Shares [company]
Pioneer Natural Resources Co. [company]
Pioneer-Standard Electronics Inc. [company]
Piper Marbury Rudnick & Wolfe [company]

Piranha [company & product]
Pitney Bowes [company]
Pitney Bowes Inc. [company]
Pitocin [product]
Piton Foundation, The [nonprofit]
Pitt-Des Moines Inc. [company]
Pittsburgh & West Virginia Railroad [company]
Pittston Co., The [company]
Pixy Stix [product]
Pizza Hut [company]
Pizza Rolls [product]
Placer Dome Inc. [company]
Plains Resources Inc. [company]
Plan for Social Excellence Inc. [company]
PlanetCAD Inc. [company]
PlanetGov.com [company]
planetrx.com [company]
Planned Parenthood [nonprofit]
Planned Parenthood Federation of America
   [nonprofit]
Planters [company]
Plantronics Inc. [company]
Planvista Corp. [company]
Plastic Card Systems [company]
Plastic Surgery Co., The [company]
Plastic Wood [product]
Plasticine [product]
Plavix [product]
Plax [product]
Playboy [product]
Playboy Playmate [product]
Playcraft [product]
Play-Doh [product]
Playmobil [product]
Playskool [product]
PlayStation [product]
Playtex [product]
Playtex Products Inc. [company]
PLC Systems Inc. [company]
Pledge [product]
Plendil [product]
Plexar [product]
Plexco [product]

Plexiglas [product]
PLM International Inc. [company]
Plug-Ins [product]
Plum Creek Timber Co. Inc. [company]
Plymouth Rubber Co. Inc. [company]
PMC Capital Inc. [company]
PMC Commercial Trust [company]
PMI Group Inc., The [company]
PNC Financial Services Group, The [company]
Pogo Producing Co. [company]
Pohlad Family Foundation, Carl and Eloise,
  The [nonprofit]
Point [company & product]
Pointe Technology Group [company]
Poison [product]
Polarfleece [product]
Polaris Industries Inc. [company]
Polaroid [company]
Polaroid Corp. [company]
Polartec [product]
Policy Management Systems Corp. [company]
Polk Bros. Foundation, The [nonprofit]
Pollock-Krasner Foundation Inc., The
  [company]
Polo [company & product]
Polo Ralph Lauren Corp. [company]
Polyair Inter Pack Inc. [company]
Polybond [product]
Polycat [product]
Poly-Fil [product]
Polygard [product]
PolyGram [company]
Poly-Lite [product]
Polymer Group Inc. [company]
PolyOne [company]
PolyOne Corp. [company]
Poly-V [company]
PolyVision Corp. [company]
Pond's [product]
Pontiac [company & product]
Pony Express [company]
Pope & Talbot Inc. [company]
Popov [product]

Poppin' Fresh, The Pillsbury Doughboy
  [product]
Pop•Secret [product]
Popsicle [product]
Pop-Tarts [product]
Popular Inc. [company]
Porsche [company & product]
Porta Potti [product]
Porta Systems Corp. [company]
Portable Church Industries [company]
Portacrib [product]
Porta-John [product]
Porter Foundation, Irwin Andrew, The
  [nonprofit]
Porter Wright Morris & Arthur [company]
Portland Gen Elec Co. [company]
Portobello Yacht Club [company]
Portosan [product]
Post Properties Inc. [company]
Post-it note [product]
PostScript [product]
Posturepedic [product]
Potash Corp. of Saskatchewan Inc. [company]
Potlatch Corp. [company]
Potomac Edison Co. [company]
Potomac Electric Power Co. [company]
Potomac Retail Enterprises [company]
Pottruck-Scott Foundation, The [nonprofit]
Powell, Goldstein, Frazer & Murphy
  [company]
PowerBar [product]
Powerbase [company & product]
PowerBook [product]
Powergen, P.L.C. [company]
PowerLight [product]
Powermate [product]
PowerPoint [product]
PowerQuest [company & product]
Powershield [product]
Powerworks [company & product]
PP [company]
PPG Industries Inc. [company]
PPL Corp. [company]

PracticeWorks Inc. [company]
Prada [product]
Pragmatic Marketing [company]
Prairie City Bakery [company]
PrairieComm [company]
Pravachol [product]
Praxair Inc. [company]
Praxis Series: Professional Assessments for Beginning Teachers, The [product]
PRBar [product]
PRC [company]
Precision Castparts Corp. [company]
Precision Drilling Corp. [company]
Prednisone [product]
Preferred Income Fund Inc. [company]
Preferred Income Opportunity Fund Inc. [company]
Prego [product]
Premarin [product]
Premdor Inc. [company]
Premier Bancorp Inc. [company]
Premier Farnell [company]
Prempro [company]
Prentiss Properties Trust [company]
Pre-Paid Legal Services Inc. [company]
Preparation H [product]
Presentation Group [company]
Presenting Solutions [company]
Presidential Realty Corp. [company]
Preston Gates & Ellis [company]
Preston Phillips Partnership [company]
Prevacid [product]
PreVision Marketing [company]
Price Pfister [company]
Priceline.com [company]
Prices Communication Corp. [company]
pricewatch.com [company]
Pride International Inc. [company]
Prilosec [product]
Primaxin [product]
Prime Group Realty Trust [company]
Prime Hospitality Corp. [company]
Prime Retail Inc. [company]

Primedia Inc. [company]
Princess [product]
Princeton Gallery [product]
Principal Financial Group [company]
Principal Technical Services [company]
Prinivil [product]
Priority Club [company]
Priority Express Courier [company]
PriorityPlus [company]
PRISM [company]
Prism [company & product]
Prison Realty Corp. [company]
Prison Realty Trust [company]
Pritikin [company & product]
Pritt [company & product]
Prize Energy Corp. [company]
Prize Tested Recipes [product]
Prizm [product]
Pro Logic [company]
Probex Corp. [company]
Procan [product]
Procardia XL [product]
Procare [product]
Process Facilities [company]
ProCollection [product]
Procter & Gamble Co., The [company]
Product 19 [product]
Product Development Technologies [company]
Pro-Fac Cooperative Inc. [company]
Professional Cutlery Direct [company]
Program Planning Professionals [company]
Progress Energy Inc. [company]
Progressive Corp., The [company]
Progressive Medical [company]
Progressive Return Fund Inc. [company]
Progressive Software Computing [company]
Project Hope [nonprofit]
ProLaw Software [company]
Prologis [company]
Prolong International Corp. [company]
Promotions by Design [company]
Promus Hotel Corp. [company]
Propective Life Corp. [company]

Properties Trust [company]
Propoxyphene N/APAP [product]
Propranolol [product]
Proprinter [product]
Propulsid [product]
ProScan [product]
Proskauer Rose [company]
Prospect Hill Foundation, The [nonprofit]
Prospect Street High Income Portfolio Inc. [company]
Pro-Tech Welding and Fabrication [company]
Protection One Inc. [company]
Protective Life Corp. [company]
Protein-29 [product]
Provena Foods Inc. [company]
Proventil [product]
Providence Homes [company]
Provident Capital Trust [company]
Provident Financial Group Inc. [company]
Providian Financial Corp. [company]
ProWalker [product]
Prozac [product]
Prudential [company]
Prudential Insurance Co. of America [company]
Prudential P.L.C. [company]
PS Business Parks, Inc. [company]
PSS World Medical Inc. [company]
Psychemedics Corp. [company]
Public Broadcasting Service (PBS) [nonprofit]
Public Service Co. of New Mexico [company]
Public Service Enterprise Group Inc. [company]
Public Services Co. of New Mexico [company]
Public Steers Trust [company]
Public Storage Inc. [company]
Public Welfare Foundation Inc. [company]
Publicis Groupe S.A. [company]
Publishers Clearing House [company]
Publix [company]
Publix Super Markets Inc. [company]
Pudding Cup [product]
Puffin Foundation Ltd., The [nonprofit]
Puget Energy Inc. [company]

Puget Sound Energy Inc. [company]
Pulitzer Inc. [company]
Pull-Ups [product]
Pulsar [company & product]
Pulte Corp. [company]
PUMA [company & product]
Pure Air [product]
Pure Premium [product]
Pure Resources Inc. [company]
Purex [product]
Purifire [company]
puritanspride.com [company]
Putnam Municipal Opportunities Trust [company]
Puttin' On The Ritz [product]
Putt-Putt [product]
Pxre Group Ltd. [company]
PYR Energy Corp. [company]
Pyramid Digital Solutions [company]
Pyrex [product]
Pyrolite [product]
QA1 Precision Products [company]
Qantas [company]
QC Optics Inc. [company]
Qestrel Cos. [company]
Qiana [product]
QIC Stream [company]
QK Healthcare Inc. [company]
QSS Group [company]
Q-tips [product]
Quad City Holdings Inc. [company]
Quaker [cereals] [product]
Quaker Chemical Corp. [company]
Quaker Oats Co., The [company]
Qualcomm [company]
Quality Imaging Products [company]
Quality Paperback Book Club [company]
qualityclick.com [company]
Quallofil [product]
Quanex Corp. [company]
Quanta Services Inc. [company]
Quantum Corp. [company]
Quarles & Brady [company]

Quarter Pounder [product]
Quattro [product]
Quebecor World, Inc. [company]
QueryObject Systems Corp. [company]
Quest Diagnostics Inc. [company]
Questar [company]
Questar Corp. [company]
Questcor Pharmaceuticals Inc. [company]
Quick Solutions [company]
Quicksilver Resources Inc. [company]
QuietJet [product]
Quik [product]
Quiksilver Inc. [company]
quill.com [company]
Quilmes Industrial [company]
Quinsana [company]
Quintiles Transnational Corp. [company]
quixtar.com [company]
Quonset [company & product]
Quorum Health Group Inc. [company]
QVC [company]
qvc.com [company]
Qwest Communications International Inc.
　[company]
Qwik Open [product]
Qwik-Gard [product]
RH Donnelley Corp. [company]
R Systems [company]
R.J. Reynolds Tobacco Holdings Inc.
　[company]
R.O.C. Taiwan Fund, The [company]
R.R. Donnelley & Sons Co. [company]
Radian Group Inc. [company]
Radiant Systems Inc. [company]
Radiologix Inc. [company]
RadioShack [company]
RadioShack Corp. [company]
Raggedy Andy [product]
Raggedy Ann [product]
Ragú [product]
Raid [product]
Railroad Co. [company]
Rainbo [product]

Rainbow Media Group [company]
Rainbow Room, The [product]
Raisinets [product]
RAIT Investment Trust [company]
Ralcorp Holding Inc. [company]
Raley's [company]
Ralgro [product]
Ralogun [product]
Ralston Purina Co. [company]
Ramblin' [product]
Ramco Gershenson Properties Trust [company]
Ram-Flx [product]
Rampart Capital Corp. [company]
Ram-X [product]
Randy River [company]
Range Resources Corp. [company]
Range Rover [product]
Ranitidine [product]
Rapid Link Communications [company]
Rapidigm [product]
Rapoport Foundation, Bernard and Audre, The
　[nonprofit]
Rapoport Foundation, Paul, The [nonprofit]
Rascal House [company]
Raskob Foundation Inc., Bill, The [nonprofit]
RateXchange Corp. [company]
Ratshesky Foundation A.C., The [nonprofit]
Ray•Ban [company & product]
Raymond James Financial Inc. [company]
Rayonier Inc. [company]
Ray-O-Vac [company & product]
Rayovac Corp. [company]
Raytheon Co. [company]
RC [company]
RCA [company]
RCM Strategic Global Government Fund Inc.
　[company]
RDO Equipment Co. [company]
RE/MAX [company]
Reacti-Gel [product]
Reader's Digest [product]
Reader's Digest Association Inc., The
　[company]

Real Estate Investment Journal [product]
Real Estate Superstars [product]
RealAudio [company & product]
ReaLemon [product]
ReaLime [product]
Realite [product]
RealNetworks Inc. [company]
Realtor [product]
Realty Income [company]
Realty Income Corp. [company]
Reasoning [product]
Reckson Associates Realty Corp. [company]
Record a Call [product]
Recycler [product]
Red Lobster [company]
Red Sage [company]
Reddi-Whip [product]
Redeye Grill [product]
Redi-Pan [product]
Redux [product]
Redwood Trust Inc. [company]
Reebok [company & product]
Reebok International Ltd. [company]
Reed Elsevier P.L.C. [company]
Reed Smith Shaw & McClay [company]
reel.com [company]
Reese Health Trust, Michael [company]
Reese's Pieces [product]
Refac [company]
Regal-Beloit Corp. [company]
Regency Centers Corp. [company]
Regions Financial [company]
Rehabcare Group Inc. [company]
REI Systems [company]
Reinhold Foundation Inc., Paul E. & Klare N., The [nonprofit]
Reinsurance Group of America Inc. [company]
Relafen [product]
Reliable Integration Services [company]
Reliable Software Technologies [company]
Reliacom [company]
Reliance Group Holdings Inc. [company]
Reliance Steel & Aluminum Co. [company]

Reliant Energy Inc. [company]
Reliant Energy, Inc. [company]
ReliaStar Financial Corp. [company]
Remington [company]
Rémy Martin [product]
Rent-A-Center Inc. [company]
Rentech Inc. [company]
Rent-Way [company]
Rent-Way Inc. [company]
ReNu [product]
Republic New York Corp. [company]
Republic Services Inc. [company]
Research Corp. [company]
Research Data Design [company]
Resmed Inc. [company]
Resortquest International Inc. [company]
Retin A [product]
Retirement Research Foundation, The [nonprofit]
Retrovir, AZT [product]
Reunion Industries Inc. [company]
Reuter Foundation, The [nonprofit]
Reuters Group P.L.C. [company]
Revelwood [company]
Revere Ware [product]
Revlon [company & product]
Revlon Inc. [company]
Reward [product]
Rex Stores [company]
Rex Stores Corp. [company]
Reynolds & Reynolds Co. [company]
Reynolds (Reynolds Wrap) [product]
Reynolds and Reynolds Co., The [company]
Reynolds Charitable Trust, Kate B., The [nonprofit]
Reynolds Foundation Inc., Z. Smith, The [nonprofit]
Reynolds Foundation, Donald W., The [nonprofit]
Reynolds Metals Co. [company]
Rezulin [product]
RFS Hotels Investors Inc. [company]
RGK Foundation, The [nonprofit]

RGS Energy Group Inc. [company]
RhoGAM [product]
Rhone-Poulenc S.A. [company]
Rica Foods Inc. [company]
Ricciardi Technologies [company]
Rice Krispies [product]
Rice Krispies Treats [product]
Rice-A-Roni [product]
Rich 'n Chips [product]
Richards Foundation, The [nonprofit]
Richardson Foundation Inc., Smith, The [nonprofit]
Richardson Foundation, Sid W., The [nonprofit]
Richfood Holdings Inc. [company]
Richmont Mines Inc. [company]
Richton International Corp. [company]
Riddell Sports Inc. [company]
Ridoline [product]
Riester-Robb [product]
Rightchoice Managed Care Inc. [company]
Ring Ding (Ring Dings) [product]
Ringling Bros. and Barnum & Bailey [company]
Rio Algom Ltd. [company]
Rio Tinto P.L.C. [company]
Riordan Foundation, The [nonprofit]
Rippel Foundation, Fannie E., The [nonprofit]
RISC System/6000 [product]
Risperdal [product]
Rit dyes [product]
Ritalin [product]
Ritchie Bros Auctioneers Inc. [company]
Rite Aid [company]
Rite Aid Corp. [company]
Ritz [company & product]
Ritz-Carlton [company]
Riunite [product]
River Cafe, The [company]
Riviera Holdings Corp. [company]
Riviera Tool Co. [company]
RJ Reynolds Tobacco Holdings Inc. [company]
RLM [company]
RMX [company]
Roach Motel [company]

Road Runner [product]
Roadway Express Inc. [company]
Robbins & Myers Inc. [company]
Robert Half International Inc. [company]
Roberts Foundation, The [nonprofit]
Roberts Realty Investors Inc. [company]
Robertson Ceco Corp. [company]
Robins Foundation, The [nonprofit]
Robins, Kaplan, Miller & Ciresi [company]
Robinson Foundation, David, The [nonprofit]
Robitussin [product]
Roca [product]
Rochester Gas & Electric Corp. [company]
Rochester Software Associates [company]
Rock Solid [product]
Rock Tenn Co. [company]
Rockefeller Brothers Fund [company]
Rockefeller Foundation, The [nonprofit]
Rockport [product]
Rock-Tenn Co. [company]
Rockwell Fund [company]
Rockwell International Corp. [company]
Rocky Road [product]
Rodbard & Associates [company]
Rogers Communication Inc. [company]
Rogers Corp. [company]
Rogers Wireless Communications Inc. [company]
Rolaids [product]
Rohm & Haas Co. [company]
Rold Gold [product]
Rolex [product]
Rollerblade [product]
Rollins Inc. [company]
Rollins Truck Leasing Corp. [company]
Rolls-Royce [company & product]
Roll-Top [company & product]
Rolodex [product]
Rondos [product]
Roper [home appliances] [company]
Roper Industries Inc. [company]
Ropes & Gray [company]
Rosarita [product]

Roscoe's House of Chicken N Waffles [company]

Rose International [company]

Rose's [lime juice] [product]

Rosenberg Foundation, The [nonprofit]

Rosenberg Foundation, Henry and Ruth Blaustein, The [nonprofit]

Rosenberg Foundation, Sunny & Abe, The [nonprofit]

Rosenman & Colin [company]

Ross Stores, Inc. [company]

Rotary Foundation of Rotary International [company]

Roth Staffing [company]

Rothschild Foundation, Judith, The [nonprofit]

Rotonics Manufacturing, Inc. [company]

Rottlund Co., Inc., The [company]

Rouge Industries Inc. [company]

Roughneck [product]

Roundy's, Inc. [company]

Rouse Cap [company]

Rouse Co. [company]

Rowan Cos. Inc. [company]

Rowe Cos. [company]

Roxicet [product]

Roy Rogers [company]

Royal & Sun Alliance Insurance Group P.L.C. [company]

Royal Ahold N.V. [company]

Royal Appliance Manufacturing Co. [company]

Royal Bank of Scotland Group P.L.C., The [company]

Royal Caribbean Cruises Ltd. [company]

Royal Dutch Petroleum Co. [company]

Royal Dutch/Shell Group [company]

Royal Group Technologies Ltd. [company]

Royalcast [product]

Royce Focus Trust Inc. [company]

Royce Micro-Cap Trust Inc. [company]

Royce Value Trust Inc. [company]

RPM [lubricating oils] [product]

RPM Inc. [company]

R-Rounds [product]

RTE [company]

RTI International Metals Inc. [company]

Rubbermaid [company]

Rubik's Cube [product]

Rubin Foundation, Shelley and Donald, The [nonprofit]

Ruby Tuesday Inc. [company]

Rudder Foundation Inc., The [nonprofit]

Ruddick Corp. [company]

Ruffles [product]

Rugrats [product]

Rural Kentucky Medical Scholarship Fund [nonprofit]

Russ Berrie & Co. Inc. [company]

Russell Corp. [company]

Russell Family Foundation, The [nonprofit]

Rust-Oleum [product]

RW3 Technologies [company]

Rx Place, The [company]

Ryder System, Inc. [company]

Ryerson Tull Inc. [company]

Ry-Krisp [product]

Ryland Group Inc., The [company]

S&H [company]

S&P Global 100 Exchange-Traded Fund [company]

S&P Global 100 Index [company]

S.C.R.E.W. Active Wear [company]

S.Y. Bancorp Inc. [company]

SA8 [product]

SAAB [company & product]

Sabatier [product]

Sabine Royalty Trust [company]

Sabre Group Inc. [company]

Sachs Foundation, The [nonprofit]

Sadia S.A. [company]

Safe Handling [company]

Safeco Corp. [company]

Safeguard Scientifics Inc. [company]

Safeway Inc. [company]

Saga Communications Inc. [company]

Saga Systems Inc. [company]

Sage Foundation, Russell, The [nonprofit]

Sahara [product]
Sailors' Snug Harbor of Boston [company]
Sakrete [product]
Saks [company]
Saks Fifth Avenue [company]
Saks Inc. [company]
SaladShooter [product]
Salans Hertzfeld Heilbronn Christy & Viener [company]
Salem [product]
Salisbury Bancorp Inc. [company]
Salomon Brothers 2008 Worldwide Dollar Government Term Trust Inc. [company]
Salomon Brothers Fund Inc., The [company]
Salomon Family Foundation Inc. [company]
Salomon Inc. [company]
Salomon Smith Barney Holdings Inc. [company]
SALT Group [company]
Salt Sense [product]
Salton Inc. [company]
Salty Dog [product]
Salty's on Alki [company]
Salvation Army, The [nonprofit]
Sam Adams (Samuel Adams) [product]
Samaritan's Purse [nonprofit]
Sames Corp. [company]
Samsonite [company]
Samuels Foundation Inc., Fan Fox and Leslie R., The [nonprofit]
San Diego Gas & Electric Co. [company]
San Francisco Music Box Co., The [company]
San Juan Basin Royalty Trust [company]
Sanborn [company]
Sandeman [company]
Sanforized [product]
Sani-Flush [product]
Sanka [product]
SANPELLEGRINO [product]
Santa Fe Energy Trust [company]
Santa Fe Intl Corp. [company]
Santa Isabel S.A. [company]
Santander Bancorp [company]

Santander Overseas Bank Inc. [company]
Santitas [product]
Sanvision Technology [company]
Sappi Ltd. [company]
Sara Lee [company]
Sara Lee Corp. [company]
Sardi's [company]
Sasakawa Peace Foundation, The [nonprofit]
Saturn [product]
Saturn Yellow [product]
Sauer-Danfoss Inc. [company]
Saul Centers Inc. [company]
Saul Ewing [company]
Save the Children [nonprofit]
Savia S.A. [company]
SBC Communications Inc. [company]
Scaife Family Foundation, The [nonprofit]
Scaife Foundation Inc., Sarah, The [nonprofit]
Scana Corp. [company]
Scandic Hotels [company]
Scania Aktiebolag [company]
ScanJet [product]
Scanoe [product]
Schawk Inc. [company]
Scherer Foundation, Karla, The [nonprofit]
Schering A.G. [company]
Schering-Plough Corp. [company]
Schick [company]
Schiff Hardin & Waite [company]
Schlitz [company]
Schlumberger Ltd. [company]
Schnader Harrison Segal & Lewis [company]
Schneider Foundation, Eulalie Bloedel, The [nonprofit]
Schnuck Markets [company]
Scholarships Foundation, The [nonprofit]
Scholastic [company]
Scholastic Aptitude Test (SAT) [product]
Scholastic Corp. [company]
Schott Foundation, Caroline & Sigmund, The [nonprofit]
Schuff Steel Co. [company]
Schulte Roth & Zabel [company]

Schultz Foundation, Arthur B., The [nonprofit]

Schumacher Group of Delaware [company]

Schusterman Family Foundation, Charles and Lynn, The [nonprofit]

Schwab Charles Corp. [company]

Schwab Family Foundation, Helen and Charles, The [nonprofit]

Schwab Foundation for Learning, The [nonprofit]

Schwan's [company]

Schweitzer Mauduit International Inc. [company]

Schwinn [company]

SCI Systems Inc. [company]

Science Applications International Corp. [company]

Scientific Atlanta Inc. [company]

Scientific Games Corp. [company]

Scientific-Atlanta, Inc. [company]

Scoma's Restaurant [company]

Scoop Fresh [product]

Scooter Pie [product]

Scooter Store [company]

Scoozi! [company]

Scope Industries [company]

Scoreboard [product]

Scorpion [company & product]

Scotch [tape] [product]

Scotch-Brite [product]

Scotchgard [product]

Scott [electronics] [product]

ScottishPower P.L.C. [company]

ScotTowels [product]

Scotts Co., The [company]

SCPIE Holdings Inc. [company]

Scrabble [product]

Scratch Guard [product]

Screen Stars [product]

Scrub Buds [product]

Scrunge [product]

Scudder Municipal Income Trust [company]

Sculpey [product]

Sea & Ski [product]

Sea Containers Ltd. [company]

Sea Nymph [product]

Sea World [company]

Seaboard Corp. [company]

Seacor Smit Inc. [company]

Seagate Technology Inc. [company]

Seagram's [company]

Sealed Air Corp. [company]

Sealy [company]

Sears [company]

Sears (Sears Roebuck) [company]

Sears, Roebuck and Co. [company]

sears.com [company]

Seaswirl [company & product]

Seat Pagine Gialle S.P.A. [company]

Seconal [product]

Second Foods [company]

Security Associates International Inc. [company]

Security Capital Corp. [company]

Security Capital Group Inc. [company]

Security Capital US Realty [company]

Security Leasing Partners [company]

Security Services and Technologies [company]

Security Solutions [company]

SecurityLink [company]

Sedgwick, Detert, Moran & Arnold [company]

Seeing Eye [product]

Sega [company]

Seiko [company]

Seitel Inc. [company]

Selas Corp. of America [company]

Seldane Select Sector SPDR Fund [company]

Select Therapeutics Inc. [company]

SelectCard [product]

Selections [product]

Selectip [product]

Selectric [product]

Self Family Foundation, The [nonprofit]

Seligman Quality Municipal Fund, Inc. [company]

Selsun Blue [product]

Semotus Solutions Inc. [company]
Sempra Energy [company]
Sempra Energy Capital [company]
Senior High Income Portfolio Inc. [company]
Sensient Technologies Corp. [company]
Sensitive Eyes [product]
Sensormatic Electronics Corp. [company]
Sensory Science Corp. [company]
Sensory Therapy [product]
Sentry Insurance Group [company]
Septra [product]
Sequa Corp. [company]
Sequoia [company]
Seracare Inc. [company]
Serengeti [company & product]
Serevent [product]
Serono [product]
Service Corp. International [company]
Service Merchandise [company]
Service Merchandise Co., Inc. [company]
ServiceMaster Co., The [company]
servicemerchandise.com [company]
Services [company]
Servin' Saver [product]
Servotronics Inc. [company]
Serzone [product]
Seven Seas Petroleum Inc. [company]
Seyfarth Shaw [company]
SFBC International Inc. [company]
Shades of You [product]
Shake 'n Bake [product]
Shame On You [product]
Shamrock logistic L.P. [company]
Shamu [company]
Shandong Huaneng Power Development
   [company]
Sharper Image, The [company]
Sharpie [product]
Shaw Communications Inc. [company]
Shaw Group Inc. [company]
Shaw Industries Inc. [company]
Shaw Pittman [company]
Shaw's Crab House [company]

Shaw's Supermarkets [company]
Shearman & Sterling [company]
Sheer Energy [product]
Sheetrock [product]
Sheffield Cellars [product]
Sheffield Pharmaceuticals Inc. [company]
Shell [company]
Shell Trans & Trading P.L.C. [company]
Shepardize [product]
Sheppard, Mullin, Richter & Hampton
   [company]
Sheraton [company]
Sherlock [company]
Sherwin-Williams [company]
Sherwin-Williams Co., The [company]
Sherwood Brands, Inc. [company]
Shine-All [product]
Ship 'n Shore [product]
Shonfeld's USA [company]
Shook, Hardy & Bacon [company]
ShopKo Stores [company]
Shopko Stores Inc. [company]
Shore.net [company]
Shout [product]
Shriners Hospitals for Children, The
   [nonprofit]
Shurgard Storage Centers Inc. [company]
Si-18 [product]
Sicomet [product]
Sidley & Austin [company]
Siebel Systems [company]
Siemens A.G. [company]
Sierra Health Foundation, The [nonprofit]
Sierra Health Services Inc. [company]
Sierra Pacific Resources [company]
Siesta air [company]
SIFCO Industries Inc. [company]
Sigi Plus [product]
Sigma Systems [company]
Sigmatel [company]
Sikkens [company]
SIL International [company]
Silastic [company]

Silgan Holdings Inc. [company]
Silhouette [product]
silhouettes.com [company]
Silicon Graphics Inc. [company]
Silicon Valley Bancshares [company]
Silk Reflections [product]
Silly Putty [product]
Silverleaf Resorts Inc. [company]
Silverline Technologies Ltd. [company]
Similac [product]
Simon Foundation Inc., William E., The
　[nonprofit]
Simon Property Group Inc. [company]
Simoniz [company & product]
Simple Recipe [product]
Simpson Thacher & Bartlett [company]
SimStar [company]
Simula Inc. [company]
Singapore Fund Inc., The [company]
Singer Foundation, Harry, The [nonprofit]
Singing Machine Co. Inc., The [company]
Singulair [company]
Singulier [company]
Sinopec Shanghai Petrochemical Co. Ltd.
　[company]
Sinutab [product]
Siragusa Foundation, The [nonprofit]
Sirius Systems [company]
Sitel Corp. [company]
Six Flags [company]
Six Flags Inc. [company]
Sizeler Property Investors Inc. [company]
Sizzler International Inc. [company]
SJW Corp. [company]
Skadden Arps [company]
Skandia A.B. [company]
Skants [product]
Skechers USA Inc. [company]
Skee-Ball [product]
Skeeter [product]
Skidgrip [product]
Ski-Doo [product]
Skillman Foundation, The [nonprofit]

Skin Bracer [product]
Skippy [product]
Skittles [product]
Sky Helicopters [company]
Sky Kennel [product]
Skyline Corp. [company]
Skyr [company & product]
SL Green Realty Corp. [company]
SL Industries Inc. [company]
Slice [product]
Slick 50 [product]
Slim-Fast [product]
SlimLine [product]
Slinky [product]
SLM Holding Corp. [company]
Sloan Foundation, Alfred P., The [nonprofit]
Slurpee [product]
Sly Fry [product]
Smacks [product]
Small Dog Electronics [company]
Smart & Final Inc. [company]
Smart [directories] [company]
Smart Start [product]
SmartDM [product]
Smarties [product]
SmartLease [company]
Smedvig Asa [company]
Smirnoff [company]
Smith & Nephew P.L.C. [company]
Smith & Wesson [company]
Smith & Wollensky [company]
Smith (A.O.) Corp. [company]
Smith Barney Intermediate Municipal Fund,
　Inc. [company]
Smith Charles E. Residential Realty Inc.
　[company]
Smith Gerber McClure & Associates [company]
Smith International Inc. [company]
Smith-Corona [company]
Smithers Foundation Inc., Christopher D., The
　[nonprofit]
Smithfield Foods Inc. [company]
Smithsonian Institution [nonprofit]

Smog Check [product]

Smogpros [product]

Smurfit-Stone Container Corp. [company]

Snack Pack [product]

SnackWell's [product]

Snap Crackle Pop [product]

Snap-on [company & product]

Snap-On Inc. [company]

Snapple [company & product]

Snell & Wilmer [company]

Snickers [product]

Sno-Caps [product]

Sno-Cat [product]

Sno-Kone [product]

Snow Crop [product]

Snugli [product]

Snyder Foundation for Animals, William, The [nonprofit]

SO HO [product]

Sobrato Family Foundation, The [nonprofit]

Sodexho Marriott Services Inc. [company]

Sofkins [product]

Soft Scrub [product]

SoftASilk [product]

Softex [product]

Softsoap [product]

Software Associates International [company]

Software Information Systems [company]

Sohio [company]

Sokalan [product]

Sola International Inc. [company]

Solarcaine [product]

Solectron Corp. [company]

Solo [product]

Solo–aire [company & product]

Solubor [product]

Solunet [company]

Solutia Inc. [company]

Sominex [product]

Sonic Automotive Inc. [company]

Sonicport Inc. [company]

Sonik Technologies [company]

Sonnenschein Nath & Rosenthal [company]

Sonoco Products Co. [company]

Sonoma Wings Foundation, The [nonprofit]

Sonos [company & product]

Sonus Corp. [company]

Sony [company]

Sony Corp. [company]

Sorbplus [product]

Soros Fellowships for New Americans, Paul & Daisy, The [nonprofit]

Soros Foundations Network, The [nonprofit]

SOS [product]

Sotheby's [company]

Sothebys Holdings Inc. [company]

Sound Retrieval System [company]

Sound-Gard [company]

Source Cap Inc. [company]

Source Capital Inc. [company]

Source Communications [company]

Sourcebooks [company]

South Carolina Electric & Gas Co. [company]

South Jersey Industries Inc. [company]

South Texas Drilling & Exploration Inc. [company]

Southdown Inc. [company]

Southern Africa Fund Inc., The [company]

Southern Banc Co. Inc., The [company]

Southern BancShares (N.C.) Inc. [company]

Southern California Edison Co. [company]

Southern Comfort [product]

Southern Co. [company]

Southern Diversified Technologies [company]

Southern Peru Copper Corp. [company]

Southern States Cooperative [company]

Southern Union Co. [company]

SouthFirst Bancshares Inc. [company]

SouthTrust Corp. [company]

Southwest Gas Corp. [company]

Southwest Georgia Financial Corp. [company]

Southwest Securities Group Inc. [company]

Southwestern Bell Telephone Co. [company]

Southwestern Energy Co. [company]

Sovereign Bancorp, Inc. [company]

Sovran Self Storage Inc. [company]

Space Needle Restaurant [company]
Spacenet [company]
Spacesaver [product]
Spackle [product]
SpaghettiOs [product]
Spain Fund Inc., The [company]
SPAM [product]
Spanlink Communications Inc. [company]
Sparks Steakhouse [company]
Spartan Stores Inc. [company]
Spartech Corp. [company]
Sparton Corp. [company]
Special K [product]
Special Olympics [nonprofit]
Speciality Equipment Cos. Inc. [company]
Specialty Laboratories Inc. [company]
Spectra [company & product]
Spectrum [hot tubs] [company & product]
Spectrum BanCorp. Inc. [company]
Spectrum Communications Cabling [company]
SpeechWorks International [company]
Speed Stick [product]
Speedcom Technologies [company]
Speedo [product]
Speedway Motorsports Inc. [company]
SpellBound [product]
Spencer Foundation, The [nonprofit]
Spencer Reed Group [company]
Spenger's Fish Grotto [company]
Spenser Communications [company]
Sperry [computer equipment] [product]
Sperry [footwear] [product]
Spherion Corp. [company]
Spiaggia Restaurant and Café [company]
Spic and Span [product]
Spider-Man [product]
Spiegel [company]
spiegel.com [company]
Spiegel/Eddie Bauer [company]
Spieker Pptys Inc. [company]
Spieker Properties Inc. [company]
Spigadoro Inc. [company]
Spinnaker Exploration Co. [company]

Spinnaker Industries Inc. [company]
Spinning [product]
Spiral [product]
Spirograph [product]
Spit Fire [product]
Sport Supply Group Inc. [company]
Sports Authority [company]
Sports Authority Inc. [company]
Sports Club Co. Inc., The [company]
Sports Illustrated [product]
Sportshape [product]
Sportster [product]
Spra-Coupe [product]
Spray 'n Vac rug [product]
Spray 'n Wash [product]
Springbok Technologies [company]
Springs Industries Inc. [company]
Sprint Corp. [company]
Sprite [product]
SPX Corp. [company]
Spyglass Hill [company]
Squeezit [product]
Squire, Sanders & Dempsey [company]
Squirt [product]
SR•D [product]
S-Rounds [product]
SRS [company & product]
SST Computing [company]
St. Joe Co. [company]
St. Joseph Light & Power Co. [company]
St. Croix Cutlery [company]
St. Joseph's [company]
St. Jude Children's Research Hospital [nonprofit]
St. Jude Medical Inc. [nonprofit]
St. Paul Cos. Inc., The [company]
Staff Leasing Inc. [company]
Stage II Apparel Corp. [company]
Stage Stores [product]
Sta-Green [product]
Stain Out [product]
Stain Stick [product]
StairMaster [product]

Stancorp Financial Group Inc. [company]
Standard Automotive Corp. [company]
Standard Commercial Corp. [company]
Standard Motor Products Inc. [company]
Standard Pacific Corp. [company]
Standard Products Co. [company]
Standard Register [company]
Standard Register Co., The [company]
Standex International Corp. [company]
Stanley [tools] [company & product]
Stanley Cup [product]
Stanley Foundation, The [nonprofit]
Stanley Works [company]
Stanley Works, The [company]
Staples [company]
Staples Inc. [company]
staples.com [company]
Sta-Prest [product]
Sta-Puf [product]
Star Gas Partners L.P. [company]
Star Struck Ltd. [company]
Starbucks [company]
Starbucks Corp. [company]
Starburst [product]
Starfire [product]
Star-Kist [product]
Starr Foundation, The [nonprofit]
Startek Inc. [company]
Starter [product]
Starwood Hotel & Resorts Worldwide Inc.
   [company]
State Bancorp Inc. [company]
State Farm Insurance Cos. [company]
State Street Corp. [company]
Staten Island Bancorp Inc. [company]
Stater Bros. [company]
Stater Bros. Holdings Inc. [company]
Station Casinos Inc. [company]
Staunton Farm Foundation, The [nonprofit]
Steadicam [product]
Steak-Umm [product]
Steam Beer [product]
Stearns & Foster [company]

Steelcase [product]
Steelcase Inc. [company]
Steeplechase Software [company]
Stein Mart [company]
Steiner Foundation, Rudolph, The [nonprofit]
Steinway Musical Instrs Inc. [company]
Stella D'oro [company & product]
Stelmar Shipping Ltd. [company]
Stepan Co. [company]
Stephan Co., The [company]
Steptoe & Johnson [company]
Steris Corp. [company]
Sterling [company]
Sterling Bancorp [company]
Sterling Capital Corp. [company]
Sterling Halite [company]
Sterling Jewelers [company]
Sterling Software Inc. [company]
Sterling Vineyards [company]
Stern Family Fund [company]
Sterno [product]
Stetson [product]
Steuben [company & product]
Stewart Information Services Corp. [company]
Sticklets [product]
Stifel Financial Corp. [company]
Stillwater Mining Co. [company]
Stilwell Financial [company]
Stilwell Financial Inc. [company]
Stirling [product]
Stoel Rives [product]
Stokely Van Camp Inc. [company]
Stolichnaya [product]
Stone & Webster Inc. [company]
Stone Container Corp. [company]
Stone Energy Corp. [company]
Stonehaven Realty Trust [company]
Stonepath Group Inc. [company]
Stoneridge Inc. [company]
Stop & Shop [company]
Stopka and Associates [company]
Storage Computer Corp. [company]
Storage Technology Corp. [company]

Storage USA Inc. [company]
StorageTek [company]
StorageTek Corp. [company]
Stormwater Research Group [company]
Stouffer's [product]
Stove Top [product]
STP [product]
Straight-Wire [product]
Strategic Global Income Fund Inc. [company]
Strategic Insight [company]
Stratesec Inc. [company]
Stratocaster [company & product]
Stratolounger [company & product]
Stratos [company & product]
streamline.com [company]
Street Glow [company]
streetTRACKS [company]
Stride Rite Corp. [company]
Stri-Dex [product]
Stroh's [product]
Stroock & Stroock & Lavan [company]
Structured Products Corp. [company]
Stryker Corp. [company]
STS Technologies Inc. [company]
Stuart Foundation, The [nonprofit]
Student Loan Corp. [company]
Sturm Ruger & Co. Inc. [company]
Style Keeper [product]
Styrofoam [product]
Subtract [product]
Suburban Propane Partners L.P. [company]
Sub-Zero [product]
Suchard [product]
Sucrets [product]
Sudafed [product]
Sudbury Foundation, The [nonprofit]
Sugar Twin [product]
Sugus [product]
Suiza Foods Corp. [company]
Sulfurkote [product]
Sullivan & Cromwell [company]
Summerlee Foundation, The [nonprofit]
Summit Bank Corp. [company]

Summit Properties Inc. [company]
Sun Chips [product]
Sun Communities Inc. [company]
Sun Gems [product]
Sun Healthcare Group Inc. [company]
Sun International Hotels Ltd. [company]
Sun Microsystems Inc. [company]
Sunair Electronics Inc. [company]
Sunbeam [company]
Sunbeam Corp. [company]
Sunburst Hospitality Corp. [company]
Suncor Energy Inc. [company]
SunGard Data Systems Inc. [company]
Sunglass Hut [company]
Sun-In hair (Sun In) [product]
Sunkist [product]
SunLife Financial Services [company]
Sun-Maid [company & product]
Sunoco Inc. [company]
Sunproof [chemicals] [company]
Sunrise Medical Inc. [company]
Sunsource Inc. [company]
Sunstone Hotel Investors Inc. [company]
SunTrust Banks Inc. [company]
Supanil [product]
Super Ball [product]
Super Big Bite [product]
Super Bowl [product]
Super Chef [product]
Super Duty [product]
Super Look [product]
Super Moist [product]
Super Single [product]
Super Soaker [product]
SuperAmerica [company]
Superba [company]
SuperBook [company & product]
Supergrip [product]
Superior [engine parts] [product]
Superior Industries International Inc.
  [company]
Superior Telecom Inc. [company]
Superior Uniform Group Inc. [company]

Superman [product]
Supermarkets General Holdings Corp.
  [company]
Supermercados Unimarc S.A. [company]
Supernumber [company]
Super-Sol Ltd. [company]
SUPERVALU Inc. [company]
SUPERVALU Retail [company]
Supp-Hose [product]
SupplyCore.com [company]
Support Technologies [company]
Suprax [product]
Supreme Industries Inc. [company]
Surdna Foundation Inc. [company]
Surefoot [product]
Sure-Lites [product]
Surfynol [product]
Sussex Bancorp [company]
Sutherland Asbill & Brennan [company]
SVI Solutions Inc. [company]
Swalm Foundation, The [nonprofit]
Swan-Creek-Farms [company]
Swanson [company & product]
Swatch [product]
Swedish Fish [product]
Sweet'n Low [product]
SweeTARTS [product]
Swidler Berlin Shereff Friedman [company]
Swift Energy Co. [company]
Swift Transportation Co. Inc. [company]
Swinney Trust, Edward F. [company]
Swiss Helvetia Fund Inc., The [company]
Swiss Miss [product]
Swissair [company]
Sybron Dental Specialties [company]
Syl-Off [product]
Symantec Corp. [company]
Symmetrel [product]
Syms Corp. [company]
Synchilla [product]
Synergistics [company]
Synergy Investment [company]
Syngenta A.G. [company]

Synovus Financial Corp. [company]
Synthroid [product]
Synygy [company]
Sysco Corp. [company]
Systech Solutions [company]
Systemax Inc. [company]
Systems Conversion [company]
Systems Design Group [company]
T. Rowe Price Group Inc. [company]
T.J.Maxx [company]
T2 Systems [company]
Tab Products Co. [company]
Tab [product]
Tabasco [product]
Taco Bell [company]
Taco Bueno [company]
Tag-It Pacific Inc. [company]
Taiwan Equity Fund Inc., The [company]
Taiwan Fund Inc., The [company]
Take To Auction.com Inc. [company]
Talbots [company]
Talbots Inc. [company]
Talisman Energy Inc. [company]
Talking Book World [company]
Talstar [company & product]
Tamagotchi [company]
Tamoxifen [product]
Tampax [product]
Tandy Corp. [company]
Tandy/RadioShack [company]
Tandycrafts Inc. [company]
Tanger Factory Outlet Centers, Inc. [company]
Tannery West [product]
Tanqueray [product]
Tara Software [company]
Targa [company & product]
Target [store] [company]
Target Corp. [company]
Taste of Texas [product]
Tastee-Freez [product]
Taster's Choice [product]
Tasty Baking Co. [company]
Tastykake [product]

Tater Tots [product]
Tatou [product]
Tauban Centers Inc. [company]
Tavern on the Green [company]
TAXOL [product]
Taylor Nelson Sofres [company]
Taylor Studios [company]
TB Woods Corp. [company]
TBA Entertainment Corp. [company]
TCF Financial Corp. [company]
TCW Convertible Securities Fund Inc.
  [company]
TD Waterhouse Group Inc. [company]
TDK Corp. [company]
TDX [company]
Team Fenex [company]
Team Inc. [company]
TeamTech International [company]
Tech Data Corp. [company]
Tech/Ops Sevcon Inc. [company]
TechBooks [company]
Teche Holding Co. [company]
TechneLite [product]
Technicolor [product]
Techniki Informatica [company]
Technitrol Inc. [company]
Technology Flavors & Fragrances Inc.
  [company]
Technology Strategy [company]
Techroline [product]
Techron [product]
TECO Energy Inc. [company]
Tectilon [product]
Tecumseh Products [product]
Teekay Shipping Corp. [company]
Teen Spirit [company]
Teflon [product]
Tefron Ltd. [company]
Tegretol [product]
Tejon Ranch Co. [company]
Teklution [company]
Tektronix Inc. [company]
Telebras HOLDRs [company]

Telecom New Zealand [company]
Telecommunications Analysis Group [company]
Telecopier [company]
Teledyne Technologies Inc. [company]
Teleflex Inc. [company]
Telefon ABL.M. Ericsson [company]
Telefonica S.A. [company]
Telegate [company]
Telekom Austria A.G. [company]
Telephone and Data Systems, Inc. [company]
Telephony Experts [company]
Teleprobe [company]
TelePrompTer [product]
Telesis [company]
Teletouch Communications Inc. [company]
Teletype [company & product]
Telmin [product]
Telstra Ltd. [company]
TelStrat International [company]
Teltronix Information Systems [company]
Telwares [company]
Temazepam [product]
Temple-Inland Inc. [company]
Templeton China World Fund Inc. [company]
Templeton Dragon Fund Inc. [company]
Templeton Foundation, John, The [nonprofit]
Templeton Vietnam and Southeast Asia Fund
  Inc., The [company]
Tempstaff [company]
Tenera Inc. [company]
Tenet Healthcare Corp. [company]
Tengasco Inc. [company]
Tennant Co. [company]
Tenneco Automotive [company]
Tenneco Automotive Inc. [company]
Tennessee Valley Authority [nonprofit]
Tenormin [product]
Tensor [product]
TEOCO [company]
Teppco Partners L.P. [company]
Teradyne Inc. [company]
Terasil [product]
Terex Corp. [company]

Tergal [product]
Terminix [company]
Terra Industries Inc. [company]
Terra Nitrogen Co. L.P. [company]
Terraclor [product]
Terramycin [product]
Terra-Tire [product]
Terremark Worldwide Inc. [company]
terrysvillage.com [company]
Tesco P.L.C. [company]
Tesoro [company]
Tesoro Petroleum Corp. [company]
Testa, Hurwitz & Thibeault [company]
TestChip Technologies [company]
Testmobile [product]
Tetoron [product]
Tetra Pak [product]
Tetra Technologies Inc. [company]
Teva [product]
Texaco [company]
Texaco Inc. [company]
Texas Biotechnology Corp. [company]
Texas Industries [company]
Texas Industries Inc. [company]
Texas Instruments [company]
Texas Instruments Inc. [company]
Texas Pacific Group Inc. [company]
Texas Pacific Land Trust [company]
Texas Steer [product]
Texas Utilities Co. [company]
Textron Inc. [company]
Thackeray Corp. [company]
Thai Capital Fund Inc., The [company]
Thai Fund Inc., The [company]
Thaumaturgix [product]
The "21" Club [company]
Thelen, Reid & Priest [company]
Theo-Dur [product]
Thera-Band [product]
Theragenics Corp. [company]
Thermagon [product]
Thermo Electron Corp. [company]
Thermo Fibergen Inc. [company]

Thermo King [company]
Thermo-Lock [company]
Thermopane [product]
Thermos [product]
Thermoscan [company & product]
Thermoview Industries Inc. [company]
Thermwood Corp. [company]
Thighmaster [product]
Think Tank Systems [company]
ThinkJet [product]
Thinsulate [product]
Third Foods [product]
Thom McAn [company]
Thomas & Betts Corp. [company]
Thomas Industries Inc. [company]
Thomas' English Muffins [product]
Thompson Hine & Flory [company]
Thompson Knight Brown Parker & Leahy
  [company]
Thompson Technologies [company]
Thompson's Water Seal [company]
Thomson Multimedia [company]
Thor Industries Inc. [company]
Thorazine [product]
Thornburg Mortgage Inc. [company]
Thoroseal [product]
ThoughtWorks [company]
Thousand Trails Inc. [company]
Three-Five Systems Inc. [company]
Thunderbird [product]
Tia Maria [product]
TIAA-CREF [product]
Tiazac [product]
Tic Tac [product]
Ticketmaster [company]
ticketmaster.com [company]
Tickle Me Elmo [product]
Tidewater Inc. [company]
Tiffany [company]
Tiffany & Co [company]
Tiger Balm [product]
tigerdirect.com [company]
Tilade [product]

Tilex [product]
Tilia International [company]
Tilt [product]
Tilt-A-Whirl [product]
Timberland [company]
Timberland Co. [company]
Tim-Bor [product]
Time Warner Inc. [company]
Times Mirror Co., The [company]
Timex [company & product]
Timken Co. [company]
Timken Co., The [company]
Timoptic [product]
Tinactin [product]
Tinker Foundation Inc., The [nonprofit]
Tinkertoy [product]
Tinopal [product]
Tiny Tiger [product]
Tioxide [product]
Tipperary Corp. [company]
Tiptronic [product]
Tirks [company & product]
Titan Corp. [company]
Titan International Inc. [company]
Titan Pharmaceuticals Inc. [company]
Titanium Metals Corp. [company]
Tivoli [product]
Tixies [product]
TJX Cos. Inc., The [company]
TKF Foundation, The [nonprofit]
TMP Worldwide Inc. [company]
TNT Post Group [company]
Toastmaster [product]
Tobias Foundation Inc., Randall L., The
    [product]
Toblerone [product]
Tobradex [product]
Toby Enterprises Inc. [company]
Tocker Foundation, The [nonprofit]
Todd Shipyards Corp. [company]
Todhunter International Inc. [company]
TOEFL [product]
Tofutti [company & product]

Tofutti Brands Inc. [company]
Together Foundation, The [nonprofit]
Toledo Edison Co. [company]
Toll Brothers [company]
Toll Brothers Inc. [company]
Toll House [product]
Tom Cat [product]
Tomkins P.L.C. [company]
Tommy Hilfiger [company]
Tommy Hilfiger Corp. [company]
TompkinsTrustco Inc. [company]
Tonka [company & product]
Tonox [product]
Too Inc. [company]
Tootsie Roll [company & product]
Tootsie Roll Industries Inc. [company]
Top Hat [company]
Top Shelf [product]
Topicort [product]
Topp Construction Services [company]
Toprol-XL [product]
Tops-2.5D [product]
Top-Sider [product]
Torayca [product]
Torch Energy Royalty Trust [company]
Torchmark Corp. [company]
Toro [company & product]
Toro Co., The [company]
Toronto-Dominion Bank [company]
Torq-Gard [product]
Torqometer [product]
Tosco Corp. [company]
Toshiba [company]
Tostitos [product]
Total [product]
Total Containment of New York [company]
Total Renal Care Holdings Inc. [company]
Total System Services Inc. [company]
Totalclaim [company & product]
Totaline [company]
Tott's [company & product]
TourBook [product]
Tournament [product]

Tower Automotive Inc. [company]
Tower Records [company]
Town & Country Trust [company]
Toy World [company]
Toyota [company]
Toyota Motor Corp. [company]
Toys "R" Us [company]
Toys "R" Us Inc. [company]
Toys That Last [product]
toysrus.com [company]
TPN Holdings P.L.C. [company]
Trace [analysis system for air conditioning]
　　[company & product]
Tracer [company & product]
Traditional Home [product]
Traffic and Weather Together [product]
Traffic Builders [product]
Trailways [product]
Trammell Crow Co. [company]
Trane [company & product]
Trans World Airlines Inc. (TWA) [company]
Trans World Entertainment Corp. [company]
Transamerica Delaware L.P. [company]
Transamerica Financing Corp. [company]
Transamerica Income Shares Inc. [company]
Transatlantic Holdings Inc. [company]
Transcanada Pipelines Ltd. [company]
Transcontinental Realty Investors Inc.
　　[company]
Transderm-Nitro [product]
Transfinancial Holdings Inc. [company]
Transicold [product]
Trans-Lux Corp. [company]
Transmedia Network [company]
Transmedia Networks Inc. [company]
Transmontaigne Inc. [company]
Transnational Financial Network Inc.
　　[company]
Transocean Sedco Forex Inc. [company]
TransPerfect Translations [company]
Transportation Components Inc. [company]
Transpro Inc. [company]
Transtechnology Corp. [company]

Transworld HealthCare Inc. [company]
TranTech [product]
Trapper Keeper [product]
Trattoria Dell' Arte [company]
Travel & Safari Clothing Co. [company]
Travelers Corporate Loan Fund Inc. [company]
TraveLodge [company]
Travenol [product]
Trav-O-Lator [product]
Trax [company]
Trazodone [product]
TRC Cos. Inc. [company]
Tredegar Corp. [company]
Trellis Fund, The [company]
Tremont Corp. [company]
Trend Micro Inc. [company]
Trenwick Group Ltd. [company]
Trex Inc. [company]
Tri Contl Corp. [company]
Triad Hospitals Inc. [company]
Triad Management Systems [company]
Triamterene/HCTZ [product]
Triarc Cos. Inc. [company]
Tribol [company & product]
Tribune Co. [company]
Tricom [company]
Tri-Com Technical Services [company]
Tricon Global [company]
Tricon Global Restaurants Inc. [company]
Tri-Continental Corp. [company]
Trident [product]
Tridil [product]
Trifari [product]
Trigon Healthcare Inc. [company]
Trilene [product]
Trimethoprim/Sulfa [product]
TriMix Foundation, The [nonprofit]
Trimline [company]
Trimox [product]
Trinet Corporate Realty Trust Inc. [company]
Trinitron [product]
Trinity Industries Inc. [company]
Trio-Tech International [company]

Triphasil [product]
Triple Point Technology [company]
TripTik [product]
Triscuit [product]
Tristar Corp. [company]
Trisun [product]
Triton Energy Ltd. [company]
Triumph [company & product]
Triumph Group Inc. [company]
Trivial Pursuit [product]
Trix [product]
Trizec Hahn Corp. [company]
Trojan [product]
Tron [company & product]
Tropical Blend [product]
Tropicana [company & product]
Troutman Sanders [company]
Truck Guard [product]
True North Communication Inc. [company]
True Temper [product]
TrueType [product]
TruGreen [product]
Trull Foundation, The [nonprofit]
Trump Hotels & Casino Resorts Inc. [company]
TruServ Corp. [company]
Trust for Public Land, The [company]
TRW [company]
TRW Inc. [company]
TRX [company]
TT [company]
Tubos de Acero de Mexico S.A. [company]
Tucker [company & product]
Tucks [product]
Tucson Osteopathic Medical Foundation, The [nonprofit]
Tuesday Morning [company]
Tuex [product]
Tuf-Edge [product]
Tuffcide [product]
Tuf-Lite [product]
Tums [product]
Tuna Helper [product]
Tupperware [product]

Tupperware Corp. [company]
Turbo Toolbox [company & product]
Turner Foundation Inc., The [nonprofit]
Turrell Fund [company]
Turtle Wax [product]
Turtles [product]
Tut Systems Inc. [company]
Tutogen Medical Inc. [company]
Tuxedo [software] [company & product]
Tuxis Corp. [company]
TV Azteca S.A. [company]
TV Guide [company & product]
TVX Gold Inc. [company]
TWA [company]
Tween [product]
Twilight Zone, The [company]
Twin Disc Inc. [company]
Twin Hills Collectables [product]
Twin Oaks [company]
Twinco [company]
Twinkies [product]
Twizzlers [product]
TXU Corp. [company]
TXU Europe [company]
Tyco Internatinal Ltd. New [company]
TyCom, Ltd. [company]
Ty-D-Bol [product]
Tygon [product]
Tylenol [product]
Tyler Technologies Inc. [company]
Tymnet [company]
Tyson Foods Inc. [company]
U S West Inc. [company]
U.S. Bancorp [company]
U.S. Energy Services [company]
U.S. Foodservice [company]
U.S. Home & Garden Inc. [company]
U.S. Industries Inc. [company]
U.S. Liquids Inc. [company]
U.S. Office Products Co. [company]
U.S. Trust Corp. [company]
U.S.B. Holding Co. Inc. [company]
UAL Corp. [company]

ubid.com [company]
Ubrandit.com [company]
UBS A.G. [company]
Ucar International Inc. [company]
UCLA [nonprofit]
Ucrete [product]
UGI Corp. [company]
U-Haul [company]
UIL Holding Corp. [company]
UL [nonprofit]
Ultimate [product]
Ultimate Warrior [product]
Ultimet [company]
Ultra [gasoline] [product]
Ultra Brite [product]
Ultra Petroleum Corp. [company]
Ultra Sheen [product]
UltraBac.com [company]
Ultracast [company & product]
Ultraflex [product]
Ultram [product]
Ultramar Diamond Shamrock Corp. [company]
Ultraray [product]
Ultrasuede [product]
Ultra-Synthet [product]
Ultratech Stepper [product]
Ultrazyme [product]
Uncle Ben's [product]
Uncola [product]
Undertaker [company]
Underwriters Laboratories Inc. [company]
Unibit [product]
Unica [company]
UniCapital Corp. [company]
Unicom Corp. [company]
Unifi Inc. [company]
Unified Western Grocers Inc. [company]
Unifirst Corp. [company]
Unigraphics Solutions Inc. [company]
Unilever N.V. [company]
Unilever P.L.C. [company]
Uni-Marts Inc. [company]
Union Bankshares Inc. [company]

Union Carbide Corp. [company]
Union Electric Co. [company]
Union Oyster House [company]
Union Pacific [company]
Union Pacific Corp. [company]
Union Planters Corp. [company]
UnionBanCal Corp. [company]
Unique Computing Solutions [company]
Uniroyal [company]
UNIS [company]
Uniscope [company & product]
Unisom [product]
UniSource Energy Corp. [company]
Unisource Worldwide Inc. [company]
Unisys [company]
Unisys Corp. [company]
Unit Corp. [company]
United Asset Management Corp. [company]
United Auto Group Inc. [company]
United Cap Fdg Partnershp L.P. [company]
United Capital Corp. [company]
United Dominion Industries Ltd. [company]
United Dominion Realty Trust Inc. [company]
United Electric Supply [company]
United Industries Corp. [company]
United Jewish Communities [company]
United Microelectronics Corp. [company]
United Mobile Homes Inc. [company]
United Negro College Fund, The [nonprofit]
United Parcel Service (UPS) [company]
United Parcel Service Inc. [company]
United Parcel Service of America Inc.
   [company]
United Park City Mines Co. [company]
United Rental Inc. [company]
United Rentals Inc. [company]
United Services Automobile Association
   (USAA) [company]
United States Cellular Corp. [company]
United States Exploration Inc. [company]
United States Fund for UNICEF [nonprofit]
United States Olympic Committee
   [nonprofit]

United States-Japan Foundation, The [nonprofit]
United Stationers Inc. [company]
United Technologies Corp. [company]
United Utils P.L.C. [company]
United Water Resources Inc. [company]
United-Guardian Inc. [company]
UnitedHealth Group Inc. [company]
UNITIL Corp. [company]
UNIVAC [company & product]
Universal [company & product]
Universal Compression Holdings Inc. [company]
Universal Corp. [company]
Universal Forest Products, Inc. [company]
Universal Health Realty Income Trust [company]
Universal Health Services Inc. [company]
Universal Software [company]
Univision Communications [company]
Univision Communications Inc. [company]
Univolt [company & product]
UNIX [product]
Uno [product]
Uno Restaurant Corp. [company]
Unocal 76 [company & product]
Unocal Corp. [company]
Unova Inc. [company]
Until There's a Cure Foundation [nonprofit]
Unum Provident Corp. [company]
UP [generators] [product]
Upjohn Institute for Employment Research [nonprofit]
Upm-Kymmene Corp. [company]
Uralane [product]
Urban Shopping Centers Inc. [company]
Urbanet [company]
URS Corp. [company]
Urstadt Biddle Properties Inc. [company]
US Airways Group Inc. [company]
US Bancorp [company]
US Can Corp. [company]
US Industries Inc. [company]

US Restaurant Properties Inc. [company]
USA ED Inc. [company]
USA Education Inc. [company]
USA Networks Inc. [company]
USA Today [product]
USC [company]
USEC Inc. [company]
USFreightways Corp. [company]
USG [company]
USG Corp. [company]
Uslife Income Fund Inc. [company]
UST Inc. [company]
USURF America Inc. [company]
USX Corp. [company]
USX Marathon Oil Co. [company]
UTI Energy Corp. [company]
UtiliCorp United Inc. [company]
Utility [product]
U-Turn [product]
Uvitex [product]
Uzi [product]
V05 [product]
V8 [product]
va.com [company]
Vacutainer [product]
Vail Resorts Inc. [company]
Valassis Communications [company]
Valero Energy Corp. [company]
Valhi Inc. [company]
Valisone [product]
Valium [product]
Valley Foundation, The [nonprofit]
Valley National Bancorp [company]
Valley National Gases Inc. [company]
Value City [company]
Value City Department Stores Inc. [company]
Value Financial Services [company]
ValuJet Airlines [company]
Valu-Rite [company]
Valve Guard [product]
Valvoline [product]
van Ameringen Foundation Inc., The [nonprofit]

Van Camp's [company]
Van Kampen [company]
Vanagon [product]
Vancenase AQ DS [product]
Vanellus [company]
Vanguard Group [company]
Vanish [product]
Vantage [product]
Varathane [product]
Varco International Inc. [company]
Varian Madical Systems Inc. [company]
Variety [product]
VariTrane [company]
Varsity, The [company]
Varsol [company]
Vaseline [product]
Vasogen Inc. [company]
Vasotec [product]
Vastera [product]
VAX [company]
Vector Group Ltd. [company]
Vectra [company]
Vectren Corp. [company]
Veetids [product]
Vegemite [product]
Veg-O-Matic [product]
Velcro [product]
Velveeta [product]
Venable, Baetjer, Howard & Civiletti [company]
Venator [company]
Venator Group [company]
Venator Group Inc. [company]
Vencor Inc. [company]
Vent-a-Ridge Tilators [product]
Ventas Inc. [company]
Venus de Milo [product]
Vera Wang [company & product]
Verapamil S.R. [company]
Veritas DGC Inc. [company]
Veritas Software Corp. [company]
VeriTru [product]
Verizon Communications [company]

Vermont Pure Holdings Ltd. [company]
Versa Climber [product]
Versace [company]
Versamid [product]
Versar Inc. [company]
Versatile Systems [company]
Versatint [product]
Versed [product]
Vertagreen [product]
Vertex Engineering Services [company]
Vespa [company & product]
Vesta Insurance Group Inc. [company]
Vestaur Securities Inc. [company]
Vetlesen Foundation, G. Unger, The [nonprofit]
Veuve Clicquot Ponsardin [company]
VF Corp. [company]
Viacom Inc. [company]
Viad Corp. [company]
Viagra [product]
Viasystems Group Inc. [company]
Vibram [product]
Vibrathane [product]
Vicks [company & product]
Vicodin [product]
Vicon Industries Inc. [company]
Vicoprofen [product]
Victoria's Secret [company]
victoriassecret.com [company]
Victory [product]
Victrola [product]
Vidal Sassoon [company & product]
Videsh Sanchar Nigam Ltd. [company]
View-Master [product]
Vinac [product]
Vinex [product]
Vinson & Elkins [company]
Vintage Petroleum Inc. [company]
Vioxx [product]
Viper [product]
Viragen Inc. [company]
Virco Manufacturing Corp. [company]
Virginia Electric & Power Co. [company]

Virginia Environmental Endowment [nonprofit]
Virginia Environmental Research Endowment [nonprofit]
Visa [company]
Visco-Static [product]
Vise-Grip [product]
VISH Inc. [company]
Vishay Intertechnology Inc. [company]
Visine [product]
Vision 1 [company]
Visqueen [company]
Vista Gold Corp. [company]
Vistabrik [product]
VistaScreen [product]
Vistronix [product]
Visx Inc. [company]
Vita Food Products Inc. [company]
Vitalis [product]
Vitamin World [company]
vitaminshoppe.com [company]
Vitavax [company]
Vitran Corp. Inc. [company]
Vitro [company]
Vivendi Universal [company]
Vivendi Universal S.A. [company]
Vlasic [company]
Vlasic Foods International Inc. [company]
VMOPERATOR [company & product]
VMS [company]
VMTAPE [company]
VNA Foundation, The [nonprofit]
Vodafone Group P.L.C. [company]
Vogler Foundation Inc., Laura B., The [nonprofit]
Voice Power Telecommunications [company]
Voicenet Inc. [company]
Voicestream Wireless Corp. [company]
Volkswagen (VW) [company]
Volt Information Sciences Inc. [company]
Voltaren [company]
Volunteers of America [nonprofit]
Volvo [company & product]
Volvo A.B. [company]

Von Liebig Foundation Inc., William J., The [nonprofit]
Vornado Operating Co. [company]
Vornado Realty Trust [company]
Vorys, Sater, Seymour & Pease [company]
Votorantim Celulose e Papel [company]
Vowel-A-Tilde [company]
VO [product]
Voyageur Arizona Municipal Income Fund Inc. [company]
Voyageur Colorado Insured Municipal Income Fund Inc. [company]
Voyageur Florida Insured Municipal Income Fund [company]
Voyageur Minnesota Municipal Income Fund Inc. [company]
VSI Holdings Inc. [company]
Vuarnet [product]
Vue Co. [company]
Vulcan [stores] [company]
Vulcan International Corp. [company]
Vulcan Materials Co. [company]
Vycor [company & product]
W.P. Stewart & Co. Ltd. [company]
W.R. Berkley Corp. [company]
W.R. Grace & Co. [company]
W.W. Grainger Inc. [company]
W2Com [company]
Wabash National Corp. [company]
Wabtec Corporate [company]
Wachovia Corp. [company]
Wackenhut Corp. [company]
Waddell & Reed Financial Inc. [company]
Wagner [company]
Wagoneer [product]
Waitt Family Foundation, The [nonprofit]
Waldenbooks [company]
Walgreen [company]
Walgreen Co. [company]
Walgreens [company]
Walk Off [product]
Walker Digital Corp. [company]
Walkman [product]

Wallace Computer Services Inc. [company]
Wallace Global Fund [company]
Wallace-Reader's Digest Funds [company]
Wal-Mart [company]
Wal-Mart Stores Inc. [company]
wal-mart.com [company]
Walt Disney World [company]
Walter Industries Inc. [company]
Walton Family Foundation Inc., The [nonprofit]
Wang [company]
Warbex [product]
Warfarin [product]
Warhol Foundation for the Visual Arts, Andy,
 The [nonprofit]
Warnaco Group Inc., The [company]
Warner-Lambert Co. [company]
Warren Memorial Foundation, The [nonprofit]
Wasa [product]
Wash a-bye Baby [product]
Wash'n Dri [product]
Washington Gas Light Co. [company]
Washington Group International Inc.
 [company]
Washington Homes Inc. [company]
Washington Mutual Inc. [company]
Washington Post Co., The [company]
Washington Real Estate Investment [company]
Washington Research Foundation, The
 [nonprofit]
Washington Savings Bank FSB, The [company]
Washington Square Health Foundation Inc.
 [company]
Waste Management Inc. [company]
Water Babies [product]
Water Club, The [company]
Water Pik [company]
Water Pik Technologies Inc. [company]
Water's Edge [company]
WaterColor Feelings [product]
Waterford [company & product]
Waterlink Inc. [company]
Waterman [company]
Waterplug [product]

Waters Corp. [company]
Watsco Inc. [company]
Watson Foundation, Thomas J., The [nonprofit]
Watson Pharmaceuticals Inc. [company]
Watson Wyatt & Co. Holdings [company]
Watts Industries Inc. [company]
Wausau Mosinee Paper Mills Corp. [company]
Wav [company]
Wave [vinyl emulsions] [product]
Wave Runner [product]
Wavecrest [product]
Wayfarer [product]
WD-40 [product]
Wear-Dated [product]
Weather Tamer [product]
Weatherford International Inc. [company]
Weathermaker [company]
Weathershield [product]
Weathertron [company]
Weaver Foundation, The [nonprofit]
Webco Industries Inc. [company]
webvan.com [company]
Wechsler [company & product]
Weddell & Reed Financial Inc. [company]
Wedgwood [product]
Wee Baby [product]
Weebok [product]
Weed Eater [product]
Weeden Foundation, The [nonprofit]
Weedwacker [product]
Weejuns [product]
Weeks Corp. [company]
Wegman's [company]
Weider Nutrition International Inc. [company]
Weight Watchers [company]
Weil, Gotshal & Manges [company]
Weill Foundation for Music Inc., Kurt, The
 [nonprofit]
Weingart Foundation, The [nonprofit]
Weingarten Realty Investors [company]
Weirton Steel Corp. [company]
Weis Markets [company]
Weis Markets Inc. [company]

Welch Foundation, Robert A., The [nonprofit]
Welch's [company & product]
Welcome Wagon [company]
Weldwood [company]
Wellbutrin [product]
Wellbutrin SR [product]
Wellco Enterprises Inc. [company]
Wellman Inc. [company]
Wellmark Foundation, The [nonprofit]
Wellpoint Health Networks Inc. [company]
Wells Fargo [company]
Wells Fargo & Co. [company]
Wellsford Real Properties Inc. [company]
Wells-Gardner Electronics Corp. [company]
Wender-Weis Foundation for Children, The
  [nonprofit]
Wendy's [company]
Wendy's International Inc. [company]
Wenner-Gren Foundation for Anthropological
  Research Inc., The [nonprofit]
Werner Enterprises Inc. [company]
Wesco Financial Corp. [company]
Wesco International Inc. [company]
Wesson [company]
West Bend [company]
West Marine [company]
West Penn Power Co. [company]
West Pharmaceutical Services Inc. [company]
West Technology [company]
Westcoast Energy Inc. [company]
Westcoast Hospitality Corp. [company]
Westcorp [company]
Western [company & product]
Western Digital Corp. [company]
Western Resources, Inc. [company]
Westfield America Inc. [company]
Westinghouse [company]
Westminster Capital Inc. [company]
Westmoreland Coal Co. [company]
Westover Scientific [company]
Westpac Banking Corp. [company]
WestPoint Stevens Inc. [company]
Westport Resources Corp. [company]

Westvaco Corp. [company]
Westwood One Inc. [company]
Wet Seal [company]
Wetzel's Pretzels [company & product]
Weyerhaeuser Co. [company]
Weylu's [company]
WGL Holdings Inc. [company]
Whaler [product]
Wheaties [product]
Wheel Horse [product]
Wherehouse Music [company]
Whirlpool [company]
Whirlpool Corp. [company]
Whiskas [product]
Whisper Quiet [product]
Whitaker Foundation, The [nonprofit]
White & Case [company]
White Foundation, Ryan, The [nonprofit]
Whitehall Foundation Inc., The [nonprofit]
Whitehall Jewellers Inc. [company]
Whitehead Foundation Inc., Lettie Pate, The
  [nonprofit]
Whitehead Foundation, Joseph B., The
  [nonprofit]
White-Westinghouse [company]
Whitman Breed Abbott & Morgan [company]
Whitman Corp. [company]
Whitman Education Group Inc. [company]
Whitney Foundation, Helen Hay, The [nonprofit]
Whole Foods Market Inc. [company]
Whole Foods Markets [company]
Wholesome Choice [company]
Whopper [product]
WHX Corp. [company]
Wicor Inc. [company]
Wiffle [product]
Wilburforce Foundation, The [nonprofit]
Wildlife Conservation Society [nonprofit]
Wiley John & Sons Inc. [company]
Wilkins Foundation, Catherine Holmes, The
  [nonprofit]
Willamette Industries Inc. [company]
Willary Foundation, The [nonprofit]

Willbros Group Inc. [company]
William Lyon Homes [company]
Williams Coal Seam Gas Royalty Trust [company]
Williams Communications Group Inc. [company]
Williams Cos. Inc., The [company]
Williams Energy Partners L.P. [company]
Williams-Sonoma Inc. [company]
Willkie Farr & Gallagher [company]
Wilmer, Cutler & Pickering [company]
Wilmington Trust Corp. [company]
Wilshire Oil Co. Of Texas [company]
Wilson Greatbatch Technologies Inc. [company]
Wilson Sonsini Goodrich & Rosati [company]
Wilson's Leather [company]
Wilsonart [company]
Winchester [company & product]
Windbreaker [product]
Windex [product]
Windham Foundation Inc., The [nonprofit]
Windmere Durable Holdings Inc. [company]
Windows [product]
Windows NT [product]
Windsurfer [product]
Wing Zone[company]
Wing-Nut [product]
Wings [product]
Winland Electronics Inc. [company]
Winn-Dixie [company & product]
Winn-Dixie Stores Inc. [company]
Winnebago [company & product]
Winnebago Industries Inc. [company]
Winnie the Pooh [product]
Winstead Sechrest W. & Minick [company]
Winston [product]
Winston & Strawn [company]
Winston Churchill Award, The [nonprofit]
Winston Foundation for World Peace, The
    [nonprofit]
Winston Hotels Inc. [company]
Winterfresh [product]
Winthrop, Stimson, Putnam & Roberts
    [company]
Winton Financial Corp. [company]

Wipro Ltd. [company]
Wireless Telecom Group Inc. [company]
Wisconsin Energy Corp. [company]
Wisconsin Power & Light Co. [company]
Wise Solutions [company]
Wiser Oil Co. [company]
Wite-Out [product]
Witness Systems [company]
Wiz [company & product]
Wm. Wrigley Jr. Co. [company]
Wm. Wycliff Vineyards [company]
Wolf [company & product]
Wolf Aviation Fund, The [company]
Wolf, Block, Schorr & Solis-Cohen [company]
Wolverine [company & product]
Wolverine Tube Inc. [company]
Wolverine World Wide Inc. [company]
Womble Carlyle Sandridge & Rice [company]
Wonder [product]
Wonder Woman [product]
Wonderbra [product]
Wonderknit [product]
Wood [magazine] [product]
Wood Family Foundation, The [nonprofit]
Woodbury [company & product]
Woodruff Foundation Inc., Robert W., The
    [nonprofit]
Woods Charitable Fund Inc. [company]
Woodside Petroleum Ltd. [company]
Woodstuff [product]
Woolite [product]
Woolworth [company]
WordPerfect [product]
Workmate [product]
WorkRite Ergonomics [company]
World Fuel Services Corp. [company]
World Series [product]
World Software [company]
World Tex Inc. [company]
World Vision [company]
World Wildlife Fund [nonprofit]
World Wireless Communications Inc.
    [company]

World Wrestling Federation (WWF) [company]
World Wrestling Federation Entertainment
  Inc. [company]
WorldPages.com Inc. [company]
Woronoco Bancorp Inc. [company]
Worthington Industries Inc. [company]
WOW [product]
WPP Group [company]
WPS Resources [company]
Wrangler [product]
WrestleMania [product]
Wright Foundation, Frank Lloyd, The [nonprofit]
Wrightco Technologies [company]
Wrigley William JR Co. [company]
Wrigley's [company & product]
Wyatt, Tarrant & Combs [company]
Wyndham International Inc. [company]
Wynn's [company & product]
Wynn's International Inc. [company]
Wytox [product]
X-Acto [product]
Xalatan [product]
Xanax [product]
Xcel Energy Inc. [company]
Xcelera Inc. [company]
Xeric Foundation, The [nonprofit]
Xerox [company]
Xerox Corp. [company]
X-Files [product]
XL Capital Ltd. [company]
X-OMAT [company]
XOR [company]
X-Tend [product]
Yahoo! [company]
yahoo.com [company]
Yahtzee [product]
Yankee Candle Inc. [company]
Yardley [company & product]
Yellow Corp. [company]
Y-Front [product]
YMCA of the USA [nonprofit]
Yodels [product]
Yoo-Hoo [company]

Yoplait [company]
York [company]
York Creek [company]
York International Corp. [company]
Yosemite Sam [product]
Young Life [company]
Youth-Dew [product]
Yukon Jack [product]
Yves Saint Laurent (YSL) [company]
YWCA of the USA [nonprofit]
Zale [company]
Zale Corp. [company]
Zamboni [company & product]
Zantac [product]
Zapata Corp. [company]
Zap-Guard [product]
Zehnder's of Frankenmuth [company]
Zemex Corp. [company]
Zenith National Insurance Corp. [company]
Zenix Income Fund Inc. [company]
Zerex [product]
Zestoretic [product]
Zestril [product]
Ziac [product]
Ziegler Cos. Inc., The [company]
Zinbardella [product]
Zions BanCorp. [company]
Ziploc [product]
Zippo [product]
Zithromax [product]
Zocor [product]
Zoloft [product]
zones.com [company]
Zovirax [product]
ZT Group International [company]
Zweig Fund Inc., The [company]
Zweig Total Return Fund Inc., The [company]
Zydone [product]
Zyloprim [product]
Zyman Marketing Group [company]
Zyprexa [product]
ZyQuest [company]
Zyrtec [product]

4

National Places of Interest

3Com Park
Aberdeen Proving Ground
Abraham Lincoln Birthplace National Historic
  Site
Acadia National Park
Adams Field
Adams National Historical Park
Addison Airport Adelphia Coliseum
Aggie Memorial Stadium
Aintree Racecourse
Air Force Research Laboratory
Air Maneuver Battle Lab
Alamodome
Albany County Airport
Albany Institute of History and Art
Albany Medical Center Hospital
Albert Einstein Medical Center
Albuquerque International Sunport
Alcatraz Island
Aleutian World War II National Historic Area
Alibates Flint Quarries National Monument
Allegheny General Hospital
Allegheny Portage Railroad National Historic
  Site
Alltel Stadium
Aloha Stadium
Alpena County Regional Airport

Altus Air Force Base
Altus Municipal Airport
Alumni Stadium
America West Arena
American Airlines Center
American Memorial Park
American Museum of Natural History
Ames Research Center
Amistad National Recreation Area
Amon C. Jones Stadium
Amon Carter Museum
Anacostia Museum Arthur M. Sackler
  Gallery
Anacostia Park
Andersen Air Force Base
Andersonville National Historic Site
Andrew Johnson National Historic Site
Andrews Air Force Base
Andrews Municipal Airport
Aniakchak National Monument & Preserve
Annapolis Naval Station
Anne Arundel Medical Center
Anniston Army Depot
Antietam National Battlefield
Antietam National Cemetery
Apostle Islands National Lakeshore
Appalachian National Scenic Trail

Appomattox Court House National Historical Park

Arches National Park

Archuleta County Airport

Arco Arena

Arizona Stadium

Arkansas Post National Memorial

Arlington House, The Robert E. Lee Memorial

Arlington International Racecourse

Armament Research, Development and Engineering Center

Army Management Staff College

Army Research Laboratory, Aberdeen

Army Research Laboratory, White Sands

Arnold Air Force Base

Arrowhead Stadium

Art Institute of Chicago, The

Art Museum, The, Princeton University

Arthur G. James Cancer Hospital

Arthur M. Sackler Gallery, Smithsonian Institution

Aspen-Pitkin County Airport/Sardy Field

Assateague Island National Seashore

Atlanta Motor Speedway

Atlanta Naval Air Station

Autzen Stadium

Badlands National Park

Ballpark in Arlington, The

Bally's at Ocean Downs

Baltimore Museum of Art, The

Baltimore/Washington International Airport

Baltimore-Washington Parkway

Bandelier National Monument

Bangor Naval Submarine Base

Bangor-on-Dee Racecourse

Bank One Ballpark

Baptist Memorial Hospital

Barksdale Air Force Base

Barnes-Jewish Hospital

Battle Command Battle Laboratory-Fort Gordon

Battle Command Battle Laboratory-Fort Huachuca

Battle Command Battle Laboratory-Fort Leavenworth

Battle Ground Stadium

Battleground National Cemetery

Bay Meadows Racetrack

Baylor University Medical Center

Beale Air Force Base

Beaver Stadium

Belmont Park

Bent's Old Fort National Historic Site

Bering Land Bridge National Preserve

Beth Israel Deaconess Medical Center

Bethel Park Stadium

Big Bend National Park

Big Cypress National Preserve

Big Hole National Battlefield

Big South Fork National River & Recreation Area

Big Thicket National Preserve

Biggs Army Airfield

Bighorn Canyon National Recreation Area

Birth of Ohio Stadium, The

Biscayne National Park

Black Canyon of the Gunnison National Park

Blackbaud Stadium

Blackstone River Valley National Heritage Corridor

Blue Grass Army Depot

Blue Ridge Parkway

Bluestone National Scenic River

Boise Air Terminal Gowen Field

Bolling Air Force Base

Booker T. Washington National Monument

Boston African American National Historic Site

Boston Harbor Islands National Recreation Area

Boston Medical Center

Boston National Historical Park

Boundary Bay Airport

Bowditch Field

Bradley Center

Bradley International Airport

Brazilian Embassy

Brices Cross Roads National Battlefield Site
Brigham and Women's Hospital
Bristol Motor Speedway
British Embassy
Bronco Stadium
Brooklyn Children's Museum, The
Brooklyn Museum, The
Brooks Air Force Base
Brown Stadium
Brown v. Board of Education National Historic
  Site
Brunswick County Airport
Bryant-Denny Stadium
Bryce Canyon National Park
Buck Island Reef National Monument
Buffalo National River
Bulldog Stadium
Burbank-Glendale-Pasadena Airport
Busch Stadium
Bush Memorial Stadium
Byrd Stadium
Cabrillo National Monument
Cajun Field
California National Historic Trail
California Palace of the Legion of Honor
California Speedway
Camden Yards
Camp Casey
Camp Castle
Camp Doha
Camp Edwards
Camp Essayons
Camp Garry Owen
Camp Giant
Camp Greaves
Camp Hovey
Camp Howse
Camp LaGuardia
Camp Mobile
Camp Nimble
Camp Page
Camp Randall
Camp Red Cloud

Camp Sears
Camp Shelby
Camp Stanley
Camp Stanton
Canaveral National Seashore
Candlestick Park
Cane River Creole National Historical Park
Cane River National Heritage Area
Cannon Air Force Base
Canterbury Park
Canyon de Chelly National Monument
Canyonlands National Park
Cape Cod National Seashore
Cape Hatteras National Seashore
Cape Henry National Memorial
Cape Krusenstern National Monument
Cape Lookout National Seashore
Capital Children's Museum
Capitol Hill Parks
Capitol Reef National Park
Capulin Volcano National Monument
Cardinal Stadium
Carl Sandburg Home National Historic Site
Carlisle Barracks
Carlsbad Caverns National Park
Carnegie Museum of Art
Carolinas Medical Center
Carrier Dome
Carter Stadium
Carter-Finley Stadium
Casa Grande Ruins National Monument
Casey Stadium
Castillo de San Marcos National Monument
Castle Clinton National Monument
Catoctin Mountain Park
Cedar Breaks National Monument
Cedars-Sinai Medical Center
Center for Earth and Planetary Studies
Central High School National Historic Site
C.F. Menninger Memorial Hospital
Chaco Culture National Historical Park
Chamizal National Memorial
Channel Islands National Park

Charles Pinckney National Historic Site
Charleston Air Force Base
Charlotte Coliseum
Charlottsville-Albemarle Airport
Chattahoochee River National Recreation Area
Cheltenham Racecourse
Chester Racecourse
Cheyenne Mountain Air Station
Cheyenne Mountain Operations Center
Chicago Midway Airport
Chickamauga and Chattanooga National
  Military Park
Chickasaw National Recreation Area
Children's Hospital [Boston]
Children's Hospital [Buffalo]
Children's Hospital [Denver]
Children's Hospital [Los Angeles]
Children's Hospital and Medical Center [Seattle]
Children's Hospital Medical Center
  [Cincinnati]
Children's Hospital of Philadelphia
Children's Hospital of Pittsburgh
Children's Memorial Hospital [Chicago]
Children's Museum [Boston]
Children's Museum of Manhattan, The
Children's National Medical Center
Chimney Rock National Historic Site
China Lake Naval Air Warfare Center,
  Weapons Division
Chiricahua National Monument
Christ Hospital
Christiansted National Historic Site
Churchill Downs
Cincinnati Art Museum
Cinergy Field
City Business [Minneapolis–St. Paul]
City of Rocks National Reserve
Clara Barton National Historic Site
Clarence Martin Stadium
Cleveland Clinic
Cleveland Hopkins International
Cleveland Museum of Art
Cleveland Stadium

Cloisters, The
College Park Airport
Colonial National Historical Park
Colonial Williamsburg
Colorado National Monument
Columbia Metropolitan Airport
Columbus Air Force Base
Columbus/West Point/Starkville
Combat Service Support Battle Lab
Comerica Park
Comiskey Park
Command and General Staff College
Commonwealth Stadium
Compaq Center
Congaree Swamp National Monument
Conseco Fieldhouse
Continental Airlines Arena
Continental Arena
Cook County Hospital
Cooper-Hewitt National Museum of Design,
  The Smithsonian Institution
Coors Field
Coronado National Memorial
Coronado Naval Leader Training Unit
Corpus Christi Army Depot
Corpus Christi International Airport
Corry Station Naval Technical Training Center
Cotton Bowl
Cougar Stadium
Cowpens National Battlefield
Craig Municipal Airport
Crane Division Naval Surface Warfare Center
Crater Lake National Park
Craters of the Moon National Monument
Cumberland Gap National Historical Park
Cumberland Island National Seashore
Cuyahoga Valley National Park
Dahlgren Naval Surface Warfare Center
Dallas Love Field
Dallas/Fort Worth International Airport
Dam Neck Fleet Combat Training Center,
  Atlantic
Darlington Speedway

Darrel Royal Memorial
Davis-Monthan Air Force Base
Dayton Aviation Heritage National Historical
   Park
Daytona International Speedway
De Soto National Memorial
Death Valley National Park
Decatur Airport
Defense Information School
DeKalb Memorial Stadium
Delaware & Lehigh National Heritage
   Corridor
Delaware Art Museum
Delaware National Scenic River
Delaware Water Gap National Recreation
   Area
Delta Center
Denali National Park & Preserve
Denver Art Museum, The
Denver Health and Hospitals
Denver International Airport
Deseret Chemical Depot
Detroit Institute of Arts, The
Detroit Metropolitan Wayne County Airport
Devens Reserve Training Area
Devils Postpile National Monument
Devils Tower National Monument
Dinosaur National Monument
Dix Stadium
Doak Campbell Stadium
Dodd Stadium
Dodger Stadium
Don Peden Stadium
Douglas Stadium
Dover Air Force Base
Dover Downs International Speedway
Dowdy-Ficklen Stadium
Doyt Perry Field
Dry Tortugas National Park
Dryden Flight Research Center
Dugway Proving Ground
Duke University Medical Center
Durango-La Plata County Airport

Dwight David Eisenhower Army Medical
   Center
Dyche Stadium
Dyess Air Force Base
Eagle County Regional Airport
Ebbets Field
Ebey's Landing National Historical Reserve
Edgar Allan Poe National Historic Site
Edison International Field
Edison National Historic Site
Edwards Air Force Base
Effigy Mounds National Monument
Eglin Air Force Base
Eielson Air Force Base
Eisenhower National Historic Site
El Malpais National Monument
El Monte Airport
El Morro National Monument
Eleanor Roosevelt National Historic Site
Ellis Island National Monument
Ellsworth Air Force Base
Elmendorf Air Force Base
Elvehjem Museum of Art, University of
   Wisconsin
Embassy of Andorra
Embassy of Antigua and Barbuda
Embassy of Australia
Embassy of Austria
Embassy of Barbados
Embassy of Belize
Embassy of Burkina Faso
Embassy of Canada
Embassy of Central African Republic
Embassy of Colombia
Embassy of Costa Rica
Embassy of Ecuador
Embassy of El Salvador
Embassy of Estonia
Embassy of Finland
Embassy of France
Embassy of Ghana
Embassy of Greece
Embassy of Grenada

Embassy of Guatemala
Embassy of Honduras
Embassy of India
Embassy of Ireland
Embassy of Israel
Embassy of Italy
Embassy of Jamaica
Embassy of Japan
Embassy of Latvia
Embassy of Lebanon
Embassy of Malaysia
Embassy of Malta
Embassy of Mexico
Embassy of Mongolia
Embassy of New Zealand
Embassy of Pakistan
Embassy of Papua New Guinea
Embassy of Paraguay
Embassy of Peru
Embassy of Portugal
Embassy of Republic of Mauritius
Embassy of Romania
Embassy of Saint Kitts and Nevis
Embassy of Saint Lucia
Embassy of Saint Vincent and the Grenadines
Embassy of Saudi Arabia
Embassy of Sierra Leone
Embassy of Spain
Embassy of Sweden
Embassy of Switzerland
Embassy of Switzerland, Cuban Annex
Embassy of the Arab Republic of Egypt
Embassy of the Argentine Republic
Embassy of the Bolivarian Republic of
  Venezuela
Embassy of the Commonwealth of Dominica
Embassy of the Commonwealth of the Bahamas
Embassy of the Czech Republic
Embassy of the Democratic and Popular
  Republic of Algeria
Embassy of the Democratic Republic of Congo
Embassy of the Democratic Socialist Republic
  of Sri Lanka

Embassy of the Dominican Republic
Embassy of the Federal and Islamic
Embassy of the Federal Republic of Germany
Embassy of the Federal Republic of Nigeria
Embassy of the Federated States of Micronesia
Embassy of the Former Socialist Federal
  Republic of Yugoslavia
Embassy of the Former Yugoslav Republic of
  Macedonia
Embassy of the Gabonese Republic
Embassy of the Grand Duchy of Luxembourg
Embassy of the Hashemite Kingdom of Jordan
Embassy of the Independent State of Samoa
Embassy of the Islamic Republic of Mauritania
Embassy of the Kingdom of Lesotho
Embassy of the Kingdom of Morocco
Embassy of the Kingdom of Swaziland
Embassy of the Kingdom of Tonga
Embassy of the Kyrgyz Republic
Embassy of the Lao People's Democratic
  Republic
Embassy of the People's Republic of China
Embassy of the Philippines
Embassy of the Republic of Afghanistan
Embassy of the Republic of Albania
Embassy of the Republic of Angola
Embassy of the Republic of Armenia
Embassy of the Republic of Azerbaijan
Embassy of the Republic of Belarus
Embassy of the Republic of Benin
Embassy of the Republic of Bulgaria
Embassy of the Republic of Burundi
Embassy of the Republic of Cameroon
Embassy of the Republic of Cape Verde
Embassy of the Republic of Chad
Embassy of the Republic of Chile
Embassy of the Republic of Côte d'Ivoire
Embassy of the Republic of Croatia
Embassy of the Republic of Cyprus
Embassy of the Republic of Djibouti
Embassy of the Republic of Equatorial Guinea
Embassy of the Republic of Georgia
Embassy of the Republic of Guinea

Embassy of the Republic of Haiti
Embassy of the Republic of Hungary
Embassy of the Republic of Iceland
Embassy of the Republic of Indonesia
Embassy of the Republic of Kazakhstan
Embassy of the Republic of Kenya
Embassy of the Republic of Korea
Embassy of the Republic of Liberia
Embassy of the Republic of Lithuania
Embassy of the Republic of Madagascar
Embassy of the Republic of Malawi
Embassy of the Republic of Mali
Embassy of the Republic of Moldova
Embassy of the Republic of Mozambique
Embassy of the Republic of Namibia
Embassy of the Republic of Nicaragua
Embassy of the Republic of Niger
Embassy of the Republic of Palau
Embassy of the Republic of Panama
Embassy of the Republic of Poland
Embassy of the Republic of Rwanda
Embassy of the Republic of Senegal
Embassy of the Republic of Seychelles
Embassy of the Republic of Singapore
Embassy of the Republic of Slovenia
Embassy of the Republic of South Africa
Embassy of the Republic of Suriname
Embassy of the Republic of the Congo
Embassy of the Republic of the Fiji Islands
Embassy of the Republic of the Gambia
Embassy of the Republic of the Marshall
  Islands
Embassy of the Republic of the Sudan
Embassy of the Republic of Togo
Embassy of the Republic of Trinidad and
  Tobago
Embassy of the Republic of Turkey
Embassy of the Republic of Uganda
Embassy of the Republic of Uzbekistan
Embassy of the Republic of Yemen
Embassy of the Republic of Zambia
Embassy of the Republic of Zimbabwe
Embassy of the Russian Federation

Embassy of the Slovak Republic
Embassy of the Solomon Islands
Embassy of the Somali Democratic Republic
Embassy of the State of Bahrain
Embassy of the State of Brunei Darussalam
Embassy of the State of Eritrea
Embassy of the State of Kuwait
Embassy of the State of Qatar
Embassy of the Sultanate of Oman
Embassy of the Syrian Arab Republic
Embassy of the Union of Burma
Embassy of the United Arab Emirates
Embassy of the United Republic of Tanzania
Embassy of Tunisia
Embassy of Turkmenistan
Embassy of Ukraine
Embassy of Uruguay
Embassy of Vietnam
Emory University Hospital
Enron Field
Eppley Airfield
Ericsson Stadium
Eugene Field House and Toy Museum
Eugene O'Neill National Historic Site
Everett Naval Station
Everglades National Park
Evergreen Speedway
Exploratorium, The
F.G. McGaw Hospital at Loyola University
Fairchild Air Force Base
Fairfax Hospital
Fairmount Park Race
Fairview-University Medical Center
Falcon Air Force Base
Falcon Stadium
Fallon Naval Air Station
Father Marquette National Memorial
Faurot Field
Federal Hall National Memorial
FedEx Field
Fenway Park
Field Museum of Natural History, The
Fine Arts Museums of San Francisco, The

Fire Island National Seashore
First Union Corp Center
Fleet Center
Flemington Speedway
Florida Citrus Bowl
Florida Hospital Medical Center
Florissant Fossil Beds National Monument
Fogg Art Museum
Folsom Field
Ford's Theatre National Historic Site
Fort A.P. Hill
Fort Belvoir
Fort Benning
Fort Bliss
Fort Bowie National Historic Site
Fort Bragg
Fort Buchanan
Fort Campbell
Fort Caroline National Memorial
Fort Carson
Fort Clatsop National Memorial
Fort Davis National Historic Site
Fort Detrick
Fort Dix
Fort Donelson National Cemetery
Fort Drum
Fort Dupont Park
Fort Eustis
Fort Frederica National Monument
Fort George G. Meade
Fort Gillem
Fort Gordon
Fort Greely
Fort Hamilton
Fort Hood
Fort Huachuca
Fort Indiantown Gap
Fort Irwin
Fort Jackson
Fort Knox
Fort Laramie National Historic Site
Fort Larned National Historic Site
Fort Leavenworth

Fort Lee
Fort Leonard Wood
Fort Lewis
Fort Matanzas National Monument
Fort McClellan
Fort McCoy
Fort McHenry National Monument and
    Historic Shrine
Fort McNair
Fort McPherson
Fort Meade
Fort Monmouth
Fort Monroe
Fort Moultrie National Monument
Fort Myer
Fort Necessity National Battlefield
Fort Point National Historic Site
Fort Polk
Fort Pulaski National Monument
Fort Raleigh National Historic Site
Fort Richardson
Fort Riley
Fort Ritchie
Fort Rucker
Fort Sam Houston
Fort Scott National Historic Site
Fort Shafter
Fort Sill
Fort Smith National Historic Site
Fort Stanwix National Monument
Fort Stewart
Fort Story
Fort Sumter National Monument
Fort Union National Monument
Fort Union Trading Post National Historic Site
Fort Vancouver National Historic Site
Fort Wainwright
Fort Washington Park
Fort Worth Naval Air Station/Joint Reserve
    Base
Fossil Butte National Monument
Fouts Field
Fox Chase Cancer Center

Foxboro Stadium
Francis E. Warren Air Force Base
Francis Scott Key Medical Center
Franklin Delano Roosevelt Memorial
Franklin Field
Franklin Institute Science Museum and
  Planetarium
Frederick Douglass National Historic Site
Frederick Law Olmsted National Historic Site
Fredericksburg & Spotsylvania National
  Military Park
Fredericksburg National Cemetery
Freer Gallery of Art, Smithsonian Institution
Fresno Air Terminal
Frick Collection, The
Friends Hospital
Friendship Hill National Historic Site
Froedtert Memorial Lutheran Hospital
Frontier Field
Garfield County Regional Airport
Gates of the Arctic National Park & Preserve
Gateway National Recreation Area
Gauley River National Recreation Area
Gaylord Entertainment Center
General Grant National Memorial Historical
  Park
George Washington Birthplace National
  Monument
George Washington Carver National
  Monument
George Washington Memorial Parkway
Georgetown University Hospital
Georgia Dome
Geotechnical Laboratory
Gettysburg National Cemetery
Gettysburg National Military Park
Giants Stadium
Gila Cliff Dwellings National Monument
Glacier Bay National Park & Preserve
Glacier National Park
Glass Bowl
Glen Canyon National Recreation Area
Glen Echo Park

Glenn Research Center
Glenwood Springs
Glenwood Springs Municipal Airport
Gloria Dei Church National Historic Site
Goddard Institute for Space Studies
Goddard Space Flight Center
Golden Gate Fields
Golden Gate National Recreation Area
Golden Spike National Historic Site
Good Samaritan Hospital
Good Samaritan Regional Medical Center
Granby-Grand County Airport
Grand Canyon National Park
Grand Portage National Monument
Grand Teton National Park
Great Basin National Park
Great Falls Park
Great Lakes Naval Training Center
Great Sand Dunes National Monument &
  Preserve
Great Smoky Mountains National Park
Greenbelt Park
Greyville Racecourse
Griffiss Business and Technology Park
Groves Stadium
Guadalupe Mountains National Park
Guilford Courthouse National Military Park
Gulfport Naval Construction Battalion Center
Gulfstream Park
Gund Arena
Gunnison County Airport
H. Lee Moffitt Cancer Center
Hagerman Fossil Beds National Monument
Haleakala National Park
Hamilton Grange National Memorial
Hampton National Historic Site
Hancock Field
Hanscom Air Force Base
Harborview Medical Center
Harpers Ferry National Historical Park
Harry S. Truman National Historic Site
Harvard Stadium
Hastings Park Racecourse

Hawaii Volcanoes National Park
Hawthorne Race
HCA Woman's Hospital of Texas
Heinz Field
Hennepin County Medical Center
Henry Ford Hospital
Henry Ford Museum and Greenfield Village
Henry Francis Du Pont Winterthur Museum
Herbert Hoover National Historic Site
Hereford Racecourse
Hersheypark Stadium
Hirshhorn Museum and Sculpture Garden,
   Smithsonian Institution
Hohokam Pima National Monument
Home of Franklin D. Roosevelt National
   Historic Site
Homestead National Monument of America
Honolulu Academy of Arts
Honolulu International Airport
Hopewell Culture National Historical Park
Hopewell Furnace National Historic Site
Horseshoe Bend National Military Park
Hospital for Joint Diseases-Orthopedic
   Institute
Hospital for Special Surgery
Hospital of the University of Pennsylvania
Hot Springs National Park
Hovenweep National Monument
Hubbell Trading Post National Historic Site
Hughes Memorial Stadium
Humphrey Metrodome
Hunter Army Airfield
Huntington Library, Art Collections, and
   Botanical Garden
Huntz Memorial Stadium
Huskie Stadium
Ice Age National Scenic Trail
Ice Palace
Immokalee Airport
Independence National Historical Park
Independent Validation and Verification Facility
Indian Stadium
Indiana Dunes National Lakeshore

Indiana University Art Museum
Indianapolis Museum of Art
Indianapolis Raceway Park
Ingleside Naval Station
Inupiat Heritage Center
Isabella Stewart Gardner Museum
Isle Royale National Park
J. Paul Getty Museum
J.B. Speed Art Museum
Jackson International Airport
Jacksonville Naval Air Station
Jacobs Field
James A. Garfield National Historic Site
Jean Lafitte National Historic Park & Preserve
Jefferson National Expansion Memorial
Jet Propulsion Laboratory
Jewel Cave National Monument
Jewish Museum, The
Jimmy Carter National Historic Site
Joe Aillet Stadium
Joe Louis Arena
John D. Rockefeller Jr. Memorial Parkway
John Day Fossil Beds National Monument
John F. Kennedy International Airport
John F. Kennedy National Historic Site
John Muir National Historic Site
John Wayne Airport
Johns Hopkins Hospital
Johnson Space Center
Johnstown Flood National Memorial
Jordan-Hare Stadium
Joshua Tree National Park
Juan Bautista de Anza National Historic Trail
Kahului Airport
Kaiser Foundation Hospital
Kalaupapa National Historical Park
Kaloko-Honokohau National Historical Park
Kansas City International Airport
Katmai National Park & Preserve
Kaufman Stadium
Keenan Stadium
Keesler Air Force Base
Kelly Air Force Base

Kelly/Shorts Stadium
Kempton Park Racecourse
Kenai Fjords National Park
Kennedy Space Center
Kennesaw Mountain National Battlefield Park
Kessler Institute for Rehabilitation
Keweenaw National Historical Park
Key Arena
Kiel Center
Kimbell Art Museum
Kings Bay Naval Submarine Base
Kings Mountain National Military Park
Kinnick Stadium
Kirtland Air Force Base
Klondike Gold Rush-Seattle Unit National
    Historical Park
Klondike Gold Rush National Historical Park
Knife River Indian Villages National Historic
    Site
Kobuk Valley National Park
Korean War Veterans Memorial
KSU Stadium
Kyle Field
L.A. Memorial Coliseum
La Guardia Airport
Lackland Air Force Base
Lackland NCO Academy
Lahey Hitchcock Clinic
Lake Chelan National Recreation Area
Lake Clark National Park & Preserve
Lake County Airport
Lake Mead National Recreation Area
Lake Meredith National Recreation Area
Lake Roosevelt National Recreation Area
Lakehurst Naval Air Systems Command
Lambeau Field
Lambert-St. Louis International Airport
Landstuhl Regional Medical Center
Lane Stadium
Langley Research Center
Las Vegas Motor Speedway
Lassen Volcanic National Park
Lava Beds National Monument

Legion Field
Lemoore Naval Air Station
Letterkenny Army Depot
Lewis & Clark National Historic Trail
Lewis Stadium
Liberty Bowl Memorial
Lightning Force Academy
Lincoln Boyhood National Memorial
Lincoln Home National Historic Site
Lincoln Memorial
Little Bighorn Battlefield National Monument
Little River Canyon National Preserve
Little Rock Air Force Base
Lockhart Stadium
Lompoc Airport
Long Beach
Long Beach Airport Daugherty Field
Long Beach Memorial Medical Center
Longfellow National Historic Site
Los Angeles Children's Museum
Los Angeles County Museum of Art
Los Angeles County-USC Medical Center
Louisiana Superdome
Louisville International Airport
Lowell National Historical Park
Lowe's Motor Speedway
Lubbock International Airport
Luke Air Force Base
Lyndon B. Johnson National Historical Park
Lyndon Baines Johnson Memorial Grove on
    the Potomac
M.H. deYoung Museum
M.M. Roberts Stadium
MacDill Air Force Base
Mackay Stadium
Madigan Army Medical Center
Madison Square Garden
Magee-Womens Hospital
Maggie L. Walker National Historic Site
Maine Acadian Culture Park
Malmstrom Air Force Base
Malone Stadium
Mammoth Cave National Park

Manassas National Battlefield Park

Manchester, NH, Manchester Airport

Manhattan Eye and Throat Hospital

Manzanar National Historic Site

Marine Corps Air Ground Combat Center

Marine Corps Air Station Cherry Point

Marine Corps Air Station Iwakuni, Japan

Marine Corps Air Station Miramar

Marine Corps Air Station New River

Marine Corps Air Station Yuma

Marine Corps Air Station, Beaufort, SC

Marine Corps Base Brig Quantico

Marine Corps Base Camp Lejeune

Marine Corps Base Camp Pendleton

Marine Corps Base Hawaii

Marine Corps Base Quantico

Marine Corps Detachment Aberdeen Proving Ground

Marine Corps Detachment Fort Gordon

Marine Corps Detachment Fort Leonard Wood

Marine Corps Detachment Lackland Air Force Base, TX

Marine Corps Detachment, Fort Sill, OK

Marine Corps Element USACGSC, Fort Leavenworth, KS

Marine Corps Logistics Base Albany, GA

Marine Corps Logistics Base Barstow, CA

Marine Corps Mountain Warfare Training Center

Marine Corps Recruit Depot Parris Island, SC

Marine Corps Recruit Depot San Diego, CA

Marine Corps Warfighting Laboratory

Marine Midland Arena

Marshall Space Flight Center

Marshall Stadium

Martin Luther King Jr. National Historic Site

Martin Memorial Medical Center

Martin Van Buren National Historic Site

Mary Hitchcock Memorial Hospital

Mary Mcleod Bethune Council House National Historic Site

Maryland General Hospital

Massachusetts Eye and Ear Infirmary

Massachusetts General Hospital

Mayo Clinic

Mayport Naval Station

McCarran International Airport

McChord Air Force Base

McConnell Air Force Base

McGhee Tyson Air National Guard Base

McGhee Tyson Airport

McGuire Air Force Base

MCI Center

McLean Hospital

Meacham International Airport

Medical University of South Carolina

Mellon Arena

Memorial Hermann Hospital

Memorial Sloan-Kettering Cancer Center

Memorial Stadium

Memphis International Airport

Meridian Naval Air Station

Merrill C. Meigs Airport

Mesa del Rey Airport

Mesa Verde National Park

Mesa, AZ, Falcon Field Airport

Methodist Hospital

Methodist Medical Center

Metropolitan Museum of Art, The

Miami International Airport

Michiana Regional Transportation Center

Michie Stadium

Michigan Speedway

Michigan Stadium

Midland International Airport

Mile High Stadium

Military Ocean Terminal, Bayonne, NJ

Military Ocean Terminal, Sunny Point, NC

Miller Park

Milwaukee Mile, The

Minneapolis Institute of Arts, The

Minneapolis-St. Paul International Airport

Minute Man National Historical Park

Minuteman Missile National Historic Site

Missoula International Airport

Missouri National Recreational River

Mitchell Athletic Complex
Moffett Federal Airfield
Mojave National Preserve
Monocacy National Battlefield
Montefiore Medical Center
Monterey Peninsula Airport
Montezuma Castle National Monument
Monticello
Montrose Regional Airport
Moody Air Force Base
Moores Creek National Battlefield
Mormon Pioneer National Historic Trail
Morristown Municipal Airport
Morristown National Historical Park
Mount Rainier National Park
Mount Rushmore National Memorial
Mount Sinai Medical Center
Mountain Home Air Force Base
Mountaineer Field
Muir Woods National Monument
Muniz Air National Guard Base
Museum of American Folk Art
Museum of Fine Arts [Boston]
Museum of Fine Arts, The [Houston]
Museum of Modern Art, The [New York]
Museum of Science [Boston]
Myrtle Beach Speedway
Naples Municipal Airport
Nashville International Airport
Nassau Coliseum
Natchez National Historical Park
Natchez Trace Parkway
Natick Soldier Center
National Air and Space Museum, Smithsonian
    Institution
National Gallery of Art
National Mall
National Museum of African Art
National Museum of American Art, The
    Smithsonian Institution
National Museum of American History
National Museum of Natural History
National Museum of the American Indian

National Park of American Samoa
National Portrait Gallery
National Postal Museum
National Rehabilitation Hospital
National Sports Center
National Zoo
Nationwide Arena
Natural Bridges National Monument
Navajo National Monument
Nazareth Speedway
Neil Armstrong Airport
Nellis Air Force Base
Nelson-Atkins Museum of Art
Network Associates Coliseum
New Bedford Whaling National Historical
    Park
New Britain Museum of American Art, The
New England Medical Center
New Hampshire International Speedway
New Hanover Airport
New Hanover International Airport
New Jersey Coastal Heritage Trail Route
New Jersey Pinelands National Reserve
New Kezar Stadium
New London Naval Submarine Base
New Mile High Stadium
New Oakland Arena, The
New Orleans Jazz National Historical Park
New River Gorge National River
New York Eye and Ear Infirmary
New York Presbyterian Hospital
New York University Medical Center
Newark International Airport
Newport Naval Education and Training Center
Newport News/Williamsburg, VA Airport
Neyland Stadium
Nez Perce National Historical Park
Nicodemus National Historic Site
Ninety Six National Historic Site
Niobrara National Scenic River
Nippert Stadium
Noatak National Preserve
Norfolk International Airport

North Carolina Speedway
North Cascades National Park
North Country National Scenic Trail
North Dakota Horse
North Island Naval Air Station
North Shore University Hospital
Northeast Telecommunications Switching
  Center
Northern Warfare Training Center
Northolt Park Racecourse
Northwestern Memorial Hospital
Norton Simon Museum
Notre Dame Stadium
Oakland International Airport
Oceana Naval Air Station
Ochsner Foundation Hospital
Ocmulgee National Monument
Offutt Air Force Base
O'Hare International Airport
Ohio Stadium
Ohio State University Medical Center
Oklahoma City National Memorial
Old Post Office Tower
Old Stone House, The
Old Sturbridge Village
Olympic National Park
Ontario International Airport California
Orange Bowl
Oregon Caves National Monument
Oregon National Historic Trail
Oriental Institute Museum, University of
  Chicago
Oriole Park at Camden Yards
Orlando Arena
Orlando International Airport
Orlando Regional Medical Center
Overmountain Victory National Historic Trail
Owen Field
Oxon Cove Park & Oxon Hill Farm
Ozark National Scenic Riverways
Pacific Bell Park
Padre Island National Seashore
Palm Beach International Airport

Palo Alto Airport of Santa Clara County
Palo Alto Battlefield National Historic Site
Papa John's Cardinal Stadium
Parker Stadium
Parkland Memorial Hospital
Paso Robles Municipal Airport
Patrick Air Force Base
PCU Lassen
PCU Mason
PCU McCampbell
Pea Ridge National Military Park
Pearl Harbor Navy Public Works Center
Pecos National Historical Park
Peirce Mill
Penn State's Milton S. Hershey Medical Center
Pennsylvania Academy of the Fine Arts
Pennsylvania Avenue National Historic Site
Pennsylvania Hospital
Pensacola Naval Air Station
Pensacola Naval Hospital
Pepsi Center
Perry's Victory & International Peace Memorial
Petersburg National Battlefield
Peterson Air Force Base
Petrified Forest National Park
Petroglyph National Monument
Philadelphia International Airport
Philadelphia Museum of Art
Philadelphia Park
Phoenix Sky Harbor International Airport
Pictured Rocks National Lakeshore
Pine Bluff Arsenal
Pinnacles National Monument
Pipe Spring National Monument
Pipestone National Monument
Piscataway Park
Pitt Stadium
Pittsburgh International Airport
Please Touch Museum
PNC Park
Pocono Downs
Pohukuloa Training Center
Point Reyes National Seashore

Pontiac Silverdome
Pony Express National Historic Trail
Pope Air Force Base
Poplar Grove National Cemetery
Port Chicago Naval Magazine National
  Memorial
Portland Art Museum
Portland International Airport
Portland International Speedway
Portsmouth Naval Shipyard
Potomac Heritage National Scenic Trail
Poverty Point National Monument
Prairie Meadows Racetrack & Casino
President's Park
Presidio of Monterey
Presidio of San Francisco
Prince William Forest Park
Princeton Airport
Princeton Stadium
Pro Player Park
Pu`uhonua O Honaunau National Historical
  Park
Puukohola Heiau National Historic Site
Qualcomm Stadium
Quinebaug & Shetucket Rivers Valley National
  Heritage Corridor
Rainbow Bridge National Monument
Raleigh Sports
Raleigh-Durham International Airport
Ralph Wilson Stadium
Randolph Air Force Base
Raymond James Stadium
Razorback W.M.
RCA Dome
Red River Army Depot
Redstone Arsenal
Redstone Scientific Information Center
Redwood National and State Parks
Rehabilitation Institute of Chicago
Rehabilitation Institute of Michigan
Reno Cannon International Airport
Renton Memorial Stadium
Rice Stadium

Richmond International Airport
Richmond International Raceway
Richmond National Battlefield Park
Rickenbacker International Airport
Rickwood Field
Rio Grande Wild and Scenic River
Robertson Stadium
Rock Creek Park
Rock Island Arsenal
Rocky Mountain Arsenal
Rocky Mountain Greyhound Park
Rocky Mountain National Park
Roger Williams National Memorial
Romney Stadium
Roosevelt Campobello International Park
Rose Bowl
Rose Garden
Rosecroft Raceway
Ross Lake National Recreation Area
Ross-Ade Stadium
Roswell Park Cancer Institute
Royal Danish Embassy
Royal Embassy of Cambodia
Royal Nepalese Embassy
Royal Netherlands Embassy
Royal Norwegian Embassy
Royal Thai Embassy
Rubber Bowl
Rush-Presbyterian-St. Luke's Medical Center
Rutgers Stadium
Rynearson Stadium
Sacramento Executive Airport
Safeco Field
Sagamore Hill National Historic Site
Saguaro National Park
Saint Croix Island International Historic Site
Saint Croix National Scenic River
Saint Paul's Church National Historic Site
Saint-Gaudens National Historic Site
Salem Maritime National Historic Site
Salina Municipal Airport
Salinas Pueblo Missions National Monument
Salt Lake City International Airport

Salt River Bay National Historic Park and
  Ecological Preserve
Sam Boyd
Samuel Wolfson Park
San Antonio International Airport
San Antonio Missions National Historical Park
San Carlos Airport
San Diego International Airport-Lindberg
San Diego Naval Medical Center
San Francisco International Airport
San Francisco Maritime National Historical
  Park
San Jose Arena
San Jose International Airport, CA
San Juan Island National Historical Park
San Juan National Historic Site
San Luis Obispo County
Sanford Stadium
Santa Ana Bowl
Santa Anita Park
Santa Barbara Municipal Airport
Santa Fe National Historic Trail
Santa Maria Public Airport
Santa Monica Mountains National Recreation
  Area
Sarasota/Bradenton International Airport
Saratoga National Historical Park
Saratoga Racetrack
Saugus Iron Works National Historic Site
Savanna Army Depot Activity
Savannah International Airport
Schoellkopf Crescent
Schofield Barracks
Schriever Air Force Base
Scott Air Force Base
Scott Stadium
Scotts Bluff National Monument
Sears Point Raceway
Seattle Kingdome
Seattle-Tacoma International Airport
Sebring, Florida, Regional Airport
Selma to Montgomery National Historic Trail
Sequoia & Kings Canyon National Parks

Sewall-Belmont House National Historic Site
Shands Hospital at the University of Florida
Shea Stadium [official name: William A. Shea
  Stadium]
Shenandoah National Park
Shepherd Center
Sheppard Air Force Base
Sheppard and Enoch Pratt Hospital
Shiloh National Cemetery
Shiloh National Military Park
Simmons Army Airfield
Sinai Samaritan Medical Center
Sitka National Historical Park
Skelly Stadium
Sleeping Bear Dunes National Lakeshore
Smithsonian Institution
Socorro Stadium
Soldier Field
Solomon R. Guggenheim Museum, The
Southwest Florida International Airport
Spartan Stadium
Spaulding Rehabilitation Hospital
Spectrum Health
Spokane International Airport
Springfield Armory National Historic Site
St. Anthony Medical Center
St. John's Mercy Medical Center
St. Joseph's Hospital and Medical Center
St. Louis Art Museum, The
St. Louis University Hospital
St. Luke's Hospital [Bethlehem, PA]
St. Luke's Hospital [Chesterfield, MO]
St. Luke's Hospital [Newburgh, NY]
St. Luke's Medical Center [Cleveland, OH]
St. Luke's Medical Center [Milwaukee, WI]
St. Petersburg-Clearwater International Airport
St. Vincent Hospital and Health Center
Stagg Memorial Stadium
Standiford Field
Stanford Stadium
Stanford University Hospital
Staples Center
Statue of Liberty National Monument

Steamboat Springs/Bob Adams Field STOL
Steamtown National Historic Site
Stennis Space Center
Stevens Field
Stones River National Battlefield
Stones River National Cemetery
Strong Memorial Hospital
Suffolk, VA Airport
Suitland Parkway
Sun Bowl Stadium
Sun Devil Stadium
Sunset Crater Volcano National Monument
Superdome
Sussex, New Jersey Regional Airport
Talladega Superspeedway
Tallahassee Regional Airport
Tampa International Airport
Target Center
Telluride Regional Airport
Temple University Hospital
Teterboro Airport
Texas Children's Hospital
Texas Heart Institute-St. Luke's Episcopal
  Hospital
Texas Motor Speedway
Texas Stadium
Thaddeus Kosciuszko National Memorial
Theodore Roosevelt Birthplace National
  Historic Site
Theodore Roosevelt Inaugural National
  Historic Site
Theodore Roosevelt Island Park
Theodore Roosevelt National Park
Thomas Gilcrease Institute of American
  History and Art
Thomas Jefferson Memorial
Thomas Stone National Historic Site
Three Rivers Stadium
Thurman Munson Memorial Stadium
Tiger Stadium
Timpanogos Cave National Monument
Timucuan Ecological & Historic Preserve
Tobyhanna Army Depot

Toledo Hospital, The
Toledo Museum of Art, The
Tompkins County Airport
Tonto National Monument
Tooele Army Depot
Touro Synagogue National Historic Site
Town & Country Sports Complex
Trans-World Dome
Travis Air Force Base
Trice Field
Tripler Army Medical Center
Tropicana Field
Truman Medical Center-West
Tucson Electric Park
Tucson International Airport
Tulane University Hospital and Clinic
Tulsa International Airport
Tumacácori National Historical Park
Tupelo National Battlefield
Turner Field
Tuskegee Airman National Historic Site
Tuskegee Institute National Historic Site
Tuzigoot National Monument
Tyndall Air Force Base
U.S. Army Aberdeen Test Center
U.S. Army Aeromedical Center
U.S. Army Air Defense Artillery School
U.S. Army Armor Center
U.S. Army Armor School
U.S. Army Aviation Center
U.S. Army Aviation Logistics School
U.S. Army Aviation School
U.S. Army Central Identification Laboratory
U.S. Army Chemical School
U.S. Army Community and Family Support
  Center
U.S. Army Engineer School
U.S. Army Engineering and Support
  Center
U.S. Army Environmental Center
U.S. Army Explosive Ordnance Disposal
  Technical Detachment
U.S. Army Infantry Center

U.S. Army Information Systems Software Center

U.S. Army Intelligence Center

U.S. Army Logistics Management College

U.S. Army Military Police School

U.S. Army Ordnance Center

U.S. Army Ordnance, Missile and Munitions Center

U.S. Army Quartermaster Center

U.S. Army Safety Center

U.S. Army School of Aviation Medicine

U.S. Army School of Engineering and Logistics

U.S. Army School of the Americas

U.S. Army Signal Center

U.S. Army Technical Center for Explosives Safety

U.S. Army Technical Test Center

U.S. Army Training Support Center

U.S. Army Transportation Center

U.S. Army War College

U.S. Army Warrant Officer Career Center

U.S. Military Academy, West Point

U.S. Naval Academy

UCLA Medical Center

UCSD Medical Center

Uilhein Soccer Park

Ulysses S. Grant National Historic Site

United Center

United States Air Force Academy

University Art Museum, Arizona State

University Hospital

University Hospital

University Hospitals and Clinics

University Hospitals of Cleveland

University Medical Center

University Museum of Archaeology and Anthropology, University of Pennsylvania, The

University of Chicago Hospitals

University of Illinois Hospital and Clinics

University of Iowa Hospitals and Clinics

University of Kentucky Hospital

University of Louisville Hospital

University of Maryland Medical System

University of Michigan Medical Center

University of New Mexico Art Museum, The

University of North Carolina Hospitals

University of Pittsburgh Medical Center

University of Texas M.D. Anderson Cancer Center

University of Texas Medical Branch Hospitals

University of Utah Hospitals and Clinics

University of Virginia Health Sciences Center

University of Washington Medical Center

University of Wisconsin Hospital and Clinics

USC Medical Center

USNS Flint

USNS Mercy

USNS Rappahannock

USNS Sioux

USS Abraham Lincoln

USS Alaska

USS Arizona Memorial

USS Arthur W. Radford

USS Bataan

USS Blue Ridge

USS Bonhomme Richard

USS Boxer

USS Bridge

USS Briscoe

USS Bulkeley

USS Bunker Hill

USS Cardinal

USS Carl Vinson

USS Carney

USS Chancellorsville

USS Charlotte

USS Chosin

USS Cleveland

USS Cole

USS Constellation

USS Constitution

USS Cowpens

USS David R. Ray

USS Decatur

USS Denver

USS Detroit

USS Donald Cook
USS Dwight D. Eisenhower
USS Elliot
USS Emory S. Land
USS Enterprise
USS Essex
USS Fife
USS Fletcher
USS Ford
USS Fort McHenry
USS Frank Cable
USS Frederick
USS Gary
USS George Washington
USS Germantown
USS Gettysburg
USS Gladiator
USS Greeneville
USS Guardian
USS Harpers Ferry
USS Harry S. Truman
USS Hawes
USS Helena
USS Heron
USS Hewitt
USS Higgins
USS Hopper
USS Hue City
USS Ingraham
USS John C. Stennis
USS John F. Kennedy
USS John S. McCain
USS Juneau
USS Kamehameha
USS Kearsarge
USS Kinkaid
USS Kitty Hawk
USS Klakring
USS Laboon
USS Lake Erie
USS Mahan
USS McFaul
USS Mitscher

USS Mount Whitney
USS Nashville
USS Nassau
USS Nicholas
USS Nimitz
USS Oak Hill
USS O'Bannon
USS O'Brien
USS Ogden
USS O'Kane
USS Oklahoma City
USS Osprey
USS Patriot
USS Peleliu
USS Peterson
USS Ponce
USS Princeton
USS Rainier
USS Ramage
USS Raven
USS Reuben James
USS Robin
USS Rodney M. Davis
USS Ronald Reagan
USS Roosevelt
USS Ross
USS Rushmore
USS Russell
USS Sacramento
USS San Francisco
USS Scott
USS Sentry
USS Shiloh
USS Simpson
USS Stethem
USS Stout
USS Stump
USS Supply
USS Tarawa
USS Taylor
USS The Sullivans
USS Theodore Roosevelt
USS Thorn

USS Ticonderoga
USS Trenton
USS Vandegrift
USS Vicksburg
USS Wasp
USS Whidbey Island
USS Winston S. Churchill
Vail/Eagle Airport
Valley Forge National Historical Park
Vance Air Force Base
Vandenberg Air Force Base
Vanderbilt Mansion National Historic Site
Vanderbilt Stadium
Vanderbilt University Hospital and Clinic
Vaught-Hemingway Stadium
Veterans Stadium
Vicksburg National Cemetery
Vicksburg National Military Park
Vietnam Veterans Memorial
Virgin Islands National Park
Virginia Beach Sportsplex
Virginia Museum of Fine Arts
Volk Field Air National Guard Base
Voyageurs National Park
Waldo Stadium
Walker Art Center
Wallace Wade Stadium
Wallops Flight Facility
Walnut Canyon National Monument
Walter Reed Army Medical Center
Walters Art Gallery
War in the Pacific National Historical Park
War Memorial Stadium
Washington Dulles International Airport
Washington Hospital Center
Washington Monument
Washington National Airport
Washita Battlefield National Historic Site
Watkins Glen International Speedway
Wausau Hospital
Wayne County's Detroit Metro Airport
Weir Farm National Historic Site
Westchester County Airport

Westover Air Reserve Base
Wheeling Downs
Whiskeytown National Recreation Area
White Sands Missile Range
White Sands National Monument
White Sands Test Facility
Whiteman Air Force Base
Whitman Mission National Historic Site
Whitney Museum of American Art
Wichita Art Museum
Will Rogers Air National Guard Base
Will Rogers World Airport
William Howard Taft National Historic Site
Williams-Brice Stadium
Wills Eye Hospital
Wilson's Creek National Battlefield
Wind Cave National Park
Wolf Trap Farm Park for the Performing Arts
Womac Army Medical Center
Women and Infants Hospital of Rhode Island
Women's Rights National Historical Park
Wood County Regional Airport
WRAL Soccer Center
Wright Brothers National Memorial
Wright-Patterson Air Force Base
Wrigley Field
Wupatki National Monument
Xcel Energy Center
Yager Stadium
Yakima Training Center
Yale Bowl
Yale Center for British Art
Yale University Art Gallery
Yale-New Haven Hospital
Yampa Valley Airport
Yankee Stadium
Yellowstone National Park
Yorktown National Battlefield
Yorktown National Cemetery
Yosemite National Park
Yucca House National Monument
Yuma Proving Ground
Zion National Park

5 News and Media

A&E [network]

AAA Going Places [magazine]

Abbeville Meridional [Louisiana newspaper]

ABC American Broadcasting Company [network]

Aberdeen American News [South Dakota newspaper]

Abilene Reporter-News [Texas newspaper]

Abingdon Argus [Illinois newspaper]

Active Dayton [Ohio newspaper]

Ada Evening News [Oklahoma newspaper]

Ada Herald, The [Ohio newspaper]

Adams County Record [Council, Idaho newspaper]

Addison County Independent [Middlebury, Vermont newspaper]

Adirondack Daily Enterprise [Saranac Lake, New York newspaper]

Adit, The [Helena, Montana newspaper]

Advertiser [Plymouth, Ohio newspaper]

Advertiser Democrat [Norway, Maine newspaper]

Advertiser, The [Lafayette, Louisiana newspaper]

Advertiser-Tribune, The [Tiffin, Ohio newspaper]

Advocate Messenger [Danville, Kentucky newspaper]

Advocate, The [Baton Rouge, Louisiana newspaper]

Advocate, The [Lone Pine, California newspaper]

Advocate, The [Provincetown, Massachusetts newspaper]

Advocate, The [Stamford, Connecticut newspaper]

Advocate/Democrat [Sweetwater, Tennessee newspaper]

Advocate-Messenger, The [Danville, Kentucky newspaper]

Advocate-Tribune [Granite Falls, Minnesota newspaper]

Afro-American Newspaper [Baltimore, Maryland newspaper]

Ag Almanac [Great Falls, Montana newspaper]

Aiken Standard [South Carolina newspaper]

Aitkin Independent Age [Minnesota newspaper]

Ajo Copper News [Arizona newspaper]

Akron Beacon Journal [Ohio newspaper]

Alamogordo Daily News [New Mexico newspaper]

Alaska Star [Eagle River, Alaska newspaper]

Albany Democrat-Herald [Oregon newspaper]

Albany Herald, The [Georgia newspaper]

Alberta Lea Tribune [Minnesota newspaper]

Albia Union-Republican [Iowa newspaper]

Albion Monitor [Sonoma County, California newspaper]

Albion Recorder, The [Michigan newspaper]

Albuquerque Journal [New Mexico newspaper]

Albuquerque Tribune, The [New Mexico newspaper]

Alcester-Hudson News [South Dakota newspaper]

Alemeda Times-Star, The [California newspaper]

Alexander City Outlook [Alabama newspaper]

Alexandria Daily Town Talk [Louisiana newspaper]

Alexandria Journal [Virginia newspaper]

Allegan County News, The [Michigan newspaper]

Allen American, The [Texas newspaper]

Allen County Times [New Haven, Indiana newspaper]

Alliance Times [Nebraska newspaper]

Alliance Times-Herald [Nebraska newspaper]

Allston/Brighton TAB [Needham, Massachusetts newspaper]

Almanac, The [Menlo Park, California newspaper]

Alpena News, The [Michigan newspaper]

Alpenhorn, The [Running Springs, California newspaper]

Alpine Avalanche [Texas newspaper]

Altus Times [Oklahoma newspaper]

Amarillo Globe News [Texas newspaper]

Amboy News [Illinois newspaper]

American Banker [Washington, D.C. newspaper]

American Health for Women [magazine]

American Homestyle & Gardening [magazine]

American Hunter, The [magazine]

American Legion [magazine]

American Legion Magazine, The

American Metal Market [New York, New York newspaper]

American Movie Classics [network]

American News [Aberdeen, South Dakota newspaper]

American Press, The [Lake Charles, Louisiana newspaper]

American Rifleman [magazine]

America's Voice [network]

Americus Times Recorder [Georgia newspaper]

Amesbury Town Online [Massachusetts website]

Amite Tangi Digest [Louisiana newspaper]

Anacortes American [Washington newspaper]

Anchorage Daily News [Alaska newspaper]

Anchorage Press [Alaska newspaper]

Andalusia Star News [Alabama newspaper]

Anderson Herald Bulletin [Indiana newspaper]

Anderson Independent-Mail, The [South Carolina newspaper]

Andover Journal-Advocate [Kansas newspaper]

Andover Townsman [Massachusetts newspaper]

Angleton Times [Texas newspaper]

Animal Planet [network]

Ann Arbor News, The [Michigan newspaper]

Annandale Advocate, The [Minnesota newspaper]

Anniston Star, The [Alabama newspaper]

Anoka County Union [Minnesota newspaper]

Antelope Valley Press [Palmdale, California newspaper]

Anthony Republican [Kansas newspaper]

Anton Community Newspapers [Mineola, New York newspaper]

Antrim County News [Bellaire, Michigan newspaper]

Apalachicola Times [Florida newspaper]

Appeal-Democrat [Marysville, California newspaper]

Arapahoe Public Mirror [Nebraska newspaper]

Arcata Eye, The [California newspaper]

Argus [Vermont newspaper]

Argus Leader [Sioux City, South Dakota newspaper]

Argus Online, The [Fremont, California website]

Arizona Business Gazette [Phoenix, Arizona newspaper]

Arizona Daily Star [Tucson, Arizona newspaper]

Arizona Daily Sun, The [Flagstaff, Arizona newspaper]

Arizona Daily Wildcat [Arizona newspaper]

Arizona Range News [Willcox, Arizona newspaper]

Arizona Republic, The [Phoenix, Arizona newspaper]

Arizona Senior World [Gilbert, Arizona newspaper]

Arizona Silver Belt [Globe, Arizona newspaper]

Arizona Tourist News [Tucson, Arizona newspaper]

Ark, The [Tiburon, California newspaper]

Arkansas Business [Little Rock, Arkansas newspaper]

Arkansas Democrat-Gazette [Arkansas newspaper]

Arkansas Tribune [Little Rock, Arkansas newspaper]

Arkansas Weekly [Batesville, Arkansas newspaper]

Arlington Heights Herald [Illinois newspaper]

Arlington Heights Journal [Illinois newspaper]

Arlington Heights Post [Illinois newspaper]

Arlington Morning News [Texas newspaper]

Arlington Town Online [Massachusetts website]

Arthur Enterprise [Nebraska newspaper]

Artvoice [Buffalo, New York newspaper]

Asbury Park Press [Neptune, New Jersey newspaper]

Ascension Citizen, The [Gonzales, Louisiana newspaper]

Asheville Citizen-Times [North Carolina newspaper]

Ashland Daily Tidings, The [Oregon newspaper]

Ashley County Ledger [Hamburg, Arkansas newspaper]

Ashley News Observer [Crossett, Arkansas newspaper]

Ashtabula Star Beacon [Ohio newspaper]

Ashton Gazette [Illinois newspaper]

Aspen Daily News [Colorado newspaper]

Aspen Times [Colorado newspaper]

Associated Press, The [national news service]

Atchison Daily Globe [Kansas newspaper]

Athens Daily Review, The [Texas newspaper]

Athens Messenger [Ohio newspaper]

Athens News, The [Ohio newspaper]

Athol Daily News [Massachusetts newspaper]

Atkins Chronicle, The [Akansas newspaper]

Atlanta Business Chronicle [Georgia newspaper]

Atlanta Daily World [Georgia newspaper]

Atlanta Journal-Constitution [Georgia newspaper]

Atlantic Herald [New Jersey newspaper]

Atmore Advance [Alabama newspaper]

Auburn Journal, The [California newspaper]

Auburn Plainsman, The [Alabama newspaper]

Augusta Chronicle, The [Georgia newspaper]

Augusta Daily Gazette [Kansas newspaper]

Aumnibus, The [Montgomery, Alabama newspaper]

Aurora News-Register [Nebraska newspaper]

Aurora Sentinel [Colorado newspaper]

Austin American [Texas newspaper]

Austin American-Statesman, The [Texas newspaper]

Austin Business Journal [Texas newspaper]

Austin Chronicle [Texas newspaper]

Austin Daily Herald [Minnesota newspaper]

Avenues [magazine]

Avon Sentinel [Illinois newspaper]

Azle News [Texas newspaper]

BA Express [Broken Arrow, Oklahoma newspaper]

Bainbridge Banter [Ohio newspaper]

Bainbridge Island Review [Washington newspaper]

Bajo El Sol [Yuma, Arizona newspaper]

Baker County Standard, The [Macclenny, Florida newspaper]

Baker Observer [Louisiana newspaper]

Bakersfield Californian [California newspaper]

Baldwin City Ledger [Kansas newspaper]

Baldwin City Signal [Kansas newspaper]

Baldwin Herald [New York newspaper]

Ball State Daily News [Muncie, Indiana newspaper]

Baltimore Business Journal [Maryland newspaper]

Baltimore Chronicle, The [Maryland newspaper]

Baltimore City Paper [Maryland newspaper]

Baltimore Sun, The [Maryland newspaper]

Baltimore Times, The [Maryland newspaper]

Bandera Bulletin, The [Texas newspaper]

Bandera Review [Texas newspaper]

Bangor Daily News [Maine newspaper]

Banks County News, The [Homer, Georgia newspaper]

Banner Press, The [Texas newspaper]

Banner-Graphic [Greencastle, Indiana newspaper]

Banner-News, The [Magnolia, Arkansas newpaper]

Bar Harbor Times [Maine newspaper]

Baraboo News Republic [Wisconsin newspaper]

Barnstable Patriot, The [Hyannis, Massachusetts newspaper]

Barre Montpelier Times [Vermont newspaper]

Barron News-Shield [Wisconsin newspaper]

Bartelsville Examiner [Oklahoma newspaper]

Barton Chronicle [Vermont newspaper]

Basta Pinoy [Boca Raton, Florida newspaper]

Bastrop Daily Enterprise [Louisiana newspaper]

Bates Student, The [Lewiston, Maine newspaper]

Batesville Guard [Arkansas newspaper]

Battalion, The [College Station, Texas newspaper]

Baxley News-Banner, The [Georgia newspaper]

Bay City News [Michigan newspaper]

Baylor County Banner [Seymour, Texas newspaper]

Bayou Business [Houma, Louisiana newspaper]

Baytown Sun, The [Texas newspaper]

BBC America [network]

BC 02 WSB [Atlanta, Georgia]

Beachcomber [Rehoboth Beach, Delaware newspaper]

Beacher, The [Michigan City, Indiana newspaper]

Beaches Leader, The [Jacksonville Beach, Florida newspaper]

Beacon Hill Times, The [Boston, Massachusetts newspaper]

Beacon News, The [Aurora, Illinois newspaper]

Beatrice Daily Sun [Nebraska newspaper]

Beaufort Gazette, The [South Carolina newspaper]

Beaumont Enterprise [Texas newspaper]

Beauregard Daily News [Louisiana newspaper]

Beaver County Times [Pennsylvania newspaper]

Beaver Press, The [Utah newspaper]

Beavercreek News-Current [Ohio newspaper]

Bedford Bulletin [New Hampshire newspaper]

Bedford Times-Press, The [Iowa newspaper]

Bee Newspapers, The [Williamsville, New York newspaper]

Bee, The [Phillips, Wisconsin newspaper]

Beeville Bee-Picayune [Texas newspaper]

Belle Fourche Post & Bee [South Dakota newspaper]

Belle Plaine Union [Iowa newspaper]

Belleville Enterprise [Michigan newspaper]

Belleville News-Democrat [Illinois newspaper]

Belleville Post [New Jersey newspaper]

Bellingham Herald, The [Washington newspaper]

Bellmore Herald [New York newspaper]

Belmont Town Online [Massachusetts website]

Beloit Daily News [Wisconsin newspaper]

Belvidere Daily Republican [Illinois newspaper]

Bennington Banner, The [Vermont newspaper]

Benton County Daily Record [Bentonville, Arkansas newspaper]

Benton Courier, The [Arkansas newspaper]

Benton Evening News [Illinois newspaper]

Benzie County Record-Patriot [Benzonia, Michigan newspaper]

Bergen Record, The [New Jersey newspaper]

Berkshire Eagle, The [Pittsfield, Massachusetts newspaper]

Berkshires Week [Berkshire County, Massachusetts newspaper]

Better Homes and Gardens [magazine]

Beulah Beacon [North Dakota newspaper]

Beverly Town Online [Massachusetts website]

Big Bear Grizzly [California newspaper]

Big Bug News, The [Prescott, Arkansas newspaper]

Big Rapids Review [Michigan newspaper]

Bigfork Eagle [Montana newspaper]

Billerica News [Massachusetts newspaper]

Billings Gazette, The [Montana newspaper]

Billings Outpost, The [Montana newspaper]

Birmingham Business Journal [Alabama newspaper]

Birmingham News [Alabama newspaper]

Birmingham Post-Herald [Alabama newspaper]

Birmingham/Bloomfield Eccentric [Michigan newspaper]

Bisbee Observer, The [Arizona newspaper]

Bismarck Tribune [North Dakota newspaper]

Bitterroot Star [Stevensville, Montana newspaper]

Black Chronicle [Oklahoma City, Oklahoma newspaper]

Black Entertainment Television [network]

Black Hills Pioneer [Spearfish, South Dakota newspaper]

Blade, The [Toledo, Ohio newspaper]

Bladen Journal [Elizabethtown, North Carolina newspaper]

Blaine Life [Coon Rapids, Minnesota newspaper]

Blairsville Dispatch [Pennsylvania newspaper]

Bland County Messenger [Virginia newspaper]

Blandinsville Star-Gazette [Illinois newspaper]

Bleckley County News, The [Cochran, Georgia newspaper]

Bloomberg Business News [Princeton, New Jersey newspaper]

Bloomberg Television [network]

Bloomer Advance [Wisconsin newspaper]

Bloomfield Democrat, The [Iowa newspaper]

Bloomfield Journal [Connecticut newspaper]

Bloomington Independent [Indiana newspaper]

Blue Mountain Panorama, The [Utah newspaper]

Blue Ridge Business [Virginia newspaper]

Blue Ridge Business Journal [Roanoke, Virginia newspaper]

Blue Springs Examiner, The [Missouri newspaper]

Bluefield Daily Telegraph [West Virginia newspaper]

Bluffton News Banner [Indiana newspaper]

Blytheville Courier News [Arkansas newspaper]

Boca Beacon [Florida newspaper]

Boca Raton News [Florida newspaper]

Boise Weekly [Idaho newspaper]

Bolingbrook Sun [Naperville, Illinois newspaper]

Bolivar Commercial, The [Cleveland, Mississippi newspaper]

Bolivar Herald-Free Press [Missouri newspaper]

Bolton Common [Massachusetts newspaper]

Bon Appetit [magazine]

Bonita Daily News [Naples, Florida newspaper]

Bonner County Daily Bee [Sandpoint, Idaho newspaper]

Boonville Daily News [Missouri newspaper]

Boothbay Register [Boothbay Harbor, Maine newspaper]

Borger News-Herald [Texas newspaper]

Boscobel Dial, The [Wisconsin newspaper]

Bossier Press-Tribune [Bossier City, Louisiana newspaper]

Boston Business Journal [Massachusetts newspaper]

Boston Herald [Massachusetts newspaper]

Boston Phoenix [Massachusetts newspaper]

Boulder City News [Colorado newspaper]

Boulder County Business Report [Colorado newspaper]

Boulder Daily Camera [Colorado newspaper]

Boulder Weekly [Colorado newspaper]

Bow Times [New Hampshire newspaper]

Box Elder News Journal [Brigham City, Utah newspaper]

Boyertown Times [Pennsylvania newspaper]

Boys' Life [magazine]

Bozeman Daily Chronicle News [Montana newspaper]

Bradenton Herald [Florida newspaper]

Bradford County Telegraph [Starke, Florida newspaper]

Bradford Era, The [Pennsylvania newspaper]

Bradley News Weekly, The [Cleveland, Tennessee newspaper]

Brainerd Daily Dispatch, The [Minnesota newspaper]

Branford Review, The [Guilford, Connecticut newspaper]

Branson Tri-Lakes Daily News [Missouri newspaper]

Brattleboro Reformer, The [Vermont newspaper]

Bravo! [network]

Braxton Citizens' News [Sutton, West Virginia newspaper]

Brazoria Facts, The [Texas newspaper]

Brentwood News [California newspaper]

Brewton Standard, The [Alabama newspaper]

Bridgeton News [New Jersey newspaper]

Bridgeville News-Star [Pennsylvania newspaper]

Brighton Argus, The [Michigan newspaper]

Bristol Herald Courier [Virginia newspaper]

Bristol Herald Courier/Bristol Virginia-Tennessean [Virginia newspaper]

Bristol Press, The [Connecticut newspaper]

Brookfield Journal, The [New Milford, Connecticut newspaper]

Brookfield News [Wisconsin newspaper]

Brookings Register [South Dakota newspaper]

Brookline TAB [Massachusetts newspaper]

Broomfield Enterprise [Colorado newspaper]

Brown County Democrat, The [Nashville, Indiana newspaper]

Brown Daily Herald [Providence, Rhode Island newspaper]

Brown Deer Herald [Wisconsin newspaper]

Brownfield News [Texas newspaper]

Brownsville Herald, The [Texas newspaper]

Brownwood Bulletin [Texas newspaper]

Brunswick Beacon [Shallotte, North Carolina newspaper]

Brunswick News, The [Georgia newspaper]

Bryan Times, The [Ohio newspaper]

Bryan-College Station Eagle, The [Texas newspaper]

Bucks County Courier Times [Levittown, Pennsylvania newspaper]

Buffalo Beat [New York newspaper]

Buffalo News, The [New York newspaper]

Buffalo Reflex [Missouri newspaper]

Bullard Weekly News [Texas newspaper]

Bulletin Online [Angleton, Texas newspaper]

Bulletin Online, The [Bend, Oregon newspaper]

Bulletin Online, The [Conroe, Texas newspaper]

Bulletin Online, The [Emporia, Kansas newspaper]

Bullhead City Bee [Arizona newspaper]

Burbank Leader [California newspaper]

Bureau County Republican [Princeton, Illinois newspaper]

Burke County Tribune [Bowbells, North Dakota newspaper]

Burlington County Times [Willingboro, New Jersey newspaper]

Burlington Free Press, The [Vermont newspaper]

Burlington Hawk Eye [Iowa newspaper]

Burnett County Sentinel [Grantsburg, Wisconsin newspaper]

Burwell Tribune [Nebraska newspaper]

Bush Blade, The [Cook Inlet, Arkansas newspaper]

Business [New York newspaper]

Business [Ohio newspaper]

Business Farmer [Wyoming newspaper]

Business First [Buffalo, New York newspaper]

Business First [Kentucky newspaper]

Business First of Columbus [Ohio newspaper]

Business First of Louisville [Kentucky newspaper]

Business Journal [Blountville, Tennessee newspaper]

Business Journal [Charleston, South Carolina newspaper]

Business Journal [Charlotte, North Carolina newspaper]

Business Journal [Colorado Springs, Colorado newspaper]

Business Journal [Greensboro, North Carolina newspaper]

Business Journal [New York newspaper]

Business Journal [Portland, Oregon newspaper]

Business Journal [Raleigh, North Carolina newspaper]

Business Journal [South Carolina newspaper]

Business Journal [Tennessee newspaper]

Business Journal of Charlotte, The [North Carolina newspaper]

Business Journal of Portland [Oregon newspaper]

Business Journal of Triad [North Carolina newspaper]

Business Journal, The [Jacksonville, Florida newspaper]

Business Journal, The [Phoenix, Arizona newspaper]

Business Journal, The [Santa Rosa, California newspaper]

Business Journal, The [Youngstown, Ohio newspaper]

Business Monthly [Saginaw, Michigan newspaper]

Business News [Houma, Louisiana newspaper]

Business News NJ [New Brunswick, New Jersey newspaper]

Business News Now [Fort Myers, Florida newspaper]

Business News, The [Dayton, Ohio newspaper]

Business News, The [Eugene, Oregon newspaper]

Business People Vermont [Williston, Vermont newspaper]

Business Report [Baton Rouge, Louisiana newspaper]

Business Report, The [Savannah, Georgia newspaper]

Business Review [Albany, New York newspaper]

Business Strategies Newspaper [Rochester, New York newspaper]

Business Times [New Haven, Connecticut newspaper]

Business Update [Grand Rapids, Michigan newspaper]

Business Week [magazine]

Butler Eagle [Pennsylvania newspaper]

Butler Warren Business Journal [Middletown, Ohio newspaper]

Butte County Valley Irrigator [Newell, South Dakota newspaper]

Butterfield Advocate [Minnesota newspaper]

Cabot Star-Herald [Arkansas newspaper]

Cache Citizen, The [Logan, Utah newspaper]

Cadillac Evening News, The [Michigan newspaper]

Caledonia Argus, The [Minnesota newspaper]

Caledonian-Record, The [Vermont newspaper]

Californian, The [Salinas, California newspaper]

Camas-Washougal Post-Record [Washington newspaper]

Cambridge Chronicle [Illinois newspaper]

Cambridge Chronicle [Massachusetts newspaper]

Camden Community News [Minneapolis, Minnesota newspaper]

Camden Hearld [Maine newspaper]

Camden News [Arkansas newspaper]

Cameron Herald [Texas newspaper]

Camp Verde Bugle [Arkansas newspaper]

Campbell Reporter [California newspaper]

Canal Traveller [Ohio newspaper]

Canandaigua Messenger [New York newspaper]

Cannon Beach Gazette [Oregon newspaper]

Cannon Falls Beacon [Minnesota newspaper]

Canton Eagle [Michigan newspaper]

Canton Observer [Plymouth, Michigan newspaper]

Canton Repository, The [Ohio newspaper]

Canyon Country Zephyr [Moab, Utah newspaper]

Canyon Courier [Conifer, Colorado newspaper]

Canyon News, The [Texas newspaper]

Cape Cod Chronicle [Massachusetts newspaper]

Cape Cod Online [Hyannis, Massachusetts website]

Cape Cod Times [Massachusetts newspaper]

Cape Cod Today [Orleans, Massachusetts newspaper]

Cape Coral Daily Breeze [Florida newspaper]

Cape Courier, The [Cape Elizabeth, Maine newspaper]

Cape Gazette [Rehoboth Beach, Delaware newspaper]

Cape May County Herald [Rio Grande, New Jersey newspaper]

Capital City Weekly [Juneau, Alaska newspaper]

Capital District [New York newspaper]

Capital District Business review [Albany, New York newspaper]

Capital Journal [Pierre, South Dakota newspaper]

Capital Times, The [Madison, Wisconsin newspaper]

Capital, The [Annapolis, Maryland newspaper]

Capitol Weekly [Augusta, Maine newspaper]

Car & Travel [magazine]

Car and Driver [magazine]

Carbon County News [Red Lodge, Montana newspaper]

Carlisle Independent [Arkansas newspaper]

Carlsbad Current-Argus [New Mexico newspaper]

Carmel Pine Cone, The [California newspaper]

Carmi Times, The [Illinois newspaper]

Carnarsie Courier [Brooklyn, New York newspaper]

Carroll County Times [Westminster, Maryland newspaper]

Carteret News-Times, The [Morehead City, North Carolina newspaper]

Carthage Press, The [Missouri newspaper]

Cartoon Network [network]

Cascade Business News [Bend, Oregon newspaper]

Casco Bay Weekly [Portland, Maine newspaper]

Cash-Book Journal [Jackson, Missouri newspaper]

Casper Star Tribune [Wyoming newspaper]

Cassville Democrat [Missouri newspaper]

Catalina Islander [Avalon, California newspaper]

Catholic Globe [Sioux City, Iowa newspaper]

Catholic Post [Peoria, Illinois newspaper]

Catoosa News [Ringgold, Georgia newspaper]

Cavalier County Republican [Langdon, North Dakota newspaper]

CBS 02 WFMY [02 Greensboro, North Carolina]

CBS [network]

Cedar Creek Pilot, The [Texas newspaper]

Cedar Key Beacon [Florida newspaper]

Cedar Rapids Gazette [Iowa newspaper]

Cedartown Standard [Georgia newspaper]

Center Republican [North Dakota newspaper]

Central Georgian [Macon, Georgia newspaper]

Central Kentucky News-Journal [Campbellsville, Kentucky newspaper]

Central Kitsap Reporter [Siverdale, Washington newspaper]

Central Virginian News [Louisa, Virginia newspaper]

Centralia Chronicle, The [Washington newspaper]

Centre Daily Times [State College, Pennsylvania newspaper]

Chadron Record [Nebraska newspaper]

Chagrin Valley Times [Chagrin Falls, Ohio newspaper]

Challis Messenger, The [Idaho newspaper]

Chanhassen Villager [Minnesota newspaper]

Chanute Tribune, The [Kansas newspaper]

Chapel Hill News [North Carolina newspaper]

Chariho Times [Rhode Island newspaper]

Char-Koosta News [Pablo, Montana newspaper]

Charles City Press [Iowa newspaper]

Charleston City Paper [South Carolina newspaper]

Charleston County Daily Times-Courier [Illinois newspaper]

Charleston Daily Mail [West Virginia newspaper]

Charleston Daily News [South Carolina newspaper]

Charleston Gazette, The [West Virginia newspaper]

Charleston Regional [South Carolina newspaper]

Charlotte Observer, The [North Carolina newspaper]

Charlotte Post [North Carolina newspaper]

Charlotte Sun Herald [Charlotte Harbor, Florida newspaper]

Chaska Herald [Minnesota newspaper]

Chatfield News [Minnesota newspaper]

Chatham Journal [Pittsboro, North Carolina newspaper]

Chattanooga Times, The [Tennessee newspaper]

Chattanoogan, The [Tennessee newspaper]

Cheboygan Daily Tribune [Michigan newspaper]

Chelsea Independent [Revere, Massachusetts newspaper]

Chelsea Standard, The [Michigan newspaper]

Cherokee County Herald [Alabama newspaper]

Cherokee Observer [Blackwell, Oklahoma newspaper]

Cherokee Villager [Arkansas newspaper]

Chester County Press [Oxford, Pennsylvania newspaper]

Chesterton Tribune [Indiana newspaper]

Chetek Alert, The [Wisconsin newspaper]

Cheyenne's Wyoming HQ [Wyoming newspaper]

Chicago Reader [Illinois newspaper]

Chicago Sun-Times [Illinois newspaper]

Chicago Tribune [Illinois newspaper]

Chickasha Daily Express [Oklahoma newspaper]

Chico Enterprise-Record [California newspaper]

Chico Examiner [California newspaper]

Chicot County Spectator [Lake Village, Arkansas newspaper]

Chino Valley Review [Prescott, Arizona newspaper]

Chinook Observer [Long Beach, Washington newspaper]

Chipley Bugle [Florida newspaper]

Chippewa Herald, The [Chippewa Falls, Wisconsin newspaper]

Choteau Acantha [Montana newspaper]

Christian Broadcasting Network [network]

Christian Science Monitor [Boston, Massachusetts newspaper]

Christian Science Monitor [national newspaper]

Chronicle [Texas newspaper]

Chronicle [West Orange, New Jersey newspaper]

Chronicle [Wisconsin newspaper]

Chronicle Independent [Camden, South Carolina newspaper]

Chronicle Online [Durham, North Carolina newspaper]

Chronicle Telegram, The [Elyria, Ohio newspaper]

Chronicle, The [Centralia, Washington newspaper]

Chronicle, The [Gaffney, South Carolina newspaper]

Chronicle, The [Willimantic, Connecticut newspaper]

Chronicle-Herald [Macon, Missouri newspaper]

Chronotype, The [Rice Lake, Wisconsin newspaper]

Cincinnati Business Courier [Ohio newspaper]

Cincinnati CityBeat [Ohio newspaper]

Cincinnati Enquirer, The [Ohio newspaper]

Cincinnati Post, The [Ohio newspaper]

Cinemax [network]

Citizen [New York newspaper]

Citizen [Connecticut newspaper]

Citizen Telegram [Rifle, Colorado newspaper]

Citizen Tribune [Morristown, Tennessee newspaper]

Citizen, The [Auburn, New York newspaper]

Citizen, The [Cincinnati, Ohio newspaper]

Citizen, The [Fayetteville, Georgia newspaper]

Citizen's Standard [Valley View, Pennsylvania newspaper]

Citizen's Voice, The [Wilkes Barre, Pennsylvania newspaper]

Citrus County Chronicle [Crystal River, Florida newspaper]

CityBusiness [Minneapolis-St. Paul, Minnesota magazine]

City Business [New Orleans, Louisiana newspaper]

City Pages [Minneapolis-St. Paul, Minnesota newspaper]

City Paper [Philadelphia, Pennsylvania newspaper]

City Weekly [Salt Lake City, Utah newspaper]

Clanton Advertiser [Alabama newspaper]

Claremore Daily Progress [Oklahoma newspaper]

Clarion Ledger [Mississippi newspaper]

Clarion, The [Palestine, Texas newspaper]

Clarion, The [Pennsylvania newspaper]

Clarion-Ledger, The [Mississippi newspaper]

Clark Eagle [New Jersey newspaper]

Clarksburg Exponent-Telegram, The [West Virginia newspaper]

Clarkston Eccentric [Michigan newspaper]

Clatskanie Chief [Oregon newspaper]

Clay Center Dispatch [Kansas newspaper]

Clayton News-Star [North Carolina newspaper]

Clayton Tribune [Georgia newspaper]

Clear Lake Mirror [Iowa newspaper]

Clearwater Tribune [Big Lake, Minnesota newspaper]

Clearwater Tribune [Orofino, Idaho newspaper]

Cleburne News [Heflin, Alabama newspaper]

Cleburne Times-Review [Texas newspaper]

Cleveland American [Oklahoma newspaper]

Cleveland Daily Banner [Tennessee newspaper]

Cleveland Free Times [Ohio newspaper]

Clewiston News [Florida newspaper]

Clifton Record Online [Texas newspaper]

Clinch Valley News [Tazewell, Virginia newspaper]

Clinton County Leader, The [Plattsburg, Missouri newspaper]

Clinton Daily Journal [Illinois newspaper]

Clinton Daily News [Oklahoma newspaper]

Clinton Herald [Iowa newspaper]

Clinton Recorder [Guilford, Connecticut newspaper]

Cloquet Journal [Minnesota newspaper]

Cloquet Pine Knot [Minnesota newspaper]

Cloverdale Reveille [California newspaper]

Clovis Independent [California newspaper]

Clovis News Journal [New Mexico newspaper]

CNBC [network]

CNN [network]

CNNfn [network]

CNNSI [network]

Coalfield Progress [Big Stone Gap, Virginia newspaper]

Coalinga's Own [California newspaper]

Coast Star, The [Manasquan, New Jersey newspaper]

Coast Weekly [Seaside, California newspaper]

Coastal Courier, The [Hinesville, Georgia newspaper]

Coastal Family [Savannah, Georgia newspaper]

Coastal Observer, The [Pawley's Island, South Carolina newspaper]

Coastal Post [Marin County, California newspaper]

Coastal View News [Carpenteria, California newspaper]

Cobb Online [Marietta, Georgia website]

Cocke County Online [Newport, Tennessee newspaper]

Cody Enterprise [Wyoming newspaper]

Coeur d'Alene Press [Idaho newspaper]

Coffee County News [Douglas, Georgia newspaper]

Coffeyville Journal, The [Kansas newspaper]

Colfax Area Express, The [Weimar, California newspaper]

Colorado Daily [Boulder, Colorado newspaper]

Colorado Springs Gazette, The [Colorado newspaper]

Coloradoan, The [Fort Collins, Colorado newspaper]

Columbia Daily Herald [Tennessee newspaper]

Columbia Daily Tribune [Missouri newspaper]

Columbia Missourian [Missouri Newspaper]

Columbia Star [South Carolina newspaper]

Columbian, The [Vancouver, Washington newspaper]

Columbine Community Courier [Littleton, Colorado newspaper]

Columbus Alive [Ohio newspaper]

Columbus Dispatch [Ohio newspaper]

Columbus Ledger-Enquirer [Georgia newspaper]

Columbus Telegram [Nebraska newspaper]

Columbus Times [Georgia newspaper]

Comedy Central [network]

Commercial Appeal, The [Memphis, Tennessee newspaper]

Commercial Record, The [South Windsor, Connecticut newspaper]

Commercial Recorder, The [Fort Worth, Texas newspaper]

Commercial-News [Danville, Illinois newspaper]

Community News [Clifton Park, New York newspaper]

Community News of Miami [Florida newspaper]

Community News, The [Aledo, Texas newspaper]

Community Press, The [Cincinnati, Ohio newspaper]

Community Times [Westminster, Maryland newspaper]

Community Times Dispatch, The [Walterboro, South Carolina newspaper]

Community Trader [Clifton Springs, New York newspaper]

Community Voice [Rohnert Park, California newspaper]

Computer News Daily/New York Times Syndicate [New York, New York newspaper]

Concord Monitor [New Hampshire newspaper]

Concord Town Online [Massachusetts website]

Connecticut Jewish Ledger [New London, Connecticut newspaper]

Connecticut Post, The [Bridgeport, Connecticut newspaper]

Connector [Niles, Michigan newspaper]

Connersville News-Examiner, The [Indiana newspaper]

Constitution-Tribune [Chillicothe, Missouri newspaper]

Consumers Digest [magazine]

Contra Costa Times [California newspaper]

Contra Costa Times [Walnut Creek, California newspaper]

Conway Daily Sun [New Hampshire newspaper]

Cook County News-Herald [Grand Marais, Minnesota newspaper]

Cook County Star [Grand Marais, Minnesota newspaper]

Cooking Light [magazine]

Coon Rapids Herald [Minnesota newspaper]

Cooperstown Crier [New York newspaper]

Coosa County News [Rockford, Alabama newspaper]

Coppell Gazette [Texas newspaper]

Coquille Valley Sentinel [Oregon newspaper]

Coral Gables Gazette [Florida newspaper]

Coraopolis Record-Star [Pennsylvania newspaper]

Corbin News-Journal [Kentucky newspaper]

Corbin Times-Tribune [Kentucky newspaper]

Cordele Dispatch [Georgia newspaper]

Cordell Beacon [Oklahoma newspaper]

Coronado Eagle [California newspaper]

Corpus Christi Caller-Times, The [Texas newspaper]

Corrigan Times [Texas newspaper]

Corsicana Daily Sun, The [Texas newspaper]

Cortez Journal, The [Colorado newspaper]

Corvallis Gazette-Times [Oregon newspaper]

Corydon Democrat, The [Indiana newspaper]

Cosmopolitan [magazine]

Cottage Grove Sentinel [Oregon newspaper]

Cottonwood County Citizen [Windom, Minnesota newspaper]

Country America [magazine]

Country Home [magazine]

Country Living [magazine]

Country Music Television [network]

Country Today, The [Eau Claire, Wisconsin newspaper]

County Bulletin [Cottage Grove, Minnesota newspaper]

County Line Reminder [Ortonville, Michigan newspaper]

County News [Cambridge, Minnesota newspaper]

Courier Herald, The [Dublin, Georgia newspaper]

Courier Journal [Kentucky newspaper]

Courier News [Elgin, Illinois newspaper]

Courier Publications [Rockland, Maine newspaper]

Courier Times, The [Sutherland, Nebraska newspaper]

Courier, The [Conroe, Texas newspaper]

Courier, The [Findlay, Ohio newspaper]

Courier, The [Houma, Louisiana newspaper]

Courier, The [Russellville, Arkansas newspaper]

Courier-Express [DuBois, Pennsylvania newspaper]

Courier-Gazette [McKinney, Texas newspaper]

Courier-Gazette [Newark, New York newspaper]

Courier-Index, The [Marianna, Arkansas newspaper]

Courier-Journal, The [Louisville, Kentucky newspaper]

Courier-News [Crestline, California newspaper]

Courier-Post, The [Cherry Hill, New Jersey newspaper]

Courier-Review [Barrington, Illinois newspaper]

Courier-Times, The [New Castle, Indiana newspaper]

Courier-Times, The [Roxboro, North Carolina newspaper]

Courier-Tribune, The [Asheboro, North Carolina newspaper]

Court TV [network]

Coventry Courier [Wakefield, Rhode Island newspaper]

Craig Daily Press [Colorado newspaper]

Crain's Chicago Business [Illinois newspaper]

Crain's Cleveland Business [Ohio newspaper]

Crain's Detroit Business [Michigan newspaper]

Crain's New York Business [New York newspaper]

Cranberry Journal-Star [Pennsylvania newspaper]

Crane Chronicle/Stone County Republican [Missouri newspaper]

Crawford County Avalanche [Grayling, Michigan newspaper]

Crescent Online, The [Evansville, Indiana website]

Crescent-News, The [Defiance, Ohio newspaper]

Crested Butte Chronicle & Pilot [Colorado newspaper]

Crested Butte Weekly [Colorado newspaper]

Crestview News Leader [Florida newspaper]

Crimson White [Tuscaloosa, Alabama newspaper]

Crittenden Press, The [Marion, Kentucky newspaper]

Crookston Daily Times [Minnesota newspaper]

Crossville Chronicle [Tennessee newspaper]

Crowley Post-Signal, The [Louisiana newspaper]

Crown Point Star [Indiana newspaper]

C-SPAN [network]

Cuba Free Press [Missouri newspaper]

Cudahy Reminder-Enterprise [Wisconsin newspaper]

Cuero Record, The [Texas newspaper]

Cullman Times, The [Alabama newspaper]

Culpeper News [Virginia newspaper]

Culpeper Star Exponent [Virginia newspaper]

Culver City News [California newspaper]

Cumberland Times-News [Maryland newspaper]

Cupertino Courier, The [California newspaper]

Curry Coast Pilot [Brookings, Oregon newspaper]

Curry County Reporter [Gold Beach, Oregon newspaper]

Custer County Chief [Broken Bow, Nebraska newspaper]

Dade County Sentinel [Trenton, Georgia newspaper]

Daily Advertiser, The [Lafayette, Louisiana newspaper]

Daily American [Somerset, Pennsylvania newspaper]

Daily American Republic [Poplar Bluff, Missouri newspaper]

Daily American, The [West Frankfort, Illinois newspaper]

Daily Ardmoreite, The [Ardmore, Oklahoma newspaper]

Daily Astorian, The [Astoria, Oregon newspaper]

Daily Banner News, The [Cambridge, Maryland newspaper]

Daily Breeze [Torrance, California newspaper]

Daily Camera, The [Colorado newspaper]

Daily Chief-Union, The [Upper Sandusky, Ohio newspaper]

Daily Citizen [Beaver Dam, Wisconsin newspaper]

Daily Citizen, The [Searcy, Arkansas newspaper]

Daily Citizen-News [Dalton, Georgia newspaper]

Daily Clay County Advocate-Press, The [Flora, Illinois newspaper]

Daily Comet, The [Thibodaux, Louisiana newspaper]

Daily Commercial Record, The [Texas newspaper]

Daily Commercial, The [Leesburg, Florida newspaper]

Daily Courier [Connellsville, Pennsylvania newspaper]

Daily Courier, The [Prescott, Arizona newspaper]

Daily Democrat [Fort Madison, Iowa newspaper]

Daily Democrat, The [Woodland, California newspaper]

Daily Dispatch, The [Douglas, Arizona newspaper]

Daily Dispatch, The [Henderson, North Carolina newspaper]

Daily Dunklin Democrat, The [Kennett, Missouri newspaper]

Daily Evening Item [Lynn, Massachusetts newspaper]

Daily Forum [Maryville, Missouri newspaper]

Daily Freeman, The [Freeman, New York newspaper]

Daily Gate City [Keokuk, Iowa newspaper]

Daily Gazette, The [Schenectady, New York newspaper]

Daily Gazette, The [Sterling, Illinois newspaper]

Daily Globe [Worthington, Minnesota newspaper]

Daily Globe, The [Shelby, Ohio newspaper]

Daily Guide [Waynesville, Missouri newspaper]

Daily Hampshire Gazette [Northhampton, Massachusetts newspaper]

Daily Herald [Chicago, Illinois newspaper]

Daily Herald [McDonough, Georgia newspaper]

Daily Herald [Provo, Utah newspaper]

Daily Herald [Roanoke Rapids, North Carolina newspaper]

Daily Herald, The [Columbia, Tennessee newspaper]

Daily Home [Talladega, Alabama newspaper]

Daily Iberian, The [New Iberia, Louisiana newspaper]

Daily Independent, The [Ashland, Kentucky newspaper]

Daily Independent, The [Ridgecrest, California newspaper]

Daily Inter Lake [Kalispell, Montana newspaper]

Daily Iowan, The [Iowa City, Iowa newspaper]

Daily Iowegian [Centerville, Iowa newspaper]

Daily Item, The [Sunbury, Pennsylvania newspaper]

Daily Jeffersonian [Cambridge, Ohio newspaper]

Daily Journal [Fergus Falls, Minnesota newspaper]

Daily Journal [Manassas, Virginia newspaper]

Daily Journal [Orem, Utah newspaper]

Daily Journal [Park Hills, Missouri newspaper]

Daily Journal of Johnson County [Franklin, Indiana newspaper]

Daily Journal Online [Tupelo, Mississippi newspaper]

Daily Journal, The [International Falls, Minnesota newspaper]

Daily Journal, The [Kankakee, Illinois newspaper]

Daily Journal, The [Prince William, Virginia newspaper]

Daily Leader, The [Brookhaven, Mississippi newspaper]

Daily Leader, The [Pontiac, Illinois newspaper]

Daily Ledger, The [Canton, Illinois newspaper]

Daily Lobo [Albuquerque, New Mexico newspaper]

Daily Local News [West Chester, Pennsylvania newspaper]

Daily Me, The [Dexter, Maine newspaper]

Daily Messenger [Clemson, South Carolina newspaper]

Daily Midway Driller, The [Taft, California newspaper]

Daily Mining Gazette, The [Houghton, Michigan newspaper]

Daily Mountain Eagle [Jasper, Alabama newspaper]

Daily Nebraskan Online [Lincoln, Nebraska newspaper]

Daily News [Eden, North Carolina newspaper]

Daily News [Iron Mountain, Michigan newspaper]

Daily News [Louisiana newspaper]

Daily News [Massachusetts newspaper]

Daily News [Newburyport, Massachusetts newspaper]

Daily News [Palatka, Florida newspaper]

Daily News [Red Bluff, California newspaper]

Daily News [Rhinelander, Wisconsin newspaper]

Daily News [Woodland Hills, California newspaper]

Daily News Journal, The [Murfreesboro, Tennessee newspaper]

Daily News Leader [Staunton, Virginia newspaper]

Daily News Online [Juneau, Alaska newspaper]

Daily News The [Jacksonville, North Carolina newspaper]

Daily News, The [Bogalusa, Louisiana newspaper]

Daily News, The [Bowling Green, Kentucky newspaper]

Daily News, The [Greenville, Michigan newspaper]

Daily News, The [Lebanon, Pennsylvania newspaper]

Daily News, The [Longview, Washington newspaper]

Daily News, The [McKeesport, Pennsylvania newspaper]

Daily News, The [Memphis, Tennessee newspaper]

Daily News-Bulletin [Brookfield, Missouri newspaper]

Daily News-Tribune [Keyser, West Virginia newspaper]

Daily Nonpareil, The [Council Bluffs, Iowa newspaper]

Daily Okeechobee News, The [Florida newspaper]

Daily Pilot [Costa Mesa, California newspaper]

Daily Post Athenian, The [Athens, Tennessee newspaper]

Daily Press [Escanaba, Michigan newspaper]

Daily Press [Hampton Roads, Virginia newspaper]

Daily Press [Victorville, California newspaper]

Daily Press, The [Ashland, Wisconsin newspaper]

Daily Progess [Oklahoma newspaper]

Daily Progress, The [Charlottesville, Virginia newspaper]

Daily Progress, The [Claremore, Oklahoma newspaper]

Daily Record [Canon, Colorado newspaper]

Daily Record [Ellensburg, Washington newspaper]

Daily Record [Parsippany, New Jersey newspaper]

Daily Record, The [Baltimore, Maryland newspaper]

Daily Record, The [Dunn, North Carolina newspaper]

Daily Record, The [Ellensburg, Washington newspaper]

Daily Record, The [Jacksonville, Florida newspaper]

Daily Record, The [Wooster, Ohio newspaper]

Daily Reflector, The [Greenville, North Carolina newspaper]

Daily Register [Portage, Wisconsin newspaper]

Daily Register, The [Harrisburg, Illinois newspaper]

Daily Reporter, The [Coldwater, Michigan newspaper]

Daily Reporter, The [Columbus, Ohio newspaper]

Daily Reporter, The [Derby, Kansas newspaper]

Daily Reporter-Herald [Loveland, Colorado newspaper]

Daily Reporter-Times [Martinsville, Indiana newspaper]

Daily Republic [Fairfield, California newspaper]

Daily Republic, The [Mitchell, South Dakota newspaper]

Daily Republican, The [Palo Alto, California newspaper]

Daily Review [Hayward, California newspaper]

Daily Review, The [Morgan City, Louisiana newspaper]

Daily Review, The [Towanda, Pennsylvania newspaper]

Daily Sentinel [Rome, New York newspaper]

Daily Sentinel, The [Grand Junction, Colorado newspaper]

Daily Sentinel, The [Pomeroy, Ohio newspaper]

Daily Sentinel, The [Scottsboro, Alabama newspaper]

Daily Siftings Herald, The [Arkadelphia, Arkansas newspaper]

Daily Southtown [Tinley Park, Illinois newspaper]

Daily Standard, The [Celina, Ohio newspaper]

Daily Star, The [Hammond, Louisiana newspaper]

Daily Star, The [Oneonta, New York newspaper]

Daily Statesman [Dexter, Missouri newspaper]

Daily Sun [The Villages, Florida newspaper]

Daily Telegram, The [Adrian, Michigan newspaper]

Daily Telegram, The [Superior, Wisconsin newspaper]

Daily Territorial, The [Tucson, Arizona newspaper]

Daily Times [Longmont, Colorado newspaper]

Daily Times [Maryville, Tennessee newspaper]

Daily Times Leader [West Point, Mississippi newspaper]

Daily Times, The [Farmington, New Mexico newspaper]

Daily Times, The [Ottawa, Illinois newspaper]

Daily Times, The [Salisbury, Maryland newspaper]

Daily Trail [Vail, Colorado newspaper]

Daily Tribune [Wisconsin Rapids, Wisconsin newspaper]

Daily Tribune News, The [Cartersville, Georgia newspaper]

Daily Tribune, The [Ames, Iowa newspaper]

Daily Tribune, The [Hibbing, Minnesota newspaper]

Daily Triplicate, The [Crescent City, California newspaper]

Daily Union, The [Junction City, Kansas newspaper]

Daily Universe, The [Provo, Utah newspaper]

Daily Variety [Los Angeles, California newspaper]

Daily Web, The [Redondo Beach, California newspaper]

Daily World, The [Aberdeen, Washington newspaper]

Daily World, The [Helena, Arkansas newspaper]

Daily World, The [Opelousas, Louisiana newspaper]

Daily-Herald, The [Provo, Utah newspaper]

Daily-Review [Morgan City, Louisiana newspaper]

Dakota Herald [Lemmon, South Dakota newspaper]

Dakota Press [Groton, South Dakota newspaper]

Dallas Business Journal [Texas newspaper]

Dallas Morning News, The [Texas newspaper]

Dallas Observer [Texas newspaper]

Dallas Times [Texas newspaper]

Dalles Chronicle [Oregon newspaper]

Dan's Papers [Bridgehampton, New York newspaper]

Danvers Town Online [Massachusetts website]

Danville News, The [Pennsylvania newspaper]

Danville Register and Bee [Virginia newspaper]

Darien News-Review [Connecticut newspaper]

Dartmouth Online [Hanover, New Hampshire website]

Davenport Leader [Iowa newspaper]

Davenport Quad-City Times [Iowa newspaper]

Davis County Clipper [Bountiful, Utah newspaper]

Davis Enterprise, The [California newspaper]

Dawg Net [Indianapolis, Indiana newspaper]

Dawson News & Advertiser [Dawsonville, Georgia newspaper]

Day, The [New London, Connecticut newspaper]

Dayton Business Reporter [Ohio newspaper]

Dayton Daily News, The [Ohio newspaper]

Daytona Beach News-Journal [Florida newspaper]

De Queen Daily Citizen [Arkansas newspaper]

Dearborn Press and Guide, The [Michigan newspaper]

Decatur Daily [Alabama newspaper]

Decatur Daily Democrat [Indiana newspaper]

Decatur Herald & Review [Illinois newspaper]

Deerfield Review [Illinois newspaper]

Deerfield Valley News [West Dover, Vermont newspaper]

DeLand Beacon [Florida newspaper]

Delano Eagle [Minnesota newspaper]

Delavan Enterprise, The [Wisconsin newspaper]

Delaware Coast Press [Rehoboth Beach, Delaware newspaper]

Delaware County Times, The [Chester, Pennsylvania newspaper]

Delaware Gazette, The [Ohio newspaper]

Delaware State News [Dover, Delaware newspaper]

Delta Business Journal [Cleveland, Mississippi newspaper]

Delta County Independent [Colorado newspaper]

Delta Democrat Times [Greenville, Mississippi newspaper]

Deming Headlight [New Mexico newspaper]

Democrat, The [Senatobia, Mississippi newspaper]

Democrat-Missourian [Harrisonville, Missouri newspaper]

Demopolis Times [Alabama newspaper]

Denton Record-Chronicle [Texas newspaper]

Denver Business Journal [Colorado newspaper]

Denver Post [Colorado newspaper]

Denver Rocky Mountain News [Colorado newspaper]

DeRidder Beauregard Daily News [Louisiana newspaper]

Derrick, The [Oil City, Pennsylvania newspaper]

Des Moines Catholic Mirror [Iowa newspaper]

Des Moines Register [Iowa newspaper]

Des Moines Today [Iowa newspaper]

Des Plaines Times [Illinois newspaper]

Deseret News [Salt Lake City, Utah newspaper]

Desert Dispatch [Barstow, California newspaper]

Desert Sun, The [Palm Springs, California newspaper]

Desert Trail, The [Twentynine Palms, California newspaper]

DeSoto County Tribune [Olive Branch, Mississippi newspaper]

Desoto Explorer [Kansas newspaper]

DeSoto Times Today [Southaven, Mississippi newspaper]

Destin Log Online [Florida website]

Detroit Free Press [Michigan newspaper]

Detroit Journal [Michigan newspaper]

Detroit Lakes Tribune, The [Minnesota newspaper]

Detroit News, The [Michigan newspaper]

Devils Lake Daily Journal [North Dakota newspaper]

DeWitt Era-Enterprise [Arkansas newspaper]

Dexter Leader [Chelsea, Michigan newspaper]

Dickinson Press [North Dakota newspaper]

Digital Missourian, The [Columbia, Missouri newspaper]

Discover [magazine]

Discovery Channel [network]

Discovery Health Channel [network]

Disney Channel [network]

Dispatch [Lexington, North Carolina newspaper]

Dispatch Record, The [Lampasas, Texas newspaper]

Dispatch, The [Moline]

Dispatch-News [Lexington, South Carolina newspaper]

Dixon's Independent Voice [California newspaper]

DIY Network

Dodge City Daily Globe [Kansas newspaper]

Dodge County News, The [Eastmas, Georgia newspaper]

Dominion Post [Morgantown, West Virginia newspaper]

Door County Advocate [Sturgeon Bay, Wisconsin newspaper]

Dorchester Reporter [Boston, Massachusetts newspaper]

Dothan Eagle, The [Alabama newspaper]

Douglas Budget [Wyoming newspaper]

Douglas County News Press [Castle Rock, Colorado newspaper]

Douglas Dispatch [Arizona newspaper]

Dover Post [Delaware newspaper]

Dowagiac Daily News [Michigan newspaper]

Downey Eagle, The [California newspaper]

Downs News & Times [Kansas newspaper]

Downtown Planet, The [Honolulu, Hawaii newspaper]

Drummer, The [Buffalo, Minnesota newspaper]

Dubuque Telegraph Herald [Iowa newspaper]

Duluth Budgeteer News [Minnesota newspaper]

Duluth News-Tribune [Minnesota newspaper]

Duluth Shipping News [Minnesota newspaper]

Duncan Banner, The [Oklahoma newspaper]

Dundalk Eagle, The [Maryland newspaper]

Duneland News [Indiana newspaper]

Dunlap Reporter, The [Iowa newspaper]

Dunn County News [Menomonie, Wisconsin newspaper]

Dunwoody Crier [Georgia newspaper]

Durango Herald Online [Colorado website]

Durant Daily Democrat, The [Oklahoma newspaper]

Durham Herald-Sun, The [North Carolina newspaper]

Duxbury Clipper [Massachusetts newspaper]

Dyersburg News/Dyer County Tennessean [Tennessee newspaper]

E! [network]

Eagle Eye Weekly [Alaska newspaper]

Eagle Press, The [Fritch, Texas newspaper]

Eagle Times Online [New Hampshire website]

Eagle Tribune [Lawrence, Massachusetts newspaper]

Eagle Tribune [North Andover, Massachusetts newspaper]

Eagle Valley Enterprise [Colorado newspaper]

East Arkansas News Leader [Wynne, Arkansas newspaper]

East Baltimore Guide, The [Maryland newspaper]

East Bay Business Times [Pleasanton, California newspaper]

East Bay Express [Berkeley, California newspaper]

East Greenwich Pendulum [Rhode Island newspaper]

East Hampton Independent, The [East Hampton, New York newspaper]

East Hampton Star [New York newspaper]

East Haven Advertiser [Milford, Connecticut newspaper]

East Orange Record [New Jersey newspaper]

East Oregorian, The [Pendleton, Oregon newspaper]

East Side Journal [Bellevue, Washington newspaper]

Eastern Arizona Courier [Safford, Arizona newspaper]

Eastern Shore News [Tasley, Virginia newspaper]

Eastside Business [Washington newspaper]

Eaton Register-Herald, The [Ohio newspaper]

Eatonton Messenger, The [Georgia newspaper]

Ebony [magazine]

Echo Press [Alexandria, Minnesota newspaper]

ECM Post Review [North Branch, Minnesota newspaper]

Eden Prairie News [Minnesota newspaper]

Edinburgh Courier [Indiana newspaper]

Editor & Publisher [New York, New York magazine]

Edmond Evening Sun [Oklahoma newspaper]

Edmond Sun [Oklahoma newspaper]

Edwardsville Intelligencer [Illinois newspaper]

Effingham Daily News [Illinois newspaper]

El Campo Leader-News, The [Texas newspaper]

El Defensor Chieftain [Socorro, New Mexico newspaper]

El Dorado News [Arizona newspaper]

El Dorado News-Times [Arkansas newspaper]

El Dorado Times, The [Kansas newspaper]

El Heraldo [Fort Lauderdale, Florida newspaper]

El Nuevo Herald [Miami, Florida newspaper]

El Observador [San Francisco, California newspaper]

El Paso Internet Courier [Texas newspaper]

El Paso Times [Texas newspaper]

El Reno Tribune [Oklahoma newspaper]

El Reportero [Huntsville, Alabama newspaper]

Elberton Star & Examiner, The [Georgia newspaper]

Elburn Herald, The [Illinois newspaper]

Elizabethton Star [Tennessee newspaper]

Elk Grove Citizen, The [California newspaper]

Elk Grove Times [Illinois newspaper]

Elk River Star News [Minnesota newspaper]

Elk Valley Times, The [Fayetteville, Tennessee newspaper]

Elkhart Truth, The [Indiana newspaper]

Elkhorn Independent [Wisconsin newspaper]

Elko Daily Free Press [Nevada newspaper]

Elko Independent [Nevada newspaper]

Elks Magazine, The [magazine]

Elle [magazine]

Ellis County Chronicle [Red Oak, Texas newspaper]

Ellis County Press [Ferris, Texas newspaper]

Ellsworth American [Maine newspaper]

Ellsworth Weekly [Maine newspaper]

Ellwood City Ledger [Pennsylvania newspaper]

Elm Grove Elm Leaves [Wisconsin newspaper]

Ely Daily Times [Nevada newspaper]

Ely Echo [Minnesota newspaper]

Emery County Progress, The [Castle Dale, Utah newspaper]

Emmitsburg Dispatch [Emmitsburg, Maryland newspaper]

Emporia Gazette, The [Kansas newspaper]

Endless Vacation [magazine]

Englewood Independent [Ohio newspaper]

Englewood Sun Herald [Florida newspaper]

Enid News and Eagle [Oklahoma newspaper]

Enon Messenger [Ohio newspaper]

Enterprise [Beaumont, Texas newspaper]

Enterprise Bulletin [Perham, Minnesota newspaper]

Enterprise Dispatch [Dassel, Minnesota newspaper]

Enterprise Ledger [Enterprise, Alabama newspaper]

Enterprise Mountaineer [North Carolina newspaper]

Enterprise, The [Blair, Nebraska newspaper]

Enterprise, The [Brockton, Massachusetts newspaper]

Enterprise, The [Stuart, Virginia newspaper]

Enterprise-Journal [McComb, Mississippi newspaper]

Enterprise-Record, The [Chico, California newspaper]

Entertainment Weekly [magazine]

Entiat Valley Explorer [Washington newspaper]

Erie Times-News, The [Pennsylvania newspaper]

ESPN [network]

ESPN Classic [network]

Essence [magazine]

Essex Reporter [Essex Junction, Vermont newspaper]

Estes Park Trail-Gazette [Colorado newspaper]

Eudora News [Kansas newspaper]

Eugene Weekly [Oregon newspaper]

Eunice News, The [Louisiana newspaper]

Eureka Herald, The [Kansas newspaper]

Evanston Review [Illinois newspaper]

Evansville Courier [Indiana newspaper]

Evansville Courier and Press [Indiana newspaper]

Evening News, The [Sault Ste. Marie, Michigan newspaper]

Evening Star, The [Auburn, Indiana newspaper]

Evening Sun, The [Hanover, Pennsylvania newspaper]

Evening Sun, The [Norwich, New York newspaper]

Evening Telegram, The [Herkimer, New York newspaper]

Evening Times, The [Little Falls, New York newspaper]

Evening Times, The [Sayre, Pennsylvania newspaper]

Evening Tribune, The [Hornell, New York newspaper]

Event, The [Salt Lake City, Utah newspaper]

Everett Independent [Massachusetts newspaper]

Everglades Echo [Naples, Florida newspaper]

Evergreen Courant, The [Alabama newspaper]

EWTN [network]

Examiner Enterprise [Bartlesville, Oklahoma newspaper]

Examiner, The [Beaumont, Texas newspaper]

Examiner, The [Independence, Missouri newspaper]

Exponent [Brooklyn, Michigan newspaper]

Exponent, The [East Grand Forks, Minnesota newspaper]

Exponent, The [Huntsville, Alabama newspaper]

Express News [San Antonio, Texas newspaper]

Express, The [Lock Haven, Pennsylvania newspaper]

Express-Times, The [Easton, Pennsylvania newspaper]

Fairbanks Daily News-Miner [Alaska newspaper]

Fairborn Daily Herald [Ohio newspaper]

Fairfax County Journal [Virginia newspaper]

Fairfield Citizen-News [Connecticut newspaper]

Fairfield County Weekly [Connecticut newspaper]

Fairfield Daily Ledger [Iowa newspaper]

Fairfield Echo [Ohio newspaper]

Fairplay Flume [Colorado newspaper]

Falls Church News-Press [Virginia newspaper]

Family Circle [magazine]

Family Handyman, The [magazine]

Familyfun [magazine]

FamilyNet [network]

Faribault County Register [Blue Earth, Minnesota newspaper]

Faribault Daily News [Minnesota newspaper]

Farm & Ranch Guide [Bismarck, North Dakota newspaper]

Farmers Press [Minnewaukan, North Dakota newspaper]

Farmersville Times [Texas newspaper]

Farmingdale Observer [New York newspaper]

Farmington Observer [Michigan newspaper]

Fauquier Citizen [Virginia newspaper]

Fauquier Times-Democrat [Virginia newspaper]

Fayette County Review [Somerville, Tennessee newspaper]

Fayetteville Free Weekly [Arkansas newspaper]

Fayetteville Observer [North Carolina newspaper]

Fayetteville Observer-Times [North Carolina newspaper]

Feather River Canyon News [Yankee Hill, California newspaper]

Federal Hill Gazette [Providence, Rhode Island newspaper]

Federal Way Mirror [Washington newspaper]

Fennimore Times [Wisconsin newspaper]

Field & Stream [magazine]

Finance and Commerce [Minneapolis, Minnesota newspaper]

Financial Times [New York City newspaper]

Finger Lakes Times [Geneva, New York newspaper]

First for Women [magazine]

Fitness [magazine]

Flare, The [Kilgore, Texas newspaper]

Flint Journal [Michigan newspaper]

Floral Park Dispatch [New York newspaper]

Florence Times Daily [Alabama newspaper]

Florida Keys Keynoter [Marathon Key, Florida newspaper]

Florida Times-Union [Jacksonville, Florida newspaper]

Florida Today [Melbourne, Florida newspaper]

Floyd County Times [Prestonsburg, Kentucky newspaper]

Floyd Press [Virginia newspaper]

Focus News [Columbia Heights, Minnesota newspaper]

Focus on the News [DeSoto, Texas newspaper]

Folio Weekly [Jacksonville, Florida newspaper]

Folsom Telegraph [California newspaper]

Fontana Herald News [California newspaper]

Food Network [network]

Foothills Sentinel [Cave Creek, Arkansas newspaper]

Forest City, The [Pennsylvania newspaper]

Forest Lake Times [Minnesota newspaper]

Forest Leaves [River Forest, Illinois newspaper]

Forest-Blade, The [Swainsboro, Georgia newspaper]

Forsyth County News, The [Cumming, Georgia newspaper]

Fort Bragg Advocate-Dispatch [California newspaper]

Fort Dodge Messenger [Iowa newspaper]

Fort Gibson Times [Oklahoma newspaper]

Fort Lauderdale Sun-Sentinel [Florida newspaper]

Fort Madison Daily Democrat [Iowa newspaper]

Fort Morgan Times [Colorado newspaper]

Fort Payne Times-Journal [Alabama newspaper]

Fort Pierce News [Florida newspaper]

Fort Worth Business Press [Texas newspaper]

Fort Worth Star-Telegram [Texas newspaper]

Forum, The [Fargo, North Dakota newspaper]

Forward Times [Houston, Texas newspaper]

Fosters Daily Democrat [Dover, New Hampshire newspaper]

Four Corners Business Journal [Colorado newspaper]

Fox Family Channel [network]

Fox News [network]

Fox Point/Bayside/River Hills Herald [New Berlin, Wisconsin newspaper]

Fox Sports [network]

Fox Television [network]

Fox Valley Press [Plainsfield, Illinois newspaper]

Foxboro Reporter [Massachusetts newspaper]

Frankfort Times [Indiana newspaper]

Franklin Banner-Tribune, The [Louisiana newspaper]

Franklin County Times [Russellville, Alabama newspaper]

Franklin Favorite [Kentucky newspaper]

Franklin Hub [New Berlin, Wisconsin newspaper]

Franklin Park Herald-Journal [Illinois newspaper]

Franklin Press, The [North Carolina newspaper]

Franklin Review Appeal [Tennessee newspaper]

Frazee Forum [Minnesota newspaper]

Frederick News-Post [Maryland newspaper]

Fredericksburg Standard [Texas newspaper]

Free Lance, The [Hollister, California newspaper]

Free Lance-Star, The [Fredericksburg, Virginia newspaper]

Free Press and Times, The [Chattanooga, Tennessee newspaper]

Free Press, The [Corning, Iowa newspaper]

Free Press, The [Kinston, North Carolina newspaper]

Free Press, The [Mankato, Minnesota newspaper]

Free Press, The [Rockland, Maine newspaper]

Free Times [Columbia, South Carolina newspaper]

Fremont Tribune [Fremont, Nebraska newspaper]

Fresno Bee, The [California newspaper]

Fresno Republican [California newspaper]

Frisco Enterprise [Texas newspaper]

FSView & The Florida Flambeau [Tallahassee, Florida newspaper]

Fulda Free Press [Minnesota newspaper]

Fulton County News, The [McConnellsburg, Pennsylvania newspaper]

Fulton Daily News [New York newspaper]

FX [network]

Gadsden Messenger [Alabama newspaper]

Gadsden Times [Alabama newspaper]

Gaffney Ledger, The [South Carolina newspaper]

Gainesville Daily Register [Texas newspaper]

Gainesville Sun [Florida newspaper]

Galesville Republican [Wisconsin newspaper]

Gallipolis Daily Tribune, The [Ohio newspaper]

Gallup Independent [New Mexico newspaper]

Galt Herald, The [California newspaper]

Galveston County Daily News [Texas newspaper]

Game Show Network [network]

Gaming Today [Las Vegas, Nevada newspaper]

Garden City Life [New York newspaper]

Garden City News [New York newspaper]

Garden City Observer [Michigan newspaper]

Garden City Telegram, The [Kansas newspaper]

Garden Island, The [Lihue, Hawaii newspaper]

Gaston Gazette, The [Gastonia, North Carolina newspaper]

Gaylord Herald Times [Michigan newspaper]

Gazette Newspapers [Gaithersburg, Maryland newspaper]

Gazette Newspapers [Long Beach, California newspaper]

Gazette Weekly, The [Levasy, Missouri newspaper]

Gazette, The [Cedar Rapids, Iowa newspaper]

Gazette, The [Colorado Springs, Colorado newspaper]

Gazette, The [Pittston, Pennsylvania newspaper]

Gazette, The [Virginia newspaper]

Gazette-Democrat [Anna, Illinois newspaper]

Gazette-Enterprise, The [Seguin, Texas newspaper]

Gazette-Journal [Reno, Nevada newspaper]

Gazette-Times [Corvallis, Oregon newspaper]

Geneseo Republic [Illinois newspaper]

Genesse County Express [Dansville, New York newspaper]

Georgetown News Democrat, The [Ohio newspaper]

Georgetown News Graphic [Kentucky newspaper]

Georgetown Town Online [Massachusetts website]

Georgia Guardian [Savannah, Georgia newspaper]

Germantown Banner-Press [Wisconsin newspaper]

Germantown News [Tennessee newspaper]

Gettysburg Times [Pennsylvania newspaper]

Gilmer Mirror [Texas newspaper]

Glades County Democrat [Moore Haven, Florida newspaper]

Gladstone Sun-News [Missouri newspaper]

Gladwin County Record [Michigan newspaper]

Glamour [magazine]

Glasgow Daily Times [Kentucky newspaper]

Gleaner Online [Kentucky newspaper]

Glen Cove Record-Pilot [New York newspaper]

Glen News [Glen Ellyn, Illinois newspaper]

Glencoe News [Illinois newspaper]

Glendale Herald [New Berlin, Wisconsin newspaper]

Glendale News-Press [California newspaper]

Glennville Sentinel [Georgia newspaper]

Glenwood Post Online [Glenwood Springs, Colorado newspaper]

GlenwoodNet [Iowa newspaper]

Globe-Gazette [Mason City, Iowa newspaper]

Gloucester County Times [Woodbury, New Jersey newspaper]

Gloucester Daily Times [Massachusetts newspaper]

Gloversville Leader-Herald, The [New York newspaper]

Goffstown News [New Hampshire newspaper]

Gold Coast Gazette [New York newspaper]

Golden Valley Enterprise [Kingman, Arizona newspaper]

Goldsboro News-Argus, The [North Carolina newspaper]

Golf Channel [network]

Golf Digest [magazine]

Golf Magazine

Goochland Gazette [Virginia newspaper]

Good Housekeeping [magazine]

Good Times [Santa Cruz, California newspaper]

Gooding County Leader [Idaho newspaper]

Goodland Daily News [Kansas newspaper]

Gorge News [Columbia Gorge, Washington newspaper]

Goshen News, The [Indiana newspaper]

Gotham Gazette [New York, New York newspaper]

Gourmet [magazine]

Grand Canyon News [Arizona newspaper]

Grand Forks Herald [North Dakota newspaper]

Grand Forks Herald [Minnesota newspaper]

Grand Forks Herald [North Dakota newspaper]

Grand Haven Tribune, The [Michigan newspaper]

Grand Island Independent [Nebraska newspaper]

Grand Rapids News [Michigan newspaper]

Grand Rapids Press [Michigan newspaper]

Grand Traverse Herald [Traverse City, Michigan newspaper]

Granite Bay View [California newspaper]

Granite State News [New Hampshire newspaper]

Grant County Herald [Minnesota newspaper]

Grant County Herald Independent [Lancaster, Wisconsin newspaper]

Grant County News [Elgin, North Dakota newspaper]

Grant County News [Hyannis, Nebraska newspaper]

Grant County Online [Kentucky newspaper]

Grant County Press [Petersburg, West Virginia newspaper]

Grass Valley Union [California newspaper]

Gray News, The [Maine newspaper]

Grayslake Review [Illinois newspaper]

Grayson County News Gazette [Leitchfield, Kentucky newspaper]

Great Bend Tribune [Kansas newspaper]

Great Neck Record [New York newspaper]

Greater Baton Rouge [Louisiana newspaper]

Greater Tulsa Reporter Newspapers [Oklahoma newspaper]

Greeley Tribune [Colorado newspaper]

Green Bay News [Wisconsin newspaper]

Green Bay News-Chronicle [Wisconsin newspaper]

Green Bay Press-Gazette [Wisconsin newspaper]

Green County Messenger [Waynesburg, Pennsylvania newspaper]

Greendale Village Life [New Berlin, Wisconsin newspaper]

Greene County Record [Stanardsville, Virginia newspaper]

Greeneville Sun, The [Tennessee newspaper]

Greenfield Observer [New Berlin, Wisconsin newspaper]

Greensburg Record-Herald [Kentucky newspaper]

Greenville Advocate [Alabama newspaper]

Greenville Herald Banner [Texas newspaper]

Greenville News, The [South Carolina newspaper]

Greenville Sun [Tennessee newspaper]

Greenwich Time [Connecticut newspaper]

Greenwood Commonwealth [Mississippi newspaper]

Greenwood Lake and West Milford News [New York newspaper]

Gresham Outlook [Oregon newspaper]

Gridley Herald, The [California newspaper]

Griffin Daily News [Georgia newspaper]

Grosse Pointe News [Michigan newspaper]

Groton Independent [South Dakota newspaper]

Grove Sun [Oklahoma newspaper]

Grove Sun Daily [Oklahoma newspaper]

Groveton News [Texas newspaper]

Grundy County Herald [Tracy City, Tennessee newspaper]

GSA Business Journal [Greenville, South Carolina newspaper]

Guernsey Gazette [Wyoming newspaper]

Gulf Herald [Pensacola, Florida newspaper]

Gunnison Country Times [Colorado newspaper]

Gurdon Times, The [Arkansas newspaper]

Gurnee Review [Illinois newspaper]

Gwinnett Daily Post [Lawrenceville, Georgia newspaper]

Haight-Ashbury Free Press [San Francisco, California newspaper]

Haleakala Times [Makawao, Hawaii newspaper]

Hales Corners Village Hub [New Berlin, Wisconsin newspaper]

Half Moon Bay Review [California newspaper]

Hamburg Item, The [Pennsylvania newspaper]

Hamilton Advocate [Missouri newspaper]

Hamilton Herald-News [Texas newspaper]

Hamilton Town Online [Massachusetts website]

Hamlin Hearld [Brockport, New York newspaper]

Hammonton Gazette, The [New Jersey newspaper]

Hampshire Review [Romney, West Virginia newspaper]

Hancock Clarion, The [Hawesville, Kentucky newspaper]

Hancock County Journal-Pilot [Carthage, Illinois newspaper]

Hannibal Courier-Post [Missouri newspaper]

Hanover Herald-Progress [Ashland, Virginia newspaper]

Harbor Watch [Burlington, Vermont newspaper]

Hardin County Independent [Elizabethtown, Kentucky newspaper]

Hardin County Index [Eldora, Iowa newspaper]

Harlan Newspapers [Harlan, Iowa newspaper]

Harlan Tribune [Iowa newspaper]

Harrison Daily Times [Arkansas newspaper]

Harrodsburg Herald [Kentucky newspaper]

Hartford Advocate [Connecticut newspaper]

Hartford Business Journal [Connecticut newspaper]

Hartford Courant [Connecticut newspaper]

Hartford News [Connecticut newspaper]

Hartselle Enquirer [Alabama newspaper]

Harvard Post, The [Massachusetts newspaper]

Hastings Tribune [Nebraska newspaper]

Havelock News [North Carolina newspaper]

Haverhill Gazette [Massachusetts newspaper]

Havre Daily News, The [Montana newspaper]

Hawaii NewsList [Hawaii newspaper]

Hawaii Tribune-Herald [Hilo, Hawaii newspaper]

Hawaiian Hard Drive [Honolulu, Hawaii newspaper]

Hawk Eye, The [Burlington, Iowa newspaper]

Haxtun-Fleming Herald [Colorado newspaper]

Hays Daily News, The [Kansas newspaper]

Hazen Star, The [North Dakota newspaper]

HBO [network]

Headlight-Herald [Tillamook, Oregon newspaper]

Health [magazine]

Hebron Herald [North Dakota newspaper]

Helena Independent Record [Montana newspaper]

Hemet News [San Jacinto, California newspaper]

Henderson Hall News [Arlington Station, Virginia newspaper]

Henderson Home News [Nevada newspaper]

Henry County Local [New Castle, Kentucky newspaper]

Henry County Standard [Paris, Tennessee newspaper]

Henry Herald, The [McDonough, Georgia newspaper]

Henryetta Daily Free-Lance [Oklahoma newspaper]

Herald & Review [Decatur, Illinois newspaper]

Herald [Rock Hill, South Carolina newspaper]

Herald and News [Klamath Falls, Oregon newspaper]

Herald and Ruralite [Sylva, North Carolina newspaper]

Herald Bulletin, The [Madison County, Indiana newspaper]

Herald Community Newspapers [Lawrence, New York newspaper]

Herald Courier, The [Bristol, Virginia newspaper]

Herald Democrat, The [Sherman, Texas newspaper]

Herald Journal, The [Logan, Utah newspaper]

Herald Leader, The [Fitzgerald, Georgia newspaper]

Herald Ledger [Eddyville, Kentucky newspaper]

Herald News [Joliet, Illinois newspaper]

Herald News, The [Fall River, Massachusetts newspaper]

Herald Review [Grand Rapids, Minnesota newspaper]

Herald Times Reporter [Manitowoc, Wisconsin newspaper]

Herald Tribune [Pasadena, California newspaper]

Herald, The [Circleville, Ohio newspaper]

Herald, The [Everett, Washington newspaper]

Herald, The [Metamora, Illinois newspaper]

Herald, The [New Britain, Connecticut newspaper]

Herald, The [Rock Hill, South Carolina newspaper]

Herald, The [Sharon, Pennsylvania newspaper]

Herald, The [Truth or Consequences, New Mexico newspaper]

Herald, The [Westchester, Illinois newspaper]

Herald-Advocate [Park Ridge, Illinois newspaper]

Herald-Chronicle, The [Winchester, Tennessee newspaper]

Herald-Citizen, The [Cookeville, Tennessee newspaper]

Herald-Coaster, The [Rosenberg, Texas newspaper]

Herald-Dispatch, The [Huntington, West Virginia newspaper]

Herald-Gazette, The [Barnesville, Georgia newspaper]

Herald-Journal [Spartanburg, South Carolina newspaper]

Herald-Leader, The [Siloam Springs, Arkansas newspaper]

Herald-Mail, The [Hagerstown, Maryland newspaper]

Herald-News, The [Dayton, Tennessee newspaper]

Herald-News, The [Joliet, Illinois newspaper]

Herald-News, The [Wolf Point, Montana newspaper]

Herald-Palladium [St. Joseph, Michigan newspaper]

Herald-Press [Palestine, Texas newspaper]

Herald-Press, The [Harvey, North Dakota newspaper]

Herald-Spectator [Niles, Illinois newspaper]

Herald-Standard [Uniontown, Pennsylvania newspaper]

Herald-Star, The [Steubenville, Ohio newspaper]

Herald-Sun, The [Durham, North Carolina newspaper]

Herald-Times [Bloomington, Indiana newspaper]

Herald-Zeitung [New Braunfels, Texas newspaper]

Hermiston Herald, The [Oregon newspaper]

Hermit's Peak Gazette [Las Vegas, New Mexico newspaper]

Hernando Today [Brooksville, Florida newspaper]

Hi Desert Star [Yucca Valley, California newspaper]

Hibbing Daily Tribune [Minnesota newspaper]

Hickory Daily Record [North Carolina newspaper]

Hicksville Illustrated News [New York newspaper]

High Country Independent Press [Belgrade, Montana newspaper]

High Country News [Paonia, Colorado newspaper]

High Plains Journal [Dodge City, Kansas newspaper]

High Point Enterprise [North Carolina newspaper]

Highland Park News [Illinois newspaper]

Highlander, The [Highlands, North Carolina newspaper]

Highlander, The [Marble Falls, Texas newspaper]

Hillsboro Free Press [Kansas newspaper]

Hillsboro Star Journal [Kansas newspaper]

Hilltop Times [Hill AFB, Utah newspaper]

Hip Fish [Astoria, Oregon newspaper]

Hippo Press [Nashua, New Hampshire newspaper]

History Channel [network]

History Channel International [network]

Hobart Gazette News [Indiana newspaper]

Hobbs News-Sun [New Mexico newspaper]

Holland Sentinel, The [Michigan newspaper]

Hollywood Reporter [California newspaper]

Holton Recorder [Kansas newspaper]

Home & Away [magazine]

Home & Garden Television [network]

Home [magazine]

Home News Tribune, The [East Brunswick, New Jersey newspaper]

Homer News [Alaska newspaper]

Hometown Publications [Moodus, Connecticut newspaper]

Honolulu Advertiser, The [Hawaii newspaper]

Honolulu Star-Bulletin [Hawaii newspaper]

Honolulu Weekly [Hawaii newspaper]

Hood County News [Granbury, Texas newspaper]

Hooker County Tribune [Mullen, Nebraska newspaper]

Hooksett Banner [New Hampshire newspaper]

Hoosier Times, The [Bloomington, Indiana newspaper]

Hope Star [Arkansas newspaper]

Houghton Lake Resorter [Michigan newspaper]

Hour, The [Norwalk, Connecticut newspaper]

Houston Business Journal [Texas newspaper]

Houston Chronicle [Texas newspaper]

Houston County News [La Crescent, Minnesota newspaper]

Houston Gazette, The [Texas newspaper]

Houston Press [Texas newspaper]

Howard Lake Herald [Minnesota newspaper]

Howe Enterprise [Texas newspaper]

Huber Heights Courier [Ohio newspaper]

Hudson Valley Business Journal [Pine Island, New York newspaper]

Hudson-Litchfield News [New Hampshire newspaper]

Hugo Daily News [Oklahoma newspaper]

Hugonian [Hugo, Minnesota newspaper]

Humboldt Independent, The [Iowa newspaper]

Hungry Horse News [Columbia Falls, Montana newspaper]

Hunterdon County Democrat [Flemington, New Jersey newspaper]

Huntington Beach News [California newspaper]

Huntington Herald-Press, The [Indiana newspaper]

Huntsville Item, The [Texas newspaper]

Huron Daily Tribune [Michigan newspaper]

Hutchinson Leader [Minnesota newspaper]

Hutchinson News, The [Kansas newspaper]

Hyde Park Herald [Chicago, Illinois newspaper]

Ida County Courier-Reminder [Ida Grove, Iowa newspaper]

Idaho Falls Post Register [Idaho newspaper]

Idaho Mountain Express and Guide [Sun Valley, Idaho newspaper]

Idaho Press Tribune [Nampa, Idaho newspaper]

Idaho State Journal, The [Pocatello, Idaho newspaper]

Idaho Statesman, The [Boise, Idaho news-paper]

Idaho World, The [Garden City, Idaho newspaper]

Idyllwild Town Crier [California newspaper]

Ile Camera, The [Grosse Ile, Michigan newspaper]

In Style [magazine]

Independent [Colorado Springs, Colorado newspaper]

Independent [Gallup, New Mexico newspaper]

Independent [Huntington Beach, California newspaper]

Independent [Marshall, Minnesota newspaper]

Independent Film Channel [network]

Independent Florida Alligator, The [Gainesville, Florida newspaper]

Independent News Herald [Clarissa, Minnesota newspaper]

Independent Press, The [Bloomfield, New Jersey newspaper]

Independent Record [Helena, Montana newspaper]

Independent Register [Brodhead, Wisconsin newspaper]

Independent Tribune [Concord, North Carolina newspaper]

Independent Voice [Dixon, California newspaper]

Independent, The [Dundee, Michigan newspaper]

Independent, The [East Hampton, New York newspaper]

Independent, The [Hillsdale, New York newspaper]

Independent, The [Livermore, California newspaper]

Independent, The [Lyndonville, Vermont newspaper]

Independent, The [Massillon, Ohio newspaper]

Independent-Messenger [Emporia, Virginia newspaper]

Index-Journal, The [Greenwood, South Carolina newspaper]

Indian Country Today [South Dakota newspaper]

Indiana Gazette, The [Pennsylvania newspaper]

Indianapolis Recorder [Indiana newspaper]

Indianapolis Star [Indiana newspaper]

Inkster Ledger Star [Michigan newspaper]

Inland Valley Daily Bulletin [Ontario, California newspaper]

Inquirer and Mirror, The [Nantucket, Massachusetts newspaper]

Inside Business [Richmond, Virginia newspaper]

Inside Online [Chicago, Illinois website]

Insider Business Journal [Brighton, Michigan newspaper]

Intelligencer [Stonington, Connecticut newspaper]

Intelligencer, The [Doylestown, Pennsylvania newspaper]

Intelligencer, The [Wheeling, West Virginia newspaper]

Inter-County Leader, The [Frederic, Wisconsin newspaper]

Inter-Mountain, The [Elkins, West Virginia newspaper]

International Channel [network]

InterTown Record [North Sutton, New Hampshire newspaper]

Investor's Business Daily [Los Angeles, California newspaper]

Iola Register [Iola, Kansas newspaper]

Iowa Falls Times-Citizen [Iowa newspaper]

Iowa State Daily [Ames, Iowa newspaper]

Ipswich Town Online [Massachusetts website]

Ironton Tribune, The [Ironton, Ohio newspaper]

Irvington Herald [Maplewood, New Jersey newspaper]

Island Gazette [Carolina Beach, North Carolina newspaper]

Island News [Key West, Florida newspaper]

Island Packet [Hilton Head, South Carolina newspaper]

Island Packet Item [Sumter, South Carolina newspaper]

Island Park News [Idaho newspaper]

Island Reporter, The [Sanibel, Florida newspaper]

Islander News, The [Key Biscayne, Florida newspaper]

Islands' Sounder, The [Friday Harbor, Washington newspaper]

Isthmus [Madison, Wisconsin newspaper]

Itasca News [Minnesota newspaper]

Item, The [Sumter, South Carolina newspaper]

Ithaca Journal [New York newspaper]

Ithaca Times [New York newspaper]

Ivanhoe Times [Minnesota newspaper]

Jackson Citizen Patriot [Michigan newspaper]

Jackson County Herald-Tribune [Edna, Texas newspaper]

Jackson County Pilot [Minnesota newspaper]

Jackson Herald, The [Georgia newspaper]

Jackson Hole Guide [Wyoming newspaper]

Jackson Hole News [Wyoming newspaper]

Jackson Independent [Louisiana newspaper]

Jackson News [Michigan newspaper]

Jackson Progressive [Mississippi newspaper]

Jackson Sun, The [Tennessee newspaper]

Jacksonville Business Journal [Florida newspaper]

Jacksonville Daily News [North Carolina newspaper]

Jacksonville Daily Progress, The [Texas newspaper]

Jacksonville News [Alabama newspaper]

Jacksonville Patriot [Arkansas newspaper]

Jamestown News [North Carolina newspaper]

Jamestown Sun, The [North Dakota newspaper]

Janesville Gazette, The [Wisconsin newspaper]

Jasper Mountain Eagle [Alabama newspaper]

Jefferson City News Tribune [Missouri newspaper]

Jefferson Post [West Jefferson, North Carolina newspaper]

Jenks Gazette [Oklahoma newspaper]

Jet [magazine]

Jewish Advocate, The [Boston, Massachusetts newspaper]

Jewish Bulletin of Northern California [San Francisco, California newspaper]

Jewish News of Greater Phoenix [Arizona newspaper]

Johnson City Record Courier [Texas newspaper]

Johnson Journal, The [Johnson County, Georgia newspaper]

Jones County News, The [Gray, Georgia newspaper]

Jonesboro Sun, The [Arkansas newspaper]

Joplin Globe, The [Missouri newspaper]

Jordan Independent [Minnesota newspaper]

Journal & Topics Newspapers [Des Plaine, Illinois newspaper]

Journal and Courier [Lafayette, Indiana newspaper]

Journal Gazette [Indiana newspaper]

Journal Gazette, The [Ft. Wayne, Indiana newspaper]

Journal Inquirer [Manchester, Connecticut newspaper]

Journal News, The [White Plains, New York newspaper]

Journal Newspapers Online [Fairfax, Virginia website]

Journal Opinion [Bradford, Vermont newspaper]

Journal Press [King George, Virginia newspaper]

Journal Record, The [Oklahoma City, Oklahoma newspaper]

Journal Review [Crawfordsville, Indiana newspaper]

Journal Star [Peoria, Illinois newspaper]

Journal Times, The [Racine, Wisconsin newspaper]

Journal Tribune [Biddeford, Maine newspaper]

Journal, The [Martinsburg, West Virginia newspaper]

Journal, The [New Ulm, Minnesota newspaper]

Journal, The [Scotia, New York newspaper]

Journal-Advocate [Sterling, Colorado newspaper]

Journal-Enterprise, The [Providence, Kentucky newspaper]

Journal-News, The [Hamilton, Ohio newspaper]

Journal-Register, The [Medina, New York newspaper]

Journal-Standard, The [Freeport, Illinois newspaper]

Junction Eagle [Texas newspaper]

Juneau Empire [Alaska newspaper]

Juno Beach Online [Florida website]

Jupiter Courier [Florida newspaper]

Ka Leo O Hawaii [Honolulu, Hawaii newspaper]

KAAL [06 Austin, Minnesota]

KABB [29 San Antonio, Texas]

KABC [07 Los Angeles, California]

KACV [02 Amarillo, Texas]

KADN [15 Lafayette, Louisiana]

KADY [63 Oxnard, California]

KAEF [23 Eureka, California]

KAET [08 Tempe, Arizona]

KAFT [13 Fayetteville, Arkansas]

KAID [04 Boise, Idaho]

KAIT [08 Jonesboro, Arkansas]

KAKE [10 Wichita, Kansas]

KAKM [07 Anchorage, Alaska]

Kalamazoo Gazette [Michigan newspaper]

Kalamazoo News [Michigan newspaper]

KALB [05 Alexandria, Louisiana]

Kalkaskian, The [Michigan newspaper]

Kalona News, The [Iowa newspaper]

KAMC [28 Lubbock, Texas]
KAMR [04 Amarillo, Texas]
KAMU [15 College Station, Texas]
Kanabec Times [Minnesota newspaper]
Kane County Chronicle [Geneva, Illinois
  newspaper]
Kanoe [Ketchikan, Alaska newspaper]
Kansas City Business Journal [Missouri
  newspaper]
Kansas City Kansan, The [Kansas City, Kansas
  newspaper]
Kansas City Star [Missouri newspaper]
KAPP [35 Yakima, Washington]
KAQY [11 Monroe, Louisiana]
KARD [14 West Monroe, Louisiana]
KARE [11 Minneapolis, Minnesota]
KARK [04 Little Rock, Arkansas]
KASA [02 Albuquerque, New Mexico]
KASN [38 Little Rock, Arkansas]
KASW [61 Phoenix, Arizona]
KATC [03 Lafayette, Louisiana]
KATN [02 Fairbanks, Alaska]
KATU [02 Portland, Oregon]
KATV [07 Little Rock, Arkansas]
Katy Times [Texas newspaper]
KAUZ [06 Wichita Falls, Texas]
KAVU [25 Victoria, Texas]
KAWB [22 Brainerd, Minnesota]
KAWE [09 Bemidji, Minnesota]
KBCI [02 Boise, Idaho]
KBDI [12 Denver, Colorado]
KBFD [32 Honolulu, Hawaii]
KBHE [09 Rapid City, South Dakota]
KBHK [44 San Francisco, California]
KBI [30 San Francisco, California]
KBIM [06 Roswell, New Mexico]
KBIN [32 Council Bluffs, Iowa]
KBJR [06 Duluth, Minnesota]
KBME [03 Bismarck, North Dakota]
KBMT [12 Beaumont, Texas]
KBNT [19 San Diego, California]
KBSI [23 Cape Girardeau, Missouri]
KBTX [03 Bryan, Texas]

KBYU [11 Provo, Utah]
KCAL [09 Los Angeles, California]
KCBA [35 Salinas, California]
KCBD [11 Lubbock, Texas]
KCBS [02 Los Angeles, California]
KCBY [11 Coos Bay, Oregon]
KCCI [08 Des Moines, Iowa]
KCCO [07 Alexandria, Minnesota]
KCCW [12 Alexandria, Minnesota]
KCDT [26 Coeur d'Ale, Idaho]
KCEC [50 Denver, Colorado]
KCEN [06 Temple, Texas]
KCET [28 Los Angeles, California]
KCFW [09 Kalispell, Montana]
KCNC [04 Denver, Colorado]
KCNG [25 Las Vegas, Nevada]
KCOP [13 Los Angeles, California]
KCOS [13 El Paso, Texas]
KCPQ [13 Tacoma, Washington]
KCPT [19 Kansas City, Missouri]
KCRA [03 Sacramento, California]
KCRG [09 Cedar Rapids, Iowa]
KCSD [23 Sioux Falls, South Dakota]
KCSM [60 San Mateo, California]
KCTF [34 Waco, Texas]
KCTS [09 Seattle, Washington]
KCTU [55 Wichita, Kansas]
KCTV [05 Kansas City, Missouri]
KCTZ [07 Bozeman, Montana]
KCVU [30 Chico, California]
KCWC [04 Riverton, Wyoming]
KDAF [33 Dallas, Texas]
KDBC [04 El Paso, Texas]
KDEB [27 Springfield, Missouri]
KDFW [04 Dallas, Texas]
KDIN [11 Des Moines, Iowa]
KDKA [02 Pittsburgh, Pennsylvania]
KDKF [31 Klamath Falls, Oregon]
KDLH [03 Duluth, Minnesota]
KDLT [05 Sioux Falls, South Dakota]
KDRV [12 Medford, Oregon]
KDSD [16 Aberdeen, South Dakota]
KDSE [09 Dickinson, North Dakota]

KDSM [17 Des Moines, Iowa]
KDTN [02 Dallas, Texas]
KDVR [31 Denver, Colorado]
Ke Alaka'i [Laie, Hawaii newspaper]
Kearney Daily Hub [Nebraska newspaper]
Kearney Hub [Nebraska newspaper]
KECI [13 Missoula, Montana]
KEDT [16 Corpus Christi, Texas]
Keene Sentinel [New Hampshire
  newspaper]
KEET [13 Eureka, California]
Keith County News [Ogallala, Nebraska
  newspaper]
Keizertimes [Keizer, Oregon newspaper]
KELO [11 Sioux Falls, South Dakota]
KEMV [06 Mountain View, Arkansas]
Kenmare News [North Dakota newspaper]
Kennebec Business Monthly [Augusta, Maine
  newspaper]
Kennebec Journal, The [Augusta, Maine
  newspaper]
Kennebunk Electronic Town Crier [Maine
  website]
Kennett Paper, The [Pennsylvania
  newspaper]
Kenosa News, The [Wisconsin newspaper]
KENS [05 San Antonio, Texas]
Kent County Daily Times, The [West
  Warwick, Rhode Island newspaper]
Kent Good Times Dispatch [Kent, Connecticut
  newspaper]
Kentucky Kernel [Lexington, Kentucky
  newspaper]
Kentucky New Era [Hopkinsville, Kentucky
  newspaper]
Kentucky Post, The Kentucky newspaper]
Kentucky Standard [Bardstown, Kentucky
  newspaper]
KENV [10 Elko, Nevada]
KENW [03 Portales, New Mexico]
Keokuk Daily Gate City [Iowa newspaper]
KEPR [19 Pasco, Washington]
KERA [13 Dallas, Texas]

Kern Valley Sun [Lake Isabella, California
  newspaper]
KERO [23 Bakersfield, California]
Kerrville Daily Times [Texas newspaper]
KESD [08 Brookings, South Dakota]
KESQ [03 Palm Springs, California]
KETA [13 Oklahoma City, Oklahoma]
KETC [09 St. Louis, Missouri]
Ketchikan Daily News [Alaska newspaper]
KETG [09 Arkadelphia, Arkansas]
KETK [56 Tyler, Texas]
KETS [02 Conway, Arkansas]
KETV [07 Omaha, Nebraska]
KEVN [07 Rapid City, South Dakota]
Kewaunee Enterprise [Algoma, Wisconsin
  newspaper]
Key West Citizen [Florida newspaper]
KEYC [12 Mankato, Minnesota]
KEYE [42 Austin, Texas]
KEYT [03 Santa Barbara, California]
KEZI [09 Eugene, Oregon]
KFAA [51 Rogers, Arkansas]
KFBB [05 Great Falls, Montana]
KFBT [33 Las Vegas, Nevada]
KFDA [10 Amarillo, Texas]
KFDM [06 Beaumont, Texas]
KFDX [03 Wichita Falls, Texas]
KFMB [08 San Diego, California]
KFME [13 Fargo, North Dakota]
KFOR [04 Oklahoma City, Oklahoma]
KFOX [14 El Paso, Texas]
KFSM [05 Fort Smith, Arkansas]
KFSN [30 Fresno, California]
KFTL [64 San Leandro, California]
KFTS [22 Medford, Oregon]
KFTY [50 Santa Rosa, California]
KFVS [12 Cape Girardeau, Missouri]
KFXF [07 Fairbanks, Alaska]
KFXK [51 Longview, Texas]
KFXO [39 Bend, Oregon]
KFYR [05 Bismarck, North Dakota]
KGAN [02 Cedar Rapids, Iowa]
KGBS [65 Austin, Texas]

KGBT [04 Harlingen, Texas]
KGEC [26 Redding, California]
KGET [17 Bakersfield, California]
KGIN [11 Grand Island, Nebraska]
KGMB [09 Honolulu, Hawaii]
KGO [07 San Francisco, California]
KGTV [10 San Diego, California]
KGUN [09 Tucson, Arizona]
KGW [08 Portland, Oregon]
KGWN [05 Cheyenne, Wyoming]
KHBS [40 Fort Smith, Arkansas]
KHET [11 Honolulu, Hawaii]
KHIN [36 Red Oak, Iowa]
KHNE [29 Hastings, Nebraska]
KHNL [08 Honolulu, Hawaii]
KHOG [29 Fayetteville, Arkansas]
KHON [02 Honolulu, Hawaii]
KHOU [11 Houston, Texas]
KHQ [06 Spokane, Washington]
KHQA [07 Quincy, Illinois]
KHSL [12 Chico, California]
KHTV [39 Houston, Texas]
KICU [36 San Jose, California]
KIDK [03 Idaho Falls, Idaho]
KIDZ [54 Abilene, Texas]
KIEM [03 Eureka, California]
KIFI [08 Idaho Falls, Idaho]
KIII [03 Corpus Christi, Texas]
KIIN [12 Iowa City, Iowa]
KIKU [20 Honolulu, Hawaii]
Kilgore News Herald, The [Texas newspaper]
Killeen Daily Herald, The [Texas newspaper]
KIMA [29 Yakima, Washington]
KIMO [13 Anchorage, Alaska]
KIMT [03 Mason City, Iowa]v
KINC [15 Las Vegas, Nevada]
KING [05 Seattle, Washington]
King City Rustler [California newspaper]
King Times [North Carolina newspaper]
Kingfisher Times & Free Press, The
  [Oklahoma newspaper]
Kingman Daily Miner [Arizona newspaper]
Kingsburg Recorder [California newspaper]

Kingsport Times-News, The [Tennessee
  newspaper]
Kinston Free Press [North Carolina
  newspaper]
KINT [26 El Paso, Texas]
KION [46 Salinas, California]
Kiowa County Press [Eads, Colorado
  newspaper]
Kiplinger's Personal Finance Magazine
  [magazine]
KIPT [13 Twin Falls, Idaho]
Kirksville Daily Express & News
  [Missouri newspaper]
KIRO [07 Seattle, Washington]
KISU [10 Pocatello, Idaho]
KITU [34 Beaumont, Texas]
KITV [04 Honolulu, Hawaii]
KIXE [09 Redding, California]
KJCT [08 Grand Junction, Colorado]
KJEO [47 Fresno, California]
KJNP [04 North Pole, Alaska]
KJRH [02 Tulsa, Oakahoma]
KJTL [18 Wichita Falls, Texas]
KJUD [08 Juneau, Alaska]
KJZZ [14 Salt Lake City, Utah]
KKCO [11 Grand Junction, Colorado]
KKTV [11 Colorado Springs, Colorado]
KKWB [65 El Paso, Texas]
KKYK [09 Little Rock, Arkansas]
KLAF [62 Lafayette, Louisiana]
KLAS [08 Las Vegas, Nevada]
KLAX [31 Alexandria, Louisiana]
KLBK [13 Lubbock, Texas]
KLCS [58 Los Angeles, California]
KLDO [27 Laredo, Texas]
KLEW [03 Lewiston, Idaho]
KLGT [23 St. Paul, Minnesota]
KLJB [18 Davenport, Iowa]
KLPA [25 Alexandria, Louisiana]
KLPB [24 Lafayette, Louisiana]
KLRN [09 San Antonio, Texas]
KLRT [16 Little Rock, Arkansas]
KLRU [18 Austin, Texas]

KLSB [19 Nacogdoches, Texas]
KLST [08 San Angelo, Texas]
KLTJ [22 Houston, Texas]
KLTL [18 Lake Charles, Louisiana]
KLTM [13 Monroe, Louisiana]
KLTS [24 Shreveport, Louisiana]
KLTV [07 Tyler, Texas]
KLVX [10 Las Vegas, Nevada]
KMAX [31 Sacramento, California]
KMBC [09 Kansas City, Missouri]
KMBH [60 Harlingen, Texas]
KMCI [38 Lawrence, Kansas]
KMEB [10 Wailuku, Hawaii]
KMEG [14 Sioux City, Iowa]
KMEX [34 Los Angeles, California]
KMGH [07 Denver, Colorado]
KMID [02 Midland, Texas]
KMIR [06 Palm Springs, California]
KMIZ [17 Columbia, Missouri]
KMOL [04 San Antonio, Texas]
KMOS [06 Warrensburg, Missouri]
KMOT [10 Minot, North Dakota]
KMOV [04 St. Louis, Missouri]
KMSB [11 Tucson, Arizona]
KMSP [09 Eden Prairie, Minnesota]
KMSS [33 Shreveport, Louisiana]
KMTR [16 Springfield, Oregon]
KMTV [03 Omaha, Nebraska]
KMVT [11 Twin Falls, Idaho]
KMXT [09 Kodiak, Alaska]
KNBC [04 Los Angeles, California]
KNBN [24 Rapid City, South Dakota]
KNCT [46 Killeen, Texas]
KNIN [09 Boise, Idaho]
KNME [05 Albuquerque, New Mexico]
KNOE [08 Monroe, Louisiana]
Knoxville News [Tennessee newspaper]
KNPB [05 Reno, Nevada]
KNSD [39 San Diego, California]
KNTV [11 San Jose, California]
KNVA [54 Austin, Texas]
KNVN [24 Chico, California]
KNVO [48 McAllen, Texas]

KNXV [15 Phoenix, Arizona]
KOAA [05 Pueblo, Colorado]
KOAA [30 Pueblo, Colorado]
KOAB [03 Bend, Oregon]
KOAC [07 Corvallis, Oregon]
KOAM [07 Pittsburg, Kansas]
KOAT [07 Albuquerque, New Mexico]
KOB [04 Albuquerque, New Mexico]
KOBF [12 Farmington, New Mexico]
KOBI [05 Medford, Oregon]
KOCB [34 Oklahoma City, Oklahoma]
KOCE [50 Huntington Beach, California]
KOCO [05 Oklahoma City, Oklahoma]
KOCV [36 Odessa, Texas]
KODE [12 Joplin, Missouri]
Kodiak Daily Mirror [Alaska newspaper]
KOED [11 Tulsa, Oklahoma]
KOET [03 Eufaula, Oklahoma]
KOFY [20 San Francisco, California]
KOIN [06 Portland, Oregon]
KOKH [25 Oklahoma City, Oklahoma]
KOKI [23 Tulsa, Oklahoma]
Kokomo Tribune [Indiana newspaper]
KOLD [13 Tucson, Arizona]
KOLN [10 Lincoln, Nebraska]
KOLO [08 Reno, Nevada]
KOLR [10 Springfield, Missouri]
KOMO [04 Seattle, Washington]
KOMU [08 Columbia, Missouri]
KOOD [09 Bunker Hill, Kansas]
KOPB [10 Portland, Oregon]
KORO [28 Corpus Christi, Texas]
KOSA [07 Odessa, Texas]
KOTA [03 Rapid City, South Dakota]
KOTI [02 Klamath Falls, Oregon]
KOTV [06 Tulsa, Oklahoma]
KOVR [13 West Sacramento, California]
KOZK [21 Springfield, Missouri]
KPAL [38 Lancaster, California]
KPAX [08 Missoula, Montana]
KPBS [15 San Diego, California]
KPDX [49 Portland, Oregon]
KPEJ [24 Odessa, Texas]

KPHO [05 Phoenix, Arizona]
KPIC [04 Roseburg, Oregon]
KPIX [05 San Francisco, California]
KPLC [07 Lake Charles, Louisiana]
KPLR [11 St. Louis, Missouri]
KPNX [12 Phoenix, Arizona]
KPOM [24 Fort Smith, Arkansas]
KPRC [02 Houston, Texas]
KPSD [13 Eagle Butte, South Dakota]
KPTS [08 Wichita, Kansas]
KPTV [12 Portland, Oregon]
KQCA [58 Sacramento, California]
KQED [09 San Francisco, California]
KQSD [11 Lowry, South Dakota]
KQTV [02 Saint Joseph, Missouri]
KRBC [09 Abilene, Texas]
KRCB [22 Rohnert Park, California]
KRCG [13 Jefferson City, Missouri]
KRCR [07 Redding, California]
KREM [02 Spokane, Washington]
KREX [05 Grand Junction, Colorado]
KREZ [06 Durango, Colorado]
KRGV [05 Weslaco, Texas]
KRIN [32 Waterloo, Iowa]
KRIS [06 Corpus Christi, Texas]
KRMA [06 Denver, Colorado]
KRMJ [18 Grand Junction, Colorado]
KRMT [41 Arvada, Colorado]
KRNV [04 Reno, Nevada]
KRON [04 San Francisco, California]
KROZ [36 Roseburg, Oregon]
KRQE [13 Albuquerque, New Mexico]
KRRT [35 San Antonio, Texas]
KRTV [03 Great Falls, Montana]
KRVU [22 Redding, California]
KRWG [22 Las Cruces, New Mexico]
KSAS [24 Wichita, Kansas]
KSAX [42 Alexandria, Minnesota]
KSBI [52 Oklahoma City, Oklahoma]
KSBW [08 Salinas, California]
KSBY [06 San Luis Obispo, California]
KSCC [36 Wichita, Kansas]
KSDK [05 St. Louis, Missouri]

KSEE [24 Fresno, California]
KSFY [13 Sioux Falls, South Dakota]
KSHB [41 Kansas City, Missouri]
KSIN [27 Sioux City, Iowa]
KSL [05 Salt Lake City, Utah]
KSLA [12 Shreveport, Louisiana]
KSMQ [15 Austin, Minnesota]
KSMS [67 Monterey, California]
KSNC [02 Great Bend, Kansas]
KSNF [16 Joplin, Missouri]
KSNG [11 Garden City, Kansas]
KSNK [08 Oberlin, Kansas]
KSNT [27 Topeka, Kansas]
KSNW [03 Wichita, Kansas]
KSPR [33 Springfield, Missouri]
KSPS [07 Spokane, Washington]
KSTP [05 St. Paul, Minnesota]
KSTU [13 Salt Lake City, Utah]
KSTW [11 Tacoma, Washington]
KSWB [69 Chula Vista, California]
KSWK [03 Lakin, Kansas]
KSWO [07 Lawton, Oklahoma]
KSYS [08 Medford, Oregon]
KTAB [32 Abilene, Texas]
KTAL [06 Shreveport, Louisiana]
KTBC [07 Austin, Texas]
KTBS [03 Shreveport, Louisiana]
KTBY [04 Anchorage, Alaska]
KTCA [02 St. Paul, Minnesota]
KTDS [10 Pierre, South Dakota]
KTEH [54 San Jose, California]
KTEJ [19 Jonesboro, Arkansas]
KTEN [10 Denison, Texas]
KTFO [41 Tulsa, Oklahoma]
KTGF [16 Great , Montana]
KTIN [21 Fort Dodge, Iowa]
KTIV [04 Sioux City, Iowa]
KTKA [49 Topeka, Kansas]
KTLA [05 Los Angeles, California]
KTMD [48 Houston, Texas]
KTMF [23 Missoula, Montana]
KTMJ [06 Junction City, Kansas]
KTNL [13 Sitka, Alaska]

KTNV [13 Las Vegas, Nevada]
KTNW [31 Richland, Washington]
KTOO [03 Juneau, Alaska]
KTRE [09 Lufkin, Texas]
KTRK [13 Houston, Texas]
KTRV [12 Nampa, Idaho]
KTSC [08 Pueblo, Colorado]
KTSF [28 Brisbane, California]
KTSM [09 El Paso, Texas]
KTTC [10 Rochester, Minnesota]
KTTV [11 Los Angeles, California]
KTTW [17 Sioux Falls, South Dakota]
KTUL [08 Tulsa, Oklahoma]
KTUU [02 Anchorage, Alaska]
KTVA [11 Anchorage, Alaska]
KTVB [07 Boise, Idaho]
KTVC [36 Eugene, Oregon]
KTVE [10 Monroe, Louisiana]
KTVF [11 Fairbanks, Alaska]
KTVK [03 Phoenix, Arizona]
KTVL [10 Medford, Oregon]
KTVM [06 Butte, Montana]
KTVN [02 Reno, Nevada]
KTVO [03 Kirksville, Missouri]
KTVQ [02 Billings, Montana]
KTVT [11 Fort Worth, Texas]
KTVU [02 Oakland, California]
KTVX [04 Salt Lake City, Utah]
KTVZ [21 Bend, Oregon]
KTWB [22 Seattle, Washington]
KTWO [02 Casper, Wyoming]
KTWU [11 Topeka, Kansas]
KTXA [21 Dallas, Texas]
KTXH [20 Houston, Texas]
KTXL [40 Sacramento, California]
KTXS [12 Abilene, Texas]
KTXT [05 Lubbock, Texas]
KUAC [09 Fairbanks, Alaska]
KUAT [06 Tucson, Arizona]
KUED [07 Salt Lake City, Utah]
KUFM [11 Missoula, Montana]
KUHT [08 Houston, Texas]
KUID [12 Moscow, Idaho]

KULC [09 Salt Lake City, Utah]
KULR [08 Billings, Montana]
KUON [12 Lincoln, Nebraska]
KUSA [09 Denver, Colorado]
KUSD [02 Vermillion, South Dakota]
KUSK [07 Prescott, Arizona]
KUSM [09 Bozeman, Montana]
KUTP [45 Phoenix, Arizona]
KUTV [02 Salt Lake City, Utah]
KVAL [13 Eugene, Oregon]
KVBC [03 Las Vegas, Nevada]
KVC [13 Austin, Texas]
KVCR [24 San Bernardino, California]
KVDA [60 San Antonio, Texas]
KVEA [52 Glendale, California]
KVEO [23 Brownsville, Texas]
KVER [04 Palm Desert, California]
KVEW [42 Kennewick, Washington]
KVIA [07 El Paso, Texas]
KVIE [06 Sacramento, California]
KVII [07 Amarillo, Texas]
KVIQ [06 Eureka, California]
KVLY [11 Fargo, North Dakota]
KVOA [04 Tucson, Arizona]
KVPT [18 Fresno, California]
KVTV [13 Laredo, Texas]
KVUE [24 Austin, Texas]
KVVU [05 Henderson, Nevada]
KVYE [07 El Centro, California]
KWBA [58 Tucson, Arizona]
KWCH [12 Wichita, Kansas]
KWCM [10 Appleton, Minnesota]
KWES [09 Midland, Texas]
KWET [12 Cheyenne, Oklahoma]
KWGN [02 Englewood, Colorado]
KWHB [47 Tulsa, Oklahoma]
KWHD [53 Englewood, Colorado]
KWHE 14 [Honolulu, Hawaii]
KWHY [22 Los Angeles, California]
KWKT [44 Waco, Texas]
KWMJ [53 Tulsa, Oklahoma]
KWQC [06 Davenport, Iowa]
KWSU [10 Pullman, Washington]

KWTV [09 Oklahoma City, Oklahoma]
KWTX [10 Waco, Texas]
KWWL [07 Waterloo, Iowa]
KWYB [18 Butte, Montana]
KXAN [36 Austin, Texas]
KXAS [05 Fort Worth, Texas]
KXII [12 Sherman, Texas]
KXJB [04 Fargo, North Dakota]
KXLF [04 Butte, Montana]
KXLT [47 Rochester, Minnesota]
KXLY [04 Spokane, Washington]
KXMA [02 Dickinson, North Dakota]
KXMB [12 Bismarck, North Dakota]
KXMC [13 Minot, North Dakota]
KXMD [11 Williston, North Dakota]
KXRM [21 Colorado Springs, Colorado]
KXTV [10 Sacramento, California]
KXTX [39 Dallas, Texas]
KXXV [25 Waco, Texas]
KYES [05 Anchorage, Alaska]
KYIN [24 Mason City, Iowa]
KYOU [15 Ottumwa, Iowa]
KYTV [03 Springfield, Missouri]
KYVE [47 Yakima, Washington]
KYW [03 Philadelphia, Pennsylvania]
KZSD [08 Martin, South Dakota]
KZTV [10 Corpus Christi, Texas]
La Canada Valley Sun [California newspaper]
La Crosse Tribune Online [Wisconsin website]
La Junta Tribune-Democrat [Colorado newspaper]
La Opinion [Los Angeles, California newspaper]
La Porte Herald-Argus, The [Indiana newspaper]
La Prensa [San Antonio, Texas newspaper]
La Prensa [San Diego, California newspaper]
La Raza [Chicago, Illinois newspaper]
LA Weekly [Los Angeles, California newspaper]
Lacrosse Tribune [Wisconsin newspaper]
Ladies' Home Journal [magazine]

Ladysmith News [Wisconsin newspaper]
Lafayette County Press [Stamps, Arkansas newspaper]
LaFollette Press [Tennessee newspaper]
LaGrange Daily News, The [Georgia newspaper]
Lahaina News [Hawaii newspaper]
Lake and Valley Clarion, The [Livingston County, New York newspaper]
Lake Charles American Press [Louisiana newspaper]
Lake City News [Florida newspaper]
Lake City Reporter [Florida newspaper]
Lake County Echo [Pequot Lakes, Minnesota newspaper]
Lake County Examiner [Lakeview, Oregon newspaper]
Lake County Leader [Polson, Montana newspaper]
Lake County News-Chronicle [Two Harbors, Minnesota newspaper]
Lake Orion Eccentric [Michigan newspaper]
Lake Powell Chronicle [Page, Arizona newspaper]
Lake Stevens Journal [Washington newspaper]
Lake Sun Leader [Camdenton, Missouri newspaper]
Lake Viking News [Missouri newspaper]
Lake Zurich Courier [Illinois newspaper]
Lakeshore Weekly News [Wayzata, Minnesota newspaper]
Lakeside Ledger [Woodstock, Georgia newspaper]
Lakeview Enterprise [Michigan newspaper]
Lakewood Journal [Washington newspaper]
Lamar Daily News, The [Colorado newspaper]
Lampasas Dispatch Record [Texas newspaper]
Lancaster News, The [South Carolina newspaper]
Lancaster Online [Pennsylvania website]
Landmark, The [Holden, Massachusetts newspaper]
Lansing State Journal [Michigan newspaper]

Lapeer County Press, The [Michigan newspaper]

Laredo Morning Times, The [Texas newspaper]

Larson Publications Newspapers [Osseo, Minnesota newspaper]

Las Cruces Bulletin [New Mexico newspaper]

Las Cruces Sun-News [New Mexico newspaper]

Las Vegas Business Press [Nevada newspaper]

Las Vegas City Life [Nevada newspaper]

Las Vegas Review-Journal [Nevada newspaper]

Las Vegas Sun [Nevada newspaper]

Lassen County News [California newspaper]

LatahEagle [Potlach, Idaho newspaper]

Laughlin Entertainer [Nevada newspaper]

Laurel Outlook [Montana newspaper]

Laurinburg Exchange, The [North Carolina newspaper]

Lawndale News [Chicago, Illinois newspaper]

Lawrence Journal-World [Kansas newspaper]

Lawson Review [Missouri newspaper]

Lawton Constitution [Oklahoma newspaper]

Leader News, The [Washburn, North Dakota newspaper]

Leader Online [Akron, Ohio website]

Leader Times [Kittanning, Pennsylvania newspaper]

Leader, The [Charlotte, North Carolina newspaper]

Leader, The [Corning, New York newspaper]

Leader-Herald, The [Gloversville, New York newspaper]

Leader-Telegram, The [Eau Claire, Wisconsin newspaper]

Leadville Herald Democrat [Colorado newspaper]

Leaf-Chronicle, The [Clarksville, Tennessee newspaper]

Learning Channel, The [network]

Leavenworth Chronicle Shopper [Kansas newspaper]

Leavenworth Echo, The [Washington newspaper]

Leavenworth Times, The [Kansas newspaper]

Lebanon Daily News [Pennsylvania newspaper]

Lebanon Daily Record [Missouri newspaper]

Lebanon Enterprise [Kentucky newspaper]

Lebanon Express [Oregon newspaper]

Lebanon Reporter, The [Indiana newspaper]

Ledger Online, The [Lynchburg, Virginia website]

Ledger, The [Lakeland, Florida newspaper]

Ledger-Independent, The [Maysville, Kentucky newspaper]

Ledger-Sentinel [Oswego, Illinois newspaper]

Lee County Examiner [North Fort Myers, Florida newspaper]

Leelanau Enterprise, The [Leland, Michigan newspaper]

Lee's Summit Journal [Missouri newspaper]

Leesburg Today [Virginia newspaper]

Leesville Daily Leader, The [Louisiana newspaper]

LeMars Daily Sentinel [Iowa newspaper]

Lennox Independent, The [South Dakota newspaper]

Lenox Time Table [Iowa newspaper]

LeRoy Pennysaver [New York newspaper]

Levittown Tribune [New York newspaper]

Lewis County Herald [Vanceburg, Kentucky newspaper]

Lewisboro Ledger [New York newspaper]

Lewisburg Tribune/Marshall Gazette [Tennessee newspaper]

Lewiston Morning Tribune [Idaho newspaper]

Lewiston Tribune [Washington newspaper]

Lewistown News-Argus [Montana newspaper]

Lewisville Leader [Texas newspaper]

Lewisville News [Texas newspaper]

Lexington Clipper-Herald [Nebraska newspaper]

Lexington Herald-Leader [Kentucky newspaper]

Lexington Town Online [Massachusetts website]

Liberty County Times [Chester, Montana newspaper]

Liberty Sun-News [Missouri newspaper]

Libertyville Review [Illinois newspaper]

Life [magazine]

Life Goes On [Columbia, Maryland newspaper]

Lifetime [network]

Lima News, The [Ohio newspaper]

Lincoln County News [Damariscotta, Maine newspaper]

Lincoln County Weekly [Damariscotta, Maine newspaper]

Lincoln Daily News [Illinois newspaper]

Lincoln Journal [Hamlin, West Virginia newspaper]

Lincoln Journal Star [Nebraska newspaper]

Lincolnwood Review [Illinois newspaper]

Lingle Guide [Wyoming newspaper]

Linton Daily Citizen [Indiana newspaper]

Lisle Sun [Naperville, Illinois newspaper]

Litchfield Enquirer [Connecticut newspaper]

Little Elm Journal [Texas newspaper]

Little Rock Free Press [Arkansas newspaper]

Littleton Independent [Colorado newspaper]

Livingston County Press [Howell, Michigan newspaper]

Livingston Enterprise, The [Michigan newspaper]

Livingston Enterprise, The [Montana newspaper]

Livonia Observer [Michigan newspaper]

L'Observateur [La Place, Louisiana newspaper]

Lockhart Post-Register [Texas newspaper]

Lodi News-Sentinel [California newspaper]

Log Cabin Democrat [Conway, Arkansas newspaper]

Logan Banner [West Virginia newspaper]

Logan Daily News, The [Ohio newspaper]

Lombardian [Lombard, Illinois newspaper]

Lompoc Record, The [California newspaper]

London News-Journal [Kentucky newspaper]

Long Beach Herald [New York newspaper]

Long Beach Press-Telegram [California newspaper]

Long Island Business [New York newspaper]

Long Island Business News [Ronkonkoma, New York newspaper]

Long Prairie Leader [Minnesota newspaper]

Longview News-Journal [Texas newspaper]

Lonoke Democrat [Arkansas newspaper]

Los Alamos Monitor [New Mexico newspaper]

Los Altos Town Crier [California newspaper]

Los Angeles Daily News [California newspaper]

Los Angeles Downtown News [California newspaper]

Los Angeles Independent [California newspaper]

Los Angeles Times [California newspaper]

Los Banos Enterprise [California newspaper]

Los Gatos Weekly Times, The [California newspaper]

Loudon County Online [Lenoir City, Tennessee website]

Loudoun Easterner [Sterling, Virginia newspaper]

Loudoun Times-Mirror, The [Leesburg, Virginia newspaper]

Louisville Cardinal, The [Kentucky newspaper]

Louisville Eccentric Observer [Kentucky newspaper]

Loveland Daily Reporter-Herald [Colorado newspaper]

Lovelock Review-Miner [Nevada newspaper]

Lovington Daily Leader, The [New Mexico newspaper]

Lowell Sun [Massachusetts newspaper]

Lubbock Online [Texas website]

Ludington Daily News [Michigan newspaper]

Lusk Herald [Wyoming newspaper]

Lynn Town Online [Massachusetts website]

Lynnfield Weekly News [Massachusetts newspaper]

Mackinac Town Crier [Mackinac Island, Michigan newspaper]

Macomb Daily, The [Michigan newspaper]

Macomb Eagle [Illinois newspaper]

Macomb Journal [Illinois newspaper]

Macon Chronicle-Herald [Missouri newspaper]

Macon Telegraph Online, The [Georgia website]

Madera County Times [California newspaper]

Madera Tribune [California newspaper]

Madill Record [Oklahoma newspaper]

Madison County Carrier [Florida newspaper]

Madison County Journal [Danielsville, Georgia newspaper]

Madison County Journal [Ridgeland, Mississippi newspaper]

Madison Daily Leader, The [South Dakota newspaper]

Madison Eagle, The [New Jersey newspaper]

Madison Press, The [London, Ohio newspaper]

Madras Pioneer [Oregon newspaper]

Mail Tribune, The [Medford, Oregon newspaper]

Main Line Times [Ardmore, Pennsylvania newspaper]

Maine Antique Digest [Waldoboro, Maine newspaper]

Maine Times [Bangor, Maine newspaper]

Malibu Times, The [California newspaper]

Malvern Daily Record [Arkansas newspaper]

Mammoth Times [Mammoth Lakes, California newspaper]

Manassas Journal Messenger [Virginia newspaper]

Manchester Enterprise [Michigan newspaper]

Manchester Times [Tennessee newspaper]

Manhasset Press [New York newspaper]

Manhattan Mercury, The [Kansas newspaper]

Manistee News Advocate [Michigan newspaper]

Mapleton Press [Iowa newspaper]

Marblehead Town Online [Massachusetts website]

Marceline Press [Missouri newspaper]

Marco Island Eagle [Florida newspaper]

Marietta Daily Journal [Georgia newspaper]

Marietta Leader, The [Ohio newspaper]

Marietta Times [Ohio newspaper]

Marin Independent [California newspaper]

Marin Independent-Journal [Novato, California newspaper]

Marion County Record [Kansas newspaper]

Marion Daily Republican [Illinois newspaper]

Mariposa Gazette [California newspaper]

Mariposa Tribune, The [California newspaper]

Marlboro Herald Advocate [Bennettsville, South Carolina newspaper]

Marlette Leader, The [Michigan newspaper]

Marshall Chronicle, The [Michigan newspaper]

Marshall Democrat-News, The [Missouri newspaper]

Marshall Gazette [Lewisburg, Tennessee newspaper]

Marshall Independent [Minnesota newspaper]

Marshalltown Times Republican [Iowa newspaper]

Marshfield Mail [Missouri newspaper]

Marshfield News-Herald [Wisconsin newspaper]

Martha Stewart Living [magazine]

Martha's Vineyard Times [Vineyard Haven, Massachusetts newspaper]

Martin County Sun [Inez, Kentucky newspaper]

Martinsville Bulletin [Virginia newspaper]

Maryland Times Press [Ocean City, Maryland newspaper]

Marysville Advocate, The [Kansas newspaper]

Marysville Journal-Tribune [Ohio newspaper]

Maryville Daily Forum [Missouri newspaper]

Mason City Globe-Gazette [Iowa newspaper]

Mason Valley News [Yerington, Nevada newspaper]

Massachusetts News [Wellesley, Massachusetts newspaper]

Massapequan Observer [Massapequa Park, New York newspaper]

Mattoon Journal-Gazette [Illinois newspaper]

Maui News [Wailuku, Hawaii newspaper]

Maywood Herald [Illinois newspaper]

McAlester News-Capital & Democrat [Oklahoma newspaper]

McAllen Monitor [Texas newspaper]

McCall's [magazine]

McCook Daily Gazette, The [Nebraska newspaper]

McDonald County Press [Pineville, Missouri newspaper]

McDowell News, The [Marion, North Carolina newspaper]

McKenzie Banner, The [Tennessee newspaper]

McKinney Messenger [Texas newspaper]

McLean County Independent [Garrison, North Dakota newspaper]

McLean County Journal [Turtle Lake, North Dakota newspaper]

McLeod County Chronicle [Glencoe, Minnesota newspaper]

McPherson Sentinel [Kansas newspaper]

Meade Co. Times-Tribune/Black Hills Press [Sturgis, South Dakota newspaper]

Meadville Tribune, The [Pennsylvania newspaper]

Medina County Gazette [Ohio newspaper]

Melrose Beacon [Minnesota newspaper]

Melrose Park Herald [Illinois newspaper]

Melrose Town Online [Massachusetts website]

Memphis Business Journal [Tennessee newspaper]

Memphis Commercial Appeal [Tennessee newspaper]

Memphis Flyer [Tennessee newspaper]

Mendocino Beacon, The [California newspaper]

Mendota Reporter [Illinois newspaper]

Menomonee Falls News [New Berlin, Wisconsin newspaper]

Men's Health [magazine]

Mequon-Thiensville Courant [New Berlin, Wisconsin newspaper]

Merced Sun-Star [California newspaper]

Mercer Island Reporter [Washington newspaper]

Mercury, The [Pottstown, Pennsylvania newspaper]

Meridian Star [Mississippi newspaper]

Merrick Herald [New York newspaper]

Merrillville Herald News [Indiana newspaper]

Merrimack River Current [Newburyport, Massachusetts newspaper]

Mesabi Daily News [Virginia, Minnesota newspaper]

Mesquite News, The [Texas newspaper]

Messenger [River Grove, Illinois newspaper]

Messenger, The [Fort Dodge, Iowa newspaper]

Messenger, The [Hartsville, South Carolina newspaper]

Messenger, The [Madisonville, Kentucky newspaper]

Messenger, The [St. Albans, Vermont newspaper]

Messenger-Inquirer [Owensboro, Kentucky newspaper]

Methow Valley News [Washington newspaper]

Metro [San Jose, California newspaper]

Metro Pulse [Knoxville, Tennessee newspaper]

Metro Santa Cruz [California newspaper]

Metro Times [Detroit, Michigan newspaper]

Metro World/Montgomery Newspapers [Delaware Valley, Pennsylvania newspaper]

Metroland [Albany, New York newspaper]

Metropolis Planet [Illinois newspaper]

Metropolitan Spirit, The [Augusta, Georgia newspaper]

Mexico Ledger [Missouri newspaper]

Miami Herald [Florida newspaper]

Miami News-Record [Oklahoma newspaper]

Miami New-Times [Florida newspaper]

Miami Today [Florida newspaper]

Miami's Community Newspapers [Florida newspaper]

Miamisburg News, The [Ohio newspaper]

Michigan Living [magazine]

Middleton Press [Connecticut newspaper]

Middletown Journal [Ohio newspaper]

Middletown Press, The [Connecticut newspaper]

Midland Daily News [Michigan newspaper]

Midland Reporter-Telegram [Texas newspaper]

Midlands Business Journal [Omaha, Nebraska newspaper]

MidWeek Magazine [Kaneohe, Hawaii newspaper]

Midweek Online [West Fargo, North Dakota website]

Midwest Messenger [Tekamah, Nebraska newspaper]

Milan News [Saline, Michigan newspaper]

Miles City Star [Montana newspaper]

Milford Cabinet and Wilton Journal [New Hampshire newspaper]

Mille Lacs County Times [Milaca, Minnesota newspaper]

Miller Press, The [South Dakota newspaper]

Milwaukee Business Journal [Wisconsin newspaper]

Milwaukee Journal Sentinel [Wisconsin newspaper]

Minden Press-Herald, The [Louisiana newspaper]

Mineola American [New York newspaper]

Mineral County Miner [Creede, Colorado newspaper]

Mineral Wells Index, The [Texas newspaper]

Mining Journal [Marquette, Michigan newspaper]

Minneota Mascot, The [Minnesota newspaper]

Minnesota Sun Publications [Bloomington, Minnesota newspaper]

Minnesota Women's Press [St. Paul, Minnesota newspaper]

Minot Daily News [North Dakota newspaper]

Mirror, The [Tonganoxie, Kansas newspaper]

Mission Times Courier [San Diego, California newspaper]

Mississippi Business Journal, The [Jackson, Mississippi newspaper]

Mississippi Press, The [Pascagoula, Mississippi newspaper]

Miss-Lou [Natchez, Mississippi magazine]

Missoula Independent [Montana newspaper]

Missoulian, The [Missoula, Montana newspaper]

Missourian, The [Washington, Missouri newspaper]

Mitchell Daily Republic, The [South Dakota newspaper]

Mitchell News-Journal [Spruce Pine, North Carolina newspaper]

Moab's Times-Independent [Utah newspaper]

Moberly Monitor-Index [Missouri newspaper]

Mobile Register Online [Alabama website]

Mobridge Tribune [South Dakota newspaper]

Modern Maturity [magazine]

Modesto Bee, The [California newspaper]

Modoc County Record, The [Alturas, California newspaper]

Mojave Valley Daily News [Bullhead City, Arizona newspaper]

Molokai Advertiser News, The [Hawaii newspaper]

Monett Times [Missouri newspaper]

Money [magazine]

Monitor, The [McAllen, Texas newspaper]

Monitor, The [Palestine, Texas newspaper]

Monroe County Advocate-Democrat [Sweetwater, Tennessee newspaper]

Monroe Evenings News, The [Michigan newspaper]

Monroe Guardian [Michigan newspaper]

Monroe Journal [Alabama newspaper]

Monroe Times, The [Ohio newspaper]

Montana Standard, The [Butte, Montana newspaper]

Montara Mountain Free Press [California newspaper]

Montclair Times, The [New Jersey newspaper]

Monte Vista Journal [Colorado newspaper]

Monterey County Herald [California newspaper]

Montevideo American News [Minnesota newspaper]

Montgomery Advertiser [Alabama newspaper]

Montgomery County Sentinel [Maryland newspaper]

Montgomery Independent [Alabama newspaper]

Montgomery Journal [Maryland newspaper]

Monticello Express, The [Iowa newspaper]

Monticello Times [Arkansas newspaper]

Monticello Times [Minnesota newspaper]

Montrose Daily Press [Colorado newspaper]

Moon Record-Star [Moon Township, Pennsylvania newspaper]

Moore American [Oklahoma newspaper]

Mooresville Times [Indiana newspaper]

Moosehead Messenger [Greenville, Maine newspaper]

Morehead News [Kentucky newspaper]

Morgan County News, The [Utah newspaper]

Morgan Messenger, The [Berkeley Springs, West Virginia newspaper]

Morgan Valley Weekly [Utah newspaper]

Morning Call, The [Allentown, Pennsylvania newspaper]

Morning Journal, The [Lorain, Ohio newspaper]

Morning News [Florence, South Carolina newspaper]

Morning News of Northwest Arkansas [Springdale, Arkansas newspaper]

Morning Sentinel [Centralia, Illinois newspaper]

Morning Sentinel, The [Waterville, Maine newspaper]

Morning Sun, The [Pittsburg, Kansas newspaper]

Morris Daily Herald [Illinois newspaper]

Morrison County Record [Little Falls, Minnesota newspaper]

Morton Grove Champion [Illinois newspaper]

Moscow-Pullman Daily News [Pullman, Washington newspaper]

Moscow-Pullman Daily News, The [Moscow, Idaho newspaper]

Motor Trend [magazine]

Motorland [magazine]

Moultrie News [Mt. Pleasant, South Carolina newspaper]

Moultrie Observer [Georgia newspaper]

Mount Airy News, The [North Carolina newspaper]

Mount Ayr Record-News [Iowa newspaper]

Mount Olive Tribune, The [North Carolina newspaper]

Mount Pleasant News [Iowa newspaper]

Mount Prospect Times [Illinois newspaper]

Mount Shasta Herald [California newspaper]

Mountain Advocate [Barbourville, Kentucky newspaper]

Mountain Democrat Online [Placerville, California newspaper]

Mountain Echo [Fall River Mills, California newspaper]

Mountain Home News [Idaho newspaper]

Mountain Lake Observer [Minnesota newspaper]

Mountain Mail [Salida, Colorado newspaper]

Mountain Messenger [Lewisburg, West Virginia newspaper]

Mountain Monthly [Cloudcroft, New Mexico newspaper]

Mountain News [Lake Arrowhead, California newspaper]

Mountain Statesman [Grafton, West Virginia newspaper]

Mountain Times [Boone, North Carolina newspaper]

Mountain Times [Timberon, New Mexico newspaper]

Mountain Times, The [Killington, Vermont newspaper]

Mountain View News, The [Spencer, Tennessee newspaper]

Mountain Xpress [Asheville, North Carolina newspaper]

Mountaineer-Progress [Phelan, California newspaper]

Mountaintop Eagle, The [Pennsylvania newspaper]

Mountrail County Record [Parshall, North Dakota newspaper]

Movie Channel, The [network]

MSNBC [network]

Mt. Pleasant Daily Tribune, The [Texas newspaper]

MTV [network]

Mundelein Review [Illinois newspaper]

Murray County News [Slayton, Minnesota newspaper]

Murray Ledger & Times, The [Kentucky newspaper]

Murrysville Star [Pennsylvania newspaper]

Muscatine Journal [Iowa newspaper]

Muskego Sun [New Berlin, Wisconsin newspaper]

Muskegon Chronicle [Michigan newspaper]

Muskegon News [Michigan newspaper]

Nando Times, The [Raleigh, North Carolina newspaper]

Napa Valley Register, The [California newspaper]

Naperville Sun [Naperville, Illinois newspaper]

Naples Daily News [Florida newspaper]

Napoleon Homestead [North Dakota newspaper]

Narragansett Times, The [Wakefield, Rhode Island newspaper]

NASA Television [website]

Nashua Telegraph [New Hampshire newspaper]

Nashville Business Journal [Tennessee newspaper]

Nashville Digest [Tennessee newspaper]

Nashville Network, The [network]

Nashville Scene [Tennessee newspaper]

Nassau Herald [New York newspaper]

Natchez Democrat, The [Mississippi newspaper]

Natchitoches Times, The [Louisiana newspaper]

National Enquirer [magazine]

National Geographic Magazine [magazine]

Navajo Hopi Observer [Flagstaff, Alaska newspaper]

Navajo Times, The [Window Rock, Arizona newspaper]

Navasota Examiner [Texas newspaper]

NBC [network]

Neb-Sandhills [Lincoln, Nebraska newspaper]

Nederland Mountain-Ear [Colorado newspaper]

Neosho Daily News [Missouri newspaper]

Neosho Post [Missouri newspaper]

Net Newspaper [Yellowstone, Wyoming newspaper]

Nevada Appeal [Carson City, Nevada newspaper]

Nevada Business Journal [Las Vegas, Nevada newspaper]

Nevada County Picayune [Prescott, Arkansas newspaper]

Nevada Daily Mail, The [Missouri newspaper]

Nevada Herald [Missouri newspaper]

Nevada Journal, The [Iowa newspaper]

Nevada Rancher [Lovelock, Nevada newspaper]

New Bay Times [Ocean Pines, Maryland newspaper]

New Berlin Citizen [Wisconsin newspaper]

New Braunfels Ferald-Zeitung, The [Texas newspaper]

New Carlisle Sun, The [Ohio newspaper]

New Castle Business Ledger [Wilmington, Delaware newspaper]

New Castle News [Pennsylvania newspaper]

New City [Chicago, Illinois newspaper]

New Gloucester News [Maine newspaper]

New Hampshire Gazette [Portsmouth, New Hampshire newspaper]

New Haven Advocate [Connecticut newspaper]

New Haven Register [Connecticut newspaper]

New Jersey Herald, The [Newton, New Jersey newspaper]

New Jersey Lawyer Weekly [Iselin, New Jersey newspaper]

New Jersey Online [website]

New London Day, The [Connecticut newspaper]

New Mexico Business Journal [Albuquerque, New Mexico newspaper]

New Mexico Jewish Link, The [Albuquerque, New Mexico newspaper]

New Milford Times [Connecticut newspaper]

New Orleans City Business [Louisiana newspaper]

New Prague Times [Minnesota newspaper]

New River Valley Current [Christiansburg, Virginia newspaper]

New Times [Miami, Florida newspaper]

New Times [Phoenix, Arizona newspaper]

New Times Broward [Palm Beach, Florida newspaper]

New Times Los Angeles [California newspaper]

New Times Weekly [San Luis Obispo, California newspaper]

New Town News [North Dakota newspaper]

New Ulm Journal [Minnesota newspaper]

New Utah [Lehi, Utah newspaper]

New Woman [magazine]

New York Daily News [New York, New York newspaper]

New York Mills Herald [Minnesota newspaper]

New York Post [New York, New York newspaper]

New York Press [New York, New York newspaper]

New York Times, The [New York, New York newspaper]

Newark Post [Delaware newspaper]

Newberg Graphic, The [Oregon newspaper]

Newberry Observer [South Carolina newspaper]

Newcastle Pacer, The [Oklahoma newspaper]

Newington Town Crier [Connecticut newspaper]

Newkirk Herald Journal [Oklahoma newspaper]

Newman Independent, The [Illinois newspaper]

Newnan Times-Herald, The [Georgia newspaper]

Newport Daily Independent [Arkansas newspaper]

Newport News-Times [Oregon newspaper]

Newport Plain Talk [Tennessee newspaper]

Newport This Week [Rhode Island newspaper]

News & Advance, The [Lynchburg, Virginia newspaper]

News & Citizen [Morrisville, Vermont newspaper]

News & Observer [Raleigh, North Carolina newspaper]

News & Record [Greensboro, North Carolina newspaper]

News & Review [Chico, California newspaper]

News and Advance [Lynchburg, Virginia newspaper]

News and Observer [Raleigh, North Carolina newspaper]

News and Record [Greensboro, North Carolina newspaper]

News and Sentinel [Colebrook, New Hampshire newspaper]

News Banner, The [West St. Tammany, Louisiana newspaper]

News Chief [Winter Haven, Florida newspaper]

News Daily [Jonesboro, Georgia newspaper]

News Democrat & Leader [Russellville, Kentucky newspaper]

News-Dispatch, The [Michigan City, Indiana newspaper]

News Enterprise [Elizabethtown, Kentucky newspaper]

News Guard, The [Lincoln City, Oregon newspaper]

News Herald, The [Franklin, Pennsylvania newspaper]

News Herald, The [Morganton, North Carolina newspaper]

News Herald, The [Panama City, Florida newspaper]

News Journal, The [Delaware newspaper]

News Letter Journal [Wyoming newspaper]

News Press, The [Stillwater, Oklahoma newspaper]

News Progress [Sullivan, Illinois newspaper]

News Record [Maplewood, New Jersey newspaper]

News Record, The [Marshall, North Carolina newspaper]

News Reporter, The [Whiteville, North Carolina newspaper]

News Tribune, The [Tacoma, Washington newspaper]

News Virginian, The [Waynesboro, Virginia newspaper]

News, The [Kingstree, South Carolina newspaper]

NEWS12 [12 Bronx, New York cable]

NEWS12 [12 Edison, New Jersey cable]

NEWS12 [12 Woodbury, New York cable]

NEWS12 [12 Yonkers, New York cable]

News-Argus, The [Goldsboro, North Carolina newspaper]

News-Banner [Bluffton, Indiana newspaper]

News-Bulletin [Belen, New Mexico newspaper]

News-Bulletin [Brookfield, Missouri newspaper]

News-Capital & Democrat [McAlester, Oklahoma newspaper]

Newsday [New York newspaper]

News-Examiner [Montpelier, Idaho newspaper]

News-Gazette [Illinois newspaper]

News-Gazette Online [Champaign-Urbana, Illinois newspaper]

News-Gazette, The [Lexington, Virginia newspaper]

News-Herald [Lenoir City, Tennessee newspaper]

News-Herald, The [Southgate, Michigan newspaper]

News-Herald, The [Willoughby, Ohio newspaper]

News-Item, The [Shamokin, Pennsylvania newspaper]

News-Journal [Daytona Beach, Florida newspaper]

News-Journal [Kentucky newspaper]

News-Journal, The [North Manchester, Indiana newspaper]

News-Journal, The [Raeford, North Carolina newspaper]

News-Leader [Fernandina Beach, Florida newspaper]

News-Press [Fort Myers, Florida newspaper]

News-Record [Harmony, Minnesota newspaper]

News-Record [Zumbrota, Minnesota newspaper]

News-Register [McMinnville, Oregon newspaper]

News-Reporter [Washington, Georgia newspaper]

News-Review [Roseberg, Oregon newspaper]

News-Review, The [Mattituck, New York newspaper]

News-Review, The [Roseburg, Oregon newspaper]

News-Star [Monroe, Louisiana newspaper]

News-Sun & Evening Star [Kendallville, Indiana newspaper]

News-Sun [Sebring, Florida newspaper]

News-Sun, The [Waukegan, Illinois newspaper]

News-Times [Newport, Oregon newspaper]

News-Times, The [Danbury, Connecticut newspaper]

News-Topic [Lenoir, North Carolina newspaper]

Newsweek [magazine]

Newsweekly [Sebewaing, Michigan newspaper]

Newton Daily News, The [Iowa newspaper]

Newton Kansan, The [Kansas newspaper]

Newtown Bee, The [Connecticut newspaper]

Niagara Gazette, The [Niagara Falls, New York newspaper]

Nick at Nite's TV Land [network]

Nickelodeon [network]

Niles Daily Star [Michigan newspaper]

Nobles County Review [Adrian, Minnesota newspaper]

Nogales International [Arizona newspaper]

Nome Nugget [Alaska newspaper]

Norfolk Daily News [Nebraska newspaper]

Norfolk Virginian-Pilot [Virginia newspaper]

Norman Transcript, The [Oklahoma newspaper]

North Adams Transcript [Massachusetts newspaper]

North Andover Town Online [Massachusetts website]

North County News [Yorktown Heights, New York newspaper]

North County Times [California newspaper]

North County Tribune [Paso Robles, California newspaper]

North Forty News [LaPorte, Colorado newspaper]

North Hills News Record [Warrendale, Pennsylvania newspaper]

North Jersey Herald & News [Passaic, New Jersey newspaper]

North Journal Star [Wexford, Pennsylvania newspaper]

North Kingstown Standard Times, The [Rhode Island newspaper]

North Lake Tahoe Bananza [Nevada newspaper]

North Little Rock Times [Arkansas newspaper]

North Platte Telegraph [Nebraska newspaper]

North Port Sun Herald [North Port, Florida newspaper]

Northbrook Star [Illinois newspaper]

Northeast Mississippi Daily Journal [Tupelo, Mississippi newspaper]

Northern Colorado Business Report, The [Fort Collins, Colorado newspaper]

Northern Express [Traverse City, Michigan newspaper]

Northern Light, The [Williams, Minnesota newspaper]

Northern New Hampshire [Colebrook, New Hampshire newspaper]

Northfield News Online [Minnesota newspaper]

Northlake Herald-Journal [Illinois newspaper]

Northwest Arkansas Times, The [Fayetteville, Arkansas newspaper]

Northwest Florida Daily News [Fort Walton Beach, Florida newspaper]

Northwest Herald, The [Crystal Lake, Illinois newspaper]

Norwalk Citizen-News, The [Connecticut newspaper]

Norwalk Reflector-Herald, The [Norwalk, Ohio newspaper]

Novato Advance [California newspaper]

Nowin Star [Irwin, Pennsylvania newspaper]

NRTA/AARP Bulletin [magazine]

Nuevo Times [Ramona, California newspaper]

Nugget Newspaper, The [Sisters, Oregon newspaper]

Nutley Journal [New Jersey newspaper]

Nyack Villager [New York newspaper]

Oak Creek Pictorial [New Berlin, Wisconsin newspaper]

Oak Creek Villager [Cottonwood, Arizona newspaper]

Oak Leaves [Oak Park, Illinois newspaper]

Oak Park Journal [Illinois newspaper]

Oak Rider, The [Tennessee newspaper]

Oakes Times [North Dakota newspaper]

Oakland Press, The [Michigan newspaper]

Oakland Tribune, The [California newspaper]

Oakmont Advance Leader Star [Oakmont, Pennsylvania newspaper]

Oberlin Herald Preview, The [Kansas newspaper]

Observer & Eccentric Newspapers [Michigan newspaper]

Observer, The [La Grande, Oregon newspaper]

Observer, The [Rio Rancho, New Mexico newspaper]

Observer, The [Springerville, Arizona newspaper]

Observer-Dispatch [Utica, New York newspaper]

Observer-Reporter [Washington, Pennsylvania newspaper]

Ocala Star-Banner [Florida newspaper]

Ocean Pines Gazette [Deale, Maryland newspaper]

Ocean Star [Point Pleasant Beach, New Jersey newspaper]

Oceana's Herald-Journal [Hart, Michigan newspaper]

Oceanside/IP Herald [New York newspaper]

Oconee Enterprise [Watkinsville, Georgia newspaper]

Octopus, The [Champaign, Illinois newspaper]

Odessa American, The [Texas newspaper]

Odyssey [network]

Ohio Observer, The [Ohio newspaper]

Ojai Valley News [California newspaper]

Okeechobee Times [Florida newspaper]

Oklahoma Gazette [Oklahoma City, Oklahoma newspaper]

Oklahoma Woman [Oklahoma City, Oklahoma newspaper]

Oklahoman Online, The [Oklahoma City, Oklahoma website]

Okmulgee Daily Times [Oklahoma newspaper]

Olathe Daily News, The [Kansas newspaper]

Old Colony Memorial [Plymouth, Massachusetts newspaper]

Oldham Era, The [Kentucky newspaper]

Olean Times Herald, The [New York newspaper]

Olney Daily Mail [Illinois newspaper]

Olympian, The [Washington newspaper]

Omaha Catholic Voice [Nebraska newspaper]

Omaha Reader [Nebraska newspaper]

Omaha World-Herald [Nebraska newspaper]

On Wisconsin [Milwaukee, Wisconsin newspaper]

Oneida Daily Dispatch [New York newspaper]

Oneida-Madison Pennysaver [Clinton, New York newspaper]

Opelika-Auburn News [Alabama newspaper]

Optic Herald [Mount Vernon, Texas newspaper]

Orange County Business Journal [Newport Beach, California newspaper]

Orange County Register [Santa Ann, California newspaper]

Orange County Review [Virginia newspaper]

Orange County Weekly [Costa Mesa, California newspaper]

Orange Leader [Texas newspaper]

Orange Transcript [New Jersey newspaper]

Oregon Live [Portland, Oregon newspaper]

Oregonian [Portland, Oregon newspaper]

Oregonian, The [Oregon newspaper]

Orem Daily Journal [Utah newspaper]

Orem Geneva Times [Orem, Utah newspaper]

Orion Gazette [Illinois newspaper]

Orlando Business Journal [Florida newspaper]

Orlando Sentinal [Florida newspaper]

Orlando Times, The [Florida newspaper]

Orlando Weekly [Florida newspaper]

Oroville Mercury-Register [California newspaper]

Osceola News Gazette [Florida newspaper]

Osceola Sentinel-Tribune [Iowa newspaper]

Osgood Journal [Versailles, Indiana newspaper]

Oshkosh Northwestern [Wisconsin newspaper]

Oskaloose Herald, The [Iowa newspaper]

Ottawa Herald, The [Kansas newspaper]

Ottumwa Courier, The [Iowa newspaper]

Ouachita Citizen, The [West Monroe, Louisiana newspaper]

Outdoor Life [magazine]

Outdoor Life Network [network]

Outer Banks Sentinel [Nags Head, North Carolina newspaper]

Outlook, The [Alexander City, Alabama newspaper]

Ovation [network]

Overton County News [Livingston, Tennessee newspaper]

Owasso Rambler [Oklahoma newspaper]

Owatonna People's Press [Minnesota newspaper]

Oxford Eagle [Mississippi newspaper]

Oxford Eagle, The [Mississippi newspaper]

Oxford Eccentric [Michigan newspaper]

Oxford Independent, The [Alabama newspaper]

Oxford Press, The [Ohio newspaper]

Oxygen [network]

Oyster Bay Enterprise-Pilot [New York newspaper]

Ozark County Times [Gainesville, Missouri newspaper]

Ozona Stockman, The [Texas newspaper]

Pacesetting Times, The [Horseshoe Bend, Arkansas newspaper]

Pacific Business News [Honolulu, Hawaii newspaper]

Pacific Coast Business Times [Ojai, California newspaper]

Pacifica Tribune [California newspaper]

Paducah Sun, The [Kentucky newspaper]

Pagosa Springs Sun [Colorado newspaper]

Pahrump Valley Times [Nevada newspaper]

Paintsville Herald, The [Kentucky newspaper]

Palacios Beacon [Texas newspaper]

Palestine Herald Press [Texas newspaper]

Palisadian-Post [Pacific Palisades, California newspaper]

Palladium-Times Online [Oswego, New York newspaper]

Palm Beach Daily News [Florida newspaper]

Palm Beach Post [Florida newspaper]

Palms West Press [Wellington, Florida newspaper]

Palo Alto Weekly [California newspaper]

Palo Verde Valley Times [Blythe, California newspaper]

Pampa News, The [Texas newspaper]

Pantagraph Online, The [Bloomington, Illinois website]

Paper Rocks, The [Boone, North Carolina newspaper]

Paper, The [Grand Rapids, Michigan newspaper]

Papillion Times, The [Nebraska newspaper]

Paradise Post [California newspaper]

Paragould Daily Press [Arkansas newspaper]

Parenting [magazine]

Parents [magazine]

Paris Beacon-News [Illinois newspaper]

Paris Express [Arkansas newspaper]

Paris News, The [Texas newspaper]

Park County Republican and Fairplay Flume [Bailey, Colorado newspaper]

Park Falls Herald [Wisconsin newspaper]

Park Rapids Enterprise [Minnesota newspaper]

Park Record [Park City, Utah newspaper]

Parkston Advance, The [South Dakota newspaper]

Parsons Sun Online [website]

Parthenon, The [Huntington, West Virginia newspaper]

Pasadena Citizen, The [Texas newspaper]

Pasadena Star-News [California newspaper]

Pasadena Weekly [California newspaper]

Pasco News [Dade City, Florida newspaper]

Patriot and Free Press, The [Cuba, New York newspaper]

Patriot Ledger, The [Quincy, Massachusetts newspaper]

Pawtucket Times [Rhode Island newspaper]

PAX TV [network]

Paynesville News [Minnesota newspaper]

Payson Roundup, The [Arizona newspaper]

PBS Public Broadcasting Service [network]

PBS17 WNED [17 Buffalo, New York]

PC Magazine

PC World [magazine]
PC/Computing [magazine]
Peabody Weekly News [Massachusetts newspaper]
Peaks News Net [Colorado newspaper]
Pecos Enterprise, The [Texas newspaper]
Pekin Daily Times [Illinois newspaper]
Pelham Weekly [New York newspaper]
Penasee Globe [Michigan newspaper]
Peninsula Clarion [Alaska newspaper]
Peninsula Daily News [Washington newspaper]
Peninsula Gateway, The [Gig Harbor, Washington newspaper]
Penn Hills Progress Star [Pennsylvania newspaper]
Pensacola News Journal [Florida newspaper]
Penthouse [magazine]
People [magazine]
Peoria Journal Star [Illinois newspaper]
Perry County Times [New Bloomfield, Pennsylvania newspaper]
Perry Daily Journal [Oklahoma newspaper]
Perryville Sun Times News [Missouri newspaper]
Peru Tribune, The [Indiana newspaper]
Petaluma Argus-Courier [California newspaper]
Peterborough Transcript [New Hampshire newspaper]
Petersburg Pilot [Alaska newspaper]
Petit Jean Country Headlight [Morrilton, Arkansas newspaper]
Petoskey News-Review [Michigan newspaper]
Petroleum News Alaska [Anchorage, Alaska newspaper]
Pharos-Tribune [Logansport, Indiana newspaper]
Philadelphia Business Journal [Pennsylvania newspaper]
Philadelphia Daily News [Pennsylvania newspaper]
Philadelphia Inquirer [Pennsylvania newspaper]
Philadelphia Online [Pennsylvania website]
Philipsburg Mail [Montana newspaper]

Phoenix New Times [Arizona newspaper]
Phoenix, The [Pennsylvania newspaper]
Picayune Item [Mississippi newspaper]
Pickens County Herald [Carrollton, Alabama newspaper]
Pictorial-Gazette [Guilford, Connecticut newspaper]
Pilot, The [Southern Pines, North Carolina newspaper]
Pilot-Independent, The [Walker, Minnesota newspaper]
Pilot-News, The [Plymouth, Indiana newspaper]
Pine Bluff Commercial [Arkansas newspaper]
Pine City Pioneer [Minnesota newspaper]
Pine Island News [Florida newspaper]
Pine River Journal [Minnesota newspaper]
Pine River Times [Bayfield, Colorado newspaper]
Pinecrest Tribune [Florida newspaper]
Pinnacle, The [Hollister, California newspaper]
Pioneer Press [Minnesota newspaper]
Pioneer Press Newspapers [Chicago, Illinois newspaper]
Pioneer Review, The [Philip, South Dakota newspaper]
Pioneer Times [Vassar, Michigan newspaper]
PitchWeekly [Kansas City, Missouri newspaper]
Pittsburgh Business Times [Pennsylvania newspaper]
Pittsburgh City Paper [Pennsylvania newspaper]
Pittsburgh Post-Gazette [Pennsylvania newspaper]
Pittsburgh Tribune-Review [Pennsylvania newspaper]
Pittsfield Gazette [Massachusetts newspaper]
Pittsfield Pigeon [Massachusetts newspaper]
Placerville Mountain Democrat [California newspaper]
Plain Dealer, The [Cleveland, Ohio newspaper]
Plain Talk [Vermillion, South Dakota newspaper]

Plainsman [Huron, South Dakota newspaper]

Plainview Daily Herald [Texas newspaper]

Plainview-Old Bethpage Herald [New York newspaper]

Plainville Daily Herald [Texas newspaper]

Plano Star Courier, The [Texas newspaper]

Platte County Record-Times [Wyoming newspaper]

Playboy [magazine]

Plaza Forum [Deerfield Beach, Florida newspaper]

Pleasanton Express [Texas newspaper]

Plum Advance Leader Star [Pennsylvania newspaper]

Plumas County News [California newspaper]

Plymouth Observer [Michigan newspaper]

Pocahontas Times, The [Marlinton, West Virginia newspaper]

Pocono Record [Pennsylvania newspaper]

Pocono Record [Stroudsburg, Pennsylvania newspaper]

Point Pleasant Register, The [West Virginia newspaper]

Point Reyes Light [California newspaper]

Point, The [South Carolina newspaper]

Polish News [Bensenville, Illinois newspaper]

Polk County Enterprise, The [Livingston, Texas newspaper]

Polk County Itemizer Observer [Dallas, Oregon newspaper]

Pompano Ledger, The [Pompano Beach, Florida newspaper]

Ponca City News [Oklahoma newspaper]

Ponchatoula Times [Louisiana newspaper]

Pope County Tribune [Glenwood, Minnesota newspaper]

Popular Mechanics [magazine]

Popular Science [magazine]

Port Arthur News [Texas newspaper]

Port Austin Times [Michigan newspaper]

Port Folio [Virginia Beach, Virginia newspaper]

Port Lavaca Wave [Texas newspaper]

Port Orchard Independent [Washington newspaper]

Port Orford Today [Oregon newspaper]

Port Planet, The [Newburyport, Massachusetts newspaper]

Port Saint Lucie News [Florida newspaper]

Port Townsend & Jefferson County Leader [Washington newspaper]

Port Washington News [New York newspaper]

Portage County Gazette [Stevens Point, Wisconsin newspaper]

Portage Journal News [Indiana newspaper]

Portales News-Tribune [Portales, New Mexico newspaper]

Porterville Recorder [California newspaper]

Portland Oregonian [Oregon newspaper]

Portland Press Herald and Maine Sunday Telegram [Maine newspaper]

Portsmouth Herald [New Hampshire newspaper]

Portuguese Times [New Bedford, Massachusetts newspaper]

Post & Mail, The [Columbia City, Indiana newspaper]

Post and Courier, The [Charleston, South Carolina newspaper]

Post Register, The [Idaho Falls, Idaho newspaper]

Post Searchlight [Bainbridge, Georgia newspaper]

Post Star [Glen Falls, New York newspaper]

Post-Bulletin Online [Rochester, Minnesota newspaper]

Post-Crescent [Appleton, Wisconsin newspaper]

Post-Dispatch [Colorado newspaper]

Post-Journal, The [Jamestown, New York newspaper]

Postland Courier [Charleston, South Carolina newspaper]

Post-Standard/Syracuse Herald-Journal [New York newspaper]

Post-Star [Glens Falls, New York newspaper]

Post-Tribune [Gary, Indiana newspaper]

Poteau Daily News & Sun [Oklahoma newspaper]

Potomac News [Woodbridge, Virginia newspaper]

Pottsville Republican [Pennsylvania newspaper]

Poughkeepsie Journal [New York newspaper]

Poway Chieftian [California newspaper]

Prairie Advocate [Lanark, Illinois newspaper]

Prairie Reader [Mankato, Minnesota newspaper]

Pratt Tribune [Kansas newspaper]

Prescott Courier [Arizona newspaper]

Prescott Journal [Wisconsin newspaper]

Prescott Valley Tribune, The [Arizona newspaper]

Press & Dakotan [Yankton, South Dakota newspaper]

Press and Sun-Bulletin [Binghamton, New York newspaper]

Press Argus-Courier [Van Buren, Arkansas newspaper]

Press Democrat, The [Santa Rosa, California newspaper]

Press Enterprise [Bloomsburg, Pennsylvania newspaper]

Press Enterprise, The [Riverside, California newspaper]

Press Journal [Vero Beach, Florida newspaper]

Press Sentinel, The [Jesup, Georgia newspaper]

Press Tribune, The [Roseville, California newspaper]

Press, The [Atlantic City, New Jersey newspaper]

Press, The [Avon Lake, Ohio newspaper]

Press, The [Elmhurst, Illinois newspaper]

Press-Citizen [Iowa City, Iowa newspaper]

Press-Enterprise [Bloomsberg, Pennsylvania newspaper]

Press-Telegram, The [Long Beach, California newspaper]

Prevention [magazine]

Prince George's Journal [Lanham, Maryland newspaper]

Prince George's Post [Upper Marlboro, Maryland newspaper]

Prince George's Sentinel [Upper Marlboro, Maryland newspaper]

Princeton Daily Clarion [Indiana newspaper]

Princeton Packet [New Jersey newspaper]

Princeton Town Topics [New Jersey newspaper]

Princeton Union-Eagle [Minnesota newspaper]

Prior Lake American [Minnesota newspaper]

Proctor Journal [Minnesota newspaper]

Progress News [Emlenton, Pennsylvania newspaper]

Progress Online [Claremore, Oklahoma website]

Progress, The [George West, Texas newspaper]

Progress-Index [Virginia newspaper]

Providence Business [Rhode Island newspaper]

Providence Business News [Rhode Island newspaper]

Providence Journal [Rhode Island newspaper]

Providence Journal-Bulletin [Rhode Island newspaper]

Providence Phoenix [Rhode Island newspaper]

Provincetown Banner [Massachusetts newspaper]

Provincetown Daily [Massachusetts newspaper]

Pueblo Chieftain, The [Pueblo, Colorado newspaper]

Pueblo Chieftain Online, The [Colorado website]

Puget Sound Business [Washington newspaper]

Puget Sound Navy News [Washington newspaper]

Pulaski County Democrat [St. Robert, Missouri newspaper]

Pulse of the Twin Cities [Minneapolis, Minnesota newspaper]

Pulse-Journal [Mason, Ohio newspaper]

Purcell Register [Oklahoma newspaper]

Purdue Exponent [West Lafayette, Indiana newspaper]

Putnam County News and Recorder [Cold Spring, New York newspaper]

Putnam Pit, The [Cookeville, Tennessee newspaper]

Putnam/Cabell Post [Winfield, West Virginia newspaper]

Quad Cities Area News [Moline, Illinois newspaper]

Quad City Times, The [Davenport, Iowa newspaper]

Quartzsite Times [Arizona newspaper]

Quay Country Sun [Tucumcari, New Mexico newspaper]

Queens Chronicle [New York newspaper]

Queens Courier, The [Bayside, New York newspaper]

Queens Gazette, The [New York newspaper]

Queens Tribune [Fresh Meadows, New York newspaper]

Quincy Herald-Whig, The [Illinois newspaper]

QVC [network]

Rabbit Creek Journal [Clipper Mills, California newspaper]

Rahway Progress [New Jersey newspaper]

Rains County Leader [Emory, Texas newspaper]

Ramona Sentinel [California newspaper]

Rancho Bernardo News Journal [California newspaper]

Range Ledger, The [Cheyenne Wells, Colorado newspaper]

Rapid City Journal [South Dakota newspaper]

Rappahannock Record [Kilmarnock, Virginia newspaper]

Ravalli Republic [Hamilton, Montana newspaper]

Rayne Acadian-Tribune [Louisiana newspaper]

Reader's Digest [magazine]

Reading Eagle-Times [Pennsylvania newspaper]

Record Herald [Waynesboro, Pennsylvania newspaper]

Record Herald, The [Washington Court House, Ohio newspaper]

Record Journal [Meriden, Connecticut newspaper]

Record Publishing [Ravenna, Ohio newspaper]

Record Review [Edgar, Wisconsin newspaper]

Record Searchlight [Redding, California newspaper]

Record, The [Kansas City, Kansas newspaper]

Record, The [North Wilkesboro, North Carolina newspaper]

Record, The [Stockton, California newspaper]

Record, The [Troy, New York newspaper]

Record-Courier, The [Gardnerville, Nevada newspaper]

Record-Courier, The [Ravenna, Ohio newspaper]

Recorder, The [Amsterdam, New York newspaper]

Recorder, The [Greenfield, Massachusetts newspaper]

Red and Black [Athens, Georgia newspaper]

Red Bluff Daily News [California newspaper]

Red Bluff News [California newspaper]

Redbook [magazine]

Redding Pilot, The [Connecticut newspaper]

Redding Record [California newspaper]

Redding Record-Searchlight [California newspaper]

Redford Observer [Michigan newspaper]

Redlands Daily Facts [California newspaper]

Redwood Gazette [Redwood Falls, Minnesota newspaper]

Reed City Herald [Michigan newspaper]

Reflector, The [Battle Ground, Washington newspaper]

Reflector-Herald [Norwalk, Ohio newspaper]

Regional Standard [Guilford, Connecticut newspaper]

Register [Texas newspaper]

Register Citizen, The [Torrington, Connecticut newspaper]

Register News [Mt. Vernon, Illinois newspaper]

Register-Guard, The [Eugene, Oregon newspaper]

Register-Herald, The [Beckley, West Virginia newspaper]

Reminder [Vernon, Connecticut newspaper]

Reminder, The [East Longmeadow, Massachusetts website]

Reno Gazette-Journal [Nevada newspaper]

Reno News & Review [Nevada newspaper]

Renville County Farmer [Mohall, North Dakota newspaper]

Report [magazine]

Reporter [Fond du Lac, Wisconsin newspaper]

Reporter, The [Vacaville, California newspaper]

Reporter-Times [Martinsville, Indiana newspaper]

Repository, The [Canton, Ohio newspaper]

Republic, The [Columbus, Indiana newspaper]

Republican and Fairplay Flume [Bailey, Colorado newspaper]

Republican Eagle [Red Wing, Minnesota newspaper]

Republican Journal, The [Belfast, Maine newspaper]

Republican-Clipper [Bethany, Missouri newspaper]

Republican-Leader [Preston, Minnesota newspaper]

Republican-Nonpareil [Central City, Nebraska newspaper]

Republic-Monitor [Perryville, Missouri newspaper]

Resort Sports Network

Reuters News Service

Revere Independent [Massachusetts newspaper]

Review, The [East Liverpool, Ohio newspaper]

Review, The [Plymouth, Wisconsin newspaper]

Revue & News, The [Alpharetta, Georgia newspaper]

Rhino Times [Greensboro, North Carolina newspaper]

Richfield Reaper, The [Utah newspaper]

Richland Beacon-News [Rayville, Louisiana newspaper]

Richland Mirror [Missouri newspaper]

Richlands News-Press [Virginia newspaper]

Richmond Register [Kentucky newspaper]

Richmond Times-Dispatch [Virginia newspaper]

Ridgefield Press, The [Connecticut newspaper]

Ritchie Gazette, The [Harrisville, West Virginia newspaper]

River Cities Reader [Davenport, Iowa newspaper]

River Reporter [Narrowsburg, New York newspaper]

Riverdale Review [Bronx, New York newspaper]

Riverfront Times [St. Louis, Missouri newspaper]

Riverview Times [St. Paul, Minnesota newspaper]

Roane County News [Kingston, Tennessee newspaper]

Roanoke Rapids Daily Herald [North Carolina newspaper]

Roanoke Times & World News [Virginia newspaper]

Roanoke Times [Virginia newspaper]

Roaring Fork Sunday [Basalt, Colorado newspaper]

Robesonian, The [Lumberton, North Carolina newspaper]

Robinson Daily News [Illinois newspaper]

Rochelle News-Leader [Illinois newspaper]

Rochester Business [New York newspaper]

Rochester Business Journal [New York newspaper]

Rochester Democrat and Chronicle [New York newspaper]

Rochester Eccentric [Michigan newspaper]

Rochester Sentinel, The [Indiana newspaper]

Rock County Star Herald [Luverne, Minnesota newspaper]

Rock Island Argus, The [Illinois newspaper]

Rockbridge Weekly [Lexington, Virginia newspaper]

Rockdale Citizen, The [Conyers, Georgia newspaper]

Rockdale Reporter, The [Texas newspaper]

Rocket-Courier [Wyalusing, Pennsylvania newspaper]

Rockford Register Star [Illinois newspaper]

Rockville Centre Herald [Rockville Centre, New York newspaper]

Rocky Mountain News [Denver, Colorado newspaper]

Rogersville Review, The [Tennessee newspaper]

Rogue River Press, The [Oregon newspaper]

Roll Call [Washington, D.C. newspaper]

Rolla Daily News [Missouri newspaper]

Rolling Meadows Review [Illinois newspaper]

Rolling Stone [magazine]

Romance Classics [network]

Rome News-Tribune [Georgia newspaper]

Rome Observer [New York newspaper]

Romulus Roman [Michigan newspaper]

Roseville Independent [Illinois newspaper]

Roslyn News [New York newspaper]

Roswell Daily Record [New Mexico newspaper]

Round Rock Leader, The [Texas newspaper]

Ruidoso News [New Mexico newspaper]

Russell Register [Jamestown, Kentucky newspaper]

Sacramento Bee [California newspaper]

Sacramento Business Journal [California newspaper]

Sag Harbor Express [New York newspaper]

Saginaw News [Michigan newspaper]

Saint Cloud Times [Minnesota newspaper]

Saint Francis Reminder-Enterprise [New Berlin, Wisconsin newspaper]

Saint Francisville Democrat [Louisiana newspaper]

Saint Martinville Teche News [Louisiana newspaper]

Saint Paul Pioneer Press [Minnesota newspaper]

Salem Evening News [Massachusetts newspaper]

Salina Journal [Kansas newspaper]

Salina Sun [Utah newspaper]

Saline Reporter [Michigan newspaper]

Salisbury Post [North Carolina newspaper]

Salon.com [Internet magazine]

Salt Lake Tribune, The [Utah newspaper]

Sampson Independent, The [Clinton, North Carolina newspaper]

San Angelo Standard-Times [Texas newspaper]

San Antonio Business Journal [Texas newspaper]

San Antonio Express-News, The [Texas newspaper]

San Bernardino County Sun, The [California newspaper]

San Diego Community Newspaper Group [California newspaper]

San Diego Daily Transcript [California newspaper]

San Diego Headline News [California newspaper]

San Diego RanchCoast News [California newspaper]

San Diego Reader [California newspaper]

San Diego Union Tribune [California newspaper]

San Francisco Business Times [California newspaper]

San Francisco Chronicle [California newspaper]

San Francisco Examiner [California newspaper]

San Francisco Bay Guardian [California newspaper]

San Francisco Times [California newspaper]

San Francisco Weekly [California newspaper]

San Gabriel Valley Tribune [West Covina, California newspaper]

San Jacinto News-Times, The [Shepherd, Texas newspaper]

San Jose Business Journal [California newspaper]

San Jose Mercury News [California newspaper]

San Luis Obispo Telegram-Tribune [California newspaper]

San Marcos Daily Record [Texas newspaper]

San Mateo County Times, The [California newspaper]

San Saba County Review, The [Texas newspaper]

Sandpoint [magazine]

Sandusky Register, The [Ohio newspaper]

Sandy Profile [Oregon newspaper]

Sanford Herald, The [North Carolina newspaper]

Sangre de Cristo Chronicle [Angel Fire, New Mexico newspaper]

Santa Barbara Independent [California newspaper]

Santa Barbara News-Press [California newspaper]

Santa Cruz County Sentinel [California newspaper]

Santa Fe New Mexican, The [New Mexico newspaper]

Santa Fe Times [New Mexico newspaper]

Santa Monica Mirror [California newspaper]

Santa Paula Times [California newspaper]

Sapulpa Daily Herald [Oklahoma newspaper]

Sarasota Herald-Tribune [Florida newspaper]

Saratoga News, The [California newspaper]

Saratogian, The [Saratoga Springs, New York newspaper]

Saugus Town Online [Massachusetts website]

Sauk Centre Herald [Minnesota newspaper]

Savage Pacer [Prior Lake, Minnesota newspaper]

Savannah Morning News [Georgia newspaper]

Savannah News [Georgia newspaper]

Sawyer County Record [Hayward, Wisconsin newspaper]

Schaumburg Times [Illinois newspaper]

Schleswig Leader [Mapleton, Iowa newspaper]

Scholastic Parent & Child [magazine]

Sci-Fi Channel [network]

Scouting [magazine]

Scranton Times, The [Pennsylvania newspaper]

Searchlight [Redding, California newspaper]

Seaside Signal [Oregon newspaper]

Seattle [Washington newspaper]

Seattle Daily Journal of Commerce [Washington newspaper]

Seattle Post-Intelligencer [Washington newspaper]

Seattle Times [Washington newspaper]

Seattle Weekly [Washington newspaper]

Sebastian Sun [Vero Beach, Florida newspaper]

Sedan Times Star [Kansas newspaper]

Sedona Red Rock News [Arizona newspaper]

Sedona Spectrum [Arizona newspaper]

Seeley Swan Pathfinder [Seeley Lake, Montana newspaper]

Self [magazine]

Selma Enterprise [California newspaper]

Selma Times Journal [Alabama newspaper]

Seminole Herald [Sanford, Florida newspaper]

Seminole Producer, The [Oklahoma newspaper]

Senior Citizens Gazette [Bakersfield, California newspaper]

Senior Times [Jamestown, Rhode Island newspaper]

Sentinel & Enterprise [Fitchburg, Massachusetts newspaper]

Sentinel [Fairmont, Minnesota newspaper]

Sentinel [Rome, New York newspaper]

Sentinel [Wisconsin newspaper]

Sentinel, The [Carlisle, Pennsylvania newspaper]

Sentinel, The [Honeoye Falls, New York newspaper]

Sentinel, The [Lewistown, Pennsylvania newspaper]

Sentinel-Courier [Cooperstown, North Dakota newspaper]

Sentinel-Echo [London, Kentucky newspaper]

Sentinel-News [Shelbyville, Kentucky newspaper]

Sentinel-Record, The [Hot Springs, Arkansas newspaper]

Sentinel-Standard [Ionia, Michigan newspaper]

Sesame Street Magazine

Seventeen [magazine]

Sewickley Herald-Star [Pennsylvania newspaper]

Seymour Tribune, The [Indiana newspaper]

Shakopee Valley News [Minnesota newspaper]

Shape [magazine]

Shawano Leader, The [Wisconsin newspaper]

Shawnee Journal Herald [Kansas newspaper]

Shawnee News-Star, The [Oklahoma newspaper]

Sheboygan Press [Wisconsin newspaper]

Shelby County Reporter [Columbiana, Alabama newspaper]

Shelby Star, The [North Carolina newspaper]

Shelbyville [Tennessee newspaper]

Shelbyville News, The [Indiana newspaper]

Shelbyville Times-Gazette, The [Tennessee newspaper]

Shenandoah.com [Strasburg, Virginia website]

Sheridan Press, The [Wyoming newspaper]

Sherman County Star [Goodland, Kansas newspaper]

Shore Journal, The [Delmarva Peninsula, Maryland newspaper]

Shore Publishing Community Newspapers [Connecticut newspaper]

Shorewood Herald [New Berlin, Wisconsin newspaper]

Showtime [network]

Sidney Daily News [Ohio newspaper]

Sidney Herald-Leader [Montana newspaper]

Sidney Sun-Telegraph, The [Nebraska newspaper]

Sierra Star [Oakhurst, California newspaper]

Sierra Sun [Truckee, California newspaper]

Sierra Vista Herald [Arizona newspaper]

Sierra Vista Herald [Bisbee, Arizona newspaper]

Siftings Herald [Arkadelphia, Arkansas newspaper]

Signal, The [Santa Clarita, California newspaper]

Sigourney News-Journal, The [Iowa newspaper]

Silicon Valley News [San Jose, California newspaper]

Silver City Daily Press & Independent [New Mexico newspaper]

Silver City Daily Press [New Mexico newspaper]

Sioux City Journal, The [Iowa newspaper]

Siskiyou Daily [Yreka, California newspaper]

Sisseton Courier, The [South Dakota newspaper]

Sisters Nugget [Oregon newspaper]

Skagit Valley Herald [Mount Vernon, Washington newspaper]

Skokie Review [Illinois newspaper]

Slate [Internet magazine]

Slidell Sentry-News [Louisiana newspaper]

Smith County Pioneer [Kansas newspaper]

Smithfield Times, The [Virginia newspaper]

Smithsonian [magazine]

Smithtown News, The [New York newspaper]

Smithville Review [Tennessee newspaper]

Smoky Mountain News [Waynesville, North Carolina newspaper]

Smyth Country News & Messenger [Marion, Virginia newspaper]

Snoqualmie Valley Record [Washington newspaper]

Snowmass Village Sun [Colorado newspaper]

Snyder Daily News [Texas newspaper]

Soap Opera Digest [magazine]

Solares Hill [Key West, Florida newspaper]

Somerset Herald [Princess Anne, Maryland newspaper]

Somersworld [New Hampshire newspaper]

Somerville Town Online [Massachusetts website]

Sonoma County Independent [Santa Rosa, California newspaper]

Sonoma Index-Tribune [California newspaper]

Sonora Union Democrat [California newspaper]

Sonoran News [North Scottsdale, Airzona newspaper]

Sound, The [Madison, Connecticut newspaper]

Sounder, The [Random Lake, Wisconsin newspaper]

Source, The [Bend, Oregon newspaper]

South Bend Tribune [Indiana newspaper]

South Boston Gazette-Virginian [Virginia newspaper]

South Boston Online [Boston, Massachusetts website]

South Boston Tribune [Boston, Massachusetts newspaper]

South County Spotlight [Scappoose, Oregon newspaper]

South Florida Business Journal [Hollywood, Florida newspaper]

South Hills Record-Star [Monroeville, Pennsylvania newspaper]

South Idaho Press, The [Burley, Idaho newspaper]

South Milwaukee Voice Graphic [New Berlin, Wisconsin newspaper]

South Plainfield Observer [Middlesex, New Jersey newspaper]

South Reporter, The [Holly Springs, Mississippi newspaper]

South Sioux City Star [Nebraska newspaper]

South Washington County Bulletin [River Falls, Wisconsin newspaper]

Southampton Press [New York newspaper]

Southeast Missourian [Cape Girardeau, Missouri newspaper]

Southern Illinoisan [Carbondale, Illinois newspaper]

Southern Living [magazine]

Southern Standard [McMinnville, Tennessee newspaper]

Southfield Eccentric [Michigan newspaper]

Southhampton Press, The [New York newspaper]

Southside Sentinel [Urbanna, Virginia newspaper]

Southwest Daily News [Louisiana newspaper]

Southwest Daily News [Sulphur, Louisiana newspaper]

Southwest Daily Times [Liberal, Kansas newspaper]

Southwest Farm Press [Overland Park, Kansas newspaper]

Southwest Florida Business [Naples, Florida newspaper]

Southwest Iowa Now [Council Bluffs, Iowa newspaper]

Southwest Journal [Minneapolis, Minnesota newspaper]

Southwest Times [Arkansas newspaper]

Southwest Times Record, The [Fort Smith, Arkansas newspaper]

Southwest Virginia Enterprise [Wytheville, Virginia newspaper]

Space Coast Press [Merritt Island, Florida newspaper]

Sparta Expositor, The [Tennessee newspaper]

Sparta News-Plaindealer [Sparta, Illinois newspaper]

Spartanburg Herald-Journal [South Carolina newspaper]

Speaking Out News [Huntsville, Alabama newspaper]

Spectator [Monroeville, Ohio newspaper]

Spectator [Raleigh, North Carolina newspaper]

Spectrum, The [New Milford, Connecticut newspaper]

Spectrum, The [St. George, Utah newspaper]

Speedvision [network]

Spencer Butte Gazette, The [Eugene, Oregon newspaper]

Spencer County Leader, The [Dale, Indiana newspaper]

Spencer Daily Reporter [Iowa newspaper]

Spokesman-Review, The [Washington newspaper]

Spooner Advocate [Wisconsin newspaper]

Sports Illustrated [magazine]

Spring Valley Tribune [Minnesota newspaper]

Springboro Sun [Ohio newspaper]

Springfield Journal [Massachusetts newspaper]

Springfield News [Oregon newspaper]

Springfield News-Leader [Missouri newspaper]

Springfield News-Sun, The [Ohio newspaper]

Springfield/Valley Advocate [Massachusetts newspaper]

St. Albans Messenger, The [Vermont newspaper]

St. Augustine Record, The [Florida newspaper]

St. Cloud Times, The [Minnesota newspaper]

St. Genevieve Sun Times [Missouri newspaper]

St. Helena Star [California newspaper]

St. James Leader-Journal [Missouri newspaper]

St. Joseph News-Express [Missouri newspaper]

St. Louis Business Journal [Missouri newspaper]

St. Louis Post-Dispatch [Missouri newspaper]

St. Maries Gazette-Record, The [Idaho newspaper]

St. Paul Pioneer Press [Minnesota newspaper]

St. Petersburg Times [Florida newspaper]

St. Tammany News Banner/Slidell Sentry-News [Louisiana newspaper]

Stamford Advocate [Connecticut newspaper]

Standard Banner [Jefferson City, Tennessee newspaper]

Standard Democrat [Sikeston, Missouri newspaper]

Standard Observer [Irwin, Pennsylvania newspaper]

Standard Press [Burlington, Wisconsin newspaper]

Standard Speaker [Hazleton, Pennsylvania newspaper]

Standard, The [Westhope, North Dakota newspaper]

Standard-Examiner [Ogden, Utah newspaper]

Standard-Journal [Milton, Pennsylvania newspaper]

Standard-Sentinel [Saluda, South Carolina newspaper]

Standard-Speaker [Hazleton, Pennsylvania newspaper]

Standard-Times [San Angelo, Texas newspaper]

Standard-Times, The [New Bedford, Massachusetts newspaper]

Stanwood/Camano, The [Washington newspaper]

Star [magazine]

Star and Wave [Cape May, New Jersey newspaper]

Star Beacon [Ashtabula, Ohio newspaper]

Star Democrat [Easton, Maryland newspaper]

Star Gazette [Hastings, Minnesota newspaper]

Star News [McCall, Idaho newspaper]

Star News [Medford, Wisconsin newspaper]

Star Press, The [Muncie, Indiana newspaper]

Star Tribune [Minneapolis-St. Paul, Minnesota newspaper]

Star Valley Independent [Afton, Wyoming newspaper]

Star, The [Kansas City, Kansas newspaper]

Star, The [Pipestone, Minnesota newspaper]

Star, The [Port Saint Joe, Florida newspaper]

Star, The [Tinley Park, Illinois newspaper]

Star-Beacon [Ashtabula, Ohio newspaper]

Star-Courier [Kewanee, Illinois newspaper]

Star-Democrat, The [Easton, Maryland newspaper]

Star-Gazette [Elmira, New York newspaper]

Star-Herald [Belton, Missouri newspaper]

Star-Herald [Scottsbluff, Nebraska newspaper]

Starkville Daily News [Mississippi newspaper]

Star-Ledger, The [New Jersey newspaper]

StarLine, The [Grand Coulee, Washington newspaper]

Star-News, The [Pasadena, California newspaper]

Star-Press [Blairstown, Iowa newspaper]

Star-Telegram [Arlington, Texas newspaper]

State [Columbia, South Carolina newspaper]

State Journal [Charleston, West Virginia newspaper]

State Journal-Register, The [Springfield, Illinois newspaper]

State News [East Lansing, Michigan newspaper]

State Port Pilot, The [Southport, North Carolina newspaper]

State, The [Columbia, South Carolina newspaper]

Staten Island Advance/Staten Island Live [New York newspaper]

Statesboro Herald [Georgia newspaper]

Statesman [Texas newspaper]

Statesman Examiner [Colville, Washington newspaper]

Statesman Journal, The [Oregon newspaper]

Statesville Record & Landmark [North Carolina newspaper]

Steamboat Pilot [Steamboat Springs, Colorado newspaper]

Steele County Press [Finley, North Dakota newspaper]

Stephenville Empire-Tribune [Texas newspaper]

Sterling Journal-Advocate [Colorado newspaper]

Stillwater News-Press [Oklahoma newspaper]

Stoneham Independent, The [Massachusetts newspaper]

Stoneham Sun [Massachusetts newspaper]

Storm Lake Times [Iowa newspaper]

Stowe Reporter [Vermont newspaper]

Straitsland Resorter [Indian River, Michigan newspaper]

Stratford Journal, The [Wisconsin newspaper]

Streator Times-Press [Illinois newspaper]

Stuart News [Florida newspaper]

Sturgis Journal [Michigan newspaper]

Style Weekly [Richmond, Virginia newspaper]

Suburban and Wayne Times, The [Wayne, Pennsylvania newspaper]

Suburban Journals, The [St. Louis, Missouri newspaper]

Suburban News [Ohio newspaper]

Suburban Newspapers of Dayton [Kettering, Ohio newspaper]

Sudbury Town Online [Massachusetts website]

Suffolk News-Herald [Virginia newspaper]

Suffolk Times [Mattituck, New York newspaper]

Sullivan County Democrat [Callicoon, New York newspaper]

Sulphur Times-Democrat [Oklahoma newspaper]

Summit Daily News, The [Frisco, Colorado newspaper]

Summit Observer [New Jersey newspaper]

Sumpter County Record-Journal [Livingston, Alabama newspaper]

Sumter County Times [Bushnell, Florida newspaper]

Sun Chronicle, The [Attleboro, Massachusetts newspaper]

Sun Herald Online [Biloxi/Gulfport, Mississippi website]

Sun Journal [Lewiston, Maine newspaper]

Sun Journal, The [New Bern, North Carolina newspaper]

Sun Journal, The [North Canton, Ohio newspaper]

Sun Newspaper [Bremerton, Washington newspaper]

Sun Newspapers [Ohio newspaper]

Sun Publications Newspapers [Naperville, Illinois newspaper]

Sun Times [Parker, Arizona newspaper]

Sun, The [Bremerton, Washington newspaper]

Sunbury News, The [Ohio newspaper]

Sundance Channel [network]

Sunflower, The [Wichita, Kansas newspaper]

Sun-Link [Hanover, Pennsylvania newspaper]

Sun-News, The [Myrtle Beach, South Carolina newspaper]

Sunnyvale Sun, The [California newspaper]

Sun-Sentinel [Fort Lauderdale, Florida newspaper]

Sunset [magazine]

Sunset, The Magazine Of Western Living

Sun-Times, The [Heber Springs, Arkansas newspaper]

Superior Express, The [Nebraska newspaper]

Superior Telegram [Wisconsin newspaper]

Suwannee Democrat [North Florida, Georgia newspaper]

Swampscott Town Online [Massachusetts website]

Sweetwater Reporter [Texas newspaper]

Swift County Monitor [Benson, Minnesota newspaper]

Syosset-Jericho Tribune [Syosset, New York newspaper]

Syracuse New Times [New York newspaper]

Tacoma Daily Index [Washington newspaper]

Tacoma News Tribune [Washington newspaper]

Taftsville Tales Weekly [Taftsville, Vermont newspaper]

Tahlequah Daily Press, The [Oklahoma newspaper]

Tahoe Daily Tribune [South Lake Tahoe, California newspaper]

Tahoe World [Tahoe City, California newspaper]

Takoma Voice [Takoma Park, Maryland newspaper]

Talk of the Town [Deary, Idaho newspaper]

Talladega Daily Home [Alabama newspaper]

Tallahassee Democrat [Florida newspaper]

Tallahassee Democrat Online [Florida website]

Tallahassee News, The [Florida newspaper]

Tampa Bay Business [Florida newspaper]

Tampa Tribune [Florida newspaper]

Taos News [New Mexico newspaper]

Taunton Daily Gazette [Massachusetts newspaper]

Taylorsville Times, The [North Carolina newspaper]

TBS Superstation [network]

Tech Source NJ [Fairfield, New Jersey newspaper]

Teen [magazine]

Tehachapi News [California newspaper]

Telegram & Gazette [Worcester, Massachusetts newspaper]

Telegram, The [Franklin, New Hampshire newspaper]

Telegram, The [Torrington, Wyoming newspaper]

Telegram-Tribune [San Luis Obispo, California newspaper]

Telegraph Herald [Dubuque, Iowa newspaper]

Telegraph, The [Alton, Illinois newspaper]

Telegraph, The [Dixon, Illinois newspaper]

Telegraph, The [Nashua, New Hampshire newspaper]

Telluride Daily Planet [Colorado newspaper]

Telluride Watch [Colorado newspaper]

Temple Daily Telegram, The [Texas newspaper]

Tempo-News [Sarasoto, Florida newspaper]

Tennessean, The [Nashville, Tennessee newspaper]

Tennessee Tribune [Nashville, Tennessee newspaper]

Terrell Tribune, The [Texas newspaper]

Texarkana Gazette [Arkansas newspaper]

Texarkana Gazette, The [Texas newspaper]

Texas City Sun [Texas newspaper]

TheStreet.com [Internet magazine]

Thief River Falls Times, The [Minnesota newspaper]

This Week [Columbus, Ohio newspaper]

This Week Community Newspapers [Burnsville, Minnesota newspaper]

Thomasville Times [North Carolina newspaper]

Thomasville Times-Enterprise [Georgia newspaper]

Three Village Times [Elmont, New York newspaper]

Tideland News [Swansboro, North Carolina newspaper]

Tiffin Advertiser-Tribune, The [Ohio newspaper]

Tifton Gazette [Georgia newspaper]

Timberjay, The [Tower, Minnesota newspaper]

Timberon Mountainer, The [New Mexico newspaper]

Time [magazine]

Times Argus, The [Barre, Vermont newspaper]

Times Citizen [Iowa Falls, Iowa newspaper]

Times Community Newspapers [Reston, Virginia newspaper]

Times Courier, The [Ellijay, Georgia newspaper]

Times Daily [Florence, Alabama newspaper]

Times Dispatch, The [Walnut Ridge, Arkansas newspaper]

Times Guardian [Canyon Lake, Texas newspaper]

Times Herald, The [Norristown, Pennsylvania newspaper]

Times Herald, The [Olean, New York newspaper]

Times Herald-Record, The [Middletown, New York newspaper]

Times Indicator [Fremont, Michigan newspaper]

Times Leader, The [Wilkes-Barre, Pennsylvania newspaper]

Times News [Nephi, Utah newspaper]

Times News, The [Lehighton, Pennsylvania newspaper]

Times Newspapers [Webster Groves, Missouri newspaper]

Times of Fountain Hills, The [Arizona newspaper]

Times Record News [Wichita Falls, Texas newspaper]

Times Record, The [Brunswick, Maine newspaper]

Times Record, The [Fort Smith, Arkansas newspaper]

Times Sentinel [Zionsville, Indiana newspaper]

Times Union [Albany, New York newspaper]

Times Union [New York newspaper]

Times West Virginian, The [Fairmont, West Virginia newspaper]

Times, The [Acadiana, Louisiana newspaper]

Times, The [Forest Lake, Minnesota newspaper]

Times, The [Hattiesburg, Mississippi newspaper]

Times, The [Munster, Indiana newspaper]

Times, The [Scotch Plains, New Jersey newspaper]

Times, The [Shreveport, Louisiana newspaper]

Times-Beacon Newspapers [Manahawkin, New Jersey newspaper]

Times-Beacon-Record Newspapers [Setauket, New York newspaper]

Times-Bulletin, The [Van Wert, Ohio newspaper]

Times-Gazette [Tennessee newspaper]

Times-Gazette, The [Greenfield, Ohio newspaper]

Times-Herald [Forrest City, Arkansas newspaper]

Times-Journal [Jackson, Ohio newspaper]

Times-Leader, The [Martins Ferry, Ohio newspaper]

Times-Leader, The [Princeton, Kentucky newspaper]

Times-Mail, The [Bedford, Indiana newspaper]

Times-News [Burlington, North Carolina newspaper]

Times-News [Hendersonville, North Carolina newspaper]

Times-News [Kingsport, Tennessee newspaper]

Times-News, The [Burlington, North Carolina newspaper]

Times-News, The [Twin Falls, Idaho newspaper]

Times-Picayune, The [New Orleans, Louisiana newspaper]

Times-Record [Valley City, North Dakota newspaper]

Times-Reporter, The [New Philadelphia, Ohio newspaper]

Times-Republican [Marshalltown, Iowa newspaper]

Times-Sentinel, The [Cheney, Kansas newspaper]

Times-Standard [Eureka, California newspaper]

Times-Union [Warsaw, Indiana newspaper]

Tinley Park Star [Illinois newspaper]

Tipp City Herald [Ohio newspaper]

Titusville Herald, The [Pennsylvania newspaper]

TNT [network]

Tobacco Valley News, The [Eureka, Montana newspaper]

Today in Batesville & Oldenburg [Indiana newspaper]

Today's Homeowner [magazine]

Today's News-Herald [Lake Havasu City, Arizona newspaper]

Today's Sunbeam [Salem, New Jersey newspaper]

Todd County Country Courier [Browerville, Minnesota newspaper]

Tomahawk Leader [Wisconsin newspaper]

Tomahawk, The [Mountain City, Tennessee newspaper]

Tombstone Tumbleweed [Arizona newspaper]

Tooele Transcript-Bulletin, The [Utah newspaper]

Topanga Messenger [California newspaper]

Topeka Capital-Journal, The [Kansas newspaper]

Topsail Voice [Hampstead, North Carolina newspaper]

Torrington Register [Connecticut newspaper]

Tower News [Minnesota newspaper]

Town-Crier [Wellington, Florida newspaper]

Townsend Star [Montana newspaper]

Tracy Press [California newspaper]

Transcript Bulletin [Tooele, Utah newspaper]

Travel & Leisure [magazine]

Travel Channel [network]

Traverse City Record-Eagle [Michigan newspaper]

Trenton Times, The [New Jersey newspaper]

Trentonian, The [Trenton, New Jersey newspaper]

Triad Business News [North Carolina newspaper]

Triangle Business Journal, The [Raleigh, North Carolina newspaper]

Tribune [Mesa, Arizona newspaper]

Tribune [St. Marys, Georgia newspaper]

Tribune Chronicle [Warren, Ohio newspaper]

Tribune Courier [Benton, Kentucky newspaper]

Tribune, The [Elkin, North Carolina newspaper]

Tribune, The [Fort Pierce, Florida newspaper]

Tribune, The [New Albany, Indiana newspaper]

Tribune, The [San Luis Obispo, California newspaper]

Tribune-Chronicle [Warren, Ohio newspaper]

Tribune-Democrat [Johnstown, Pennsylvania newspaper]

Tribune-Phonograph [Abbotsford, Wisconsin newspaper]

Tribune-Review [Greensburg, Pennsylvania newspaper]

Tribune-Star [Terra Haute, Indiana newspaper]

Tri-City Herald [Washington newspaper]

Tri-County News [Heron Lake, Minnesota newspaper]

Tri-County Press [Cuba City, Wisconsin newspaper]

Tri-County Times [Fenton, Michigan newspaper]

Tri-County Weekly [Jamesport, Missouri newspaper]

Trinity Broadcasting Network

Trinity Standard, The [Texas newspaper]

Tripp Star-Ledger [South Dakota newspaper]

Tri-Valley Herald [Pleasanton, California newspaper]

Tropolitan, The [Troy, Alabama newspaper]

Trotwood Independent [Ohio newspaper]

Troy Daily News [Ohio newspaper]

Troy Eccentric [Michigan newspaper]

Troy Messenger [Troy, Alabama newspaper]

Trumbull Times [Colorado newspaper]

Tucson Citizen [Arizona newspaper]

Tucson Weekly [Arizona newspaper]

Tullahoma News [Tennessee newspaper]

Tullahoma News Leader [Tennessee newspaper]

Tulsa Free Press [Oklahoma newspaper]

Tulsa Today [Oklahoma newspaper]

Tulsa World Online [Oklahoma website]

Turlock Journal [California newspaper]

Turner Classic Movies (TCM) [network]

Tuscaloosa News, The [Alabama newspaper]

Tuscola County Advertiser [Caro, Michigan newspaper]

TV Guide [magazine]

Twin Cities Business [Minneapolis, Minnesota newspaper]

twi-ny [New York, New York website]

Tyler County Booster, The [Woodville, Texas newspaper]

Tyler Tribute Online [Minnesota newspaper]

U.S. News & World Report [magazine]

Uintah Basin Standard [Roosevelt, Utah newspaper]

UIS Journal [Springfield, Illinois newspaper]

Ukiah Daily, The [California newspaper]

Underwood News [North Dakota newspaper]

Union Boundary [Tulsa, Oklahoma newspaper]

Union City Daily Messenger [Tennessee newspaper]

Union County Advocate [Henderson, Kentucky newspaper]

Union Daily Times, The [South Carolina newspaper]

Union Democrat, The [Sonora, California newspaper]

Union Leader [New Jersey newspaper]

Union Leader, The [Manchester, New Hampshire newspaper]

Union, The [Grass Valley, California newspaper]

Union-Bulletin [Washington newspaper]

Union-News [Springfield, Massachusetts newspaper]

Union-Sun & Journal, The [Lockport, New York newspaper]

United Press International (UPI) [news service]

University Daily Kansan, The [Lawrence, Kansas newspaper]

Univision [network]

Unravel the Gavel [New Hampshire newspaper]

Up and Coming Magazine [Fayetteville, North Carolina newspaper]

UPN (United Paramount Network)

Upper Dauphin Sentinel [Millersburg, Pennsylvania newspaper]

Urban Tulsa [Tulsa, Oklahoma newspaper]

Urbana Daily Citizen [Ohio newspaper]

USA Network

USA Today [national newspaper]

UT Wire [Charlotte, North Carolina newspaper]

Utah Statesman Online [Logan, Utah website]

Uvalde Leader News [Texas newspaper]

Vacaville Reporter [California newspaper]

Vail Daily News [Colorado newspaper]

Vailsburg Leader, The [New Jersey newspaper]

Valdosta Daily Times [Georgia newspaper]

Vallejo Times-Herald, The [California newspaper]

Valley Advocate [Hatfield, Massachusetts newspaper]

Valley Courier [Alamosa, Colorado newspaper]

Valley Herald [Aspinwall, Pennsylvania newspaper]

Valley Independent [Pennsylvania newspaper]

Valley Independent, The [Monessen, Pennsylvania newspaper]

Valley Journal [Carbondale, Colorado newspaper]

Valley Journal [Lake Benton, Minnesota newspaper]

Valley Morning Star, The [Harlingen, Texas newspaper]

Valley News [Bristol, Connecticut newspaper]

Valley News [White River Junction, Vermont newspaper]

Valley News and Salina Sun [Gunnison, Utah newspaper]

Valley News Dispatch [Tarentum, Pennsylvania newspaper]

Valley Press-Banner [Felton, California newspaper]

Valley Reporter, The [Waitsfield, Vermont newspaper]

Valley Roadrunner [Valley Center, California newspaper]

Valley Stream Herald [New York newspaper]

Valley Times-News [West Point, Georgia newspaper]

Valley Times-News, The [Lanett, Alabama newspaper]

Valparaiso News [Indiana newspaper]

Van Buren Press Argus-Courier [Arkansas newspaper]

Van Horn Advocate [Texas newspaper]

Van Zandt News [Canton, Texas newspaper]

Vancouver Business Journal [Washington newspaper]

Vandalia Drummer News [Ohio newspaper]

Vanguard, The [Mobile, Alabama newspaper]

Vanity Fair [magazine]

Venice Godolier [Florida newspaper]

Ventura County Star [California newspaper]

Verde Independent [Cottonwood, Arizona newspaper]

Verde Valley Online [Cottonwood, Arizona website]

Vermont Life [Montpelier, Vermont newspaper]

Vermont Sports [Waterbury, Vermont newspaper]

Vermont Times [Shelburne, Vermont newspaper]

Vernal Express [Vernal, Utah newspaper]

Vernon Hills Review [Illinois newspaper]

Vernon Publishing Newspapers [Versailles, Missouri newspaper]

Vero Beach Press Journal [Florida newspaper]

Versailles Republican [Indiana newspaper]

VFW Magazine

VH1 [network]

VIA Magazine

Vicksburg Post, The [Mississippi newspaper]

Victoria [magazine]

Victoria Advocate [Texas newspaper]

Victoria Advocate, The [Texas newspaper]

Victoria Gazette [Minnesota newspaper]

Vida en el Valle [Fresno, California newspaper]

View Neighborhood Newspapers [Las Vegas, Nevada newspaper]

Village Herald [Lynbrook, New York newspaper]

Village Sun [Islamorada, Florida newspaper]

Village Voice [Hot Springs, Arizona newspaper]

Village Voice, The [New York, New York newspaper]

Villager Journal [Cherokee Village, Arkansas newspaper]

Ville Platte Gazette [Louisiana newspaper]

Vincennes Sun-Commercial [Indiana newspaper]

Vineyard Gazette [Edgartown, Massachusetts newspaper]

Virginia Pilot, The [Norfolk, Virginia newspaper]

Virginian Review [Covington, Virginia newspaper]

Virginian Review [Virginia newspaper]

Virginian-Pilot [Norfolk, Virginia newspaper]

Virtual Times, The [Redwood City, California newspaper]

Vogue [magazine]

Voice, The [New Baltimore, Michigan newspaper]

Voices News [Southbury, Connecticut newspaper]

Voice-Tribune, The [Louisville, Kentucky newspaper]

Volante [Vermillion, South Dakota newspaper]

WAAY [31 Huntsville, Alabama]

Wabash Plain Dealer [Indiana newspaper]

WABC [07 New York, New York]

WABG [06 Greenville, Mississippi]

WABI [05 Bangor, Maine]

WABU [68 Boston, Massachusetts]

WABW [14 Albany, Georgia]

WACH [57 Columbia, South Carolina]

Waco Tribune-Herald [Texas newspaper]

Waconia Patriot [Minnesota newspaper]

WACS [25 Dawson, Georgia]

WACX [55 Orlando, Florida]

WACY [32 Green Bay, Wisconsin]

Wadena Pioneer Journal [Minnesota newspaper]

WAFB [09 Baton Rouge, Louisiana]

WAFF [48 Huntsville, Alabama]

WAGA [05 Atlanta, Georgia]

WAGM [08 Presque Isle, Maine]

WAGT [26 Augusta, Georgia]

Waikiki News [Honolulu, Hawaii newspaper]

WAKA [08 Montgomery, Alabama]

Wake Weekly, The [Wake Forest, North Carolina newspaper]

Wakonda Times [South Dakota newspaper]

WALA [10 Mobile, Alabama]

WALB [10 Albany, Georgia]

Walker Messenger [LaFayette, Georgia newspaper]

Wall Street Journal [national newspaper]

Walla Walla [Washington newspaper]

Wallkill Valley Times [Walden, New York newspaper]

Wallowa Country Chieftain [Enterprise, Oregon newspaper]

Walpole Times, The [Massachusetts newspaper]

Walton Sun, The [Santa Rosa Beach, Florida newspaper]

Walton Tribune, The [Georgia newspaper]

WAMI [69 Miami, Florida]

WAND [17 Decatur, Illinois]

Wanderer, The [Mattapoisett, Massachusetts newspaper]

WANE [15 Fort Wayne, Indiana]

WAOW [09 Wausau, Wisconsin]

Wapakoneta Daily News [Ohio newspaper]

WAPK [30 Kingsport, Tennessee]

WAPT [16 Jackson, Mississippi]

Warren Sentinel, The [Front Royal, Virginia newspaper]

Warwick Beacon [Rhode Island newspaper]

Wasatch County Courier, The [Heber City, Utah newspaper]

Wasatch Wave [Heber, Utah newspaper]

Washington Business Journal [Washington, D.C. newspaper]

Washington City Paper [Washington, D.C. newspaper]

Washington Evening Journal, The [Iowa newspaper]

Washington Post [Washington, D.C. newspaper]

Washington Times [Washington, D.C. newspaper]

Washington Times-Herald [Indiana newspaper]

Wasilla Frontiersman [Alaska newspaper]

Watauga Democrat [Boone, North Carolina newspaper]

WATE [06 Knoxville, Tennessee]

Waterbury Republican-American [Connecticut newspaper]

Waterford Eccentric [Michigan newspaper]

Waterfront News [Fort Lauderdale, Florida newspaper]

Waterloo Courier [Iowa newspaper]

Waterloo-Cedar Falls Courier [Iowa newspaper]

Watertown Daily Times [Wisconsin newspaper]

Watertown Daily Times, The [New York newspaper]

Watertown Public Opinion [South Dakota newspaper]

Watertown Tab & Press [Needham, Massachusetts newspaper]

WATL [36 Atlanta, Georgia]

WATM [23 Johnstown, Pennsylvania]

Watsonville Register-Pajaronian [California newspaper]

Waukesha Freeman [Wisconsin newspaper]

Waukon Standard [Iowa newspaper]

Waunakee Tribune [Wisconsin newspaper]

Wausau Daily Herald, The [Wisconsin newspaper]

Waushara Argus [Wisconsin newspaper]

Wauwatosa News-Times [Wisconsin newspaper]

WAVE [03 Louisville, Kentucky]

Wave of Long Island [Rockawave, New York newspaper]

Wave, The [Bethany Beach, Delaware newspaper]

WAVY [10 Portsmouth, Virginia]

Waxahachie Daily Light [Texas newspaper]

Waycross Journal-Herald [Georgia newspaper]

Waycross Online [Georgia website]

Wayland Town Online [Massachusetts website]

Wayne County Journal-Banner [Piedmont, Missouri newspaper]

Wayne Eagle [Michigan newspaper]

Wayne Independent, The [Honesdale, Pennsylvania newspaper]

Wayne Suburban & Wayne Times, The [Pennsylvania newspaper]

WAZT [10 Woodstock, Virginia]

WB (Warner Brothers) [network]

WBAK [38 Terre Haute, Indiana]

WBAL [11 Baltimore, Maryland]

WBAY [02 Green Bay, Wisconsin]

WBBH [20 Fort Myers, Florida]

WBBJ [07 Jackson, Tennessee]

WBBM [02 Chicago, Illinois]

WBCC [68 Cocoa, Florida]

WBDC [50 Washington, District of Columbia]

WBFF [45 Baltimore, Maryland]

WBFS [33 Miami, Florida]

WBGN [66 Pittsburgh, Pennsylvania]

WBGU [27 Bowling Green, Ohio]

WBIQ [10 Birmingham, Alabama]

WBKO [13 Bowling Green, Kentucky]

WBKP [05 Calumet, Michigan]

WBNA [21 Louisville, Kentucky]

WBNG [12 Binghamton, New York]

WBNS [10 Columbus, Ohio]

WBNX [55 Cleveland, Ohio]

WBOC [16 Salisbury, Maryland]

WBOY [12 Clarksburg, West Virginia]

WBQP [12 Pensacola, Florida]

WBRA [15 Roanoke, Virginia]

WBRC [06 Birmingham, Alabama]

WBRE [28 Wilkes-Barre, Pennsylvania]

WBRZ [02 Baton Rouge, Louisiana]

WBTV [03 Charlotte, North Carolina]

WBTW [13 Florence, South Carolina]

WBVT [39 Burlington, Vermont]

WBZ [04 Boston, Massachusetts]

WCAG [33 LaGrange, Georgia]

WCAU [10 Philadelphia, Pennsylvania]

WCAX [03 Burlington, Vermont]

WCBB [10 Lewiston, Maine]

WCBI [04 Columbus, Mississippi]

WCBS [02 New York, New York]

WCCB [18 Charlotte, North Carolina]

WCCO [04 Minneapolis, Minnesota]

WCES [20 Augusta, Georgia]

WCET [48 Cincinnati, Ohio]

WCEU [15 Daytona Beach, Florida]

WCFC [38 Chicago, Illinois]

WCFE [57 Plattsburgh, New York]

WCGT [16 Columbus, Georgia]

WCHS [08 Charleston, West Virginia]

WCIA [03 Champaign, Illinois]

WCIV [04 Charleston, South Carolina]

WCJB [20 Gainesville, Florida]

WCLP [18 Chatsworth, Georgia]

WCMH [04 Columbus, Ohio]

WCML [06 Alpena, Michigan]

WCMU [14 Mount Pleasant, Michigan]

WCMV [27 Cadillac, Michigan]

WCMW [21 Manistee, Michigan]
WCNC [06 Charlotte, North Carolina]
WCNY [24 Syracuse, New York]
WCOV [20 Montgomery, Alabama]
WCPB [28 Salisbury, Maryland]
WCPO [09 Cincinnati, Ohio]
WCSC [05 Charleston, South Carolina]
WCSH [06 Portland, Maine]
WCTE [22 Cookeville, Tennessee]
WCTI [12 New Bern, North Carolina]
WCTV [06 Tallahassee, Florida]
WCVB [05 Needham, Massachusetts]
WCVE [23 Richmond, Virginia]
WCVN [54 Covington, Kentucky]
WCYB [05 Bristol, Virginia]
WDAF [04 Kansas City, Missouri]
WDAM [07 Hattiesburg, Mississippi]
WDAY [06 Fargo, North Dakota]
WDBD [40 Jackson, Mississippi]
WDBJ [07 Roanoke, Virginia]
WDCA [20 Washington, District of Columbia]
WDCN [08 Nashville, Tennessee]
WDCO [29 Macon, Georgia]
WDCP [35 University Center, Michigan]
WDCQ [19 University Center, Michigan]
WDEF [12 Chattanooga, Tennessee]
WDFX [34 Dothan, Alabama]
WDHN [18 Dothan, Alabama]
WDIV [04 Detroit, Michigan]
WDJT [58 Milwaukee, Wisconsin]
WDKA [49 Paducah, Kentucky]
WDRB [41 Louisville, Kentucky]
WDRL [24 Roanoke, Virginia]
WDSE [08 Duluth, Minnesota]
WDSI [61 Chattanooga, Tennessee]
WDSU [06 New Orleans, Louisiana]
WDTN [02 Dayton, Ohio]
WDTV [05 Bridgeport, West Virginia]
WDWB [20 Detroit, Michigan]
WDZL [39 Hollywood, Florida]
Weakley County Press [Martin, Tennessee
  newspaper]
WEAO [49 Kent, Ohio]

WEAR [03 Pensacola, Florida]
Weather Channel [network]
Weatherford Daily News [Oklahoma
  newspaper]
Weatherford Democrat [Texas newspaper]
WEAU [13 Eau Claire, Wisconsin]
WECT [06 Wilmington, North Carolina]
WEDH [24 Hartford, Connecticut]
Wednesday Journal [Oak Park, Illinois
  newspaper]
WEDU [03 Tampa, Florida]
WEEK [25 Peoria, Illinois]
Weekly Alibi [Albuquerque, New Mexico
  newspaper]
Weekly Eagle [Lewisburg, Tennessee
  newspaper]
Weekly Journal, The [Moscow, Pennsylvania
  newspaper]
Weekly Planet [Tampa, Florida newspaper]
Weekly Post, The [Locust, North Carolina
  newspaper]
Weekly Post, The [Rainsville, Alabama
  newspaper]
Weekly Vista, The [Bella Vista, Arkansas
  newspaper]
Weekly, The [Norcross, Georgia newspaper]
WEHT [25 Evansville, Indiana]
Weight Watchers Magazine
Weimar Mercury [Texas newspaper]
Weirs Times, The [New Hampshire
  newspaper]
Weirton Daily Times [West Virginia
  newspaper]
Weiser Signal American [Idaho newspaper]
WEIU [51 Charleston, Illinois]
WEKW [52 Keene, New Hampshire]
Wellesley Town Online [Massachusetts website]
Wellington Daily News [Kansas newspaper]
Wellsville Daily Reporter [New York
  newspaper]
WEMT [39 Johnson City, Tennessee]
WENH [11 Durham, New Hampshire]
WENY [36 Elmira, New York]

WESH [02 Orlando, Florida]

West Allis Star [West Berlin, Wisconsin newspaper]

West Bend Daily News [West Bend, Wisconsin newspaper]

West Bloomfield-Lakes Eccentric [Michigan newspaper]

West Central Tribune [Willmar, Minnesota newspaper]

West Hartford News [Connecticut newspaper]

West Haven Voice [Connecticut newspaper]

West Hawaii Today [Kailua-Kona, Hawaii newspaper]

West Liberty Index [Iowa newspaper]

West Milton Record [Ohio newspaper]

West Orange Times, The [Winter Garden, Florida newspaper]

West Plains Daily Quill [Missouri newspaper]

West Point News [Nebraska newspaper]

West Proviso Herald [Illinois newspaper]

West Side Leader [Akron, Ohio newspaper]

West Yellowstone News [Montana newspaper]

Westbury Times [New York newspaper]

Westchester Today [New York newspaper]

Western Nebraska Observer [Kimball, Nebraska newspaper]

Western News, The [Libby, Montana newspaper]

Western Star, The [Lebanon, Ohio newspaper]

Westfield Leader, The [New Jersey newspaper]

Westlake Picayune [Texas newspaper]

Westland Eagle [Michigan newspaper]

Westland Observer [Michigan newspaper]

Weston Democrat, The [West Virginia newspaper]

Weston Forum, The [Connecticut newspaper]

Westport News [Connecticut newspaper]

Westword [Denver, Colorado newspaper]

WETA [26 Washington, D.C.]

Wethersfield Post [Connecticut newspaper]

WETK [33 Burlington, Vermont]

WETM [18 Elmira, New York]

Wetzel Chronicle/Tyler Star News [New Martinsville, West Virginia newspaper]

WEVU [07 Fort Myers, Florida]

WEVV [44 Evansville, Indiana]

WEWS [05 Cleveland, Ohio]

WEYI [25 Clio, Michigan]

WFAA [08 Dallas, Texas]

WFBC [40 Greenville, South Carolina]

WFFT [55 Fort Wayne, Indiana]

WFGC [61 West Palm Beach, Florida]

WFGX [35 Fort Walton Beach, Florida]

WFHL [23 Decatur, Illinois]

WFIE [14 Evansville, Indiana]

WFLA [08 Tampa, Florida]

WFLD [32 Chicago, Illinois]

WFLX [29 West Palm Beach, Florida]

WFMJ [21 Youngstown, Ohio]

WFMZ [69 Allentown, Pennsylvania]

WFOR [04 Miami, Florida]

WFPT [62 Frederick, Maryland]

WFRV [05 Green Bay, Wisconsin]

WFSB [03 Hartford, Connecticut]

WFSG [56 Panama City, Florida]

WFSU [11 Tallahassee, Florida]

WFTC [29 Minneapolis, Minnesota]

WFTS [28 Tampa, Florida]

WFTV [09 Orlando, Florida]

WFUM [28 Flint, Michigan]

WFVT [55 Charlotte, North Carolina]

WFXB [43 Myrtle Beach, South Carolina]

WFXG [54 Augusta, Georgia]

WFXL [31 Albany, Georgia]

WFXR [27 Roanoke, Virginia]

WFYI [20 Indianapolis, Indiana]

WGAL [08 Lancaster, Pennsylvania]

WGBA [26 Green Bay, Wisconsin]

WGBH [02 Boston, Massachusetts]

WGBY [57 Springfield, Massachusetts]

WGCU [30 Fort Myers, Florida]

WGEM [10 Quincy, Illinois]

WGFL [53 Gainesville, Florida]

WGGB [40 Springfield, Massachusetts]

WGHP [08 High Point, North Carolina]

WGMB [44 Baton Rouge, Louisiana]
WGME [13 Portland, Maine]
WGN [09 Chicago, Illinois]
WGNO [26 New Orleans, Louisiana]
WGNT [27 Portsmouth, Virginia]
WGNX [46 Atlanta, Georgia]
WGTE [30 Toledo, Ohio]
WGTU [29 Traverse City, Michigan]
WGTV [08 Atlanta, Georgia]
WGVK [52 Kalamazoo, Michigan]
WGVP [44 Valdosta, Georgia]
WGVU [35 Grand Rapids, Michigan]
WGXA [24 Macon, Georgia]
WHA [21 Madison, Wisconsin]
WHAG [25 Hagerstown, Maryland]
Wharton Journal-Spectator [Texas newspaper]
WHAS [11 Louisville, Kentucky]
WHBQ [13 Memphis, Tennessee]
WHDH [07 Boston, Massachusetts]
Wheaton Sun [Naperville, Illinois newspaper]
WHEC [10 Rochester, New York]
Wheeling Countryside [Illinois newspaper]
Wheeling News-Register [West Virginia
  newspaper]
Whidbey News Times [Washington newspaper]
WHIO [07 Dayton, Ohio]
White Lake Beacon [Whitehall, Michigan
  newspaper]
Whitefish Bay Herald [Wisconsin newspaper]
Whitefish Pilot [Montana newspaper]
Whittier Daily News [California newspaper]
WHIZ [18 Zanesville, Ohio]
WHKY [14 Hickory, North Carolina]
WHLA [31 La Crosse, Wisconsin]
WHNS [21 Greenville, South Carolina]
WHNT [19 Huntsville, Alabama]
WHO [13 Des Moines, Iowa]
WHOA [32 Montgomery, Alabama]
WHP [21 Harrisburg, Pennsylvania]
WHRO [15 Norfolk, Virginia]
WHSV [03 Harrisonburg, Virginia]
WHTJ [41 Charlottesville, Virginia]
WHTM [27 Harrisburg, Pennsylvania]

WHWC [28 Menomonie, Wisconsin]
WHYY [12 Philadelphia, Pennsylvania]
WIAT [42 Birmingham, Alabama]
WIBW [13 Topeka, Kansas]
Wichita Business Journal [Kansas newspaper]
Wichita Eagle [Kansas newspaper]
Wichita Eagle, The [Kansas newspaper]
Wickenburg Sun [Arizona newspaper]
WICS [20 Springfield, Illinois]
WICZ [40 Binghamton, New York]
WIFR [23 Rockford, Illinois]
Wilkes-Barre Times Leader [Pennsylvania
  newspaper]
WILL [12 Urbana, Illinois]
Willamette Week [Portland, Oregon
  newspaper]
Williamson Daily News [West Virginia
  newspaper]
Williamsport Sun-Gazette [Pennsylvania
  newspaper]
Willimantic Chronicle [Connecticut
  newspaper]
Williston Daily Herald [North Dakota
  newspaper]
Williston Pioneer, The [Florida newspaper]
Willow Glen Resident [California
  newspaper]
Wilmette Life [Illinois newspaper]
Wilmington Morning Star, The [North
  Carolina newspaper]
Wilmington News-Journal [Ohio newspaper]
Wilson County News, The [Floresville, Texas
  newspaper]
Wilson Daily Times [North Carolina
  newspaper]
Wilson World, The [Lebanon, Tennessee
  newspaper]
Wilton Bulletin, The [Connecticut
  newspaper]
WILX [10 Lansing, Michigan]
Winchester News [Virginia newspaper]
Winchester Star, The [Virginia newspaper]
Winchester Sun, The [Kentucky newspaper]

Windsor Journal [Windsor Locks, Connecticut newspaper]

Windsor Locks Journal [Bristol, Connecticut newspaper]

Winfield Daily Courier [Kansas newspaper]

Winfield News [Indiana newspaper]

WINK [11 Fort Myers, Florida]

Winnetka Talk [Illinois newspaper]

Winona Daily News [Minnesota newspaper]

Winona Post [Minnesota newspaper]

Winslow Mail, The [Arizona newspaper]

Winsted-Lester Prairie Journal [Minnesota newspaper]

Winston County Journal [Louisville, Mississippi newspaper]

Winston-Salem Journal [North Carolina newspaper]

Winterset Madisonian [Iowa newspaper]

Winthrop Independent [Massachusetts newspaper]

WIPB [49 Muncie, Indiana]

WIS [10 Columbia, South Carolina]

WISC [03 Madison, Wiscosin]

Wiscasset Newspaper [Maine newspaper]

Wisconsin State Journal [Wisconsin newspaper]

Wise County Messenger [Decatur, Texas newspaper]

WISH [08 Indianapolis, Indiana]

WISN [12 Milwaukee, Wisconsin]

WITF [33 Harrisburg, Pennsylvania]

WITI [06 Milwaukee, Wiscosin]

WITN [07 Washington, North Carolina]

WIVB [04 Buffalo, New York]

WIXT [09 Syracuse, New York]

WJAC [06 Johnstown, Pennsylvania]

WJAL [68 Chambersburg, Pennsylvania]

WJAR [10 Cranston, Rhode Island]

WJBF [06 Augusta, Georgia]

WJBK [02 Detroit, Michigan]

WJCT [07 Jacksonville, Florida]

WJET [24 Erie, Pennsylvania]

WJFW [12 Rhinelander, Wisconsin]

WJHG [07 Panama City, Florida]

WJHL [11 Johnson City, Tennessee]

WJLA [07 Washington, District of Columbia]

WJRD [49 Tuscaloosa, Alabama]

WJSP [28 Columbus, Georgia]

WJSU [33 Tuscaloosa, Alabama]

WJSU [40 Birmingham, Alabama]

WJTV [12 Jackson, Mississippi]

WJWB [17 Jacksonville, Florida]

WJWJ [16 Beaufort, South Carolina]

WJXT [04 Jacksonville, Florida]

WJXX [25 Jacksonville, Florida]

WJZ [13 Baltimore, Maryland]

WJZY [46 Charlotte, North Carolina]

WKAG [43 Hopkinsville, Kentucky]

WKAR [23 East Lansing, Michigan]

WKAS [25 Ashland, Kentucky]

WKBD [50 Detroit, Michigan]

WKBN [27 Youngstown, Ohio]

WKBT [08 La Crosse, Wisconsin]

WKBW [07 Buffalo, New York]

WKCF [18 Orlando, Florida]

WKEF [22 Dayton, Ohio]

WKFT [40 Fayetteville, North Carolina]

WKGB [53 Bowling Green, Kentucky]

WKHA [35 Hazard, Kentucky]

WKJG [33 Fort Wayne, Indiana]

WKLE [46 Lexington, Kentucky]

WKMA [35 Madisonville, Kentucky]

WKMG [06 Orlando, Florida]

WKMJ [68 Louisville, Kentucky]

WKMR [38 Morehead, Kentucky]

WKMU [21 Murray, Kentucky]

WKNO [10 Memphis, Tennessee]

WKNT [40 Bowling Green, Kentucky]

WKOH [31 Owensboro, Kentucky]

WKON [52 Owenton, Kentucky]

WKOP [15 Knoxville, Tennessee]

WKOW [27 Madison, Wisconsin]

WKPC [15 Louisville, Kentucky]

WKPD [29 Paducah, Kentucky]

WKPI [22 Pikeville, Kentucky]

WKPT [19 Kingsport, Tennessee]

WKRC [12 Cincinnati, Ohio]

WKRG [05 Mobile, Alabama]

WKRN [02 Nashville, Tennessee]

WKSO [29 Somerset, Kentucky]

WKTV [02 Utica, New York]

WKYC [02 Cleveland, Ohio]

WKYT [27 Lexington, Kentucky]

WKYU [24 Bowling Green, Kentucky]

WKZT [23 Elizabethtown, Kentucky]

WLAE [32 New Orleans, Louisiana]

WLAJ [53 Lansing, Michigan]

WLBT [03 Jackson, Mississippi]

WLBZ [02 Bangor, Maine]

WLED [49 Littleton, New Hampshire]

WLEF [36 Park Falls, Wisconsin]

WLEX [18 Lexington, Kentucky]

WLFI [18 West Lafayette, Indiana]

WLIO [35 Lima, Ohio]

WLIW [21 Plainview, New York]

WLJT [11 Martin, Tennessee]

WLKY [32 Louisville, Kentucky]

WLMT [30 Memphis, Tennessee]

WLNE [06 Providence, Rhode Island]

WLNS [06 Lansing, Michigan]

WLNY [55 Melville, New York]

WLOS [13 Asheville, North Carolina]

WLOX [13 Biloxi, Mississippi]

WLPB [27 Baton Rouge, Louisiana]

WLRN [17 Miami, Florida]

WLS [07 Chicago, Illinois]

WLTX [19 Columbia, South Carolina]

WLTZ [38 Columbus, Georgia]

WLUC [06 Negaunee, Michigan]

WLUK [11 Green Bay, Wiscosin]

WLVI [56 Boston, Massachusetts]

WLVT [39 Bethlehem, Pennsylvania]

WLWT [05 Cincinnati, Ohio]

WLYH [15 Harrisburg, Pennsylvania]

WMAQ [05 Chicago, Illinois]

WMAR [02 Baltimore, Maryland]

WMAZ [13 Macon, Georgia]

WMBB [13 Panama City, Florida]

WMBD [31 Peoria, Illinois]

WMC [05 Memphis, Tennessee]

WMDT [47 Salisbury, Maryland]

WMEA [26 Portland, Maine]

WMEB [12 Bangor, Maine]

WMEC [22 Macomb, Illinois]

WMED [13 Calais, Maine]

WMEM [10 Presque Isle, Maine]

WMFE [24 Orlando, Florida]

WMGC [34 Binghamton, New York]

WMGM [40 Linwood, New Jersey]

WMGT [41 Macon, Georgia]

WMHT [17 Schenectady, New York]

WMOR [32 Tampa, Florida]

WMPB [67 Baltimore, Maryland]

WMPN [29 Jackson, Mississippi]

WMPT [22 Annapolis, Maryland]

WMSN [47 Madison, Wisconsin]

WMSY [52 Marion, Virginia]

WMTV [15 Madison, Wisconsin]

WMTW [08 Auburn, Maine]

WMUR [09 Manchester, New Hampshire]

WMVS [10 Milwaukee, Wisconsin]

WMVT [36 Milwaukee, Wisconsin]

WNAC [64 Providence, Rhode Island]

WNBC [04 New York, New York]

WNCN [17 Raleigh, North Carolina]

WNCT [09 Greenville, North Carolina]

WNDS [50 Derry, New Hampshire]

WNDU [16 South Bend, Indiana]

WNDY [23 Indianapolis, Indiana]

WNEM [05 Saginaw, Michigan]

WNEO [45 Kent, Ohio]

WNEP [16 Scranton, Pennsylvania]

WNET [13 New York, New York]

WNGS [67 Buffalo, New York]

WNGT [48 Toledo, Ohio]

WNIN [09 Evansville, Indiana]

WNIT [34 Elkhart, Indiana]

WNJB [58 New Brunswick, New Jersey]

WNJN [50 Montclair, New Jersey]

WNJS [23 Camden, New Jersey]

WNJT [52 Trenton, New Jersey]

WNJU [47 Teterboro, New Jersey]

WNNE [31 White River Junction, Vermont]

WNOL [38 New Orleans, Louisiana]

WNPB [24 Morgantown, West Virginia]
WNPI [18 Norwood, New York]
WNSC [30 Rock Hill, South Carolina]
WNTZ [48 Natchez, Mississippi]
WNUV [54 Baltimore, Maryland]
WNVC [56 Fairfax, Virginia]
WNVT [53 Falls Church, Virginia]
WNWO [24 Toledo, Ohio]
WNYE [25 Brooklyn, New York]
WNYO [49 Buffalo, New York]
WNYT [13 Albany, New York]
WOAY [04 Oak Hill, West Virginia]
WOFL [35 Lake Mary, Florida]
WOGX [51 Lake Mary, Florida]
WOI [05 Des Moines, Iowa]
WOIO [19 Cleveland, Ohio]
WOKR [13 Rochester, New York]
WOLF [56 Scranton, Pennsylvania]
WOLO [25 Columbia, South Carolina]
Woman's Day [magazine]
Woman's World [magazine]
WOOD [08 Grand Rapids, Michigan]
Wood River Journal, The [Hailey, Idaho newspaper]
Woodburn Independent [Oregon newspaper]
Woodbury Bulletin [Cottage Grove, Minnesota newspaper]
Woodbury Bulletin [Wisconsin newspaper]
Woodbury Voices [Colorado newspaper]
Woodland Hills Progress-Star [Forest Hills, Pennsylvania newspaper]
Woodstock Independent, The [Illinois newspaper]
Woodstock Times [New York newspaper]
Woonsocket Call [Rhode Island newspaper]
Worcester Business Journal [Massachusetts newspaper]
Worcester County Messenger [Pocomoke City, Maryland newspaper]
Worcester Phoenix [Massachusetts newspaper]
Worcester Telegram & Gazette [Massachusetts newspaper]
World, The [Barre, Vermont newspaper]

World, The [Coos Bay, Oregon newspaper]
WOSU [34 Columbus, Ohio]
WOTV [41 Battle Creek, Michigan]
WOUB [20 Athens, Ohio]
WOUC [44 Athens, Ohio]
WOWK [13 Huntington, West Virginia]
WOWT [06 Omaha, Nebraska]
WPBA [30 Atlanta, Georgia]
WPBF [25 Palm Beach Gardens, Florida]
WPBN [07 Traverse City, Michigan]
WPBS [16 Watertown, New York]
WPBT [02 Miami, Florida]
WPBY [33 Huntington, West Virginia]
WPDE [15 Florence, South Carolina]
WPEC [12 West Palm Beach, Florida]
WPGA [58 Macon, Georgia]
WPHL [17 Philadelphia, Pennsylvania]
WPIX [11 New York, New York]
WPLG [10 Miami, Florida]
WPMI [15 Mobile, Alabama]
WPMT [43 York, Pennsylvania]
WPNE [38 Green Bay, Wisconsin]
WPRI [12 East Providence, Rhode Island]
WPSD [06 Paducah, Kentucky]
WPSG [57 Philadelphia, Pennsylvania]
WPSX [03 University Park, Pennsylvania]
WPTA [21 Fort Wayne, Indiana]
WPTD [16 Dayton, Ohio]
WPTO [14 Oxford, Ohio]
WPTV [05 West Palm Beach, Florida]
WPTY [24 Memphis, Tennessee]
WPTZ [05 Plattsburgh, New York]
WPVI [06 Philadelphia, Pennsylvania]
WPXI [11 Pittsburgh, Pennsylvania]
WPXT [51 Portland, Maine]
WQAD [08 Moline, Illinois]
WQEC [27 Quincy, Illinois]
WQED [13 Pittsburgh, Pennsylvania]
WQLN [54 Erie, Pennsylvania]
WQOW [18 Eau Claire, Wisconsin]
WQPT [24 Moline, Illinois]
WQRF [39 Rockford, Illinois]
WRAL [05 Raleigh, North Carolina]

WRAZ [50 Raleigh, North Carolina]
WRBL [03 Columbus, Georgia]
WRBW [65 Orlando, Florida]
WRC [04 Washington, District of Columbia]
WRDW [12 Augusta, Georgia]
WREG [03 Memphis, Tennessee]
WRET [49 Spartanburg, South Carolina]
WREX [13 Rockford, Illinois]
WRGB [06 Schenectady, New York]
WRHM [20 Wausau, Wisconsin]
WRIC [08 Richmond, Virginia]
WRJA [27 Sumter, South Carolina]
WRLH [35 Richmond, Virginia]
WRNN [62 Kingston, New York]
WROC [08 Rochester, New York]
WRSP [55 Springfield, Illinois]
WRTV [06 Indianapolis, Indiana]
WSAV [03 Savannah, Georgia]
WSAW [07 Wausau, Wisconsin]
WSAZ [03 Huntington, West Virginia]
WSBE [36 Providence, Rhode Island]
WSBK [38 Boston, Massachusetts]
WSBN [47 Norton, Virginia]
WSBT [22 South Bend, Indiana]
WSEC [14 Springfield, Illinois]
WSEE [35 Erie, Pennsylvania]
WSET [13 Lynchburg, Virginia]
WSFA [12 Montgomery, Alabama]
WSFX [26 Wilmington, North Carolina]
WSIL [03 Carterville, Illinois]
WSIU [08 Carbondale, Illinois]
WSJK [02 Sneedville, Tennessee]
WSJV [28 South Bend, Indiana]
WSKG [46 Binghamton, New York]
WSLS [10 Roanoke, Virginia]
WSMV [04 Nashville, Tennessee]
WSOC [09 Charlotte, North Carolina]
WSPA [07 Spartanburg, South Carolina]
WSST [55 Cordele, Georgia]
WSVN [07 Miami, Florida]
WSWS [66 Opelika, Alabama]
WSYT [68 Syracuse, New York]
WSYX [06 Columbus, Ohio]

WTAE [04 Pittsburgh, Pennsylvania]
WTAJ [10 Altoona, Pennsylvania]
WTAP [15 Parkersburg, West Virginia]
WTAT [24 Charleston, South Carolina]
WTBS [17 Atlanta, Georgia]
WTCI [45 Chattanooga, Tennessee]
WTEN [10 Albany, New York]
WTGL [52 Orlando, Florida]
WTHI [10 Terre Haute, Indiana]
WTHR [13 Indianapolis, Indiana]
WTIC [61 Hartford, Connecticut]
WTKR [03 Norfolk, Virginia]
WTLH [49 Tallahassee, Florida]
WTLV [12 Jacksonville, Florida]
WTLW [44 Lima, Ohio]
WTMJ [04 Milwaukee, Wisconsin]
WTNZ [43 Knoxville, Tennessee]
WTOC [11 Savannah, Georgia]
WTOG [44 St. Petersburg, Florida]
WTOK [11 Meridian, Mississippi]
WTOL [11 Toledo, Ohio]
WTOM [04 Traverse City, Michigan]
WTOV [09 Steubenville, Ohio]
WTRF [07 Wheeling, West Virginia]
WTSP [10 St. Petersburg, Florida]
WTTE [28 Columbus, Ohio]
WTTV [04 Indianapolis, Indiana]
WTTW [11 Chicago, Illinois]
WTVA [09 Tupelo, Mississippi]
WTVC [09 Chattanooga, Tennessee]
WTVD [11 Durham, North Carolina]
WTVF [05 Nashville, Tennessee]
WTVG [13 Toledo, Ohio]
WTVH [05 Syracuse, New York]
WTVI [42 Charlotte, North Carolina]
WTVJ [06 Miami, Florida]
WTVM [09 Columbus, Georgia]
WTVP [47 Peoria, Illinois]
WTVQ [36 Lexington, Kentucky]
WTVR [06 Richmond, Virginia]
WTVS [56 Detroit, Michigan]
WTVT [13 Tampa, Florida]
WTVW [07 Evansville, Indiana]

WTVX [34 West Palm Beach, Florida]
WTWO [02 Terre Haute, Indiana]
WTXF [29 Philadelphia, Pennsylvania]
WTXL [27 Tallahassee, Florida]
WUFT [05 Gainesville, Florida]
WUHF [31 Rochester, New York]
WUNC [04 Chapel Hill, North Carolina]
WUPA [69 Atlanta, Georgia]
WUPL [54 Metairie, Louisiana]
WUPN [48 Winston-Salem, North Carolina]
WUPW [36 Toledo, Ohio]
WUSA [09 Washington, District of Columbia]
WUSF [16 Tampa, Florida]
WUTB [24 Baltimore, Maryland]
WUTR [20 Utica, New York]
WUTV [29 Grand Island, New York]
WUXP [30 Nashville, Tennessee]
WVAH [11 Charleston, West Virginia]
WVAN [09 Savannah, Georgia]
WVBT [43 Portsmouth, Virginia]
WVEC [13 Norfolk, Virginia]
WVER [28 Rutland, Vermont]
WVIA [44 Pittston, Pennsylvania]
WVII [07 Bangor, Maine]
WVIR [29 Charlottesville, Virginia]
WVIT [30 West Hartford, Connecticut]
WVIZ [25 Cleveland, Ohio]
WVLT [08 Knoxville, Tennessee]
WVPT [51 Harrisonburg, Virginia]
WVSX [59 Ghent, West Virginia]
WVTA [41 Windsor, Vermont]
WVTB [20 St. Johnsbury, Vermont]
WVTM [13 Birmingham, Alabama]
WVVA [06 Bluefield, West Virginia]
WVVH [23 Wainscott, New York]
WWAY [03 Wilmington, North Carolina]
WWBT [12 Richmond, Virginia]
WWCI [10 Vero Beach, Florida]
WWCP [08 Johnstown, Pennsylvania]
WWHO [53 Chillicothe, Ohio]
WWJ [62 Detroit, Michigan]
WWL [04 New Orleans, Louisiana]
WWLP [22 Springfield, Massachusetts]

WWMT [03 Kalamazoo, Michigan]
WWNY [07 Watertown, New York]
WWOR [09 Secaucus, New Jersey]
WWPB [31 Hagerstown, Maryland]
WWTI [50 Watertown, New York]
WWTV [09 Traverse City, Michigan]
WWUP [10 Sault Sainte Marie, Michigan]
WXEL [42 West Palm Beach, Florida]
WXGA [08 Waycross, Georgia]
WXIA [11 Atlanta, Georgia]
WXII [12 Winston-Salem, North Carolina]
WXIN [59 Indianapolis, Indiana]
WXIX [19 Cincinnati, Ohio]
WXLV [45 Winston-Salem, North Carolina]
WXMI [17 Grand Rapids, Michigan]
WXOW [19 La Crosse, Wisconsin]
WXTX [54 Columbus, Georgia]
WXVT [15 Greenville, Mississippi]
WXXA [23 Albany, New York]
WXXI [21 Rochester, New York]
WXXV [25 Gulfport, Mississippi]
WXYZ [07 Detroit, Michigan]
WYBE [35 Philadelphia, Pennsylvania]
WYES [12 New Orleans, Louisiana]
WYFF [04 Greenville, South Carolina]
WYFX [62 Youngstown, Ohio]
WYIN [56 Merrillville, Indiana]
WYMT [57 Hazard, Kentucky]
Wyoming Tribune Eagle [Cheyenne, Wyoming
  newspaper]
Wyoming Webworks News [Cheyenne,
  Wyoming newspaper]
WYOU [22 Scranton, Pennsylvania]
WYOW [34 Eagle River, Wisconsin]
WYTV [33 Youngstown, Ohio]
WYZZ [43 Bloomington, Illinois]
WZDX [54 Huntsville, Alabama]
WZPX [43 Grand Rapids, Michigan]
WZTV [17 Nashville, Tennessee]
WZVN [26 Fort Myers, Florida]
XETV [06 San Diego, California]
Yakima Herald-Republic [Washington
  newspaper]

Yale Daily News [New Haven, Connecticut
    newspaper]
Yale Herald [New Haven, Connecticut
    newspaper]
Yankee Trader [Long Island, New York
    newspaper]
Yankton Daily Press & Dakotan [South Dakota
    newspaper]
Yellow Springs News [Ohio newspaper]
Yellowstone Net Newspaper [Belgrade,
    Montana newspaper]
YM [magazine]
York County Coast Star [Saco, Maine
    newspaper]
York Daily Record [York County, Pennsylvania
    newspaper]
York Dispatch, The [Pennsylvania newspaper]
York News Times [Nebraska newspaper]
York Sunday News [Pennsylvania newspaper]
York Weekly [Maine newspaper]
Your Community Shopper [Ardmore,
    Tennessee newspaper]
Ypsilanti Courier [Michigan newspaper]
Ypsilanti Press [Michigan newspaper]
Yuma Daily Sun [Arizona newspaper]
Yuma Sun [Arizona newspaper]
ZDTV [network]
Zephyr [Galesburg, Illinois newspaper]

Political, Governmental, and International Associations and Institutions

6

8th Day Center for Justice
AARP (American Association of Retired Persons)
Academia Mexicana de Derecho Internacional
Academic Council on the United Nations System, The
Academie Europeenne des Sciences, des Arts et Des Lettres
Academy of Criminal Justice Sciences
Academy of Mining Sciences
Academy of Model Aeronautics
Academy of Motion Picture Arts & Sciences
ACC Network on Rural Development and Food Security
ACC Subcommittee on Drug Control (ACC/SDC)
ACC Subcommittee on Nutrition (ACC/SCN)
ACC Subcommittee on Oceans and Coastal Areas
ACC Subcommittee on Statistical Activities (ACC/SSA)
ACC Subcommittee on Water Resources (ACC/SWR)
Accounting and Auditing Policy Committee (AAPC)
Acoustic Neuroma Association
Acoustical Society of America

Acronym Institute, The
Action Internationale Contre la Faim
Actionaid
Actors' Equity Association
Adirondack Mountain Club
Administration for Children and Families
Administration on Aging
Administrative Committee of the Federal Register
Administrative Committee on Coordination (ACC)
Adult Literacy Organization of Zimbabwe, The
Advanced Technology Program Advisory Commission on Intergovernmental Relations
Aerospace Industries Association of America Inc.
Aerospace Medical Association
AFL-CIO (American Federation of Labor–Congress of Industrial Organizations)
Africa Faith And Justice Network
Africa Fund, The
Africa Genetics Association
African American Islamic Institute
African Medical and Research Foundation Inc., The
African Methodist Episcopal Church
African Methodist Episcopal Zion Church

African-American Institute, The
African-American Labor Center
Afro-Asian Peoples' Solidarity Organization
AFS-Intercultural Programs Inc.
Agence Internationale Pour le Developpement
Agency for Healthcare Research and Quality (AHRQ)
AgExport Services Division
Aggressive Skaters Association
Agricultural History Society
Agricultural Marketing Service
Agricultural Research Service (ARS)
Agudath Israel World Organization
Aiesec International
Air and Waste Management Association
Air Combat Command
Air Courier Association
Air Education and Training Command
Air Force Association
Air Force Materiel Command
Air Force Mobility Command
Air Force Research Laboratory
Air Force Reserve Command
Air Force Reserve Officer Training Corps (AFROTC)
Air Force Sergeants Association
Air Force Space Command: 14th Air Force Flying Tigers
Air Force Special Operations Command (AFSOC)
Air Line Pilots Association
Air Movement & Control Association International Inc.
Air National Guard
Air Transport Association of America
Aircraft Mechanics Fraternal Association (AMFA)
Aircraft Owners and Pilots Association
Airline Ambassadors International Inc.
Al-Anon Family Group Headquarters Inc.
Alateen
Albert Schweitzer Fellowship
Albert Schweitzer Institute for the Humanities

Alberta Teachers' Association
Alcoholics Anonymous (A.A.)
Alexander Graham Bell Association for the Deaf
Alianza Espiritualista Internacional
All India Women's Conference
All Pakistan Women's Association
Alliance For Communities In Action
Alliance Internationale de Tourisme
Alliance to End Childhood Lead Poisoning
All-India Boy Scouts Association
All-Nigerian United Nations Students And Youth Association
Alpha Kappa Alpha Sorority
Alternative Agricultural Research and Commercialization Center (AARC)
Altrusa International Inc.
Aluba (Asociacion de Lucha Contra Bulimia y Anorexia)
Alzheimer's Association
Amalgamated Transit Union
Amateur Softball Association
American Academy of Allergy, Asthma and Immunology
American Academy of Arts and Letters
American Academy of Family Physicians
American Academy of Forensic Sciences
American Academy of Mechanics
American Academy of Political and Social Science
American Aging Association
American Agricultural Economics Association
American Alliance for Health, Physical Education, Recreation and Dance
American Anthropological Association
American Antiquarian Society
American Anti-Vivisection Society, The
American Art Therapy Association Inc.
American Association for Clinical Chemistry Inc.
American Association for Health Education
American Association for Higher Education

American Association for Laboratory Animal Science

American Association for Respiratory Care

American Association for the Advancement of Science (AAAS)

American Association for World Health

American Association of College Registrars and Admissions Officers (AACRAO)

American Association of Colleges for Teacher Education

American Association of Community Colleges

American Association of Consumer Sciences

American Association of Family and Consumer Sciences

American Association of Kidney Patients

American Association of Museums

American Association of Naturopathic Physicians

American Association of Petroleum Geologists

American Association of Physics Teachers

American Association of Retired Persons (AARP)

American Association of State Highway and Transportation Officials (AASHTO)

American Association of University Professors (AAUP)

American Association of University Women (AAUW)

American Astronomical Society

American Atheists

American Automobile Association (AAA)

American Bankers Association (ABA)

American Baptist Churches-USA National Ministries

American Bar Association (ABA)

American Battle Monuments Commission

American Bible Society

American Booksellers Association

American Business Women's Association

American Camping Association, The

American Cancer Society

American Catholic Historical Society

American Ceramic Society, The

American Chemical Society

American Cetacean Society, The

American Chain Association (ACA)

American Chiropractic Association

American Civil Liberties Union (ACLU)

American Collectors Association

American College of Surgeons

American Collegiate Hockey Association (ACHA)

American Committee On Africa

American Community Cultural Center Association

American Concrete Pressure Pipe Association (ACPPA)

American Congress on Surveying and Mapping (ACSM)

American Contract Bridge League

American Correctional Association

American Council for Judaism

American Council of the Blind

American Council of Life Insurance

American Council Of Young Political Leaders

American Council On Consumer Interests

American Council on Education

American Counseling Association

American Cutting Horse Association

American Dental Association

American Diabetes Association

American Drug Free Powerlifting Association

American Economic Association

American Education Research Association

American Electronics Association

American Electroplaters and Surface Finishers Society (AESF)

American Farm Bureau Federation

American Federal of Television and Radio Artists (AFTRA)

American Federation of Arts

American Federation of Government Employees

American Federation of Government Employees

American Federation of Labor and Congress of Industrial Organizations
American Federation of Musicians of the United States and Canada
American Federation of Police and Concerned Citizens
American Federation of State, County and Municipal Employees (AFSCME)
American Federation of Teachers
American Film Marketing
American Forces Information Service
American Foreign Law Association Inc.
American Foreign Service Association
American Forest Foundation
American Forests
American Forum For Global Education, The
American Foundation for the Blind
American Foundrymen's Society Inc.
American Friends Service Committee
American Gaming Association
American Gas Association
American Genetic Association
American Geographical Society
American Geographical Society, The
American Geriatrics Society
American Group Pshychotherapy Association
American Health Care Association
American Heart Association
American Heart Association (AHA)
American Historical Association
American Historical Association
American Home Workers Association
American Horse Council Inc.
American Horse Shows Association Inc.
American Horticultural Society
American Hospital Association
American Humane Society
American Humanist Association
American Immigration Lawyers Association
American Indian and Alaska Native Affairs Desk (OJP)
American Indian Law Alliance
American Industrial Health Council

American Industrial Hygiene Association
American Institute of Architects, The
American Institute of Biological Sciences
American Institute of Certified Public Accountants
American Institute of Chemical Engineers
American Institute of Chemists, The
American Institute for Foreign Study
American Institute of Mining, Metallurgical and Petroleum Engineers, The
American Institute of Physics
American Insurance Association
American Iron and Steel Institute
American Jail Association
American Jewish Committee, The
American Jewish Congress
American Jewish Historical Society
American Jewish World Service
American Judges Association
American Kennel Club (AKC)
American Legion Auxiliary
American Legion, The
American Library Association (ALA)
American Lung Association
American Lutheran Church
American Management Association
American Marketing Association (AMA)
American Mathematical Society
American Medical Association (AMA)
American Medical Student Association (AMSA)
American Medical Women's Association
American Medical Women's Association Inc.
American Medical Writers Association
American Mensa Ltd.
American Meteorological Society
American Mideast Business Association
American Model United Nations (AMUN)
American Montessori Society
American Montessori Society
American Morgan Horse Association
American Mothers Inc.
American Motorcyclist Association (AMA)
American Museum of Natural History

American Nuclear Society
American Numismatic Association
American Nurses Association
American Ornithologists' Union
American Osteopathic Association
American Parkinson Disease Association
American Payroll Association (APA)
American Pharmaceutical Association
American Philatelic Society
American Philosophical Society
American Physical Society, The
American Physical Therapy Association (APTA)
American Planning Association
American Planning Association
American Planning Association
American Plastics Council
American Police Hall of Fame
American Political Science Association
American Postal Workers Union
American Psychiatric Association
American Psychiatric Nurses Association
American Psychoanalytic Association, The
  (APA)
American Psychological Association (APA)
American Psychological Association (Apa)
American Public Health Association
American Public Works Association
American Pulpwood Association Inc.
American Red Cross
American Rental Association
American Resort Development Association
American School Counselor Association
American Sign Language Teachers Association
American Social Health Association
American Society for Biochemistry and
  Molecular Biology
American Society for Engineering Education
American Society for Investigative Pathology
American Society for Nutritional Sciences
American Society for Photogrammetry and
  Remote Sensing
American Society for Public Administration
  (ASPA)

American Society for Quality
American Society for Testing and & Materials
American Society for the Prevention of Cruelty
  to Animals (ASPCA)
American Society of Agronomy
American Society of Appraisers
American Society of Association Executives
American Society of Bakery Engineers
American Society of Civil Engineers
American Society of Clinical Pathologists
American Society of Dowsers Inc.
American Society of Heating, Refrigerating and
  Air-Conditioning Engineers Inc.
American Society of International Law, The
American Society of Journalists and Authors
American Society of Magazine Editors
American Society of Mechanical Engineers
American Society of Media Photographers
American Society of Naval Engineers
American Society of Newspaper Editors
American Sociological Association
American Speech-Language-Hearing
  Association
American Sportfishing Association (ASA)
American Sportscasters Association
American Statistical Association
American Stock Exchange (Amex)
American Sun Protection Association (ASPA)
American Symphony Orchestra League
American Theological Library Association
American University In Cairo, The
American Veterans Committee
American Veterans of World War II, Korea and
  Vietnam (AMVETS)
American Veterinary Medical Association
American Watchmakers-Clockmakers Institute
American Water Resources Association
American Water Works Association (AWWA)
American Welding Society
American-Arab Antidiscrimination Committee
Americans for Democratic Action Inc.
Americans for Middle East Understanding Inc.
Americans for Peace Now

American-South African People's Friendship
Association

America's Community Bankers

Ames Research Center

AMIDEAST (America-Mideast Educational
and Training Services)

Amnesty International

Amnesty International USA

Amurt-Ananda Marga Universal Relief Team

AMVETS (American Veterans of World War
II, Korea and Vietnam)

Anacostia Museum Arthur M. Sackler
Gallery

Anglican Communion

Anglican Consultative Council, The

Animal and Plant Health Inspection
Service

Animal Protection Institute

Animal Welfare Institute

Anti-Apartheid Movement in Austria

Anti-Defamation League

Anti-Slavery International

Antitrust Division

Anuvrat Global Organization (Anuvibha)

APA - The Engineered Wood Association

APMI International

Appalachian Regional Commission

Arab Association For Arts, Culture And
Information, The

Arab International Association for Tourism And
Automobile Clubs

Arab Office for Youth and Environment

Arab Society for the Protection of Industrial
Property

Arab Society of Certified Accountants

Arab Towns Organization

Arab Women Solidarity Association

Arc, The

Archaeological Institute of America

Architects Designers Planners For Social
Responsibility

Architectural and Transportation Barriers
Compliance Board (Access Board)

Archivio Disarmo Centro Di Documentazione
Sulla Pace E Sul Disarmo

Arctic Research Commission

Argentinas

Argentine-North American Association For the
Advancement Of Science, The

Armed Forces Communications and Electronics
Association

Armed Forces Communications and Electronics
Association

Armed Forces Radiobiology Research Institute
(AFRRI)

Armed Forces Retirement Home

Armed Forces Staff College

Armenian General Benevolent Union

Armenian International Women's Association

Armenian Relief Society Inc.

Army Digitization Office (ADO)

Army Medical Department (AMEDD)

Army Research Laboratory (ARL)

Army Review Boards Agency (ARBA)

Arthritis and Musculoskeletal Interagency
Coordinating Committee

Arthritis Foundation

Article 19, The International Centre Against
Censorship

ArtsEdge

ASAE—The Society for Engineering in
Agricultural, Food, and Biologicalsystems

Asean Confederation of Women's
Organizations

Asia Society, The

Asian American Journalists Association

Asian Cultural Forum On Development
(ACFOD)

Asian Environmental Society

Asian Pacific Youth Forum

Asian Women's Institute, The

Asian Youth Council

ASM International

Asociacion Argentina Para la Infancia

Asociacion Argentina Pro-Naciones Unidas de
Cordoba

Asociacion Ciudadanos del Mundo
Asociacion Cristiana Femenina de Buenos Aires
Asociacion Cubana de las Naciones Unidas
Asociacion Cultural Sejekto de Costa Rica
Asociacion de Promocion de la Educacion
Popular
Asociacion Guatemalteca Pro Naciones Unidas
Asociacion Guias Argentinas
Asociacion Iberoamericana de Periodistas
Especializados y Tecnicos (Aipet
Asociacion Internacional de Hidatidologia
Asociacion Latinoamericana de Instituciones
Financieras de Desarrollo
Asociacion Latinoamericana para los Derechos
Humanos (ALDUH)
Asociacion Mexicana para las Naciones Unidas
Asociacion Mundial de Vivienda Rural
Asociacion Nacional de Amas de Casa Rurales
de Colombia
Asociacion Nacional de Locutores de Mexico
A.C
Asociacion Napguana
Asociacion Panamena por los principios univer-
sales de las Naciones Unidas
Asociacion Para las Naciones Unidas en Espana
Asociacion Pro Naciones Unidas de Argentina
Asociacion Pro Naciones Unidas del Peru
Asociacion Regional Liberal en Pro de los
Derechos Humanos, Economicos, Sociales y
Politicos
Asociatia Pentru Natiunile Unite Din Romania
Assemblee Parlementaire de la Francophonie
Assemblies of God
Asset Forfeiture Program
Associated Country Women of the World
Associates of the National Agricultural Library
Association
Association Burkinabe des Communicatrices
(Abc)
Association Centrafricaine pour les Nations
Unies (Acanu)
Association Congolaise pour les Nations Unies

Association de Conseil D'organisation de
Recherche et de Developpement (ACORD)
Association des Amis Marocains des Nations
Unies Club Unesco
Association des Etats Generaux Etudiants de
l'Europe
Association des Etudes Internationales
Association for Applied Psychophysiology and
Biofeedback (AAPB)
Association for Better Living and Education
(ABLE)
Association for Childhood Education
International
Association for Clinical Pastoral Education
Association for Computational Linguistics
Association for Couples in Marriage
Enrichment
Association for Education in Journalism and
Mass Communication
Association for Information and Image
Management International
Association for Investment Management and
Research
Association for Promotion Of International
Cooperation
Association for Quality and Participation
Association for Research and Enlightenment
(A.R.E.)
Association for Systems Management (ASM)
Association for the Gifted
Association for the Protection of Nature and
the Environment
Association for the Study of Afro-American
Life and History Inc.
Association for Women in Communications
Association for Women in Psychology
Association for Women in Science (AWIS)
Association for World Education
Association Francaise pour les Nations Unies
Association Francois-Xavier Bagnoud
Association Guineenne pour les Nations Unies
Association Internationale des Charites

Association Internationale des Juristes
Democrates

Association Internationale des Universites du
Troisieme Age

Association Internationale pour la Defense de la
Liberte Religieuse

Association Internationale pour la Protection de
la Propriete Industrielle

Association Luxembourgeoise pour les Nations
Unies

Association Malienne pour les Nations Unies

Association Marocaine d'etudes et de
Recherches Internationales

Association Mondiale des Amis de L'enfance

Association Mondiale pour L'ecole Instrument
de Paix

Association Mongole pour les Nations
Unies

Association Montessori International

Association of American Buddhists

Association of American Geographers

Association of American Medical Colleges
(AAMC)

Association of American Publishers

Association of American Railroads

Association of American Universities

Association of America's Public Television
Stations

Association of Arab-American University
Graduates Inc.

Association of Certified Fraud Examiners

Association of College and Research Libraries
(ACRL)

Association of Collegiate Schools of
Architecture (ACSA)

Association of Communications Enterprises
(ASCENT)

Association of Conservation Engineers

Association of Consulting Chemists &
Chemical Engineers Inc.

Association of Consulting Engineers

Association of Energy Engineers (AEE)

Association of Flight Attendants

Association of Former International Civil
Servants

Association of Fundraising Professionals

Association of Government Accountants

Association of Home Appliance Manufacturers

Association of Illinois Electric Cooperatives
(AIEC)

Association of Information Technology
Professionals (AITP)

Association of Jesuit Colleges and Universities

Association of Jewish Libraries

Association of Junior Leagues International Inc.

Association of Management Consulting Firms

Association of Operating Room Nurses
(AORN)

Association of Pet Dog Trainers (APDT)

Association of Professional Engineers

Association of Progressive Rental Organizations

Association of Research Libraries

Association of Surfing Professionals

Association of the Bar of the City of New York

Association of the United States Army

Association of Torah-Observant Messianics

Association of Vineyard Churches

Association of Women Entrepreneurs of Small
Scale Industries

Association of Women's Health, Obstetric and
Neonatal Nurses (AWHONN)

Association of World Citizens

Association on American Indian Affairs

Association Rissalat At-Taleb

Association Senegalaise pour les Nations Unies

Association Tunisienne des Jeunes Medicins
sans Frontieres

Association Tunisienne des Meres

Association Tunisienne pour les Nations Unies

Association Zairoise pour les Nations Unies

Associazione Centro Solidarieta Genova

Associazione Noi per Loro

Associazione Volontari per il Servizio
Internationale

Astronomical Society of the Pacific

Athletes United for Peace (Aup)

Athletic Trainers' Associations
Attorney General
Australian Medical Association (AMA)
Australian Mines & Metals
Australian National Sports Fishing Association
Authors League of America
Autism Society of America
Automotive Hall of Fame
Automotive Wholesalers of Illinois
AZA (American Zoo and Aquarium Association)
Azad Muslim Welfare Complex Bangladesh
Baha'i International Community
Baha'i of the United States, National Spiritual
  Assembly
Bakery, Confectionery and Tobacco Workers
  International Union
Balkan-Ji-Bari International
Ballistic Missile Defense Organization
  (BMDOLINK)
Bangladesh Mahila Samity
Baptist World Alliance
Barbecue Industry Association
Bellevue Hospital Center
Benevolent and Protective Order of the Elks of
  the U.S.A.
Beyond War Foundation
Bibliographical Society of America
BIFMA International
Big Brothers/Big Sisters of America
Bildner Center For Western Hemisphere
  Studies
Billy Graham Evangelistic Association
Birlesmis Milletler Turk Dernegi
Black Economic Development Conference Inc.
Black Economic Research Center
Blinded Veterans Association
Blindness, Research to Prevent
Blue Cross and Blue Shield Association
B'nai B'rith International
Board
Board of Governors of the Federal Reserve
  System
Board of Veterans' Appeals

Bobek Charity Foundation of the Republic of
  Kazakhstan
Bochasanwasi Shree Akshar Purusottam
  Sanstha
Boy Scouts of America
Boys & Girls Clubs of America
Brahma Kumaris World Spiritual University
Brain Injury Association
Bread For the World Institute
Brehon Law Society
Bridge, Tunnel and Turnpike Association
British American Security Information Council
British Automatic Sprinkler Association
British Columbia Automobile Association
  (BCAA)
British Columbia Shopping Centre Association
British Contract Furnishing Association
  (BCFA)
British Furniture Manufacturers Ltd.
  (BFM)
British Marine Equipment Council
British Standards Institute
Brookings Institution, The
Brooks Bird Club Inc., The
Brothers Of Charity
Building Owners and Managers Association
  (BOMA)
Building Owners and Managers Association
  International
Bureau of Alcohol, Tobacco, and Firearms
Bureau of Economic Analysis (BEA)
Bureau of Engraving and Printing
Bureau of Export Administration
Bureau of Indian Affairs (BIA)
Bureau of International Labor Affairs
Bureau of Justice Assistance
Bureau of Justice Statistics
Bureau of Labor Statistics
Bureau of Land Management (BLM)
Bureau of Legislative Affairs
Bureau of Prisons
Bureau of the Census
Bureau of the Public Debt

Business and Institutional Furniture
　Manufacturer's Association
Business and Professional Women
Business Council for International
　Understanding
Business Council for the United Nations
Business Executives For National Security Inc.
Business Marketing Association
Business Products Industry Association (BPIA)
Business Technology Association (BTA)
Cairo Institute for Human Rights Studies
California Association of Nurserymen
California Chiropractic Association
California Library Association
California Nuisance Wildlife Control
　Operators Association
Camara De Comercio, Industria y Produccion
　de la Republica Argentina
Cambodian Network Council
Camp Fire Boys and Girls
Campaign for the Earth Foundation
Can Manufacturers Institute (CMI)
Canadian Association of Home Inspectors
　(CAHI)
Canadian Automobile Association
Canadian Historical Association (CHA)
Canadian Institute of Strategic Studies. The
Canadian Mental Health Association
Canadian Paint and Coatings Industry (CPCA)
Canadian Psychological Association
Canadian Voice of Women for Peace
Canadian Wood Council, The
Capitol Newswire International News Service
CARE Inc. (Co-Operative for Assistance &
　Relief Everywhere Inc.)
Caribbean Conservation Association
Caribbean Family Planning Affiliation Ltd.
Caribbean Human Rights Network
Caritas Internationalis (International
　Confederation of Catholic Charities)
Carnegie Council on Ethics and International
　Affairs
Carnegie Endowment for International Peace

Carpet and Rug Institute
Catholic Charities USA
Catholic Daughters of the Americas
Catholic International Education Office
　(OIEC)
Catholic Near East Welfare Association
Catholic Relief Services
Catholic War Veterans of the U.S.A. Inc.
Center for Cost and Financing Studies
Center for Defense Information
Center for Earth and Planetary Studies (CEPS)
Center for Economic and Social Studies for the
　Third World
Center for Information Technology
Center for International Cooperation, The
Center for International Health And
　Cooperation, The
Center for International Policy
Center for Marine Conservation
Center for Nutrition Policy and Promotion
Center for Organization and Delivery Studies
Center for Outcomes and Effectiveness
　Research
Center for Practice and Technology Assess-
　ment
Center for Primary Care Research
Center for Psychology and Social Change
Center for Quality Measurement and
　Improvement
Center for Scientific Research and Middle East
　Strategic Studies
Center for Scientific Review (CSR)
Center for the Study Of Southern Culture
Center for UN Reform Education
Center for Women's Global Leadership
Center of Concern
Centers for Disease Control and Prevention
　(CDC)
Central Collegiate Hockey Association
　(CCHA)
Central Committee for Conscientious
　Objectors
Central Intelligence Agency (CIA)

Centre D'expertises Socio-Politiques en Europe
Centre for Development and Population
  Activities
Centre for International Peacebuilding, The
Centre for Science and Environment (CSE)
Centre for Training and Rehabilitation of
  Destitute Women
Centre for War/Peace Studies
Centre National de Co-Operation au
  Developpement (CNCD)
CEO Institute
Cerebral Palsy Associations Inc., United
Chamber of Commerce of the U.S.
Chemical Manufacturers Association, Inc.
Chemical Specialties Manufacturers Association
  (CSMA)
Chief Financial Officers Council
Chief Information Officers Council
Child Welfare League of America Inc.
Child Welfare League of Trinidad and Tobago
Childhope
Children of the Earth
Children's Aid Society, The
Children's Atelier, The
Children's Book Council
Children's Fund For Southern Africa Inc.
Chlorine Institute Inc., The
Christian Children's Fund
Christian Church (Disciples of Christ)
Christian Democrat International
Christian Embassy of Campus Crusade for
  Christ
Christian Methodist Episcopal Church
Christian Mission for the United Nations
  Community
Christian Motorcyclists Association
Christian Peace Conference
Christians Associated for Relationship with
  Eastern Europe (CAREE)
Christophers, The
Church Medical Center of Russia
Church of England
Church of Jesus Christ of Latter-day Saints

Church of the Brethren
Church Women United
Church World Service
Churches of Christ
Citizen Diplomacy of San Diego
Citizens Foundation, The
Citizens' Stamp Advisory Committee
Civic Assembly of Women of the Philippines
Civil Air Patrol, National Headquarters
Civil Division
Civil Rights Division
Cleaning Equipment Trade Association (CETA)
Club International Pour la Recherche de la Paix
Coalition Against Trafficking in Women
Coalition for Peace Action
Coalition of Visionary Retailers
Coastal Conservation Association
Coastal Ocean Program (COP)
Coin Laundry Association
College Art Association (CAA)
College Association for the Research of the
  Principle (CARP)
College Band Directors National Association
College Board, The
College Fund/UNCF, The
College of Cardinals
Colonial Athletic Association (CAA)
Comite Europeen du Beton, The
Comite Francais des Organisations Non-
  Gouvernamentales pour la Liaison et
  l'Information des Nations Unies
Comite Internacional de la Bandera de la Paz
Commission for the Defense of Human Rights
  in Central America (CODEHUCA)
Commission Internationale de L'eclairage
Commission of Fine Arts
Commission of the Churches on International
  Affairs
Commission to Study the Organization of
  Peace
Commitment
Committee for Citizens' Rights (Dhaka)
Committee for Economic Development

Committee for International Co-Operation in National Research in Demography

Committee for Purchase from People Who Are Blind or Severely Disabled

Committee for the Implementation of Textile Agreements

Committee for the National Institute For the Environment

Committee on Foreign Investment in the United States

Commodity and Marketing Programs

Commodity Credit Corporation

Commodity Futures Trading Commission (CFTC)

Common Cause

Common Heritage Institute

Commonwealth Broadcasting Association (CBA)

Commonwealth Medical Association

Commonwealth Pharmaceutical Association

Communications Coordination Committee for the U.N.

Communications Workers of America

Community Associations Institute

Community Development Financial Institutions Fund

Community Dispute Resolution

Community Oriented Policing Services (COPS)

Community Relations Service

Compliance Review Staff Administration

Comprehensive Nuclear-Test-Ban Treaty Organization (CTBTO)

Computing Services & Software Association (CSSA)

Comunicacion Cultural A.C.

Comunita Incontro

Concern Worldwide

Confederacion Latinoamericana de Cooperativas de Ahorro y Credito (COLAC)

Confederation des Unions Syndicales des Travailleurs Grecs de la Fonction

Confederation Internationale des Anciens Prisonniers de Guerre

Confederation of Independent Trade Unions in Bulgaria

Conference of European Churches

Congregation de Notre Dame

Congregation of Our Lady of Charity of the Good Shepherd

Congregation of the Mission

Congregation of the Sisters of St. Joseph of Peace

Congregations of St. Joseph

Congress of Racial Equality (CORE)

Congressional Budget Office (CBO)

Consejo Argentino Para las Relaciones Internacionales

Consejo Indio de Sudamerica

Consejo Latinoamericano de Mujeres Catolicas

Consortium on Peace Research Education and Development

Consultative Committee on Administrative Questions (CCAQ)

Consultative Committee on Programme and Operational Questions (CCPOQ)

Consultative Council of Jewish Organizations

Consumer Education and Research Centre (CERC)

Consumer Electronics Manufacturers Association

Consumer Federation of America

Consumer Product Safety Commission (CPSC)

Consumers International

Consumers Union

Contact Lens Manufacturers Association (CLMA)

Continental Basketball Association (CBA)

Control System Integrators

Coolidge Center for Environmental Leadership

Cooperation Internationale Pour le Developpement et la Solidarite

Cooperative Baptist Fellowship

Cooperative for American Relief Everywhere (CARE)

Cooperative State Research, Education and
  Extension Service
Coordinadora Nacional de Jubilats i
  Pensionistes de Catalunya
Co-Ordinating Board Of Jewish Organizations
Coordinating Council on Juvenile Justice and
  Delinquency Prevention
Corporation for National Service
Corrections Program Office (OJP)
Cotton, Oilseeds, Tobacco and Seeds Division
Council for Advancement and Support of
  Education (CASE)
Council for Exceptional Children, The
Council for Responsible Genetics
Council for Security Cooperation in the Asia-
  Pacific
Council for Better Business Bureaus
Council of Economic Advisers
Council of Fleet Specialists
Council of International Programs USA
Council of State Governments, The
Council on Economic Priorities
Council on Environmental Quality
Council on Foreign Relations
Council on Hemispheric Affairs
Council on International and Public Affairs
Council on International Educational Exchange
Council on Social Work Education
Council on Ocean Law
Counterpart International Inc.
Country Music Association (CMA)
Cousteau Society Inc., The
Covenant House
Credit Union National Association Inc.
Crime Mapping Research Center
Criminal Division
Critical Infrastructure Assurance Office (CIAO)
Croatian Club for International Cooperation
  (CCIC)
CSA/USA, Celiac Sprue Association/United
  States of America Inc.
Cultural Survival Inc.
Customs Brokers Council of Australia (CBCA)

Dairy, Livestock and Poultry Division
Data for Development
Dayemi Complex Bangladesh
Daytop Village Foundation Inc.
Defence for Children International
Defenders of Wildlife
Defense Acquisition University
Defense Advanced Research Projects Agency
  (DARPA)
Defense Automatic Addressing System Center
  (DAASC)
Defense Civilian Personnel Management
  Service (CPMS)
Defense Commissary Agency (DeCA)
Defense Contract Audit Agency (DCAA)
Defense Finance and Accounting Service
  (DFAS)
Defense Information Systems Agency (DISA)
Defense Intelligence Agency (DIA)
Defense Legal Services Agency
Defense Logistics Agency (DLA)
Defense Manpower Data Center (DMDC)
Defense Nuclear Facilities Safety Board
Defense Prisoner of War/Missing Personnel
  Office
Defense Security Cooperation Agency (DSCA)
Defense Security Service (DSS)
Defense Systems Management College
Defense Technical Information Center (DTIC)
Defense Technology Security Administration
Defense Threat Reduction Agency (DTRA)
Delaware River Basin Commission
Delta Air Line Pilots Association
Delta Kappa Gamma Society International,
  The
Delta Sigma Theta Sorority Inc.
Democratic Club
Department of Agriculture
Department of Commerce
Department of Defense
Department of Defense Field Activities
Department of Defense Human Resources
  Field Activity

Department of Defense National Performance
 Review Activities
Department of Education
Department of Energy
Department of Health and Human Services
Department of Housing and Urban
 Development (HUD)
Department of Justice (DOJ)
Department of Labor (DOL)
Department of State
Department of the Air Force
Department of the Army
Department of the Interior
Department of the Navy
Department of the Navy Environmental
 Program
Department of the Treasury
Department of Transportation
Department of Veterans Affairs
Departmental Representative to the Defense
 Nuclear Facilities Safety Board (DNFSB)
Depaul University-School for New
 Learning, The
Deutsche Gesellschaft Fuer Die Vereinten
 Nationen
Deutscher Frauenrat - Lobby Der Frauen-
 Bundesvereinigung Gemischter
Deutscher Frauenring E.V.
Deutschland (Ijab) E.V.
Developing Countries Farm Radio Network
Development Studies Association
Dhaka Ahsania Mission
Dhammakaya Foundation, The
Dharma Realm Buddhist Association
Diocese of the Armenian Church Of America
Direct Marketing Association
Director General of Foreign Service and
 Director of Personnel
Directorate for Command, Control,
 Communications and Computer System (J-6)
Directorate for Intelligence (J-2)
Directorate for Manpower and Personnel (J-1)
Directorate for Operations

Directorate of Management
Disabled American Veterans
Disabled People's International
Distilled Spirits Council of the United States
 (DISCUS)
Diversion Control Program
Division of Coal Mine Workers' Compensation
Division of Federal Employees' Compensation
Division of Longshore and Harbor Workers'
 Compensation
DLA Environmental and Safety Policy Office
 (CAAE)
DLA Office of Operations Research and
 Resource Analysis (DORRA)
Dominican Leadership Conference (DLC)
DPMA: The Association of Information
 Systems Professionals
Drug Courts Program Office (OJP)
Drug Enforcement Administration (DEA)
Drug Enforcement Administration
Drug, Chemical & Allied Trades Association
 Inc., The
Dryden Flight Research Center
Ducks Unlimited Inc.
E&P Forum International Association of Oil
 and Gas Producers
Earth Ethics Research Group Inc.
Earth Society Foundation, The
Earthaction
Earthjustice Legal Defense Fund
Earthstewards Network,The
Earthtrust
Earthwatch
Eastern Collegiate Roller Hockey Association
 (ECRHA)
Eastern Orthodox
Eastern Regional Organization for Public
 Administration
Eastern Rite
Eastern Surfing Association
Eastern Technology Council
Economic and Social Commission for Asia and
 the Pacific (ESCAP

Economic and Social Commission for Western Asia (ESCWA)

Economic Commission for Africa (ECA)

Economic Commission for Europe (ECE)

Economic Commission for Latin America and the Caribbean (ECLAC)

Economic Development Administration

Economic Research Service

Economics and Statistics Administration

Economists Allied for Arms Reduction

Edison Electric Institute

Education Development Center Inc.

Education International (Internationale de l'Education)

Educational Theatre Association

Egyptian Organization for Human Rights

Egyptian Society of Human Rights Supporters Cultural Club, The

Egyptian United Nations Association

Eleanor Roosevelt Centre at Val-Kill (ERVK), The

Electoral Reform Society of Great Britain and Ireland

Electric Auto Association

Electric Power Supply Association

Electronic Industries Alliance (EIA)

Electrochemical Society, The

Electronic Industries Association

Electronic Messaging Association (EMA)

Electronics Representatives Association

Elizabeth Seton Federation Inc., The

Employees' Compensation Appeals Board (ECAB)

Employment and Training Administration

Employment Standards Administration

Endangered Species Committee

Endometriosis Association

Energy Efficiency and Renewable Energy Network (EE)

Energy Efficient Lighting Association (EELA)

Energy Information Administration (EIA)

Energy Sciences Network

Energy Society of Pakistan

English International Association of Lund, The

English-Speaking Union of the United States

Entomological Society of America

Entre les Peuples (MOBRAP)

Envelope Manufacturers Association (EMA)

Environment and Natural Resources Division

Environmental Information Services (EIS)

Environmental Law Institute

Environmental Protection Agency (EPA)

Environmental Studies Program Information System

Epidemiology Program Office

Episcopal Church

Equal Employment Opportunity Commission (EEOC)

Equal Employment Opportunity Office

Esperanto League for North America, The

European Academy of Arts Sciences and Humanities

European Advisory Council for Technology Trade

European and Mediterranean Commission on Water Planning

European Calling Card Services Association (ECCSA)

European Chemical Industry Council

European Competitive Telecommunications Association (ECTA)

European Express Organisation

European Federation of Conference Towns

European Federation of Employees in Public Services

European Federation of National Associations Working with the Homeless

European Union of Public Relations

European Wind Energy Association

Evangelical Covenant Church, The

Evangelical Lutheran Church in America

Evangelical United Brethren Church

Executive Office for Immigration Review

Executive Office for Immigration Review

Executive Office for U.S. Attorneys

Executive Office for U.S. Trustees

Executive Office for Weed and Seed [OJP]
Executive Office of the President
Executive Women's Golf Association (EWG)
Exhibit Designers and Producers Association
Experience, The
Experiment in International Living, The
Experimental Aircraft Association (EAA)
Exploration Geophysicists, Society of
Explorers Club, The
Export Administration Review Board
Export-Import Bank of the United States
Fairness & Accuracy in Reporting
Family Campers & RVers
Family Federation for World Peace and
  Unification International (Ffwpui)
Family Planning Association of Tanzania
Family Service America Inc.
Family, Career and Community Leaders of
  America
Farm and Foreign Agriculture Services
Farm Credit Administration
Farm Service Agency
Federacio Catalana d'Escolitisme i Guitage
  (Fceg)
Federacion Argentina de Apoyo Familiar
Federacion Argentina de Mujeres Universitarias
  —Asociacion Buenos Aires
Federacion de Mujeres Progresistas
Federacion Nicaraguense de Asociaciones de
  Profesionales &Quotcontapro
Federal Accounting Standards Advisory Board
  (FASAB)
Federal Aviation Administration (FAA)
Federal Bar Association
Federal Bureau of Investigation (FBI)
Federal Bureau of Prisons
Federal Communications Commission
  (FCC)
Federal Credit Policy Working Group
  (FCPWG)
Federal Crimes Victims Division
Federal Deposit Insurance Corp. (FDIC)
Federal Election Commission (FEC)

Federal Emergency Management Agency
  (FEMA)
Federal Energy Management Program
Federal Energy Regulatory Commission
  (FERC)
Federal Executive Board
Federal Executive Institute and Management
  Development Centers
Federal Financial Institutions Examination
  Council
Federal Financial Managers Council (FFMC)
Federal Financing Bank
Federal Highway Administration
Federal Housing Finance Board
Federal Interagency Committee for the
  Management of Noxious and Exotic Weeds
Federal Interagency Committee on Education
Federal Interagency Council on Statistical
  Policy
Federal Labor Relations Authority
Federal Laboratory Consortium for Technology
  Transfer
Federal Law Enforcement Training Center
Federal Library and Information Center
  Committee
Federal Managers Association
Federal Maritime Commission
Federal Mediation and Conciliation Service
Federal Mine Safety and Health Review
  Commission
Federal Reserve Bank of Atlanta
Federal Reserve Bank of Boston
Federal Reserve Bank of Chicago
Federal Reserve Bank of Cleveland
Federal Reserve Bank of Dallas
Federal Reserve Bank of Kansas City
Federal Reserve Bank of Minneapolis
Federal Reserve Bank of New York
Federal Reserve Bank of Philadelphia
Federal Reserve Bank of Richmond
Federal Reserve Bank of San Francisco
Federal Reserve Bank of St. Louis
Federal Reserve System

Federal Retirement Programs
Federal Retirement Thrift Investment Board
Federal Trade Commission (FTC)
Federation Abolitionniste Internationale
Federation Aeronautique Internationale
Federation des Associations Feminines du
  Cameroun
Federation Internationale des Associations de
  Personnes Agees
Federation Internationale des Corps et
  Associations Consulaires
Federation Internationale des Droits de
  L'homme
Federation Internationale des Femmes des
  Carrieres Juridiques
Federation Internationale des Organisations de
  Correspondance et d'echanges
Federation of Afro-Asian Insurers & Reinsurers
Federation of American Women's Clubs
  Overseas
Federation of American-Arab Organizations
Federation of American Scientists (FAS)
Federation of Associations of Former
  International Civil Servants
Federation of European Twine and Rope
  Industries
Federation of Jewish Men's Clubs Inc.
Federation of National Committee in
  International Christian Youth Exchange
Federation of Peace and Conciliation
Federation of the Elderly
Federation of World Volunteer Firefighters
  Associations
Federazione Italiana Comunita Terapeutiche
  (FICT)
FedStats
FedWorld Information Network
Feline and Canine Friends Inc.
Fellowship of Reconciliation
Femmes Chef d'entreprises Mondiales
Filium (Asociacion Para la Prevencion del
  Maltrato del Hijo)
Filter Manufacturers Council (FMC)

Financial Crimes Enforcement Network
Financial Management Association
  International
Findhorn Foundation
Fleet Reserve Association
Fondazione Filippo Turati
Food and Agriculture Organization of the
  United Nations (FAO)
Food and Drug Administration (FDA)
Food and Nutrition Service
Food for the Hungry International
Food Safety and Inspection Service
Force Structure, Resources and Assessment
  Directorate (J-8)
Ford Foundation, The
Foreign Agricultural Service Administration
Foreign Claims Settlement Commission of the
  United States
Foreign Policy Association
Foreign Service Institute
Forest & Fishery Products Division
Foresta Institute for Ocean and Mountain
  Studies
Forum for International Trade Training (FITT)
Forum of Democratic Leaders in the Asia-
  Pacific
Forum on the Problems of Peace and War
Fossil Fuels Policy Action Institute
Foundation
Foundation Ecology and Life
Foundation for Amity and National Solidarity
Foundation for Health Education and Drug
  Awareness Inc. (FHEDA)
Foundation for the Establishment of an
  International Criminal Court
Foundation for the Rights of the Family
Foundation for the Support of the United
  Nations
Four Directions Council
Four-H Club
Fourth Freedom Forum
Fragrance Foundation, The
Franciscans International

Franklin & Eleanor Roosevelt Institute, The

Franklin Delano Roosevelt Memorial
  Commission

Fraternite Notre Dame Inc.

Freedom House

Freedom of Information Center

French Institute/Alliance Française

French-American Chamber of Commerce

Friedrich Ebert Stiftung

Friedrich-Naumann Stiftung

Friends of Animals Inc.

Friends of the Earth

Friends of the United Nations

Friends World Committee for Consultation

Friendship Force, The

Fukuoka International Ms. Association, The

Fulbright Association Inc., The

Fully Informed Jury Association

Functional Cost and Profit Analysis (FCA)

Fund for New Priorities in America

Fund for Peace, The

Fundacion Augusto C. Sandino (FACS)

Fundacion Casa de la Cultura, el Arte y La
  Ciencia

Fundacion Habitat y Desarrollo (Fundacion
  Habitat)

Fundacion Mundial Hastinapura

Fusen Heishi No Kai

Gabonese Association Of Business Women

Gaelic Athletic Association

Galilee Society for Health Research and
  Services

Gateway to Government Food Safety
  Information

Genealogical Society, National

General Accounting Office (GAO)

General Confederation of Trade Unions

General Conference of Seventh Day Adventists

General Federation of Women's Clubs

General Services Administration (GSA)

Geological Society of America Inc.

Georgetown International Relations
  Association Inc.

Gerakan Pramuka Indonesia (Indonesian Scout
  Movement)

German American National Congress, The
  (Deutsch-Amerikanischer National
  Kongress—D.A.N.K.)

German Peace Society-United War Resisters

Gideons International, The

Girl Scouts of the Philippines

Girl Scouts of the USA

Girls Inc.

Glenn Research Center

Global Alliance for Women's Health

Global Commission to Fund the United
  Nations, The

Global Committee of Parliamentarians on
  Population and Development

Global Cooperation for a Brighter Society
  International (GCS)

Global Education Associates

Global Education Motivators Inc.

Global Family

Global Forum of Spiritual and Parliamentary
  on Human Survival

Global Fund for Women

Global Futures Network

Global Information Network

Global Kids

Global Network Against Weapons and Nuclear
  Power in Space

Global Nomads International

Global Policy Forum

Global Resource Action Center for the
  Environment (GRACE)

Globetree

Goddard Institute for Space Studies

Goddard Space Flight Center

Gold Wing Road Riders Association (GWRRA)

Good Neighbors International

Government Information Xchange (GIX)

Government National Mortgage Association
  (Ginnie Mae)

Government Printing Office (GPO)

Government-Wide Registration Service

Grain Inspection, Packers and Stockyards Administration

Gran Fraternidad Universal (Fundacion Dr Serge Raynaud de la Ferriere)

Grand Council of the Crees (Feyou Istchee)

Grand Encampment of Knights Templar

Graphic Communications International Union

Gray Panthers

Gray Panthers Project Fund Inc.

Greek Association for the United Nations

Greek Committee for International Democratic Solidarity

Greek Committee for International Detente and Peace

Greek League for Women's Rights

Greek National Council Against Drugs

Greek Orthodox Archdiocese of America

Greek Orthodox Church

Greeley Foundation, The

Greenpeace

Greenpeace International Council

Group of 78, The

Group of Thirty: Consultative Group on International Economic & Monetary

Guide Dog Foundation for the Blind Inc.

Gulf Coast Lacrosse Association (GCLA)

Hadassah

Hadassah, the Women's Zionist Organization of America

Hague Appeal for Peace

Hague International Model United Nations, The

Handgun Control Inc.

Hawaii Coffee Association

Headquarters United States Air Force

Health Care Financing Administration

Health Care Organization for Africa

Health Industry Distributors Association (HIDA)

Health Industry Manufacturers Association (HIMA

Health Insurance Association of America

Health Resources and Services Administration

Healthcare Convention & Exhibitors Association (HCEA)

Heartland Alliance for Human Needs and Human Rights

Helen Keller International Inc.

Helicopter Association International

Helpage International

Heritage Africa

Heritage Foundation, The

Heritage Preservation Association

Heroees y Martires

Hessische Stiftung Friedens- Und Konfliktforschung (Hsfk)

High Performance Computing and Communications (HPCC)

High Technology Crime Investigation Association (HTCIA)

Himpunan Perserikatan Bangsa-Bangsa

Hirshhorn Museum and Sculpture Garden

Histophila

Home Automation Association

Homework Center

Honda Sport Touring Association

Hope '87-Hundreds of Original Projects for Employment

Horror Writers Association

Horticultural and Tropical Products Division (H&TP)

Hostelling International—American Youth Hostels

Hotel Employees and Restaurant Employees International Union

Housewives in Dialogue

Howard League for Penal Reform

Human Resources Professionals Association of Ontario (HRPAO)

Human Rights Advocates International

Human Rights Advocates Inc.

Human Rights Foundation For Civil Society

Human Rights Internet

Human Rights Watch

Humane Society of the United States

Humanistic Institute for Co-Operation With
  Developing Countries, The (Hivos)
Humanitarian and Politological Centre &
  Strategy
Hunger Project, The
IAEKM (International Association of
  Electronic Keyboard Manufacturers)
Iamvlichos
Illinois and Michigan Canal National Heritage
  Corridor Commission
Illinois Bridal & Party Association Ltd.
Illinois Manufacturers' Association
Illinois State Florists' Association
IMARK Group
Immigration and Naturalization Service (INS)
Implement Workers of America
Import Administration (IA)
Independent Bankers Association of America
Independent Oil and Gas Association of West
  Virginia
Independent Order of Odd Fellows, Sovereign
  Grand Lodge
Independent Peace Movement (A.K.E.)
Independent Pet and Animal Transportation
  Association International (IPATA)
Independent Validation and Verification Facility
  [NASA]
Indian Arts and Crafts Board
Indian Committee of Non-Governmental
  Organizations
Indian Council of World Affairs
Indian Federation of United Nations
  Associations
Indian Law Resource Center
Indigenous World Association
Indonesian Committee on Religion and Peace
Indonesian Students Association for
  International Studies (ISAFIS)
Indoor Tanning Association (ITA)
Industrial and Power Association
Industrial College of the Armed Forces
Industry Council for Development
Information Resources Management College

Information Security Oversight Office
Information Systems Audit and Control
  Association (ISACA)
Information Systems Coordination Committee
  (ISCC)
Information Technology Association of New
  Zealand (ITANZ)
Information Technology Industry Council
Institute for Creation of Spiritual
  Consciousness in Politics And Economy
  (ISPW)
Institute for Defense and Disarmament Studies
Institute for Development Training
Institute for Families And Children
Institute for Independent Education
Institute for International Cooperation of the
  German Adult Education
Institute for International Economic
  Cooperation and Development (ICEPS)
Institute for Mediterranean Affairs
Institute for Public Affairs of the Orthodox
  Union
Institute for Research and Advice on Mental
  Deficiency
Institute for Science and International Security
  (ISIS)
Institute for Security and Cooperation in Outer
  Space
Institute for Telecommunications Sciences
Institute of Clean Air
Institute of Cultural Affairs International
  (ICAI)
Institute of General Semantics
Institute of Global Education
Institute of Industrial Engineers
Institute of Internal Auditors, The
Institute of International Container Lessors
Institute of International Education
Institute of International Relations, The
Institute of Makers of Explosives
Institute of Management Accountants
Institute of Management Consultants
Institute of Mathematical Statistics

Institute of Navigation, The
Institute of Social and Economic Research
Institute of Social Studies Trust
Institute of World Affairs
Instituto de Relaciones Internacionales e
  Investigaciones Para la Paz
Instituto Iberoamericano de Derecho
  Aeronautico y del Espacio y de la Aviacion
Instituto Peruano de Polemologia
Instituto Social y Politico de la Mujer (Ispm)
Integrated Bar of the Philippines
Interaction
Interagency Alternative Dispute Resolution
  Working Group (IADRWG)
Inter-Agency Benchmarking and Best Practices
  Council
Interagency Commission on Crime and
  Security in U.S. Seaports
Interagency Committee on Employment of
  People with Disabilities
Inter-Agency Committee on Sustainable
  Development (IACSD)
Inter-Agency Committee on Women and
  Gender Equality (IACWGE)
Inter-Agency Procurement Services Office
  (IAPSO)
Inter-Agency Electronic Grants Committee
  (IAEGC)
Interagency Savings Bonds Committee
Inter-American Housing Union
Inter-American Parliamentary Group on
  Population and Development
Inter-American Press Association
Inter-American Statistical Institute
Interex—International Association of Hewlett-
  Packard Computing Professionals
Interfaith Center on Corporate
  Responsibility
Internal Revenue Service (IRS)
International Abolitionist Federation
International Academy for Ecological
  Reconstruction
International Academy of Architecture

International Academy of Ecology and Life
  Protection Sciences (MANEB)
International Academy of Informational
  Processes and Technologies
International Advertising Association. Inc.
International Agency for the Prevention of
  Blindness
International Alliance of Women
International and American Associations for
  Dental Research
International Arabian Horse Association
  (IAHA)
International Association Against Drug
  Trafficking and Drug Abuse, The
International Association Against Noise
International Association Against Painful
  Experiments on Animals
International Association for Bridge and
  Structural Engineering (IABSE)
International Association for Community
  Development
International Association for Counselling
International Association for Housing Science
  (IAHS)
International Association for Hydrogen
  Energy
International Association for Maternal and
  Neonatal Health (IAMANEH)
International Association for Near-Death
  Studies (IANDS)
International Association for Religious
  Freedom
International Association for Research in
  Income and Wealth
International Association for Sufism
International Association for Suicide
  Prevention and Crisis Intervention
International Association for the Exchange of
  Students for Technical Experience (IAESTE)
International Association for Volunteer Effort
International Association for Water Law
International Association of Administrative
  Professionals

International Association of Arson Investigators (IAAI)

International Association of Auto Theft Investigators (IAATI)

International Association of Bridge, Structural and Ornamental Ironworkers

International Association of Broadcasting

International Association of Business Communicators (IABC)

International Association of Chiefs of Police

International Association of Crafts & Small & Medium-Sized Enterprises

International Association of Democratic Lawyers

International Association of Drilling Contractors

International Association of Educators for World Peace

International Association of Fire Chiefs

International Association of Firefighters

International Association of Fire Fighters (IAFF)

International Association of Gay Square Dance Clubs

International Association of Gerontology

International Association of Independent Tanker Owners (Intertanko)

International Association of Islamic Banks (Economics & Development)

International Association of Jazz Educators

International Association of Jewish Lawyers and Jurists

International Association of Judges

International Association of Lawyers Against Nuclear Arms

International Association of Logopedics and Phoniatrics

International Association of Machinists and Aerospace Workers

International Association of Mayors of Northern Cities

International Association of Peace Foundations

International Association of Ports and Harbors (IAPH)

International Association of Residential and Community Alternative

International Association of Schools of Social Work

International Association of the Soap & Detergent Industry

International Association of Universities of the Third Age

International Association of University Presidents

International Association of Women in Radio and Television

International Association of Women Judges

International Association of Women Police, The

International Association of Young Lawyers

International Association on Water Quality

International Astronautical Federation

International Atomic Energy Agency (IAEA)

International Bank for Reconstruction and Development (IBRD)

International Bar Association

International Basketball Association

International Board on Books for Young People

International Botted Water Association (IBWA)

International Broadcasting Bureau (IBB)

International Brotherhood of Electrical Workers

International Brotherhood of Painters and Allied Trades

International Brotherhood of Teamsters

International Bureau of Education (IBE)

International Cartographic Association

International Cat Association, The (TICA)

International Catholic Child Bureau (BICE)

International Catholic Migration Commission (ICMC)

International Catholic Organizations Information Center

International Catholic Union of the Press

International Center for Dynamics of Development

International Center for Innovation and Synthesis

Internation Center of Photography

International Center of Sociological, Penal & Penitentiary Research & Studies

International Center of Studies for the Protection of Human Rights

International Centre for Science and High Technology (ICS)

International Centre for Settlement of Investment Disputes (ICSID)

International Centre for Study and Development

International Centre for Trade Union Rights (ICTUR)

International Centre of Roerichs

International Chamber of Commerce (ICC)

International City/County Management Association (ICMA)

International Civil Aviation Organization (ICAO) - Montreal, Canada

International Civil Service Commission (ICSC)

International College of Surgeons

International Commission for the Prevention of Alcoholism and Drug Dependency

International Commission of Jurists

International Commission on Irrigation & Drainage

International Commission on Occupational Health

International Committee for Peace, Disarmament and Ecological Security at Seas and Oceans

International Committee of Catholic Nurses and Medico + Socio Associations

International Committee of Youth Organizations of the CIS

International Communication Association Online

International Computer Security Association (ICSA)

International Computing Centre (ICC)

International Confederation of Christian Family Movements

International Confederation of Free Trade Unions

International Confederation of Midwives

International Conference of Labour Historians

International Co-Operative Alliance

International Copper Association

International Council for Adult Education

International Council for Caring Communities Inc. (ICCC)

International Council for Commercial Arbitration

International Council of Aircraft Owner and Pilot Associations

International Council of Jewish Women

International Council of Museums

International Council of Nurses

International Council of Psychologists

International Council of Scientific Unions

International Council of Shopping Centers (ICSC)

International Council of Voluntary Agencies

International Council of Women

International Council on Alcohol And Addictions

International Council on Education For Teaching

International Council on Jewish Social & Welfare Services

International Council on Management Of Population Programmes (ICOMP)

International Council on Social Welfare

International Court of Justice (ICJ)

International Criminal Tribunal for Rwanda (ICTR)

International Criminal Tribunal for the Former Yugoslavia (ICTY)

International Cultures Mission

International Cystic Fibrosis Association

International Defensive Pistol Association (IDPA)

International Dental Federation

International Desalination Association

International Development Association
(IDA)

International Diabetic Athletes Association
(IDAA)

International Diving Educators Association
(IDEA)

International Driving Tests Committee
(CIECA)

International Educational Development Inc.

International Electrotechnical Commission

International Facility Management Association
(IFMA)

International Federation for East Timor

International Federation for Home
Economics

International Federation for Housing And
Planning

International Federation for Hydrocephalus
and Spina Bifida

International Federation for Information and
Documentation

International Federation for Medical &
Biological Engineering

International Federation for Protection of
Rights of Ethnic, Religious, Linguistic

International Federation of Action by
Christians for the Abolition of Torture

International Federation of Agricultural
Producers

International Federation of Airline Pilots
Associations

International Federation of Automatic
Control

International Federation of Beekeepers'
Associations

International Federation of Business &
Professional Women

International Federation of Catholic
Universities

International Federation of Clinical Chemistry
(IFCC)

International Federation of Disabled Workers
& Civilian Handicapped

International Federation of Employees in
Public Services

International Federation of Essential Oils and
Aroma Trades

International Federation of Freight Forwarders
Associations

International Federation of Liberal and Radical
Youth

International Federation of Library
Associations and Institutions (IFLA)

International Federation of Library
Associations and Institutions

International Federation of Medical Students'
Associations

International Federation of Non-Government
Organizations for the Prevention of Drug and
Substance Abuse

International Federation of Operational
Research Societies

International Federation of Organic Agriculture
Movements

International Federation of Pharmaceutical
Manufacturers Associations

International Federation of Pharmaceutical
Wholesalers (IFPW)

International Federation of Physical Medicine
and Rehabilitation

International Federation of Red Cross and Red
Crescent Societies

International Federation of Settlements and
Neighbourhood Centres

International Federation of Social Workers

International Federation of Surgical Colleges

International Federation of Surveyors

International Federation of Training and
Development Organisations

International Federation of Translators

International Federation of University Women

International Federation of Women Lawyers

International Federation of Workers'
Educational Associations

International Federation on Ageing
International Fellowship of Reconciliation
International Film and Television Exchange Inc.
International Finance Corp. (IFC)
International Fund for Agricultural Development (IFAD)
International Fund for Social Progress
International Graphoanalysis Society
International Health Awareness Network
International Hotel Association
International House New York
International Human Rights Association of American Minorities
International Human Rights Internship Program
International Human Rights Law Group
International Humanist and Ethical Union
International Immigrants Foundation
International Information Center for Terminology
International Informatization Academy
International In-line Skating Association
International Institute for Educational Planning (IIEP)
International Institute of Administrative Sciences
International Institute of Higher Studies in Criminal Sciences
International Institute of Humanitarian Law
International Institute of Integral Human Sciences, The
International of Non-Aligned Studies
International Institute of Rural Reconstruction
International Institute on Ageing (INIA)
International Iron & Steel Institute
International Juridical Organization for Environment and Development
International Kolping Society
International Labour Organization (ILO)
International Law Association (ILA)
International League for Human Rights

International League for the Rights and Liberation of Peoples
International League of Societies for Persons with Mental Handicaps
International Lesbian and Gay Association
International Mahavir Jain Mission
International Map Trade Association (IMTA)
International Maritime Organization (IMO)
International Mass Retail International Modeling & Talent Association
International Mission, Ministry Of Churches Of Christ
International Model United Nations Association
International Model United Nations Association
International Monetary Fund (IMF)
International Motor Contest Association (IMCA)
International Movement A.T.D. Fourth World (Aide à Toute Détress)
International Movement For Fraternal Union Among Races And Peoples (UFER)
International Narcotic Enforcement Officers Association
International Network of Engineers and Scientists for Global Responsibility
International Network of Peace Museums
International Ocean Institute
International Oil Working Group Inc.
International OM Association
International Organization for the Development of Freedom of Education
International Organization for the Elimination of all Forms of Racial
International Organization for Unification of Terminological Neologisms
International Organization of Employers
International Organization of Good Templars (IOGT)/Youth Federation (IGTYF)
International Organization of Indigenous Resource Development
International Organization of Journalists

International Peace Academy
International Peace Bureau
International Peace Information Service
International Peace Organization
International Peace Research Association
International Petroleum Industry
  Environmental Conservation
International Photographic Council
International Physicians for the Prevention of
  Nuclear War Inc.
International Planned Parenthood Federation
International Police Association
International Precious Metals Institute
International Presentation Association
International Presentation Association of the
  Sisters of the Presentation
International Press Institute
International Prisoners Aid Association
International Progress Organization
International Public Policy Institute
International Public Relations Association
International Publishers Association
International Reading Association
International Real Estate Federation
International Real Estate Institute
International Relief Friendship Foundation
  Inc., The
International Religious Foundation, The
International Religious Liberty Association
  (IRLA)
International Reprographic Association (IRgA)
International Rescue Committee Inc.
International Research and Training Institute
  for the Advancement of Women (INSTRAW)
International Road Federation
International Romani Union
International Save the Children
  Alliance, The
International Schools Association
International Scientific Council for Island
  Development (INSULA)
International Secretariat Committee of Nuclear
  Free Zone Local Authorities

International Senior Citizens Association
  Inc., The
International Shinto Foundation, The
International Social Science Council
International Social Security Association (ISSA)
International Social Service
International Society for Community
  Development
International Society for Human Rights
International Society for Intercultural
  Education, Training and Research
International Society for Mangrove Ecosystems
International Society for Photogrammetry &
  Remote Sensing
International Society for Prosthetics And
  Orthotics
International Society for Research On
  Aggression
International Society for Traumatic Stress
  Studies, The
International Society of Aboriculture
International Society of City and Regional
  Planners
International Society of Explosives Engineers
International Society of Friendship and Good
  Will
International Society of Nursing in Cancer
  Care
International Society of Postmasters of the
  Americas
International Society of Radiographers &
  Radiological Technicians
International Society of Weighing &
  Measurement
International Sociological Association
International Statistical Institute
International Students, Inc.
International Studies Association
International Study Center for Children and
  Families
International Sustainable, Social and Economic
  Responses (ISSER)
International Telecommunication Union (ITU)

International Television Association (ITVA)
International Trade Administration
International Trade Centre UNCTAD/WTO (ITC)
International Training Centre of the ILO (ITC/ILO)
International Tunnelling Association
International Union for Health Promotion and Education
International Union for Land-Value Taxation and Free Trade
International Union for the Scientific Study of Population
International Union of Architects
International Union of Biological Sciences
International Union of Building Centres
International Union of Commercial Agents and Brokers (IUCAB)
International Union of Economists
International Union of Electronic, Electrical, Salaried, Machine and Furniture Workers
International Union of Local Authorities
International Union of Nutritional Sciences
International Union of Operating Engineers
International Union of Psychological Science (IUPSYS)
International Union of Socialist Youth
International Union of Students
International Union of Technical Associations and Organizations
International Union of Tenants
International Union of Young Christian Democrats
International Union, United Automobile Aerospace and Agricultural Implement
International Urban Development Association
International Webmasters Association
International Wildlife Coalition
International Women's Anthropology Conference
International Women's Health Coalition
International Women's Tribune Centre Inc.

International Work Group for Indigenous Affairs
International Yan Xin Qigong Association
International Young Christian Workers
International Youth and Student Movement for the United Nations (ISMUN)
International Youth League
Internationaler Jugendaustausch-Und Besucherdienst Des Bundes-Republik
Internet Developers Association
Internet Society
Inter-Parliamentary Union
INTERPOL
Iota Phi Lambda Sorority Inc.
IPS (Inter Press Service)
Iranian Trade Association
Islamic Chamber of Commerce Industry & Commodity Exchange
Islamic Council of Europe
Islamic Heritage Society, Inc.
Islamic/African Relief Agency
Istituto Sindacale per la Cooperazione con i Paesi in Via di Sviluppo
Izaak Walton League of America
J. William Fulbright Foreign Scholarship Board, The
James Madison Memorial Fellowship Foundation
Jane Addams Conference
Japan Council Against A and H Bombs (Gensuikyo)
Japan Well-Aging Association
Japanese Consumers' Co-Operative Union
Japan-United States Friendship Commission
Jascaa International
Jatiya Tarun Sangha
Jet Propulsion Laboratory
Jewellers Association of Australia Ltd.
Jewish Braille Institute of America Inc., The
Jewish Community Centers Association of North America
Jewish War Veterans of the USA
Jewish Women International

Jigyansu Tribal Research Centre
John Birch Society
Johnson Foundation, The
Johnson Space Center
Joint Board for the Enrollment of Actuaries
Joint Chiefs of Staff
Joint Inspection Unit (JIU)
Joint Inter-Agency Meeting on Computer-Assisted Translation and Terminology (JIAM-CATT)
Joint Military Intelligence College
Joint United Nations Information Committee (JUNIC)
Joint United Nations Programme on HIV/AIDS (UNAIDS)
Jonas Salk Foundation, The
Jordan Trade Association
Journalists' Union Of Russia
Junior Achievement Inc.
Junior Chamber International
Junior State of America
Justice Information Center
Justice Management Division
Juvenile Products Manufacturers Association (JPMA)
Juventudes de la ONU-Youths of the UN
Kennedy Space Center [NASA]
Kenya Freedom from Hunger Council for National Development
Kiwanis International
Knights of Columbus
Korean Assembly for the Reunion of Ten Million Separated Families
Korean International Volunteer Organization
Kulturel Information and Koordination (KIK)
La Leche League International Inc.
Laborers' International Union of North America
Lama Gangchen World Peace Foundation, The
Langley Research Center [NASA]
L'association Pour le Progres et la Defense des Droits des Femmes Maliennes
Latin American Studies Association (LASA)

Latter-day Saint Student Association (LDSSA)
Lawyers Alliance for World Security (LAWS)
Lawyers Committee for Human Rights
Lawyers' Committee on Nuclear Policy, The
Lead Industries Association
Leadership Conference of Women Religious/Conference of Major Superiors of Men
League for Industrial Democracy
League for the Defence of Human Rights
League of Women Voters of the U.S.
Lebanese Association Of Human Rights
Lebanon Family Planning Association
Legacy International
Legal Services Corp.
Legion of Christ
Legion of Good Will
Lesotho Chamber of Commerce and Industry
Lesotho Workcamps Association
Lester B. Pearson Canadian International Peacekeeping Training Centre, The
Leukemia and Lymphoma Society
Liberal International
Liberty International
Library and Information Technology Association (LITA)
Life and Peace Institute
Life Education International
Lifebridge Foundation, The
Liga de Amas de Casa, Consumidores y Usuarios de la Republicana Argentina
Lignin Institute, The
L'information des Nations Unies
Links Inc., The
Lions Club of Dar Es Salaam
Lions Clubs International (International Association of Lions Clubs, The)
Logistics Directorate (J-4)
Lord Byron/New Frontiers
Loretto Community (Sisters of Loretto and Co-Members)

Luggage and Leather Goods Manufacturers of America

Lutheran Church-Missouri Synod

Lutheran Immigration and Refugee Service

Lutheran World Federation, The

Maarts Youth Organization

Magazine Publishers of America

Magnet Schools of America

Malaysian Chinese Association (MCA)

Manufacturers' Agents National Association (MANA)

Manufacturers Association of Israel

Manufacturers of Emission Controls Association

Manufacturing Extension Partnership

Map International

Marangopoulos Foundation for Human Rights

March of Dimes Birth Defects Foundation

Marga Institute

Marie Curie Fellowship Association

Marine Corps Association

Marine Corps League

Marine Expeditionary Units

Marine Mammal Commission

Marine Technology Society

Marine Trades Association of Baltimore County

Market Access Compliance (MAC)

Marshall Space Flight Center [NASA]

Martin Luther King, Jr. Center, The

Maryknoll Fathers and Brothers C.F.M.S.A. (Catholic Foreign Mission Society of America)

Maryknoll Sisters of St. Dominic Inc.

Maryland United for Peace and Justice

Masons, Ancient and Accepted Scottish Rite, Northern Masonic Jurisdiction, Supreme Council 33

Masons, Ancient and Accepted Scottish Rite, Southern Jurisdiction, Supreme Council

Masons, Royal Arch, General Grand Chapter International

Mathematical Association of America

Mathematical Association of America (MAA)

Mechanical Contractors Association of America (MCAA)

Medecins Sans Frontieres

Medical Action for Global Security

Medical Group Management Association (MGMA)

Medical Library Association (MLA)

Medical Mission Sisters

Medical Women's International Association

Medicare Payment Advisory Commission (MedPAC) (formerly the Physician Payment Review Commission and the Prospective Payment Assessment Commission)

Mediterranean Women's Studies Centre

Meetings Industry Association of Australia

Mega Cities Project Inc.

Mennonite Central Committee

Mercy International Association

Messianic Jewish Alliance Of America

Metal Finishing Suppliers' Association (MFSA)

Metalworking Resource Group

Metro Manila Council Of Women Balikatan Movement Inc.

MFPA - Multifunction Peripheral Association

Midwest Model United Nation Inc.

Migrantes

Migratory Bird Conservation Commission

Mike Monroney Aeronautical Center

Military Chaplains Association of the U.S.A.

Millennium Institute

Minerals Management Service

Mining and Metallurgical Society of America

Mining Health & Safety Research Program

Minority Business Development Agency

Minority Rights Group, The

Mississippi River Parkway Commission

Missouri Fox Trotting Horse Breed Association

Moa Foundation New York Inc.

Mobilization For Survival

Model Aeronautics Association of Canada (MAAC)

Modern Buddhism of America, Inc.

Modern Language Association (MLA)
Modern Language Association of America
Modern Woodmen of America
Moffett Federal Airfield [NASA]
Moose International Inc.
Moral Re-Armament Inc.
Mormon Church
Moscow Public Science Foundation (MPSF)
Moscow Research Center for Human Rights
Mothers Against Drunk Driving (MADD)
Mountbatten Centre for International
   Studies, The
Mouvement Burkinabe de Lutte Contre le
   Racisme, L'Apartheid et pour l'Amitie
Mouvement du Nid, le (Asbl)
Mouvement Mondial des Meres
Movement for a Better World
Movimento Democratico das Mulheres
   Portuguesas (M.D.M.)
Mufid Humanity University
Mugarik Gabe
Multilateral Investment Guarantee Agency
   (MIGA)
Muscular Dystrophy Association (MDA)
Muscular Dystrophy Association of Canada
Music Teachers National Association
Muslim Students Association
Muslim World League (MWL)
NAFSA: Association of International Educators
Narcotics Officers Associations
National Aboriginal and Torres Strait Islander
   Catholic Council
National Abortion and Reproductive Rights
   Action League (NARAL)
National Abortion Federation
National Academy of Recording Arts and
   Sciences Inc.
National Adult Baseball Association
National Aeronautic Association
National Aeronautics and Space Administration
   (NASA)
National Agricultural Library
National Agricultural Statistics Service

National Air and Space Museum
National Air Traffic Controllers Association
National Aircraft Resale Association
National Alliance of Black School Educators
National Alliance of Senior Citizens
National Alliance of Third World Journalists
National Arboretum
National Asphalt Pavement Association
National Assembly for Youth Development
National Association for Business Economists
National Association for Female Executives
National Association for Gifted Children
   (USA)
National Association for the Advancement of
   Colored People
National Association for The Advancement of
   Colored People
National Association for the Advancement of
   Colored People (NAACP)
National Association for the Advancement of
   Minorities in Technology
National Association for the Education of
   Young Children
National Association for Women in Education
National Association of Black & White Men
   Together
National Association of Black Journalists
National Association of Broadcast Employees
   and Technicians
National Association of Chain Drug Stores
National Association of Charterboat Operators
National Association of College and University
   Residence Halls (NACURH)
National Association of College Stores
National Association of Colleges and
   Employers
National Association of Colored Women's
   Clubs Inc.
National Association of Composers/USA
National Association of Credit Management
   (NACM)
National Association of Home Builders
   (NAHB)

National Association of Human Rights Workers

National Association of Industrial Technology

National Association of Insurance and Financial Advisors

National Association of Insurance Commissioners

National Association of Intercollegiate Athletics (NAIA)

National Association of International Broadcasters

National Association of Legal Professionals

National Association of Letter Carriers

National Association of Life Underwriters

National Association of Manufacturers

National Association of Mothers' Centers

National Association of Negro Business and Profeeional Women's Club Inc., The

National Association of Parliamentarians

National Association of Precollege Directors (NAPD)

National Association of Professional Organizers

National Association of Professional Pet Sitters (NAPPS)

National Association of Purchasing Management (NAPM)

National Association of Purchasing Management (NAPM)

National Association of Resale and Thrift Shops

National Association of Retired Federal Employees

National Association of Rocketry

National Association of Science Writers

National Association of Securities Dealers (NASD)

National Association of Social Workers

National Association of State Information Resource Executives (NASIRE)

National Association of Teachers of Singing

National Association of the Deaf

National Association of the Remodeling Industry (NARI)

National Association of Victims of Child Abuse Laws

National Association of Victims Support Schemes

National Association of Watch and Clock Collectors

National Association of Women Business Owners

National Association of Women in Construction (NAWIC)

National Association of Women Judges

National Association of Women Lawyers

National Association to Advance Fat Acceptance

National Auctioneers Association

National Audobon Society

National Automobile Club

National Auto Sport Association

National Baptist Convention of the USA Inc.

National Bioethics Advisory Commission

National Bipartisan Commission on the Future of Medicare

National Black Business Trade Association

National Black MBA Association

National Business Center (NBC)

National Business Education Association

National Cancer Institute (NCI)

National Career Development Association

National Catholic Educational Association, The

National Cattlemen's Beef Association

National Cemetery Administration (NCA)

National Center for Chronic Disease Prevention and Health Promotion

National Center for Education Statistics (NCES)

National Center for Environmental Health

National Center for Health Education (NCHE)

National Center for Health Statistics

National Center for HIV, STD and TB Prevention

National Center for Infectious Diseases

National Center for Injury Prevention and Control

National Center for Research Resources (NCRR)

National Centrum Voor Ontwikkelingssamenwerking

National Child Labor Committee

National Climatic Data Center (NCDC)

National Clubhouse Association

National Coalition of 100 Black Women

National Coffee Association of U.S.A.

National Collegiate Conference Association

National Commission for the Certification of Crane Operators (NCCCO)

National Commission on Libraries and Information Science

National Committee for Habitat, The

National Committee on American Foreign Policy

National Committee on United States-China Relations

National Communication Association

National Communications System

National Concrete Masonry Association

National Conference for Community and Justice, The

National Conference of Black Lawyers

National Conference of Christians And Jews

National Congress Of Neighborhood Women

National Consumers League

National Cooperative Business Association

National Cooperative Business Association

National Council for Geographic Education

National Council for International Health

National Council for International Visitors (NCIV)

National Council for Research On Women

National Council for The Social Studies

National Council of Catholic Women

National Council of German Women's Organizations

National Council of Jewish Women

National Council of La Raza

National Council of Negro Women Inc.

National Council of Saemaul-Undong Movement

National Council of the Churches of Christ in the USA

National Council of Women of Canada, The

National Council of Women of The United States Inc.

National Council of Ymcas of Japan, The

National Council on Alcoholism and Drug Dependence

National Council on Crime and Delinquency

National Council on Disability

National Council on Family Relations

National Council on Islamic Affairs

National Council on the Aging (NCOA)

National Court Appointed Special Advocate Association (CASA)

National Credit Union Administration (NCUA)

National Criminal Justice Reference Service (OJP)

National Criminal Justice Reference Service

National Cultures Centre

National Cutting Horse Association

National Defense Industrial Association (NDIA)

National Defense Industrial Association (NDIA)

National Defense University

National Depressive and Manic-Depressive Association (DMDA)

National Drug Intelligence Center

National Easter Seal Society, The

National Economic Council

National Education Association

National Education Association

National Education Association/World Confederation of Organizations of the Teaching Profession

National Educational Research Policy and Priorities Board

National Electrical Contractors Association

National Emergency Medicine Association (NEMA)

National Emergency Number Association

National Endowment for the Arts

National Endowment for the Humanities (NEH)

National Environmental Satellite, Data and Information Service (NESDIS)

National Eye Institute

National Federation of Federal Employees

National Federation of Music Clubs

National Federation of the Blind

National Federation of Women's Clubs of the Philippines

National Federation of Youth Organizations in Bangladesh

National FFA Organization

National Field Selling Association

National Fire Academy (NFA)

National Fire Protection Agency

National Fire Sprinkler Association

National Flag Protection

National Flood Insurance Program

National Food Processors Association

National Foreign Trade Council

National Foundation on the Arts and the Humanities

National Gallery of Art

National Gambling Impact Study Commission

National Gay and Lesbian Task Force

National Genealogical Society

National Geophysical Data Center (NGDC)

National Governors' Association (NGA)

National Governors' Association

National Grange of the Order of Patrons of Husbandry

National Ground Water Association

National Guard Associations

National Heart, Lung and Blood Institute (NHLBI)

National Highway Traffic Safety Administration (NHTSA)

National Houseware Manufacturers Association

National Human Genome Research Institute (NHGRI)

National Hydrogen Association

National Ice Cream & Yogurt Retailers

National Imagery and Mapping Agency (NIMA)

National Immunization Program

National Indian Youth Council

National Institute for Allergy and Infectious Diseases (NIAID)

National Institute for Occupational Safety and Health

National Institute of Child Health and Human Development

National Institute of Corrections (FBOP)

National Institute of Dental and Craniofacial Research (NIDCR)

National Institute of Diabetes and Digestive and Kidney Disease (NIDDK)

National Institute of Drug Abuse

National Institute of Environmental Health Sciences (NIEHS)

National Institute of General Medical Sciences (NIGMS)

National Institute of Justice (OJP)

National Institute of Mental Health (NIMH)

National Institute of Neurological Disorders and Stroke (NINDS)

National Institute of Nursing Research

National Institute of Standards and Technology

National Institute on Aging

National Institute on Disability and Rehabilitation Research

National Institute on Early Childhood Development and Education

National Institute on Educational Governance, Finance, Policy-Making and Management

National Institute on Postsecondary Education, Libraries and Lifelong Learning (PLLI)

National Institute on Student Achievement, Curriculum and Assessment

National Institute on the Education of At-Risk Students

National Institutes of Health (NIH)
National Investigations Committee on UFOs
National Interfraternity Conference
National Italian American Coordinating
　Association
National Junior College Athletic Association
　(NJCAA)
National Junior Horticultural Association
National Kitchen and Bath Association (NKBA)
National Labor Relations Board (NLRB)
National Law Enforcement and Corrections
　Technology Center
National League of Cities
National Legal Aid and Defender Association
National Lesbian & Gay Journalists Association
National Library of Education
National Lumber and Building Material
　Dealers Association (NLBMDA)
National Marine Fisheries Service (NMFS)
National Mediation Board
National Mental Health Association
National Multiple Sclerosis Society
National Museum of African Art
National Museum of American Art
National Museum of American History
National Museum of Natural History
National Museum of the American Indian
National Muzzle Loading Rifle Association
National Naval Officers Association
National Neurofibromatosis Foundation
　Inc., The
National Nuclear Security Administration
National Occupational Information
　Coordinating Committee
National Ocean Service (NOS)
National Oceanic and Atmospheric
　Administration (NOAA)
National Oceanographic Data Center (NODC)
National Onsite Wastewater Recycling
　Association, Inc
National Organization for Victim Assistance
National Organization for Women (NOW)
National Paint & Coatings Association, The

National Park Foundation
National Parks and Conservation Association
　(NPCA)
National Peace Foundation
National Performance Review (NPR)
National Pest Control Association
National Portrait Gallery
National Postal Museum
National Press Club
National Press Photographers Association
National Professional Media Women
National Propane Gas Association
National PTA (National Congress of Parents
　and Teachers)
National Quality Program
National Railroad Passenger Corporation
　(Amtrak)
National Rehabilitation Association
National Research and Development Centers
　[Department of Education, U.S.]
National Restaurant Association
National Retail Federation
National Reye's Syndrome Foundation
National Rifle Association (NRA)
National Right to Life Committee Inc.
National Roofing Contractors Association
National Roofing Contractors Association
National Rural Development Partnership
　(NRDP)
National Safety Council
National Science Foundation, The
　(NSF)
National Science Teachers Association
National SCRABBLE Association
National Sculpture Society
National Security Agency/Central Security
　Service
National Security Council
National Service Conference of the American
　Ethical Union
National Small Business United
National Society for the Blind and Physically
　Handicapped, The

National Society of the Daughters of the American Revolution
National Society of Professional Engineers
National Society of the Sons of the American Revolution
National Softball Association
National Space Society
National Speakers Association
National Stereoscopic Association
National Student Speech Language Hearing Association
National Stuttering Association
National Tay-Sachs & Allied Diseases Association
National Technical Information Service (NTIS)
National Technical Services Association (NTSA)
National Technical Services Association (NTSA)
National Telecommunications and Information Administration
National Tooling & Machining Association
National Transportation Safety Board
National Trust for Historic Preservation
National Tuberous Sclerosis Association, The
National U.S.-Arab Chamber Of Commerce
National Urban League Inc.
National Volleyball Association (NVA)
National War College
National Weather Service (NWS)
National Wildlife Federation
National Wildlife Federation
National Woman's Party
National Women's Conference Center Inc.
National Woman's Christian Temperance Union
National Writers Union
National Zoo
Natural Resources Conservation Service
Natural Resources Defense Council, Inc.
Nature Conservancy, The
Navy League of the United States

NDIA (National Defense Industrial Association)
Near East Foundation, The
Nebraska Autobody Association
Nederlandse Vereniging Voor de Verenigde Naties
Neighborhood Cleaners Association International
Nepal Committee for Peace and Development
New Humanity Inc.
New York Academy of Sciences
New York Association for American-Russian Relations
Newspaper Association of America
Newspaper Association of American
Newspaper Society, The
Nexus-International Broadcasting Association
NGO Committee on Disarmament
Nigerian Centre for Research and Documentation (NICERSOC)
Nipponzan Myohoji Dai Sangha
No to Alcoholism and Drug Addiction/No to Alcohol and Narcotics (NAN)
Nord-Sud Xxi
Norfil Foundation, Inc.
North American Christian Peace Conference
North American Congress on Latin America
North American Electric Reliability Council (NERC)
North American Equipment Dealers Association
North American Mission Board Southern Baptist Convention
North American Scottish Athletics Association
North Carolina Fisheries Association
Northeast Organic Farming Association (NOFA)
Northern California Association of Law Libraries (NOCALL)
Northern Forum, The
Northwest Power Planning Council

Nuclear Age Peace Foundation, The

Nuclear Control Institute

Nuclear Regulatory Commission (NRC)

Nuevos Derechos del Hombre (New Human Rights)

Occupational Safety and Health Administration (OSHA)

Occupational Safety and Health Review Commission

Oesterreichische Liga Fuer Die Vereintennationen

Office and Professional Employees International Union

Office for Civil Rights

Office for Outer Space Affairs (OOSA)

Office for State and Local Domestic Preparedness Support (OJP)

Office for the Coordination of Humanitarian Affairs (OCHA)

Office for Victims of Crime (OJP)

Office for Victims of Crime

Office of Acquisition and Property Management

Office of Administration

Office of Administrative Law Judges

Office of Advocacy

Office of Aircraft Services

Office of American Indian Trust (OAIT)

Office of Attorney Recruitment and Management

Office of Bilingual Education and Minority Languages Affairs (OBEMLA)

Office of Civilian Health and Medical Program of the Uniformed Services

Office of Community Planning and Development

Office of Dispute Resolution

Office of Economic Adjustment

Office of Economic Impact and Diversity (ED)

Office of Educational Research and Improvement (OERI)

Office of Elementary and Secondary Education (OESE)

Office of Environment, Safety and Health (EH)

Office of Environmental Management (EM)

Office of Environmental Policy and Compliance

Office of Fair Housing and Equal Opportunity

Office of Federal Contract Compliance Programs

Office of Fossil Energy

Office of General Counsel

Office of Global Programs

Office of Government Ethics

Office of Governmentwide Policy

Office of Health Care Information

Office of Hearings and Appeals

Office of Housing

Office of Independent Oversight & Performance Assurance (OA)

Office of Indian Education

Office of Information and Privacy

Office of Information Technology Integration

Office of Inspector General

Office of Intelligence (IN)

Office of Intelligence Policy and Review

Office of Intergovernmental Affairs

Office of International Affairs

Office of International Information Programs (IIP)

Office of Justice Programs

Office of Justice Programs

Office of Juvenile Justice and Delinquency Prevention (OJP)

Office of Labor-Management Standards

Office of Legal Counsel

Office of Legislative Affairs

Office of Legislative and Congressional Affairs

Office of Management and Administration

Office of Management and Budget (OMB)

Office of Migrant Education

Office of National AIDS Policy

Office of National Drug Control Policy

Office of Navajo and Hopi Indian Relocation

Office of Naval Research (ONR)

Office of Nuclear Energy, Science, and Technology (NN)

Office of Oceanic and Atmospheric Research

Office of Personnel Management

Office of Policy Development

Office of Policy, Management and Budget

Office of Postsecondary Education (OPE)

Office of Procurement and Assistance Management

Office of Professional Responsibility

Office of Public Affairs

Office of Reform Assistance and Dissemination

Office of Research and Technology Applications (ORTA)

Office of Satellite Data Processing and Distribution

Office of Science and Technology

Office of Science and Technology Policy

Office of Security and Emergency Operations (SO)

Office of Small and Disadvantaged Business Utilization

Office of Special Counsel (OSC)

Office of Special Education and Rehabilitative Service

Office of Special Education Programs

Office of Technology Policy

Office of the Associate Attorney General

Office of the Attorney General

Office of the Budget

Office of the Comptroller of the Currency

Office of the Deputy Attorney General

Office of the First Lady

Office of the Inspector General

Office of the Naval Inspector General

Office of the Ombudsperson

Office of the Pardon Attorney

Office of the Permanent Representative to the United Nations

Office of the Secretary of Defense

Office of the Secretary of Energy Advisory Board (AB)

Office of the Secretary

Office of the Solicitor General

Office of the Special Trustee for American Indians

Office of the Under Secretary of Defense (Comptroller)

Office of the Under Secretary of Defense for Acquisition and Technology (ACQWeb)

Office of the Under Secretary of Defense for Personnel and Readiness

Office of the Under Secretary of Defense for Policy

Office of the United Nations High Commissioner for Human Rights

Office of the Vice President of the United States

Office of Tribal Justice

Office of Under Secretary for Public Diplomacy and Public Affairs

Office of Vocational and Adult Education (OVAE)

Office of Women's Business Ownership

Office of Worker and Community Transition (WT)

Office of Workers' Compensation Programs

Offshore Marine Service Association

Offshore Minerals Management Program (OMM)

Ohio High School Athletic Association (OHSAA)

Olof Palme Peace Foundation, The

Olympic Committee, United States

One Day Foundation, The

Online News Association

Operation Friendship International Youth Venture

Operation Peace Through Unity

Operation Smile International

Operational Plans and Interoperability Directorate (J-7)

Operative Plasterers' & Cement Masons' International Association

Opportunities Industrialization Centers International Inc.

Optimist International

Optometric Association

Orbicom-International Network of Unesco Chairs in Communications, The

Order of Eastern Star, General Grand Chapter

Order of Saint Augustine

Ordre des Chevaliers Hospitaliers de Saint-Jean de Jerusalem

Organisation Internationale Pour la Protection des Animaux-Oipa

Organisation Mondiale des Experts-Conseils-Arbitres (OMECA)

Organisation Panafricaine des Femmes

Organization for Defending Victims Of Violence

Organization for Flora Neotropica

Organization for Industrial Spiritual & Cultural Advancement (OISCA)

Organization for International Economic Relations

Organization for the Prohibition of Chemical Weapons (OPCW)

Organization of African Trade Union Unity

Organization of American Historians, The

Organization of American States (OAS)

Organization of Islamic Capitals And Cities

Osaka Junior Chamber, Inc.

Osterreichischer Informationsdienst Fuer Entwicklungspolitik

Osterreichisches Lateinamerika — Institut

Overeaters Anonymous Inc.

Overseas Press Club of America

Overseas Private Investment Corp.

Ovum Pacis — Women's International Peace University, The

Oxfam

Oxfam America

Pacific Air Forces

Pacific Seafood Processors Association

Pact Inc.

Pakistan Crescent Youth Organization (PCYO)

Pakistan Lions Youth Council

Pakistan Students Association International

Pakistan United Nations Association

Pakistan Women Lawyer's Association

Pan Pacific and Southeast Asia Women's Association International

Pan-African Institute for Development

Pan-African Movement, The

Pan-American Development Foundation, The

Panel of External Auditors of the United Nations, the Specialized Agencies and the International Atomic Energy Agency

Panpacific and Southeast Asia Women's Association of the U.S.A.

Paper, Allied-Industrial, Chemical and Energy Workers International Union

Paraplegic and Quadriplegic Association

Parents Without Partners

Parents, Families and Friends of Lesbians and Gays

Parliamentarians For Global Action

Pasture Systems and Watershed Management Research Lab (PSWMRL)

Pate Institute for Human Survival

Patent and Trademark Office

Pathways to Peace

Pax Christi International

Pax World Service

PCMCIA

Peace Action

Peace and Cooperation

Peace Brigades International

Peace Center of Iran

Peace Child International

Peace Committee 2000

Peace Corps

Peace Education Foundation, The

Peace History Society

Peace Links

Peace Research Institute Dundas

Peace Studies Institute Manchester College

Peacefund Canada

Peaceways

Pearl S. Buck Foundation, The

Pearson Centre

Pension Benefit Guaranty Corporation
Pentacostal Holiness Church
People for the American Way
People to People Committee on Disability
People to People International
Peres Center for Peace, The
Perhaps Kids Meeting Kids Can Make a
Difference
Permanent Committee for the Oliver Wendell
Holmes Devise
Pertubohan Bangsa-Bangsa Bersatu Singapura
Pet Food Institute [PFI]
Pet Food Manufacturers' Association
Pet Sitters International
PGA-Professional Golfers' Association of
America
Pharmaceutical Maintenance and Operations
Network
Phelps Stokes Fund
Philadelphia Yearly Meeting of the Religious
Society of Friends
Philippine Human Rights Information Center
(Philrights)
Philippine Medical Women's Association
Photographic Society of America
Photonics Industry and Technology
Development Association
Physicians for Peace
Pilot International Inc.
Plan International
Planetary Association for Clean Energy
Planetary Citizens
Planetary Society, The
Planned Parenthood Federation of America Inc
Plant Genome Information Resource (PGDIC)
Plastics Export Promotion Council
Plenty International
Plumbing-Heating-Cooling Contractors
Association
Police Officers Associations (POA)
Police, International Association of Chiefs of
Polish National Commission for Unesco
Politik Und Sicherhei

Polskie Towarzystwo Przyjaciol Onz
Polyurethane Manufacturers Association
Population & Community Development
Association
Population Action International
Population Communications International
Population Council, The
Population Institute, The
Por Desarollo
Portrait of an American Family Association
Postal Rate Commission
Presbyterian Church
President's Commission on the Celebration of
Women in American History
President's Committee on Employment of
People with Disabilities
President's Council on Integrity and Efficiency
President's Council on Sustainable
Development
President's Foreign Intelligence Advisory Board
Prevent Blindness America
Princess Elizabeth Foundation
Princeton Middle East Society, The
Printing Industries of New England (PINE)
Prison Fellowship International
Private Health Association Of Lesotho
(PHAL)
Procedural Aspects of International Law
Institute
Product Development and Management
Association (PDMA)
Production Estimates and Crop Assessment
Division
Professional and Technical Association
Professional Bowler Association (PBA)
Professional Photographers of America, Inc
Professionals' Network for Social
Responsibility, The (PNSR)
Progetto Domani: Cultura E Solidarieta
Program for Appropriate Technology in Health
Programme for Promoting Nuclear Non-
Proliferation
Project Concern International

Project Ploughshares
Promoting Enduring Peace
Proutist Universal, Inc.
Public Health Practice Program Office
Public Health Service (PHS)
Public Relations Society Of America Inc.
Publique
Publishing Triangle
Pugwash Conference on Science and World
  Affairs, The
Puppeteers of America
Quota International Inc.
Ra'ad Rehabilitation Goodwill Complex
Rabita Council International
Radda Barnen
Radin Institute for Family Health Education
  and Promotion (RIFHEP)
RadTech International North America
Railroad Retirement Board
Rainforest Alliance
Rainforest Foundation International, The
Ralph Bunche Institute on the United
  Nations
Ramblers' Association
Reach Out and Read National Training Center
  (ROR)
Reader's Digest Association
Recording Industry Association of America
  (RIAA)
Recreation Vehicle Industry Association (RVIA)
Reform Party Constituency Associations
Refugee Policy Group
Regulatory Information Service Center
Rehabilitation International
Rehabilitation Services Administration
Reinforcing Iron Workers
ReliefWeb
Rencontre Nationale Avec le Peuple D'afrique
  du Sud
Rene Dubos Center for Human Environments
  Inc., The
Research, Action and Information Network for
  Bodily Integrity of Women

Reserve Officers Association of the United
  States
Resource Center for the United Nations,
  (RCUN)
Retail Tobacco Dealers of America
Retail, Wholesale and Department Store Union
Retired Officers Association
Ribbon International, The
RID-USA (Remove Intoxicated Drivers)
Risk Management
Rissho Kosei-Kai
Robert F. Kennedy Memorial Center for
  Human Rights
Rockefeller Foundation, The
Role Playing Gamers Association (RPGA)
Romanian Independent Society for Human
  Rights
Rotary Club of Kathmandu
Rotary International
Royal College of Nursing of the UK
Rural Business-Cooperative Service
Rural Community Development
Rural Housing Service
Rural Utilities Service
Rurality-Environment-Development
  Association International
Russian Association of International Relations
Russian Committee of Cooperation with Latin
  America
Russian Federation Peace Committee
Russian Peace Foundation, The
Russian-American University
Sacramento Area Commerce and Trade
  Organization
SAE (Society of Automotive Engineers)
Sail Training Association
Saint Lawrence Seaway Development
  Corporation
Salesian Mission
Salvation Army Inc., The
Save the Children (UK) Zimbabwe
Save the Children Federation
Save the Children Fund, The

Save-the-Redwoods League
Scaffold Industry Association
School Associations
School of Diplomacy and International Relations
School Sisters of Notre Dame
Science for Peace
Scientist Church of Christ
Scolaires
Scottish Educational Trust for United Nations and International Affairs
Scout Association of Ireland (SAI)
Screen Actors Guild
Seattle Professional Engineering Employees Association (SPEEA)
Secretariado Nacional d Instituciones Privadas de Bienestar Social
Secretary of State
Secretary of the Interior
Securities and Exchange Commission (SEC)
Seeing Eye Inc., The
Selective Service System
Semiconductor Equipment and Materials International (SEMI)
Senior Executive Service
Servas International
Service Employees International Union
Servicio Paz y Justicia en America Latina-Serpaj-Al
Seventh-day Adventist Church
Shannon Centre for International Co-Operation
Share International Foundation Inc., The
Shared Interest
Sheet Metal and Air Conditioning Contractors' National Association (SMACNA)
Sheet Metal Workers' International Association (SMWIA)
Shriners of North America and Shriners Hospitals for Children, The
Sickle Cell Disease Association of America

Sierra Club
Sierra Leone United Nations Association
SIETAR International (The International Society for Intercultural Education Training and Research)
Simon Wiesenthal Center
Simplified Tax and Wage Reporting System (STAWRS) [Department of the Treasury, U.S.]
Sindicato Dos Jornalistas
Singapore Furniture Industries Council
Sisters of Mercy of the Americas
Small Agency Council (SAC)
Small Business Administration (SBA)
Smart Card Industry Association
Smithsonian Institution
SMYAL, Sexual Minority Youth Assistance League
Soap and Detergent Association
Social Agenda
Social Security Administration (SSA)
Social Service National Coordination Council
Sociales y Politicos A.C
Socialist International Women
Socialist Women of Austria
Sociedad de Estudios Internacionales
Societa Italiana per l'organizzazione Internazionale
Societe de Legislation Comparee
Society for Integrative and Comparative Biology
Society for International Development
Society for Public Health Education Inc.
Society for the Preservation and Encouragement of Barber Shop Quartet Singing in America Inc. (SPEBSQSA)
Society for the Psychological Study Of Social Issues
Society of Actuaries
Society of American Foresters
Society of Architectural Historians
Society of Biblical Literature
Society of Experimental Test Pilots, The

Society of Flight Test Engineers

Society of Illustrators

Society of Motion Picture & Television
  Engineers

Society of Naval Architects and Marine
  Engineers, The

Society of Plastics Engineers

Society of Professional Journalists (SPJ)

Society of Zoologists

Sociologists for Women in Society

Software and Information Industry Association

Soil and Water Conservation Society

Soka Gakkai International

Solar Cookers International

Solidaridad Internacional Fundacion Espanola
  para la Cooperaction (SI)

Solid Waste Association of North America

Songwriters Guild of America, The

Sons of Italy in America, Order of

Soroptimist International of the Americas

Sos – Kinderdorf International

South And Meso American Indian Rights
  Center

South Asian Journalists Association

Southeastern Collegiate Hockey Association
  (SCHA)

Southeastern Lumber Manufacturers
  Association

Southern Africa Committee

Southern African Research and Documentation
  Centre

Southern Baptist Convention, Christian Life
  Commission

Southern Early Childhood Association

Southern Forest Products Association

Special Forces Association

Special Libraries Association (SLA)

Special Olympics International

Specialty Equipment Market Association
  (SEMA)

Spina Bifida Association of America

Spiritual Frontiers Fellowship International

Sports Car Club of America Inc.

Sri Chinmoy Centre

St. Joan's International Alliance

St. John's Community Services

Stanley Foundation, The

State Compensation and Assistance
  Division

State Justice Institute

STAT-USA

Steel Manufacturers Association

Steel Tank Institute

Stel Trade

Stennis Space Center [NASA]

Stiftung Wissennschaft Und Politik
  Forschunginstitut Fuer Internationale

Strategic Plans and Policy Directorate (J-5)

Structural Engineers Association

Substance Abuse and Mental Health Services
  Administration

Subtropical Agricultural Research Laboratory

Sunray Meditation Society

Sunsat Energy Council

SuperZoo 2000

Support Centers International

Surface Mount Technology Association

Surgical Aid to Children of the World

Survival International

Susila Dharma International

Susquehanna River Basin Commission

Svenska Fn-Forbundet

Symphony for United Nations

Synagogue Council of America

Synergos Institute, The

Syrian Family Planning Association

Syrian Orthodox Church in America

Tanzania Scouts Association

Tanzania Young Men's Christian Association

TASH (The Association for Persons with
  Severe Handicaps)

Tax Division

Tax Foundation

Teachers Insurance and Annuity Association-
  College Retirement Equities Fund (TIAA-
  CREF)

Teachers of English to Speakers of Other Languages

Technology and Culture

Telecommunications Industry Association (TIA)

Temple of Understanding, The

Tennessee Valley Authority

Tennessee Valley Authority (TVA)

Textile Trade Policy Group

Thanks-Giving Foundation, The

Thanks-Giving Square

Theosophical Society in America, The

Therapy Center for Dependent Individuals (Kethea)

Third World Movement Against the Exploitation Of Women

Time Capsule Inc.

Tin Can Sailors Inc.

Toastmasters International

Together Foundation for Global Unity

Tokyo Junior Chamber Inc.

TOUGHLOVE International

Tourette Syndrome Association

Toyota Land Cruiser Association

Trade and Development Agency

Trade Compliance Center

Trade Information Center

Trade Policy Committee

TransAfrica Forum

Transnational Immigration & Refugee Group Inc.

Transnational Radical Party

Travel Agents, American Society of (ASTA)

Travel and Tourism Research Association (TTRA)

Travelers Aid International

Treasury Management Association

Trees for the Future

TRICARE Military Health System

Trickle Up Program Inc.

Trilateral Commission, The

Trinidad & Tobago Institute of International Affairs, The

Tripoli Rocketry Association

Trocaire-The Catholic Agency for World Development

Trust of Programmes for Early Childhood, Family and Community Education

Tubists Universal Brotherhood Association

Tubular Exchanger Manufacturers Association

U.S. Air Forces in Europe

U.S. Army Corps of Engineers

U.S. Army Financial Management

U.S. Attorneys

U.S. Commercial Service

U.S. Fire Administration (USFA)

U.S. Fish and Wildlife Service

U.S. Marshals Service

U.S. Military Academy

U.S. Parole Commission

U.S. Patents Database at CNIDR (Center for Networked Information Discovery and Retrieval)

U.S. Peace Council

U.S. Societies & Associations

U.S. Trustee Program

Uganda Girl Guides Association

Umoja Wa Wanawake Tanzania

UN Assoc. of the Republic of Croatia

Unda (International Catholic Association for Radio and Television)

Unesco Etxea (Unesco Centre-Basque Country)

UNICEF, U.S. Committee for

Union Democratica de Pensionistas y Jubilados de Espana (U.D.P.)

Union des Foires Internationales

Union Iberoamericana de Colegios y Agrupaciones de Abogados

Union Internationale de la Navigation Fluviale

Union Internationale de l'industrie du Gaz

Union Internationale des Huissiers de Justice et Officers Judiciaires

Union Nationale de la Femme Tunisienne

Union of American Hebrew Congregations

Union of Concerned Scientists

Union of International Associations

Union of Needletrades, Industrial and Textile
Employees

Union of Spiritual Communities of
Christ, The

Union of Tanzania Workers, The

Union of Technical Assistance for Motor
Vehicles and Road Traffic (Unatac)

Union Professionnelle des Experts Maritimes

Unitarian Universalist Association

United Association

United Association of Journeymen and
Apprentices of the Plumbing and Pipe Fitting
Industry of the United States and Canada

United Brotherhood of Carpenters and Joiners
of America

United Cerebral Palsy Association

United Church Board for World Ministries

United Church of Christ

United Church of Christ Commission for
Racial Justice

United Church of Christ/Office for Church in
Society

United Daughters of the Confederacy

United Earth

United Food and Commercial Workers
International Union

United International Union of Automobile,
Aerospace and Agricultural

United Jewish Communities

United Methodist Church

United Methodist Church, General Board of
Church And Society

United Methodist Church, General Board Of
Global Ministries

United Mine Workers of America

United Nations (UN)

United Nations Association

United Nations Association in Canada

United Nations Association of Australia

United Nations Association of Bangladesh

United Nations Association of Barbados

United Nations Association of Belarus

United Nations Association of Bhutan

United Nations Association of Bulgaria

United Nations Association of China

United Nations Association of Cyprus

United Nations Association of Denmark

United Nations Association of Ethiopia

United Nations Association of Finland

United Nations Association of Georgia

United Nations Association of Ghana

United Nations Association of Hungary

United Nations Association of Iceland

United Nations Association of Israel

United Nations Association of Jamaica

United Nations Association of Japan

United Nations Association of Kenya

United Nations Association of Latvia

United Nations Association of Lebanon

United Nations Association of Lesotho

United Nations Association of Lithuania

United Nations Association of Mauritius

United Nations Association of Nepal

United Nations Association of New Zealand

United Nations Association of Nigeria

United Nations Association of Norway

United Nations Association of Russian
Federation

United Nations Association of Slovakia

United Nations Association of Slovenia

United Nations Association of Sudan

United Nations Association of Tanzania

United Nations Association of Thailand

United Nations Association in the Democratic
Socialist Republic of Sri Lanka

United Nations Association of the Isle of Man

United Nations Association of the Philippines

United Nations Association of the Republic of
Korea

United Nations Association of the United
Kingdom

United Nations Association of the United
States of America

United Nations Association of Turkey

United Nations Association of Uganda

United Nations Association of Yemen

United Nations Association of Yugoslavia

United Nations Association of Zambia

United Nations Association of Zimbabwe

United Nations Board of Auditors

United Nations Centre for Human Settlements (UNCHS)

United Nations Children's Fund (UNICEF)

United Nations Commission on International Trade Law (UNCITRAL)

United Nations Common Supplier Database (UNCSD)

United Nations Compensation Commission (UNCC)

United Nations Conference on Trade and Development (UNCTAD)

United Nations Convention to Combat Desertification (UNCCD)

United Nations Development Fund for Women (UNIFEM)

United Nations Development Programme (UNDP)

United Nations Educational, Scientific and Cultural Organization (UNESCO)

United Nations Environment Programme (UNEP)

United Nations Framework Convention on Climate Change (UNFCCC)

United Nations High Commissioner for Refugees, (UNHCR)

United Nations Industrial Development Organization (UNIDO)

United Nations Institute for Disarmament Research (UNIDIR)

United Nations Institute for Training and Research (UNITAR)

United Nations International Drug Control Programme (UNDCP)

United Nations International School (UNIS)

United Nations Interregional Crime and Justice Research Institute (UNICRI)

United Nations Joint Staff Pension Fund (UNJSPF)

United Nations Malaysia Association

United Nations Non-Governmental Liaison Service (NGLS)

United Nations of Yoga

United Nations Office at Geneva (UNOG)

United Nations Office at Nairobi (UNON)

United Nations Office at Vienna (UNOV)

United Nations Office for Project Services (UNOPS)

United Nations Population Fund (UNFPA)

United Nations Postal Administration (UNPA)

United Nations Relief and Works Agency for Palestine Refugees in the Near East (UNRWA)

United Nations Research Institute for Social Development (UNRISD)

United Nations Staff College (UNSC)

United Nations University (UNU)

United Nations Volunteers (UNV)

United Neighborhood Centers Of America

United Ostomy Association

United Pentacostal Church Inc.

United Schools International

United States Amateur Ballroom Dancers Association

United States Catholic Mission Association

United States Chemical Safety and Hazard Investigation Board

United States Chess Federation

United States Combined Training Association

United States Committee for Refugees

United States Committee for Unicef

United States Committee for Unifem

United States Customs Service

United States Fencing Association (USFA)

United States Holocaust Memorial Museum

United States Institute of Peace

United States International Development Cooperation Agency

United States International Trade Commission (USITC)

United States Marine Corps

United States Marshals Service

United States Mint

United States National Central Bureau
United States Naval Academy
United States Naval Institute
United States Nuclear Waste Technical Review
  Board
United States Ombudsman Association
United States Parole Commission
United States Postal Service (USPS)
United States Secret Service
United States Servas Inc.
United States Ski and Snowboard Association
  (USSA)
United States Specialty Sports Association
  (USSSA)
United States Student Association
United States Tennis Association (USTA)
United States Trade Representative
United States Youth Soccer Association
  (USYSA)
United Steelworkers of America
United Synagogue of Conservative
  Judaism, The
United Transportation Union
United Way International
United Way of America
Unitek Research Institute
Universal Children's Gardens
Universal Esperanto Association
Universal Federation of Travel Agents
  Associations
Universal Postal Union (UPU)
University Center for Peace Research
Unveiling Ministries, The
Urban Assembly, The
Ursuline Sisters Congregation of Tildonk
US Army Warrant Officer Association
USA Jobs
Us-Asia Institute
Usenix Association
USO (United Service Organizations)
Vaka — Peace Mouvement
Valve Manufacturers Association
Verbaende in Deutschland

Verband der Akademikerinnen Osterreichs
  (Vao)
Vereniging Voor de Verenigde Naties
Verification Technology Information Centre
Veterans Against Nuclear Arms
Veterans Benefits Administration (VBA)
Veterans Day National Committee
Veterans' Employment and Training Service
Veterans for Peace Inc.
Veterans Health Administration (VHA)
Veterans of Foreign Wars of the U.S.
Video Software Dealers Association (VSDA)
Vietnam Veterans of America Foundation
Vietnamese Students Association
Violence Against Women Office (OJP)
Virginia Gildersleeve International Fund For
  University Women
Voice of America (VOA)
Volunteers in Service to America (VISTA)
Volunteers of America
Vulcan Riders Association
Wage and Hour Division
Wainwright House
Wallops Flight Facility
War & Peace Foundation, The
War Resisters International
War Resisters League
Washington Legal Foundation
Water Environment Federation
Water Management Research Laboratory
  (WMRL)
Water Quality Association
Waterless Printing Association
Wellstart International
West Indian Student's Association
Western Association of Fastener Distributors
  (WAFD)
Western Front Association (WFA)
Western Governors' Association
Western Home Furnishings
White House Commission on Presidential
  Scholars
White House News Photographers' Association

White House Office
White House Office for Women's Initiatives and Outreach
White Sands Missile Range (WSMR)
White Sands Test Facility
William J. Hughes Technical Center
Wisconsin Education Association Council (WEAC)
Wittenberg Center For Alternative Resources, The
Women and Business
Women for International Peace and Arbitration
Women in International Trade [Department of Commerce, U.S.]
Women Lawyer's Association of the Philippines Inc.
Women of Reform Judaism
Women of Vision
Women, Law And Development International
Women's Action for New Directions
Women's American O.R.T. (Organization for Educational Resources and Technological Training) Inc.
Women's American ORT
Women's Branch, Union of Orthodox Jewish Congregations of America
Women's Caucus for Art
Women's Commission for Refugee Women and Children
Women's Educational and Industrial Union
Women's Environment and Development Organization (WEDO)
Women's Federation for World Peace International Inc.
Women's Federation for World Peace, International
Women's Foreign Policy Council
Women's Institute for Freedom of the Press
Women's International Democratic Federation
Women's International League for Peace and Freedom
Women's International Zionist Organization

Women's International League for Peace and Freedom
Women's League for Conservative Judaism
Women's Missionary Society African Methodist Episcopal Church
Women's National Basketball Association (WNBA)
Women's National Book Association
Women's Overseas Service League
Women's Peace Network (Madre/W.P.N.)
Women's Union of Russia, The
Women's United Soccer Association (WUSA)
Women's World Banking
Women's World Summit Foundation, The
WomenWatch
Won Buddhism
Workers of America
World Academy of Art and Science
World Africa Chamber of Commerce
World Alliance of Young Men's Christian Associations
World Assembly of Muslim Youth
World Association for Educational Research
World Association for Element Building and Prefabrication
World Association for Psychosocial Rehabilitation
World Association for Small and Medium Enterprises
World Association of Former U.N. Internes and Fellows Inc., The
World Association of Girl Guides and Girl Scouts
World Association of Industrial and Technological Research Organizations
World Association of Newspapers
World Association of Women Journalists & Writers
World Bank Group
World Blind Union
World Chiropractic Alliance
World Christian Life Community
World Coal Institute

World Community Foundation, The
World Confederation for Physical Therapy
World Confederation of Jewish Community
  Centers
World Confederation of Labour
World Conference of Mayors for Peace
  Through Inter-City Solidarity Officers
World Conference on Religion and Peace
World Congress Alternatives And Environment
World Conservation Union, The
World Council for Curriculum And Instruction
World Council of Churches
World Council of Conservative Synagogues
World Council of Credit Unions
World Council of Independent Christian
  Churches, The
World Council of Peoples for the United
  Nations
World Economy, Ecology & Development
  Association
World Education Fellowship, The
World Energy Council
World Family Organization
World Federalist Association
World Federalist Movement
World Federation for Mental Health
World Federation of Democratic Youth
World Federation of Methodist and Uniting
  Church Women
World Federation of Occupational Therapists
World Federation of the Deaf
World Federation of Therapeutic Communities
  Inc.
World Federation of Trade Unions
World Federation of Ukrainian Women's
  Organizations
World Federation of UNESCO Clubs Centres
  and Associations
World Federation of United Nations
  Associations (WFUNA)
World Food Programme (WFP)
World Future Society
World Futures Studies Federation

World Game Institute
World Goodwill
World Health Organization (WHO)
World Human Dimension
World Hunger Year
World Information Clearing Center (WICC)
World Information Transfer Inc.
World Intellectual Property Organization
  (WIPO)
World Islamic Call Society
World Jewish Congress
World Jurist Association
World League for Freedom and Democracy
  (WLFD)
World Leisure and Recreation Association
World Lithuanian Youth Association, The
World LP Gas Association, The
World Management Council
World Meteorological Organization (WMO)
World Muslim Congress
World Organization for Early Childhood
  Education (OMEP)
World Organization of Building Officials
World Organization of Jews From Arab
  Countries
World Organization of the Scout Movement
World Ort Union
World Peace Council
World Peace Foundation, The
World Peace Prayer Society, The
World Policy Institute, The
World Psychiatric Association
World Resources Institute
World Safety Organization
World Science Fiction Society
World Society for Ekistics
World Society for the Protection Of Animals
World Society of Victimology
World Student Christian Federation
World Teleport Association
World Tourism Organization
World Trade Organization (WTO)
World Union for Progressive Judaism

World Union of Catholic Women's
  Organizations
World Veterans Federation
World Vision International
World Vision International Zimbabwe
World Wildlife Fund
World Without War Council, Inc.
World Women Parliamentarians for Peace
World Young Women's Christian Association
World Youth Service and Enterprise (WYSE)
World's Woman's Christian Temperance Union
Worldwatch Institute
Worldwatch Institute
Worldwide Consultative Association of Retired
  Generals and Admirals
Worldwrite
Wyndom Foundation, The
Yachay Wasi
YMCA of the USA
Yokohama International Human Rights Center
Young Men's Christian Association (YMCA)
Young President's Organization
Young Women's Christian Association (YWCA)
Young Women's Christian Association (YWCA)
Young Women's Christian Association of
  Nigeria
Young Women's Christian Association of the
  U.S.A.
Young Women's Christian Association of the
  United States of America
Youth Challenge (Yc)
Youth Charter for Sport
Yugoslav Un Association
Zero Population Growth
Zimbabwe Council of Churches
Zimbabwe Red Cross Society
Zionist Organization of America
Zionist Organization of America
Zonta International

7

Sports Teams

Air Force Falcons
Akron Zips
Alabama A&M Bulldogs
Alabama Birmingham Blazers
Alabama Crimson Tide
Alabama State Hornets
Albany Danes
Alcorn State Braves
American Eagles
Anaheim Angels
Appalachian State Mountaineers
Arizona Cardinals
Arizona Diamondbacks
Arizona State Sun Devils
Arizona Wildcats
Arkansas Pine Bluff Golden Lions
Arkansas Razorbacks
Arkansas State Indians
Army Black Knights
Army Cadets
Atlanta Braves
Atlanta Falcons
Atlanta Hawks
Auburn Tigers
Austin Peay Governors
Ball State Cardinals
Baltimore Orioles

Baltimore Ravens
Baylor Bears
Belmont Bruins
Bethune Cookman Wildcats
Boise State Broncos
Boston Bruins
Boston Celtics
Boston College Eagles
Boston Red Sox
Boston Terriers
Bowling Green Falcons
Bradley Braves
Brigham Young Cougars
Brown Bears
Bucknell Bison
Buffalo Bills
Buffalo Bulls
Buffalo Sabres
Butler Bulldogs
Cal Poly Mustangs
Calgary Flames
California Bears
California State Fullerton Titans
California State Northridge Matadors
Campbell Camels
Canisius Golden Griffins
Carolina Hurricanes

Carolina Panthers
Centenary Gents
Centenary Ladies
Central Connecticut Blue Devils
Central Connecticut Lady Blue Devils
Central Florida Golden Knights
Central Michigan Chippewas
Charleston Southern Bucs
Charlotte 49ers
Charlotte Hornets
Charlotte Sting
Chattanooga Lady Mocs
Chattanooga Moccasins
Chicago Bears
Chicago Blackhawks
Chicago Bulls
Chicago Cubs
Chicago Fire
Chicago State Cougars
Chicago White Sox
Cincinnati Bearcats
Cincinnati Bengals
Cincinnati Reds
Citadel Bulldogs
Clemson Lady Tigers
Clemson Tigers
Cleveland Browns
Cleveland Cavaliers
Cleveland Indians
Cleveland Rockers
Cleveland St. Vikings
Coastal Carolina Chanticleers
Coastal Carolina Lady Chanticleers
Colgate Red Raiders
College of Charleston Cougars
Colorado Avalanche
Colorado Buffaloes
Colorado Rapids
Colorado Rockies
Colorado State Rams
Columbia Lions
Columbus Blue Jackets
Columbus Crew

Connecticut Huskies
Coppin State Eagles
Cornell Big Red
Creighton Bluejays
D.C. United
Dallas Burn
Dallas Cowboys
Dallas Mavericks
Dallas Stars
Dartmouth Big Green
Davidson Wildcats
Dayton Flyers
Delaware Fighting Blue Hens
Delaware State Hornets
Denver Broncos
Denver Nuggets
Denver Pioneers
Depaul Blue Demons
Detroit Lions
Detroit Pistons
Detroit Red Wings
Detroit Shock
Detroit Tigers
Detroit Titans
Drake Bulldogs
Drexel Dragons
Duke Blue Devils
Duquesne Dukes
East Carolina Lady Pirates
East Carolina Pirates
East Tennessee State Buccaneers
Eastern Illinois Panthers
Eastern Kentucky Colonels
Eastern Michigan Eagles
Eastern Washington Eagles
Edmonton Oilers
Elon Phoenix
Evansville Aces
Fairfield Stags
Fairleigh Dickinson Knights
Florida A&M Rattlers
Florida Atlantic Owls
Florida Gators

Florida International Golden Panthers
Florida Marlins
Florida Panthers
Florida State Seminoles
Fordham Rams
Fresno State Bulldogs
Furman Paladins
Gardner-Webb Bulldogs
George Mason Patriots
George Washington Colonials
Georgetown Hoyas
Georgia Bulldogs
Georgia Southern Eagles
Georgia State Panthers
Georgia Tech Yellow Jackets
Golden State Warriors
Gonzaga Bulldogs
Grambling Lady Tigers
Grambling Tigers
Green Bay Packers
Hampton Pirates
Hartford Hawks
Harvard Crimson
Hawaii Rainbow Warriors
Hawaii Rainbow Wahines
High Point Panthers
Hofstra Flying Dutchmen
Holy Cross Crusaders
Houston Astros
Houston Comets
Houston Cougars
Houston Rockets
Howard Bison
Idaho State Bengals
Idaho Vandals
Illinois Chi Flames
Illinois Fighting Illini
Illinois State Redbirds
Indiana Fever
Indiana Hoosiers
Indiana Pacers
Indiana State Sycamores
Indianapolis Colts

Iona Gaels
Iowa Hawkeyes
Iowa State Cyclones
IUPUI Jaguars
Jackson State Tigers
Jacksonville Dolphins
Jacksonville Jaguars
Jacksonville State Gamecocks
James Madison Dukes
Kansas City Chiefs
Kansas City Royals
Kansas City Wizards
Kansas Jayhawks
Kansas State Wildcats
Kent State Golden Flashes
Kentucky Wildcats
Lafayette Leopards
Lamar Cardinals
LaSalle Explorers
Las Vegas Outlaws
Lehigh Engineers
Lehigh Mountain Hawks
Liberty Flames
Liberty Lady Flames
Long Beach State 49ers
Long Island Blackbirds
Los Angeles Clippers
Los Angeles Dodgers
Los Angeles Galaxy
Los Angeles Kings
Los Angeles Lakers
Los Angeles Sparks
Louisiana State Tigers
Louisiana Tech Bulldogs
Louisiana Tech Lady Techsters
Louisville Cardinals
Loyola Chi Ramblers
Loyola Marymount Lions
Loyola Greyhounds
Maine Black Bears
Manhattan Jaspers
Marist Red Foxes
Marquette Golden Eagles

Marshall Thundering Herd
Maryland Eastern Shore Fighting Hawks
Maryland Terrapins
Massachusetts Minutemen
Massachusetts Minutewomen
McNeese State Cowboys
McNeese State Cowgirls
Memphis Tigers
Mercer Bears
MetroStars
Miami Dolphins
Miami Fusion
Miami Heat
Miami Hurricanes
Miami RedHawks
Miami Sol
Michigan State Spartans
Michigan Wolverines
Middle Tennessee State Blue Raiders
Mighty Ducks of Anaheim
Milwaukee Brewers
Milwaukee Bucks
Minnesota Golden Gophers
Minnesota Lynx
Minnesota Timberwolves
Minnesota Twins
Minnesota Vikings
Minnesota Wild
Mississippi Rebels
Mississippi State Bulldogs
Mississippi Valley State Devils
Missouri Tigers
Monmouth (NJ) Hawks
Montana Grizzlies
Montana State Bobcats
Montreal Canadiens
Montreal Expos
Morehead State Eagles
Morgan State Golden Bears
Mt. St. Mary's Mountaineers
Murray State Racers
Nashville Predators
Navy Midshipmen

Nebraska Cornhuskers
Nevada Wolf Pack
New England Patriots
New England Revolution
New Hampshire Wildcats
New Jersey Devils
New Jersey Nets
New Mexico Lobos
New Mexico State Aggies
New Orleans Privateers
New Orleans Saints
New York Giants
New York Islanders
New York Jets
New York Knicks
New York Liberty
New York Mets
New York Rangers
New York Yankees
Niagara Purple Eagles
Nicholls State Colonels
Norfolk State Spartanettes
Norfolk State Spartans
North Carolina A&T Aggies
North Carolina Asheville Bulldogs
North Carolina State Wolfpack
North Carolina Tar Heels
North Carolina Wilmington Seahawks
North Texas Eagles
Northeastern Huskies
Northern Arizona Lumberjacks
Northern Illinois Huskies
Northern Iowa Panthers
Northwestern State Demons
Northwestern Wildcats
Notre Dame Fighting Irish
Oakland Athletics
Oakland Golden Grizzlies
Oakland Raiders
Ohio Bobcats
Ohio State Buckeyes
Oklahoma Sooners
Oklahoma State Cowboys

Oklahoma State Cowgirls
Old Dominion Lady Monarchs
Old Dominion Monarchs
Oral Roberts Golden Eagles
Oregon Ducks
Oregon State Beavers
Orlando Magic
Orlando Miracle
Ottawa Senators
Pacific Tigers
Panthers Wright State Raiders
Penn State Nittany Lions
Pennsylvania Quakers
Pepperdine Waves
Philadelphia 76ers
Philadelphia Eagles
Philadelphia Flyers
Philadelphia Phillies
Phoenix Coyotes
Phoenix Mercury
Phoenix Suns
Pittsburgh Panthers
Pittsburgh Penguins
Pittsburgh Pirates
Pittsburgh Steelers
Portland Fire
Portland Pilots
Portland State Vikings
Portland Trail Blazers
Prairie View Panthers
Princeton Tigers
Providence Friars
Providence Lady Friars
Purdue Boilermakers
Quinnipiac Braves
Radford Highlanders
Rhode Island Rams
Rice Owls
Richmond Spiders
Rider Broncs
Robert Morris Colonials
Rutgers Scarlet Knights
Sacramento Kings

Sacramento Monarchs
Sacramento State Hornets
Sacred Heart Pioneers
Sam Houston State Bearkats
Samford Bulldogs
San Antonio Spurs
San Diego Chargers
San Diego Padres
San Diego State Aztecs
San Diego Toreros
San Francisco 49ers
San Francisco Giants
San Francisco Lady Dons
San Jose Earthquakes
San Jose Sharks
San Jose State Spartans
Santa Clara Broncos
Seattle Mariners
Seattle Seahawks
Seattle Storm
Seattle SuperSonics
Seton Hall Pirates
Siena Saints
South Alabama Jaguars
South Carolina Gamecocks
South Carolina State Bulldogs
South Florida Bulls
Southeast Louisiana Lady Lions
Southeast Louisiana Lions
Southeast Missouri State Indians
Southern Illinois Saluki
Southern Jaguars
Southern Methodist Mustangs
Southern Mississippi Golden Eagles
Southern Utah Thunderbirds
Southwest Missouri State Bears
Southwest Texas State Bobcats
St. Bonaventure Bonnies
St. Francis Terriers [NY]
St. Francis Red Flash [PA]
St. John's Red Storm
St. Joseph's Hawks
St. Louis Billikens

St. Louis Blues
St. Louis Cardinals
St. Louis Rams
St. Mary's Gaels
St. Peter's Peacocks
Stanford Cardinal
Stephen F. Austin State Lumberjacks
Stephen F. Austin State University Ladyjacks
Stetson Hats
Stony Brook Seawolves
Syracuse Orangemen
Syracuse Orangewomen
Tampa Bay Buccaneers
Tampa Bay Devil Rays
Tampa Bay Lightning
Tampa Bay Mutiny
Temple Owls
Tennessee Lady Volunteers
Tennessee Martin Skyhawks
Tennessee State Lady Tigers
Tennessee State Tigers
Tennessee Tech Eaglettes
Tennessee Tech Golden Eagles
Tennessee Titans
Tennessee Volunteers
Texas A&M Aggies
Texas Arlington Lady Mavericks
Texas Arlington Mavericks
Texas Christian Horned Frogs
Texas El Paso Miners
Texas Longhorns
Texas Rangers
Texas San Antonio Roadrunners
Texas Southern Tigers
Texas Tech Red Raiders
Toledo Rockets
Toronto Blue Jays
Toronto Maple Leafs
Toronto Raptors
Towson Tigers
Troy State Trojans
Tulane Green Wave
Tulsa Golden Hurricane

UAB Blazers
UC Irvine Anteaters
UC Santa Barbara Gauchos
UCF Knights
UCLA Bruins
UL Lafayette Ragin' Cajuns
UL Monroe Indians
UMBC Retrievers
UMKC Kangaroos
UNLV Runnin' Rebels
USC Trojans
USC Women of Troy
Utah Jazz
Utah Starzz
Utah State Aggies
Utah Utes
Valparaiso Crusaders
Vancouver Canucks
Vancouver Grizzlies
Vanderbilt Commodores
Vermont Catamounts
Villanova Wildcats
Virginia Cavaliers
Virginia Commonwealth Rams
Virginia Military Institute Keydets
Virginia Tech Hokies
Wagner Seahawks
Wake Forest Demon Deacons
Washington Capitals
Washington Huskies
Washington Mystics
Washington Redskins
Washington State Cougars
Washington Wizards
Weber State Wildcats
West Virginia Mountaineers
Western Carolina Catamounts
Western Carolina Lady Catamounts
Western Illinois Westerwinds
Western Illinois Fighting Leathernecks
Western Kentucky Hilltoppers
Western Kentucky Ladytoppers
Western Michigan Broncos

Wichita State Shockers
William & Mary Tribe
Winthrop Eagles
Wisconsin Badgers
Wisconsin Green Bay Phoenix
Wofford Lady Terriers
Wofford Terriers
Wyoming Cowboys
Wyoming Cowgirls
Xavier Musketeers
Yale Bulldogs
Youngstown State Penguins